RESEARCH IN THE HISTORY OF ECONOMIC THOUGHT AND METHODOLOGY

RESEARCH IN THE HISTORY OF ECONOMIC THOUGHT AND METHODOLOGY

Founding Editor: Warren J. Samuels (1933–2011)
Series Editors: Luca Fiorito, Scott Scheall, and
Carlos Eduardo Suprinyak

Recent Volumes:

RESEARCH IN THE HISTORY OF ECONOMIC THOUGHT
AND METHODOLOGY   VOLUME 34A

RESEARCH IN THE HISTORY OF ECONOMIC THOUGHT AND METHODOLOGY

EDITED BY

LUCA FIORITO
University of Palermo, Palermo, Italy

SCOTT SCHEALL
Arizona State University Downtown Phoenix Campus, Phoenix, AZ, USA

CARLOS EDUARDO SUPRINYAK
Universidade Federal de Minas Gerais, Belo Horizonte, Brazil

Emerald

United Kingdom – North America – Japan
India – Malaysia – China

Emerald Group Publishing Limited
Howard House, Wagon Lane, Bingley BD16 1WA, UK

First edition 2016

British Library Cataloguing in Publication Data
A catalogue record for this book is available from the British Library

ISBN: 978-1-78560-960-2
ISSN: 0743-4154 (Series)

Printed and bound by CPI Group (UK) Ltd, Croydon, CR0 4YY

ISOQAR certified
Management System,
awarded to Emerald
for adherence to
Environmental
standard
ISO 14001:2004.

Certificate Number 1985
ISO 14001

INVESTOR IN PEOPLE

CONTENTS

PART II
ESSAYS

LIST OF CONTRIBUTORS

Daniele Besomi	Université de Lausanne, Lausanne, Switzerland
Peter J. Boettke	George Mason University, Fairfax, VA, USA
Christopher J. Coyne	George Mason University, Fairfax, VA, USA
Erwin Dekker	Erasmus University Rotterdam, Rotterdam, The Netherlands; George Mason University, Fairfax, VA, USA
Massimo Di Matteo	University of Siena, Siena, Italy
Andrew Farrant	Dickinson College, Carlisle, PA, USA
Luca Fiorito	University of Palermo, Palermo, Italy
Nicola Giocoli	University of Pisa, Pisa, Italy
Jan Horst Keppler	Université Paris-Dauphine, Paris, France
Hansjörg Klausinger	WU, Vienna University of Economics and Business, Austria
Paul Lewis	King's College London, London, UK
Patrick Newman	George Mason University, Fairfax, VA, USA
Gabriel Oliva	Universidade de São Paulo, São Paulo, Brazil
Maria Pia Paganelli	Trinity University, San Antonio, TX, USA
Salim Rashid	Universiti Utara Malaysia, Kedah, Malaysia
Scott Scheall	Arizona State University Downtown Phoenix Campus, Phoenix, AZ, USA

Solomon Stein	George Mason University, Fairfax, VA, USA
Virgil Henry Storr	George Mason University, Fairfax, VA, USA
Carlos Eduardo Suprinyak	Universidade Federal de Minas Gerais, Belo Horizonte, Brazil
Janek Wasserman	University of Alabama, Tuscaloosa, AL, USA

EDITORIAL BOARD

INTRODUCTION

In our Introduction to the most recent volume of *Research in the History of Economic Thought and Methodology (RHETM)*, we promised several changes to the focus and format of the journal — historically, one of the preeminent outlets in the field. If that Volume (33, published in April 2015) amounted to something of a stopgap between the journal's former format and the vision of the new editorial team, then the current issue — the first of two issues to be published in 2016's Volume 34 — represents the first florescence of this vision.

In *The Postwar Austrian Diaspora*, edited by our own Scott Scheall, we offer the first of an ongoing series of symposia dedicated to single themes in the history of economic thought and methodology. This first symposium considers the initial devolution and eventual evolution of the Austrian School of economics following the escape of its most prominent members from a Vienna facing impending Nazi annexation and an otherwise rapidly disintegrating Central European scene in the 1930s. The symposium features contributions from several respected historians of the Austrian School, including Hansjörg Klausinger, Virgil Storr, Paul Lewis, and Peter Boettke. Of particular note is the contribution of the young Brazilian scholar, Gabriel Oliva, a chapter entitled "The Road to Servomechanisms: The Influence of Cybernetics on Hayek from *the Sensory Order* to the Social Order," winner of the first annual Warren Samuels Prize for Interdisciplinary Research in the History of Economic Thought and Methodology, an award named after *RHETM*'s late founder (and continuing inspiration). Such monothematic symposia will be a permanent feature of future issues and the Samuels Prize-winning essay will appear in the first issue of each new annual volume moving forward.

The present issue also features general research essays from several eminent authors in the field, including the world-renowned Adam Smith scholar Maria Pia Paganelli and her co-author Andrew Farrant, Nicola Giocoli, and Daniele Besomi (past winner [2011] of the History of Economics Society's Best Article Prize[1]).

Our "From the Vault" section continues *RHETM*'s tradition of publishing historically and philosophically significant, but otherwise unavailable, newly discovered archival materials. The distinguished historian of economic thought, Salim Rashid, contributes "A New Document from Thomas Mun's Age." Meanwhile, our "Reviews" section features a review by Jan Horst Keppler of Damien Bazin, Lynn Urch, and Rowland Hill's new (2011) English translation of Heinrich von Stackelberg's (1934) *Market Structure and Equilibrium*.

We are excited about this novel fourfold format. We have several symposia in the works for future issues and we (hope and) anticipate that *RHETM* will become the leading outlet in the field for this kind of focused research. Of course, in addition to the most interesting and finest quality symposia materials, we will continue to seek out and publish only the best general research articles, archival documents, and review essays.

Finally, we would like to acknowledge the contributions of those who work so hard to lighten our shared editorial burden. In particular, our new Publisher, Kieran Booluck, and his teams of layout designers, marketers, copyeditors, and web designers at Emerald Publishing Group, facilitate our responsibilities and make the publication of such lovely — and intellectually stimulating — issues possible. We should also thank the members of our Editorial Board, generally, for their continuing support of our mission and, more specifically, for the work that each Board member unhesitatingly contributed to the evaluation of this year's Samuels Prize nominees.

Luca Fiorito
Scott Scheall
Carlos Eduardo Suprinyak
Editors

NOTE

1. Published in *RHETM* Volume 28, Part 1: See Besomi, Daniele (2010), "Periodic crises": Clément Juglar between theories of crises and theories of business cycles, in Jeff E. Biddle, Ross B. Emmett (ed.) *A Research Annual (Research in the History of Economic Thought and Methodology, Volume 28 Part 1)* Emerald Group Publishing Limited, pp.169–283.

PART I
THE POSTWAR AUSTRIAN DIASPORA – A SYMPOSIUM ON AUSTRIAN ECONOMICS IN THE WAKE OF WORLD WAR II

INTRODUCTION TO A SYMPOSIUM ON AUSTRIAN ECONOMICS IN THE IMMEDIATE POSTWAR PERIOD

Scott Scheall

The Austrian School is unique in the history of economic thought. This is true, of course, for many reasons, but I will resist the temptation to enumerate all of the respects in which, to my mind, the Austrian School is special. Suffice it to say — and most relevant to the theme of the present symposium — that the Austrian School is unique in that, just at the height of their international renown, for reasons utterly unconnected to economic science, the members of the School were driven by the mounting Nazi menace from their home base in Vienna to sundry locations scattered across the globe. At around the same time, moreover, the members of the School were, in the eyes of many within the economics discipline, seemingly rebuked in two debates of supreme consequence for both economic science and policy. Though he may have won the initial skirmish, F. A. Hayek, of course, was seen to ultimately "lose" the war with Keynes, while the combined forces of Hayek and Ludwig von Mises were judged to have been finally and roundly defeated by the market socialists, especially, Oskar Lange and Abba Lerner, in the famous Socialist Calculation Debates.

Research in the History of Economic Thought and Methodology, Volume 34A, 3−7
Copyright © 2016 by Emerald Group Publishing Limited
ISSN: 0743-4154/doi:10.1108/S0743-41542016000034A001

Yet, with varying degrees of success, the expatriated Viennese members of the School adapted to these altered environmental conditions both within and without the field of economics so that, after several decades in the wilderness, a reformed Austrian School ultimately emerged, first, in the United States, and, later, in other parts of the world, including — somewhat ironically — in several former Habsburg domains large swaths of which had just emerged from the Eastern Bloc (and Yugoslavia). The present symposium highlights several fascinating aspects of the fall and rise (such as it has been) of the Austrian School of economics.

Hansjörg Klausinger details the history of the *Nationalökonomische Gesellschaft* (*NOeG*; Austrian Economic Association) from its foundation near the end of the Great War through then-President Hans Mayer's infamous and disgraceful expulsion from the Association of non-Aryan members following the *Anschluss Österreichs* in 1938, to Mayer's death in 1955. Klausinger extracts this history from a deft comparison of various archival materials with the extant textual literature on the Association's activities. Of special interest, Klausinger provides a comprehensive accounting (or, at least, as comprehensive as the available evidence allows) of the papers presented at the meetings of the *NOeG* during the years when the economists of Vienna were considered so eminent in the discipline as to attract a constant stream of renowned foreign scholars. Beyond this, an irony of history emerges from Klausinger's investigation: Why did Mayer take the fateful option to expel his non-Aryan colleagues only to then effectively terminate the Association's activities through the war years? Why not simply do the second without doing the first (and thus preserve more or less intact his liberal bona fides)?

Erwin Dekker argues that, beyond scattering its affiliates far and wide, the Second World War had the effect of obscuring, at least for a time and to some degree, the Austrian School's traditional notion of the legitimate moral responsibilities of the engaged social scientist. Dekker points out that, in tension with the narrow positivistic interpretation it is typically given; Max Weber's famous doctrine of *Wertfreiheit* is itself an ethical commitment. Thus, by mostly ignoring in their postwar work the social responsibilities of the "moral scholar," the Austrians in fact moved against, rather than in harmony with, Weber's principles, properly understood. Concomitant with this change in the image of the proper role of the social scientist was a shift in the conception of economic knowledge. Where once the value of economic reasoning was considered in light of the (always circumscribed) insight it provided into the pressing issues of the day, in the postwar world, Austrian economists would pursue economic knowledge more for its own sake than as a prophylactic against ill-judged policymaking.

Solomon Stein and Virgil Storr also dig into various Weberian themes, and Ludwig von Mises makes his most extensive appearance in the present symposium, in their co-authored contribution. Stein and Storr argue that similarities between Mises and Weber extend far beyond long-acknowledged methodological connections to parallel conceptions of social objects. The authors explore the similar treatments of the market that appear in Mises and Weber. Mises regarded the market as the resultant of myriad decisions taken by sovereign consumers. For Weber, the market was a social order grounded in the pursuit of economic advantage by calculating individuals. Stein and Storr argue further that affinities extend to similar conceptions of the popular hostility toward markets as grounded in perceptions of its "impersonal" character. Moreover, Stein and Storr show, both Mises and Weber treated the market as embedded within, rather than co-extensive with, society.

Janek Wasserman's chapter focuses on the networks of Austrian-School economists as they existed in pre-*Anschluss* Vienna and later, after the Second World War, in the United States. Wasserman challenges the prevailing notion that the Viennese School, such as it was, all but disappeared in the postwar era, only to be ultimately usurped in both the public and professional imaginations by a neo-Austrian School largely the creation of Mises' American acolytes. Wasserman shows that, in their post-emigration years, certain less renowned (or, at least, less renowned than Hayek) members of the fourth and final generation of the Viennese school − in particular, Gottfried Haberler, Fritz Machlup, and Oskar Morgenstern − continued to advance older Austrian themes, while preserving the former Viennese network perhaps as tightly as dispersion could permit in the pre-Internet age.

The two subsequent contributions each fill a significant lacuna in the extant historical literature on the development of Hayek's thought after the war. The influence of Viennese biologist and creator of general system theory, Ludwig von Bertalanffy, on Hayek's later thought has long been acknowledged. However, the personal and intellectual relationship between Bertalanffy and Hayek has never been explored with the understanding and attention to historical detail that Paul Lewis brings to his chapter. Lewis argues that, through his engagement with Bertalanffy's work, Hayek was able to clarify important aspects of his theoretical psychology, especially his conception of mind as an emergent property of the structure of neuronal activities. Beyond this, Lewis shows that Bertalanffy's general system theory afforded Hayek a conceptual framework with which to articulate his ideas concerning complex phenomena.

Similarly, the influence of the nascent development of cybernetics on Hayek's writings on complexity has long been recognized but rarely examined in detail. In his chapter — awarded the first annual Warren Samuels Prize for Interdisciplinary Research in the History of Economic Thought and Methodology by the esteemed members of our Editorial Board — Gabriel Oliva explores the early history of cybernetics, its origins in Norbert Wiener's wartime association with the American military, and its postwar development by Wiener and the participants of the Macy Conferences. Oliva shows how these early "first-order" cybernetic ideas sanctioned Hayek's framing of his theoretical psychology — especially his account of purposeful behavior — and, ultimately, his social theory, as implications of evidence drawn from the natural sciences. He further compares and contrasts Hayek's reliance on cybernetics with the arguments of certain early cyberneticians such as Wiener and Garret Hardin concerning Hayek-like conceptions of economy and society as self-regulating systems.

Finally, Peter Boettke, Christopher Coyne, and Patrick Newman offer an extensive history of the School and review of the relevant literature. Beginning with a discussion of its late nineteenth century advent in the writings of Carl Menger and his first disciples, Eugen Böhm-Bawerk and Friedrich Wieser, the authors track the vicissitudes in the Austrian School's prospects into the modern era, through its interwar zenith, near-immediate eclipse and subsequent quiescence despite the best efforts of Mises and Hayek, and its postwar revival, particularly in the work of Israel Kirzner, Ludwig Lachmann, and Murray Rothbard. Of particular interest, Boettke, Coyne, and Newman address the "Kirznerian conundrum," identified by the latter-day Austrian scion, that Mises and Hayek made their most significant contributions to economics and social theory — in fact, precisely those contributions with which they are now most intimately associated — during those years immediately after the Second World War when the School was, in terms of its professional and public reputation, at its lowest ebb. Beyond this, the contemporary association of Austrian economics with libertarian politics, Boettke, Coyne, and Newman show to be merely the latest display of a tendency — indeed, in earlier manifestations during more politically dangerous times, a right duty — to communicate with multiple audiences, including fellow economists, the general public, and, especially, policymakers. The political allegiances — and, more to the point, the readiness to engage with practical affairs — typically associated with Austrian economists are a vestige of the environment in which the School first appeared, and of the subsequent history of the Habsburg Empire and First Austrian Republic.

The present symposium serves to improve our understanding of the post-war history of the Austrian School of economics. We learn in these chapters how the Austrians managed to preserve, and gradually adapt and extend their intellectual network, despite a cataclysm rarely, if ever, surpassed in the history of human drama — and one that has never been eclipsed in the more humdrum history of *ideas*. We learn further how the Austrians — especially Hayek and his fellow fourth-generation compatriots — adapted their ideas and arguments to new contexts geographical, social, and intellectual. It was not merely the physical setting that shifted after the war. As Hayek especially, but also Mises, Machlup, Morgenstern, and Haberler all in their unique ways came to realize, the foundations of economic science they had learned in Vienna had also shifted — and seismically so — during the war. For a few, Machlup and Haberler, in particular, this meant something like compromise with the emerging mainstream. Beyond his seminal contribution to the development of game theory, for Morgenstern, it mostly meant withering criticism of all things non-Morgenstern. For Mises, it meant retrenchment, reiteration, and reinforcement, albeit to a new audience of American admirers. For Hayek, it meant a fairly radical reformulation of economics (and the social sciences more generally) as concerned, in the first instance, with the discovery and coordination of subjective knowledge.

The Austrian School of economics celebrates its sesquicentennial in 2021. If the past (and present) is indeed prologue, one might with some considerable confidence issue the following pattern prediction: It will be devastating criticism joined to an attitude open to appropriate compromise, reiteration, and reinforcement of the best ideas of the past married to a constant inclination to improve these ideas via reformulation that, if any-thing, will secure the survival of the Austrian School through another 150 years.

THE *NATIONALÖKONOMISCHE GESELLSCHAFT* (AUSTRIAN ECONOMIC ASSOCIATION) IN THE INTERWAR PERIOD AND BEYOND

Hansjörg Klausinger

ABSTRACT

The Nationalökonomische Gesellschaft *(Austrian Economic Association,* NOeG*) provides a prominent example of the Viennese economic circles and associations that more than academic economics dominated scientific discourse in the interwar years. For the first time this chapter gives a thorough account of its history, from its foundation in 1918 until the demise of its long-time president, Hans Mayer, 1955, based on official documents and archival material. The topics treated include its predecessor and rival, the* Gesellschaft österreichischer Volkswirte, *its foundation in 1918 soon to be followed by years of inactivity, the relaunch by Mayer and Mises, the survival under the NS-regime and the expulsion of its Jewish members and the slow restoration after 1945. In particular, an attempt is made to provide a list of the*

Research in the History of Economic Thought and Methodology, Volume 34A, 9–43
ISSN: 0743-4154/doi:10.1108/S0743-41542016000034A002

papers presented to the NOeG, *as complete as possible, for the period 1918–1938.*

Keywords: History of economic thought; Austrian school of economics; Vienna economic circles; University of Vienna

JEL classifications: A14; B13; B25

INTRODUCTION

In many disciplines the intellectual discourse in interwar Vienna was characterised by the existence of interlocking ('extramural') circles and associations outside academia. In economics the most famous such institutions[1] were Ludwig Mises's private seminar, the *Geist-Kreis* organised by Friedrich A. Hayek and Herbert Fürth and the *Nationalökonomische Gesellschaft* (Austrian Economic Association, in short *NOeG*). There were also others in neighbouring disciplines where participants of the economics circles were active, for example the Schlick Circle (or Vienna Circle of logical positivism), Karl Menger's Mathematical Colloquium and the circle of the legal theorist Hans Kelsen. Yet, due to their largely informal nature little has been preserved of these circles in the form of written documents and much of what we know today (or, i.e. believe to know) relies on oral tradition or on the memories and reminiscences of their members.[2]

This is also true of the subject of this chapter, the activities of the *NOeG* during the interwar period and beyond. In the following the conventional stories about the history of the *NOeG*, as told, for example by Mises, Hayek and other participants, shall be taken as a point of departure and contrasted to what can be learnt from existing archival records. These records consist on the one hand of the documents preserved in the various Austrian offices in charge of supervising this kind of private associations (e.g. the branches of the police department like the *Vereinsbehörde*), which unfortunately rarely include more than just the results of the annual elections to the board, and on the other hand of correspondence and other contemporary documents, such as, for example the diary kept by the Austrian economist Oskar Morgenstern. These documents will be used to reconstruct the history of the *NOeG*, that is, of its institutions, its activities – in particular of the papers presented in sessions of the *NOeG*, its relation with the Viennese *Zeitschrift für Nationalökonomie* and – the most delicate issue – how it fared after the *Anschluss* and under the rule of National Socialism (NS) and afterwards.

Accordingly the structure of the chapter after sketching the conventional story of the *NOeG* is primarily chronological. It starts with the pre-history of the *NOeG*, that is, its predecessor and later on competitor, the *Gesellschaft österreichischer Volkswirte*. Then it turns to the foundation of the *NOeG* in 1918 and its long period of inactivity through the 1920s. Next the circumstances leading to its revival in 1927 are examined. For the period 1927–1938 we look both at the scientific activities and the evolution of the internal organisation. The following sections deal with the fate of the *NOeG* and its members under the reign of the NS, 1938–1945, and with its restoration after 1945. This story of the *NOeG* essentially ends with Hans Mayer's death because not much can be learnt of its activities in the following decade from the existing sources, possibly due to the diminished nature of such activities. The concluding section shows the extent to which the history of the *NOeG*, 1918–1956, mirrors the history of academic economics in Austria in general.

SOME STORIES TOLD ABOUT THE *NOeG*

Hitherto most of what has been written on the early history of the *NOeG* is based on the memories of contemporaries, expressed in scattered remarks in diverse recollections and reminiscences. The basic sources used in the secondary literature – which often relegates discussion of the *NOeG* to footnotes – are the autobiographical accounts by Mises (1978) and Hayek (1983, 1994, undated) and the summary of oral interviews by Craver (1986).[3]

Simply due to his age, Mises is the only one of our informants who was able to tell his story of the beginnings of the *NOeG*: According to his recollections (Mises, 1978, p. 98f.) he was the one who initiated an informal discussion circle 'for the friends of economic inquiry'[4] that was to evolve into the *NOeG*, starting in March 1908. He mentions as participants besides himself Karl Pribram, Emil Perels and Else Cronbach, all in their late twenties and all, except Pribram, affiliated with the Vienna Chamber of Commerce.[5] During the war, he recounts, due to mistakes in the selection of participants the atmosphere of the circle deteriorated and it eventually discontinued. When he returned to Vienna after (or, in fact, during) the war, a more formal organisation proved necessary, so Mises initiated the foundation of a private association, the *Nationalökonomische Gesellschaft*. However, the working of the *NOeG* ran into difficulties because of the presence of the newly appointed Vienna professor Othmar Spann, with whom cooperation turned out as impossible. When Spann was excluded from the *NOeG* — Mises gives no date — its activities could be started anew, now for reasons of academic courtesy with the presidency bestowed on the other Viennese economics professor, Hans Mayer and Mises as his deputy. According to Mises, the *NOeG* was dominated by the participants of his own seminar, anyway, and its attraction only diminished when he left Vienna for Geneva in 1934.

Hayek, a generation younger, is another witness of the Austrian economics community and the *NOeG*. He remembers (Hayek, 1983, p. 410f., undated, p. 44f. and 51) that after the war the association still existed, besides the Mises seminar, and that he had even attended some meetings. Yet when he returned from his trip to the United States, in 1924, the association had expired — Hayek largely lays the blame on the evils of the inflation period. However, in the next years it became urgent to bridge the evolving gap between the followers of Mayer and of Mises, who personally were not on good relations, as the younger members of the Mises seminar had to turn to Mayer for the support of an academic career. It is noteworthy that in Hayek's account it was he — Hayek — who took the initiative that led to the revival of the *NOeG*. According to him 'the nucleus' of the *NOeG* was formed by the members of the Mises seminar, although it also comprised members of the Mayer seminar and in addition some industrialists and senior civil servants.[6]

Apart from some details added by other participants like Furth (1989) and by the interviews collected in Craver (1986, p. 17), the recollections of Mises and Hayek provide most of the evidence on which the secondary literature on the *NOeG* has been based up to now.[7] As it turns out, not all of this evidence is incontrovertible.

THE PRE-HISTORY OF THE *NOeG*: THE *GESELLSCHAFT DER ÖSTERREICHISCHEN VOLKSWIRTE*

Looking at the history of associations of professional economists in Austria, it must be acknowledged that indeed before and then for a long time besides the *NOeG* there existed another association, namely the

Gesellschaft österreichischer Volkswirte, that is, the Association of Austrian Economists (henceforth: *Gesellschaft*).[8]

The *Gesellschaft* was founded in 1874, on the model of the German *Volkswirtschaftlicher Kongress* of 1858 and with a similarly liberal outlook. Yet, when already in one of the first annual assemblies — in contrast to the free-trade ideas of its founders — a majority of the members voted for a protectionist tariff, its activities soon came to a halt in 1877. It took a decade until it was reconstructed under modified bylaws with the goal of providing a forum for discussion for professional economists of various orientations and for businessmen and public servants alike. Its first president was Lorenz von Stein (1888–1890), followed by Karl Theodor von Inama-Sternegg (1891–1896), Eugen von Philippovich (1897–1909) and Ernst von Plener (1910–1925), all of whom might be classified as adhering to what Plener (1915, p. 123) called the 'historical or social-ethical schools' rather than to 'exact theory'. Members of the Austrian school proper were also prominently represented at the board: Eugen von Böhm-Bawerk (1894–1902), Robert Meyer (1890–1914), Friedrich von Wieser (1908/1909) and also Richard Lieben (1894–1915).[9] Michael Hainisch, the future President of the First Republic of Austria, was another notable member of the board. On the eve of WWI the *Gesellschaft* had attained approximately 270 members, signifying the intended width of its outreach.

From the beginning the papers presented at the monthly sessions of the *Gesellschaft* were destined to be published, first in a bulletin and starting in 1892 in a journal, the *Zeitschrift für Volkswirtschaft, Sozialpolitik und Verwaltung*, the 'organ of the *Gesellschaft*'. The *Zeitschrift* was closely linked to the *Gesellschaft* with regard to its editors, too. Böhm-Bawerk, Inama-Sternegg and Plener served as the founding editors and kept this position for the rest of their lives. After the turn of the century Philippovich and Wieser entered the board and Walter Schiff worked as managing editor. When Inama-Sternegg died in 1909, he was replaced in 1911 by Robert Meyer; after the deaths of Meyer and Böhm-Bawerk (1914) and Philippovich (1917) Plener and Wieser were left, only to see the *Zeitschrift* through to its final volume. At the end of the war publication was discontinued.

After the war, when the *Gesellschaft* was rivalled by the *NOeG*, Plener remained its president until 1925 and was succeeded by Richard Reisch. The journal was revived eventually, in 1921, in a new form, titled *Zeitschrift für Volkswirtschaft und Sozialpolitik*, no longer formally linked to the *Gesellschaft* and split up from its public law section, which was continued in 1920 as *Zeitschrift für öffentliches Recht* with Kelsen as its editor. In addition to the remaining editors of its predecessor, Plener and Wieser, Reisch and Spann entered the editorial board and the position of managing editor was filled by F. X. Weiss. In the course of the next years, Plener was replaced after his death (1923) by Mayer, and Wieser (1925) by Richard Schüller.[10] After the first four volumes of the new series had appeared regularly from 1921 to 1924, the fifth volume stretched over three years (1925–1927) and thereafter the publication of the journal once more was stopped.

THE FOUNDATION OF THE *NOeG* 1918 AND ITS INACTIVITY THROUGH THE 1920s

At the eve of WWI, in the *Gesellschaft* and at the editorial board of the *Zeitschrift* as well as in academic economics the deaths of important members led to a piecemeal replacement of the older generation of Austrian economists[11]: The decease of Böhm and Philippovich, the retirement of Menger and the temporary leave of Wieser at Vienna and the chairs to be filled before and during the war at Graz, Prague and other 'provincial' universities created room for a younger generation of economists (not all affiliated with the Austrian school). Such members of a younger generation were, for example Spann in Vienna (who succeeded Philippovich), Joseph Schumpeter in Graz, Mayer in Prague or Alfred Amonn in Czernowitz. Although quite diverse in their approaches, they possibly shared the desire for a more theoretically oriented forum for economic debate than offered by the existing *Gesellschaft*.

There is not much known about the specific circumstances that gave rise to the foundation of the *Nationalökonomische Gesellschaft*. Therefore we must rely on what has been preserved in the official documents.[12] Accordingly, the first step occurred still during the war, when on March 28, 1918 the provincial government of Lower Austria (then still including the capital Vienna) was notified of the formation of the *Verein* in a letter signed by Mayer and Mises. The actual foundation is to be dated with the constituent general assembly held on June 19, 1918. The elected board was composed of Schumpeter (president), Mayer (vice-president), Karl Pribram (secretary), Mises (treasurer) and the ordinary members Amonn, Moritz Dub, Victor Grätz and Spann.[13] The seat of the *NOeG* was in Vienna, at the Chamber of Commerce. According to the bylaws its purpose consisted in fostering theoretical economics by organising presentations and discussions and by publishing papers. In contrast to the existing *Gesellschaft*, the *NOeG* distinguished itself by a different purpose, namely the furthering of economic *theory*, and a smaller scale — typically the papers were presented to an audience of 20–30 persons, and membership must have been far below that of the *Gesellschaft*, although it was not restricted to academic economists.

Beyond these formalities, little is known about the *NOeG*'s activities in its first years. Evidently, in 1918/1919 the problems of survival after the end of the war, the scarcity of food, the deranged means of transportation, or the Spanish influenza that ravaged Austria, must have gravely interfered with its working. The only information available is that unearthed from the Mises papers and utilised in his Mises biography by Hülsmann (2007). In particular, in December 1918, Schumpeter, still in Graz, apologised for not being able to attend a session of the *NOeG* in Vienna, because of transportation problems.[14] Furthermore in January 1920 Mises presented what was to become his famous paper on economic calculation in a socialist commonwealth (Mises, 1920) in a session of the *NOeG*, with Schumpeter, Amonn and the socialists Max Adler and Helene Bauer among the audience, of which he later reported in a letter to Emil Lederer.[15]

From 1920 onwards for years to come there is no evidence bequeathed of any specific activity of the *NOeG*: Although requested by Austrian law, no annual general assembly took place, neither were papers presented nor published.[16] This torpor might have been due to a variety of reasons: First, in 1918 when the *NOeG* was founded, most of its leading members resided in Vienna or had close ties to the University of Vienna.[17] Yet, in the course of the years this was no longer so: Although Mises and Spann were still present, Schumpeter — after a rather disastrous stint as Secretary of Finance in the first cabinet of the Austrian Republic — had withdrawn from academia (into a still more disastrous career in the Vienna banking business), Mayer had left for his chair at Prague (now located in foreign territory) and later on switched to Graz succeeding Schumpeter, while Amonn followed Mayer in Prague.[18] Second, with the onset of the Austrian hyperinflation, which lasted from August 1921 to September 1922, it might have become difficult for the association to secure the financial means required just for keeping its activities going.[19] And thirdly,[20] Spann who in these years started developing his own specific approach of 'universalism' became more and more inimical to traditional economics and to the teachings of the Austrian school in particular. It can be easily imagined, thus, that a scientific association dependent for its everyday working on two personalities as idiosyncratic as Spann's and Mises', its only active Vienna members, would not have easily survived. In fact, there are no signs of life from the *NOeG* throughout most of the 1920s.

THE RELAUNCH IN 1927

Things changed, but not necessarily for the better, with the appointment in 1923 of Hans Mayer to the economics chair at the University of Vienna from which Wieser had retired. After a short period of 'benign neglect' the adverse approaches pursued by Mayer and Spann sparked a bitter and long controversy. At the same time, although both considered themselves followers of the Austrian school, the relationship between Mayer and Mises also exhibited mutual resentments. This made all three – Mayer, Mises and Spann[21] – look for an institutional setting, beyond their respective private seminars, in order to facilitate the pursuit of their respective approaches and to demonstrate more visibly their claim for leadership in the Austrian economics community. In the mid-1920s, incidentally, there existed two vehicles that might have furthered these intentions. On the one hand, there was the idea to found a new or revive one of the old existing economics associations. On the other hand, there was the need to reorganise the Viennese *Zeitschrift*.

Turning first to the *Zeitschrift*, it had eventually stopped appearing in 1927.[22] The underlying difficulties were twofold: First, the journal had increasingly run into financial distress so that finally its publisher, Deuticke, refused to continue publication without serious adaptations. Second, tensions among the editors had increased to an extent that cooperation appeared impossible. The main point of controversy was the extent to which Spann believed himself justified to use the *Zeitschrift* as an outlet for propagating his universalistic approach in contrast to the more traditional varieties of (individualistic) economics favoured by the other three editors, Mayer, Reisch and Schüller. Furthermore, in the view of the other editors some of Spann's attacks – for example on Max Weber in Spann (1923) – had transgressed the limits of legitimate critique.

In the end, the problem was solved by terminating the cooperation with Spann. In order to do so, the journal could not be continued under its old name but a new one had to be chosen: *Zeitschrift für Nationalökonomie*. The financial difficulties were resolved by switching to a new publisher, from Deuticke to the Vienna branch of the Berlin publisher Julius Springer, and by the acquisition of subsidies from various sources.[23] Henceforth, Mayer, Reisch and Schüller made up the board of editors and

Oskar Morgenstern and Paul Rosenstein-Rodan were installed as managing editors – and indeed over the years the journal became ever more the domain of Morgenstern rather than Mayer. Eventually after lengthy negotiations the first issue was produced in September 1929.

With regard to the economics association the plans of the acting persons may only be glimpsed from scattered remarks in the diary of Morgenstern, who observed the events from his position as Mayer's assistant at the university. Apparently activities in this regard had started already in 1924: At first Mayer intended to gain the support of Wieser and Reisch for using the *Gesellschaft* for his purposes,[24] possibly as a reaction to rumours that Spann was up to establishing an 'Aryan Economic Association'.[25] Both projects came to nought.

In the event, the *NOeG* was revived successfully in 1927. Before, in 1926, the Vienna police department had inquired into its fate because the association had failed for many years to provide information on its activities (assemblies, elections and so on), yet Mises was able to console the officers. Preparations for a new start began in April 1927[26] in order to find a forum for discussion for the two strands of Austrian economics represented by Mayer and Mises and their respective followers, and at the same time to get rid of Spann and his pupils.[27]

On 16 December 1927, eventually a general assembly was convened and members of the board elected. The board consisted of Mayer (president), Mises (vice-president), Hayek (secretary), Machlup (treasurer), and Richard Strigl[28] and Rosenstein-Rodan as ordinary members.[29] This was followed, on the same day, by the first paper presented to the revived association by Mises. Morgenstern reported:[30]

> On Friday there was the first session of the *Nationalökonomische Gesellschaft* in the *Café Landtmann* .... Mayer even arrived on time. Mises's paper was long, bad and loquacious, as such not a good start .... Then a dispute between him [Mises] and Mayer evolved, in which Mayer proved a skilled and dangerous debater.

Apart from revealing Morgenstern's prejudices, his account set the tone for things to come: often the discussions in the *NOeG* were to become both exciting and bad-tempered.

1927–1938: YEARS OF HIGH THEORY?

Although there is some justification for Mises' assertion (in his *Recollections*) that in the years to come the *NOeG* was dominated by members of the Mises circle, like for example Haberler, Hayek and Machlup, at the outset the board and the membership of the *NOeG* were finely balanced between Mayer and Mises. For example, the sessions were chaired by Mayer and Mises, and occasionally also by Reisch and Schüller,[31] and although for example Hayek with regard to his scientific affinities was closer to Mises than Mayer, he like other young Austrians – Haberler or Morgenstern – ultimately depended on Mayer's backing for his academic career.[32]

However, in the 1930s the composition of the board and the balance between Mayer and Mises shifted towards the former, mainly due to emigration. This can be ascertained by looking at the elections to the board in the 1930s. In 1932 four ordinary members were added to the board: Haberler, Morgenstern, Karl Schlesinger and Strigl. In 1933, when Hayek's professorship at the LSE had become definitive, he gave up the position of secretary for that of ordinary member; he was replaced by Machlup, and Machlup as treasurer by Morgenstern. In 1934 Ewald Schams and Victor Bloch were elected to the board, while in 1935 Machlup's departure for the United States necessitated another change, Morgenstern was elevated to the position of secretary and Bloch of treasurer. In 1936 Mayer's assistant Alexander Mahr was included among the members as was Reinhard Kamitz in January 1938, when Haberler left. So just before the *Anschluss* the board consisted of Mayer, Mises (who had remained vice-president all the time despite his leave for Geneva in 1934), Morgenstern, Bloch, Kamitz, Mahr, Schams, Schlesinger and Strigl.[33]

Unfortunately, apart from the composition of the board, little is known about other aspects of the association, for example the existing documents do not include membership lists and there is almost no evidence on the finances of the association: One might speculate that part of the costs has been borne by Mayer's economics department or by the Chamber of Commerce; in any case, the funds provided for the *Zeitschrift* were not directly available for covering the *NOeG*'s expenses.

In effect, the *NOeG* as an association was able to fulfil some useful functions that complemented the existing circles: It offered a broader audience in contrast to that of the circles, which were more strictly limited in number, and therefore bridged the gap between circles with otherwise little overlap in membership. Furthermore by representing a more formal contact than private circles could have provided it facilitated the invitation of visitors from abroad and thereby made its members familiar with important ideas from outside the Austrian school.

The most important activity of the *NOeG*, however, consisted in organising sessions where members or guests, from Austria and from abroad, were invited to present their papers. As regards the time and place of these presentations, although not strictly fixed, they usually took place on Friday, and the first sessions were held unceremoniously in the basement of a coffeehouse near the University (the *Café Landtmann*), yet in mid-1928 relocated to a room provided free of charge by the Austrian Banking Association.[34] The papers to be presented were apparently expected to be more than merely work in progress but to have reached a rather definitive stage. Many of them subsequently were published in the *Zeitschrift*, some also in other journals. Notably, the association – in contrast to its individual members – had no ambition to enter into public debates on topics of economic policy. Although at times papers on economic policy were presented, their impact did not transgress the limits of scientific discussion and virtually none of them left a mark in the ongoing controversies, for example in the Austrian newspapers.

Ideally, one might be able to supplement the early history of the *NOeG* by a complete list of the sessions and the papers presented. Unfortunately, this is not possible due to the lack of any documentation by the *NOeG* itself. In contrast, a variety of other sources must be utilised. These are, first, the references to the papers ultimately published in the *Zeitschrift* or elsewhere; second, the reports of contemporaries, like Morgenstern, Rosenstein, or Haberler, preserved in correspondence or (in Morgenstern's case) in a diary;[35] and third, the scattered hints in the recollections and autobiographical material left by the actors themselves and in the secondary literature. This attempt is further complicated by the fact that the sheer number of circles present in interwar Vienna makes it difficult to identify in retrospect on which specific occasion a paper had been presented. Taking all these caveats into account, the following tries to provide a picture of the activities of the *NOeG* as accurate and complete as possible. (For a list of papers see the appendix.)

Doing some statistics, of the 56 presentations of which we know 22 were published henceforth, the vast majority (15) in the Viennese *Zeitschrift*, two in *Weltwirtschaftliches Archiv* and one in *Archiv für Sozialwissenschaft und Sozialpolitik*, *Zeitschrift für die gesamte Staatswissenschaft* and in the *Economic Journal*, respectively; two appeared as separate booklets. Turning to the presenters, among the Austrians the list is led by Hayek (with eight papers), whose activities extended well into the period when he taught at LSE, Morgenstern and Mises (4), Rosenstein-Rodan (3), the mathematician Karl Menger, Haberler, Felix Kaufmann, Machlup and Strigl (2) and

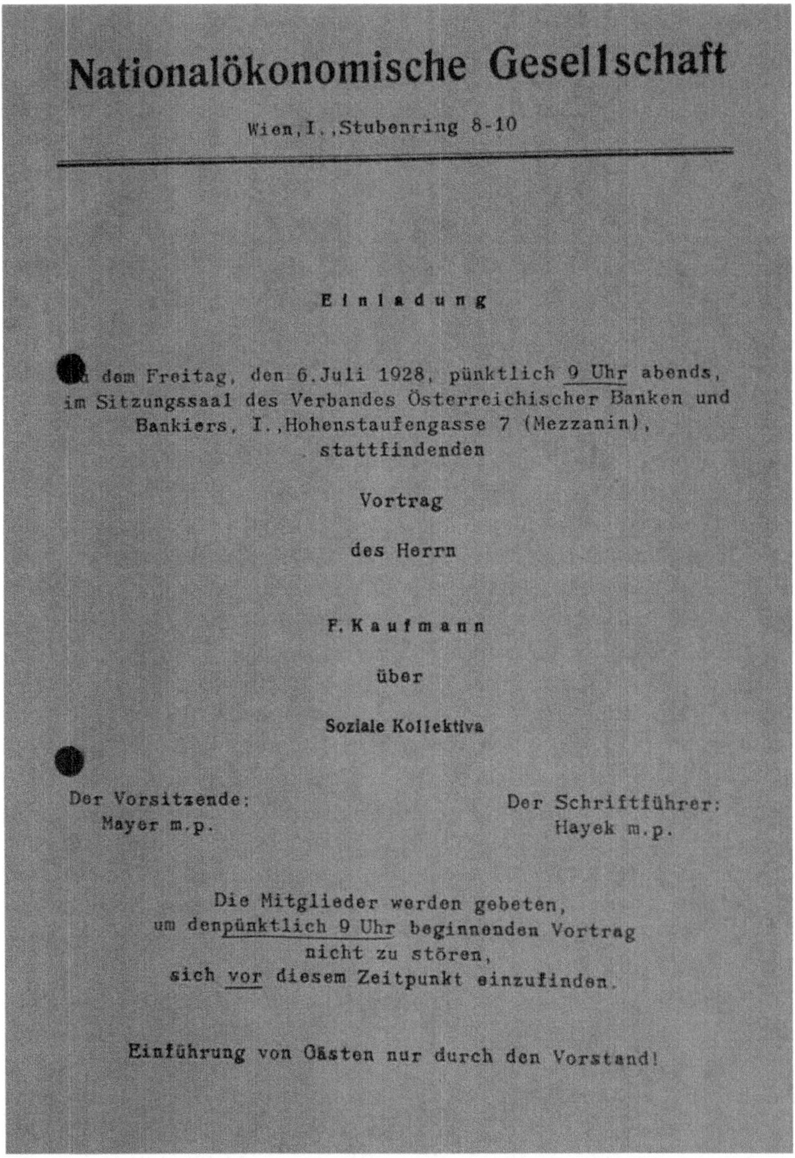

Nationalökonomische Gesellschaft

Wien, I., Stubenring 8-10

E i n l a d u n g

zu dem Freitag, den 6. Juli 1928, pünktlich 9 Uhr abends, im Sitzungssaal des Verbandes Österreichischer Banken und Bankiers, I., Hohenstaufengasse 7 (Mezzanin), stattfindenden

Vortrag

des Herrn

F. K a u f m a n n

über

Soziale Kollektiva

Der Vorsitzende:
Mayer m.p.

Der Schriftführer:
Hayek m.p.

Die Mitglieder werden gebeten,
um denpünktlich 9 Uhr beginnenden Vortrag
nicht zu stören,
sich vor diesem Zeitpunkt einzufinden.

Einführung von Gästen nur durch den Vorstand!

Fig. 1. Invitation to the July 6 1928 Session of the *NOeG*.
Source: OMP, correspondence *NOeG*.

one paper presented by Mahr, Karl Polanyi, Karl Pribram, Schlesinger and Gerhard Tintner. From Germany the most active speaker was Wilhelm Röpke (with four papers), others who presented one paper were Siegfried Budge, Adolph Löwe, Fritz Neumark, Otto Veit and Wilhelm Vleugels.[36] Other European countries were represented by Adam Heydel (of Krakow, Poland), the Dutchman Johan Koopmans, and from the German-speaking parts of the former Empire, Oskar Engländer (Prague) and Alexander Bilimovic (Laibach). The only British speaker was Lionel Robbins, while visitors from the United States included Frank Knight, Jacob Viner, Howard Ellis and Edward S. Mason. In their reminiscences some of the participants recall the presence of additional visitors from abroad:[37] For example Mayer (1952, p. 251) also refers to Laurits V. Birck, Oskar Lange, Redvers Opie and C. A. Verrijn Stuart;[38] Furth (1989) adds Alan Sweezy and Hugh Gaitskell;[39] and drawing on interviews Craver (1986, p. 18) includes Joan Robinson and Umberto Ricci.[40]

For reasons of space it is not feasible to discuss all the papers presented separately, nor is it easy to select the most important ones from this highly competitive field. Choosing those papers most likely still known to present-day economists, one might start with the two contributions by Karl Menger, which due to their thoroughly formal character must be regarded as 'outliers' in this series. In the first paper Menger (1934, 1935) dealt with the paradox that arises from applying the notion of expected utility to the famous St. Petersburg game. According to Menger (1979, p. 259f.), the paper had already been written in 1923, presented to the *NOeG* in 1927 (so it must have been the second paper after its revival, in December), but submitted to the *Zeitschrift* only years later at Morgenstern's behest, because Mayer had advised against publishing the talk. The second paper on the laws of return, presented in December 1935 and published the following year (Menger, 1936a, 1936b), drew on Mises' claim, allegedly put forward in his *Grundprobleme* (Mises, 1933, p. 2 and 145f.), that the principle of diminishing returns could be proved by means of pure logic, that is, a priori. Menger refuted this thesis, yet apparently without shaking Mises's belief into apriorism. Another deservedly famous paper that resulted from a presentation at the *NOeG* was Viner's 'Cost curves and supply curves' (1931), which for the first time examined algebraically and graphically the relationship between short-run and long-run cost curves. Famously, he had given a student the impossible task of drawing the figures such that the envelope of the U-shaped short-run average cost curves should run through their minima (Viner, 1950). Of the Austrian contributions one might point to papers on the methodology of the social sciences by Kaufmann,

Morgenstern's paper on the Pigovian cost controversy, his and Rosenstein-Rodan's attempts at integrating time into the economic theory of equilibrium, Haberler's on international economics, and finally to Hayek's papers on intertemporal equilibrium and on economics and knowledge.[41] Notably, Hans Mayer, the association's president, did not present a single paper.

Finally, the available sources may provide some insights into the evolution of the *NOeG* sessions throughout the 1930s, for example on the general climate of the debates, specific tensions among its members and the evolving participation of prominent economists from abroad. For this we have mostly to draw on Morgenstern's notes. From the beginning he noticed the recurring tensions in the debates between Mayer and Mises and, as time went by, the bad temper that Mayer all too often exhibited in the discussions, especially when he felt his own contributions insufficiently recognised. A typical example is provided by the description given by Herbert Fürth in a letter to Haberler:[42]

> Mayer was classical: he spoke for half an hour about Strigl's sacrilege, who although he had praised his [Mayer's] article on imputation, had not praised it sufficiently; and he believed that this could only be explained by the fact that Strigl had not read the article at all because it was not a thick book, although it contained more effort and knowledge than others' books.

Morgenstern also regularly complained about the lack of understanding of most of the participants as soon as 'exact theory' or formal mathematical reasoning was concerned, as demonstrated in particular towards the presentations by Karl Menger.[43]

The extent to which Mises' statement that after he himself had left Vienna for Geneva in 1934 the *NOeG* 'slowly began to die' (Mises, 1978, p. 99) is correct, cannot be ascertained for sure because of the paucity of sources for this period. However, observers at home and abroad appear to confirm his view: Hayek in two letters of 1935/1936 spoke about the 'decay of Viennese economics' and Ilse Mintz-Schüller, a member of the Mises circle, regretted at the end of 1934 that the *NOeG* had ceased to organise presentations.[44] In fact, after 1934 it was not only the absence of Mises, besides Mayer the crucial person at the top, that made itself felt badly, but also the emigration of leading figures of the younger generation. Furthermore, another important figure in the Austrian economics community, Oskar Morgenstern, apparently lost interest in the *NOeG*, being more concerned both with the research within his own Institute and with his participation in other circles, for example Schlick's and Menger's. In this regard, the members of the Austrian school remaining in Vienna, Strigl, Schönfeld or Schams, were only imperfect substitutes for those who had left. In addition, one might conjecture that after 1934, with the civil war of February and the ensuing proclamation of the corporate state, the ties with English-speaking economists loosened, especially of course with those leaning to the left.[45] All this may have contributed to a decline in the number and the quality of sessions, and to their more parochial nature.

AFTER THE *ANSCHLUSS*, 1938–1945

The occupation of Austria by Nazi Germany (the *Anschluss*) effected on 13 March 1938 gave rise to the persecution of all persons considered as 'enemies of the movement' by the NS and to the *Gleichschaltung* (forcible coordination) of all governmental or civil organisations. The way that Mayer and the *NOeG* reacted to this challenge made them infamous.[46]

According to the files, on 18 March 1938 the (non-Jewish) members of the board present in Vienna met and resolved that all members of Jewish descent should be excluded from the association. The next day the *Vereinsbüro* was notified by a letter signed by Kamitz, and Mayer sent the following notice to the members of the *NOeG*:[47]

> In consideration of the changed situation in German Austria I am informing you that under the respective laws now applicable also to this state, all non-Aryan members are leaving the *NOeG*.

As noted, at the time the board had consisted of Mayer, Mises, Morgenstern, Bloch, Kamitz, Mahr, Schams, Schlesinger and Strigl. Morgenstern was not present in Vienna but just spent his time as a visiting professor in the United States. Of the Jewish members, Mises was in Geneva, Bloch was still living in Vienna (he fled to London in 1939), and Schlesinger had committed suicide, in Vienna, on March 12, the day of the invasion.[48]

As regards the Viennese *Zeitschrift* so closely affiliated with the *NOeG*, Mayer soon brought it into line with the new regime: He greeted the new rulers in an editorial (Mayer, 1938), ousted the now unwelcome co-editors Reisch and Schüller and replaced the managing editor Morgenstern by Mahr. After 1939 the journal appeared only on a limited scale and the changes effected by Mayer meant a loss of reputation that weighed heavily on the journal well into the time after the war.

In retrospect, Mayer defended his actions as the only means to sustain those valuable institutions of the Austrian economics community (the *NOeG* and the *Zeitschrift*) in the face of the danger of abolition by the Nazis, as threatened by the *Stillhaltekommissar* Albert Hoffmann (Mayer, 1952, p. 252):[49]

> The liquidation of the *NOeG* would have meant the loss, perhaps never to be made up for, of an institution with a well-known scientific tradition that had an important role to play just in those times when all science was to be politicized.

What is true, however, is that the forcible coordination of the existing associations in Austria was a long drawn out process, directed by a specific office, the *Stillhaltekommissar*. The standard prescriptions for the reconstruction under the new German law requested the inclusion of an 'Arierparagraph', that is, a paragraph that excluded non-Aryans from membership, and the adaptation of the decision process to the *Führer* principle. The *NOeG* adjusted its bylaws accordingly in July 1940, and the NS office accepted them within one day's notice and approved the reconstruction of the *NOeG*. Mayer's pre-emptive behaviour in 1938 is thus to be explained most probably as an attempt to appease the new regime. Indeed, he could as well have followed the example of the *Gesellschaft österreichischer Volkswirte*, which under its vice-president Ernst Mosing, the successor of Reisch,[50] was liquidated and deleted from the *Vereinsregister*.[51]

Having formally secured the continuing existence of the *NOeG*, apparently under Mayer's presidency it did not display any activities in the following years. In fact, in August 1944 the office in charge inquired whether the *NOeG* would still exist at all. Yet, there had been a general assembly in December 1943 that confirmed a new composition of the board: It now was made up of Mayer (president), Adolf Günther (vice-president), who had succeeded Othmar Spann at the economics chair of the University of Vienna in 1939, Mahr (secretary), Josef Sznahovich (deputy secretary),[52] Kamitz (treasurer), Wilhelm Weber (deputy treasurer)[53] and Felix Klezl-Norberg (auditor).[54] In his notification Mayer hastened to indicate the political affiliations of the members. So he added 'Parteigenosse' (member of the NSDAP) to the names of Günther, Kamitz and Weber, and characterised himself in parentheses as 'political attitude: national socialist'. In September 1944 there was a final change in the board: Somewhat cryptically Mayer announced that the then acting director of the *NOeG*, Alexander Mahr, due to professional strain had been replaced by Rudolf Starke, member of the board of the Julius Meinl AG (and 'Parteigenosse').

Beyond these formalities there is no indication that the *NOeG* did any substantial business during the NS period.

THE RESTORATION AFTER 1945

With the end of the NS regime, the situation of economics within the law faculty at the University of Vienna was almost restored to that before 1938:[55] the professors appointed after the *Anschluss* were dismissed, Degenfeld-Schonburg, who had been retired, was reinstated, Spann – in a curious compromise – again became a member of the faculty but was barred from teaching, and of course Mayer kept his chair. Although as shown above with regard to the *NOeG* and the *Zeitschrift*, and in addition on some other occasions, he had proved his ability to adapt to the new rulers somewhat excessively, after 1945 he managed to present himself as a victim of the regime and also played some role in the denazification of the Austrian universities. 1946/1947 he was elected dean of the law faculty. After the faculty had granted him the permission to keep the chair for one additional year (*Ehrenjahr*), he retired in 1950 and continued to lecture for some more years as honorary professor. Moreover, in 1951, he had succeeded in pushing the appointment of his hand-picked successor, Alexander Mahr.

After 1945, the *NOeG* was kept dormant for a few years, and it took until January 1949 that Mayer – again responding to an official inquiry if the association still existed – initiated its reconstruction. (Already earlier the *Gesellschaft österreichischer Volkswirte* had been revived when its liquidation was officially annulled in 1946; in November 1945, a provisional board of the *Gesellschaft* had been constituted with Mosing, Mayer [!], Degenfeld and the statistician Wilhelm Winkler[56] as its members.) With regard to the *NOeG* in a meeting of the general assembly, held on 20 January 1949, the old bylaws were reinstated and a new board was elected. The enlarged board now consisted of Mayer (president), Mosing (first vice-president), Mahr (second vice-president), Weber (secretary), Leo Illy (formerly: Schönfeld, treasurer) and the ordinary members Ernst John, Klezl-Norberg, Ernst Lagler and Schams. The next day Mayer sent a letter to the relevant office of the police department (*Sicherheitsdirektion*), in which he applied for the reconstruction of the *NOeG* and – somewhat ambiguously – maintained that it had been 'suspended' during the war; the motion was granted within a month. In the next years the board was still more enlarged by including in 1949 Hans Bayer, Degenfeld-Schonburg, Kamitz, Richard Kerschagl and Wilhelm Taucher[57] – signifying that the outreach of the association be broadened beyond the University of Vienna. Degenfeld deceased in 1952 and Illy in 1953, he was replaced at the board by Karl Heinz Werner.[58] Finally in 1954 Weber, who embarked on a Rockefeller Fellowship, was replaced as treasurer by Josef Sznahovich and Theodor Pütz[59] was appointed to the board. Beyond these formalities it might be conjectured that due to lack of financial means the *NOeG*'s scientific output must have been rather restricted. As far as this can be surmised from the available evidence, presentations of papers at the *NOeG* started only in 1954, yet at a slower pace than before the war.

As regards the *Zeitschrift*, its publication had almost petered out during the war, with only five issues from 1941 to 1944, and it stopped appearing for a few years after 1945. With Hans Mayer still the main editor the first post-war issue came out in 1948, but for the following years the *Zeitschrift* could not regain its former stature, both in quality and quantity, and contained more special than regular issues. In 1952 and 1955 the *Zeitschrift* printed the proceedings of two conferences organised by the International Economic Association, apparently thanks to the support of Helene Lieser, a member both of the *NOeG* and formerly of the Mises seminar and now at the IEA.[60] On the occasion of Mayer's 70th and 75th birthday, respectively, two *Festschriften* were published as issues of the *Zeitschrift*.[61] In 1953 a new editorial board had been installed, still chaired by Mayer and including as members, besides his successor at the University of Vienna, Mahr, Luigi Einaudi (Rome), Jean Marchal (Paris), Valentin Wagner (Basle) and Otto von Zwiedineck-Südenhorst (Munich); the position of managing editor was filled by Werner.

We conclude our investigation with Mayer's death in 1955. In its aftermath a general assembly of the *NOeG* was convened not only to seek a successor for Mayer but also for an important restructuring of the Austrian economic societies. As resolved in a joint session the *Gesellschaft* was dissolved and then its members incorporated into the *NOeG*, whose full name was amended to 'Nationalökonomische Gesellschaft (Gesellschaft östereichischer Volkswirte)'. The new and once more enlarged board comprehended both members of the *NOeG* and the former *Gesellschaft*. Mahr was elected president, following the deceased Mayer; the other members were Mosing and Pütz (vice-presidents), Peter Meihsl (secretary), Sznahovich (treasurer), Bayer, John, Kamitz, Kerschagl, Klezl-Norberg, Lagler, Slawtscho Sagoroff, Taucher, Weber and Wilhelm Zeller.[62] In the *Zeitschrift* Mahr succeeded Mayer as the main editor and he co-opted

Haberler and Morgenstern into the editorial board. When Werner left the University, he was replaced as managing editor by Weber and Sznahovich. In the years that followed Mahr struggled to return to a regular schedule,[63] to attract prominent economists as authors and to fill the journal with articles of more than local interest, but in sum failed in his endeavour to bring the *Zeitschrift* back to its glorious pre-war era.

After Mahr's death in 1972 he was succeeded both in the *NOeG* and in the *Zeitschrift* by Weber.[64] Of the activities of the *NOeG* in these three decades of the post-war period little of scientific substance has been preserved, on the one hand for lack of evidence and on the other hand, one might speculate, for lack of any activities remotely comparable to those of the interwar years.

CONCLUDING REMARKS

Summing up the early history of the Austrian Economic Association, it is evident that its evolution − also due to the contemporary economic and political events it had to cope with − was rather in fits and starts, stretching over widely different phases. Yet, its success was also to a large degree dependent on the persons on the top of the association, for better or worse.

The beginning of the *NOeG* may be likened to a flake in the pan, when a bunch of 'young turks' in the Austrian economics community, most of them only recently appointed to a chair and representing widely differing approaches, opted for a new institution for eliciting discussion. Apparently, its distinguishing feature should have consisted in its focus on theoretical economics and its smaller and (compared with the existing *Gesellschaft*) younger audience. However, this attempt rapidly failed, probably not only due to external circumstances (post-war poverty, inflation, the dispersion of the community), but also because of internal tensions.

When the three-pronged conflict within the Viennese economics community, between the 'prima donnas' Mayer, Mises and Spann, had reached a crucial phase in the 1920s, it turned out that Mayer and Mises − perhaps driven by those young Austrian economists who were in need of good relations with both the academic and the extramural leaders of the school − were able to join forces in reviving the *NOeG*. Although tensions between Mayer and Mises never ceased, the next years, judged by the quality of the papers presented, must be considered

the most prosperous phase in its existence. Not only was it characterised
by a lively debate within the community, with numerous contributions to
what then appeared as the cutting-edge of scientific progress – for example incorporating time and uncertainty into the theory of equilibrium,
but also frequent visits by eminent economists from abroad, like Knight,
Viner and Robbins.

Yet, in the course of the 1930s observers noticed signs of decline. After
1934 the combined effects of the emigration of the younger generation of
the Austrian school, the alienation of Morgenstern and the loosening ties
to visitors from English-speaking countries may have contributed to the
diminished role played by the *NOeG*. At last, the personal character of
Hans Mayer, his excessive self-esteem as a theorist and extreme sensitivity
to criticism, made him not the first choice for chairing sessions or otherwise
leading such an association. So, if history had not intervened, the activities
of the *NOeG* perhaps might have, once more, slowly petered out.

However, the events of the *Anschluss* put the *NOeG* to a crucial test.
Those responsible, primarily Mayer, opted to adapt the activities of the
NOeG to the NS system, which in a first and, as it appears, pre-emptive
step meant the exclusion of its Jewish members. Afterwards, having secured
the formal survival of the association, apparently Mayer just embarked on
a strategy of 'muddling through'. During the rule of the NS the *NOeG* did
not display any discernable activities, scientific or otherwise. Yet, whatever
Mayer's motives,[65] in the eyes of the emigrants and former friends (like
e.g. Robbins) his reputation and that of 'his' association was forever
tarnished.

Presently, we lack the documents to fully appreciate the evolution of the
NOeG in the decades after the war. In any case, it took Mayer a long time
both to get the *Zeitschrift* and the *NOeG* going again. Both the membership of the *NOeG* and the authorship of the journal became still more local,
mostly consisting of the dignitaries of the Austrian economics community,
supplemented by one or the other contributors from abroad (but almost
none from English-speaking countries). This did not change much under
Mayer's successor Alexander Mahr. It is no coincidence that a repatriated
emigrant like the Austrian economist Josef Steindl remembered this period
as that when the teaching of economics in Austria had 'reached its lowest
point' (Steindl, 1988, p. 401).

In any case, as becomes not only evident from a glance at the list of
papers in the appendix, as regards the history of the *NOeG* (and also other
Viennese economic circles) there are still gaps to be filled by future
research.

NOTES

1. In fact, informal circles and associations formally constituted under Austrian law often merged one into the other. For example, in the 1920s out of the informal 'Schlick Circle' evolved an association, the 'Verein Ernst Mach'.

2. The literature on the Vienna circles, even if restricted to economics, is not even remotely comprehensible. See for example most recently Craver (2012), Dekker (2014) and Wright (2015), and the retrospectives from Engel-Janosi (1974), Browne (1981), Haberler (1981) or Furth (1989).

3. In addition see Robbins (1971) and Menger (1994). On the unreliability of memory in this regard see Caldwell (2007).

4. Mises' biographer Hülsmann (2007, p. 364) speaks of 'a student circle'.

5. Karl Pribram (1877–1973), acquired a lectureship (*Habilitation*) at the University of Vienna in 1907 and was appointed extraordinary professor in 1914; his posthumously published *magnum opus* is Pribram (1983). Emil Perels (1880–1944) had studied in Vienna and participated in the Böhm-Bawerk seminar; after WWI he became the predecessor of Mises as the director of the *Abrechnungsamt*, the very office, where Hayek after his doctorate was to find his first employment. Else Cronbach (1879–1913) studied in Vienna, but acquired her doctorate of *Staatswissenschaften* in Berlin (as then women were not admitted to a comparable degree in Austria).

6. Note that although the term is sometimes used in the literature (and also by Hayek, undated, p. 45), there is no clear description of the nature or the members of a 'Mayer circle'.

7. See, for example Müller (1993, p. 158), Leube (1998, p. 308f.), Hennecke (2000, p. 75), Feichtinger (2001, p. 187f.), Leonard (2010, p. 107f., 2011, p. 87f.) or Schulak and Unterköfler (2011, p. 108ff.), Hülsmann (2007) follows Mises' recollections but adds information from materials in the Mises Archive.

8. On the following see Patzauer (1915) and Plener (1915), various issues of the *Mitgliederverzeichnis und Bericht über die Generalversammlung der Gesellschaft österreichischer Volkswirte* and the files preserved at the *Wiener Stadt- und Landesarchiv* ('Vereinsakt, Gesellschaft österreichischer Volkswirte').

9. The co-author of Auspitz and Lieben (1889); see Mises (1919).

10. Reisch and Schüller were students of Carl Menger (Hayek, 1934, p. 405, 1992a, p. 77), Reisch (1866–1938), lecturer for financial law and economics and 1922–1932 President of the Austrian central bank, Schüller (1870–1972), senior official at the Austrian Ministry of Trade and honorary professor of economics.

11. See on this Klausinger (2015b).

12. The following draws on the files preserved at the *Vereinsbehörde, Landespolizeidirektion Wien* ('Vereinsakt, Nationalökonomische Gesellschaft').

13. Moritz Dub (1865–1927) was an economic journalist of the leading Viennese daily, *Neue Freie Presse* (see Mises, 1927); the industrialist Victor Grätz (1877–1939, London) was later to become a member of the Mises seminar.

14. Letter, Schumpeter to Mises, 9 December 1918, Mises Archive 51: 130f. (Hülsmann, 2007, p. 362n.).

15. See Hülsmann (2007, pp. 373–379) and letter, Mises to Lederer, 14 January, 1920, Mises Archive 73: 52ff. (quoted in Hülsmann, 2007, p. 378n.).

16. However, Hayek remembers to have visited some sessions of the *NOeG* when he studied in Vienna, at the most until 1923 (Hayek, undated, p. 44).

17. For example, at the time of the foundation Spann, Mises and Mayer had been members of the Scientific Committee for the War Economy at the Austrian-Hungarian ('k.u.k.') War Ministry (Pinwinkler, 2003, pp. 84–89).

18. On the redeployment of these chairs see Klausinger (2015b).

19. This is Hayek's explanation, see above.

20. This is Mises's explanation, see above.

21. John van Sickle, of the Rockefeller Foundation, aptly labelled them 'the prima donnas' (Leonard, 2010, p. 79).

22. On the *Zeitschrift für Nationalökonomie* in the interwar period see Rothschild (2004) and, with some inaccuracies, Corneo (2005). The following is based on documents of the *Springer Archiv*, as summarised in Klausinger (2015a, pp. 285–287).

23. In 1929 subsidies were provided by the Ministry of Education, the Chamber of Commerce, the Austrian Banking Association and the Austrian National Bank.

24. See Morgenstern's diary (=OM-D), 26 December 1924, in Oskar Morgenstern Papers, box 12 (=OMP 12).

25. See OM-D, 18 December 1924 and 13 January 1925, OMP 12.

26. See letter, Haberler to Morgenstern, 6 April 1927, OMP 2: 'Mayer and Mises are going to revive the economics association'.

27. Ferdinand Degenfeld-Schonburg, newly appointed to the third economics chair at the University of Vienna in October 1927, was also sidelined by Mayer and Mises and never played a role in the *NOeG*.

28. Richard Strigl (1891–1942) worked at the Vienna Labour Office, taught at the University of Vienna and later at the Vienna *Hochschule für Welthandel*. He also cooperated with Morgenstern at the Institute (Hayek, 1944).

29. Although Hayek was elected secretary, from the available evidence the special role that he assigned to himself in his recollections cannot be confirmed.

30. See OM-D, 18 December 1927, OMP 12.

31. On chairing the sessions see OM-D, 8 March 1930, OMP 13.

32. In particular, with regard to their habilitations at the University of Vienna, Haberler in 1927, Morgenstern in 1928/1929 and Hayek in 1929 see Klausinger (2012).

33. Karl Schlesinger (1889–1938) was an industrialist and a participant in the Vienna economic and mathematical circles, his role in furthering a mathematical approach to general equilibrium analysis has been highlighted by Weintraub (1985, pp. 64–69); Ewald Schams (1899–1955) worked as a civil servant, he was an outsider among the Austrians in his leaning towards mathematical economics (Hayek, 1992b); Victor Bloch (1883–1968) was a banker and a member of the Mises seminar; Reinhard Kamitz (1907–1993) in 1938 acted as the deputy director of Morgenstern's Institute of Business Cycle Research – in the Second Republic of Austria he served as Minister of Finance 1952–1960 and President of the Austrian National Bank 1960–1968.

34. On the location see Furth (1989, p. 251) and OM-D, 22 June 1928, OMP 12. See also the announcement of the session of July 28, 1928, with Kaufmann speaking, reproduced in Fig. 1.

35. Unfortunately, the evidence becomes thinner over time, as apparently Morgenstern – our prime witness – got increasingly less interested in these sessions (there is also a large gap in his diary from summer 1933 to the end of 1934), and as many participants had left Vienna, for example Haberler, Hayek, Machlup and Rosenstein.

36. According to Hülsmann (2007, p. 613f.) in December 1931 Mises invited the German economist Charlotte von Reichenau (misspelled "Reichmann" by Hülsmann) to a talk at the *NOeG*, which she accepted. It is, however, not in the records.

37. Vienna at the time was an attractive destination for economists from abroad and conversely Austrian economists regularly visited British and American universities. For example, Fleck (2015, pp. 147–149) in a study of the fellowships awarded to social scientists by the Rockefeller Foundation finds that in the interwar period 25 fellows from Vienna studied abroad while 19 fellows – among them eight economists – from foreign countries visited Austrian universities.

38. Most of whom placed contributions in the *Zeitschrift*, see Birck (1929), Lange (1932), Opie (1935), Verrijn Stuart (1932) and Vleugels (1929).

39. See Sweezy (1934); according to Mises (Hülsmann, 2007, p. 675n.) Gaitskell when in Vienna had worked on a translation of Böhm-Bawerk's capital theory, and he also pursued this issue later on, see Gaitskell (1936, 1938).

40. See Robinson (1936) and, for example, Ricci (1929).

41. See, for example, Kaufmann (1929, 1931), Morgenstern (1928, 1931, 1934), Rosenstein-Rodan (1929), Haberler (1930a, 1930b), and Hayek (1928) for published papers. Hayek's presentation of September 1935 could be a predecessor of Hayek (1937), which he presented in London 1936.

42. Letter, Fürth to Haberler, 14 March 1936, Gottfried Haberler Papers, box 67 (= GHP 67).

43. See for example OM-D, 31 December 1935, OMP 13. On Mayer's and Mises' hostility towards the use of mathematics see Leonard (2004).

44. See letters, Hayek to Machlup, January 1935, Fritz Machlup Papers, box 43 (= FMP 43), Hayek to Haberler, 3 June 1936, GHP 67, and Ilse Mintz-Schüller's note in a letter, Max Mintz to Machlup, 9 December 1934, FMP 53.

45. Hugh Gaitskell, the future leader of the Labour Party, who had been an eyewitness to civil war in Vienna, might be a case in point.

46. See, for example Robbins (1971, p. 91), whose 'love affair with Vienna, its setting and its culture ... [was] only terminated on the morrow of Anschluss when, to his eternal shame, Hans Mayer, the senior Professor of Economics in the University of Menger, Wieser, and Böhm-Bawerk, whom I myself had more than once heard denouncing Hitler and all his works, instead of closing it down as he could honourably have done, expelled the Jewish members from the famous *Nationalökonomische Gesellschaft* of which he was President'. By the way, it was not only Robbins, but most of the emigrated Austrians who after Mayer's behaviour under the NS regime considered the relationship with him as irrevocably destroyed.

47. As quoted in Mises (1978, p. 99).

48. From the documents, at the crucial meeting only the presence of Mayer, the president, and Kamitz, the secretary, can be taken for certain.

49. Furthermore, Mayer, rather disingenuously, argued that the ejection of the non-Aryan members had not done much harm to them because most had already left the country (*ibid.*, p. 251f.).

50. Reisch had resigned for health reasons in 1937, he died in 1938. Ernst Mosing (1882–1959), was a banker and industrialist.

51. Unfortunately, in the relevant archive holdings (*Österreichisches Staatsarchiv, Archiv der Republik*, Gruppe 04b, 'Stiko'), unlike those of the Austrian Institute for Business Cycle Research, neither the files for the *NOeG* nor for the *Gesellschaft* have been preserved.

52. There is no archival evidence on Josef Sznahovich's affiliation with Mayer and the University of Vienna, except that his dissertation, supervised by Mayer and Degenfeld, contains a eulogy on Mayer as the founder of modern (Austrian) economics (Sznahovich, 1950, 2n.).

53. Wilhelm Weber (1916–2005) started working as assistant for Mayer (and later on for Mahr) in 1939 until 1957, interrupted by his service in the army, 1940–1944. After his habilitation in 1950 he was to become extraordinary professor for economics and public finance in 1957 and full professor in 1963.

54. Felix Klezl-Norberg (1885–1972) worked at the Austrian Statistical Office (as vice-president since 1936) and taught at the University of Vienna.

55. For more details see Klausinger (2015a, pp. 295–298).

56. Wilhelm Winkler (1884–1984) worked at the Austrian Statistical Office until 1938 and taught as professor of statistics at the University of Vienna from 1929 until 1955 (interrupted by his forced retirement between 1938 and 1945); Winkler and Klezl-Norberg (see above) were rivals in both institutions (Pinwinkler, 2003).

57. Ernst John (1909–1997) had already been on the staff of the Austrian Institute for Business Cycle Research under Morgenstern, and after 1945 became vice-president of its successor, the *Wifo* (*Österreichisches Institut für Wirtschaftsforschung*). Ernst Lagler (1903–1974) had worked before the war as an assistant of Degenfeld and was to become extraordinary professor at the University of Vienna in 1951. At the time Hans Bayer (1903–1965) – another former assistant of Mayer – Richard Kerschagl (1896–1976) and Wilhelm Taucher (1892–1962) occupied economics chairs at the University of Innsbruck, the Vienna *Hochschule für Welthandel* and the University of Graz, respectively.

58. Karl Heinz Werner (*1919) had been Mayer's assistant since 1943 and wrote his habilitation thesis on Mayer's favourite topic, the problem of imputation (Werner, 1950).

59. Theodor Pütz (1905–1994) was Degenfeld's successor at the University of Vienna.

60. See *Zeitschrift* 13 (3), 1952, and 15 (1–2), 1955.

61. See *Zeitschrift* 12 (2–4), 1949, and 14 (2–4), 1954.

62. The new appointees Peter Meihsl, Sławtscho Sagoroff (1898–1970) and Wilhelm Zeller, all at a time worked as statisticians, Meihsl and Zeller (as vice-president) at the Austrian Statistical Office and Sagoroff had been appointed professor of statistics at the University of Vienna in 1954.

63. In 1956 two issues were filled by reprints from its predecessor, the *Zeitschrift für Volkswirtschaft und Sozialpolitik*, and by a register (*Zeitschrift* 15 (3, 4), 1956).

64. Weber's most notable contribution to Austrian economics consisted in organising a memorial conference on Menger's *Grundsätze* in Vienna and his co-editorship of the volume arising from it (Hicks & Weber, 1973).
65. On Mayer's motives see the discussion in Klausinger (2015a).

ACKNOWLEDGEMENTS

Paper presented at the Meeting of the European Society for the History of Economic Thought (ESHET) in Rome, May 2015, and published in a preliminary version as *WU Department of Economics Working Paper* No. 195. I am grateful to Manfred Nermuth, President of the *NOeG* 2013/14, for his support of this investigation and for making the *Vereins*-files available for research. For many helpful comments I am indebted to two anonymous referees. For the permission to quote I thank the David M. Rubenstein Rare Book and Manuscript Library of Duke University with regard to the papers of Oskar Morgenstern, and Helmuth F. Furth with regard to the correspondence of Gottfried Haberler and J. Herbert Furth. I am also grateful to Jörg Guido Hülsmann for the copy of a letter, Schumpeter to Mises, 9 December 1918, preserved in the Mises Archive — Translations from German sources are by the author.

REFERENCES

American Economic Association. (Ed.). (1952). *Readings in price theory*. Chicago, IL: Irwin.

Auspitz, R., & Lieben, R. (1889). *Untersuchungen über die Theorie des Preises*. Leipzig: Duncker & Humblot. Reprint Düsseldorf: Verlag Wirtschaft und Finanzen 1993.

Bilimovic, A. (1938). Einige Bemerkungen zur Theorie der Planwirtschaft. *Zeitschrift für Nationalökonomie, 9*, 147−166.

Birck, L. V. (1929). Kalkulationen und Preisberechnungsmethoden. *Zeitschrift für Nationalökonomie, 1*, 99−113.

Browne, M. St. (1981). Erinnerungen an das Mises-Privatseminar. *Wirtschaftspolitische Blätter, 28*(4), 110−120.

Caldwell, B. (2007). Life writings: On-the-job training with F. A. Hayek. In E. R. Weintraub & E. L. Forget (Eds.), *Economists' lives: biography and autobiography in the history of economics* (pp. 342−354). London: Duke University Press.

Corneo, G. (2005). Editorial − The journal of economics, 75 years ago and now. *Journal of Economics, 84*, iii−vi.

Craver, E. (1986). The emigration of the Austrian economists. *History of Political Economy, 18*, 1−32.

Craver, E. (2012). How ideas migrate. In H. M. Krämer, H. Kurz, & H.-M. Trautwein (Eds.), *Macroeconomics and the history of economic thought: Festschrift in honour of Harald Hagemann* (pp. 158–164). London: Routledge.

Dekker, E. (2014). The Vienna circles: Cultivating economic knowledge outside academia. *Erasmus Journal for Philosophy and Economics, 7*(2), 30–53.

Ellis, H. S. (1935). Die Bedeutung der Produktionsperiode für die Krisentheorie. *Zeitschrift für Nationalökonomie, 6,* 145–169.

Engel-Janosi, F. (1974). *... aber ein stolzer Bettler: Erinnerungen aus einer verlorenen Generation.* Graz: Styria.

Feichtinger, J. (2001). Wissenschaft zwischen den Kulturen: Österreichische Hochschullehrer in der Emigration 1933–1945. Frankfurt: Campus.

Fleck, C. (2015). Akademische Wanderlust im Wandel. In M. Grandner & T. König (Eds.), *Reichweiten und Außensichten: Die Universität Wien als Schnittstelle wissenschaftlicher Entwicklungen und gesellschaftlicher Umbrüche* (650 Jahre Universität Wien: Aufbruch ins neue Jahrhundert, Vol. 3, pp. 127–151). Göttingen: Vienna University Press.

Furth, J. H. (1989). Erinnerungen an Wiener Tage. *Wirtschaftspolitische Blätter, 36*(2), 247–253.

Gaitskell, H. T. N. (1936). Notes on the period of production – Part I. *Zeitschrift für Nationalökonomie, 7,* 577–595.

Gaitskell, H. T. N. (1938). Notes on the period of production – Part II. *Zeitschrift für Nationalökonomie, 9,* 215–244.

Haberler, G. (1930a). Transfer und Preisbewegung. *Zeitschrift für Nationalökonomie, 1,* 547–554. (English translation, Transfer and price movements, Haberler, 1985, chapter 6.).

Haberler, G. (1930b). Die Theorie der komparativen Kosten und ihre Auswertung für die Begründung des Freihandels. *Weltwirtschaftliches Archiv, 32,* 349–370. (English translation, The theory of comparative costs and its use in the defense of free trade, Haberler, 1985, chapter 1.).

Haberler, G. (1981). Mises's private seminar. *Wirtschaftspolitische Blätter, 28*(4), 121–126.

Haberler, G. (1985). A. Y. C. Koo (Ed.), *Selected essays of Gottfried Haberler.* Cambridge, MA: MIT Press.

Hayek, F. A. (1928). Das intertemporale Gleichgewichtssystem der Preise und die Bewegungen des 'Geldwertes'. *Weltwirtschaftliches Archiv, 28,* 33–76. (English translation, Intertemporal price equilibrium and movements in the value of money, Hayek, 1999, chapter 5).

Hayek, F. A. (1929). *Das Mieterschutzproblem: Nationalökonomische Betrachtungen.* Vienna: Steyrermühl.

Hayek, F. A. (1931). *Prices and Production.* London: Routledge.

Hayek, F. A. (1934). Carl Menger. *Economica,* N. S. 1, 393–420. Revised reprint, Hayek, 1992, 61–96.

Hayek, F. A. (1935a). The maintenance of capital. *Economica,* N. S. 2, 241–276.

Hayek, F. A. (1935b). Preiserwartungen, monetäre Störungen und Fehlinvestitionen. *Nationalökonomisk Tidsskrift, 73,* 176–191. (English translation, Price expectations, monetary disturbances, and malinvestments, Hayek, 1999, chapter 7.).

Hayek, F. A. (Ed.). (1935c). *Collectivist economic planning.* London: Routledge & Sons.

Hayek, F. A. (1937). Economics and knowledge. *Economica, 4,* 33–54.

Hayek, F. A. (1944). Richard von Strigl. *Economic Journal, 54*, 284–286. Reprinted, Hayek, 1992, 168–170.

Hayek, F. A. (1983). Nobel prize-winning economist. In A. Alchian (Ed.), *Transcript of an interview conducted in 1978 under the auspices of the oral history program.* University Library, UCLA, 1983. Oral History transcript No. 300/224. Department of Special Collections, Charles E. Young Research Library, UCLA.

Hayek, F. A. (1992a). P. G. Klein (Ed.), *The fortunes of liberalism. (The Collected Works of F. A. Hayek*, Vol. 4). Chicago, IL: University of Chicago Press.

Hayek, F. A. (1992b). Ewald Schams (1899–1955). In Hayek, 1992a, 166–168.

Hayek, F. A. (1994). St. Kresge & L. Wenar (Eds.), *Hayek on Hayek: An autobiographical dialogue.* London: Routledge.

Hayek, F. A. (1999). St. Kresge (Ed.), *Good money. Part I: The new world. (The collected works of F. A. Hayek*, Vol. 5). Chicago, IL: University of Chicago Press.

Hayek, F. A. (undated). Inductive base. Material collected for Hayek biography by W. W. Bartley III. (Copyright the Estate of F. A. Hayek).

Hennecke, H.-J. (2000). *Friedrich August von Hayek: Die Tradition der Freiheit.* Düsseldorf: Verlag Wirtschaft und Finanzen.

Heydel, A. (1929). Zur Problematik des Begriffes der Produktivität. *Zeitschrift für Nationalökonomie, 1*, 237–249.

Hicks, J., & Weber, W. (1973). *Carl Menger and the Austrian school of economics.* Oxford: Clarendon Press.

Howson, S. (2011). *Lionel Robbins.* Cambridge: Cambridge University Press.

Hülsmann, J. G. (2007). *Mises: The last knight of liberalism.* Auburn: Ludwig von Mises Institute.

Kaufmann, F. (1929). Soziale Kollektiva. *Zeitschrift für Nationalökonomie, 1*, 294–308.

Kaufmann, F. (1931). Was kann die mathematische Methode in der Nationalökonomie leisten? *Zeitschrift für Nationalökonomie, 2*, 754–779.

Klausinger, H. (2012). The Austrian economists and academic politics in the inter-war period: a preliminary investigation. In H. M. Krämer, H. Kurz, & H.-M. Trautwein (Eds.), *Macroeconomics and the history of economic thought: Festschrift in honour of Harald Hagemann* (pp. 118–130). London: Routledge.

Klausinger, H. (2015a). Hans Mayer, last knight of the Austrian school, Vienna branch. *History of Political Economy, 47*, 271–305.

Klausinger, H. (2015b). Die Krise der Nationalökonomie an der Universität Wien nach 1917. In H.-M. Trautwein (Ed.), *Studien zur Geschichte der ökonomischen Theorie* (pp. 117–175). Berlin: Duncker & Humblot.

Koopmans, J. G. (1933). Zum Problem des Neutralen Geldes. In F. A. Hayek (Ed.), *Beiträge zur Geldtheorie* (pp. 211–359). Vienna: Springer. Reprint 2007.

Lange, O. (1932). Die allgemeine Interdependenz der Wirtschaftsgrößen und die Isolierungsmethode. *Zeitschrift für Nationalökonomie, 4*, 52–78.

Leonard, R. (2004). Between worlds, or an imagined reminiscence by Oskar Morgenstern about equilibrium and mathematics in the 1920's. *Journal of the History of Economic Thought, 26*, 285–310.

Leonard, R. (2010). *Von Neumann, Morgenstern and the creation of game theory: from chess to social science, 1900–1960.* Cambridge, MA: Cambridge University Press.

Leonard, R. (2011). The collapse of interwar Vienna: Oskar Morgenstern's community, 1925–1950. *History of Political Economy, 43*, 83–130.

Leube, K. L. (1998). Über Kontinuitäten und Diskontinuitäten in der österreichischen Schule der Nationalökonomie. In K. Acham, K. W. Nörr, & B. Schefold (Eds.), *Erkenntnisgewinne, Erkenntnisverluste: Kontinuitäten und Diskontinuitäten in den Wirtschafts-, Rechts- und Sozialwissenschaften zwischen den 20er und 50er Jahren* (pp. 301–324). Stuttgart: Steiner.

Löwe, A. (1928). Über den Einfluß monetärer Faktoren auf den Konjunkturzyklus. In K. Diehl (Ed.), *Schriften des Vereins für Sozialpolitik,* vol. 173, part 2: *Beiträge zur Wirtschaftstheorie, Konjunkturforschung und Konjunkturtheorie* (pp. 355–370). Munich: Duncker & Humblot.

Machlup, F. (1931a). *Börsenkredit, Industriekredit und Kapitalbildung.* Vienna: Springer. Reprint 2002. (English translation, Machlup, 1940.)

Machlup, F. (1931b). Begriffliches und Terminologisches zur Kapitalstheorie. *Zeitschrift für Nationalökonomie, 2,* 632–639.

Machlup, F. (1940). *The stock market, credit and capital formation.* London: Hodge.

Mahr, A. (1931). Abstinenztheorie und Lehre von der Minderschätzung der Zukunftsgüter. *Zeitschrift für Nationalökonomie, 2,* 62–74.

Mayer, H. (1938). [Editorial]. *Zeitschrift für Nationalökonomie, 9,* 145–146.

Mayer, H. (1952). Selbstdarstellung. In N. Grass (Ed.), *Österreichische Rechts- und Staatswissenschaften der Gegenwart in Selbstdarstellungen* (pp. 233–272). Innsbruck: Wagner.

Menger, K. (1934). Das Unsicherheitsmoment in der Wertlehre. *Zeitschrift für Nationalökonomie, 5,* 459–485. (English translation, Menger, 1967.)

Menger, K. (1935). Bemerkungen zu meinem Aufsatz "Das Unsicherheitsmoment in der Wertlehre". *Zeitschrift für Nationalökonomie, 6,* 283–285.

Menger, K. (1936a). Bemerkungen zu den Ertragsgesetzen. *Zeitschrift für Nationalökonomie, 7,* 25–56. (English translation, Menger, 1954.)

Menger, K. (1936b). Weitere Bemerkungen zu den Ertragsgesetzen. *Zeitschrift für Nationalökonomie, 7,* 388–397.

Menger, K. (1954). The logic of the laws of return: A study in meta-economics. In O. Morgenstern (Ed.), *Economic activity analysis* (pp. 419–481). New York, NY: Wiley. Abbreviated and revised reprint, Menger, 1979, chapter 23.

Menger, K. (1967). The role of uncertainty in economics. In M. Shubik (Ed.), *Essays in mathematical economics in honour of Oskar Morgenstern* (pp. 211–231). Princeton, NJ: Princeton University Press. Abbreviated and revised reprint as Menger, 1979, chapter 22.

Menger, K. (1979). *Selected papers in logic and foundations, didactics, economics* (Vienna Circle Collection, Vol. 10). Dordrecht: Reidel.

Menger, K. (1994). L. Golland, B. McGuinness, & A. Sklar (Eds.), *Reminiscences of the Vienna circle and the mathematical colloquium* (*Vienna Circle Collection,* Vol. 20). Dordrecht: Kluwer.

Mises, L. (1919, November 14). Richard Lieben als Nationalökonom. *Neue Freie Presse,* 3.

Mises, L. (1920). Die Wirtschaftsrechnung im sozialistischen Gemeinwesen. *Archiv für Sozialwissenschaft und Sozialpolitik, 47,* 86–121. (English translation, Economic calculation in the socialist commonwealth, in Hayek (Ed.), 1935c, 87–130).

Mises, L. (1927, January 9). Moritz Dub und die volkswirtschaftliche Journalistik in Österreich. *Neue Freie Presse,* 10.

Mises, L. (1933). *Grundprobleme der Nationalökonomie: Untersuchungen über Verfahren, Aufgaben und Inhalt der Wirtschafts- und Gesellschaftslehre*. Jena: Fischer.

Mises, L. (1978). *Notes and recollections*. Spring Mills: Libertarian Press.

Morgenstern, O. (1928). Qualitative und quantitative Konjunkturforschung. *Zeitschrift für die gesamte Staatswissenschaft, 85*, 54–88.

Morgenstern, O. (1931). Offene Probleme der Kosten- und Ertragstheorie. *Zeitschrift für Nationalökonomie, 2*, 481–522.

Morgenstern, O. (1934). Das Zeitmoment in der Wertlehre. *Zeitschrift für Nationalökonomie, 5*, 433–458. (English translation, The time moment in economic theory, in Morgenstern, 1976, 169–183).

Morgenstern, O. (1976). A. Schotter (Ed.), *Selected economic writings of Oskar Morgenstern*. New York, NY: New York University Press.

Müller, K. H. (1993). The ideal worlds of Austria's political economists. In P. Weibel & F. Stadler (Eds.), *The cultural exodus from Austria* (pp. 153–168). Vienna: Löcker.

Opie, R. (1935). Professor Pigou's theory of unemployment. *Zeitschrift für Nationalökonomie, 6*, 289–314.

Patzauer, H. (1915). Chronik der Gesellschaft österreichischer Volkswirte (1875–1915), Vereinsleitung 1888–1915, Verzeichnis der Vorträge 1888–1915. *Jahrbuch der Gesellschaft österreichischer Volkswirte, 1915*, 160–179.

Pinwinkler, A. (2003). *Wilhelm Winkler (1884–1984) – eine Biographie. Zur Geschichte der Statistik und Demographie in Österreich und Deutschland*. Berlin: Duncker & Humblot.

Plener, E. (1915). Vierzig Jahre Gesellschaft österreichischer Volkswirte. *Jahrbuch der Gesellschaft österreichischer Volkswirte, 1915*, 118–130.

Pribram, K. (1937). Gleichgewichtsvorstellungen in der Konjunkturtheorie. *Zeitschrift für Nationalökonomie, 8*, 129–145.

Pribram, K. (1983). *A history of economic reasoning*. Baltimore, MD: Johns Hopkins University Press.

Ricci, U. (1929). Das Sparen in der Individualwirtschaft. *Zeitschrift für Nationalökonomie, 1*, 222–236.

Robbins, L. (1934). Remarks upon certain aspects of the theory of cost. *Economic Journal, 44*, 1–18.

Robbins, L. (1971). *Autobiography of an economist*. London: Macmillan.

Robinson, J. (1936). The long-period theory of employment. *Zeitschrift für Nationalökonomie, 7*, 74–93.

Röpke, W. (1929). *Die Theorie der Kapitalbildung*. Tübingen: Mohr Siebeck.

Rosenstein-Rodan, P. (1929). Das Zeitmoment in der mathematischen Theorie des wirtschaftlichen Gleichgewichtes. *Zeitschrift für Nationalökonomie, 1*, 129–142.

Rothschild, K. W. (2004). The end of an era: The Austrian *Zeitschrift für Nationalökonomie* in the interwar period. In I. Barens, V. Caspari, & B. Schefold (Eds.), *Political events and economic ideas* (pp. 247–260). Cheltenham: Edward Elgar.

Schlesinger, K. (1931). Das "Rätsel" der französischen Geldpolitik. *Zeitschrift für Nationalökonomie, 2*, 387–407.

Schulak, E. M., & Unterköfler, H. (2011). *The Austrian school of economics: its ideas, ambassadors, and institutions*. Auburn: Ludwig Mises Institute.

Spann, O. (1923). Bemerkungen zu Max Webers Soziologie. *Zeitschrift für Volkswirtschaft und Sozialpolitik, 3*, 761–770.

Steindl, J. (1988). Zeitzeuge. In F. Stadler (Ed.), *Vertriebene Vernunft II. Emigration und Exil österreichischer Wissenschaft* (pp. 399–401). Vienna: Jugend & Volk.

Strigl, R. (1934). Lohnfonds und Geldkapital. *Zeitschrift für Nationalökonomie, 5,* 18–41.

Strigl, R. (1936). Zurechnung und Ertragsgestaltung. *Zeitschrift für Nationalökonomie, 7,* 360–387.

Sweezy, A. (1934). The interpretation of subjective value theory in the writings of the Austrian economists. *Review of Economic Studies, 1,* 176–185.

Sznahovich, J. (1950). *Die österreichische Übergangswirtschaft in den Jahren nach dem Zweiten Weltkrieg.* Unpublished doctoral thesis. University of Vienna.

Tintner, G. (1935). Die Nachfrage im Monopolgebiet. *Zeitschrift für Nationalökonomie, 6,* 536–538.

Verrijn Stuart, C. A. (1932). Die Wirkungen von Veränderungen in der Kaufkraft des Goldes auf das Wirtschaftsleben. *Zeitschrift für Nationalökonomie, 3,* 508–537.

Viner, J. (1931). Cost curves and supply curves. *Zeitschrift für Nationalökonomie, 3,* 23–46. Reprinted in American Economic Association (Ed.), 1952, 198–226.

Viner, J. (1950). Supplementary note. In R. V. Clemence (Ed.), *Readings in economic analysis* (pp. 31–35). Cambridge: Addison-Wesley. Reprinted in American Economic Association (Ed.), 1952, 227–232.

Vleugels, W. (1929). Volkswirtschaftslehre als Wirtschaftslehre. *Zeitschrift für Nationalökonomie, 1,* 309–320.

Weintraub, E. R. (1985). *General equilibrium analysis: Studies in appraisal.* Cambridge: Cambridge University Press.

Werner, K. H. (1950). *Die ökonomische Ertragsrechnung als Grundlage des Verteilungsproblems.* Habilitation thesis. University of Vienna.

Wright, C. E. (2015). *A cross-sectional network analysis of the Viennese interwar intellectual community.* Working Paper. University of Wollongong (Australia).

ARCHIVAL SOURCES

David M. Rubenstein Rare Book and Manuscript Library, Duke University: Oskar Morgenstern Papers (OMP).

Hoover Institution Archives, Stanford University: Gottfried Haberler Papers (GHP), Fritz Machlup Papers (FMP).

Wilhelm Röpke-Institut at Erfurt Digitalized version of the Wilhelm Röpke Papers (WRP) deposited in Cologne.

Landespolizeidirektion Wien, Vereinsbehörde. "Vereinsakten."

Österreichisches Staatsarchiv, Archiv der Republik. Gruppe 04b, "Stillhaltekommissar."

Wien-Bibliothek, Tagblatt-Archiv.

Wiener Stadt- und Landesarchiv. "Vereinsakten."

APPENDIX

Table A1. Papers Presented at the *NOeG*, 1918−1938.

Date	Author	Title of Paper	Documentation
Dec 1918	n/a	n/a	S: Letter, Schumpeter to Mises, 9 Dec 1918, cited in Hülsmann (2007, p. 362n.)
Jan 1920	Ludwig Mises	Die Wirtschaftsrechnung im sozialistischen Gemeinwesen [Economic calculation in the socialist commonwealth]	P: Mises (1920); S: Hülsmann, (2007, pp. 373−379)
(...)			
16 Dec 1927	Ludwig Mises	n/a	S: OM-D, 18 Dec 1927, OMP 12
Dec 1927	Karl Menger	Das Unsicherheitsmoment in der Wertlehre [The role of uncertainty in economics]	P: Menger (1934, 1967); S: Menger (1967, p. 259f.)
5 Jan 1928	Oskar Morgenstern	Qualitative und quantitative Konjunkturforschung [Qualitative and quantitative business cycle research]	P: Morgenstern (1928); S: OM-D, 18 Dec 1927, OMP 12
Mar 1928	Friedrich A. Hayek	Intertemporales Gleichgewicht [Intertemporal equilibrium]	P: Hayek (1928); S: Letter, Rosenstein to OM, 20 Mar 1928, OMP 3
16 Mar 1928	Adam Heydel	Zur Problematik des Begriffes der Produktivität [On the problem of the notion of productivity]	P: Heydel (1929); S: FAH to OM, 16 Mar 1928, OMP 3
26 Mar 1928	Adolph Löwe	Gibt es eine monetäre Konjunkturtheorie? [Is there a monetary theory of the business cycle?]	R: Löwe (1928); S: FAH to OM, 16 Mar 1928, OMP 3
Apr 1928	Wilhelm Vleugels	n/a	R: Vleugels (1929); S: FAH to OM, 16 Mar 1928, OMP 3
22 June 1928	Paul Rosenstein-Rodan	Das Zeitmoment in der mathematischen Theorie des wirtschaftlichen Gleichgewichts [The time element in the mathematical theory of economic equilibrium]	P: Rosenstein (1929); S: OMP-D, 24 June 1928, OMP 13

Table A1.   (*Continued*)

Date	Author	Title of Paper	Documentation
28 July 1928	Felix Kaufmann	Soziale Kollektiva [Social collectives]	P: Kaufmann (1929); S: Announcement in OMP 3, folder *NOeG*
18 Dec 1928	Friedrich A. Hayek	Das Mieterschutzproblem [The problem of rent control]	P: Hayek (1929); S: OM-D, 20 Dec 1928, OMP 13
15 Feb 1929	Oskar Morgenstern	Über Ratenzahlungen [On instalment payments]	S: OMP 1, folder 'Biographical material'; OM-D, 16 Feb 1929, OMP 13
22 Feb 1929	Wilhelm Röpke	Die Theorie der Kapitalbildung [The theory of capital formation]	P: Röpke (1929)
22 Mar 1929	Ludwig Mises	(Über Methodologie [On methodology])	S: OM-D, 23 Mar 1929, OMP 13
10 May 1929	Paul Rosenstein-Rodan	Liberalismus und Grenznutzentheorie [Liberalism and marginal utility theory]	S: OM-D, 11 May 1929, OMP 13
1929	Alexander Mahr	(Über den Zinssatz [On the rate of interest])	R: Mahr (1931); S: OM-D, 7 Jan 1930, OMP 13
6 Dec 1929	Gottfried Haberler	Transfer und Preisbewegung [Transfer and price movements]	P: Haberler (1930a); S: OM-D, 7 Dec 1929, OMP 13
20 Dec 1929	Paul Rosenstein-Rodan	n/a	S: OM-D, 21 Dec 1929, OMP 13
9 Jan 1930	Oskar Morgenstern	Offene Probleme der Ertragstheorie [Open problems in the theory of returns]	P: Morgenstern (1931); S: OMP 1, folder 'Biographical material'; OM-D, 11 Jan 1930, OMP 13
7 Feb 1930	Oskar Morgenstern	Offene Probleme der Ertragstheorie II [Open problems in the theory of returns II]	S: OM-D, 8 Feb 1930, OMP 13
7 Mar 1930	Gottfried Haberler	Komparative Kosten [Comparative costs]	P: Haberler (1930b); S: GHP, box 64; OM-D, 8 Mar 1930, OMP 13
25 Apr 1930	Fritz Machlup	Verdrängt die Börse den Kredit? [Does the stock exchange displace credit?]	S: Machlup (1931a, p. v); OM-D, 26 Apr 1930, OMP 13

Table A1. (*Continued*)

Date	Author	Title of Paper	Documentation
30 May 1930	Frank Knight	(Über die Unmöglichkeit der Wertfreiheit [On the impossibility of value freedom])	S: OM-D, 29 and 31 May 1930, OMP 13
20 June 1930	Felix Kaufmann	Über die mathematische Methode [On the mathematical method]	P: Kaufmann (1931); S: OM-D, 23 June 1930, OMP 13
26 Sep 1930	Jacob Viner	Cost curves and supply curves	P: Viner (1931); S: OM-D, 25 and 28 Sep 1930, OMP 13
11 Oct 1930	Karl Schlesinger	Französische Geldpolitik [French monetary policy]	P: Schlesinger (1931); S: OM-D, 14 Oct 1930, OMP 13
19 Dec 1930		Discussion Machlup-Haberler-Hayek (on capital theory)	P: Machlup (1931b); S: OM-D, 21 Dec 1930, OMP 13
13 Feb 1931	Friedrich A. Hayek	Preise in der Konjunktur (Über Krisentheorie) [Prices in the business cycle (On the theory of crises)]	R: Hayek's LSE lectures of Jan 1931 (Hayek, 1931); S: OM-D, 15 Feb 1931, OMP 13; Furth (1989)
16 Apr 1931	Oskar Engländer	Kritik der Preistheorien [Critique of price theories]	S: OM-D, 17 Apr 1931, OMP 13
23 June 1931	n/a	n/a	S: OM-D, 25 June 1931, OMP 13
16 Oct 1931	Ludwig Mises	(Über die Währungslage [On the state of foreign exchanges])	S: OM-D, 16 Oct 1931, OMP 13; Hülsmann (2007, p. 645).
1932	Charlotte von Reichenau	n/a	S: Hülsmann (2007, p. 613f.)
29 Apr 1932	Edward S. Mason	Can a socialist state act rationally?	R: Part of Mason's Lowell Lectures 1932; S: OM-D, 2 May 1932
23 Sept 1932	Richard Strigl	Lohnfonds und Geldkapital [Wage fund and money capital]	P: Strigl (1934); S: OM-D, 24 Sep 1932, OMP 13
11 Nov 1932	Siegfried Budge	Neutrales Geld [Neutral money]	S: OM-D, 13 Nov 1932, OMP 13
16 Dec 1932	Karl Polanyi	n/a	S: OM-D, 18 Dec 1932, OMP 13
20 Mar 1933	Otto Veit	Devisenbewirtschaftung [Exchange controls]	S: OM-D, 22 Mar 1933, OMP 13

Table A1. (*Continued*)

Date	Author	Title of Paper	Documentation
7 Apr 1933	Lionel Robbins	Remarks upon certain aspects of the theory of cost	P: Robbins (1934); S: Howson (2011, p. 236); OM-D, 14 Apr 1933, OMP 13
9 June 1933	Johan G. Koopmans	Neutrales Geld [Neutral money]	R: Koopmans, 1933; S: OM-D, 10 Jun 1933, OMP 13
23 June 1933	Oskar Morgenstern	Das Zeitproblem in der ökonomischen Theorie [The time moment in economic theory]	P: Morgenstern (1934); S: OMP 1, folder 'Biographical material'; OM-D, 30 June 1933, OMP 13
14 Sep 1933	Friedrich A. Hayek	Konstanthaltung des Kapitals [The maintenance of capital]	R: Hayek (1935a); S: OM-D, 15 Sep, 1933, OMP 13
(…)			[Gap in OM-D]
18 Jan 1935	Wilhelm Röpke	n/a	S: OM-D, 18 Jan 1935, OMP 13
1 Feb 1935	Howard S. Ellis	Die Bedeutung der Produktionsperiode für die Krisentheorie [The role of the period of production in the theory of crises]	P: Ellis (1935); S: OM-D, 20 Jan and 2 Feb 1935, OMP 13
April 1935	Friedrich A. Hayek	100% Banking	S: Furth (1989)
14 June 1935	Fritz Neumark	n/a	S: OM to GH, 13 June 1935, GHP 65
6 Sep 1935	Wilhelm Röpke	Theoretische Streitfragen der Expansionspolitik [Theoretical questions of expansionist policy]	R: WR-Papers DVD 7/ 13, 193 – 205; S: OM-D, 7 Sep 1935, OMP 13; OM to GH, 10 Sep 1935, OMP 5; WR to Herbert von Beckerath, 14 Apr 1936, WR-Papers P1/408.
20 Sep 1935	Gerhard Tintner	Monopol [Monopoly]	R: Tintner (1935); S: OM-D, 22 Sep 1935, OMP 13
Sep 1935	Friedrich A. Hayek	Wissen und Wirtschaftswissenschaft [Knowledge and economics]	R: Hayek (1937); S: Furth (1989)

Table A1.   (*Continued*)

Date	Author	Title of Paper	Documentation
30 Dec 1935	Karl Menger	Das Ertragsgesetz [The law of returns]	P: Menger (1936a); S: OM-D, 31 Dec 1935, OMP 13
13 Mar 1936	Richard Strigl	(Ertragstheorie [The theory of returns])	R: Strigl (1936); S: Herbert Fürth to GH, 14 Mar 1936, GHP 67
2 Oct 1936	Friedrich A. Hayek	(Über Voraussicht [On foresight])	R: Hayek (1935b); S: OM-D, 4 Oct 1936, OMP 13
23 Oct 1936	Karl Pribram	Gleichgewichtsvorstellungen in der Konjunkturtheorie [On notions of equilibrium in the theory of the business cycle]	P: Pribram (1937).
Sept/Nov 1936	Wilhelm Röpke	n/a	S: WR to GH, 7 Nov 1936, GHP 66
Dec 1937	Friedrich A. Hayek	(Wirtschaftspolitik [Economic policy])	S: Furth (1989)
17 Feb 1938	Alexander Bilimovic	Einige Bemerkungen zur Theorie der Planwirtschaft [Some remarks on the theory of a planned economy]	P: Bilimovic (1938)

Notes and abbreviations: P, Published paper; R, Related lecture or paper; S, Sources where the presentation is referred to; FAH, Friedrich A. Hayek; GH, Gottfried Haberler; OM, Oskar Morgenstern; WR, Wilhelm Röpke; ( ), Title referred from documents; [ ], English translation of a German title; n/a, Author or title could not be ascertained from the documents.

THE MORAL SCHOLAR AND THE A-MORAL SCIENTIST: THE RESPONSIBILITY OF THE SOCIAL SCIENTIST IN AUSTRIAN ECONOMICS BEFORE AND AFTER THE MIGRATION

Erwin Dekker

ABSTRACT

In this chapter it is argued that when the Austrian revival takes place in the 1970s and 1980s the image of economics as an analytical science which can be methodologically kept clean from value judgments, and the economist as a pure truth-seeker shapes modern Austrian economics at the expense of an idea of a socially involved, embedded scholar with a responsibility toward society which was characteristic of the pre-WWII Austrian school. The neglect of that part of the Austrian heritage is important not only for how we understand the role and responsibility of the social scientist but also because it alters what we consider to be relevant and valid economic knowledge. The chapter demonstrates that insight into economic processes was excluded from what was considered

Research in the History of Economic Thought and Methodology, Volume 34A, 45–71
ISSN: 0743-4154/doi:10.1108/S0743-41542016000034A003

*valid economic knowledge and how social relevance of knowledge was no
longer a goal in the postwar Austrian School. The chapter identifies
alternative currents in the modern Austrian school to this general trend
and suggests ways forward to think about the appropriate institutions to
promote relevance and the moral conduct of (Austrian) economics.*

Keywords: Austrian school of economics; WertFreiheit; Max Weber;
economic knowledge; insight

In the final days of 1948 Joseph Schumpeter addresses the American
Economic Association in his presidential lecture. His speech is not only an
exemplary statement of the professional confidence of the economics profession at the time, but also a radical break with economics as it was practiced in the German-speaking world in which Schumpeter came of age. His
own work had always been sweeping in scope, from his theory of the entrepreneur to his reflections on imperialism and the future prospects of the
modern tax state, to his magnum opus on the future of capitalism
Capitalism, Socialism and Democracy (Schumpeter, 1943/1976). If we were
to believe his address, however, there was to be no more of that.
Economics would be a purely analytic science, free from special interests,
value judgments and ideology. Schumpeter presents economic science as a
technique; a technique for truth-finding, not one for formulating economic
policy. Economists concerned with the latter are in fact a danger to the
reputation of the science: "most of us, not content with their scientific task,
yield to the call of public duty and to their desire to serve their country and
their age, and in doing so bring into their work their individual schemes of
values" (Schumpeter, 1949, p. 346).
   Schumpeter wants to stay as far from any values as possible, toward an
almost complete relativism: "I share the conviction that there is no sense in
saying that the world of ideas of bourgeois liberalism is 'superior' in any
relevant sense to the world of ideas of the middle ages, or the world of
ideas of socialism to that of bourgeois liberalism," only to continue that
the progress in economic science itself does not reflect any practical
improvement in economic policy making, "actually, I further believe that
there is no reason other than personal preference for saying that more wisdom or knowledge goes into our policies than went into those of the

Tudors or Stuarts or, for that matter, into Charlemagne's" (Schumpeter, 1949, p. 349). Schumpeter's work, admittedly, always carries the mark of the provocateur, but the break he advocates with the type of social science with which he came of age, and which he practiced for all his life — he would pass away about a year later — is remarkable. This analytical economics pursued for truth's sake only, is far from the verbal debates about the feasibility of socialism and the future of liberalism that animates so much of his work. Yet at the same time it captures much of what becomes the standard image of economics in the postwar world, the emphasis on technique, the disciplinary autonomy, and the pursuit of positive economics only.

We will argue here that when the Austrian revival takes place in the 1970s and 1980s this image of economics as an analytical science which can be methodologically kept clean from value judgments, and the economist as a pure truth-seeker shapes modern Austrian economics at the expense of an idea of a socially involved, embedded scholar with a certain responsibility toward society which was characteristic of the original Austrian school. So that Schumpeter's transformation, although less extreme, also takes place within the Austrian School. While contributors to the so-called Austrian revival are critical of many of the assumptions underlying neoclassical theory of the time, the Austrian revival of the 1970s and 1980s leaves the self-image of economics and the economist largely intact. The neglect of that part of the Austrian heritage is important not just for how we understand the role and responsibility of the social scientist, but also, as this chapter will demonstrate, because it alters what we consider to be relevant and valid economic knowledge.

This contrast between the interwar work and that of the Austrian revival is readily apparent, at least prima facie, from an examination of the titles of the interwar books of Ludwig von Mises with the works in the "Austrian revival." His first book is a reflection on nationalism and the causes of WWI (*Nation, Staat und Wirtschaft*, 1919), his second book deals with the appeal and feasibility of socialism (*Gemeinwirtschaft*, 1922), his third with inflation and the possibility of a stable currency (*Die Geldtheoretische Seite des Stabilisierungsproblem*, 1923), the fourth one with the fortunes and possibilities of liberalism (*Liberalismus*, 1927), the next two with monetary policies, the business cycle and interventionism more generally, then after a book on epistemology, his magnum opus "*Nationalökonomie*" (1940) in the 1940s, to be followed by "*Omnipotent Government*" (1944a) and "*Bureaucracy*" (1944b). His work, in other words, was a continuous engagement with the major intellectual currents of his day.[1] That is a very different type of scholarship than the Austrian books that are published in the wake of Kirzner's *Competition and Entrepreneurship* (1973): Dolan's collection of papers of the first meeting at South Royalton *The Foundations of Austrian Economics* (Dolan, 1976b), Brian Loasby's *Choice, Complexity and Ignorance* (1976), Gerald O'Driscoll's *Economics as a Coordination Problem* (1977), the collection of essays by Ludwig Lachmann *Capital, Expectations and the Market Process* (1978a), and the NYU conference volume edited by Mario Rizzo *Time, Uncertainty and Disequilibrium* (1979). They are primarily theoretical books, concerned with Austrian economic *theory*, and methodological issues in economics more generally. There are exceptions, both in the inter-war period, and in the revival to this general trend, but it nonetheless suggests that something quite fundamental has shifted.

   This chapter will analyze this shift by first examining the ideas on the responsibility of the scholar in the pre-WWII Austrian school. Then it will proceed to contextualize these ideas in particular in relation to the work of Max Weber, whose influence and relevance for the Austrian School has repeatedly been emphasized (Boettke & Storr, 2002; Prendergast, 1986). It will then contrast this older view with the self-image of the economist in neoclassical economics and the Austrian revival in sections three and four. Section five will consider some alternative conceptualizations of the role and responsibility of the scholar in the modern Austrian tradition, which are closer to the older strand.

THE RESPONSIBILITY OF THE SCHOLAR: FROM MENGER TO HAYEK

Within the Austrian tradition there is a largely neglected strand that conceptualizes the role of the scholar and his responsibility toward the society, economy or state that he studies. Carl Menger states that responsibility clearly in his book on method: "But never, and this is the essential point in the matter under review, may science dispense with testing for their suitability those institutions which have come about 'organically'. It must, when careful investigation so requires, change and better them (...). No era may renounce this 'calling'." (Menger, 1883/2009, p. 234). His statement comes at the end of a thoughtful discussion of common law and the important role of the historical school in drawing attention toward the unconscious wisdom[2] contained in that tradition. Menger warns for the possibility of erring in two ways when dealing with common law. Erring in one direction the jurist or law scholar might propose "immature or hasty reforms," but erring in the other direction he might treat the common law with too much respect, and fail to see that it no longer serves its purpose. It is typical of Menger's forward-looking perspective that he believes that his generation is more likely to err in the direction of too much caution, than in the direction of too much desire for reform. In that sense Menger, is close to the optimistic liberals of the nineteenth century, much of that optimism has already disappeared when Friedrich von Wieser makes his most important contributions (Dekker, 2016).

That being said, Wieser's idea of the responsibility of the scholar is very much in line with that of Menger. He is concerned with the same two errors of overcautiousness and the zeal of the reformer. And while he warns against overcautiousness and too much belief in natural powers, something for which he faults the classical economists, he sees the primary danger in the zeal of the reformer. He lists numerous examples of this urge: the many failed reforms of the French revolution, the attempt to form a world language in the form of Esperanto, and the desire of technical experts to rationally reform society (Wieser, 1910, pp. 143–4). Instead Wieser argues, social reforms take time, and they need to grow from within, or at least be supported by important parts of society. As has been the case with the tradition of freedom in Britain.

More generally Wieser's work contains a strong idea that the scholar should possess certain qualities that allow him to recognize both the good and the bad, and to deal with them accordingly: "[Theory] should be equally remote from optimism and pessimism. It should appraise both the lights and the shadows. It should discern the community of interests but no less should it recognize power, the conflict of motives and the economic evil" (Wieser, 1924/1967, p. 9). That idea is closely tied to the frequent comparisons that we find in the work of Wieser between the economist and the doctor, who are both engaged in making the right diagnosis.

That same analogy is present in the work of Eugen von Böhm-Bawerk. The economist should be engaged in providing the right diagnosis, and where possible prescribing a cure, or at least making sure that the wrong cure is not applied (Böhm-Bawerk, 1892/1924, p. 137). In an essay, entitled "Our tasks" – the opening essay of the newly establish journal *Volkswirtschaft, Sozialpolitik und Verwaltung* – he describes the task of the scholar as consisting of a certain aloofness, and resistance to the latest fashion:

> Here, I think, is again a point at which theory can and should be of great service to praxis. Based on centuries of experience that are embodied and put to use by theory, professionally trained, to soberly and dispassionately examine the facts and extract from the changing phenomena the permanent core, theory [sic] has a far greater capacity, to diagnose the whims of fashion as just that, than the practitioner, standing in the middle of it all. (Böhm-Bawerk, 1892/1924, p. 142)[3]

Once again we see the emphasis on diagnosis in this quote, but also notice the moral character that this endeavor has for him. The scholar should do this soberly and dispassionately, and as he concludes: "I hope [that our journal] will honestly serve the concerns of our age, and thus will provide a few building blocks for the lasting construction of science" (Böhm-Bawerk, 1892/1924, p. 143).

It is tempting to think of this combination of this call for political, social and economic relevance combined with an explicitly moral (dispassionate and aloof) stance as a phenomenon of the age, as something that befits the German and Austrian professors of the late nineteenth century, close as they were to statesmen. As is well known both Wieser and Böhm-Bawerk occupied important political positions, and the great prestige of professors in the German world around 1900 is quite exceptional (Fourcade-Gourinchas, 2001). But the interwar generation of the Austrian scholars continues this tradition. Not just in the way they engage with the "concerns of their age" as we saw in our brief survey of the work of Mises in the introduction, but also in how they conceptualized their role as scholars. To illustrate this we will discuss here the campaign mounted in the *Neue Wiener Tagblatt* during the 1930s by members of the Austrian school. The discussion of the role of the scholar in the work of Mises and Hayek's work of the interwar period, will be postponed until the next section.

In the early 1930s a group of Austrian economists decide to engage in journalistic effort to inform the public about the solutions to the economic crisis and to influence public policy. The two main contributors to this effort were Fritz Machlup and Oskar Morgenstern (Klausinger, 2005, pp. 19–20). The campaign, as Klausinger describes it, consisted of two parts. One part, performed by Machlup, consisted of a series of weekly columns entitled *Two minutes of Economics* (*Zwei Minuten Volkwirtschaft*) which ran for over two years. Machlup himself described the series as "a means to spread economic understanding [in the sense] of public enlightenment" (Machlup quoted in Klausinger, 2005, p. 26). The other part was more concerned with economic issues of the day, but the subtitle for the pieces, *A Contribution to Economic Sense* (*Ein Beitrag zur wirtschaftlichen Vernunft*), which was originally used, demonstrates a goal that is similar to the one Machlup had in mind. These Austrian economists felt that they were contributing to the spread of economic knowledge, an economic enlightenment, among the public and engaging with the relevant issues of their day. That was not restricted to Machlup, who at the same time taught at an institute for adult education, but extended to Gottfried Haberler, Hayek writing from London, Ludwig von Mises, Erich Schiff, Richard Strigl, Martha Stephanie Braun, and even the later politically far more withdrawn Morgenstern were contributors to the series.

WERTFREIHEIT, VALUE-RELEVANCE, AND RESPONSIBILITY: THE MORAL SCHOLAR

The idea that scholarly activity is moral and that the scholar should be concerned with the social relevance of his ideas runs counter to most interpretations of the Wertfreiheit doctrine. The idea of Wertfreiheit is strongly associated with the work of Max Weber. While Weber's idea has sometimes been anachronistically interpreted as making a positivist analytical argument about the split between facts and values, this was certainly not the case. Even the sociologist Talcott Parsons, who is now frequently associated with positivist sociology, was well aware that Weber's purpose was different. As Parsons explains in his interpretation of Weber's work, Weber was not arguing that the scientists abstains from all value-commitments, on the contrary Weber felt that scientists upheld certain values: "The point is rather that *in his role* as scientist a particular sub-value system must be paramount for the investigator, that in which conceptual clarity, consistency and generality on the one hand, empirical accuracy and verifiability on the other are the valued outputs of the process of investigation" (Parsons, 1965, p. 50).

Even though Parson acknowledges the importance of value-commitments for the scientist, the one he ascribes to Weber have a definite positivist ring to them: consistency, generality, and verifiability. That is however, not at all how Weber describes the important value-commitments of the scientist. Weber, famously, thinks of science as a vocation, and he time and again emphasizes the importance of a passion in the scientist for his subject and for finding the truth (see particularly Weber, 1919/2012). That passion should, however, be guided and tempered by certain values, in particular Weber emphasizes intellectual honesty, "sobriety of judgment" and the willingness to present "inconvenient facts." Or as he puts it at the end of his essay on the meaning of ethic-neutrality: "I simply wish to point out that if anyone, then the professional 'thinkers' are under a special obligation to keep a cool head when confronted with the dominant ideals – even the most majestic ones – at any given time; and this means that they should be able 'to swim against the current' if necessary" (Weber, 1917/2012, p. 334). Notice that Weber argues that the scholar will not only be confronted with inconvenient facts, but also with social ideals.

It must be a very similar ideal that Mises has in mind when he writes in the preface of his *Nation, State and Economy*:

> Even if we were in a position to see interrelations clearly and to recognize where devel-
> opments are heading, it would be impossible for us to confront the great events of our
> day objectively and not let our view be blurred by wishes and hopes. Standing in the
> middle of battle, one strives in vain to keep cool and calm. It exceeds human capacity
> to treat the vital questions of one's time *sine ira et studio* [without anger and partiality].
> (Mises, 1919/1983, p. i)

It is important to see that this objectivity is not a methodological guideline that one follows, but instead an ideal for which "one strives", something which in the circumstances of 1919 is particularly difficult.

Such striving requires, as Weber realized all too well, restraint on the part of the scholar. It is tempting to mix our value judgments with our analysis, and it might even make us more popular with the public or our students, as he suggests. It might also be very difficult to eliminate our own value judgments from our evaluation of a situation, but the mere fact that it is difficult does not relieve us of our duty: "the 'vocation' loses the only really significant meaning that it still retains today if one does not fully exercise that specific form of *self-restraint* which it requires" (Weber, 1917/2012, p. 307). It is thus a moral quality of scholarly work if it aspires to be value-free, even if that ideal might prove hard to achieve.

And moral values, argues Weber, are not just important for the scholar in the fulfilment of his professional task and responsibility, they also guide his scholarship. This is what some commentators have called the value-relevance thesis of Weber. The questions that are most relevant, most pressing, those that are judged to possess the most "cultural significance" are the ones that should be pursued. This judgment about the cultural significance is not just important for it helps guide our analysis beforehand (what would later be called the context of discovery by Popper), but it also helps scholars to understand the significance of the conclusions of their analysis[4] (Silverman, 1984, p. 921). If we could just quote from the first of Mises interwar books it is now appropriate to quote the first line of the introduction of his second interwar book: "Socialism is the watchword and catchword of our day. The socialist idea dominates the modern spirit. The masses cling to it, it expresses the thoughts and feelings of all; it has set its seal upon our time. When history comes to tell our story it will write above the chapter: *The Epoch of Socialism*" (Mises, 1922/1951, p. 26). Mises makes an argument about the cultural significance of socialism, and the ideals he is confronting, an argument which serves to justify why he devotes an entire book to it. That is equally evident from the title of the book's final chapter "The Historical Significance of Modern Socialism."

The Weberian understanding of the role and responsibility of the scholar are also prominent in Hayek's work. Although his primary goal in the late 1930's is understanding the rise of scientism in the social sciences, rather than formulating an idea about the moral obligations of the scholar, his work is very close to this latter concern. In *The Trend of Economic Thinking*, his inaugural lecture at the LSE, he argues that the origin of economics, as well as the passions of individual economists are directed at alleviating social ills. To underline that idea he approvingly quotes Pigou: "It is not wonder, but the social enthusiasm which revolts from the sordidness of mean streets and the joylessness of withered lives, that is the beginning of economic science" (quoted in Hayek, 1933, p. 123). That in itself is not a problem argues Hayek, in fact it helped economists to make progress: "In criticizing proposals for improvement, they accepted the ethical postulates on which such proposals were based and tried to demonstrate that these were not conducive to the desired end and that, very often, policies of a radically different nature would bring about the desired result" (Hayek, 1933, p. 123). But caution is in order, argues Hayek, for while economics sometimes can suggest the most appropriate means to pursue an agreed upon end, just as often economics tells us that certain ends cannot be achieved, or can only be achieved at an excessively high price.

In that sense the study of economics is a sobering exercise, or as Hayek expresses it in a hopeful reflection on the situation of the 1930s:

> It is, indeed, one of the interesting facts of the present time that a growing number of economists of the younger generation who have not the slightest sentimental attachment to conservatism – and many of whom began as socialists – feel more and more compelled by their reasoning to take a conservative attitude towards many problems – or rather an attitude which, a generation ago, would have been called conservative. (Hayek, 1933, p. 135)

The study of the economy will actually have moral, humbling effects according to Hayek. It will be hard to refrain from attempts to "reconstruct the world," and the economist's reluctance to do so will make him unpopular with the public, but:

> If he [the economist] recognizes the circumstances from which they [the dislike and suspicion] spring, he will be able to bear them with patience and understanding, confident that he possesses in his scientific knowledge a solvent for differences which are really intellectual, and that although, at present, his activities have little effect, yet in course of time they will come to be recognized as serving more consistently than the activities of those he opposes, the ends which they share in common. (Hayek, 1933, p. 137)

One might of course disagree with Hayek about the limits of what can be achieved through economic policy, but what he argues is that economics helps us to find out what can and cannot be achieved in the first place. It is precisely this function that Weber also envisions for economics, in a passage that might as well have been written by Hayek,[5] Weber argues that the purpose of his course on economics is:

> Understanding the economic causes of social phenomena and understanding the difficulties in realizing the socially desired solution. Promoting this insight into the real power structure and not the fruitless attempt to suppress the pursuit of a certain social activity is the only means of forestalling a really dubious dilettantism, i.e. one which in ignorance of the economic causes of a specific illness applies quack remedies to the symptoms. [The course would therefore] not place the main emphasis on the demonstration of ways and means for the solution of the great problems of the age, but on the contrary – and keeping to these limits requires a certain resignation – to expose the full extent of the economic difficulties, in this way seeking to ensure that the consequence of these was properly appreciated and the practical questions properly posed. (Weber quoted in Hennis, 1991, pp. 36–37, 1994, p. 122, translation slightly altered)

The elements emphasized by the Austrians are all there: the personal restraint, the responsibility to explore the realm of the possible, and the idea that economics can be a corrective to lay understanding.

Together these elements could contribute to, what Weber scholar Wilhelm Hennis has identified as, Weber's overarching goal: "cooperation in the political education of our nation, guiding its members to improved powers of judgement" (Hennis, 1991, p. 38; Weber, 1909/2012a). Hennis, based on Weber, makes an insightful distinction between the idea that what scientists do is simply the augmentation of positive knowledge and the augmentation of our power of judgment. That difference can in fact be easily found, even in Weber's most mature statements on the subject, which have traditionally been most frequently interpreted in a positivist manner. In his 1917 essay on the subject, he distinguishes between the calculating purpose of science, in which it helps to decide between different means and its function of providing insight:

> But fortunately, science can contribute to even more than that; we are able to offer you a third benefit: achieving *clarity* (...). If you take this or that position, then scientific experience tells us that you must apply such and such *means* in order to implement your position in practice (...) Does the end 'justify' the means or not? The teacher can confront you with the necessity of this choice. (...) In terms of its meaning, this or that practical standpoint can be derived with inner consistency, and therefore with *integrity*, from such and such an ultimate fundamental position (...), if you remain *true to yourself*, you will necessarily arrive at such and such ultimate, inner consequences in terms of meaning. (Weber, 1919/2012, pp. 349–50, emphasis added)

This is not an argument for political arguments from the scholar, but it does underline the edifying role that the scholar can have. The scholar can test a position for inner consistency, he can demonstrate the ultimate consequences of a position and confront the individual with the necessity of choice.

It is similarly noteworthy that Weber is concerned with the meaning and use of science of our personal lives (rather than some public value), and thus he concludes his observations on providing clarity:

> In that way, we can, if we are competent enough, compel the individual – or at least help him – to give *an account to himself of the ultimate meaning of his own conduct.* (...) Here, too, I am tempted to say that a teacher who succeeds in doing this is acting in the service of 'moral forces' – that is to say: assuming the duty of creating clarity and a sense of responsibility. (Weber, 1919/2012, p. 350)

Weber's view on the responsibility of the scholar is thus more than just the notion that he should adhere to certain scholarly values, but also that the scholar should judge the (cultural) significance of the facts he is investigating, and that he has a role in laying out the options for action, and pointing out the responsibilities that the actor has. By doing so, the social scientist could contribute to the improvement of the powers of judgment in society (at least when at type of knowledge is valued in return by society). An important part of that task relates to an awareness of the limits of scientific knowledge on the one hand, and in demonstrating what cannot be practically achieved on the other hand.

Seen in this light the work on socialism by Mises and Hayek appears in a fresh light. Superficially it might read like a simple condemnation of socialism, and there are certainly traces of that, but the more interesting part is aimed at providing clarity. It hopes to demonstrate that the aims of the socialists cannot be achieved by socialist means. This is particularly true of Mises original book *Socialism* (1922/1951). But it is also the reason why

Hayek's book "The Road to Serfdom" (1944) is dedicated to "the socialists of all parties." Even so, Hayek admits that his book is also a "political book," which is inspired by certain (non-scholarly) values and ideals. When he describes his goal in the preface, he is, however, still very close to a Weberian exercise in providing clarity: "I have come to regard the writing of this book as a duty which I must not evade, this was mainly due to a peculiar and serious feature of the discussions of problems of future economic policy at the present time, of which the public is scarcely sufficiently aware" (Hayek, 1944, p. vii). What we see here, is Hayek balancing different values: the cultural significance of totalitarianism, his desire to fight it, and his scholarly values.

In the Weberian perspective and in the Austrian tradition Wertfreiheit is thus an ethical commitment of the scholar, an ideal, among others, for which he the scholar should strive. That idea is very different from the methodological or even logical interpretation that the "value-freedom" postulate would receive within modern economics, including the Austrian revival.

ECONOMICS AS TECHNIQUE, THE ECONOMIST AS TECHNOCRAT

The advent of the idea that economics is primarily a technique, as exemplified by Schumpeter's address, is perhaps nowhere more evident than in Terence W. Hutchison's book *The Significance and Basic Postulates of Economic Theory* (1938). Its primary concern is the formulation of a demarcation criterion between science and non-science. Behind this goal lies the ultimate aim of overcoming dissent in economics. For the lack of a clear scientific criterion that marks of objective scientific knowledge from the rest is the cause of: "the ferocious and interminable character of the many controversies that rage among economists themselves on the one hand, and on the other hand much of the uncertainty as to the significance of their results with which economists face the outside world" (Hutchison, 1938, p. 4). In good positivist spirit, Hutchison does not only hope to demarcate science from value judgments, but also from philosophy: "'scientists' have definite, agreed, and relatively conclusive criteria for the testing of propositions, and theories which 'philosophers' do not accept" (Hutchison, 1938, p. 7). The demarcation criterion or "test" that distinguishes between science and pseudo-science ("there is one criterion by which the scientist can keep his results pure from the contamination of pseudo-science and there is one test with which he can always challenge the pseudo-scientist – a test which at once ensures precision and exposes the vague concepts and unsupported generalizations on which the pseudo-scientist always relies") is the appeal to fact.

Many of these arguments are also to be found in Friedman's article on "The Methodology of Positive Economics." He, for example, shares Hutchison's belief that we can clearly distinguish between positive and normative economics. Friedman, more importantly, also makes the next step in suggesting that from positive economic knowledge we can infer the consequences of different policies and typically decide which one is better or preferable (Friedman, 1953, pp. 5–7). That idea became the shared understanding of the role of the economist within the postwar economic profession. Policy makers, could decide based on a social welfare function what the desirable ends were and economists would be able to calculate the most efficient means of achieving them. There was some dispute about the possibility of finding the appropriate welfare function, but the distinction between positive and normative knowledge and hence the division of labor between the economist and the politician was widely accepted.[6]

But even Hutchison realizes that this textbook image of the economist as technocratic character is too simple (see also Blaug, 1992, pp. 128–131). In his next book *Positive Economics and Policy Objectives* he does not fundamentally challenge the by then widely accepted value-freedom thesis in its positivist interpretation. But he does realize that economics is more than just calculating the most efficient means to achieve a certain end. Hutchison argues that one of the tasks of the economist is emphasizing the need to choose. He does not only quote Popper ("Progress rests ... with the clarity of our conception of our ends, and with the realism of their choice"), but he also, at least implicitly, realizes that Weber's argument is one about moral responsibility, when he quotes him to the extent that: "The social sciences ... are the least fitted to presume to save the individual the difficulty of making a choice" (Hutchison, 1964, p. 166). It is unclear, however, how such a statement relates to the idea that economists can advise on the best means to achieve policy objectives determined by politicians.[7]

It was clear at the time of the appearance of Hutchinson's work that something fundamental was shifting. This is evident in both Frank Knight's extensive review essay of the book and in Fritz Machlup criticism of Hutchison's work (Knight, 1940; Machlup, 1955). Both Knight and Machlup realize that Hutchison's idea of a demarcation criterion will remove any notion of judgment of the evidence in support of or in contention with a particular theory. That is, it eliminates the human element from science. Against which Machlup argues: "the data of 'observation', are themselves results of interpretations of *human* actions by *human* actors" (Machlup, 1955, p. 16). For Machlup, however, this remains primarily a methodological difference between the natural and the social sciences. Knight's conception is closer to that of Weber and the older Austrian tradition. Knight argues: "The social action which the study of economics has as its function to guide, or at least to illuminate, is essentially that of making 'rules of the game', in the shape of law, for economic relationships" (Knight, 1940, p. 28).[8] This position might be said to lay somewhere between the idea of Weber and the technocratic vision. It tends more toward the former in the sense that it hopes to illuminate, and it tends more toward the latter where it constructs the "rules of the game." Ultimately, however, Knight is closer to the Weberian position. This becomes especially evident when he argues that economics will typically not lead one to be able to predict economic behavior or to control that behavior. Instead he argues:

> Concrete and positive answers to questions in the field of economic science or policy depend in the first place on judgments of value and as to procedure on a broad, general education in the cultural sense, and on "insight" into human nature and social values, rather than on the findings of any possible positive science. From this point of view the need is for an interpretative study (*verstehende Wissenschaft*). (Knight, 1940, p. 31)

What is especially noteworthy is Knight's idea of first illumination and here "insight" which help us understand the world, rather than predict or control it. Such understanding, however, requires an interpretation of the world around us, and thus the need, as Weber put it, for "sobriety of judgment." It is telling that Knight in his rejoinder to Hutchison describes economics as a craft, instead of a science (Knight, 1941). A craft that requires experience and that does not primarily rely on impersonal techniques.

AUSTRIAN ECONOMICS AS AN ALTERNATIVE TECHNIQUE? WERTFREIHEIT MISUNDERSTOOD

When Austrian economics re-emerges in the 1970s, and the 1980s, there are two strategies that are being pursued. One is that of trying to engage in "academic dialogue" and the other to start an alternative "Austrian movement" (Vaughn, 1994; Chapter 5). But in both streams, as I will argue here,

the role and responsibility of the scholar or social scientist is not challenged. Instead the important contributors to this Austrian revival were
primarily concerned with setting up an alternative body of economic *theory*
to the prevailing neoclassical economics. It was the period in which
Thomas Kuhn's theory of paradigms was very popular, and it was not long
before Austrian economics presented itself as an alternative paradigm to
neoclassical economics (Dolan, 1976a). This had various consequences for
the face of Austrian economics afterwards, not all of which we can explore
here. But the idea of an alternative paradigm stimulated a focus on theory
and theoretical foundations. Hence Austrian economics is typically presented as similar in structure to neoclassical economics, but different in the
fundamental assumptions: (radical) subjectivism, different assumptions
regarding time, and competition is thought of as a process, rather than an
end-state. These are typically supplemented by some negative characteriza-
tions drawn in contrast to neoclassical economics such as a distrust of
aggregates and less reliance on the equilibrium concept (Egger, 1978;
Kirzner, 1980/1990; Lachmann, 1978b).

In this process the role of the economist is left unchallenged.[9] That itself
might have been influenced by Kuhn's theory of paradigms which was able
to account for different perspectives within a *science*. Thus Austrian economists, could easily present themselves as scientists, despite the fact that
there was fundamental disagreement with the neoclassical economists. This
in contrast with the positivist period of the immediate postwar years during
which science was believed to be identical with consensus. However that
may be, while Israel Kirzner and Murray Rothbard both reflected, in the
first volume of modern Austrian economics, on the role of value judgments
in economics, and the (perceived) relationship between Austrian economics
and free market economics, neither of them questioned the positivist interpretation of the fact-value distinction (as logical principle and methodological rule, rather than moral value) or a critical reflection on the idea of the
economist as policy adviser, dominant within the neoclassical framework.

Kirzner's essay on the method of Austrian economics praises Knight for
his criticism of Hutchison, but contrary to what one might expect he does
so merely for the importance of purposeful action and not for the other
arguments in Knight's critique, such as the social nature of science, the
goal of illumination and critique and the importance of a sense of judgment. Instead he focuses on the description and explanation of human
action in terms of purposes: "When Lachmann called upon economists to
make the world intelligible in terms of human decisions and purposes, I
take it that he was telling us the following: It is the task of science to

describe and explain reality" (Kirzner, 1976a, p. 44). That is a narrow reading of Lachmann, because for him the notion of intelligibility entails something much closer to Weber's verstehen. Kirzner furthermore emphasizes that economics is a science that can arrive at definite truths if the right methodology is applied (Kirzner, 1976a, p. 47). In an essay in the same volume Kirzner considers the Wertfreiheit doctrine, which he mainly interprets through the work of Robbins who has demonstrated: "that the economist's value judgments have nothing at all to do with his concerns as a scientific investigator" and, "Robbins was able to show that *Wertfreiheit* emerges as an implication of this definition of economics" (Kirzner, 1976b, pp. 76–77).[10] This could not be further from the Weberian conception of the importance of values and the recognition that value-freedom is itself the most important scholarly value, instead of the result of some instrumental method or the result of pure logical reasoning.

Rothbard, although as usual more provocative in his writing, accepts the by-then standard positivist notion of the fact-value split, which distinguishes between scientific knowledge and "individual value judgments, [which are] ultimately arbitrary and solely a creature of individual whim" (Rothbard, 1976a, p. 89).[11,12] And although Rothbard is well aware of the temptation to engage in value judgments, and could thus pursue an understanding of value-freedom as a moral goal to aspire to, he instead focuses on the split between value judgments as they can be logically demonstrated, to show that others have overstepped the boundary. That argument is interesting in itself, but it removes the knower and his sense of judgement completely from the picture. That idea is a direct outcome of Rothbard's understanding of praxeology as a logical system based on deduction: "since praxeology begins with a true axiom, A, all the propositions that can be deduced from this axiom must also be true" (Rothbard, 1976b, pp. 19–20).[13] That brings us to a more general issue, and a possible objection to my argument so far, and that is the position of Mises on these issues and the importance of his position for the Austrian revival.

Mises emphasizes, starting in the 1930s, that praxeology is a logical system from which a priori truths can be derived seems at odds with Weber's idea of the moral scholar who weighs the evidence. Take the following quote from his "Epistemological Problems of Economics:"

> Therefore, when one reaches the conclusion, strictly by adherence to the canons of scientific procedure, that private ownership of the means of production is the only practicable form of social organization, this is neither an apology for capitalism nor an improper attempt to lend the authority of science to the support of liberalism. (...)

> Liberalism has nothing to do with world views, metaphysics, or value judgments. (Mises, 1933/1978, pp. 40–1)

The emphasis on scientific procedure, on the one hand, obscures the role of scholar in the process of interpretation and evaluation of our knowledge. The extent to which Mises thinks that objective science can take us in the political domain, on the other hand, eliminates the need for a kind of political or economic enlightenment. And thus we find in Mises work a recurring frustration that his opponents are unwilling to accept his conclusions: "Whoever wished to combat liberal economic policy was compelled to challenge the character of economics as a science. Enemies arose against it for political reasons" (Mises, 1933/1978, p. 4).

This is also evident from the fact that Mises looks upon economic knowledge as a technology and he tends to emphasize the instrumental value of economic knowledge, which he compares to a technology that helps man to act (Mises, 1933/1978, p. 39). Those conceptions, which deviate from his views in the 1920s, are already more in line with postwar ideas of economics as a technique and the economist as engineer, than they are with the Weberian idea of the morally motivated and responsible scholar.

When Mises', and by implication Kirzner's and Rothbard's, methodological position was challenged, within the Austrian revival, this indeed resulted in a heated debate over the Scientific (capital S) status of Austrian economics and the dangers of giving up that claim (Storr, 2011). And when scholars made attempts to reconcile Mises a priori methodology with other methodological positions, this typically involved a rethinking of the role and responsibility of the scholar (Boettke & Storr, 2002; Lavoie, 1986). It is to such alternative conceptualizations within the postwar development of Austrian economics that we will now turn.

ALTERNATE CURRENTS WITHIN THE AUSTRIAN REVIVAL

When Don Lavoie challenges Mises deductive a priori method he recognizes that Mises methodology has all the characteristics of a scientific technique:

> Mises sometimes present his apriori science as what Imre Laktos called a Euclidean system, a privileged category of knowledge, uniquely certain and immune to all criticism. It was built from a set of self-evident axioms from which strictly deductive arguments can be cranked out mechanically. (Lavoie, 1986, pp. 195–6)

The demarcation criterion is here not an appeal to fact, as in Hutchison's
early work, but to the logic that underlies the deductive system, but it is a
demarcation criterion nonetheless. Lavoie is well aware of the implications
of such a conception of science and truth. When he contrasts his favored
hermeneutics approach, with the Euclidean method of Mises system, he
argues: "Hermeneutics is an approach that bases its assessment of what is
scientific by reliance on the pragmatic judgments of systematicity, coherence, clarity, etc., by members of the scientific community" (Lavoie, 1986,
p. 197).[14] Lavoie reintroduces the human knower, as he is present in the
process of interpreting and evaluating the evidence. A role that necessarily
entails a certain professional responsibility.

One might expect to find similar arguments in the work of Ludwig
Lachmann, who was an important contributor to the Austrian revival, and
whose work inspired much of Lavoie's contributions. But even though
Lachmann deviated from both Kirzner and Rothbard in the importance he
attached to the idea of equilibrium, and the extent, or extremes, to which
he believed subjectivism should be taken, otherwise his writings hardly
question the role and responsibility of the social scientist. For Lachmann it
seems clear that we are after truth for truth's sake. To some extent that is
surprising, for especially his arguments in favor of hermeneutics later in his
life make him return to the insights of Weber, and to a recognition of the
varied skills that the hermeneutic economist needs (reminiscent of Knight's
idea of economics as a craft).

That is different in the work of Hayek's PhD student G.L.S. Shackle,
which was developed largely in isolation from the Austrian revival.
Intellectually Shackle is indebted to both Hayek and Keynes, a combination that might seem odd from the perspective of the Austrian revival, but
that in Shackle's subjectivist perspective with its focus on uncertainty is
quite natural. His work in which the uncertainty and choice that individuals face are central is characterized by an awareness of the role and
responsibility of the scholar. Shackle's work, focused as it is on that limitations of our knowledge and the uncertainty about the future, is highly
reflexive about the epistemological position of the scholar:

> A discipline, a region of the world of thought, should seek to *know itself*. Like an
> individual human being, it has received from its origins a stamp of character, a native
> mode of response to the situations confronting it. Right responses, "responsibility,"
> will require of the profession as of the individual an insight into the powers and
> defects of the tool which history has bequeathed to it. (Shackle, 1972, p. 24)

This quote is interesting for its emphasis on responsibility as well as the
awareness of the limitations of what the scholar can know. The latter is

very much in line with Hayek's thought: "If we are to understand how society works, we must attempt to define the general nature and range of our ignorance concerning it. Though we cannot see in the dark, we must be able to trace the limits of the dark areas" (Hayek, 1960, p. 23; see also Hayek, 1975). Shackle realizes that those limitations create a "responsibility" for the scholar, and as he observes for the profession as a whole, to be aware of the limitations of one's theories and tools. Above we saw Hayek's emphasis on the limitations of what economics can achieve, and the explorations of those limits characterizes Shackle's most important book "Epistemics and Economics" (1972). As he explains:

> Theories which tell us what *will* happen are claiming too much: too much of independence from their turbulent surroundings, too much capacity to remain upright in the gales of politics, diplomacy and technical chance and change, too much internal simplicity for even the world of business itself. Kaleidic theories give insight: preparedness for what cannot, in its nature, be known for sure or exactly in detail, but which need not spring a total surprise. (Shackle, 1972, p. 73)

The crucial term in much of Shackle's book is *insight*. He contrasts the ability to generate insight with the ability to predict or control, and argues that economic theories are typically more able to provide the former. As he argues in praise of Böhm-Bawerk's theory of capital structure: "Böhm-Bawerk's conception illustrates our claim that a theory's power to give insight is independent of its aptness in framing policy" (Shackle, 1972, p. 69). The insight that he refers to is the idea that capital is inextricably bound up with time. It is an insight that helps us understand production, the price of capital goods and the behavior of businesses men. That is the same type of insight into the world that the Viennese economists were attempting to promote in their campaign in the *Neue Wiener Tagblatt*. Even in Kirzner's work there are moments when he emphasizes the insight that economics generates: "In the Austrian view, a thorough training in neoclassical economics simply does not equip one with a *sensitive understanding* of how the market economy works" (Kirzner, 1980/1990, p. 112, emphasis added). An interpretation along these lines would suggest that Kirzner's theory of the entrepreneur is precisely such a theory which provides insight, without directly being a guide for public policy. Kirzner, however, was reluctant to embrace a wider notion of economic knowledge and insisted on the "fundamental conception of what makes a science of economics possible" (Kirzner, 1994, p. 319).

Weber's idea of the political education of a nation is also taken up by another strand within Austrian postwar thought. This strand has emphasized the ability of economic knowledge to inform public debates. The most notable book in this strand is Henry Hazlitt's "Economics in One Lesson" (Hazlitt, 1946), with its one lesson to mind the long-run consequences of economic policies. It emphasizes the interconnectedness of the economic system and the invisible consequences of economic policies, much in line with Weber's idea that a primary purpose of social science is to demonstrate how difficult it is to achieve socially desired results. In a similar vein a more recent pamphlet initiated by Dan Klein argues for the appreciation of the economist and his role in the deliberative process of individual and political decision making. Klein emphasizes that economics generates not just empirical facts and logical truths, but also insights that can help "the everyman." Although Klein's argument is directed at his colleagues who "favor liberty," he is aware that such enlightenment need not be partisan, but is primarily helpful in forming judgments: "For judgement on economic matters, economists can be the source of deeper insights and can prompt deeper values, having an influence like that which a parent has on a child" (Klein, 2001, p. 35).[15] Like some of the authors discussed above, Klein emphasizes that the study of knowledge and the recognition of the knowledge problem itself should make us rethink what the economist can contribute (Klein, 1999). But more importantly perhaps, both Klein and Hazlitt recognize that the goal of economic thought is relevance. Hazlitt's book is clearly aimed at the general public, Klein argues that economists should address the "everyman." In other words they argue that economics is an argument in the broader social conversation, to which they hope to contribute, much in line with the interwar work of the Austrian school.

More generally one could say that in the years following the initial revival part of the scholarly tradition has resurfaced within the Austrian school, although without much explicit consideration. The debate about subjectivism within Austrian economics was primarily a theoretical affair (Vaughn, 1994). From that debate, especially in the work of Lavoie and his followers, it became clear that more was at stake than just a theoretical reorientation. But the alternative, hermeneutic, notion of science that Lavoie was arguing for was, as well as the task of contributing to public enlightenment, or the political judgment of our nation as Weber put it, departs from the widely accepted notion of what it means to do economic science. It is therefore likely to be met with suspicion. It removes the scholar from the safe ivory tower, and requires the ability of economists to contribute to public and social deliberation without promoting partisan truths. That was, of course, Weber's point, and why he was so committed to the *moral value* of "Wertfreiheit."

CONCLUDING REMARKS: RESPONSIBILITY AND INSTITUTIONS

This chapter has traced the conception of the role and responsibility of the scholar and social scientist in the original Austrian school and in the Austrian revival. The chapter has demonstrated that this conception is closely tied up with what is considered economic knowledge and how certain we believe this knowledge to be. If we think of the student of the economy as a scientist than this typically reflects a restricted idea of what economic knowledge is, but a great certainty about the validity of that knowledge, and when we think of him as scholar, or indeed a student, we typically find a broader idea of economic knowledge, about which we can be somewhat less certain (Boettke & Horwitz, 2005; Dekker, 2016).[16] If we think of the economist as a scientist we emphasize his ability to *discover* the truth, if we think of him as a student or scholar we emphasize that he can *generate* insight and illumination. Weber's idea of Wertfreiheit as the most important moral ideal for the scholar only has a place in this latter conception, because in the former economic knowledge is the outcome of a technical procedure.

In the Austrian revival the scientific image of the economist prevailed, despite the fact that in the original Austrian economists the scholarly idea was dominant. That should make us wonder what can account for this difference. Above we have already considered the dominance of the scientific idea of economics in neoclassical economics as practiced during the first decades after WWII. But there is in fact another very important difference between the original Austrian economists and the Austrian revival, and that is the institutional context. Although it was certainly not true that Austrian economics was part of the mainstream of the economics discipline in the 1970s and 1980s it was mainly practiced in the research universities of that day and age. In the interwar years, on the contrary, the Viennese circles (Kreise) were the predominant institutional setting of that period (Dekker, 2014). These circles, at a certain distance of the university, tended to create a more direct relation between the scholar and his society. Academic institutions of the postwar period, however, increased the distance between society and the scholar. That distance was praised for it, supposedly, granted the greatest autonomy to the scholar, and the least possibility for the influence of non-scientific values.

It is this ingrained belief that Don Lavoie tries to undercut in an article about the role of academics and academies in our society. For Lavoie the central problem is not the lack of detachment of the scholar, but an excess of detachment. The scholar, he argues, has become detached from the world and detached from other disciplines. This he contrasts with the ideal of being open and engaging in conversation, what he calls dialogical openness: "For while value-freedom suggests that to be a scholar requires one suppress ones' own point of view, openness makes it clear that what we are really doing is risking our point of view against those of others" (Lavoie, 1995, p. 390). Lavoie's argument is in line with that of Weber about the value-relevance, and the engagement with what is culturally relevant, but it is also at odds with it, in the sense that it argues for more moral involvement of the scholar with the beliefs of the individuals he studies and engages.

More interesting than this difference is the fact that both Lavoie and Weber react to, and criticize the institutional practices of their contemporaries. And, obviously a lot has changed in the institutional practices since Weber wrote. Weber directs his criticism at his contemporaries who are preaching instead of teaching in the classroom, Lavoie directs his criticism at those who have withdrawn from the world and for whom academic concerns have trumped cultural significance. Their contributions both raise the question what the appropriate institutional setting is, in which scholarly work thrives best. Both Weber and Lavoie refer to moral qualities and ideals, but pay less attention to where these might flourish. Realizing that value-freedom as well as relevance are moral ideals, among other scholarly ideals (Lavoie praises patience, empathy and openness) is a first step. The next step should be to ask what institutions promote these qualities.

NOTES

1. For further testament to this involvement see the volume of collected inter-war writings (Mises, 2002).
2. The translation by Nock translates "unreflectirte" with unintended, but that translation seems more inspired by Hayek's reading of Menger.
3. My translation: "Hier, glaube ich, ist wieder ein Punkt, an dem die Theorie der Praxis wichtige Dienste leisten kann und soll. Gestützt auf die hundertjährigen Erfahrungen, die sich in ihr verkörpern und verwerten, berufsmäßig geübt, nüchtern und leidenschaftslos die Tatsachen zu untersuchen und aus dem Wandel der Erscheinungen den dauernden Kern herauszulösen, besitzt die Theorie eine weit größere Befähigung, die Wetterlaunen der Mode als solche zu diagnostizieren, als der Praktiker, der mitten in der Tagesströmung steht."
4. One way to think about this is the difference that McCloskey and Ziliak have recently drawn to the difference between statistical and real-world significance, or the oomph of results (Ziliak & Mccloskey, 2008).

5. See in particular, Hayek on quack remedies in "The Trend of Economic Thinking" (1933, pp. 126–7).

6. The work at the Cowles Commission at the time was also of great importance in establishing this image of the economist as objective scientist (Koopmans, 1957; Marschak, 1947; Mirowski, 2002).

7. Hutchison, is has to be noted, is very aware that there are usually multiple policy objectives, and part of his idea of judgment relies on the idea that alternative means will succeed differently in achieving this plurality of objectives.

8. Knight recognizes that there might be a pure realm of economic theory for which this is not the case: "Our own discussion so far has accepted this view that preferences themselves are simply facts, the only question being as to how these facts are known. It must now be emphasized that this position is possible only for a treatment limited to the character of 'pure' economics, completely divorced from any consideration of criticism or guidance of social action" (Knight, 1940, p. 22).

9. One might venture that given the already existing concerns about the "unscientificness" of Austrian economics, it was considered bad strategy to challenge the role of economists as scientists.

10. Kirzner repeats this interpretation in the 1990s (Kirzner, 1994).

11. Rotbard, as is well known, believes that ethics can in fact be an objective science too, but for the purpose of the argument he accepts in this essay that this is not the case.

12. This idea present in Robbins, Friedman and others is in direct contrast with Max Weber, who does not regard values as personal whims at all: "From the point of view of the demand for the 'value-freedom' of empirical analysis, it is therefore far from sterile, let alone absurd to discuss valuations: but if discussions of that kind are to be useful, one has to realize what their true purpose is" (Weber, 1917/2012, p. 312).

13. Later work by Rothbard self-consciously puts scholarship in the function of political goals, and thus clearly violates the values of scholarship as laid out by Weber.

14. Prendergast in a paper on Alfred Schutz and the Austrian school describes this distinction very neatly: "science as a system of decision rules and evidence criteria, rather than a system of true and justified beliefs" (Prendergast, 1986, p. 7)

15. The metaphor of the parent and the child is somewhat unfortunate. In the pamphlet Klein moves back and forth between arguing that economists should make people 'willing to see' certain basic economic insights (a more paternalistic view) and a call for engagement with public discourse.

16. See also Dan Klein's arguments for the greater robustness at the cost of absolute certainty (Klein, 2012, especially chapter 16).

ACKNOWLEDGMENT

The author would like to thank an anonymous referee, Pete Boettke, Solomon Stein, Arjo Klamer, and Pavel Kuchař for valuable suggestions and comments. While working on this chapter Erwin Dekker was a postdoctoral fellow with the F. A. Hayek Program for Advanced Study in Philosophy, Politics, and Economics at the Mercatus Center and the Department of Economics at George Mason University.

REFERENCES

Blaug, M. (1992). *The methodology of economics.* Cambridge: Cambridge University Press.

Boettke, P. J., & Horwitz, S. (2005). The limits of economic expertise: Prophets, engineers, and the state in the history of development economics. *History of Political Economy,* *37*(Annual Suppl.), 10−39.

Boettke, P. J., & Storr, V. (2002). Post-classical political economy: Polity, society and economy in Weber, Mises and Hayek. *American Journal of Economics and Sociology,* *61*, 161−191.

Böhm-Bawerk, E. v. (1892/1924). Unsere Aufgaben. In *Gesammelte Schriften von Eugen von Böhm Bawerk* (pp. 129−143). Wien: Hölder-Pichler-Tempsky.

Dekker, E. (2014). Vienna circles: Cultivating economic knowledge outside academia. *Erasmus Journal for Philosophy and Economics,* *7*(2), 30−53.

Dekker, E. (2016). *The Viennese students of civilization: The meaning and context of Austrian economics reconsidered.* Cambridge: Cambridge University Press.

Dolan, E. G. (1976a). Austrian economics as extraordinary science. In *The foundations of modern Austrian economics* (pp. 3−18). Menlo Park, CA: Institute for Humane Studies.

Dolan, E. G. (1976b). *The foundations of modern Austrian economics.* Kansas City, KS: Sheed Andrews and McNeel.

Egger, J. B. (1978). The Austrian method. In L. M. Spadaro (Ed.), *New directions in Austrian economics* (pp. 19−39). Kansas City, KS: Sheed Andrews and McNeel.

Fourcade-Gourinchas, M. (2001). Politics, institutional structures, and the rise of economics: A comparative study. *Theory and Society,* *30*(3), 397−447.

Friedman, M. (1953). The methodology of positive economics. In *Essays in positive economics* (pp. 3−46). Chicago, IL: University of Chicago Press.

Hayek, F. A. (1933). The trend of economic thinking. *Economica,* (40), 121−137.

Hayek, F. A. (1944). *The road to Serfdom.* Chicago, IL: The University of Chicago Press.

Hayek, F. A. (1960). *The constitution of liberty.* Chicago, IL: The University of Chicago Press.

Hayek, F. A. v. (1975). The pretence of knowledge. *The Swedish Journal of Economics,* *77*(4), 433−442.

Hazlitt, H. (1946). *Economics in one lesson.* New York, NY: Harper & Brothers.

Hennis, W. (1991). The pitiless "sobriety of judgement": Max Weber between Carl Menger and Gustav von Schmoller—The academic politics of value freedom. *History of the Human Sciences,* *4*, 27−59.

Hennis, W. (1994). The meaning of "Wertfreiheit" on the background and motives of Max Weber's 'postulate. *Sociological Theory,* *12*, 113−125.

Hutchison, T. W. (1938). *The significance and basic postulates of economic theory.* London: Macmillan and Co.

Hutchison, T. W. (1964). *Positive economics and policy objectives.* Chicago, IL: University of Chicago Press.

Kirzner, I. M. (1973). *Competition and entrepreneurship*. Chicago, IL: University of Chicago Press.

Kirzner, I. M. (1976a). On the method of Austrian economics. In E. G. Dolan (Ed.), *The foundations of modern Austrian economics* (pp. 40–51). Kansas City, KS: Sheed Andrews and McNeel.

Kirzner, I. M. (1976b). Philosophical and ethical implications of Austrian economics. In E. G. Dolan (Ed.), *The foundations of modern Austrian economics* (pp. 75–88). Kansas City, KS: Sheed Andrews and McNeel.

Kirzner, I. M. (1980/1990). The "Austrian" perspective on the crisis. In S. Littlechild (Ed.), *Austrian economics* (Vol. 1, pp. 191–202). Aldershot: Edward Elgar.

Kirzner, I. M. (1994). Value-freedom. In P. J. Boettke (Ed.), *The Elgar companion to Austrian economics* (pp. 312–319). Aldershot: Edward Elgar.

Klausinger, H. (2005). Die Austroliberalen und die Kampagne in "Neuen Wiener Tagblatt," 1931–1934. In *Wirtschaftspolitische Beiträge in kritischer Zeit (1931–1934)* (pp. 11–36). Marburg: Metropolis Verlag.

Klein, D. B. (1999). *What do economists contribute?* New York, NY: New York University Press.

Klein, D. B. (2001). *A plea to economists who favour liberty: Assist the everyman*. London: The Institute of Economic Affairs.

Klein, D. B. (2012). *Knowledge and coordination*. Oxford: Oxford University Press.

Knight, F. H. (1940). What is truth in economics. *Journal of Political Economy, 48*, 1–32.

Knight, F. H. (1941). The significance and basic postulates of economic theory: A rejoinder. *Journal of Political Economy, 49*(5), 750–753.

Koopmans, T. C. (1957). *Three essays on the state of economic science*. New York, NY: McGraw-Hill.

Lachmann, L. M. (1978a). Capital, expectations, and the market process. Economic theory. Kansas City, KS: Sheed Andrews and McNeel.

Lachmann, L. M. (1978b). Lachmann – An Austrian stock-taking. In L. M. Spadaro (Ed.), *New directions in Austrian economics* (pp. 1–18). Kansas City, KS: Sheed Andrews and McNeel.

Lavoie, D. (1986). Euclideanism versus hermeneutics: A reinterpretation of Mises apriorism. In I. M. Kirzner (Ed.), *Subjectivism, intelligibility and economic understanding* (pp. 192–210). New York, NY: New York University Press.

Lavoie, D. (1995). The "objectivity" of scholarship and the ideal of the university. In P. J. Boettke & M. J. Rizzo (Eds.), *Advances in Austrian economics 2B* (pp. 371–403).

Loasby, B. J. (1976). *Choice, complexity, and ignorance: An enquiry into economic theory and the practice of decision-making*. Cambridge: Cambridge University Press.

Machlup, F. (1955). The problem of verification in economics. *Southern Economic Journal, 22*, 1–21.

Marschak, J. (1947). Economic structure, path, policy, and prediction. *American Economic Review, 37*(2), 81–84.

Menger, C. (1883/2009). *Investigations into the method of the social sciences*. Auburn: Mises Institute.

Mirowski, P. (2002). *Machine dreams: Economics becomes a cyborg science*. Cambridge: Cambridge University Press.

Mises, L. v. (1919). *Nation, Staat und Wirtschaft, Beiträge zur Politik und Geschichte der Zeit*.

Mises, L. v. (1919/1983). *Nation, state and economy: Contributions to the politics and history of our time*. New York, NY: New York University Press.

Mises, L. v. (1922). *Die Gemeinwirtschaft: Untersuchungen über den Sozialismus*. Jena: Gustav Fischer Verlag.

Mises, L. v. (1922/1951). *Socialism: An economic and sociological analysis*. New Haven, CT: Yale University Press.

Mises, L. v. (1927). *Liberalismus*. Jena: Verlag von Gustav Fischer.

Mises, L. v. (1940). *Nationalökonomie: Theorie des Handelns und Wirtschaftens*. Geneva: Editions Union.

Mises, L. v. (1944a). *Omnipotent government: The rise of the total state and total war*. Yale, CT: Yale University Press.

Mises, L. v. (1944b). *Bureaucracy*. New Haven, CT: Yale University Press.

Mises, L. v. (1978). *Epistemological problems of economics*.

Mises, L. v. (2002). *Selected writings of Ludwig von Mises: Between two world wars*. Indianapolis, IN: Liberty Fund.

Mises, L. v., & Klein, F. (1923). *Die geldtheoretische Seite des Stabilisierungsproblems*. München: Verlag von Duncker & Humblot.

O'Driscoll, G. P. (1977). *Economics as a coordination problem: The contributions of Friedrich Hayek*. Kansas City, KS: Sheed Andrews and McNeel.

Parsons, T. (1965). Evaluation and objectivity in social science: An interpretation of Max Weber's contribution. *International Social Science Journal*, *17*, 46−63.

Prendergast, C. (1986). Alfred Schutz and the Austrian school of economics. *American Journal of Sociology*, *92*, 1.

Rizzo, M. J. (1979). Time, uncertainty and disequilibrium: Exploration of Austrian themes. Mario Rizzo. Lexington, MA: Lexington Books.

Rothbard, M. N. (1976a). Praxeology, value judgments and public policy. In E. G. Dolan (Ed.), *The foundations of modern Austrian economics* (pp. 89−111). Kansas City, KS: Sheed Andrews and McNeel.

Rothbard, M. N. (1976b). Praxeology: The methodology of Austrian economics. In E. G. Dolan (Ed.), *The foundations of modern Austrian economics* (pp. 19−39). Kansas City, KS: Sheed Andrews and McNeel.

Schumpeter, J. A. (1943/1976). *Capitalism, socialism, and democracy*. London: George Allen & Unwin.

Schumpeter, J. A. (1949). Science and ideology. *The American Economic Review*, *39*(2), 346−359.

Shackle, G. L. S. (1972). *Epistemics and economics: A critique of economic doctrines*. Cambridge: Cambridge University Press.

Silverman, P. B. (1984). *Law and economics in interwar Vienna: Kelsen, Mises, and the regeneration of Austrian liberalism*. Chicago, IL: University of Chicago.

Storr, V. H. (2011). On the hermeneutics debate: An introduction to a symposium on Don Lavoie's "The interpretive dimension of economics-science, hermeneutics, and praxeology." *Review of Austrian Economics*, *24*, 85−89.

Vaughn, K. I. (1994). *Austrian economics in America*. Cambridge: Cambridge University Press.

Weber, M. (1909/2012a). Review of Adolf Weber's the tasks of economic theory as science. In H. H. Bruun & S. Whimster (Eds.), *Max Weber: Collected methodological writings* (pp. 269−272). New York, NY: Routledge.

Weber, M. (1917/2012). The meaning of "value freedom." In H. H. Bruun & S. Whimster (Eds.), *Max Weber: Collected methodological writings* (pp. 304–334). New York, NY: Routledge.

Weber, M. (1919/2012). Science as profession and vocation. In H. H. Bruun & S. Whimster (Eds.), *Max Weber: Collected methodological writings* (pp. 335–353). New York, NY: Routledge.

Wieser, F. v. (1910). *Recht und Macht: Sechs Vorträge.* Leipzig: Verlag von Duncker & Humblot.

Wieser, F. v. (1924/1967). *Social economics.* New York, NY: Augustus M. Kelley Publishers.

Ziliak, S. T., & Mccloskey, D. (2008). *The cult of statistical significance.* Ann Arbor, MI: University of Michigan Press.

THE NATURE OF THE MARKET IN MISES AND WEBER

Solomon Stein and Virgil Henry Storr

ABSTRACT

Max Weber and the Austrian School of Economics share many of the same intellectual influences as well as a similar commitment to a social science characterized by methodological individualism, methodological subjectivism, and value-freedom. Although many of the links between Weber and the Austrian school have been explored, one area of agreement between Weber and Mises that is yet to be explored is their shared understanding of the nature of the market. This chapter attempts to close this gap by examining the pictures of the market in Weber's Economy and Society *and Mises'* Human Action. *We find that both portrayals share important features. These include similarities regarding (i) the nature of the market; (ii) the market's autonomous logic; (iii) the impersonality of the market; and (iv) the market in society.*

Keywords: The market; society; Ludwig von Mises; Max Weber; Austrian economics

Research in the History of Economic Thought and Methodology, Volume 34A, 73–91
ISSN: 0743-4154/doi:10.1108/S0743-41542016000034A014

INTRODUCTION

Max Weber and the Austrian School of Economics share many of the same intellectual influences as well as a similar commitment to a social science characterized by methodological individualism, methodological subjectivism and value-freedom. Weber was deeply influenced by the Austrians. Weber read and appreciated the economic and methodological writings of Carl Menger, the founding figure of the Austrian school. Additionally, Weber (1978, p. 78, 100) favorably references Ludwig von Mises's *Theory of Money and Credit* (1912) and Mises' (1935[1920]) essay on the problem of economic calculation under socialism.[1] Weber also deeply influenced the Austrian school. Mises, for instance, engaged in a systematic albeit critical study of Weber's methodological and economic positions in both *Epistemological Problems of Economics* (1960[1933]) and *Human Action* (1996[1949]). Mises also recognized the continuity between his work and that of Weber on the epistemic status of the social sciences, even though Weber was (in Mises' view) mistaken. As Mises (1960[1933], p. 79) summarized, "if it is possible today to approach the logical problems of sociology with better conceptual tools, this is primarily due to the work that Max Weber devoted to the logical problems of history."

While sympathetic to Weber's project, Mises believed that the conceptual system developed in Weber was marred by a single but important error. Weber treats economic theory as an ideal-typical generalization of action which, according to Mises, gives rise to historicism. Mises, however, views theoretical conceptions within economics as logically necessary relationships that are omnipresent and effective wherever the relevant assumptions are met. Mises attributes this error in Weber to the total dominance of historicism in the German university system at the time that Weber was writing. Although Weber stands like the biblical Noah, "righteous in his generation," for Mises (1960[1933], p. 83), "the reason why Weber fell into [methodological] misconception can be easily understood and explained from his personal history and from the state in which the knowledge of the findings of sociological investigation existed in his day in the German Reich, and especially at the universities."

Mises' student Alfred Schütz attempted to resolve Mises' criticisms of Weber's method of ideal-types in *The Phenomenology of the Social World* (1967). As Mises (1960[1933], p. 84, f. 27) footnotes,

Max Weber's epistemology has been continued and revised by Alfred Schütz in a way which also seeks to dispose of the judgment of the logical character of economic propositions to which I objected. Schütz's penetrating investigations, based on Husserl's system, lead to findings whose importance and fruitfulness, both for epistemology and historical science itself, must be valued very highly. However, an evaluation of the concept of the ideal type, as it is newly conceived by Schütz, would exceed the scope of this treatise. I must reserve dealing with his ideas for another work.

This promised future analysis of Schütz, however, appears to never have been written.

The absence of that evaluation of the attempted synthesis in Schütz is all the more vexing given that, once the question of the precise epistemic status of economic theory is resolved, the methodological characteristics of Mises' and Weber's theories are in agreement. There are, in fact, multiple parallels in terms of their emphasis on understanding social life as the results of meaningful action by individuals, studied in a way that is neutral with respect to the normative evaluation of conduct in favor of understanding the meanings held by the actors themselves. Consider, for instance, Weber's discussion of the importance of methodological individualism in understanding even collectivist societies. As Weber (1978, p. 18) describes,

> It is a tremendous misunderstanding to think than an "individualistic" *method* should involve what is in any conceivable sense an individualistic system of *values* .... Even a socialistic economy would have to be understood sociologically in exactly the same kind of "individualistic" terms: that is, the terms of the action of individuals, the types of officials found in it, as would be the case with a system of free exchange analyzed in terms of the theory of marginal utility or a "better", but in this respect similar theory.

This of course, is precisely the approach Mises takes in *Socialism* (1981[1951]).

The existence of a methodological connection between the Weberian project in interpretive sociology and the system developed by Mises has been pointed out by their intellectual descendants (see Boettke & Storr, 2002; Holton & Turner, 1989; Lachmann, 1951, 1971, 1977; Storr, 2013; Swedberg, 1998).[2] While Mises does not systematically engage Weber's theoretical contributions to substantive economic and sociological analysis, Weber's substantive contributions have influenced several of Mises' intellectual descendants.[3]

Ludwig Lachmann, in particular, developed his Austrian economics along consciously Weberian lines. In *The Legacy of Max Weber*, Lachmann (1971) uses Weber's methodological writings as a point of departure to develop an interpretive understanding of human action based on analysis of "the plan" pursued by each individual. Further, Lachmann advances the Austrian research program in understanding institutional evolution along Weberian lines by constructing a general theory of institutions that emphasizes the role of institutions as "means of orientation" (Lachmann, 1971, p. 49) for inter-plan coordination., The hermeneutic or interpretive turn in Austrian econom-ics (Ebeling, 1986; Lavoie, 1986; Prychitko, 1995; Storr, 2011) is a similar project in refining the study of Austrian economics as a science of meanings along Weberian lines. Likewise, Boettke and Storr (2002) argue for a more complete integration of the Austrian tradition following from Mises and Hayek, and the work in economic sociology that draws upon Weber (such as Granovetter, 2001; Holton & Turner, 1989; Swedberg, 1998). For Boettke and Storr (2002), reconnecting these two intellectual communities would enrich both groups theoretical and empirical work. Additionally, Storr (2013) argues for an explicitly Weberian approach to the study of culture by econo-mists. Drawing upon Weber's *The Protestant Ethic and the Spirit of Capitalism* (2010[1905]), Storr outlines a program of cultural study in under-standing the "spirits" that animate economic activity in various cultures, and argues that this is superior to the quantitative, aggregative approaches typical of empirical work among mainstream economists. Moreover, empirical work that embodies this interpretive approach to economic understanding within Austrian economics has frequently taken the form of analytic narrative, such as Chamlee-Wright (1997), Storr (2004), Leeson (2009), Skarbek (2014), Stringham (2015), and Grube and Storr (2015).

One area of agreement between Weber and Mises that is yet to be explored is their shared understanding of the nature of the market. The rest of this chapter explores the conceptual relationships between Mises and Weber's discussions of the nature of the market itself. The section "The Nature of the Market in Human Action" presents Mises' conception of the market as a process ultimately directed by consumer sovereignty. The sec-tion "The Nature of the Market in Max Weber" discusses Max Weber's view of the market as a social order based in purely calculative considera-tions. The section "Mises and Weber on the Market: Conceptual Similarities," then, shows the deep conceptual similarities between these pictures of the market, particularly the relationship of the market to other social structures. The final section concludes.

THE NATURE OF THE MARKET IN *HUMAN ACTION*

The Market as a Social System

In *Human Action*, Mises (1996[1949]) presents society as a conceptual whole, the entire meaningful totality of phenomena that arise as a result of deliberative coordination between acting individuals. The inherent hetero-geneity of productive factors, Mises argues, make each individual actor pre-fer cooperation and the benefits of comparative advantages to isolation.[4] Subjective feelings of community and solidarity, for Mises, become an out-growth of this process of cooperation rather than its source. As Mises (1996[1949], p. 144) writes,

> Within the frame of social cooperation there can emerge between members of society feelings of sympathy and friendship and a sense of belonging together …. However, they are not, as some have asserted, the agents that have brought about social relation-ships. They are the fruits of social cooperation, they thrive only within its frame; they did not precede the establishment of social relations and are not the seed from which they spring.

Society, like the individual acts of cooperation that comprise it, is a means by which individuals seek to achieve their personal ends. To best reach those private ends, individuals choose to serve as means by which others can engage in the pursuit of their personal ends.

The market is the process within society that results from this individual pursuit of ends through serving as means to the ends of others. Since the benefits that result from the division of labor reflected in the market pro-cess are the proximate cause of social life,[5] for Mises, the market process is concomitant (though not coextensive) with society. The market process is the fundamental phenomenon of society. As Mises (1996[1949], p. 257) explains, "The market alone puts the whole social system in order and pro-vides it with sense and meaning." And, experientially, "The market is the focal point to which the activities of the individuals converge. It is the cen-ter from which the activities of the individuals radiate" (Mises, 1996[1949], p. 258). The market is able to serve as this orienting structure because one result of the market process is the existence of the price structure, which enables individuals to engage in economic calculation.

For Mises, prices and the calculation they enable serve to render the market intelligible. While each action taken in the market reflects coopera-tion to reap the benefits of the division of labor, the knowledge that indivi-duals require in order to accomplish those ends are heterogeneous, subjective, and constantly changing. Only the existence of prices, particu-larly in terms of money, allows each individual confronting the myriad nexus of potential activities to determine what, in their judgment, is the most suitable action. Economic calculation is, thus, the indispensable fea-ture of market organizations. "The market is real," argues Mises (1996 [1949], p. 259), "because it can calculate." Individual action based in

economic calculation serves as the fundamental unit of analysis. The simultaneous playing-out of these myriad individual choices in the market process comes to be reflected in the price structure, which in turn informs
subsequent calculation. A similar reciprocal pattern of meanings relates the
market process with society as a totality. The individual acts of coordination in the market (ultimately, the want-satisfying outputs of those actions)
are the basis for the establishment of society, while society in its totality
provides the surrounding institutional features that facilitate the maximal
realization of the benefits of market interaction.

Mises develops his analysis of the market process and the social life
oriented around it from two perspectives. One perspective is concerned
with the identification of the logical categories and their relations in the
market, thereby rendering the operation of the market intelligible in terms
of these categories. The other perspective attempts to understand the
experience of acting individuals within the market process and the society
around it. Ultimately these two perspectives converge. For Mises, the logical interrelationships among individuals acting within the market are seen
to be generative of the experience of action in the market for individual
actors. The central organizing insight that explains this convergence is the
recognition that the ultimate determination of the structure of economic
organization rests in the choices of consumers, what Mises (1996[1949],
p. 269) refers to as "the Sovereignty of the Consumers."

Consumer Sovereignty and Market Perception

Understanding the market process as directed by consumer sovereignty
requires movement beyond initial appearances, which would place the
locus of control with entrepreneurs. Making sense of the coordinated
activities that occur in the market, however, requires understanding the
purposes and plans of those entrepreneurs. Directly (for final goods) or
ultimately (for intermediate goods) the efforts expended during the production of these final and intermediate goods is for consumption. It is
the "buying and abstention from buying" of the various goods and services available in the market that determines market activity (Mises, 1996
[1949], p. 270). Far from playing a controlling role, the entrepreneur can
only succeed by making use of resources in a way that allows for the
satisfaction of more (or the more urgently felt) wants of consumers. The
ends for which each individual actor chooses to participate in the vast

skein of specialization under the division of labor are the given (though hardly fixed) elements of the market process.

The market system is oriented to maximally satisfy the demands of acting individuals in their catallactic roles as consumers. As suggested above, each individual acting in their other catallactic roles (producer, entrepreneur, capitalist, etc.) seeks to most effectively meet consumer demand in order to acquire the resources to most effectively meet her own demand as a consumer. Moreover, the broader social structure that is continually resulting from the operations of the market process is also selected, through competition, to make the best use of the scarce factors of production for this goal. As Mises (1996[1949], p. 311) explained,

> The resultant of these endeavors is not only the price structure but no less the social structure, the assignment of definite tasks to the various individuals. The market makes people rich or poor, determines who shall run the big plants and who shall scrub the floors, fixes how many people shall work in the copper mines and how many in the symphony orchestras.

Dissatisfaction with the outcomes of the market process, thus, primarily represents dissatisfaction with the content of the desires expressed by individuals in their consumption habits. "'The moralists' and the sermonizers' critique of profits," Mises (1996[1949], p. 299) contends, "misses the point. It is not the fault of the entrepreneurs that the consumers − the people, the common man − prefer liquor to Bibles and detective stories to serious books, and that governments prefer guns to butter."

For Mises, recognition that what is produced as well as the techniques of production that are employed is driven by the actions of the consumers in the market process implies also that the features of the market serve as a mirror for how individuals in their catallactic role as consumers approach choices among market alternatives. This view of the market is far from romantic. According to Mises (1996[1949], pp. 270−271), consumers are

> ... merciless bosses, full of whims and fancies, changeable and unpredictable. For them nothing counts other than their own satisfaction. They do not care a whit for past merit and vested interests. If something is offered to them that they like better or that is cheaper, they desert their old purveyors. In their capacity as buyers and consumers they are hard-hearted and callous without consideration for other people .... [Entrepreneurs] are not free to spend money which the consumers are not prepared to refund to them in paying more for the products. In the conduct of their business affairs they must be unfeeling and stony-hearted because the consumers, their bosses, are themselves unfeeling and stony-hearted.

In Mises' view, consumers rather than the capitalists and entrepreneurs are the true unsentimental monsters in the market process.[6]

This immense generative power rests in consumers as a whole. Each individual contributes to this power only in proportion to their own command over resources. As such, in a society of non-negligible size, the power of even the richest individual wealth holders is vanishingly small. Acting individuals, thus, experience the market process as an automatic, natural and exogenous process that is totally outside one's control. Because individuals rarely see past this initial appearance to understand the catallactic relationships that are in place, Mises argues, they erroneously reach conclusions that are self-contradictory. For instance, according to Mises (1996[1949], p. 315), the market,

> ... appear[s] to the individual as something given which he himself cannot alter. He does not always see that he himself is a part, although a small part, of the complex of elements determining each momentary state of the market. Because he fails to realize this fact, he feels himself free, in criticizing the market phenomena, to condemn with regard to his fellow men a mode of conduct which he considers as quite right with regard to himself. He blames the market for its callousness and disregard of persons and asks for social control of the market in order to "humanize" it. He asks on the one hand for measures to protect the consumer against the producer. But on the other hand he insists even more passionately upon the necessity of protecting himself as a producer against the consumers.

Mises (1996[1949], p. 319) asserts that economics is unique in its capacity to demonstrate how the various forms of catallactic "split-personality" lead to spurious conclusions and problematic economic policies.

Mises, however, argues that it is also important to pay attention to how individuals perceive of market outcomes when attempting to understand the market process. While stressing that productive activity is constrained to meet the demands of consumers, these market constraints are not of the same character as restrictions enforced using the police power of a state. The producer is formally free to deviate in the use of resources subject only to technical limitations, provided the costs required to do so are paid. That this price is too high, or that the constraints imposed by consumer sovereignty are binding more generally, is of the same as being "constrained" by the laws of gravitation. Contrary to the identification of wage labor with slavery, the catallactic relationships that govern the individual as a producer of labor and the conditions of the labor market are nothing like slavery. As Mises (1996[1949], p. 634) summarizes,

> What makes the worker a free man is precisely the fact that the employer, under the pressure of the market's price structure, considers labor a commodity, an instrument of

earning profits. The employee is in the eyes of the employer merely a man who for a consideration in money helps him to make money. The employer pays for services rendered and the employee performs in order to earn wages. There is in this relation between employer and employee no question of favor or disfavor. The hired man does not owe the employer gratitude; he owes him a definite quantity of work of a definite kind and quality.

In a theme that will be stressed more in section 4, the "commodification" demanded by the market process and, ultimately, by individuals in their capacity as consumers is one of the sources of the welfare improvements brought about by the Industrial Revolution.

THE NATURE OF THE MARKET IN MAX WEBER

The Market as a Pure System of Purely Rational Action

Weber's most detailed treatment of the market as an ideal type appears is in a fragmentary chapter of his posthumously collected magnum opus, *Economy and Society* (1978). In this chapter, Weber presents market activity as a pure type of social relationship characterized by a totally rational social action. For Weber, action in the market is governed exclusively by the deliberate pursuit of economic advantage. The market itself presents itself as "a coexistence and sequence of rational consociations" (Weber, 1978, p. 635), coming into existence with the initiation of bargaining ("the market's most distinctive feature, viz., dickering" (Weber, 1978, p. 635)) between two potential exchange partners, and terminating with the completion of the exchange. The individuals engaged in an exchange are related only insofar as their deliberate pursuit of economic gain makes the proposed exchange of commodities mutually beneficial. The realization of those gains eliminates the basis for interaction. The terms of exchange that result in each of these instances is social action because it is oriented to the interests of a vast number of third parties along with the participants.

Deliberate pursuit of one's personal economic advantage requires considering the interests of these third parties, each of whom is a source of an alternative exchange opportunity that will be forgone if the present bilateral negotiation results in an exchange. The greater the extent to which economic activity is based in the deliberate pursuit of economic advantages (contrasted with say, the performance of traditional productive roles), the more any bilateral exchange is dominated by the considerations of all the members of the market community (Weber, 1978, p. 636). Introducing a monetary unit to reflect in quantitative terms these otherwise incomparable alternatives (i.e., economic calculation) enables the maximally deliberate consideration by all parties. Moreover, the use of money is inherently a social act since it is predicated on the expectation that one's future potential exchange partners will also accept money in exchange for other resources.

The scope of the market community for Weber is, thus, delineated by those individuals whose interests are reflected in the determination of the prices in each individual exchange interaction as well as those who share a reciprocal set of expectations expressed in the use of money. No other characteristics of each individual are required, or even relevant, for orienting others in their deliberate acquisition of economic advantages. The market community is a peculiar sort and is "the exact counterpart to any consociation through rationally agreed or imposed norms" (Weber, 1978, p. 636). Dickering may be the *action* most distinct to the market, but the most distinct *feature of market relations* is their impersonality. As Weber (1978, p. 636) writes,

> The market community as such is the most impersonal relationship of practical life into which humans can enter with one another .... The reason for the impersonality of the market is its matter-of-factness, its orientation to the commodity and only to that. Where the market is allowed to follow its own autonomous tendencies, its participants do not look towards the persons of each other but only toward the commodity; there are no obligations of brotherliness or reverence, and none of those spontaneous human relations that are sustained by personal unions.

It is worth noting here that this discussion of the impartiality of the market in Weber echoes Mises' discussion of the "unfeeling and stony-hearted" entrepreneurs and consumers who people markets.

According to Weber, the extent to which each individual exchange must be socially oriented toward yet other members of the market community makes the impersonality of market relations inevitable. Given the nature and scope of the knowledge that market actors would need to possess in order to have any other considerations beyond those reflected in prices, epistemic limitations alone are sufficient to restrict the orientation of third parties to the ultimate disposition of the commodities at issue. Since the deliberate orientation toward economic advantage requires taking into account these commodity-focused third party interests, even the individuals directly involved in the potential exchange are best able to pursue their own personal economic advantage by restricting their considerations to the commodities to be exchanged.

Within the market community, Weber identifies the emergence of certain norms of conduct that serve to ensure the smooth operation of each instance of exchange. The strict adherence to contract, particularly the finality of a completed transaction, serves both to secure for each party the benefits expected from the exchange itself, and to preclude any need to continue (or re-initiate) a direct relationship with that particular counterparty. For those spheres outside of the market community, the market's ability to deliver precisely the benefits being sought continuously demonstrates the definite advantages of adopting a market orientation. The internal logic of a situation in which the deliberate pursuit of economic gain by market participants would also be enhanced with the erosion of restrictions on exchange activity interacts with this promise of material returns to give the market a consistently expansionary posture. The result is, thus, "the continuous onslaught of the market community" (Weber, 1978, p. 638) against social institutions that would preclude exchanges. The combination of all of these features of market relationships, for Weber, gives to the social orders conditioned primarily by the market community a sense of being teleologically ordained.

Social Opposition to the Market Community

Weber has also attempted to explain why certain social forces are at odds with and are likely to resist the expansion of market communities. According to Weber, the market constellation of self-reinforcing elements is resisted by established social groups who previously controlled the access to and meanings of economic resources. For Weber (1978, p. 638), "the freedom of the market is typically limited by sacred taboos or through monopolistic consociations of status groups which render exchange with outsiders impossible." The continual expansion driven by the logic of the market community, however, erodes this control of economic resources by certain social groups. This diagnosis bears a strong resemblance to Weber's discussions of the perpetual expansion of bureaucratic administration. Both bureaucracy and markets are, in their spheres, unrivaled in the technically efficient operation of their functions. Both bureaucracy and markets, for Weber, generate an additional internal pressure to increase control. As a result, both bureaucracy and markets in their particular spheres come to displace alternatives that represent intermingling between deliberate and non-deliberate considerations, such as the organization of economic activity by tradition.

Only in cases where social action is based in purely charismatic authority, according to Weber, is this displacement of non-deliberate by purely deliberate and calculative considerations resisted. Since the charismatic group is totally removed from the day-to-day acquisition of economic advantages, they are instead oriented toward the exceptional historical moment represented by the presence of the charismatic leader. These situations of purely charismatic organization, Weber explains, are the antipode to the market's wholly deliberate orientation. Contrary to the stable and self-reinforcing nature of the pure market relations, charismatic orders are inherently unstable, and the resulting social forms cannot maintain the same indifference to the everyday. The ethical norms fostered by these groups, either as rationalized religious systems of ethics or established as a new traditional order of status groups, eventually faces the opposition to the commodity-orientation of market action. Every increase in the degree of importance given to deliberate economic considerations decreases the scope for actors to deviate from the impersonal interests of the entire market community to acknowledge obligations stemming from their particular non-market social relationships.

The logic of social action in the market, the impersonality dictated by that logic, and the opposition to traditional or religious ethics regarding economic conduct all color Weber's conceptual understanding of the interactions between those communities and the market community as intellectual systems. As an ideal type for understanding actual social action that takes place within the market sphere, however, Weber's other discussions in *Economy and Society* suggest it may be in need of modification. In particular, even as features such as price determination are likely governed by the impersonally considered interests of deliberate pursuit of advantage, social relationships that are experienced as personal can nevertheless form and have meaning within the market community (Goodwin, 1996; Price & Arnould, 1999; Storr, 2008). Conceptually, space for these subjectively personal relationships is a result of deviations from the strict conditions of the pure market relationship. For instance, the extension of social interaction from a temporally limited and isolated act of exchange to one with any kind of repeated interaction must take on some additional meaning, and "cannot be exclusively confined to the technically necessary activities" (Weber, 1978, p. 41). The deliberate acquisition of monopoly by market participants, Weber explains, can result in group formation. But, these too are unlikely to be strictly impersonal as Weber suggests.[7]

MISES AND WEBER ON THE MARKET: CONCEPTUAL SIMILARITIES

The accounts of the market found in Mises and Weber can be seen as reflecting a shared conception of the important questions regarding market activity and the lines along which answers can be found.[8] This section will highlight some of the key elements of this conception and their presence in both Mises and Weber. These include similarities regarding (i) the nature of the market; (ii) the market's autonomous logic; (iii) the impersonality of the market; and (iv) the market in society.

The Nature of the Market

Mises and Weber see the market as the conceptual label used to render intelligible a particular kind of individual activity. Yet, both Mises and Weber have a view of the market as more than "just" a bucket into which certain activities can be sorted. The interrelationships between all the various acts that occur in markets have emergent properties, most obvious in Mises' work in his description of the price system. For Mises (1996[1949], pp. 257–258),

> ... the forces determining the – continually changing – state of the market are the value judgments of these individuals [in society] and their actions as directed by these value judgments. The state of the market at any instant is the price structure, i.e. the totality of the exchange ratios as established by the interaction of those eager to buy and those eager to sell.

Moreover, the market has sociological elements as well as economic elements. Weber (1978, p. 635), for instance, has focused on the norms that ensure the effective operation of exchanges, even in situations where there is almost no chance of legal enforcement. As Weber (1978, pp. 328–329) explains,

> Agreements on the stock exchange, for example, take place between professional traders in such forms as in the vast majority of cases to exclude "proof" in cases of bad faith: the contracts are oral, or are recorded by marks and notations in the trader's own notebook. Nevertheless, a dispute practically never occurs. Likewise, there are organizations pursuing purely economic ends the rules of which nevertheless dispense entirely, or almost entirely, with legal protection from the state .... As a result of the peculiar subjective attitude of the participants, cartel contracts often had not even any effective

conventional guarantee. However, they often functioned nonetheless for a long time and quite efficiently in consequence of the convergent interests of all the participants.

The passage of time is also inherent in thinking about the market for both Mises and Weber. Mises takes the continual change, referred to in passing above, as fundamental to the market. "Not that prices are fluctuating," Mises (1996[1949], p. 217) argues, "but that they do not alter more quickly could fairly be deemed a problem requiring explanation." Similarly, Weber (1978, p. 635) viewed the market as a "sequence of rational consociations;" that it is sequential, of course, includes the passage of time. Additionally, the subjective orientations that make the norms of exchange conduct self-enforcing are, for Weber, the result of expectations about future market activity. As Weber (1978, p. 637) writes,

> It is normally assumed by both partners to an exchange that each will be interested in the future continuation of the exchange relationship, be it with this particular partner or with some other, and that he will adhere to his promises for this reason and avoid at least striking infringements of the rules of good faith and fair dealing.

Finally, both Mises and Weber view individuals as acting in the market on the basis of self-interest. "Market behavior," Weber (1978, p. 636) states, "is influenced by rational, purposeful pursuit of interests," and, similarly, Mises (1996[1949], p. 257) argues that in the market, "everybody acts on his own behalf."

The Market's Autonomous Logic

Mises and Weber offer similar descriptions of the logical relationships the constitute the market process. Consumer sovereignty is one such logical relationship for Mises. As Mises (1996[1949], p. 271) writes, "the consumers determine ultimately not only the prices of the consumers" goods, but no less the prices of all factors of production. They determine the income of every member of the market economy. Weber (1978, p. 636), similarly, argues that "the more rationally [any exchange] is considered, the more it is directed by the actions of all parties potentially interested in the exchange." These relations, they agree, give additional meaning to the systematic outcomes of market activity that are absent in other social relationships. Instances of bilateral exchange outside of the market community, Weber (1978, p. 638) points out, are often a matter of "who will cheat whom," rather than oriented mainly toward the interests of third parties. Similarly, outside of market interactions, seeing outcomes as ultimately the result of consumer sovereignty would be meaningless. For both Mises and Weber, these relations reside autonomously in the system insofar as they are generated by the nature of these interactions and are meaningful primarily or entirely within it. Serving to further differentiate the market sphere from other spheres is the development of monetary calculation, indispensable to market action and alien in all other contexts. Recall, Mises (1996[1949], p. 259) argued that "the market economy calculates in terms of money prices. That it is capable of such calculation was instrumental in its evolution and conditions its present-day operation. The market economy is real because it can calculate." Similarly, Weber (1978, p. 86) explained that "Calculation in terms of money, and not its actual use, is thus the specific means of rational, economic provision."

The Impersonality of the Market

According to both Weber and Mises, the market's logic, and the particular values revealed in the market, reflected in prices, and rendered commensurable by monetary calculation, are distinctive in content as well as form. In comparison to non-market relationships, the relative devaluation of considerations unrelated to the efficient provision of goods and services is subjectively experienced as the market having an "impersonal" orientation. As a claim about the basic operation of market activity, neither Weber nor Mises dispute this understanding. Recall that for Weber this is the basis for the antagonism of other social bodies toward markets. As Mises (1996 [1949], p. 313) describes, individuals as consumers "choose the captains of industry and business [based] exclusively [on] their qualification to adjust production to the needs of the consumers. They do not bother with other features and merits." Similarly, Weber (1978, pp. 636–637) notes that "the market community as such is the most impersonal relationship of practical life into which humans can enter with one another ... the market is fundamentally alien to any type of fraternal relationship." When Mises discusses the impersonality of the market, however, as discussed above he is either keen to emphasize this is the direct result of consumers' demands for goods and services regardless of "personal" considerations, or to stress the implications of economic activity being impersonal for the political and social liberty afforded to individuals. Though the level of generality differs, both Weber and Mises identify intellectual hostility toward markets with this "impersonal" character.

The Market in Society

Although both Mises and Weber stress the impersonal nature of market relations, (fortunately) both Weber and Mises acknowledge that the market is embedded in society as a whole. As mentioned above, Weber introduces personal relationships into various discussions of the market either alongside the autonomous logic of market exchange or, as in the case of the groups formed as a result of deliberate acquisition of monopoly, directly in the operation of that logic. Additionally, among other features, the attitude of social elites toward economic activity, and the social classes associated with the market is explicitly included among the economically conditioned features of political life (Weber, 1978, p. 193). Mises' approach arguably embeds society within the market, at least insofar as the benefits of coordination that result from market activity come to be the basis for (potentially all) social relations. Moreover, the impersonal character of the market, in Mises, does not mean that individuals themselves are stripped of personality but that their personality is mostly reflected in their consumption choices. As Mises (1996[1949], p. 233) acknowledges, consumer choices are "widely influenced by metaphysical, religious, and ethical considerations, by aesthetic value judgments, by customs, habits, prejudices, tradition, changing fashions, and many other things."

CONCLUSION

The relationship between the work of Mises and Weber is properly seen as extending beyond the methodological commitments to substantive conceptions of social concepts. The centrality of the idea of "market process" to the evolution of the Austrian school in the post-war era makes the nature of the market a natural topic with which to illustrate these conceptual links. In other areas such as comparative economic systems, the analysis of bureaucracy, and even the charismatic orientation of artistic genius, a more complete analysis of the similarities and differences between Mises and Weber remains unwritten.

The nature of the market is also of interest in its own right. The identification of the autonomous logic that governs market relationships as "impersonal" in both Mises and Weber stands in tension with other passages where individuals acting and experiencing the market do so in a personal way. Clearly the significance of features outside the market's autonomous logic, and the existence of personal relationships within market activity do not render the "impersonal" logic of market activity moot. But, the theoretical treatments of these extra-market features are underdeveloped compared to the treatment of the market's logic in isolation. The positive research program suggested by the gap between the theory of the market's logic and the theory that renders actual experiences in the market meaningful presents one path along which Austrian economists have "just gotten on with it" in recent years.[9]

NOTES

1. Weber explicitly cites *The Theory of Money and Credit* as his preferred exposition of monetary theory (Weber, 1978, p. 78). Additionally, Weber's discussion of Neurath's proposal for the replacement of prices with calculation in-kind are in substantial agreement with Mises' evaluation of socialist economic calculation, which Weber also makes note of as having appeared in print between the composition and printing of his own analysis (Weber, 1978, p. 100).

2. For instance, Lachmann (1977, p. 94) stated in his review of Mises' *Human Action*, "in reading this book we must never forget that it is the work of Max Weber that is being carried on here."

3. There are a few favorable references to Weber substantive economics and sociology throughout Mises' work, and the Weberian origins of Mises' thought echo throughout the development of post-war Austrian economics, insofar as *Human Action* is a (if not *the*) central text to that tradition.

4. Mises sees this exogenous heterogeneity as necessary for the creation of a perpetually extant structure of cooperation rather than a series of joint production efforts dissolved upon completion of a project. However, it seems likely that endogenous heterogeneity resulting from specialization and learning in the course of joint projects conducted by homogenous agents would necessitate some form of permanent cooperative organization.

5. And, at least from the viewpoint of the individual, the final cause as well.

6. One is of course equally free to make other moral judgments regarding action in the market, while still affirming that consumer sovereignty is what shapes that action. One individual's callous lack of sentiment is another's iconoclasm in the face of stifling social taboos.

7. The administrative staff of such an organization, for instance, has an interest in perpetuating the identity of the group even if the economic advantages for which it was formed have ceased to exist.

8. The extent of their agreement cannot be explained only through appeal to their shared methodological foundations: the view of the market given in textbook neoclassical economics, after all, is also methodologically individualist and methodologically subjectivist and yet quite distinct from either vision here.

9. See, for instance, Chamlee-Wright, 1997; Chamlee-Wright & Storr, 2010; Storr, 2004; Storr & John, 2011; Grube and Storr 2015).

REFERENCES

Boettke, P. J., & Storr, V. H. (2002). Post-classical political economy: Polity, society, and economy in Weber, Mises and Hayek. *American Journal of Economics and Sociology*, *61*(1), 161–191.

Chamlee-Wright, E. (1997). *The cultural foundations of economic development: Urban female entrepreneurship in Ghana*. New York, NY: Routledge.

Chamlee-Wright, E., & Storr, V. H. (Eds.). (2010). *The political economy of hurricane Katrina and community rebound*. Cheltenham: Edward Elgar.

Ebeling, R. (1986). Toward a hermeneutical economics: Expectations, prices, and the role of interpretation in a theory of the market process. In I. M. Kirzner (Ed.), *Subjectivism, intelligibility, and economic understanding* (pp. 39–55). New York, NY: New York University Press.

Goodwin, C. (1996). Communality as a dimension of service relationships. *Journal of Consumer Psychology*, *5*(4), 387–415.

Granovetter, M. (2001). A theoretical agenda for economic sociology. In G. Collins (Ed.), *Economic sociology at the millenium*. New York, NY: Russell Sage.

Grube, L., & Storr, V. H. (Eds.). (2015). *Culture and economic action*. Cheltenham: Edward Elgar.

Holton, R. J., & Turner, B. S. (1989). *Max Weber on economy and society*. New York, NY: Routledge.

Lachmann, L. M. (1951). The science of human action. *Economica*, *18*(72), 412–427.

Lachmann, L. M. (1971). *The legacy of Max Weber*. Berkeley, CA: The Glendessary Press.

Lachmann, L. M. (1977). *Capital, expectations, and the market process: Essays on the theory of the market economy*. Menlo Park, CA: Institute for Human Studies.

Lavoie, D. (1986). Euclideanism versus hermeneutics: A reinterpretation of misesian apriorism. In I. M. Kirzner (Ed.), *Subjectivism, intelligibility and economic understanding* (pp. 192–210). New York, NY: New York University Press.

Leeson, P. T. (2009). *The invisible hook: The hidden economics of pirates*. Princeton, NJ: Princeton University Press.

Mises, L. (1935[1920]). Economic planning in the socialist commonwealth. In F. A.Hayek (Ed.), *Collectivist economic planning* (pp. 87–130). London: Routledge.

Mises, L. (1960[1933]). *Epistomological problems of economics*. New York, NY: D Van Nostrand Co.

Mises, L. (1981[1951]). *Socialism: An economic and sociological analysis*. Indianapolis, IN: Liberty Press.

Mises, L. (Ed.). (1996[1949]). *Human action*. Cambridge, MA: Yale University Press.

Price, L. L., & Arnould, E. J. (1999). Commercial friendships: Service provider-client relationships in context. *Journal of Marketing*, *63*, 38–56.

Prychitko, D. L. (1995). *Individuals, institutions, interpretations: Hermeneutics applied to economics*. Aldershot: Avebury.

Schütz, A. (1967). *The phenomenology of the social world*. Evanston, IL: Northwestern University Press.

Skarbek, D. (2014). *The social order of the underworld: How prison gangs govern the American penal system*. Oxford: Oxford University Press.

Storr, V. H. (2004). *Enterprising slaves and master pirates: Understanding economic life in the bahamas*. New York, NY: Peter Lang.

Storr, V. H. (2008). The market as a social space: On the meaningful extraeconomic conversations that occur in markets. *Review of Austrian Economics, 21*(2), 135–150.

Storr, V. H. (2011). On the hermeneutics debate: An introduction to a symposium on Don Lavoie's 'the interpretive dimension of economics—Science, hermeneutics, and praxeology.' *Review of Austrian Economics, 24*(2), 85–89.

Storr, V. H. (2013). *Understanding the culture of markets.* New York, NY: Routledge.

Storr, V. H., & John, A. (2011). The determinates of entrepreneurial alertness and the characteristics of successful entrepreneurs. In E. Chamlee-Wright (Ed.), *Annual proceedings of the wealth and well-being of nations* (pp. 87–107). Beloit, WI: Beloit College Press.

Stringham, E. (2015). *Private governance: Creating order in economic and social life.* Oxford: Oxford University Press.

Swedberg, R. (1998). *Max Weber and the idea of economic sociology.* Princeton, NJ: Princeton University Press.

Weber, M. (2010[1905]). *The protestant ethic and the spirit of capitalism.* [*S. Kalberg, trans.*]. New York: Oxford University Press.

Weber, M. (1978). *Economy and society.* Berkeley, CA: University of Berkeley Press.

"UN-AUSTRIAN" AUSTRIANS? HABERLER, MACHLUP, AND MORGENSTERN, AND THE POST-EMIGRATION ELABORATION OF AUSTRIAN ECONOMICS

Janek Wasserman

ABSTRACT

Historians of economic thought have begun to reintegrate "un-Austrian" Austrians back into discussions of Austrian Economics, yet many scholars have argued that the Austrian School dissolved after emigration, with only Mises and his followers left to carry on the legacy. This chapter argues that a renewed focus on the networks established by the Austrians themselves, before and after emigration, reveals a distinctly different picture of Austrian Economics. Focusing on their shared interest in international trade theory and business cycle theory and their continued contributions to economic methodology, we see the émigré Austrians advancing Austrian ideas while also reconstituting and elaborating new Austrian affiliations. Ultimately, we find ourselves in

Research in the History of Economic Thought and Methodology, Volume 34A, 93–124
ISSN: 0743-4154/doi:10.1108/S0743-41542016000034A004

agreement with Herbert Furth that Austrian Economics is far broader
than Hayek, Mises, and their acolytes would have it, and that it is vital
to understand and preserve this more diverse tradition by investigating
more closely the works of Haberler, Machlup, Morgenstern, and others.

Keywords: Oskar Morgenstern; Gottfried Haberler; Fritz Machlup;
Rockefeller foundation; trade theory; economic methodology

> You know that I consider Hayek the "Dean" of the Austrian School; nevertheless, he
> still is only one of many members, and has no authority to excommunicate those who
> are not fully in agreement with his views. Moreover, the sentences you quote don't con-
> tradict my opinion about Auspitz, Lieben, and Schumpeter: sure, they can be included
> in the school only "with qualifications" or "not wholly" – but that is very different
> from calling them "un-Austrian"! Incidentally – would you deny that you, too – like
> every original thinker – has absorbed "many other influences" besides Menger, Boehm,
> and Wieser?
>   — J. Herbert Furth to Fritz Machlup, 21 July 1979 (Furth, 1979b)

While historians of economic thought have begun to reintegrate "un-
Austrian" Austrians back into discussions of Austrian Economics (Zanotti
and Cachanosky, 2015), scholars have typically argued that the original
Austrian School dissolved "in the wilderness" of emigration (Klausinger,
2006a). For some historians, the decline of the school owed to the remarkable ability of the Austrian émigrés to assimilate into the American academy and adapt to their new surroundings (Craver, 1986a, 1986b; Krohn,
1988; Spaulding, 1968). Austrian economists entered the mainstream and
therefore ceased to be "Austrian." The retrospective self-descriptions of the
native Austrians, in which they claimed not to represent a national tradition, reinforced this interpretation. The distance maintained between the
Austrian émigrés and American Austrians around Mises further bolstered
the conclusions that the old Austrian school was gone and that Misesians
had created a new Austrian Economics. This chapter argues that a renewed
focus on the networks established by the Austrians themselves reveals a different picture of Austrian Economics – in Vienna but more crucially in the
United States. Focusing on their shared interest in various elements of international economics – namely, international trade, business cycle, monetary,
and financial theory – we see the émigré Austrians extending and advancing
"traditional" Austrian ideas after emigration while also reconstituting and

elaborating their Austrian affiliations. The Misesians therefore represent but a branch of a renovated Austrian network in the United States.

With the exception of Friedrich Hayek, the "fourth generation" of the Austrian School, which included luminaries such as Gottfried Haberler, Fritz Machlup, and Oskar Morgenstern, has received little attention from students of Austrian Economics. The cohort's post-emigration work in particular has not appeared in collections, nor has it attracted scholarly research. For example, the three-volume *Austrian Economics* (Littlechild, 1990), contains but one article from this cohort (excluding Hayek). One can search the pages of *The Quarterly Journal of Austrian Economics* and *The Review of Austrian Economics* in vain for articles drawing from this group.[1] This neglect is somewhat surprising given the readiness of American Austrians to solicit interviews, lectures, and memoirs by the Viennese about past and present Austrian Economics (cf. Haberler, 1979, 2000; Machlup, 1980) and the references made to the significance of the fourth generation in promotional materials.

The argument for the omission of these "un-Austrian" Austrians usually follows from an ahistorical rendering of the Austrian idea. After the Austrian "revival" of the early 1970s, fourth-generation Austrians placed some distance between themselves and the predominantly American Austrians. This decision also led Austrian-born economists to downplay the "Austrianness" of their later work. The combination of self-ascribed American Austrians and self-effacing Viennese Austrians has led even sensitive observers to downplay the significance of émigré Austrian economists. Vaughn (1994) offers a clear version of this interpretation: "To be sure, other Austrian émigrés to the United States were actively involved in academic pursuits. ... However, despite the fact that they were working on issues that could be considered 'Austrian', as the term later came to be used, none of these economists thought of himself as an 'Austrian' economist except by nationality (p. 92)." This approach – which on the one hand recognizes the ongoing "Austrian" character of the work of the fourth generation, while on the other excludes them from consideration in a study on "the migration of a tradition" – forecloses discussion of a more diverse tradition of Austrian Economics.

This chapter will pick up the investigation of the Austrian tradition where Vaughn and others have left off by exploring the continued relevance of Austrian ideas in much of the work of the fourth generation. It will examine the significant ways that those Austrians continued to see themselves as part of a broader intellectual tradition. First, it will look at how the "un-Austrian" Austrians disappeared from Austrian Economics during the period of rebirth. To counteract this selective, *post facto* definition of Austrianness, the chapter will then trace what it meant to be Austrian in previous decades, particularly at the time of emigration. Being Austrian did not necessarily mean subscribing to a set of core propositions; instead, it entailed a skeptical and confrontational methodological style and direct interaction with other Austrian works. By focusing on style and interaction, we will move away from standard definitions of Austrian Economics, offered retrospectively by the fourth generation (Hayek, 1968; Machlup, 1982) and American Austrians (Rizzo, 1982; Klein, 2008). The Austrian School offered no static body of theory to the fourth generation, and no texts were beyond criticism. Before emigration, the fourth generation had traveled broadly and was exposed to a far wider array of influences than their predecessors, altering the connections to Menger, Böhm-Bawerk, and Wieser. Their work reflected this more transnational and ecumenical quality, yet it remained part of a broader heritage. As Machlup himself noted, he did not even consider himself part of a school until the mid-1930s when Luigi Einaudi, a close friend of the younger Austrians, referred to a distinctive movement coming out of Vienna (Leijonhufvud, 1977, pp. 27–29).

Following the lead of Klausinger (2002, 2006a, 2006b, 2015), we will then look at the subjects that preoccupied the Austrians and served as a basis for subsequent work. By no means exhaustive, this discussion will focus on the continued Austrian elements in the post-emigration work of the fourth generation in areas like international trade, business cycle, monetary, and financial theory. Drawing on the ideas of actor-network theory and the sociology of scientific knowledge, we will explore how the Austrian collective constituted itself through interpersonal connections, publications, conferences, correspondence, and institutions in which they participated – and often conflicted (Collins, 1998; Dekker, 2014; Latour, 2005). By positing an alternative to the Lakatosian model of a scientific research program grounded in core propositions, which has been employed to define the Austrian school in the past (Machlup, 1982; Rizzo, 1982), we can better see the processes through which Austrians made their science. Lastly, we will look at the ways in which Haberler, Machlup, and Morgenstern (along with Hayek) endeavored to resuscitate the Austrian approach after World War II – in the United States, Austria, and transnationally. Despite later claims to the contrary, the Austrian émigrés did not solely see themselves as Austrian by nationality, they also saw themselves as part of an ongoing tradition.

To preempt potential criticisms, I will offer a few caveats. This chapter does not deny the significance of the Misesian strand of Austrian

Economics, nor does it claim that libertarian Austrians represent a false deviation from the "true" school. It recognizes that the predominant interpretation of Austrian Economics and its history follows a relatively straight line from Menger through Böhm-Bawerk, to Mises and Hayek, to Lachmann, Rothbard, and Kirzner, and onto the present. Those that practice Austrian Economics today draw upon this rich lineage and have sustained and elaborated a distinctive economic approach. This chapter merely challenges the teleological assumptions of this interpretation and argues that Austrian Economics will be improved by articulating additional areas of concern and conflict within the tradition.

PROLOGUE: THE REBIRTH OF AUSTRIAN ECONOMICS AND THE EFFACEMENT OF THE FOURTH GENERATION

In the 1970s, a series of developments contributed to the reestablishment of Austrian Economics as a vibrant field of study, yet they also effaced certain dimensions of the tradition. In conferences and panels, articles and books, and academic programs at New York University and George Mason University, the Austrian approach gained greater attention than it had in decades. Through interviews with the Austrian émigré economists and closer engagement with emergent conservative and libertarian associations, a sizable American audience came to know about the ideas of Carl Menger, Ludwig von Mises, and Friedrich Hayek. This newfound interest in the Austrian School precipitated a search for a usable past, which produced an authorized version of Austrian Economics. This consensus interpretation had the ironic effect of effacing the Austrianness of the fourth generation of the original school – including Haberler, Hayek, Machlup, and Morgenstern – particularly, its post-emigration work. The promotional materials for the George Mason program (n.d.) reflect the canonized history:

> Carl Menger founded the Austrian School in Vienna in 1871 with his pathbreaking *Principles of Economics*. The ideas of Menger were further developed by two of his students, Eugene [sic] Böhm-Bawerk and Friedrich von Wieser. During the early twentieth century, the works of the Austrians were widely acclaimed and many of the ideas were absorbed into the mainstream of economic thought. This popularity grew in the twenties and thirties due to the works of such Austrians as Ludwig Mises, Friedrich Hayek and Lionel Robbins. After the war, the Austrian tradition was spread further by many

of Mises' most prominent students, such as Fritz Machlup, Oskar Morgenstern, and Gottfried Haberler, who taught at New York University, Princeton, and Harvard. In 1974, Friedrich Hayek won the Nobel Prize for his contributions to economic science, an event which helped spark the tremendous revival of interest in the Austrian School which has been seen in recent years.

The timeline presented is a curious one. First, it misrepresents members of the fourth generation as "students" of Mises. While Machlup took classes with Mises, the influences revealed in his university notebooks (n.d.) suggest no overarching influence from Mises. Like Machlup, Haberler took courses with Mises, but his early work did not betray a major impact from Mises's theories. Morgenstern never studied with Mises at all. While it recognizes the role of Austrian émigré economists in spreading the tradition, it suggests they spread ideas inspired by Mises, rather than their own original contributions. It overlooks the fourth generation's work in the interwar era, suggesting that Mises, Robbins, and Hayek were the true exemplars. This interpretation fit well with the self-presentation of the postwar Mises circle, which viewed itself as a marginal movement of true believers, yet it diminished the role of the individuals most responsible for bringing Austrian ideas across the Atlantic.

Coinciding with the American rebirth, the *Encyclopedia of Social Sciences* commissioned Fritz Machlup to write an encyclopedia entry on Austrian Economics that would provide a clear outline of the school's precepts (1982). Early drafts (Machlup, 1979a) hewed closely to the developing consensus. Machlup offered a brief history of the movement, eight core propositions of the school, and a discussion of "Austrian Economists," "non-Austrian Austrians," and "un-Austrian Austrians." Machlup shared the piece with his friend and fellow Austrian Herbert Furth, who called into question Machlup's overall thesis, which overlooked the contributions of the fourth generation and presented a somewhat teleological account of the movement – from Menger to Mises to the libertarians of American Austrian Economics. In challenging Machlup's portrayal, Furth presented an alternate history of the movement that included a far broader range of Austrian thinkers and economic trends.

That this revisionist task fell to Furth makes sense, given his vital role in maintaining connections between the Austrian émigrés after emigration. Born in Vienna in 1899, he became close friends with Friedrich Hayek upon arrival at the University of Vienna in 1918. The two participated in the Association of German-Democratic Students that year and later formed the *Geistkreis*, a circle of young intellectuals that included most future members of the fourth generation. He and Haberler became brothers-in-law in the 1920s. Furth practiced law until the Anschluss, when, as a Jew, he fled Austria for the United States, where he took a position at Lincoln University. In the early 1940s he became an employee of the Federal Reserve Bank, where he worked until retirement.

Despite his friendship with Hayek, Furth did not consider himself an economist while in Austria; he was never a member of the Miseskreis, for example. Ironically, it was only in American exile that he became an economist. In his work, he drew closer to Haberler and Machlup, as the three men began more intensive study of international finance and monetary policy. The three of them engaged in spirited discussions about balances of payments, the dollar shortage, the gold exchange standard, and inflation. Despite their diverging policy prescriptions and political affiliations, they constituted a node of economic inquiry deeply indebted to Austrian ideas.

Given his longstanding connection to the Austrian tradition and his reputation for sharp opinions and voluminous responses, Furth was an ideal critic for Machlup's article. Furth (1979a, 1979b) expressed several reservations. First, he disagreed that a "verbal approach" characterized Austrian Economics, since many members had used mathematics to advance economic knowledge. By Machlup's logic, Morgenstern would be "un-Austrian," a position he and others, including Menger (1972), the son of the school's founder, rejected. Furth also refused to grant that Joseph Schumpeter did not belong to the tradition. He accused Machlup of overrating Mises − "a narrow-minded dogmatic fanatic" − and of mistakenly asserting the centrality of political individualism to the movement. He argued that the principles of consumer sovereignty and political individualism were controversial within the school and only represented the views of Mises and his followers. As these disagreements evince, Furth believed that the Austrian School represented a broader series of interests than Machlup admitted.

In his response Furth had not only challenged Machlup's account but also Hayek's (1968). Hayek had written an account of the school that emphasized the non-mathematical articulations of value presented by Menger, Böhm-Bawerk, and Wieser. He highlighted the division of the tradition into two tracks, one following Böhm-Bawerk − which remained closer to Menger's fundamentals in its analysis of capital and interest − and the other tracking Wieser − wherein the calculability and comparability of utility loomed large. Mises continued the Böhm-Bawerk tradition and Hans Mayer advanced the Wieser approach. The controversial figure of

Joseph Schumpeter, arguably the greatest economist of the third generation, did not fit Hayek's schema. After lauding Böhm-Bawerk for his
"thorough command of the whole of economic literature (p. 460)," he
excluded Schumpeter on similar grounds: Schumpeter "although much
indebted to Böhm-Bawerk, absorbed so many other influences (particularly
that of the Lausanne school) that he cannot be wholly regarded as a member of this group (p. 461)." According to Hayek, for the former economist,
broad knowledge made him a better Austrian; for the latter, it exempted
him. In the concluding paragraph, Hayek acknowledged the existence of a
fourth generation, yet he sidestepped any consideration of their significance: "Most of these men, however, did the greater part of their work
outside Austria (p. 461)." His list of 33 representative Austrian works contained only one article, by Hayek himself, written by a member of his generation. For Hayek, the Austrian school reached its zenith in the "golden
age" before the Great War, divided in the 1920s and then dissipated in
the 1930s.

Machlup (1979b) pushed back against Furth's criticisms in his answer.
He claimed that he was following the conventions of the existing literature
on the School. He stood by the exclusion of Schumpeter, using Hayek's
language verbatim. He refused to recognize the compatibility of mathematical approaches with the Austrian School, and he denied that he overrated
Mises. The one concession he made was to create a separate "controversies" section of the article, where he located Mises's more problematic ideas.

Furth was not satisfied by Machlup's justifications. The epigraph for
this article comes from Furth's final answer to Machlup, which coyly
demonstrated the absurdity of Machlup's position. Furth rejected that
any one person, be it Hayek, be it Mises, had the right to include or
exclude members. Additionally, Hayek's logic for excluding Schumpeter –
that Schumpeter took on too many other influences – produced the
ironic consequence of excising the entire fourth generation, *including
Machlup*, from Austrian Economics! After all, who hadn't taken on other
influences throughout their careers? Furth cautioned against presenting
the Misesian strand of the School as the rightful heir to the Austrian man-
tle. Furth argued that the usually cautious and precise Machlup had suc-
cumbed to the false belief that Austrian Economics required a unified
definition, an interpretation that flew in the face of historical reality.
Furth demanded a closer investigation of the diverse nature of the
Austrian School that he – and Machlup, too – had known in Vienna
and beyond.

POST-WWI AUSTRIAN ECONOMICS: DISCONTINUITY, INSTABILITY AND INTERNATIONALIZATION

To better understand the difference of opinion between Hayek and Machlup on one side and Furth on the other, we must return to the interwar years to investigate the rifts within the School. We will look at the state of economics in Austria in the interwar period and the kind of research that members of the School conducted and how their work began to diverge. The years immediately following the Great War represented a period of transition in Austrian economics. Younger Austrians were exposed to a broad range of approaches while facing diminished academic prospects. This led them to seek research opportunities abroad to further their careers. Their work increasingly bore an international stamp that the earlier generations' arguably did not possess. They also established significant connections in the transnational academy, particularly in the United States, which would later facilitate emigration and new collaborations.

For Austrian students interested in the tradition of Carl Menger, the 1920s were a challenging time. Menger, though still living in Vienna, had long since retired. Böhm-Bawerk and Eugen Philippovich had passed away during the war, leaving Friedrich von Wieser as the lone representative with a tenured academic appointment. Even before his retirement in 1922, however, his interests had shifted to sociology (Hayek, 1926). After Wieser's departure, the economics faculty consisted of the Marxist economic historian Carl Grünberg, the universalist Othmar Spann, and Wieser's student, Hans Mayer. Despite concerns about his productivity, Mayer received his appointment ahead of Alfred Amonn and Ludwig Mises because of support from Wieser and Spann (Klausinger, 2015; Leonard, 2012, pp. 77–92). Joseph Schumpeter was not even considered, since he permanently left the Austrian academy after his stint in the first postwar government. Mises struggled to overcome antipathies against him in the academy that likely owed to his Jewish origins, his difficult personality, and his political liberalism (Caldwell, 2008, pp. 145–6; Craver, 1986a, p. 5). While Mises taught courses as an untenured *Privatdozent* that the fourth generation attended, it was not until the mid-1920s that they were permitted to join his *Privatseminar*, for students had to possess a Ph.D. (Haberler, 1981, p. 122). With so many forceful personalities as instructors, the fourth generation received an eclectic education. Machlup's university notebooks (n.d.) reveal the lack of methodological focus in economics instruction. In courses with Spann and Wieser,

Machlup read books by Spann, Schumpeter, Philippovich, Hume, Kant, Knut Wicksell, Irving Fisher, and Arthur Spiethoff. Likewise, Oskar Morgenstern, Paul Rosenstein-Rodan, and Erich Voegelin struggled to accommodate their bickering advisers, Spann and Mayer (Morgenstern, 1923; Voegelin, 1925).

Despite the vibrancy of the Viennese intellectual environment and the high level of intellectual debate in seminars, discussion groups, and societies like the *Geistkreis*, Mises's *Privatseminar* and the *Nationalökonomische Gesellschaft*, the situation for the Austrian economists was unpropitious in the 1920s. There were no jobs in the academy and very few in finance or economics. The ubiquitous anti-Semitism of the Austrian academy made it even more difficult to find success, with scholars like Spann actively thwarting dissertation and habilitation attempts by Jewish students and those (like Morgenstern) suspected of Jewish origins. These circumstances encouraged younger Austrian scholars to seek academic opportunities abroad. This is not to say that these scholars planned or wished to leave Austria permanently, only that they were willing to explore international options. Hayek headed to the United States in 1922–23. Others followed suit thereafter. After the 1924 establishment of the Laura Spelman Rockefeller Memorial Fund fellowships, Viennese economists formed a strong working relationship with the Rockefeller Foundation (RF) (Craver, 1986b; Fleck, 2011, p. 58). Furth, Haberler, Machlup, Morgenstern, Rosenstein-Rodan, Gerhard Tintner, and Voegelin received fellowships in the next decade to study abroad.

The RF interaction helps explain the increasing internationalization and heterodoxy of the younger Austrian School that is often associated with the "dissolution" phase of the 1930s. Fellowships, which lasted one or two years, introduced the Austrians to new research trends in the Europe and the United States, particularly the business cycle research conducted at the Cambridge (United Kingdom) Economic Service, the Harvard Economic Service, and the National Bureau of Economic Research. While Schumpeter and Mises – in *Theorie der wirtschaftlichen Entwicklung* and *Theorie des Geldes und der Umlaufsmittel*, respectively – had deduced the mechanisms of the trade cycle, empirical research loomed larger for the younger generation as a result of these transatlantic connections. Haberler, Hayek, Machlup, and Morgenstern all employed statistics in their work from the 1920s, even as they maintained a healthy skepticism toward these data. Synthetic tendencies and a growing methodological skepticism toward empiricism appear clearly in the early works of this generation, such as Hayek's *Geldtheorie und Konjunkturtheorie* (1929), Morgenstern's *Wirtschaftsprognose* (1928a), and Haberler's *Sinn der Indexzahlen* (1927). These confrontations between deductive and inductive approaches, combined with a growing mistrust of statistical data, pressed the younger thinkers beyond the theoretical deductions of the previous generation (Caldwell, 2008, pp. 133–164; Klausinger, 2011; Leonard, 2012, pp. 93–109). While none of the young Austrians ever embraced inductive theories of economic knowledge, they recognized the need to confront the empiricist challenge. Meanwhile extended absences from Vienna accentuated the intellectual discontinuity between generations of the Austrian School. This is not to say that the fourth generation broke with their predecessors – they did much to continue Austrian work on capital, interest, production, and the business cycle. Nevertheless, a shift in the meaning of Austrian Economics was already underway in the mid-1920s, and the transatlantic exchange had a lot to do with it.

The work conducted by the Austrians, often in conjunction with the Rockefeller-sponsored Institut für Konjunkturforschung, reinforced these new tendencies. The institute was founded in 1927 by Mises and directed by Hayek until 1930, when he was succeeded by Oskar Morgenstern. As Hayek described in a grant proposal to the RF: "The first aim of the Institute has been to prepare and issue a regular economic service .... The Institute has however planned, in accordance with its original aims, to undertake several special investigations into problems connected with business cycles of a more general character (cited in Van Sickle, 1930)." Recognizing the importance that the RF attached to empirical research, Hayek tried to garner support for his institute by linking its work to the other international forecasting centers, even though his preference lay more with theoretical work "of a more general character." The RF responded positively, providing a five-year grant totaling $20,000 beginning in 1931. This was $1,000 per annum more than Hayek requested, with the extra funds earmarked for Morgenstern and Hayek, since "these two men are among the ablest of the younger economists in the German speaking countries, and there is some danger that they will be drawn away from Vienna unless conditions can be made for [sic] attractive for them (Van Sickle, 1930)." The RF was right to fear a brain drain, for Hayek left Vienna for London in 1931. After his departure, Haberler assisted Morgenstern with the institute. Likewise, Morgenstern had regular employment requests, declining positions at Berkeley and Kiel (Morgenstern, 1932). The RF renewed its support in 1936 for two years at $6,000 per annum and again for three years in 1938, though it would cancel payment after the Anschluss.

Hayek's departure signaled the beginning of the migration of the Austrian School. As will be discussed in the subsequent section, one can reasonably argue that the center of the Austrian School ceased to reside in

Vienna by the early 1930s, as Haberler, Hayek, Machlup, and Mises all either left the capital permanently or spent extended periods abroad. Nevertheless, Morgenstern dedicated himself to carrying on the tradition he had learned from Wieser and Mayer, particularly the former (1927b). Morgenstern, playing a larger role in Viennese economic circles, distanced himself critically from Mises and some of his fourth-generation colleagues in his search for more exact formulations of economic theory. Under his leadership, the Institut began its transition toward mathematical economics (Klausinger, 2006b). He invited an impressive array of scholars to contribute to its activities, including Haberler, Abraham Wald, and Gerhard Tintner (Sigmund, 2015, pp. 248–53). He attracted commissions from the League of Nations, the International Chamber of Commerce, and the Bank for International Settlements. After Mises's departure for Switzerland in 1934, Morgenstern also reshaped the economics seminar associated with the school, inviting more contributions from mathematicians. Neither Morgenstern nor his collaborators viewed their work as a fundamental break from the Austrian tradition, however. As Karl Menger stressed in a retrospective article celebrating the centenary of the Austrian School (1972), participants in the Mathematical Colloquium of the early 1930s sought better mathematical expressions of the verbal concepts of the earlier Austrians, striving to demonstrate the compatibility of modern mathematics and marginalist economics. He cited the works of Morgenstern, Karl Schlesinger, John Von Neumann, Wald, and Menger himself as examples of this synthetic work. As a further justification for this interpretation, he argued that the earlier Austrians, including his father, had recognized the need for advanced math (algebra and differential equations), yet their lack of training doomed such efforts (pp. 21–22). While increasingly critical of Mises, Mayer, Hayek, and Haberler in the coming decades, Morgenstern still positioned his work against theirs, thereby carrying the debates of the School into emigration. In other words, though the center of Austrian thought shifted, the turmoil of the 1930s stimulated creative elaborations within the School abroad.

DEPRESSION AND INTERREGNUM: AUSTRIANS BETWEEN VIENNA AND THE UNITED STATES

The Great Depression and the rise of European fascism had profound effects on the Austrians, their home country, and their intellectual output.

By 1938, most members of the fourth generation had left Central Europe. A mere two years later, almost all had established themselves in the Anglophone world. The preceding years therefore represented a transitional period. Not only were the Viennese preoccupied with their academic prospects and the political travails of the day, but they were also rethinking their economic theories as a consequence of these historical events. Even as the Austrians diverged geographically and intellectually, and as the coherence of the collective attenuated, the individuals relied on their Austrian ideas and connections for intellectual and personal sustenance. In its continued academic and institutional connections and the intensification of its correspondence and personal interactions, the Austrian school reconfigured itself – less as a single-minded economic collective and more as a political and ideological network. One can rightly argue that the traditional Austrian school declined "in the wilderness" of emigration (Klausinger, 2006a). It is nevertheless vital to explore the important ways in which Austrians elaborated and transformed their heritage, and how Austrian ideas continued to have relevance in a new transatlantic context. The new challenges that the post-emigration moment offered introduced new opportunities for Austrian intellectual entrepreneurship, which led the Austrians into new areas of institutional, ideological, and political activity.

Owing to the Depression, fourth-generation Austrians devoted increased attention to topical economic matters: business cycles; international trade; deflation; monetary and capital theory; interventionism; and laissez-faire. With the upsurge of protectionist and autarkic policies in the 1930s, they investigated the dynamics of international economics, which drew them into conversation and conflict with economists around the globe. Consequently, Austrians engaged with multiple audiences. Undoubtedly, their prescriptions diverged (Klausinger, 2006b); nevertheless, discussion and conflict with one another informed many of their works. And, more often than not, they continued to support one another's work and their shared concerns.

As early as 1930, third- and fourth-generation Austrians began to leave their home country in search of better employment prospects. Many benefited from Rockefeller support in putting down new roots. Paul Rosenstein-Rodan left for London in 1930, receiving a subvention from the RF at University College. He also taught at the RF-sponsored London School of Economics for seventeen years. Friedrich Hayek departed Vienna in 1931 for LSE. In 1934, Haberler took a position with the League of Nations Economic Section in Geneva, where he worked with Arthur Loveday, adviser to the RF on business cycle research. Haberler followed Joseph Schumpeter to Harvard in 1936. During the war, he attempted to get Hayek an appointment to the New School. Mises also went to Geneva in 1934, join-ing William Rappard's *Institut Universitaire*. Fritz Machlup spent a semester as a Rockefeller fellow at Harvard in 1935 before receiving an appointment at the University of Buffalo. From Buffalo, Machlup negotiated (in vain) an offer for Ludwig Mises at UCLA. Morgenstern found himself in the United States as a Carnegie Visiting Professor when the Anschluss occurred in March 1938. Deciding not to return to Europe, he wrote to American collea-gues in search of a job. He eventually accepted a position at Princeton University. While many Austrian economists − including close associates such as Alexander Gerschenkron, Martha Steffy Brown, Walter Fröhlich, and Erich Schiff − were still in Austria as late as 1938, those most associated with the Austrian tradition were quite successful in their emigration efforts, especially when compared with other Austrian scientists (Rockefeller Fellowship, 1938; Spaulding, 1968).

With many Austrians on the move during the 1930s, the center of grav-ity of the school shifted from the work of Mises and the Privatseminar to Haberler, Hayek, Machlup, and Morgenstern. This owed to creative and intellectually influential publications by Haberler, Hayek, and Machlup, and the institutional and organizational skills of Haberler and Morgenstern. Morgenstern and Haberler attracted international interest for trade cycle the-ory through their involvement with various League of Nations activities and the international network of trade cycle institutes supported by the RF. Haberler also published significant works on international trade that com-bined "pure theory" with policy recommendations. Instead of separating the theoretical and practical, he "tried to apply the theoretical analysis to every question arising from trade policy" (Haberler, 1936a, p. vii). Haberler chose to build out from Austrian theoretical foundations into policy advice. The lasting significance of this work owed to Haberler's reinterpretation of com-parative costs in terms of opportunity cost (Baldwin, 1982). These elabora-tions built directly on the works of Wieser and Böhm-Bawerk. His policy prescriptions, which advocated against protectionist tariffs and for freer trade, fit well within the Austrian tradition. His call for greater attention to "simplifying assumptions" in economic theory inspired future work by him and Machlup (Haberler, 1936a, p. 211).

The initial version of *International Trade*, published in German in 1933, helped establish Haberler's reputation as a significant economist. It attracted the attention of Arthur Loveday and the Economic and Financial Section of the League of Nations. The League commissioned him to write a work "coordinat[ing] the analytical work then being done on the problem of the recurrence of periods of depression" (Haberler, 1937, p. v).

Prosperity and Depression was a synthetic work as much as an original piece of research, in which Haberler argued that most of the approaches to business cycles could be reconciled and that "the differences between the theories analyzed is not so radical as is sometimes believed" (p. 2). Haberler struck a pose of a neutral arbiter between various theoretical undertakings and placed distance between himself and any one approach, including the Austrian. Haberler offered a substantive criticism of the "over-investment" school of Mises, Hayek, Machlup, and Strigl for their inattention to the possibility and effects of a secondary deflation. He also took Mises to task for his notion of free banking, yet Haberler generally endorsed the explanatory power of Austrian theory over others (pp. 57–59). In composing the book, Haberler leaned heavily on Hayek and Machlup. Hayek was critical yet supportive at the outset, saying that Haberler was off to an "outstanding start (1934)." Machlup was even more effusive, calling the finished work "masterful" (Machlup, 1934).

In later editions Haberler (1946) distanced himself from the monetarists and Keynesians, leveling a particularly harsh criticism against the latter, thereby hewing closer to his Austrian roots. This criticism emerged from an earlier article on the Keynesian multiplier (Haberler, 1936c). Hayek lavished praise on this interpretation, suggesting that Haberler should aid him in a concerted attack on Keynes's theory (Hayek, 1936). Other members of the Austrian school were also appreciative. No less an authority than Joseph Schumpeter regarded Haberler's work as a "masterly presentation of the modern material" that ranked as one of the most significant recent contributions to economic theory. The *London Times* also acknowledged the work's significance: "But in a mere two years he has done what might have taken some men a lifetime" (cited in Officer, 1982, p. 149).

The success of *Prosperity and Depression* in reorienting international trade theory and macroeconomics (Boianovsky, 2000; Boianovsky & Trautwein, 2006) opened up new opportunities for collaboration between Haberler, Machlup, and Morgenstern. Hayek, Machlup and Haberler's correspondence intensified in the period after 1933. They exchanged spirited letters during the Frank Knight-Austrian debates over capital theory. Machlup and Haberler built off of one another's work over the next decades. For example, Machlup mentioned his debt to Haberler (along with Hayek and the Miseskreis) in the acknowledgments to the English edition of *The Stock Market, Credit and Capital Formation* (1940a, 1940b, p. viii). Haberler referred favorably to Machlup's analysis of the role of short-term loans in the creation of inflation and cyclical upswings (Haberler, 1946, pp. 57–67). Both men recognized the need to clarify, qualify, and elaborate

Austrian theory to make it more robust and more useful as a policy tool. Their letters are filled with advice and suggestions for further improvement.

The interaction between the works of Haberler and Morgenstern was less overt and less significant overall, manifesting more in their correspondence than in acknowledgments in one another's scholarly output. In the concluding chapter of *Prosperity*, Haberler referenced the work of Morgenstern (among others) in his renewed call for greater attention to the issues of international trade and their relevance for business cycles. Haberler observed that business cycle theory tends to consider (national) economies as closed systems with few significant exogenous influences. Contemporary economic events belied this theoretical assumption. He argued for more comparative research between national economies and greater focus on the ways in which the fluctuations within one national economy impact others. These considerations developed out of Haberler's knowledge of the work Morgenstern and his colleagues were conducting at the Institut für Konjunkturforschung.

Haberler and Morgenstern were intimate friends since the early 1920s, so their nearly simultaneous rise to prominence was especially gratifying. As Haberler made his name in international trade theory and macroeconomics, Morgenstern established himself as one of the leading European researchers on trade cycles. While he did not produce any major works on trade cycle theory or international trade, in his role as the director of the Institut, Morgenstern was a central organizer of international trade cycle research. The RF esteemed him highly, which opened up many research opportunities for him and his associates. The RF provided monies for larger comparative studies of economic conditions in the Habsburg successor states and programs in mathematical economics. He built the Viennese Institut from a humble operation into an internationally recognized one. The little center, which never had a staff of more than eleven, became the envy of all the European institutes, even eliciting complaints from fellow directors about Morgenstern's ambition, political involvement and policy advice (Rockefeller Fellowship, n.d.). Despite this resentment, the RF maintained "a warm place in [its] heart for the little group down in Vienna which ... is justified by their performance (Van Sickle, 1933)."

The clearest evidence of continued interactions between Haberler, Morgenstern, and the others comes from a series of three meetings conducted during the summer of 1936 in Geneva, Annecy, and Vienna, respectively. In a time when fewer and fewer international scientific conferences took place in Europe, these gatherings played an important role in fostering the exchange of ideas. Austrians played central roles in these meetings, and their ideas gained a broad audience. Haberler and Morgenstern were the central figures, and their theoretical considerations loomed large in the discussions. The origins of these conferences dated back over a year to the publication of *Prosperity and Depression*. In a 1935 report, Tracy Kittredge of the RF identified several areas for further economic research, including business cycle research, international trade, and banking and monetary policy. A collaborator and supporter of the Austrians, he expressed his argument in language informed by Austrian economics:

> There is substantial agreement that the most urgent task before the economists of the world today is to complete the analysis of contemporary economic phenomena with a view to making available for future practical programs definite knowledge of the results of previous governmental attempts to modify and control economic processes. The gap between economic theory and economic life is still very wide. Regardless of theoretical considerations, the populations of the world are insisting on governmental action. Governments are forced to undertake vast programs without adequate preparation or sufficient knowledge of the processes involved, or of the possible and unpredictable repercussions of their actions. (Rockefeller Fellowship, n.d.)

The discussion of government planning and interventions, and the emphasis on market processes reflected Kittredge's familiarity with Hayek and Mises's work. His attention to the insufficiency of economic knowledge demonstrated a familiarity with Morgenstern's pessimistic account of economic forecasting. His desire to elaborate economic theory and connect it to policy also reflected the shift underway in the fourth generation of Austrians. Fittingly, Kittredge recommended Haberler, Mises, and Morgenstern for a potential conference, as well as other sympathetic economists, such as Robbins, Frisch, and Rist (Rockefeller Fellowship, n.d.).

This conference would fall between two others, likewise sponsored by the RF. The League of Nations Financial and Economic Section had planned a conference to discuss international trade and business cycles, with Haberler's *Prosperity and Depression* serving as the centerpiece (Van Sickle, 1935). Meanwhile the European business cycle institutes — about a dozen centers across the continent — had scheduled their biennial meeting in Vienna, with Morgenstern serving as host. After consulting with Morgenstern and Loveday, the RF scheduled their event between the others in the French town of Annecy. The list of invitees represented a who's who of European economists.[2] Austrians and those sympathetic to Austrian ideas played prominent roles at the conference. In addition to the participation of Haberler, Morgenstern, and Mises, Wilhelm Röpke provided commentary on the program and attended. Even Joseph Schumpeter, the prodigal Austrian, was invited but had to decline in order to complete his own book on business cycles (Schumpeter, 1936).

The Austrians dominated the proceedings at these conferences and came away positively disposed to the direction of international economics. Unsurprisingly, Haberler valued the Geneva conference most highly, since it placed him at the center of the discussion. He wrote to Machlup, who was in the United States at the time and could not attend, of the fruitful developments out of the meetings (Haberler, 1936b, 1936d). For the Austrians as a collective, the Annecy conference was more significant, as it raised important questions about economics to which they had long devoted themselves. In the agenda for the conference, the organizers posed three overarching themes: (1) Is there such a thing as a "world economy"? If so, what forces act on it? (2) How can these forces be measured and analyzed? (3) What deficiencies exist in the research on economic change and how can they be remedied? The ensuing discussion focused on the relative importance of research at the national and international levels and on the reliability of currently available economic data.

The Austrians contributed to discussion of all three questions, and they spoke almost as one, especially on the latter two points. Morgenstern embraced the use of new statistical reporting, yet he stressed theory: "purely scientific research work" was "of basic importance ("Record", 1936)." Given the diversity of statistical sources and the variability across national borders, Morgenstern advocated for better data collection at the national level, more international coordination, and a continued skepticism regarding empirical information. Haberler concurred, noting the gaps in historical economic data. Mises highlighted the unreliability of information coming from non-industrial nations and the danger of focusing too much on the rapid changes associated with industrial development rather than the "glacier-like" changes of agricultural society. Morgenstern supported Mises's observations. Most significantly, Morgenstern and Mises made common cause in their criticism of Ohlin and Lipinski, who believed that the members of these institutes had a proper role to play in policy decisions. Morgenstern argued instead that the institutes had to investigate the *impacts* of government policy. Mises amplified these points, maintaining that it was too easy for governmental committees to "capture" economic experts by rigging the composition of those commissions. Therefore, experts should remain outside the policy realm, criticizing government interventions. Economic experts should coordinate their actions internationally to make sure that the best ideas and research achieved broad circulation ("Record", 1936).

Of course, the common purpose shown at the 1936 by Austrian economists should not be read as intellectual or theoretical consensus. Morgenstern, in his pursuit of "exaktes Denken" expressed through mathematical economics, had departed significantly from Mises and Hayek. Later he would diverge from Haberler, too. His diaries of the 1930s include repeated negative comments on all of these figures and their works. Haberler likewise had frequent disparaging comments in letters to Morgenstern and Machlup about Mises and Hayek in the late 1930s, lamenting the "unworldly" theorizing of each (cf. Haberler, 1936d, 1941, 1946). Machlup tried to strike a conciliatory tone between factions. Hayek defended himself against Haberler and chided Morgenstern. Mises lectured Machlup on proper Austrian treatment of monopolies and periods of production (cf. Mises, 1937). What is striking in all of these exchanges and disagreements is that the fourth-generation Austrians continued to define themselves with and against one another. This kind of conflict, characteristic of knowledge collectives (Collins, 1998), suggests a continued awareness of a shared tradition and purpose.

The preceding discussion of the Austrian School during the 1930s reveals that the Austrians shifted and reoriented their research interests and affiliations with one another, yet an Austrian intellectual network continued to thrive. While figures like Mises and, to a lesser extent, Hayek moved from the center to the periphery, they still served as important colleagues and interlocutors for the others. The most significant reorientation within the Austrian field was a shift from cross-generational to intra-generational interaction. The Austrians of the fourth generation made fewer references as a whole to the work of Menger, Wieser, and Böhm-Bawerk, or to Schumpeter and Mises. However, they continued to reference one another, and they developed their ideas intersubjectively at conferences, in meetings, and during visits. In the subsequent decades even as the Austrians assimilated in the United States and entered mainstream economic discussions, they still maintained a sense of their Austrianness, both in their commitment to certain ideas and approaches and to the restoration of Austrian Economics in the land of their birth.

AUSTRIANS IN AMERICA

The Austrians of the fourth generation made a quick adjustment to their new American surroundings, introducing their ideas to the American academy. The Austrians directed their energies to engaging an Anglo-American audience, which effaced some of their earlier influences and obscured their Austrian intellectual debts. The argument that they therefore disappeared into the mainstream and the Austrian School declined is persuasive from this vantage, yet there are significant reasons to temper that assessment. First, much of the Austrians' earliest American output developed out of prior concerns and preexisting connections. Morgenstern, for example, extended some of his earlier work on trade cycle theory (Morgenstern, 1927a, 1927b, 1928b), employing Haberler's insights in *Prosperity and Depression* and his ongoing work on game theory in a new article (Morgenstern, 1943). Haberler revised and translated some of his earlier German language work (Haberler, 1936a), providing an introduction to an American audience of Austrian and European work. To recover the rest of these "neo-Austrian" developments, we need to examine the interpersonal, institutional, and intellectual connections that the Austrians fashioned after emigration.

Machlup's American work and activities best exemplify a combination of old and new commitments, of Austrian preservation and elaboration and American assimilation. He entered into the debate between Frank Knight and Friedrich Hayek over capital theory, clarifying and defending the Austrian theory (Machlup, 1935). Subsequently, his American research drew inspiration from Haberler's international trade theory. As we have seen, Haberler focused on potential shortcomings in the application of "pure" trade theory – namely, imperfect competition and frictional costs. Without a better understanding of the influence of these factors, Haberler maintained, trade theory and policy would be severely limited. Machlup used this admonition as a springboard. In his investigations of duopoly, oligopoly, pliopoly, and other market conditions, he elaborated and confirmed the findings of earlier Austrian theories about value and the production process. Significantly, his work reaffirmed freer trade policies over protectionism and interventionism, identifying labor unions and wage controls as the major cause of market disruptions (Machlup, 1937, 1939a, 1942, 1943a, 1943b). Nonetheless, the seriousness with which he took issues of competition within the market process opened a new fault line between Machlup and Mises. In their correspondence, Mises chided Machlup for overemphasizing the significance of monopolistic phenomena in capitalist economies (Mises, n.d.).[3]

Machlup published several articles that followed directly from Haberler's work in the 1930s and 1940s, reflecting a closer interaction between the two men. In "The Theory of Foreign Exchange," he argued that the use of curve analysis, that is, opportunity cost curves, could be applied in the theory of foreign exchanges. In a footnote, he acknowledged that "much of the subject matter present here is based on Professor Haberler's *International Trade*" (1939b, p. 375). By presenting the ways that (Austrian) value theory facilitates economic analysis, Machlup advanced the marginalist tradition. Foreign exchange theory needed updating in light of new stabilization mechanisms and economic doctrines. This meant that new theories had to take monetary policies into consideration. Again, this assertion followed from Haberler's position in *Prosperity and Depression* that different business cycle theories could be reconciled in a more robust trade theory. The authors that Machlup cited extended beyond his fellow Austrians – including John Maynard Keynes, Arthur Gayer, Jacob Viner, and Thomas Balogh – suggesting an international orientation of his work. Nevertheless, Haberler and Hayek featured prominently in the discussion, the latter for his recent discussions of monetary policy in *Monetary Nationalism and Internationalism* (Machlup, 1939b, p. 375; Hayek, 1937). After devoting much of the preceding decade to perfect and imperfect competition, Machlup trained his focus on frictional costs and the importance of price elasticity in international trade. The shared interests of Haberler and Machlup also manifested in increased correspondence and participation on panels together at the American Economic Association. Haberler noted the convergence approvingly in a letter, expressing excitement that they "are moving in the same direction" (Haberler, 1942).

Machlup's methodological investigations of the postwar years continued to draw on his Austrian intellectual background and the work of his fellow fourth-generation Austrians. In turn, he influenced his longstanding friends, especially Haberler. Haberler made use of Machlup's "semantic" discussions of the balance of payments, equilibrium, and the dollar shortage to clarify his own arguments. In an article critical of the multiplier concept, he deployed Machlup's semantic formulations first presented in *International Trade and the National Income Multiplier* (Haberler, 1947; Machlup, 1943b). Haberler then published his *Survey of International Trade Theory* (1961a) in Machlup's International Finance Section series. He provided Machlup with the only copy of the manuscript, asking for suggestions from his friend before publication (1961b).

These examples demonstrate the dense Machlup-Haberler interactions, especially between 1934 and 1946. Their connections remained strong into the 1960s, as they wrote regularly and met often – at their respective Cambridge, Baltimore, and Princeton homes and at economics conferences. They also participated together in significant postwar international

institutions, such as Hayek's Mont Pèlerin Society and Machlup's Bellagio
Group on international finance. Machlup and Haberler were the driving
force behind the latter group, which gathered together economists, bankers,
and government officials to discuss matters of international monetary policy (Bellagio Group, n.d.).

While Machlup and Haberler remained intimately involved with one
another's activities and maintained contact with Hayek and Mises through
Mont Pèlerin, Morgenstern diverged from the others. The personal ties
between Morgenstern and Haberler – and, to a lesser extent, with Machlup
and even Mises – prevented a complete rupture from his fellow Austrians.
Moreover, his need to define his thinking *against* his fellow Austrians suggested his continued engagement with their thought. Like them, he sought
clear expression of economic theory. His frustration owed to their unwilling-
ness to embrace mathematics and logic, the only tools open to contemporary
economists seeking greater precision. Nevertheless, it was the Austrians –
more than Americans or Keynesians – with whom Morgenstern grappled in
his economic thinking, which implied that Austrianism was still the most formidable school of economic thought for him.

Morgenstern's attention shifted to game theory in the early 1940s, and
he became involved in an array of government programs as an adviser
(Leonard, 2012). His work with Von Neumann on game theory and his
operations and logistics work with Harold Kuhn at Mathematica show few
traces of his earlier concerns.[4] Nonetheless, Morgenstern (1944, p. 7) maintained that innovations in game theory would advance economics by building on the subjectivist impulses of the marginal utility school: "We believe
that it is necessary to know as much as possible about the behavior of the
individual and about the simplest forms of exchange. This standpoint was
actually adopted with remarkable success by the founders of the marginal
utility school, but nevertheless it is not generally accepted. Economists frequently point to much larger, more 'burning' questions, and brush everything aside which prevents them from making statements about these."
Through mathematical expressions of economic behavior, Morgenstern
hoped to shed light on the earlier Austrians' descriptions of exchange and
value. He also hoped to win the whole economics profession to the marginal utility standpoint through game theory.

Moreover, Morgenstern still produced occasional works on international
trade and on the methodology of economics that showed familiarity with
the works of his fellow Austrians, as he elaborated some of his earliest,
Austrian-inspired ideas. In particular, he used his skepticism regarding economic observation and forecasting to level sustained critiques of

macroeconomic approaches to international economics (Morgenstern, 1950). This placed Morgenstern's work in a closer relationship to his fellow Austrians. Morgenstern's *Accuracy of Economic Observations* continued the theoretical work that he had begun in the late 1920s in *Wirtschaftsprognose*. In identifying the shortcomings of statistical data gathering and quantitative economic observation more generally, Morgenstern challenged the positivist optimism of midcentury econometricians and statistical economists. He distinguished clearly between the explanatory power of mathematical economics and the haziness of statistical economics (Boumans, 2012). Even with his close identification with mathematical economics, Morgenstern nonetheless took a skeptical view of the subfield, arguing for greater humility in the face of so much uncertainty.

Morgenstern applied this skepticism in his deconstruction of midcentury economic data, arguing that not only were the findings of many economists wrong, but their very facts were fatally flawed. Morgenstern (1948) attacked contemporary economics for its reliance on "unanalyzed global aggregates." While he recognized the desirability of describing aggregates, he felt that their "phenomenology" had not been explored, meaning that economists needed to analyze the composition and changes to the individual elements that comprised the aggregate. This phenomenological reference introduced another Austrian, Alfred Schütz, into American methodological discussions.

In subsequent work, Morgenstern exposed the problems in several of the key data used by international economists: gold points and GNP. Morgenstern (1955) dissected the incoherence of gold statistics, arguing that their "utter uselessness" rendered any calculation of balance of payments impossible. Countries measured their reserves in different fashions, they defined inflows and outflows inconsistently, and they recorded different data in their tables. When assembled, the gold movement data from the nations of the world simply did not add up. According to Morgenstern, since it was impossible to say anything definitive about international gold movements, one of the best measured quantities in economics, there was little hope for more comprehensive quantitative work in international economics. In the revised version of *Accuracy* (1963), he devoted chapters to the reliability of business accounts and national production statistics, assessing each of these sets negatively. These conclusions placed Morgenstern in conversation with Machlup on the incoherence of the concept of the balance of payments. Although Machlup (1950) stressed inconsistencies in the definition of the term rather than the unreliability of data, both Austrians urged greater caution from their fellow economists.

Morgenstern also continued to work on international trade theory. He drew direct inspiration from earlier work by the Vienna school and the proposals advanced at the 1936 conferences. In correspondence with Haberler, Morgenstern referred to the need for more systematic study of international business cycles. Both men recognized the sterility of purely theoretical studies à la Hayek's *Pure Theory of Capital*. These exchanges enriched Morgenstern's financial transactions work (1959) and partially accounts for how long it took to complete (nearly two decades), its prohibitive length (nearly 600 pages), *and* its narrowed scope. While Morgenstern initially planned to offer a more comprehensive study of international business cycles, a want of reliable data restricted the book to an investigation of interest and exchange rates. His conclusions about the state of international trade cycle theory struck a resoundingly Austrian chord: "The reader will quickly observe that a curious dilemma results: either we should reject most of our data in order to salvage large parts of previously abstracted and widely accepted theory, or, accepting the data we should modify the latter, chiefly by depriving it of much of its intended precision (p. vii)." Morgenstern favored the former approach, arguing that only from our accumulated theoretical knowledge can current economic problems be adequately formulated. He then summarized the current status of business cycle research, rehearsing Haberler's typology from *Prosperity and Depression*. Finally, he called for more and better data gathering to make international investigations easier. He advocated comparative analysis into the "world economy" and the use of game theory to understand trade interactions. These techniques would help draw business cycle and international trade theory out of their current impasse. These proposals all resembled the suggestions offered at the 1936 Annecy conference by Haberler, Mises, and him.

While Machlup and Morgenstern's works did not influence one another much, the two men grew much closer after Machlup moved to Princeton in 1960. One of the first ways that Morgenstern and Machlup rekindled their affiliation was by organizing a reunion of Ludwig Mises's *Privatseminar* on the occasion of his eightieth birthday at Princeton in September 1961. Interestingly, Machlup took a different attitude toward the Austrian School here than he would twenty years later. Morgenstern and Machlup invited Haberler, Hayek, Herbert Furth, Erich Schiff, Walter Fröhlich, Martha Steffy Brown, Ilse Mintz, and several other émigrés to attend. They deliberately separated their "family reunion" from a celebration in New York organized by Mises's American students. Machlup (1961a) intimated to Lawrence Fertig that the inclusion of the American Misesians would dilute the Austrianness of the planned festivity:

How many "friends of the family" can one invite to a family reunion before it becomes just a party? The "family" which we have in mind was the group of people who gathered around Mises every other Friday during practically all of the 1920s and the early 1930s. The idea was to reconvene this group (plus wives and widows) to the extent that the members live in the United States. Only the most important postwar friends could be added if this was really to be the reunion that we had in mind. As soon as there are more than a sprinkling of postwar friends the original idea is lost.

Machlup drew a distinction between the earlier Austrian school and the contemporary American Austrian one. He did not explicitly favor one or the other, but he made it clear that he saw them as different and unrelated, save for a shared connection to Mises. The inclusion of "friends" would disrupt the "family," which intimated that the American Misesians were not full Austrians. In the letter, Machlup suggested that the earlier school was not unified intellectually; instead, their affiliation owed to a more fundamental, familial bond. At the reunion, though the focus was on the historical connection of the Austrians rather than on a shared ideological patrimony, the tributes to Mises suggested that the Austrians continued to view themselves as part of a collective (Machlup, 1961b).

Postwar institution building further reinforces the idea that the Austrians saw themselves engaged in a common project for the renewal and elaboration of transatlantic social sciences. The fourth-generation economists took great pains to reestablish the Austrian tradition of economics in their homeland and Europe more generally. As early as 1948 they returned to Vienna, hoping to restore the city to intellectual greatness. As Hayek (1946) wrote to the RF, "There is clearly an opportunity to preserve Vienna as an intellectual center, and the Austrians themselves are trying hard to get the help of those people who during the interwar period have left Austria .... I am naturally most interested in seeing the tradition in Economics preserved." Hayek proposed "to get some of the Austrian economists who are now located in the United States or in England to go to Vienna for a short concentrated course." He mentioned the names of Haberler, Machlup, Morgenstern, Mises, Schumpeter, Eric Voegelin and Gerhard Tintner. Haberler and Morgenstern eventually joined Hayek for a seminar in 1948 (Machlup and Voegelin had to withdraw at the last moment). That these three men spearheaded the effort to restore Austrian economics is striking, since they are often presented as the most divergent among the fourth generation. The reports they filed described the humble yet promising conditions of the social sciences in Vienna. Hayek expressed disappointment with the absence of Mises and Schumpeter, since they would have further extended the survey of economics provided to Austrian students. After castigating the deplorable state of economics at Austrian universities, all three economists applauded the RF-supported Institut für Wirtschaftsforschung (WiFo), the successor to Hayek and Morgenstern's institute, for reviving economic research. They all stressed the need for a 15- or 20-year plan for restoring Viennese prominence. As Hayek (1948) opined, it would only take the return of one or two accomplished scholars as endowed professors "completely to alter the atmosphere." What comes through in the reports is that Austrian Economics represented a broad tradition that was alive and well in its American form. Restoration in Austria was a matter of individual, institutional, and political will.

In the wake of the 1948 visit, the Austrian émigrés struggled to elevate the stature of the social sciences in postwar Austria, as they strived to enlist support for new research centers. Hayek and Morgenstern both expected economics, as they understood it, to play an integral role in these new institutions. Hayek, Morgenstern, and the sociologist Paul Lazarsfeld established an Institute for Advanced Studies (IHS) in Vienna in the 1950s and early 1960s (Fleck, 2000). After some initial struggles, the IHS became one of the leading European centers of social scientific research. A large number of émigrés, including economists, made their way back to Vienna to teach summer courses and serve as visiting professors. Morgenstern, Haberler, and Tintner all participated, with Tintner permanently returning to Vienna.

Through his interventions with the RF and Ford Foundation, Machlup assisted in the formation of a new comparative economics project, the Wiener Institut für internationale Wirtschaftsvergleiche (WIIW), which was affiliated with the IHS and WiFo. Machlup's efforts to conduct comparative economic studies of Western and Eastern European countries can be seen as a direct descendent of Morgenstern's work in the Habsburg successor states during the 1930s. Finally, Hayek, Machlup, Haberler, Karl Popper, and others frequently attended the Forum Alpbach to aid in the revitalization of the social sciences and philosophy in Austria and Europe. They sought money from the Rockefeller and Ford Foundations on the Forum's behalf. Although none of these institutions restored "Austrian Economics" in its original home, they demonstrated a commitment to the preservation and elaboration of the Austrian tradition. Its representatives had diverged from the many of the concerns of the first and second generations, and their work showed little similarity with the Misesian branch. They had also embraced new ideas and approaches in American emigration. Nevertheless, they remained Austrian, not just in their national origins, but also in their respective self-identifications as economists and scientists. This manifested in their correspondence, their scholarly output, and their intellectual entrepreneurship as institution builders.

CONCLUSION

This chapter has argued that "un-Austrian" Austrians and their ideas deserve greater attention and application within contemporary Austrian Economics. Contrary to conventional accounts, the Austrians of the fourth generation did not disappear into the American mainstream and give up their Austrian commitments. By tracing networks of interactions, institutions and affiliations, this chapter demonstrates the flexibility and adaptability of the Austrian tradition. While the connections between scholars shifted and intellectual interests changed, a commitment to methodological individualism and subjectivism, a distrust of statistical economics, and a focus on the primacy of theoretical economics remained paramount. Particularly in international trade theory and business cycle theory and debates about economic methodology, émigré Austrians extended and advanced Austrian ideas after emigration, while also reconstituting and elaborating their Austrian affiliations. Ultimately, we find ourselves in agreement with Herbert Furth: Austrian Economics is far broader than Hayek, Mises, and their libertarian acolytes would have it, and it is vital to preserve this more diverse tradition.

NOTES

1. There are three articles total: Klausinger (2006b), Connell (2007, 2013).
2. The names include: D.H. Robertson; Lionel Robbins; Loveday; Jan Tinbergen; Bresiani-Turroni; Oskar Anderson; L. Dupriez; Rist; Bertil Ohlin; Haberler; Morgenstern; Rappard; E. Lipinski; Alvin Hansen; Wesley Mitchell; John M. Clark; Jacob Viner; J.B. Condliffe; H.D. Henderson; N.F. Hall; L. Lorwin; P.W. Martin; Wilhelm Röpke; Schumpeter; Mises.
3. Cf. Mises to Machlup, June 29, 1937, June 15, 1939, and April 8, 1943.
4. Thanks to one of the article's reviewers for suggesting the inclusion of these details.

ACKNOWLEDGMENT

I would like to thank the Botstiber Institute for Austrian-American Studies and the Rockefeller Archive Center for a fellowship and grant-in-aid, respectively, which supported the research for this chapter. Additional thanks go to Professors Guenter Bischof and Hansjörg Klausinger. Bischof invited me to talk at the Center Austria in March and to present early findings at a workshop in Vienna in June. Klausinger provided me his invaluable insight into interwar Viennese economics and suggested the topic of international economics and the Austrian School in comments on another paper. A final thanks goes to the two excellent reviewers of this chapter for *RHETM*, who provided extensive critical and constructive commentary.

REFERENCES

Baldwin, R. E. (1982). Gottfried Haberler's contribution to international trade theory and policy. *Quarterly Journal of Economics, 97*(1), 141–148.

Bellagio Group. (n.d.). *Box 282, Folder 1-Box 285, Folder 8*. Fritz Machlup Papers, Hoover Institution Archives, Palo Alto, CA.

Boianovsky, M. (2000). In search of a canonical history of macroeconomics in the interwar period: Haberler's *prosperity and depression* revisited. *Revista Brasileira de Economia, 54*(3), 303–331.

Boianovsky, M., & Trautwein, H.-M. (2006). Haberler, the league of nations, and the quest for consensus in business cycle theory in the 1930s. *History of Political Economy, 38*(1), 45–89.

Boumans, M. (2012). Observations in a hostile environment: Oskar Morgenstern on the accuracy of economic observations. *History of Political Economy, 44*(Suppl.), 114–136.

Caldwell, B. (2008). *Hayek's challenge: An intellectual biography of F.A. Hayek*. Chicago, IL: University of Chicago Press.

Collins, R. (1998). *The sociology of philosophies*. Cambridge, MA: Harvard University Press.

Connell, C. (2007). Fritz Machlup's methodology and the theory of the growth of the firm. *Quarterly Journal of Austrian Economics, 10*(4), 300–312.

Connell, C. (2013). Fritz Machlup and the Bellagio group. *Quarterly Journal of Austrian Economics, 16*(3), 255–298.

Craver, E. (1986a). The emigration of the Austrian economists. *History of Political Economy, 18*, 1–32.

Craver, E. (1986b). Patronage and the directions of research in economics. *Minerva, 24*, 205–222.

Dekker, E. (2014). Vienna circles: Cultivating economic knowledge outside academia. *Erasmus Journal for Philosophy and Economics, 7*(2), 30–53.

Fleck, C. (2000). Wie Neues nicht entsteht. *Österreichische Zeitschrift für Geschichtswissenschaften, 11*, 129–177.

Fleck, C. (2011). *A transatlantic history of the social sciences*. New York, NY: Bloomsbury.

Furth, J. H. (1979a). *Letter from Herbert Furth to Fritz Machlup, 6/27/79*. (Box 39, Folder 9). Fritz Machlup Papers. Hoover Institution Archives, Palo Alto, CA.

Furth, J. H. (1979b). *Letter from Herbert Furth to Fritz Machlup, 7/21/79*. (Box 39, Folder 9). Fritz Machlup Papers. Hoover Institution Archives, Palo Alto, CA.

George Mason University. (n.d.). *Austrian economics (pamphlet). (Box 26, Folder 28).* Friedrich Hayek Papers. Hoover Institution Archives, Palo Alto, CA.

Haberler, G. (1927). *Der Sinn der Indexzahlen.* Tübingen: Mohr.

Haberler, G. (1933). *Der internationale Handel: Theorie der weltwirtschaftlichen Zusammenhänge.* Berlin: Springer.

Haberler, G. (1936a). *The theory of international trade.* London: William Hodge.

Haberler, G. (1936b). *Letter from Haberler to Machlup, 8/1936. (Box 41, Folder 4).* Fritz Machlup Papers. Hoover Institution Archives, Palo Alto, CA.

Haberler, G. (1936c). Mr. Keynes' theory of the "Multiplier": A methodological criticism. *Zeitschrift für Nationalökonomie, 7*(3), 299–305.

Haberler, G. (1936d). *Letter from Haberler to Machlup, 11/11/36. (Box 41, Folder 4).* Fritz Machlup Papers. Hoover Institution Archives, Palo Alto, CA.

Haberler, G. (1937). *Prosperity and depression.* Geneva: League of Nations.

Haberler, G. (1941). *Letter from Haberler to Machlup, 4/8/41. (Box 41, Folder 4).* Fritz Machlup Papers. Hoover Institution Archives, Palo Alto, CA.

Haberler, G. (October 26, 1942). *Letter from Haberler to Machlup. (Box 41, Folder 4).* Fritz Machlup Papers. Hoover Institution Archives, Palo Alto, CA.

Haberler, G. (1946). *Prosperity and depression* (3rd ed.). Lake Success: League of Nations.

Haberler, G. (1947). The foreign trade multiplier: A comment. *American Economic Review, 37*(5), 898–906.

Haberler, G. (1961a). *A survey of international trade theory.* Princeton, NJ: Princeton University Press.

Haberler, G. (1961b). *Letter from Haberler to Machlup, 1/25/1961. (Box 41, Folder 7).* Fritz Machlup Papers. Hoover Institution Archives, Palo Alto, CA.

Haberler, G. (January 3, 1979). *Interview with Gottfried Haberler at AEI.* Gottfried Haberler Papers. Hoover Institution Archives, Palo Alto, CA.

Haberler, G. (1981). Mises's private seminar. *Wirtschaftspolitische Blätter, 28*(4), 121–126.

Haberler, G. (2000). *Between Mises and Keynes: An interview with Gottfried von Haberler (1900–1995).* Austrian Economics Newsletter, Spring 2000.

Hayek, F. A. (1926). Friedrich Freiherr v. Wieser. *Jahrbücher für Nationalökonomie und Statistik, 70*(6), 513–530.

Hayek, F. A. (1929). *Geldtheorie und Konjunkturtheorie.* Vienna: Hölder-Pichler-Tempsky.

Hayek, F. A. (September 4, 1934). *Letter from Hayek to Haberler. (Box 16).* Gottfried Haberler Papers. Hoover Institution Archives, Palo Alto, CA.

Hayek, F. A. (March 15, 1936). *Letter from Hayek to Haberler. (Box 16).* Gottfried Haberler Papers. Hoover Institution Archives, Palo Alto, CA.

Hayek, F. A. (1937). *Monetary nationalism and internationalism.* Geneva: Graduate Institute of International Studies.

Hayek, F. A. (October 31, 1946). *Letter from Hayek to J.H. Willits. (RG 1.1, Series 700, Box 2, Folder 15).* Rockefeller Archive Center, Sleepy Hollow, NY.

Hayek, F. A. (1948). *Report on visits to Austria and Switzerland.* (RG 1.1, Series 700, Box 2, Folder 15). Rockefeller Archive Center, Sleepy Hollow, NY.

Hayek, F. A. (1968). Economic thought VI: The Austrian school. In *International encyclopedia of the social sciences* (pp. 458–462). New York, NY: Macmillan.

Klausinger, H. (2002). *The Austrian school of economics and the gold standard mentality in Austrian economic policy in the 1930s* (Working paper). Center for Austrian Studies, Minneapolis, MN.

Klausinger, H. (2006a). 'In the wilderness': Emigration and the decline of the Austrian school. *History of Political Economy*, 38, 617–664.

Klausinger, H. (2006b). From Mises to Morgenstern: Austrian economics during the Ständestaat. *Quarterly Journal of Austrian Economics*, 9(3), 25–43.

Klausinger, H. (2011). Hayek's Geldtheoretische Untersuchungen. *European Journal of the History of Economic Thought*, 18(4), 579–600.

Klausinger, H. (2015). Hans Mayer, last Knight of the Austrian school, Vienna branch. *History of Political Economy*, 47(2), 271–305.

Klein, P. (2008). The mundane economics of the Austrian school. *Quarterly Journal of Austrian Economics*, 11(3/4), 165–187.

Krohn, C.-D. (1988). Die Emigration der Österreichischen Schule der Nationalökonomie in die USA. In F. Stadler (Ed.), *Vertriebene Vernunft II* (pp. 402–415). Vienna: Lit-Verlag.

Latour, B. (2005). *Reassembling the social: An introduction to actor-network theory*. Cambridge, MA: Harvard University Press.

Leijonhufvud, A. (March 16, 1977). *Interview with Professor Machlup. (Box 113, Folder 6)*. Fritz Machlup Papers. Hoover Institution Archives, Palo Alto, CA.

Leonard, R. (2012). *Von Neuman, Morgenstern, and the creation of game theory*. Cambridge: Cambridge University Press.

Littlechild, S. (Ed.). (1990). *Austrian economics* (Vols. 1–3), Brookfield, VT: Elgar.

Machlup, F. (November 4, 1934). *Letter from Machlup to Haberler. (Box 23)*. Gottfried Haberler Papers. Hoover Institution Archives, Palo Alto, CA.

Machlup, F. (1935). Professor Knight and the "period of production". *Journal of Political Economy*, 43(5), 577–624.

Machlup, F. (1937). Monopoly and competition: A classification of market positions. *American Economic Review*, 27(3), 445–451.

Machlup, F. (1939a). Evaluation of the practical significance of the theory of monopolistic competition. *American Economic Review*, 29(2), 227–236.

Machlup, F. (1939b). The theory of foreign exchanges. *Economica*, 6, 375–397.

Machlup, F. (1940a). Correspondence with Ludwig von Mises. (Box 53, Folder 27). Fritz Machlup Papers. Hoover Institution Archives, Palo Alto, CA.

Machlup, F. (1940b). *The stock market, credit, and capital formation*. London: Hodge.

Machlup, F. (1942). Competition, pliopoly and profit. *Econometrica*, 9(33/34), 1–23. 153–173.

Machlup, F. (1943a). The division of labor between government and private enterprise. *American Economic Review*, 33(1), 87–104.

Machlup, F. (1943b). *International trade and the national income multiplier*. Princeton, NJ: Princeton University Press.

Machlup, F. (1950). Three concepts of the balance of payments and the so-called dollar shortage. *Economic Journal*, 60, 46–68.

Machlup, F. (1961a). *Letter from Machlup to Lawrence Fertig, 7/5/61. (Box 53, Folder 28)*. Fritz Machlup Papers. Hoover Institution Archives, Palo Alto, CA.

Machlup, F. (1961b). *Speech, 10/17/61. (Box 93, Folder 18)*. Fritz Machlup Papers. Hoover Institution Archives, Palo Alto, CA.

Machlup, F. (1979a). *Austrian economics (Early drafts). (Box 39, Folder 9)*. Fritz Machlup Papers. Hoover Institution Archives, Palo Alto, CA.

Machlup, F. (1979b). *Letter from Machlup to Herbert Furth, 7/16/79. (Box 39, Folder 9)*. Fritz Machlup Papers. Hoover Institution Archives, Palo Alto, CA.

Machlup, F. (1980). An interview with professor Fritz Machlup. *Austrian Economics Newsletter, 3*(1), 9–12.

Machlup, F. (1982). Austrian economics. In *Encyclopedia of economics* (pp. 38–43). New York, NY: McGraw-Hill.

Machlup, F. (n.d.). *Notebooks. (Box 76, Folder 1)*. Fritz Machlup Papers. Hoover Institution Archives, Palo Alto, CA.

Menger, K. (1972). Österreichischer Marginalismus und mathematische Ökonomie. *Zeitschrift für Nationalökonomie, 32*(1), 19–28.

Mises, L. (June 29, 1937). *Letters from Mises to Machlup. (Box 53, Folder 27)*. Fritz Machlup Papers. Hoover Institution Archives, Palo Alto, CA.

Mises, L. (n.d.). *Letters from Mises to Machlup. (Box 53, Folder 27)*. Fritz Machlup Papers. Hoover Institution Archives, Palo Alto, CA.

Morgenstern, O. (1923). *Diaries*. (Box 12). Oskar Morgenstern Papers. Durham, NC: Rubenstein Library, Duke University.

Morgenstern, O. (1927a). International vergleichende Konjunkturforschung. *Zeitschrift für die gesamte Staatswissenschaft, 83*(2), 261–290.

Morgenstern, O. (1927b). Friedrich von Wieser (1851–1926). *American Economic Review, 17*(4), 669–674.

Morgenstern, O. (1928a). *Wirtschaftsprognose: Eine Untersuchung ihrer Voraussetzungen und Möglichkeiten*. Vienna: Springer.

Morgenstern, O. (1928b). Qualitative und quantitative Konjunkturforschung. *Zeitschrift für die gesamte Staatswissenschaft, 85*(1), 12–20.

Morgenstern, O. (November 2, 1932). *Letter from Morgenstern to Tracy Kittredge*. (RG 1.1, Series 705, Box 4, Folder 36). Rockefeller Archive Center, Sleepy Hollow, NY.

Morgenstern, O. (1943). On the international spread of business cycles. *Journal of Political Economy, 51*(4), 287–309.

Morgenstern, O. (1944). *Theory of games and economic behavior*. Princeton, NJ: Princeton University Press.

Morgenstern, O. (1948). Demand theory reconsidered. *Quarterly Journal of Economics, 62*, 165–201.

Morgenstern, O. (1950). *On the accuracy of economic observations*. Princeton, NJ: Princeton University Press.

Morgenstern, O. (1955). *The validity of international gold movement statistics*. Princeton, NJ: Princeton University Press.

Morgenstern, O. (1959). *International financial transactions and business cycles*. Princeton, NJ: Princeton University Press.

Officer, L. H. (1982). Prosperity and depression—and beyond. *Quarterly Journal of Economics, 97*(1), 149–159.

Record of the Discussions at the Conference called by the Rockefeller Foundation to consider the Desirability and Feasibility of Encouraging Coordination of Economic Research upon Problems of Economic Change. (1936). (RG 3, Series 910, Box 4, Folder 31). Rockefeller Archive Center, Sleepy Hollow, NY.

Rizzo, M. (1982). Mises and Lakatos: A reformulation of Austrian methodology. In I. Kirzner (Ed.), *Method, process, and Austrian economics* (pp. 53–73). Lexington, MA: D.C. Heath and Company.

Rockefeller Fellowship. (1938). *Tentative and very incomplete list of displaced Austrian scholars and scientists.* (RG 2, Series 705, Box 184, Folder 1320). Sleepy Hollow, NY: Rockefeller Archive Center.

Rockefeller Fellowship. (n.d.). *Program Files, Business Cycle Conference.* (RG 3, Series 910. Box 4, Folder 29). Rockefeller Archive Center, Sleepy Hollow, NY.

Schumpeter, J. (April 11, 1936). *Letter from Schumpeter to John Van Sickle.* (RG 3, Series 910, Box 4, Folder 29). Rockefeller Archive Center, Sleepy Hollow, NY.

Sigmund, K. (2015). *Sie nannten sich Der Wiener Kreis: Exaktes Denken am Rand des Untergangs.* Wiesbaden: Springer.

Spaulding, E. W. (1968). *The quiet invaders.* Vienna: Österreichischer Bundesverlag für Unterricht, Wissenschaft und Kunst.

Van Sickle, J. (October 13, 1930). *Letter from Van Sickle to Edmund Day.* (RG 1.2, Series 705, Box 4, Folder 36). Rockefeller Archive Center, Sleepy Hollow, NY.

Van Sickle, J. (May 1, 1933). *Letter from Van Sickle to Edmund Day.* (RG 1.2, Series 705, Box 4, Folder 36). Rockefeller Archive Center, Sleepy Hollow, NY.

Van Sickle, J. (October 30, 1935). *Letter from Van Sickle to Arthur Loveday.* (RG 3, Series 910. Box 4, Folder 29). Rockefeller Archive Center, Sleepy Hollow, NY.

Vaughn, K. I. (1994). *Austrian economics in America.* New York, NY: Cambridge University Press.

Voegelin, E. (1925). Die Zeit in der Wirtschaft. *Archiv für Sozialwissenschaft und Sozialpolitik, 53,* 186–211.

Zanotti, G. J., & Cachanosky, N. (2015). Implications of Machlup's interpretation of Mises's epistemology. *Journal of the History of Economic Thought, 37,* 111–138.

SYSTEMS, STRUCTURAL PROPERTIES AND LEVELS OF ORGANISATION: THE INFLUENCE OF LUDWIG VON BERTALANFFY ON THE WORK OF F.A. HAYEK

Paul Lewis

ABSTRACT

The purpose of this chapter is to examine the influence exerted on the thought of F.A. Hayek by the work of the biologist and founder of system theory, Ludwig von Bertalanffy. The author's methodology includes textual analysis and archival work. It is argued first of all that Bertalanffy provided Hayek with a conceptual framework in terms of which he could articulate the philosophical significance of his theoretical psychology. In particular, Bertalanffy's work afforded Hayek a set of concepts that helped him to articulate the relationship between mental and physical events − that is, between mind and body − implied by his theory. The second part of the chapter builds on the first by exploring how Hayek subsequently applied the abstract conceptual framework or ontology set out by Bertalanffy to the economy. In this way, Bertalanffy's ideas helped Hayek to articulate and shape his emerging

Research in the History of Economic Thought and Methodology, Volume 34A, 125−159
ISSN: 0743-4154/doi:10.1108/S0743-41542016000034A005

view of the economy as a complex adaptive system, which consists of different 'levels of organisation', which displays 'structural' or 'emergent properties', and which evolves over time on the basis of those group-level properties.

Keywords: Hayek; emergence; system theory; organisation; cultural evolution; group selection

INTRODUCTION

This chapter examines the influence exerted on the thought of F.A. Hayek by the work of the biologist and founder of systems theory, Ludwig von Bertalanffy. The background to the chapter is provided by the fact that several distinguished commentators have observed that Bertalanffy's ideas helped to shape Hayek's thinking from the late 1940s onwards, as Hayek was developing his account of the mind, and the market, as complex adaptive systems. For example, the editor of Hayek's *Collected Works*, Bruce Caldwell, reports that Bertalanffy 'read and commented on a manuscript version of *The Sensory Order*', stating that, 'Hayek probably owes occasional references to the findings of "theoretical biology" to him' (Caldwell, 2004, p. 278, n. 14). Later, Caldwell alludes to Hayek's efforts to apply Bertalanffy's work, in particular his notion of 'higher level regularities', to the economy. Caldwell concludes that, while Hayek's emerging views on complexity were shaped by a number of people, 'He was, perhaps, closest to the system theorist Bertalanffy' (2004, p. 362). A similar view has been expressed by the complexity theorist Barkley Rosser, who writes that, '[M]uch of Hayek's investigations of complexity involved cybernetics (Wiener) and its close relative, general systems theory (von Bertalanffy), with a strong influence from Warren Weaver as well' (2010). The same broad theme was echoed by the Austrian economist and historian of thought Karen Vaughn, who describes Hayek in the 1950s as being 'deeply immersed' in Bertalanffy's work on 'the complexity of biological systems' (1999a, p. 249). Finally, the neuroscientist Fuster (2011, p. 5) describes 'the dynamic systems theory of von Bertalanffy' as an intellectual current shaping Hayek's theoretical psychology, arguing that it laid the ground for Hayek's 'acceptance of a cortical dynamics in which the whole is more than the sum of the parts and [is] irreducible to them'.

Insightful though these remarks are their authors do not elaborate in detail on the nature and significance of Bertalanffy's influence on Hayek.

Hence, one is left with a series of interesting, but also somewhat tantalising, claims about Bertalanffy's precise role in the development of Hayek's thought. The claims are fascinating because they point to a potentially important influence on the development of Hayek's post-war thinking about the mind and the market. But they are also tantalising because they raise, but leave unanswered, several questions: What did Hayek's references to 'theoretical biology' involve and what is their import for his psychology and his economics? What is 'system theory' and what lessons, if any, did Hayek draw for his economics from his study of biological 'systems'? What is a 'higher level regularity' and what did Hayek's efforts to use that concept entail? What bearing, if any, does the idea that in certain systems 'the whole is more than the sum of its parts' have for Hayek's thought?

This chapter seeks to build on the valuable work carried out by the scholars mentioned above by exploring, in more detail than hitherto, the nature and significance of Bertalanffy's influence on Hayek. The section entitled, 'Von Bertalanffy, Organismic Biology and System Theory' carries out essential preliminary work by setting out the key tenets of Bertalanffy's thought. Having done so, we are then in a position to consider in the section on 'Bertalanffy's Influence, Part I: Hayek's Theoretical Psychology' how Bertalanffy's ideas helped to shape Hayek's work on the mind. As we shall see, Bertalanffy's work provided Hayek with a conceptual framework in terms of which he could articulate the philosophical significance of his theoretical psychology. In particular, Bertalanffy's work afforded Hayek a set of concepts that enabled him to articulate the relationship between mental and physical events – that is, between mind and body – implied by his theory. In 'The Influence of Bertalanffy II: Hayek's Economics', we build on that analysis by exploring how Hayek subsequently applied the abstract conceptual framework or ontology set out by Bertalanffy to the economy, in order to articulate and shape his emerging view of the economy as a complex adaptive system, which consists of different 'levels of organisation', and which displays 'structural' or 'emergent properties', on the basis of which it evolves over time. The final section summarises and draws conclusions.

VON BERTALANFFY, ORGANISMIC BIOLOGY AND SYSTEM THEORY

Ludwig von Bertalanffy was a theoretical and applied biologist and the founder of system theory. Born in 1901, Bertalanffy grew up in Vienna, where he attended the University of Vienna and was a student of Moritz Schlick. He studied botany and philosophy, and also worked at an experimental institute of biology. Through Schlick, Bertalanffy was introduced to the work of the Vienna Circle, whose meetings he attended and whose goal of a unified science he came to support. However, as we shall see, Bertalanffy was far less enamoured with the reductionism to which the members of the Vienna Circle subscribed, arguing that the mechanistic and atomistic approaches associated with reductionism were incapable of explaining complex biological phenomena. Bertalanffy was awarded his PhD in 1926 and published his first book, *Kritische Theorie der Formbildung* (*Modern Theories of Development: An Introduction to Theoretical Biology*), in 1928 (Bertalanffy, 1933). Over the course of his career, Bertalanffy worked as a theoretical and applied biologist at a variety of academic institutions in Europe and north America, achieving widespread recognition for his research on the comparative physiology of metabolism and growth, and for developing a practical method for diagnosing cancerous cells, as well as for his ideas about the nature of biological systems. He was nominated for the Nobel Prize in physiology in 1972 but died before a decision about the award could be made.[1]

When Bertalanffy began writing in the mid-1920s, biology was in the thrall of the so-called mechanism-vitalism controversy, and it is will be useful both for understanding Bertalanffy's work, and also its significance for Hayek, briefly to outline that debate. Inspired by classical physics and by philosophers such as Descartes, advocates of the mechanistic approach argued that the best way of understanding biological phenomena was to break them down into their smallest constituent parts and to analyse them in terms of the properties of those isolated individual components. Mechanism presupposes, therefore, that the world is atomistic, consisting of nothing more than the sum of its individual material parts. To use a phrase commonly employed in the interwar years, the mechanistic approach portrays the world as a *mosaic* of separate, independent atoms (Allen, 2005, p. 265, 270, 275; Haraway, 2004, p. 6; Hayek, 1952, p. 76, [1969] 2014, pp. 316–317). On this view, biology would ultimately become a branch of physics, with explanations of biological phenomena being couched in terms of the behaviour of isolated elementary physical particles.

The problem with this approach, Bertalanffy argued, was that it ignored the way in which the behaviour of the individual parts is affected by the relations into which they enter. As a result, it failed to do justice to the profound importance of those relations for the properties and behaviour of biological entities (Bertalanffy, 1933, pp. 31–43, 1950a, p. 148, 1952, pp. 12–13). For Bertalanffy, it is only when physio-chemical materials are organised so as to form a particular structure that the key properties of living organisms obtain: '[I]t is the particular manner of composition of the materials and processes, their spatial and temporal organisation, which constitutes what we call life' (Bertalanffy, 1933, p. 51, 35). On this view, as Bertalanffy (1933, p. 35) puts it in a phrase to which we shall return below, 'life *is* more than a heap of physical and chemical processes and has its "own laws"'. The problem with reductionist approaches is that, by attempting to explain biological phenomena solely in terms of the behaviour of their isolated parts, they neglect what Bertalanffy thought was the hallmark of living things, namely the way in which the behaviour of the parts, and therefore of the biological organism as a whole, is affected by how the parts relate to and interact with each other (1933, p. 51).

The advocates of vitalism argued contrary to the mechanists that, far from being explicable in terms of isolated atomic causal processes, biological phenomena can be understood only by postulating the existence of a supernatural force, existing independently of the material world, that gives life to the biological world. However, according to Bertalanffy, while vitalism 'recognises the character of organic order and wholeness' of the biological world, thereby avoiding the major failing of mechanism, the fact that it attributes the existence of biological phenomena to a metaphysical life-giving force implies that it portrays biological organisms as being 'governed, as it were, by a host of goblins, who invent and design the organism [and] control its processes' (1952, pp. 7–8). In doing so, Bertalanffy argues, 'Vitalism means nothing less than a renunciation of a scientific explanation of biological data' (Bertalanffy, 1933, p. 46, 45).

Bertalanffy sought to transcend the terms of this debate, and thereby to overcome its limitations, by developing what he called an 'organismic' conception of the biological world that would make it possible (a) to do justice to the importance of the structural relations obtaining between the parts of an organism for its properties and behaviour, thus avoiding the shortcomings of the mechanistic approach, while also (b) facilitating the scientific but non-reductionist analysis of biological phenomena, thereby avoiding the metaphysical excesses of vitalism (Bertalanffy, 1933, p. 46, also see 1952, pp. 9–54). At the heart of this new approach were four closely related concepts: the notions of a 'system' and of 'organisation'; the concept of 'structural' or 'emergent' properties; and the idea that the world is 'hierarchical', in the sense that is composed of entities existing at different 'levels of organisation'. Taken together, these concepts form an intellectual framework that underwrites a non-reductionist approach to biology that seeks to find biological laws that are quite distinct from, and irreducible to, the laws of physics and chemistry. Given that, as we shall also see, these concepts all proved to be important in the development of Hayek's thought, it is worth elaborating briefly on each of them.

A *system* is a set of parts or elements that are related to one another in a particular way. It is, in Bertalanffy's words, 'a complex of elements in mutual interaction' (1952, p. 11, also see 1950a, p. 143). The set of relations that characterises a particular kind of system is its *structure*. Systems, then, are entities that arise through the organised relationship of their parts. Bertalanffy uses the notion of 'organisation' to denote the way in which individual parts must stand in certain relations to one another, forming a particular structure, if a certain kind of system − such as a living system − is to obtain. As Bertalanffy puts it, 'organisms are organized things', so that '[t]he problem of life is that of *organization* ... the character-istics of life are characteristics of a system arising from, and associated with, the organization of materials and processes' (1933, p. 46, 1952, p. 12, also see 1933, p. 49).

When individual elements are arranged into structures, their behaviour is different compared to what it is when they are isolated from one another. This is significant because it implies that, taken as a whole, sys-tems can display properties that are quite different from the properties of their individual component parts taken in isolation. In such cases, Bertalanffy writes, 'the actual whole shows properties that are absent from its parts' (1952, p. 12, also see p. 147). 'The properties of a living cell', for example, 'are very different from properties of the component proteins' (1952, p. 147; also see p. 12). Following the terminology of the famous zoologist and psychologist Conwy Lloyd Morgan (1926-27), Bertalanffy refers to these novels, system-level properties as *emergent properties* (1952, p. 197, also see 1933, p. v, 52).[2]

The notion of emergence suggests, moreover, that reality is stratified in the sense that there is a hierarchical structure of ontologically distinct systems − 'a hierarchy of levels' or 'hierarchical order', as Bertalanffy (1952, p. 26, 37, 1933, p. 49) variously describes it − each of which has its own distinctive, irreducible properties (Bertalanffy, 1952, p. 23, 197). On this view, therefore, nature consists of a nested hierarchy of organised sys-tems, varying from the atomic to the molecular to the cellular to the orga-nismic to the group, each with its own properties. And what this implies, for Bertalanffy, is that there are distinct ('higher level') biological laws describing the behaviour of emergent biological systems that cannot be reduced to, or replaced without loss of understanding by, the ('lower level') laws of physics and chemistry (Bertalanffy, 1933, pp. 8–10, 28–66, 1950a, pp. 139–140, 1952, pp. 148–157, 181, 197).

It is worth noting explicitly that, as it is used by Bertalanffy, the term 'organisation' is not synonymous with 'designed' or 'consciously planned'. On the contrary, Bertalanffy contends that the relational organisation of the elements that characterises organised wholes is an example of a 'spontaneous order', whereby the biological 'process as a whole carries order within itself, representing a self-regulating steady state' (1952, p. 145, 34).[3] In this respect, as in others, Bertalanffy argues that organismic biology constitutes an advance over vitalism in particular, which 'being at one with the machine theory [i.e., the mechanistic approach] in analysing the vital processes into occurrences running along their separate lines, believed these to be coordinated by an immaterial, transcendent entelechy' (1933, pp. 177–178, also see 1950a, pp. 153–154). This spontaneous order arises, Bertalanffy continues, through competition: 'Every whole is based upon the competition of its elements, and presupposes the "struggle between its parts"... The latter is a general principle of organisation in simple physio-chemical systems as well as in organisms and social units' (Bertalanffy, 1950a, pp. 153–154; also see p. 162).[4]

As Bertalanffy notes, in an aspect of his work that will also be relevant for understanding his influence on Hayek, the emergence of order in the biological world constitutes something of a puzzle from the point of view of second law of thermodynamics. The latter states that the amount of entropy or disorder in the universe is increasing and implies that physical interactions should proceed towards the least-ordered state possible (i.e. the state of maximum entropy). It follows that order is the least probable state of affairs and chaos the most likely. Set against this expectation of increasing disorder, the fact that biological evolution has clearly displayed a tendency to produce increasingly complex and more highly organised forms of life appears anomalous. One of Bertalanffy's signal contributions to theoretical biology was to deal with this apparent anomaly. He did do by pointing out that the second law of thermodynamics applies only to systems that are *closed* in the sense of being isolated from their surroundings. Biological systems, in contrast, are an example of what Bertalanffy termed an *open* system; they interact with the environment around them and can therefore maintain themselves in a continual, non-equilibrium steady state by importing matter and energy from the world around them and exporting their entropy or waste to it. Hence, according to Bertalanffy, open systems 'need not approach maximum entropy and disorder and a standstill of processes in thermodynamic equilibrium. Instead, spontaneous order, and even an increase in order, can appear in such systems' (Bertalanffy, 1952, p. 145, also see 1950a, pp. 154–157, 1950b, pp. 25–27, 1952, pp. 112–113, 123–146).[5]

In the late 1930s and 1940s, Bertalanffy extended this emphasis on the importance of the relational organisation of phenomena into 'wholes' exhibiting emergent properties from the biological to the physical, psychological and social realms. His goal was to develop a trans-disciplinary framework – couched in terms of concepts such as 'system', 'organisation', 'level' and 'emergence' – that was applicable to all phenomena of organised complexity, independent of their substance or spatio-temporal sphere of existence. Bertalanffy summarised the worldview or ontology underpinning his approach, along with the associated epistemology, as follows:

> Reality, in the modern conception, appears as a tremendous hierarchical order of organised entities, leading, in a superposition of many levels, from physical and chemical to biological and sociological systems. Unity of science is granted, not by a utopian reduction of all sciences to physics and chemistry, but by the structural uniformities of the different levels of reality ... When emphasising general structural isomorphies of different levels, [systems theory] asserts, at the same time, their autonomy and possession of specific laws. (Bertalanffy, 1950a, pp. 164–165; also see pp. 139–143)

Bertalanffy termed his framework, general system theory. And, as indicated above, system theory adopts a holistic approach that – in contrast to reductionist approaches inspired by classical mechanics – emphasises (i) the explanatory significance of the relations that obtain between the elements or parts of physical, biological and social systems for our understanding of the latter's properties and behaviour, (ii) the way in which, based upon their emergent properties, systems interact with their environment, leading to continual evolution, and (iii) the epistemological independence ('autonomy') of the different disciplines (Hammond, 2003, pp. 103–141).[6]

BERTALANFFY'S INFLUENCE, PART I: HAYEK'S THEORETICAL PSYCHOLOGY

Hayek's Theoretical Psychology: The Sensory Order

As a preliminary to considering Bertalanffy's influence on Hayek's theoretical psychology, we consider first of all the account of the working of the mind set out in Hayek's principal work on that topic, namely his 1952 book *The Sensory Order* (Hayek, 1952). The task Hayek sets himself in that book is to explain why the phenomenal (subjective, mental) picture of the world provided by our senses differs from the physical order revealed to us by the natural sciences. The starting point for Hayek's analysis is the fact that there is no simple, one-to-one correspondence between the order of our sense experiences, in which events are classified according to their sensory qualities (colour, sound, etc.), and the physical or scientific order, in which events are classified according to their relations with other events. Objects that resemble each other in sensory terms may display very different physical relations to each other, while objects that appear altogether different to us may display very similar physical properties. There are, in Hayek's terminology, two different orders: a physical order, which is revealed to us by the natural sciences; and a phenomenal, or mental, or sensory, order which we experience as individuals. The task of theoretical psychology, as Hayek understands it, is to show how the neurons of which the human central nervous system is composed form a classificatory structure that is capable of discriminating between different physical stimuli so as to give rise to the sensory order that we actually experience (Hayek, 1952, pp. 2–8, 13–19, 37–40).

For Hayek, the human central nervous system consists of a hierarchical network of inter-connected nerve fibres. Each neuron is connected to many – but not all – others by means of linkages known as axons, so that the nervous system has structure in which the position of any one neuron is defined by its connections to other nerve fibres. Neurons can generate outgoing electrical impulses or 'firings' if they are stimulated sufficiently by incoming impulses, and it is through the transmission of such impulses that neurons interact with each other (Hayek, 1952, pp. 42, 55–64). For Hayek, it is the structure of the connections between the nerve fibres that governs people's cognitive processes and which accounts for the key features of our mental experiences (Hayek, 1952, p. 12). The (primary) nerve impulse generated by a particular external stimulus will in turn stimulate neurons connected to those along which that primary impulse is transmitted. In this way, the external stimulus leads to the generation within the central nervous system of an induced pattern of (secondary) nerve impulses, characteristic not only of the external stimulus currently being experienced but also of the other external stimuli that have typically accompanied it in the past. Hayek refers to this train or wake of (secondary) impulses as the *following* of the initial nerve impulse. And it is by classifying external events according to the extended pattern of nerve firings or followings they trigger that the central nervous system differentiates them from each other and thereby creates distinct sensory data. Two external events are classified as the same, and are experienced as having the same sensory qualities, if they stimulate the same configuration of neurons and so trigger an identical set of neural events or following (Hayek, 1952, pp. 48–54, 62–78).

For Hayek, then, the human mind is a vast network of inter-connected neurons that acts as an instrument of classification, discriminating between incoming stimuli and thereby creating the sensory qualities we experience (Hayek, 1952, p. 16, 35). 'What we call "mind"', Hayek (1952, p. 16) writes, 'is thus a particular order of a set of events taking place in some organism and in some manner related to but not identical with the physical order of events in the environment'.[7] It is against this background that Bertalanffy's influence on Hayek's theoretical psychology can be understood.

Bertalanffy's Influence on Hayek's Theoretical Psychology

The first reference to Bertalanffy in Hayek's published writings comes in chapter 2 of *The Sensory Order*, in a section where Hayek is discussing what he means by the definition of the mind, quoted immediately above, to which his theory gives rise. In a series of four paragraphs (2.27–2.30), Hayek elaborates on his account of the nature of the relationship between mental and physical events by drawing on Bertalanffy's work.[8] The first of the four paragraphs begins as follows:

> The apparent paradox that certain relations between non-mental events should turn them into mental events resolves itself as soon as we accept the definition of the mind as a peculiar order. (Hayek, 1952, p. 46)

This sentence refers to the relationship between mental and physical events (i.e. to the mind–body problem). Hayek elaborates on how that relationship can be understood by alluding to the notion of structural or emergent properties:

> Any individual neural event may have physical properties which are similar or different from other such events if investigated in isolation. But, irrespective of the properties which those events will possess by themselves, they will possess others solely as a result of their position in the order of inter-connected neural events ...[A]n order of events is something different from the properties of the individual events ...[T]he peculiar properties of the elementary neural events which are the terms of the mental order have nothing to do with that order itself. What we have called physical properties of those events are those properties which will appear if they are placed in a variety of experimental relations to different other kinds of event. The mental properties are those which they possess only as a part of the particular structure and which may be largely independent of the former ... That a particular order of events or objects is something

different from all the individual events taken separately is the significant fact behind the endless and unprofitable talk about 'the whole being greater than the mere sum of its parts'. Of course an order does not arise from the parts being thrown together in a heap, and one arrangement of a given set of parts may constitute something different from another arrangement of the same set of parts. An order involves elements *plus* certain relations between them ...[I]t is only when we understand how the elements are related to each other that the talk about the whole being more than the parts becomes more than an empty phrase. All that theoretical biology has in this respect to say on the significance of structural properties as distinct from the properties of the elements, and about the significance of 'organization', is directly applicable to our problem. (Hayek, 1952, pp. 46–47)

Hayek distinguishes here between the physical properties of neural events — that is, of nerve firings — and their mental properties. The physical properties, he tells us, are those that neural events possess in isolation ('by themselves'). Hayek distinguishes such physical properties from the mental properties of neural events, such as their capacity to give rise to certain kinds of sensory experience. The mental properties of neural events, he states arise only when people's nerve fibres, and the neural events to which they give rise when they fire, form part of a set or order of 'inter-connected neural events'. More specifically, as we have seen, it is only because people's nerve fibres are organised into a structure such that some stimuli gave rise to different 'followings' that discrimination between stimuli, classification and, therefore, sense perception is possible. As Hayek puts it, 'The mental properties [of neural events] are those which they possess only as part of the particular structure ... we call mind' (1952, p. 47; also see p. 53).

In the second half of the passage reproduced above, Hayek discusses in more detail the nature of these mental properties, and their relations to physical (neural) events, stating that, 'All that theoretical biology has in this respect to say on the significance of structural properties as distinct from the properties of the elements, and about the significance of "organisation", is directly applicable to our problem'. The significance of this appeal to 'structural properties' and 'organisation' is of course that it indicates that, for Hayek, mental properties are emergent properties that arise only when people's neurons are organised into a structure of the kind described above. Hence, Hayek's remark that the mental order 'does not arise from the parts being thrown together in a heap' but rather 'involves certain elements plus certain relations obtaining between them'.

It is worth noting at this juncture that the material contained in the four paragraphs in question cannot be found in an earlier manuscript version of *The Sensory Order*, namely *What is Mind?* (Hayek, 1945).[9] It appears, therefore, that Hayek added these paragraphs between drafting *What is Mind?* in 1945 and completing the final manuscript of *The Sensory Order* in 1952. Significantly, correspondence between Bertalanffy and Hayek indicates that Hayek read the German version of Bertalanffy's *Problems of Life* (1952), which had been published in German in the early 1940s, in 1947, and that Hayek sent Bertalanffy a copy of the manuscript for *The Sensory Order* in April 1950.[10] Bertalanffy sent his comments on the manuscript to Hayek in June of the same year (Hayek Archive Box 12, folder 4; Bertalanffy Archive letter B50; also see Hayek (1952, pp. viii–ix). Moreover, in a footnote situated at the end of the paragraphs in question, Hayek refers to the German version of Bertalanffy's *Problems of Life* (1952), in which Bertalanffy uses the notion of emergent properties, and its correlates such as 'levels of organisation', to clarify various issues in theoretical biology and gestalt psychology. In addition, both the bibliography of *The Sensory Order* and also correspondence between the two men indicates that Hayek read some of Bertalanffy's other writings, mostly notably his 1950 *British Journal for the Philosophy of Science* paper on system theory, where Bertalanffy discusses structural or emergent properties and levels of organisation in terms that closely resemble those used by Hayek, during the period when he was writing the final manuscript of *The Sensory Order* (Bertalanffy, 1950a; Hayek, 1952, p. 195). The fact that the four paragraphs in which Hayek develops these ideas were added to the manuscript of *The Sensory Order* only after the initial draft of *What is Mind?* was written, taken together with the fact that the works by Bertalanffy referenced by Hayek contain accounts of the very concepts and ideas – in particular the notions of internal relations, organisation and structural properties – that Hayek himself discusses in the passages, often using similar terminology to Bertalanffy, indicates that the addition of these passages is attributable to the influence of Bertalanffy.[11]

What we can see here, then, is Hayek drawing on Bertalanffy's work in order to explain the account of the relationship between mental and physical events – that is, the relationship between mind and body – implied by his theoretical psychology. On this line of interpretation, Hayek drew on Bertalanffy's work in order to give an account of the philosophical significance of his theoretical psychology. In particular, as we have seen, Hayek portrays mental phenomena, not as consisting of distinctive 'mental stuff' that exists independently of the physical and biological world, but rather as a structural or emergent property of the structured array of neurons found in the human brain.

The Interpretive Significance of Bertalanffy's Ideas for Understanding Hayek: Appreciating the Philosophical Implications of Hayek's Theoretical Psychology

The significance of this interpretation of Bertalanffy's influence on Hayek is underlined towards the end of *The Sensory Order*, where Hayek draws out some of the implications of his theory of the mind for various philosophical issues. In particular, in paragraphs 8.40–8.43, which like those quoted in the previous section were added to Hayek's manuscript only after *What is Mind?* had been drafted, Hayek discusses the topics of dualism and materialism in the philosophy of mind, writing as follows:

8.40. Because the account of the determination of mental qualities which has been given here explains them by the operation of processes of the same kind as those we observe in the material world, it is likely to be described as a 'materialistic' theory. Such a description in itself would matter very little if it were not for certain erroneous ideas associated with the term materialism which not only prejudice some people against a theory thus described but, what is more important, would also suggest that it implies certain conclusions which are almost the opposite of those which in fact follow from it. In the true sense of the word 'materialistic' it might even be argued that our theory is less materialistic than the dualistic theories which postulate a distinct mind 'substance'.

8.41. The dualistic theories are a product of the habit, which man has acquired in his early study of nature, of assuming that in every instance where he observed a peculiar and distinct process it must be due to the presence of a corresponding peculiar and distinct substance. The recognition of such a peculiar material substance came to be regarded as an adequate explanation of the process produced.

8.42. It is a curious fact that, although in the realm of nature in general we no longer accept as an adequate explanation the postulate of a particular substance possessing the capacity of producing the phenomena we wish to explain, we still resort to this old habit where mental events are concerned. The mind 'stuff' or 'substance' is a conception formed in analogy to the different kinds of matter supposedly responsible for the different kinds of material phenomena. It is, to use an old term in its literal sense, the result of a 'hylomorphic' manner of thinking. Yet in whatever manner we define substance, to think of mind as a substance is to ascribe to mental events some attributes for whose existence we have no evidence and which we postulate solely on the analogy of what we know of material phenomena.

8.43. In the strict sense of the terms employed an account of mental phenomena which avoids the conception of a distinct mental substance is therefore the opposite of materialistic, because it does not attribute to mind any property which we derive from our acquaintance with matter. In being content to regard mind as a peculiar order of events, different from the order of events which we encounter in the physical world, but determined by the same kind of forces as those that rule in that world, it is indeed the only theory which is not materialistic.

Taken at face value, these passages seem rather puzzling. In particular, how can it be, as Hayek argues in paragraph 8.40, that a theory which tries to account for mental phenomena in terms of physical processes be *less* materialist than one which postulates a distinct mental substance? In a similar vein, what does Hayek mean when he states in paragraph 8.43 that an explanation of mental phenomena which does not postulate a distinct mental substance is the *opposite* of materialistic?

These passages become much more intelligible once they are read against the background provided by the work of Bertalanffy, and his efforts to use the notions of organisation and emergence to overcome the mechanism-vitalism controversy and thereby to develop an emergentist account of biological phenomena. The problem that bedevils both mechanism and vitalism, Bertalanffy and Hayek argue, is that both approaches view the material world as being essentially atomistic in nature. On this view, physical particles only enter into external relations with one another; their properties remain unchanged by the relations in which they are involved. The possibility that physical particles might enter into internal relations with each other and thereby form organised structures – such as the human brain – that have their own distinctive (emergent) properties is therefore ruled out of court not only by mechanism but also, because it shares the same underlying atomistic worldview, by vitalism. As the historian of biology Donna Haraway has put it, Bertalanffy 'saw vitalism as part of the mechanistic paradigm rather than opposed to it because both were limited by the same images and metaphors', in particular by the fact that in the case of vitalism the atomistic worldview 'is not challenged by a wider meaning of organization or by a refusal to operate from the additive perspective' (Haraway, 2004, p. 38, 28; also see pp. 26–29, 38–39, 61–63, 118, 137). In Bertalanffy's words:

> [I]t is the defect of vitalism that it does not free itself properly from mechanism ...
> [B]oth mechanism and vitalism rest on the [atomistic] machine theory, they only differ
> in the kind of hypothetical entities they choose to assume in order to meet its deficien-
> cies. The only way out is to reject this analogy as a sufficient basis for biological theory.
> (Bertalanffy, 1933, pp. 44–45; also see pp. 98, 188)

Bertalanffy's goal in developing organicism was to transcend the commitment to an atomistic worldview that was common to the mechanistic and vitalistic approaches. He did so by invoking the notions of structural properties, and levels of organisation, in order to carve out the conceptual space for an emergentist perspective on the relationship between the physical, biological and mental worlds (Bertalanffy, 1933, pp. 28–32, 50, 62, 1952,

p. xi, 9–22, 170–171) (Hammond, 2003, pp. 36–40, 103–105, 111–115; Haraway, 2004, pp. xi–xii, xix, 19, 26–29, 38–39, 61–63, 137, 176–177).

Viewed against this background, the meaning of the passages from *The Sensory Order* quoted above can now be clarified and the two questions posed after the quotation answered. First, when Hayek writes in paragraph 8.40 that, 'In the true sense of the word "materialistic" it might even be argued that our theory is less materialistic than the dualistic theories which postulate a distinct mind "substance"', his point is that what one might call 'true materialism' is not the same as 'atomism'; by acknowledging the possibility that micro-physical particles can become organised into ordered structures that exhibit emergent (mental) properties (say), one can acknowledge that there is more to mind than (mere, atomistic) micro-physical particles without having to postulate a 'distinct mind "substance"'. This approach is 'less materialistic' than that adopted by mechanism and vitalism precisely because it avoids the atomistic picture of the material world presupposed by those perspectives, a worldview whose shortcomings drove the vitalists in particular into postulating the existence of distinctive mental 'stuff'. It is also telling in this respect that, writing in the Epilogue to the third volume of *Law, Legislation and Liberty*, in a remark to which we shall return below, Hayek acknowledges explicitly the significance of Bertalanffy's approach, writing that the efforts of Cartesian dualists and vitalists 'to account for one unexplained order by analogy with another equally unexplained, has now been replaced by system theory, originally developed by yet another Viennese friend, Ludwig von Bertalanffy, and his numerous followers. This has brought out the common features of those diverse complex orders which are also discussed by information and communication theory and semiotics' (1979, pp. 158–159, also see Hayek, 1973, p. 31).[12] Second, when Hayek writes in paragraph 8.43 that his account of mental phenomena is the opposite of materialistic precisely because it does not attribute to mind properties possessed by material substances, his point is that his account portrays mental properties as emergent properties of the structured arrangement – 'the peculiar order' – of neurons found in the human brain. Therefore, like all emergent properties, the (mental) properties possessed by an emergent 'whole' such as the mind are quite different from the (material) properties possessed by the constituent parts (in this case, the individual nerve fibres) of which that whole is composed.[13]

It appears, therefore, that in the late 1940s, Hayek read the works of Bertalanffy and, through doing so, was able to develop his appreciation of how the organisation of elements into a structure in which they stand in certain relations to one another can give rise to structural properties that are quite distinct from the properties of those elements taken in isolation. More specifically, as argued above, Hayek's theoretical psychology portrays mental phenomena as an emergent property of the structured array of neurons found in the human brain. And as both the opening sentence of paragraph 2.27 of *The Sensory Order* and also our reading of paragraph 8.40–43 suggest, this enabled Hayek to come up with an effective way of conceptualising the nature of the mind–body relationship, the task of understanding which was something that Hayek had come to view as the problem to which his account of the mind in *The Sensory Order* was in fact the solution.

Hayek mentions Bertalanffy's notion of a 'system' only once in *The Sensory Order* (see Hayek, 1952, p. 83, to which reference we return below). However, he does explicitly deploy that concept in one of his other, unpublished papers on theoretical psychology, on which he was working in the early 1950s. The paper in question is entitled, 'Within Systems and About Systems' (Hayek, n.d.). In it, Hayek attempted to develop the theoretical framework set out in *The Sensory Order* into a general theory of communication between two systems, each of which is a classificatory apparatus of the kind described in his work on theoretical psychology. The influence of Bertalanffy can be seen in this unfinished manuscript, with Hayek explicitly stating that, 'The term system will … be used here in the sense in which it is used in von Bertalanffy's "General System Theory"', that is 'in the sense of a coherent structure of causally connected physical parts' (Hayek, n.d., p. 4).[14] Systems of this kind, Hayek continues, are 'organised' into 'a structure' that has a 'hierarchy of levels' (p. 5, 7, 10). What this demonstrates is that Hayek was aware of, and was using, Bertalanffy's concept of 'system' in the early 1950s. This will turn out to be significant when we consider, in the next section of the chapter, how Bertalanffy's ideas helped to shape Hayek's thinking in the 1950s and 1960s, not on the topic of theoretical psychology, but on economics and social theory.

THE INFLUENCE OF BERTALANFFY II:
HAYEK'S ECONOMICS

We move on now to consider Hayek's writings on the problem of social order, in particular his answer to the question – which he first posed in his 1937 paper, 'Economics and Knowledge' ([1937] 2014) – of how order arises in decentralised market economies when the knowledge required for people to form mutually compatible plans is dispersed throughout the economy as a whole. Hayek first made significant progress towards answering this question in his 1945 paper on 'The Use of Knowledge in Society' ([1945] 2014). He argued there that, when individuals form and implement plans based on their knowledge of their local circumstances, they generate changes in relative prices that afford other people an indication of that knowledge, enabling them to amend their plans so as to take that knowledge into account even though they are not directly aware of it (Hayek, [1945] 2014, pp. 98–102). However, as Hayek hints in his 1945 paper (see [1945] 1948, p. 88), and as he argues more systematically and explicitly in his later writings on the political theory and the philosophy of law, plan co-ordination is facilitated not only by the information conveyed by relative price signals but also by the knowledge provided by various social norms and rules (including both the formal legal rules of property, tort and contract law, and also by informal norms of honesty and promise-keeping). The fact that people act in accordance with the same general guidelines about how to interpret and respond to circumstances of various kinds helps them to form reasonably accurate expectations of each other's conduct, thereby enabling them to devise plans that have a decent chance of coming to fruition. Perhaps most notably, by facilitating enforceable contracts, legal rules enable people to formulate and embark upon plans of action confident that the contributions that other people must make for those plans to be brought to a successful conclusion will actually be forthcoming (Fleetwood, 1995; Vaughn, 1999b).[15]

The significance of all this for our present purposes is that, especially from the early 1960s, Hayek's efforts to articulate and develop his insights into the working of the market economy were informed and shaped, at least in part, by Bertalanffy's work. During this period, Hayek was attempting to reformulate his ideas about economic theory so that they incorporated his developing understanding of complex phenomena (Caldwell, 2004, pp. 297–306, 2014). What is especially noteworthy for the argument being advanced here is that, as Hayek wrote to Karl Popper in 1960, he was attempting to restate his insights into the working of the economy using 'the conception of higher level regularities', adding that:

> I suspect it is really what Bertalanffy with his General Systems Theory was after and the conception itself was of course already implied in my 'Degrees of Explanation'. It

continues to become clearer, though I have not yet got an altogether satisfactory formulation of what I am after. (Hayek to Popper, February 27th 1960, Hayek Collection,
Box 44, folder 2, Hoover Institution Archives, quoted in Caldwell, 2014, p. 18)[16]

Elsewhere in the same letter, Hayek writes of his efforts that: 'Though I do
not mean to concentrate mainly on methodology, The New Look at
Economic Theory which I am taking and which may result in a book of
that title inevitably began with an attempt to restate my views on the nature of economic theory, and the conception of higher level regularities
which I then formed continues to occupy me and seems fruitful far beyond
the field of economics' (quoted in Kresge, 1994, p. 28).[17] The allusion to 'A
New Look at Economic Theory' is a reference both to a book on economics that Hayek was planning to write in the late 1950s and also to a set of
lectures he delivered at the University of Virginia in 1961. In a section of
the lectures entitled, 'Higher Level Regularities', Hayek discusses how such
regularities describe the 'general character of an order', in particular the
fact that in such an order there will obtain 'certain relations between its
parts'. He does not, however, develop the idea in much more detail in those
lectures, beyond pointing out the limitations of the knowledge social scientists are likely to be able to obtain about such systems (Hayek, [1961]
2014, pp. 381–382).[18]

A more significant attempt to use Bertalanffy's ideas to understand the
economy can arguably be found in Hayek's important 1967 essay, 'Notes
on the Evolution of Systems of Rules of Conduct' ([1967a] 2014). Although
he does not mention Bertalanffy by name, Hayek in that essay employs
Bertalanffy's notion of a 'system', and his distinction between different
levels of reality, to express the idea that the coordinative power of the market economy is an emergent property, or higher level regularity, that arises
when people's (inter)actions are governed and structured (organised) by
particular sets or systems of rules.[19]

Hayek argues first of all that the coordinative power of the price
mechanism, which he christens 'the overall order of actions', is an emergent
property that arises when people's interactions are structured by a set of
rules that includes both formal legal rules and informal social norms
(Hayek, [1967a] 2014, p. 282). It is an emergent property because it is possessed only by a particular 'whole' (p. 282), namely the free market economy that is formed by a group of people whose interactions are governed
by a set of rules of that kind:

The overall order of actions in a group is ... more than the totality of regularities obser-
vable in the actions of the individuals and cannot be reduced to them ... It is more than

the mere sum of its parts but presupposes also that those elements are related to each other in a particular manner. (Hayek, [1967a] 2014, p. 282)[20]

Hayek underlines the emergent nature of the overall order of actions later in the chapter, arguing that in such cases 'some regularity in the behaviour of the elements produces ... a wholly different regularity in the actions of the whole' that 'cannot be ... reduced to the regularities of the parts' (pp. 289, 286).[21] In the first place, then, Hayek employs the idea of 'higher level' regularities, derived from Bertalanffy, to develop and articulate his view that the coordinative power of the market is an emergent property that is irreducible to the 'lower level' properties of individual people.[22]

Moreover, this emergent property is generated by a *system* of rules in Bertalanffy's sense of that term. That is to say, for Hayek, the emergent property, the overall order of actions, is the result of the causal *interaction* of several different rules, rather than being simply the *sum* of their separate effects. We can see this most clearly in Hayek's remark that, '[S]ystems of rules of conduct will develop as wholes' ([1967a] 2014, p. 283):

> The evolutionary selection of different rules of individual conduct operates through the viability of the order it will produce, and any given rules of individual conduct may prove beneficial as part of one set of such rules, or in one set of external circumstances, and harmful as part of another set of rules or in another set of external circumstances. (Hayek, [1967a] 2014, p. 280; also see p. 73, 1973, pp. 59–61, 1979, p. 167, as well as [1962] 2014, p. 246, [1965] 2014, p. 267)

Just as Bertalanffy argues that the elements of a system behave differently when they are part of that system compared to when they are in isolation, thereby giving rise to emergent, system-level properties, so Hayek analogously contends that the rules in terms of which social systems are defined have a different impact on social outcomes depending on the other rules with which they interact. On Hayek's account, therefore, there is an intricate rule *structure*, with certain rules complementing each other in the sense that, taken together, they give rise to emergent capacities that are not possessed by any of them taken alone. For example, as noted above, the existence of the overall order of actions requires both formal legal rules and also informal moral rules; one of those types of rules alone will not suffice to generate the overall order of actions (Hayek, 1960, p. 36, 158). And it is this insight – that the outcomes to which sets of complementary rules give rise are emergent, rather than additive – which Hayek attempts to capture using the notion of 'system'. Hayek's discussion of rule systems can thus be seen to be a specific instance, or application, of Bertalanffy's concept.[23]

The notion of a 'system' in the sense in which that concept is defined by Bertalanffy is also important for Hayek's attempt to deal with the next task he sets himself, namely that of explaining how a set — or, as Hayek also terms it — a 'system' of rules of the kind required to generate the overall order of actions comes to prevail ([1967a] 2014, p. 279).[24] Hayek's explanation takes the form of a theory of cultural evolution, whereby the rules in question are the product of a process of competition between different groups of people. Significantly, the groups in question are defined by reference to the system of rules to which their members subscribe, and the trait that forms the basis for the competition between those groups is the emergent property or overall order of actions to which each system gives rise. As Hayek puts it, '[W]hat may be called the natural *selection* of rules will operate on the basis of the greater or lesser efficiency of the resulting *order of the group*' ([1967a] 2014, p. 279):

> It is the resulting overall order of actions but not the regularity of the actions of the separate individuals as such which is important for the preservation of the group ... [and] the selection process of evolution will operate on the order as a whole. (Hayek, [1967a] 2014, p. 280, 283)

The different sets of rules structure the actions of the members of the various groups and, in virtue of their collective capacity to underpin the emergent capacity to coordinate people's plans, determine the success of those groups in the process of competition through which selection occurs. Those groups whose activities were structured by a set of rules that gives rise to the emergent capacity effectively to coordinate people's actions were able to generate the wealth required to sustain higher populations, while groups that did not adhere to such rules declined in size and ultimately were eliminated. Ultimately, therefore, groups exhibiting the emergent property in question came to predominate. For Hayek, then, it is in virtue of their capacity to generate the emergent causal power to coordinate people's actions without centralised direction that groups — and, more specifically, the systems of rules that characterise them — are selected in the process of social evolution (Gaus, 2006; Lewis, 2015).[25]

Hayek elaborates on these issues in another essay originally published in 1967, namely 'The Results of Human Action but not of Human Design' ([1967b] 2014). In the course of discussing, the process of cultural selection through which the system of rules that sustains the spontaneous market order or catallaxy itself emerges, Hayek argues that a key insight in the history of social theory, which he attributes to the Austrian economist Carl Menger, was the realisation that 'the problem of the origin or formation and that of the manner of functioning of social institutions was essentially the same':

> [T]he institutions did develop in a particular way because the co-ordination of the actions of the parts which they secured proved more effective than the alternative institutions with which they had completed and which they had displaced. The theory of the evolution of traditions and habits which made the formation of spontaneous orders possible therefore stands in a close relation to the theory of the evolution of the particular kinds of spontaneous orders which we call organisms, and has in fact provided the essential concepts on which the latter was built. (Hayek, [1967b] 2014, p. 298)

Hayek adds a footnote to this passage, where he writes that, 'It is interesting to compare this with the insight from the biological field stressed by Ludwig von Bertalanffy, *Problems of Life* ... p. 134', before quoting Bertalanffy as follows:

> What are called structures are slow processes of long duration, functions are quick processes of short duration. If we say that a function such as the contraction of a muscle is performed by a structure, it means that a quick and short process wave is superimposed on a long-lasting and slowly running wave. (Bertalanffy, 1952, p. 134; quoted in Hayek, [1967b] 2014, p. 298, n. 16)

The passage from Bertalanffy is to be found in a section of *Problems of Life* entitled, 'The System Conception of the Organism – A Basis for Exact Biology' (Bertalanffy, 1952, pp. 132–146; also see Haraway, 2004, p. 39, 185). Bertalanffy argues in that section that the (static) study of the functions served by certain biological systems within the organism cannot be divorced from the (dynamic) processual account of how those organised systems arise and maintain themselves over time. This is, of course, analogous to the point that Hayek wishes to make with regard to social (rule) systems, namely that the (static) functional account of how certain systems of social rules underwrite the emergent capacity to coordinate people's actions is inextricably bound up with the (dynamic) account of the process through which those systems of rules emerge over time, because it is precisely in virtue of their effectiveness in generating such a capacity that those systems come to prevail in the process of evolutionary competition.[26]

Hayek is drawing here on Bertalanffy in support of his (Mengerian) claim that the static and dynamic aspects of the analysis of order must be combined if the possibility of market order is to be understood as fully as possible. Not for nothing does Hayek refer on several occasions to the importance of the 'twin ideas of evolution and spontaneous order' (Hayek, [1967a] 2014, p. 299, also see [1966] 1991, p. 81, 1979, p. 158). On Hayek's account, these two concepts intimately related because, as we have seen, he believes that it is only though an evolutionary account of the development of those systems of rules which sustain the emergent capacity to coordinate people's actions that it is possible to obtain a satisfactory account of how the spontaneous order of the market. But Bertalanffy's contribution is arguably more significant than simply that of providing an illustration of how natural scientists engage in a form of theorising analogous to that proposed by Menger and Hayek. For some of the key components of the analytical framework in terms of which Hayek articulates and develops his Mengerian insight about the need to combine static and dynamic analysis – the conceptual glue that holds the notions of spontaneous order and evolution together, if you will – are, as we have seen, ones that Hayek obtains from Bertalanffy, in particular the notion of emergent or structural properties and the concept of a 'system'.[27] What we can see here, then, is that Hayek used Bertalanffy's ideas to express and develop Menger's insight about the intimate connection between the origin and manner of functioning of social institutions in a modern idiom, namely the language of system theory.[28]

It is worth elaborating on one final aspect of Hayek's contention that cultural change proceeds via the selection of groups that adhere to systems of rules that underwrite the overall order of actions. A corollary is that groups that are characterised by rules which do not yield that emergent property will gradually wither away, as of course will the associated sets of rules. Therefore, as Hayek notes, cultural evolution can also be thought of as proceeding via the 'selective evolution of rules and practices', involving in particular the 'selective elimination of less suitable conduct' (1979, p. 154, 1960, p. 26, also see 1979, p. 155, 157, 159). On this view, order arises from the elimination of systems of rules that are *not* conducive to order. As Hayek puts it:

> [N]ot every system of rules of conduct will produce an overall order of the actions of a group of individuals ... The classical instance in which the very regularity of the behaviour of the elements produces 'perfect disorder' is the second law of thermodynamics, the entropy principle. It is evident that in a group of living beings many possible rules of individual conduct would also produce only disorder or make the existence of the group as such impossible. A society of animals or men is always a number of individuals observing such common rules of conduct as, in the circumstances in which they live, will produce an order of actions. (Hayek, [1967a] 2014, p. 279, also see [1966] 1968, p. 169, 1973, p. 44)

It seems likely that this passage bears the influence of Bertalanffy's work on systems, in particular his notion of a system that is *open* in the sense of being able to import energy from its surroundings. As noted above,

Bertalanffy developed that concept in order to understand how, in an apparent violation of the second law of thermodynamics, the biological world displays a tendency to produce increasingly complex and more highly organised forms of life. Significantly, Hayek had long been aware of Bertalanffy's work on this topic, writing in *The Sensory Order* of the 'recent and most promising work of L. von Bertalanffy [on]..."open systems"' (Hayek, 1952, p. 83).[29] It seems reasonable to conclude, therefore, that the references to thermodynamics and entropy that Hayek makes in the course of his exposition of his theory of group selection are derived from Bertalanffy's work, constituting another way in which – and, *a fortiori*, further evidence that – Bertalanffy's work on systems influenced Hayek's thinking on cultural evolution.

What we can see in these two 1967 essays is that Hayek used system theory, which he had originally come across through his work on the philosophy of mind, to help him articulate 'the common features of ... diverse complex orders' in other domains, most notably in this case the market as an spontaneous order or catallaxy (1979, pp. 158–159). Bertalanffy's conceptual framework – in particular, the notions of emergent or structural properties, of distinct 'levels' of reality, and of (open) 'systems' – provided Hayek with a means of expressing and developing his insights into the working of the economy, in particular by helping him to articulate his view that the market order or catallaxy rests on a system of rules that has itself arisen spontaneously, through a process of evolution centring on the capacity of those rules to generate the emergent property to coordinate people's actions. While as Hayek often notes, the development of evolutionary biology was informed by the ideas of political economists, what we see here is Hayek re-appropriating for economics the ideas developed by theoretical biologists like Bertalanffy, using the notions of 'system', of 'levels of organisation' and of 'structural' or 'emergent' properties, first of all to help him frame the nature and philosophical significance of his theoretical psychology, before subsequently deploying them to express his emerging understanding of the economy as a complex system, using terminology that he believed would render his ideas both more precise and also more intelligible to his audience. As Hayek put it in the Epilogue to the third volume of *Law, Legislation and Liberty*, 'My colleagues in the social sciences find my study on *The Sensory Order* uninteresting or indigestible ... But the work on it helped me greatly to clear my mind on much that is very relevant to social theory. My conception of evolution, of a spontaneous order and of the methods and limits of our endeavours to explain complex phenomena have been formed largely in the course of work on that book. As I was using the work I had done in my student days on theoretical psychology in forming my views on the methodology of the social science[s], so the working out of my earlier ideas on psychology with the help of what I had learnt in the social science helped me greatly in all my later scientific developments' (Hayek, 1979, pp. 199–200, n. 26, also see 1979, p. xii, 158).[30]

CONCLUSION

The argument advanced above is that Ludwig von Bertalanffy influenced the post-war work of F.A. Hayek in two related ways. First, in the late 1940s and early 1950s, Bertalanffy's work helped Hayek to articulate the philosophical significance of his theoretical psychology, in particular the fact that for Hayek the mind is an emergent property of the organised arrangement of neurons found in the human brain.

Second, in Hayek's hands, the conceptual framework provided by general system theory proved, as Bertalanffy intended, abstract enough to be applicable to phenomena situated at a number of different 'levels' of reality. In particular, having in the course of writing *The Sensory Order* used Bertalanffy's ideas to help draw out and express some of the philosophical implications of his theory of mind, Hayek in the 1950s and 1960s applied system theory to help him analyse the working of society and thereby articulate and develop his emerging vision of the economy as a complex system. Perhaps most importantly, Hayek used the notions of a 'system' (of rules), and of higher level emergent properties, in particular to provide a conceptual framework and a language that enabled him to unite, in a coherent and fruitful way, the 'twin ideas of evolution and spontaneous order' by which he set such great store.

Bertalanffy's work was not, of course, the only influence that helped shape Hayek's efforts to develop an account of the economy as a complex adaptive system. For example, the influence of Warren Weaver, in particular his distinction between organised and disorganised complexity, has been well documented (Caldwell, 2014, pp. 14–15).[31] Nevertheless, the account developed above suggests that Bertalanffy too played a significant role in the development of Hayek's post-war thought. If this chapter has served to make the nature of Bertalanffy's contribution clearer, then it will have served its purpose.

NOTES

1. For more on Bertalanffy's life, see Davidson (1983, pp. 45–69), Hammond (2003, pp. 108–111) and Pouvreau (2009).

2. Emergent properties can be contrasted with what are variously called *resultant*, *aggregate* or *summative* properties. These are the properties of wholes that are possessed by the individual elements of which those wholes are composed. Resultant properties are possessed by the individual elements irrespective of how they are related to one another, obtaining both when those elements are taken in isolation and also when they form an unstructured aggregate or 'heap'. The paradigm of a resultant property is mass. The mass of a water molecule, for example, is simply the mass of its constituent atoms (Bertalanffy, 1933, pp. 32–34, 1950a, p. 147, 1952, p. 10, 14).

3. It is interesting to note that Hayek first used the term 'spontaneous order' in his 1955 Cairo Lectures on 'The Political Ideal of the Rule of Law' (see Hayek, [1955] 2014, p. 161; also see Caldwell, 2014, p. 14).

4. Hayek was quite aware of the fact that, as used by Bertalanffy, the term 'organisation' was being used in a very sense different to that intended by Hayek in his criticisms of constructive rationalism: 'The biologist will generally speak without hesitation of "organisation" without implying design …[B]iology has from its beginnings been concerned with that special kind of spontaneous order which we call an organism' (Hayek, 1973, p. 27, 37).

5. Hence, Bertalanffy's definition of an 'organism': 'A living organism is a hierarchical order of open systems which maintains itself in the exchange of [its] components by virtue of its system conditions' (1952, p. 129).

6. Bertalanffy introduced the term 'general system theory' at a seminar held at the University of Chicago in 1937. Other important figures in the founding of systems theory, many of whom were associated with the University of Chicago, were the economist Kenneth Boulding, the mathematician and game theorist Anatol Rapoport, the neurophysiologist and behavioural scientist Ralph Gerard, and the psychologist James Grier Miller (Boulding, 1983, pp. 18–19; Davidson, 1983, pp. 179–181; Pouvreau, 2009, pp. 53–54). It is worth noting at this juncture that in May 1954, in a letter that also bore the name of Kenneth Boulding, Bertalanffy wrote to Hayek to invite him to join in forming 'an International Society for the development, encouragement, and promotion of General System Theory'. April 1955 saw Bertalanffy invite Hayek to attend in December 1955 the inaugural meeting of what by then was called 'The Society for the Advancement of General Systems Theory', held in Atlanta, Georgia (Hayek Archives, Box 12–14 Bertalanffy). No response from Hayek to these letters has been found. For more on the development of the Society, see Hammond (2003, pp. 245–267, especially pp. 245–250) and Pouvreau (2009, pp. 127–130, 137–139, 144–147, 158–160).

7. We shall elaborate on this point below, when we consider Hayek's reflections on the account of the relationship between mental and physical phenomena to which his theoretical psychology gives rise.

8. Hayek also references the work of the English philosopher of biology, Woodger (1929), who — like Bertalanffy — discusses emergent properties and levels of organisation. Given that references to Woodger are less extensive than those to

Bertalanffy in Hayek's writings, and given too that Hayek almost certainly came across Woodger's work through his reading of Bertalanffy, he will not be discussed further here. For more, see Lewis (2016a).

9. The origins of *The Sensory Order* are to be found in a paper Hayek wrote as a student in 1920, entitled *Beiträge zur Theorie der Entwicklung des Bewusstseins*, or 'Contributions to a Theory of How Conscious Develops' (Hayek, 1920). That paper contains most of the key elements of the theoretical psychology set out in *The Sensory Order* (Lewis, 2016a, Section 3.1). However, while Hayek felt that he had been able to set out the key principles of his theoretical psychology in that early essay, it was not until after he had resumed work on his manuscript in the late 1940s that he was able (a) to state clearly and precisely the problem addressed by his theory and also (b) to derive in a reasonably complete fashion the theory's broader philosophical implications. More specifically, so far as issue (a) is concerned, it was only after reading the work of the gestalt psychologists in the 1940s that Hayek was able to define the terms 'mind' and 'body' in such a way as to show precisely how his theory bore upon the age-old problem that falls under the 'traditional heading … of the "relation" between mind and body, or between mental and physical events' (1952, p. 1; also see Hayek, 1994, p. 138) (De Vecchi, 2003, pp. 140–147; also see Lewis, 2016a, Section 4). The principal significance of Bertalanffy's work for Hayek's theoretical psychology concerns issue (b), consisting – it will be argued below – in how it afforded Hayek a set of concepts – such as the notions of (levels of) 'organisation', of 'structural' or 'emergent' properties, and of 'systems' – that enabled him to articulate the wider philosophical significance of his account of the mind as a relational order. Moreover, as we shall also see, in providing Hayek with the conceptual tools required to express, at a high level of abstraction, the nature of the human mind (viewed as a relational order), Bertalanffy's ideas also constituted a set of abstract concepts that were used by Hayek to identify and highlight the commonalities between the mind and other relational orders such as the market. In doing so, Bertalanffy's work helped Hayek to articulate and develop his insight that spontaneous orders are ubiquitous, being found in many parts of the natural and social world (Caldwell, 2014, p. 2, 24–25, 35; Lewis & Lewin, 2015).

10. Both Hayek and Bertalanffy attended the European Forum Alpbach in August 1947, with Bertalanffy giving a talk on system theory at that event (Pouvreau, 2014, p. 176, 197; Wirth, 2015, p. 14). Given that their correspondence began in late 1947, and given that both men were present at the symposium, it seems reasonable to conclude that it was at that symposium that the two men first met.

11. This claim should not be taken to imply that the role played by the notion of emergence in particular in Hayek's theoretical psychology is solely attributable to Bertalanffy. First, as already noted, in writing the passage from *The Sensory Order* discussed above, Hayek also drew on the work of Bertalanffy's fellow organicist biologist Joseph Woodger. Second, and more importantly, the notion of emergence had been apparent in Hayek's theoretical psychology long before he read Bertalanffy, entering into his thought as early as the *Beiträge* (via the work of the German psychologist Wilhelm Wundt) and also later through his reading of the gestalt psychologists. What Hayek's reading of Bertalanffy did, then, was to enable

him to refine and articulate his understanding of emergence in a clearer and more sophisticated way (rather than prompt him to use the concept for the first time) (Lewis, 2016a).

12. In a footnote accompanying this passage, Hayek (1979, p. 200, n. 33) references Bertalanffy's (1969) book on systems theory.

13. In a 1947 letter to Hayek, Bertalanffy responds to an earlier – alas, unseen – letter from Hayek who, having read some of Bertalanffy's work on systems theory, had commented on the similarities between 'vitalism' in biology and 'wholism' in sociology. At the very least, this indicates that Hayek was familiar both with the vitalism–mechanism debate at the time when he was working on *The Sensory Order*, and also with the scope for 'organismic' approaches that emphasised the importance of organising relations and structural properties to transcend this opposition. Bertalanffy writes as follows: 'I am delighted that you are interested in my "systems theory", and I am very much looking forward to discussing this in more detail. Even your preliminary remarks regarding sociology and economics are highly valuable to me. I can see that, terminologically, I have to be far more careful in these matters, even though I am sure that we are entirely of one mind on the issue itself. Particularly important to me is your advice on the terms "individualistic" and "liberalist", as is your note that the mystical "holism-concept" in sociology logically equates to "vitalism". On the other hand, I expect that one will be able to define the matter in such a way that "organisation" (and "over-organisation") actually signify roughly the opposite of the regular meaning, that is "mechanisation" of social life ... An edifying example of the expression itself running counter to the actual situation. Do please keep the copy of "Theoretical Biology" as long as you would like' (Hayek Archives, Bertalanffy 12–14 box). I am very grateful to Eva Peters for translating Bertalanffy's letter from the original German.

14. In a footnote on the same page, Hayek writes, 'L. von. Bertalanffy, 19' (Hayek, n.d., p. 4, n. 3). The absence both of a date for the Bertalanffy reference, and also of a bibliography in Hayek's manuscript, makes it hard if not impossible to be sure on which Bertalanffy essay or book Hayek was drawing. Given, however, that Bertalanffy offers definitions of 'system' consistent with that used by Hayek in several places, the absence of a precise reference is probably unimportant (see, e.g. Bertalanffy, 1950a, p. 143, 1952, p. 11).

15. As Hayek puts it in *Law, Legislation and Liberty*, 'What makes men members of the same civilisation and enables them to live and work together in peace is that in the pursuit of their individual ends the particular monetary impulses which impel their efforts towards concrete results are guided and restrained by the same abstract rules. If emotion or impulse tells them what they want, the conventional rules tell them how they will be able and be allowed to achieve it' (Hayek, 1976, p. 12; also see Hayek [1968] 1968, p. 72).

16. In his 1955 essay on 'Degrees of Explanation', Hayek mentions 'general system theory', along with cybernetics and the theory of automata, as one of the recent intellectual developments exploring complex phenomena ([1955] 2014, p. 211). For more on the significance of cybernetics for the development of Hayek's thought, see Lewis (2016b) and Oliva (2016).

17. The notion that reality is hierarchical, displaying distinct 'levels of organisation', was, as we have seen, a notable feature of Bertalanffy's work. Additional

evidence of Hayek's interest in this idea can be found in the form of teaching notes he produced for a seminar class on 'Scientific Method and the Study of Society', held at the University of Chicago in late 1952. These included a chart listing phenomena at different 'levels of organisation' – the very title of chapter 2 of Bertalanffy's *Problems of Life* (1952, p. 23) – ranging from the gene to the cell to individuals to society, along with the corresponding fields of study (genetics, physiology, etc.) (see Hayek Archive, Box 63, folder 13; also see Caldwell, 2004, pp. 298–299). The distinction between these different levels of organisation, coupled with the fact that in Hayek's chart each is allocated its own field of study, suggests that Hayek followed Bertalanffy in viewing the world as hierarchical in nature, with entities at lower levels of organisation forming the building blocks out of which higher level entities, possessing their own higher level or emergent properties, are formed. As Hayek later put it, 'Societies differ from simpler complex structures by the fact that their elements are themselves complex structures' ([1967a] 2014, p. 288).

18. See Caldwell (2014, pp. 16–19) for a discussion of the book project to which Hayek refers and to the Virginia lectures.

19. Hayek does show that he is aware of Bertalanffy's notion of a system, both in *The Sensory Order* (1952, p. 83) and also in 'Within Systems and about Systems' (n.d., p. 4).

20. In Hayek's view, it is precisely because statistics 'treats the individual elements which it counts as if they were not systematically connected' and so 'deliberately disregards the fact that the relative position of the different elements in a structure may matter' that it is incapable of advancing the understanding of social order ([1964] 2014, p. 265).

21. Elsewhere in the essay, Hayek underscores the irreducibility of the emergent power to coordinate people's actions by noting that 'it is at least conceivable that the same overall order of actions may be produced by different sets of rules of individual conduct'. It is possible to make sense of this possibility, Hayek contends, only by acknowledging that 'the system of rules of individual conduct and the order of actions that results from the individuals acting in accordance with them are not the same thing' (that is, by acknowledging the existence of an ontological distinction between rules and individual actions, on the one hand, and the emergent power to coordinate people's plans, on the other) (Hayek, [1967a] 2014, p. 279, 287–279; also see Hayek, [1966] 1968, p. 169). Hayek makes a similar point in *The Errors of Constructivism*, writing that, 'The order of society is therefore a factual state of affairs which must be distinguished from the regularity of the conduct of individuals' ([1970] 2014, p. 344).

22. There is no evidence that there was any correspondence between Hayek and Bertalanffy in the 1960s. However, the two men did attend some of the same conferences. First, in June 1960, both attended the 'Symposium on the Principles of Self-Organization', sponsored by the Information Systems Branch of the US Office of Naval Research and held at the University of Illinois. However, neither Hayek nor Bertalanffy presented a paper and the few references to them in the conference's Transactions are devoid of intellectual content (see Foerster & Zopf, 1962, p. x, 132, 261, 382, 283, 399). Second, and more significantly, both men participated in the 1968, at Alpbach symposium, so-called because it was held at Alpbach in the

Austrian Tirol. The participants in the symposium, which was organised by the writer Arthur Koestler, were concerned to remedy 'the insufficient emancipation of the life sciences from the mechanistic concepts of nineteenth century physics, and the resulting crudely reductionist philosophy' (Koestler, 1969, p. 2). Accordingly, they shared a common interest in exploring the potential of the organismic paradigm, with its emphasis on organisation, emergence, and the hierarchical ordering of the natural and social worlds, in variety of different disciplinary contexts. Indeed, in addition to Hayek and Bertalanffy, participants in the 1968 symposium included another of the principal architects of organismic biology, namely the Viennese developmental biologist Paul Weiss (Haraway, 2004, pp. 4–5, 15–16, 38, 131–133, 183–184). The paper Hayek presented at the symposium was 'The Primacy of the Abstract'. Frustratingly, and tantalisingly, for the purposes of the present essay, the first footnote in the version of the chapter published in the conference proceeding contains the following comments from the editors of the volume: 'On the original programme of the conference, Professor Hayek was scheduled to give a paper on "Group Behaviour and Individual Behaviour" and the applications of the hierarchic concept in the social sciences. In the preamble to his presentation, he explained why he preferred to talk on "The Primacy of the Abstract" instead. This also explains why, except for references in passing, social science in the narrower sense was not discussed at the Symposium. *Eds*'. (Koestler & Smythies, 1969, p. 309, n. 1). The editors' comments were, perhaps unsurprisingly, excised from the version of the paper that was published in Hayek's ([1969] 1978) volume, *New Studies in Politics, Philosophy and Economics* (Hayek, [1969] 1978, p. 35). Nor do they appear in the version of the essay reprinted as in Hayek's *Collected Works* (Hayek, [1969] 2014). One can, of course, speculate that had Hayek written on the topic intended for him, he would have presented a variation on, or development of, his 1967 paper, 'Notes on the Evolution of Systems of Rules of Conduct', which is – as we have seen – the essay in which Hayek focussed most explicitly on the importance of higher level emergent properties (as part of his account of group selection and cultural evolution) (Gaus, 2006; Lewis, 2012, 2015). But it would have been fascinating to see how Hayek might have developed that work, and to learn how his fellow conferees would have responded to his paper in the discussion that followed, given that – as already noted – they were present at the symposium several scholars who had carried out pioneering work on hierarchical levels of organisation and structural properties in biology from the 1920s onwards. As it is, the significant recorded interaction between Bertalanffy and Hayek at the symposium is limited to a debate about the merits of Darwinian evolutionary theory (see Koestler & Smythies, 1969, pp. 79–80; also see Pouvreau, 2009, pp. 188–189).

23. Hayek's use of the notion of a 'system' of rules to understand how social order is possible also informs his jurisprudence. In the latter, Hayek argues that judges should try to discover those laws that are implied by, or complementary to, the laws that are already in force, thereby helping to reinforce the prevailing system of rules and to sustain the emergent order of actions that supervenes on that rule system (Hayek, 1973, pp. 94–123, 1976, pp. 31–44, 70–73, 157–158, n. 4, 1979, pp. 157–160, 207, n. 62; also see Mack, 2006). It is also noteworthy in this regard that, in discussing how systems of complementary rules are required for the emergent order of (just) actions is to obtain, Hayek contrasts his (organicist) approach

with the old atomistic view of the world as a mosaic of independent, atomistic parts: 'The idea that we are not fully free to pick and choose whatever combination of features we want our society to possess, or to fit them together into a viable whole, that is, that we cannot build a desirable order like a mosaic by selecting whatever particular parts we like best, and that many well-intentioned measures may have a long train of unforeseeable and undesirable consequences, seems to be intolerable to modern man' (Hayek, 1979, p. 59; also see p. 48, 51).

24. Also see Hayek (973, pp. 65–67, 74–75, 96–106, 1976, pp. 24–29, 1979, pp. 157–160, 207, n. 62).

25. It is also noteworthy in this regard that, by the late 1960s, Hayek was applying these ideas, about group selection on the basis of the emergent properties sustained by systems of rules, back to his theoretical psychology. '[W]hat we call mind', Hayek ([1967a] 2014, pp. 321–322), 'is essentially … a system of abstract rules of action' (also see Hayek, [1969] 2014, p. 49). This system of rules, Hayek argues, evolves through a process of competition whereby systems of rules, and the groups of neurons in which those rules are embodied, are selected – or not, as the case may be – in virtue of their emergent capacity to classify the world, and to dispose people to act, in ways that enable a person successfully to navigate his/her environment: '[I]t is by a selection among mechanisms producing different action patterns that the system of rules of action is built up on which rests what we regard as an interpretation of the external world by the mind … As the organism plays with a great many action patterns of which some are confirmed and retained as conducive to the preservation of the species, corresponding structures of the nervous system producing appropriate dispositions will first appear experimentally and then either be retained or abandoned' (Caldwell, 2004, p. 307; Hayek, [1967b] 2014, p. 321, also see Hayek, [1962] 2014, pp. 146–147). This process of neuronal group selection on the basis of the emergent properties that supervene on the system of rules governing the behaviour of the relevant group of neurons is, of course, analogous to the process of group selection that Hayek believes accounts for the development of rule-governed social systems such as the market economy.

26. Another way of expressing Hayek's point is as follows. For Hayek, while it is important and interesting to develop give a static or synchronic account of how, when people's actions are governed by a particular system of rules, there arises the emergent property known as the overall order of actions, such analyses take the existence of the rules as given. Ultimately, therefore, they provide an incomplete answer to the question of how social order is possible in decentralised market economies, because they do not explain the origins of the requisite rule system. A fuller explanation of the possibility of order requires a dynamic or diachronic account of how the relevant system of organising rules comes to exist. As Hayek puts it, while it is the case that 'for the explanation of the functioning of the social order at any one time the rules of individual conduct must be assumed to be given … these rules of conduct have themselves developed as part of a larger whole' and the existence of such wholes, or systems of rules, 'can be made intelligible only by … a theory of their evolution' ([1967a] 2014, p. 284, 287). And, of course, it is precisely such a theory that Hayek's analysis of group selection is meant to provide. For more on this, see Lewis (2015, Sections 3.2–3.3). Hayek's emphasis on the need

to give an evolutionary account of how systems of rules come into being also differentiates his account of complex systems from that offered by advocates of cybernetics, who tended to treat structures as static or given rather than giving a dynamic account of how they come to be established (Lewis, 2016a, n. 14, 2016b).

27. If this claim is correct, then it implies that those commentators — such as Vanberg (1986, p. 97), Paul (1988, p. 261), and Hodgson (1993, p. 177) — who have called into question the compatibility of Hayek's work on spontaneous order with his evolutionary theory of group selection are mistaken. For excellent accounts of various influences on Hayek's evolutionary theory other than Bertalanffy, see Caldwell (2000) and Angner (2002).

28. Hence, also Hayek's remark that 'for the understanding of the methodological problems of the social sciences a study of the procedures of geology or biology is much more instructive than that of physics. In all of these fields the structures or steady states ... can be fully accounted for only by considering also circumstances which are not properties of the structures themselves but particular facts of the environment in which they have developed and exist' (Hayek, [1967a] 2014, p. 287). The reference to 'steady states' found here, which comes from another paragraph where Hayek discusses Menger's claim that function and evolution are intimately bound together, also reflects the influence of Bertalanffy, who used it in the section of *Problems of Life* on which Hayek drew to distinguish physical equilibria, in which the lower levels parts as well as the higher level structures they form remain constant over time, from biological systems such as the organism, which 'persists as a whole' over time whilst being maintained in that higher level 'steady state' only through processes that involve the 'continuous change, formation, growth, wearing out, and death of systems of the next lower level ...[for example] of cells in a multicellular organism' (Bertalanffy, 1952, pp. 124–125). As Bertalanffy puts it in the sentence immediately following the one cited by Hayek and reproduced in the main text, 'A living organism is an object maintaining itself in an orderly flow of events wherein the higher systems appear persistent in the exchange of the subordinate ones' (Bertalanffy, 1952, pp. 134–135; also see pp. 124–136).

29. In a footnote, Hayek refers to the German version of Bertalanffy's (1952) book (Hayek, 1952, p. 83, n. 1). In addition, the bibliography of *The Sensory Order* contains references to Bertalanffy's 1950 *Science* article on 'The Theory of Open Systems in Physics and Biology' (Bertalanffy, 1950b; also see Hayek, 1952, p. 195).

30. There is some evidence to indicate that the influence between Hayek and Bertalanffy flowed in both directions. In his 1950 paper on systems theory, Bertalanffy references Hayek's *Road to Serfdom* in a passage where he describes what he sees as the (then) contemporary 'tendency to consider a society, an economy, or a nation, as a whole which is superordinated to its parts'. Bertalanffy continues as follows: 'This conception is at the basis of all the various forms of collectivism, the consequences of which are often disastrous for the individual and, in the history of our times, profoundly influence our lives' (1950a, p. 135). Elsewhere, Bertalanffy favourably cites Hayek's notion of 'explanation of the principle' arguing that 'there are degrees in scientific explanation and that in complex and theoretically little-developed fields we have to be satisfied with what the economist Hayek has justly termed "explanation in principle"' (Bertalanffy, 1969, p. 36, also see 1969, p. 47, 113).

31. It is worth noting that, in Weaver's (1948) account, 'organisation' is under-stood as being present in systems which 'involve dealing simultaneously with a size-able number of factors which are integrated into an organic whole' (p. 539). After having introduced the notion of organised complexity, Weaver proceeds to discuss various possible ways of analysing those systems, such as statistics, computing and operations research (pp. 539–542). It is noteworthy, however, that nowhere in the article does Weaver discuss the notion of emergence or its correlates, structural properties and levels of organisations. While Weaver was influential in shaping Hayek's views on complexity in general, perhaps most notably by providing a scien-tifically grounded rationale for Hayek's scepticism about the usefulness of statistical methods for the study of the social world, he does not appear to have had a signifi-cant impact on Hayek's views about the way that complex systems display emergent properties. In a similar vein, the population geneticist Sewall Wright, who was one of the early exponents of group selection, who attended seminars organised by Hayek at Chicago in the 1950s, and whose work was cited by Hayek (1979, p. 202, n. 37; Caldwell, 2004, p. 299, 314–315), explicitly disavowed the notion of emer-gence, arguing that it 'can have no place in scientific analysis of the problem [of evo-lution]' (Wright, 1931, p. 154).

ACKNOWLEDGEMENTS

I am very grateful to Virgil Storr, Gabriel Oliva, two anonymous referees, and participants in the NYU Colloquium on Market Institutions and Economic Processes, the 15th Summer Institute for the Study of the History of Economic Thought, held at the University of Richmond, the Philosophy, Politics and Economy Workshop at George Mason University, and the Southern Economic Association annual conference (New Orleans), for very helpful comments on an earlier version of the chapter. I am grate-ful also to Bruce Caldwell for providing access to unpublished material from the Hayek archives and to the Bertalanffy Center for the Study of Systems Science (Vienna) for granting me access to Hayek's letters to Bertalanffy. I am indebted to Eva Peters for translating those letters. The early stages of the research for this chapter were carried out whilst the author was a Visiting Fellow of Peterhouse, Cambridge. I am grateful to the Master and Fellows of Peterhouse for their support and hospitality. Financial support from the Earhart Foundation is also thankfully acknowl-edged. None of the above should be held responsible for any errors and infelicities remaining in the chapter.

REFERENCES

Allen, G. E. (2005). Mechanism, vitalism and organicism in late nineteenth and twentieth-century biology: The importance of historical context. *Studies in the History and Philosophy of Biological and Biomedical Sciences, 36,* 261–283.

Angner, E. (2002). The history of Hayek's theory of cultural evolution. *Studies in the History and Philosophy of Biological and Biomedical Sciences, 33,* 695–718.

Bertalanffy, L. v. (1933 [1928]). *Modern theories of development: An introduction to theoretical biology.* (Trans. and adapted from the original, 1928 German edition by J. H. Woodger). London: Oxford University Press.

Bertalanffy, L. v. (1950a). An outline of general system theory. *British Journal for the Philosophy of Science, 1,* 134–165.

Bertalanffy, L. v. (1950b). The theory of open systems in physics and biology. *Science, 111,* 23–29.

Bertalanffy, L. v. (1952). *Problems of life: An evaluation of modern biological thought.* London: Watts & Co.

Bertalanffy, L. v. (1969). *General system theory: Foundations, development, applications.* New York, NY: George Braziller.

Boulding, K. E. (1983). Introduction. In M. Davidson (Ed.), *Uncommon sense: The life and thought of Ludwig von Bertalanffy, father of general systems theory.* Los Angeles, CA: J.P. Tarcher, Inc.

Caldwell, B. (2000). The emergence of Hayek's ideas on cultural evolution. *Review of Austrian Economics, 13,* 5–22.

Caldwell, B. (2004). *Hayek's challenge: An intellectual biography of F.A. Hayek.* Chicago, IL: The University of Chicago Press.

Caldwell, B. (2014). Introduction. In F. A. Hayek (2014).

Davidson, M. (1983). *Uncommon sense: The life and thought of Ludwig von Bertalanffy, father of general systems theory.* Los Angeles, CA: J.P. Tarcher, Inc.

De Vecchi, N. (2003). The place of gestalt psychology in the making of Hayek's thought. *History of Political Economy, 35,* 135–162.

Fleetwood, S. (1995). *Hayek's political economy: The socio-economics of order.* London: Routledge.

Foerster, H. v., & Zopf, G. W. Jr. (Eds.). (1962). *Principles of self-organization.* Oxford: Pergamon Press.

Fuster, J. (2011). Hayek in today's cognitive neuroscience. *Advances in Austrian Economics, 15,* 3–11.

Gaus, J. (2006). Hayek on the evolution of society and mind. In E. Feser (Ed.), *The Cambridge companion to Hayek.* Cambridge: Cambridge University Press.

Hammond, D. (2003). *The science of synthesis: Exploring the social implications of general systems theory.* Boulder, CO: The University Press of Colorado.

Haraway, D. (2004). *Crystals, fabrics, and fields: Metaphors that shape embryos.* Berkeley, CA: North Atlantic Books.

Hayek. (1920). *Contributions to a theory of how conscious develops.* Unpublished paper. Hayek Archives.

Hayek, F. A. (n.d.). *Within systems and about systems: A statement of some problems of a theory of communication.* Typescript. Hoover Institution, Hayek Archives, box 104, folder 22.

Hayek, F. A. ([1937] 2014). Economics and knowledge. In F. A. Hayek (2014).

Hayek, F. A. ([1945] 2014). The use of knowledge in society. In F. A. Hayek (2014).

Hayek, F. A. ([1955] 2014). Degrees of explanation. In F. A. Hayek (2014).

Hayek, F. A. ([1961] 2014). A new look at economic theory. In F. A. Hayek (2014).

Hayek, F. A. ([1962] 2014). Rules, perception and Intelligibility. In F. A. Hayek (2014).

Hayek, F. A. ([1964] 2014). The theory of complex phenomena. In Hayek (2014).

Hayek, F. A. ([1965] 2014). Kinds of rationalism. In Hayek (2014).

Hayek, F. A. ([1966] 1968). The principles of a liberal social order. In F. A. Hayek (Ed.),
Studies in philosophy, politics and economics. London: Routledge and Kegan Paul.

Hayek, F. A. ([1966] 1991). Dr. Bernard Mandeville (1670–1733). In W. W. Bartley & S.
Kresge (Eds.), *The collected works of F.A. Hayek, volume 3: The trend of economic
thinking.* Chicago, IL: The University of Chicago Press.

Hayek, F. A. ([1967a] 2014). Notes on the evolution of systems of rules of conduct. In F. A.
Hayek (2014).

Hayek, F. A. ([1967b] 2014). The results of human action but not of human design. In F. A.
Hayek (2014).

Hayek, F. A. ([1968] 1968). The confusion of language in political thought. In F. A. Hayek
(Ed.), *Studies in philosophy, politics and economics.* London: Routledge and
Kegan Paul.

Hayek, F. A. ([1969] 1978). The primacy of the abstract. In F. A. Hayek (Ed.), *New studies in
philosophy, politics, economics and the history of ideas.* London: Routledge &
Kegan Paul.

Hayek, F. A. ([1969] 2014). The primacy of the abstract. In F.A. Hayek (2014).

Hayek, F. A. ([1970] 2014). The errors of constructivism. In F.A. Hayek (2014).

Hayek, F. A. (1945). *What is mind?* Unpublished paper. Hayek archives.

Hayek, F. A. (1952). *The sensory order: An inquiry into the foundations of theoretical psychology.* London: Routledge & Kegan Paul.

Hayek, F. A. (1960). *The constitution of liberty.* London: Routledge.

Hayek, F. A. (1969). The primacy of the abstract. In A. Koestler & J. Smythies (Eds.), Beyond
reductionism: New perspectives in the life sciences. The alpbach symposium 1968.
London: Hutchinson of London.

Hayek, F. A. (1973). *Law, legislation and liberty: A new statement of the liberal principles of justice and political economy* (Vol. 1). London: Routledge.

Hayek, F. A. (1976). *Law, legislation and liberty: A new statement of the liberal principles of justice and political economy. Volume II: The mirage of social justice.* London: Routledge.

Hayek, F. A. (1979). *Law, legislation and liberty: A new statement of the liberal principles of justice and political economy. Volume III: The political order of a free people.*
London: Routledge.

Hayek, F. (1994). Hayek on Hayek: An autobiographical dialogue. In S. Kresge & L. Wenar
(Eds.), *Collected Works of F.A. Hayek.* Chicago, IL: The University of Chicago Press.

Hayek, F. A. (2014). In B. Caldwell (Ed.), *The collected works of F.A. Hayek, Volume 15: The
market and other orders.* Chicago, IL: The University of Chicago Press.

Hodgson, G. M. (1993). *Economics and evolution: Bringing life back into economics.*
Cambridge: Polity Press.

Koestler, A. (1969). *The alpbach symposium: Opening remarks.* In A. Koestler & J. Smythies
(Eds.), Beyond reductionism: New perspectives in the life sciences. The alpbach symposium 1968. London: Hutchinson of London.

Koestler, A., & Smythies, J. (Eds.). (1969). *Beyond reductionism: New perspectives in the life sciences. The alpbach symposium 1968.* London: Hutchinson of London.

Kresge, S. (1994). Introduction. In S. Kresge & L. Wenar (Eds.), *Hayek on Hayek: An autobiographical dialogue.* Chicago, IL: The University of Chicago Press.

Lewis, P. A. (2012). Emergent properties in the work of Friedrich Hayek. *Journal of Economic Behavior and Organisation, 82,* 368–378.

Lewis, P. A. (2015). Notions of order and process in Hayek: The significance of emergence. *Cambridge Journal of Economics, 39,* 1167–1190.

Lewis, P. A. (2016a). The emergence of "Emergence" in the work of F.A. Hayek: An historical analysis. *History of Political Economy, 48,* 111–150.

Lewis, P. A. (2016b). *The influence of cybernetics of the work of F.A. Hayek.* Unpublished paper. Department of Political Economy, King's College London.

Lewis, P. A., & Lewin, P. (2015). Orders, orders everywhere ... On Hayek's *the market and other orders. Cosmos and Taxis, 2*(2), 1–17. Retrieved from https://cosmosandtaxis. files.wordpress.com/2015/03/ct_vol2_issue2_lewislewin.pdf

Mack, E. (2006). Hayek on justice and the order of actions. In E. Feser (Ed.), *The Cambridge companion to Hayek.* Cambridge: Cambridge University Press.

Morgan, C. L. (1926-27). A concept of the organism, emergent and resultant. *Proceedings of the Aristotelian Society, 27,* 141–176.

Oliva, G. (2016). The Road to Servomechanisms: The Influence of Cybernetics on Hayek from 'The Sensory Order' to the Social Order. In L. Fiorito, S. Scheall, & C. E. Suprinyak (Eds.), *Research in the History of Economic Thought and Methodology* (Vol. *34A*). Bingley, UK: Emerald Group Publishing Limited.

Paul, E. F. (1988). Liberalism, unintended orders, and evolutionism. *Political Studies, 36,* 251–272.

Pouvreau, D. (2009). *The dialectical tragedy of the concept of wholeness: Ludwig von Bertalanffy's biography revisited.* Litchfield Park, AZ: ISCE Publishing.

Pouvreau, D. (2014). On the history of Ludwig von Bertalanffy's "General Systemology", and on its relationship to cybernetics, part II: Contexts and developments of the systemological hermeneutics instigated by Bertalanffy. *International Journal of General Systems, 43,* 172–245.

Rosser, J. B. (2010). How complex are the Austrians? *Advances in Austrian Economics, 14,* 165–179.

Vanberg, V. (1986). Spontaneous market order and social rules. *Economics and Philosophy, 2,* 75–100.

Vaughn, K. (1999a). Hayek's theory of the market order as an instance of the theory of complex, adaptive systems. *Journal des Economistes et des Etudes Humaines, 9,* 241–256.

Vaughn, K. I. (1999b). Hayek's implicit economics: Rules and the problem of order. *Review of Austrian Economics, 11,* 128–144.

Weaver, W. (1948). Science and organized complexity. *American Scientist, 36,* 536–544.

Wirth, M. (2015). A window to the world: The European forum alpbach 1945 to 2015 (E. Lueger, Trans.). Vienna: The European Forum Alpbach.

Woodger, J. (1929). *Biological principles.* London: Kegan Paul, Trench, Trubner & Co., Ltd.

Wright, S. (1931). Evolution in mendelian populations. *Genetics, 16,* 97–159.

THE ROAD TO SERVOMECHANISMS: THE INFLUENCE OF CYBERNETICS ON HAYEK FROM *THE SENSORY ORDER* TO THE SOCIAL ORDER

Gabriel Oliva

ABSTRACT

This chapter explores the ways in which cybernetics influenced the works of F. A. Hayek from the late 1940s onward. It shows that the concept of negative feedback, borrowed from cybernetics, was central to Hayek's attempt to explain the principle of the emergence of human purposive behavior. Next, the chapter discusses Hayek's later uses of cybernetic ideas in his works on the spontaneous formation of social orders. Finally, Hayek's view on the appropriate scope of the use of cybernetics is considered.

Keywords: Cybernetics; F. A. Hayek; Norbert Wiener; Garrett Hardin; Ludwig von Bertalanffy

JEL classifications: B25; B31; C60

Research in the History of Economic Thought and Methodology, Volume 34A, 161–198
ISSN: 0743-4154/doi:10.1108/S0743-41542016000034A006

When I began my work I felt that I was nearly alone in working on the evolutionary formation of such highly complex self-maintaining orders. Meanwhile, researches on this kind of problem — under various names, such as autopoiesis, cybernetics, homeostasis, spontaneous order, self-organisation, synergetics, systems theory, and so on — have become so numerous that I have been able to study closely no more than a few of them. (Hayek, 1988, p. 9)

INTRODUCTION

Recently, the new approach of complexity economics has gained a significant number of followers. Some authors, such as Colander, Holt, and Rosser (2004), claim that a "new orthodoxy" is gradually emerging inside the mainstream of economics and that this orthodoxy will be founded on the vision of the economy as a complex system. The optimism of these authors regarding the growth of complexity economics might be regarded as an overstatement but, given the current trends in economics discussed by them, it is nevertheless reasonable to expect that the complexity approach will have an important role in the future of economics.

These new developments enhance the relevance of investigating the early interactions between economists and complexity theorists. Among the first economists to emphasize the centrality of the issue of complexity to the study of social phenomena was the Austrian F. A. Hayek (Barbieri, 2013; Gaus, 2006; Rosser, 1999). However, in the 1950s, when Hayek began to explicitly incorporate elements of complexity into his work, "complexity theory" as it then existed was rather different from what we understand by the term today. At that time, the peculiar scientific movement of cybernetics was arguably the most important complexity-related development (Mitchell, 2009, pp. 295—300).[1]

It is widely recognized in the literature that Hayek formed his views on complexity with great influence from cybernetics[2] (Caldwell, 2004a; Rosser, 2010; Vaughn, 1999b). This belief is justified for various reasons. First, there was explicit and positive reference to the contributions of cybernetics in Hayek's works from the 1950s onward. Moreover, Hayek maintained contact with some of the individuals associated with this approach such as Heinrich Klüver,[3] Garrett Hardin,[4] and Ilya Prigogine.[5] Despite the widespread recognition of the relevance of the Hayek-cybernetics connection, to my knowledge, there has been no work that explores in detail how cybernetics is related to Hayek's ideas. This chapter aims to fill this gap in the literature.

For several reasons, our investigation will start with Hayek's book on "theoretical psychology", *The Sensory Order* (1952). First, *The Sensory Order* (TSO) was the first work in which Hayek made references to authors associated with cybernetics. Second, the book's introduction was written by the Gestalt psychologist Heinrich Klüver, who was an active participant of the Macy Conferences of cybernetics. Finally and most importantly, we will see that the ideas of cybernetics do not appear in a peripheral way, but constitute a central part of the argument of the book. Surprisingly, this fact has not been noted by previous commentators.

In the next section, we will provide a brief exposition of some basic concepts of cybernetics. The section "Cybernetics in the Sensory Order" carries out an exploration of the influences from this discipline on TSO. We will focus mainly on Hayek's attempt to explain the emergence of purposive behavior. In the section "Cybernetics in the Social Order," we analyze Hayek's uses of cybernetics in his later works on social theory. It will be shown, specifically, how he tried to address the "knowledge problem" that he had formulated decades before by using new concepts and ideas drawn from this theory. We will also consider in this section Hayek's view on the appropriate scope of the use of cybernetics. Final remarks and conclusions are made in the last section.

CYBERNETICS: BASIC CONCEPTS AND IDEAS

Cybernetics − a neo-Greek expression that means "steersman" − was defined by Wiener (1948a, p. 11) as the entire field of control and communication in the animal and the machine. Though cybernetics started by being closely associated in many ways with physics,[6] it does not depend in any essential way on the laws of physics. *Au contraire*, the cyberneticians saw it as having its own foundations, which could be used to understand the workings of the most diverse kinds of systems − physical, biological, and socioeconomic. With a single set of concepts, we would be able represent automatic pilots, radio sets, and cerebellums and draw useful parallelisms between machine, brain, and society (Ashby, 1956, pp. 1−4).

One of the main concepts employed by cybernetics is that of feedback. Consider a machine composed of two different parts (M_1 and M_2). Each part receives inputs (I_1 and I_2) and converts them into outputs (O_1 and O_2) according to well-defined transformation functions (f_1 and f_2). In isolation, M_1 and M_2 could be represented as in Fig. 1.

Though we have full knowledge of the parts of the system, we still cannot determine the behavior of the system as a whole unless we specify the way these parts are coupled. It could be the case that the parts are independent of each other, so that the analysis of the whole is reducible to the analysis of its parts in isolation, as in Fig. 1. But it could also be the case that one part's output is connected to the other's input. If M_1's output is linked to M_2's input, but not the other way around, then we say that M_1 dominates M_2 (Fig. 2). When both outputs are connected to both inputs, *feedback* may be said to be present (Figs. 3–4).

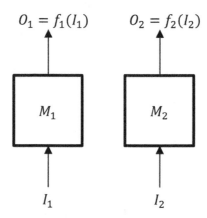

Fig. 1. System with Isolated Parts.

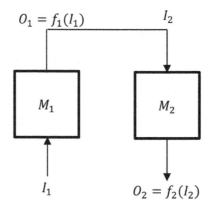

Fig. 2. System in which M_1 Dominates M_2.

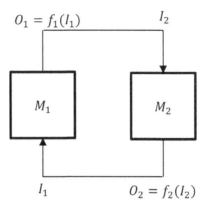

Fig. 3. Feedback System.

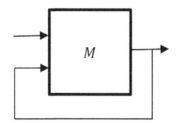

Fig. 4. Feedback System Seen as a Whole.

There are two different kinds of feedback: negative and positive. Negative feedback is self-correcting, that is, it tends to bring the system back to a previous state after an exogenous shock. Therefore, when the feedback of a system is negative, the system tends to be stable. Positive feedback, on the other hand, is self-reinforcing. This means that a shock is magnified by the operation of the feedback mechanism, leading the system away from the previous status quo. The system, thus, exhibits explosive behavior.

One example of the operation of negative feedback is given by the temperature regulation process that occurs in the interior of homoeothermic or warm-blooded animals. If the temperature of the animal is too high, the organism reacts taking measures to ensure that more heat is liberated from the body to the environment (through the flushing of the skin and the evaporation of increasing sweat) and less heat is generated inside the body (by reducing the metabolism). Similarly, if the temperature of the animal is too low, the organism takes measures in the opposite direction such as shivering, increasing muscular activity, and secreting adrenaline (Ashby, 1960, p. 59). Therefore, by means of negative feedback, the body is able to keep its temperature within limits. In general, a system which regulates variables in order to maintain the stability of its internal conditions is said to display the property of *homeostasis*.[7]

But cybernetics shall not live by feedback alone. As Wiener's definition of the field suggests, other essential concepts include communication, control, and information. The concept of control is tightly linked to that of feedback. Control systems are those that regulate the behavior of other systems. This can be done by means of an open loop process, by which the control system's outputs are generated based solely on inputs, or by a closed loop process, in which feedback from the system's output is also used. For this reason, closed loop control systems are also called feedback control systems or *servomechanisms*.

In feedback control systems, there is a desirable state (desirable variable), an actual state (controlled variable), and a measure of the difference between these two (error). The actual state is influenced by a manipulated variable, determined by the action of the controller, and also by disturbances or exogenous shocks. The error of the system is fed back to the controller, which acts on the manipulated variable in order to approach the desired state (Ahrendt & Taplin, 1951, p. 5) (Fig. 5).

The two last fundamental concepts of cybernetics are the intertwined ones of communication and information. Communication may be broadly defined as the exchange or transmission of information. In this connection, three different levels of communication problems can be pointed out: (a) the technical problem of accurately transmitting symbols of communication, (b) the semantic problem of conveying precisely a desirable meaning

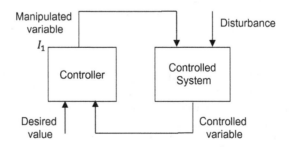

Fig. 5.   The Components of a Feedback Control System. *Source*: Adapted from
Ahrendt and Taplin (1951, p. 5).

by the transmitted symbols, and (c) the effectiveness problem of affecting the conduct of the receptor of communication in a desired way (Weaver, 1964, p. 4). Claude Shannon's seminal article "A Mathematical Theory of Communication" (1948) explicitly deals only with the technical problem. As he puts it:

> The fundamental problem of communication is that of reproducing at one point either exactly or approximately a message selected at another point. Frequently the messages have meaning; that is they refer to or are correlated according to some system with certain physical or conceptual entities. These semantic aspects of communication are irrelevant to the engineering problem. (Shannon, 1948, p. 379)

If we restrict ourselves to the technical problem of communication, information can be precisely measured. What it measures is the uncertainty associated with a specific probability distribution. Thus, the information conveyed by a degenerate probability distribution − for example, two possible events with $p_1 = 1$ and $p_2 = 0$ − is zero, once the outcome is known with certainty. The exact measure of information proposed by Shannon (1948) is given in Eq. (1).

$$H = -k \sum_{i=1}^{n} p_i \log(p_i) \quad \text{with } k > 0 \tag{1}$$

In his paper, Shannon proved that this was the only equation that satisfied a set of desired properties.[8] Because this formula is the same as the expression for entropy in statistical mechanics, he used the terms information and entropy interchangeably.[9] The unit of measurement of information is determined by the choice of the base of the logarithm. If the base two is chosen, then it will be measured in bits (binary units). Using this expression, Shannon was able to give formulas for the channel capacity of a transmission line (in bits per second) and the amount of redundancy needed in order to send with fidelity a given signal through a noisy channel.

Wiener was working at the same time on similar lines as Shannon's and reached almost the same conclusions as him (Wiener, 1948a, pp. 60−94). There were, though, two significant differences between them. First, unlike Shannon, Wiener was eager to extend the concept of information to semantic and effectiveness problems. Second, while Shannon quantified information as positive entropy, Wiener thought *negative* entropy was the appropriate definition of information. Though from a strictly mathematical point of view this difference was only a matter of the sign of the expression, it had important implications for the newly created field of cybernetics.

In equating information with negative entropy, Wiener conceived the amount of information of a system as a universal measure of its degree of organization, in the same way entropy measured a system's degree of disorganization (Wiener, 1948a, p. 11). Order – in the mechanical, living, and social worlds – could only be created maintained if a sufficient quantity of information is produced so as to oppose the tendency of increasing entropy.

Defined in this way, information fit neatly into Wiener's general cybernetic framework. Negative feedback control systems are regulated by information which "is fed back to the control center [and] tends to oppose the departure of the controlled from the controlling quantity" (Wiener, 1948a, p. 118). Thereby, (closed-loop) control was reinterpreted by Wiener as communication (of information) with (negative) feedback, thus putting together all the conceptual pieces of cybernetics.

The historical origins of cybernetics can be traced to Wiener's work during World War II,[10] when the allies were seeking more effective methods to defend themselves against air attacks. Invited by Vannevar Bush, Norbert Wiener – who would later found cybernetics – started working with the engineer Julian Bigelow for the National Defense Research Committee (NDRC) on how to design a better way to control anti-aircraft artillery. In order to accomplish that, firing would have to aim at the best prediction of the future position of the enemy's plane based on the information available about its past path.

This prediction was not a simple matter because the pilots were trained to take evasive actions, such as zigzag courses, to avoid the allied artillery. Predicting the course of the planes, then, would require a *simulation* of the pilot's reaction to the shooting, for which Wiener and Bigelow employed servomechanisms. Unsurprisingly, after a while, they would find a problem with their prototype: sometimes the mechanism overcompensated its course corrections and oscillated violently due to positive feedback. Because of the urgency of the wartime needs and the practical difficulties involved in ensuring that the feedback mechanism would be of the negative type, Wiener's wartime project was terminated in 1943 without being effectively used by the allied forces (Conway & Siegelman, 2005, p. 88).

The end of Wiener's period in the military was immediately followed by the beginning of his work to take to the next level the analogy between servomechanisms and human behavior. He and Bigelow teamed up with the physiologist Arturo Rosenblueth in order to draw connections between the feedback mechanism they encountered in their anti-aircraft project and the one found in the electrical networks of the human brain.

Rosenblueth, Wiener, and Bigelow (1943) interpreted all goal-directed action as being governed by a negative feedback processes. As a goal is being pursued, the course of action is constantly corrected by comparing the current distance from the goal with its anticipated position. If, for example, my goal is to pick up a pencil, my movements will be guided by the feedback provided by "the amount by which we have failed to pick up the pencil at each instant" (Wiener, 1948a, p. 7). In this view, a pathological condition such as purpose tremor (also called intention tremor) is interpreted as being caused by a malfunction of the feedback mechanism, leading the ill individual to undershoot or overshoot his target in an uncontrollable oscillation.

From this discussion, the authors drew some very interesting conclusions. First, there is no contradiction in systems being deterministic and teleological at the same time if a negative feedback mechanism is present. Second, teleology and purposeful behavior in general are possible both in the realms of the human and the machine. Goal-seeking behavior, thus, should not be viewed as a distinctly human feature. Third, as a consequence, organisms and machines could be described with the same vocabulary and studied by the same methods (Fig. 6). As Gerovitch (2002) summarizes it, Wiener, Rosenblueth, and Bigelow "undermined the philosophical oppositions between teleology and determinism, between voluntary acts and mechanical actions, and ultimately between men and machines" (p. 62).

In 1942, Rosenblueth presented the ideas he was developing with Wiener and Bigelow in a conference on "Cerebral Inhibition," sponsored by the

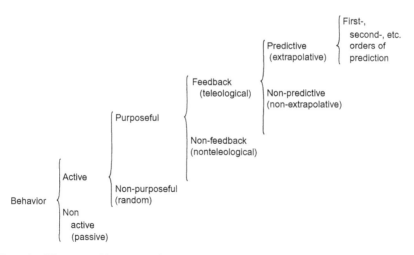

Fig. 6. The Classification of Behavior (Rosenblueth, Wiener, & Bigelow, 1943, p. 11).

Josiah Macy Foundation.[11] Rosenblueths's talk made quite an impact on the diversified audience, composed of psychiatrists like Warren McCulloch and social scientists such as Gregory Bateson and Margaret Mead.[12]

McCulloch would soon become a leading figure of the cybernetics movement. At that time, he was working with his younger colleague Walter Pitts in a project that aimed at understanding the brain as an electrical machine that performed logical calculations in a way similar to digital computers. The new ideas of circular causation and communication presented by Rosenblueth in the conference were fundamental to the paper McCulloch and Pitts would publish the next year. In this work, they conclude that systems with negative feedback can generate purposive behavior and that "activity we are wont to call mental are rigorously deducible from present neurophysiology" (McCulloch & Pitts, 1943, p. 132).

Similar ideas were being developed independently by the English psychiatrist William Ross Ashby, who would also join the cybernetics club later. In a sequence of three articles, Ashby (1945, 1947a, 1947b) aimed to understand the phenomena of self-organization and to apply his theory to the analysis of the brain. His conclusion was that "a machine can be at the same time (a) strictly determinate in its actions, and (b) yet demonstrate a self-induced change of organization" (Ashby, 1947a, p. 125). In fact, he maintained that the brain was an important example of such a machine.

Cybernetics would rapidly develop into a hot new field of research and would drag the attention of scholars from the most diverse areas of knowledge. From 1946 to 1953, some of these scholars gathered around in a series of 10 meetings – the Macy Conferences – specifically devoted to discuss the new interdisciplinary field of control and communication that would become known as cybernetics. This group of researchers included prominent figures in the fields of mathematics (Norbert Wiener, John von Neumann, Walter Pitts), engineering (Julian Bigelow, Claude Shannon, Heinz von Forster), philosophy (Filmer Northrop), neurophysiology (Arturo Rosenblueth, Ralph Gerard, Rafael Lorente de Nó), psychiatry (Warren McCulloch, Lawrence Kubie, Henry Brosnin), psychology (Heinrich Klüver, Kurt Lewin, Alex Bavelas, Joseph Licklider), biology (W. Ross Ashby, Henry Quastler), linguistics (Roman Jakobson, Charles Morris, Dorothy Lee), and the social sciences (Gregory Bateson, Lawrence Frank, Paul Lazarsfeld, Margaret Mead) (Heims, 1993, pp. 255–256).

Limited space precludes us from going through a more detailed inspection of the history of the cybernetics movement.[13] Suffice it to say that the influence of cybernetics extended far beyond the limits of the Macy Conferences, reaching some highly unsuspected audiences. In this context, it did not take long before the Austrian economist F. A. Hayek took note of cybernetic ideas and began to employ them in his works.

CYBERNETICS IN THE SENSORY ORDER

The Sensory Order and the Quest for Purposive Behavior

In 1945, a year after publishing his popular book *The Road to Serfdom*, Hayek's journey on the road to servomechanisms would begin. This was the year he started to work on his book on theoretical psychology, *The Sensory Order*, which was based on a manuscript Hayek himself had written as a law student in 1920.

One important motivation for writing this book was to counter behaviorism, a doctrine that conceived psychology as the science of environmentally determined behavior and opposed the use of concepts that made reference to "mental" states (Caldwell, 2004b, pp. 246–248). Hayek, on the other hand, held the view that the facts of the social sciences could not be described in terms of the external environment and the physical properties of things, but only through the (subjective) belief that individuals formed about the objects of their environment.[14] One of his main tasks in TSO was to justify the use of mentalist concepts in the social sciences using arguments drawn from the natural sciences.

In the period between his first manuscript and the completion of the book, there were independent works that corroborated the conclusions previously reached by Hayek and which also provided him with conceptual tools to think through the problems he wanted to address. Among these works, we can highlight those authored by Wiener, Rosenblueth, McCulloch, Pitts, and Ashby, pioneer researchers in the field that would become known as cybernetics. As we will see, these works, grounded in the findings of the natural sciences, provided Hayek with fundamental evidence he would use in his explanation of purposive behavior.

Hayek's starting point in TSO is the existence of two different orders: the physical and the sensory order. In the physical order, objects are classified as similar or different according to their producing similar or different external events. But in the sensory order, objects are classified according to their sensory properties (colors, sounds, etc.). That these are two distinct orders is shown by the fact that there is no one-to-one correspondence between them.[15] Objects classified as of the same kind in the sensory order may be classified as of different kinds in the physical order and vice-versa (Hayek, 1952, pp. 1–3).

What Hayek wanted to explain was how "the existence of a phenomenal world which is different from the physical world" (Hayek, 1952, p. 28) could be reconciled with the fact that ultimately the sensory order is a part of the physical order, that is, the brain is made of physical matter which obeys the same laws of physics as any other physical event. The constitution of mind, then, was to be explained by means of physics: "We want to know the kind of process by which a given physical situation is transformed into a certain phenomenal picture" (Hayek, 1952, p. 7).

This is a particular way of formulating what in philosophy is known as the mind-body problem. Indeed, Hayek (1952, p. 1) himself used the expression "mind-body problem" to describe what he would tackle in TSO. Two aspects of this problem are often emphasized by philosophers of mind: those of qualia and intentionality. Qualia refer to subjective features of conscious experience; feelings and sensations that are only accessible to the person himself. Intentionality denotes the directedness shown by many mental phenomena that have meaning in the sense that they are about something else.

> Qualia are considered philosophically problematic insofar as it is difficult to see how their subjectivity can be explained in terms of the objective features of the brain and nervous system. [...] Intentionality is problematic insofar as it is difficult to see how processes in the brain could have any more intrinsic meaning than squiggles of ink on paper or noises generated by the larynx. (Feser, 2006, pp. 308–309)

Let us consider first how Hayek dealt with qualia. According to him, the central nervous system displays a structure of fibers that enables the *classification* of neural impulses, converting them into the order of sensory qualities. For Hayek, then, the emergence of qualities is not due to original attributes of individual impulses, but results from the whole system of neural connections through which this impulse is transmitted. This "structure of fibers" or "system of neural connections" is developed in the course of the evolution of the species and the development of the individual:

> [...] it is thus the position of the individual impulse or group of impulses in the whole system of such connexions which gives it its distinctive quality; that this system of connexions is acquired in the course of the development of the species and the individual by a kind of 'experience' or 'learning'; and that it reproduces therefore at every stage of its development certain relationships existing in the physical environment between the stimuli evoking the impulses. (Hayek, 1952, p. 53)

Hayek's solution to the problem of qualia, then, presupposes the concept of classification. As Feser (2006) noted however, classification "seem[s] clearly to be an intentional process, insofar as the classifications performed are taken to have meaning or significance rather than being mere mechanical operations" (p. 299). Therefore, in Hayek's thought, the existence of qualia presupposes the existence of intentionality,[16] which we will now consider.

Consider first Hayek's take on the relatively simple problem of intentional body movements. He fully endorsed the explanation of motor coordination given by cybernetics (as illustrated by Wiener's example of picking up a pencil). For him, (negative) feedback is present in the interaction between the proprioceptive (sense of strength of movement and relative position of nearby body parts) and exteroceptive (perception of the outside world) impulses.

> The choice of a kind of behaviour pattern and its continued control, modification, and adjustment while it takes place, will be a process in which the various factors act successively to produce the final outcome. [...] In connexion with these continuous adjustments, made while the movement proceeds, the interaction between the exteroceptive and the proprioceptive impulses and the operation of the 'feed-back' principle become of special significance. [...] [A]t first the pattern of movement initiated will not be fully successful. The current sensory reports about what is happening will be checked against expectations, and the difference between the two will act as a further stimulus indicating the required corrections. The result of every step in the course of the actions will, as it were, be evaluated against the expected results, and any difference will serve as an indicator of the corrections required. (Hayek, 1952, p. 95)

In fact, in a footnote placed in the same page as the above-quoted passage, Hayek refers his readers to the works of Wiener (1948a, 1948b), McCulloch (1948), and Ashby (1947a, 1947b, 1948, 1949), all of whom were important members of the cybernetics movement. Not only did he expresses approval of these authors' descriptions of the working of body movements, he also endorsed their vision that purposeful behavior is not a peculiar attribute of living beings, but could also be found in some types of machines.

According to Hayek, a system displays purposive behavior if: (i) it can make some kind of representation (or "model") of the possible and desirable outcomes of different courses of action in a given existing situation and (ii) its actions are the result of a process of selection among the different courses of action that have desirable outcomes. In the case of the human brain, patterns of impulses in the nervous system form a model of the environment that pre-selects, from among the effects of alternative courses of action, the desirable ones. Then, the effective course of action that takes the "path of least resistance" (i.e., the course whose representation is associated with more attractive and less repellant qualities) is chosen from among these pre-selected courses of action. Moreover, this model (which determines what is possible, pre-selected, and selected) constantly evolves with experimentation and the contrast between expectation and reality (Hayek, 1952, pp. 124–126).

The human brain, though, is not unique in its capacity of generating purposive behavior. Much more simple organisms and machines exist and can be built which, by acting according to (i) and (ii), also display purposiveness. Here Hayek has in mind machines such as Wiener's anti-aircraft gun.

> That such guidance by a model which reproduces, and experimentally tries out, the possibilities offered by a given situation, can produce action which is purposive to any desired degree, is shown by the fact that machines could be produced on this principle (and that some, such as the predictor for antiaircraft guns, or the automatic pilots for aircraft, have actually been produced) which show all the characteristics of purposive behavior. (Hayek, 1952, p. 126)

Such machines are very primitive in comparison to the human brain. For instance, they can take account of much fewer facts in their environment, they do not have the capacity of learning from experience, and they do not display the feature of consciousness. But regarding purposiveness, Hayek sees them as differing from the human brain in degree, but not in kind.[17] He, however, maintained that a fully satisfactory explanation of human purposiveness required further research:

> [...] it should be pointed out, however, that in one respect in which the task which we are undertaking is most in need of a solid foundation, theoretical biology is only just beginning to provide the needed theoretical tools and concepts. An adequate account of the highly purposive character of the action of the central nervous system would require as its foundation a more generally accepted biological theory of the nature of adaptive and purposive processes than is yet available. (Hayek, 1952, p. 80)

Hayek, therefore, did not believe that the "highly purposive" behavior of the human brain could be adequately explained solely by means of the concept of negative feedback. He nevertheless endorsed it as providing a good, even though not fully satisfactory, explanation of relatively *simple* purposeful behavior. Before we move on, it is important to clarify that I do not contend that Hayek drew his fundamental views on purposive behavior from cybernetics. In fact, it seems that his views were already formed before he had any contact with the ideas of this intellectual movement.[18] What I do contend is that Hayek's use of negative feedback in TSO was important because it gave scientific evidence in favor of his theory of the existence of multiple degrees of purposiveness, ranging from simple machines to the human brain.

In the beginning of the twentieth century, behaviorism was very influential in psychology, and its proponents claimed that mentalist descriptions of events – like those of subjectivist economists – had no place in rigorous scientific analysis. One of Hayek's tasks in TSO was to show that a description of human behavior in subjective terms could be scientifically legitimate. In order to support this claim, Hayek would tackle the mind-body problem, using both philosophical arguments and *scientific* ones he borrowed from, among other sources, cybernetics. By identifying human purposive behavior as having the same nature as the behavior of negative feedback systems, Hayek was able to claim that the existence of subjective qualities and purposes was grounded in the rigorous findings of the natural sciences.[19]

Purposive Behavior Once Again: The Within Systems' Manuscript

Did Hayek succeed in giving a satisfactory solution to the mind-body problem? Not quite, for there is a clear gap in his thesis. This gap lies in his claim that the difference between simple purposive systems such as Wiener's anti-aircraft machine and more complex ones like the human brain was only a matter of degree. In what sense could both be regarded as the same kind of phenomena, if human purposiveness displays important features such as communicating meaning, which seems to be lacking in any conceivable machine?

Although Hayek sketched an explanation of the emergence of purposive behavior in general, he did not explain – not even in principle – the "higher" types of purpose that we encounter in the human brain, but not in simple machines. As we have already pointed out, Hayek showed awareness of this problem in TSO when he wrote that:

> An adequate account of the highly purposive character of the action of the central nervous system would require as its foundation a more generally accepted biological theory of the nature of adaptive and purposive processes than is yet available. (Hayek, 1952, p. 80)

As Birner (2009, pp. 188–190) has shown, Karl Popper's reaction to TSO just after it had been published makes explicit this weakness in

Hayek's position. In a letter to Hayek in the same year the book was published, Popper writes:

> I am not sure whether one could describe your theory as a casual theory of the sensory order. I think, indeed, that one can. But then, it would also be the sketch of a casual theory of the mind. But I think I can show that a causal theory of the mind cannot be true (although I cannot show this of the sensory order); more precisely, I think I can show the impossibility of a casual theory of the human language [...]. I am now writing a paper on the impossibility of a casual theory of the human language, and its bearing upon the body-mind problem, which must be finished in ten days. (Hayek Collection, Box 44, Folder 1)

In the promised article, published in 1953, Popper argued that a causal theory of the human mind could not explain some of the functions displayed by human language. Drawing from the psychologist and linguist Karl Bülher, Popper said that it was possible to distinguish at least four different functions of language. From the lower to the higher level, they were: (1) the expressive or symptomatic function; (2) the stimulative or signal function; (3) the descriptive function; and (4) the argumentative function. One of the main theses of the paper was that "Any causal physicalistic theory of linguistic behaviour can only be a theory of the two lower functions of language" (Popper, 1953).

Hayek's theory of the mind was a causal physicalistic one that claimed that all mental phenomena (including linguistic behavior) could be in principle – though not in practice – reduced to physical ones. In order to counter Popper's claims, Hayek would have to further elaborate his theory with the aim of providing an explanation of the principle of these phenomena. It seems that it was this that motivated him to write the unfinished manuscript entitled "Within Systems and About Systems: A Statement of Some Problems of a Theory of Communication":

> If our aim is to be achieved, we must succeed in producing models which produce in kind such mental functions as "thinking" or "having an intention" or "haming" [sic], or "describing", or "communicating a meaning", or "drawing an inference" and the like [...]. It will be sufficient if we can construct an instance which possesses all the characteristics which are common to all the instances to which we commonly apply any one of these terms. (Hayek Collection, Box 129, Folder 7, p. 3)

In this chapter, he postulates systems (which could be organisms or machines) capable of the same process of classification he described in TSO. After a long preliminary discussion of the features of the system and of its isolated interaction with its environment, Hayek proceeds to analyze the communication between two systems of the kind described. These two systems possessed identical structures and differed only in their respective short-term memories. Hayek's strategy here is to consider this simple case in order to provide an explanation of the principle for the first three of the four levels of langue discussed by Popper.

A system expressing its inner state to another similar system (the first function of language) involves no greater complication than a system interacting with its environment. In the same way that a classifying system can learn to interpret and predict events in its environment, it can also learn to interpret and predict the actions of a system expressing its inner state. The second function of language (the stimulative one) is performed when a system communicates a signal which regularly causes a particular response from another system (or a response belonging to a particular class).

Again, the situation in this second case is not significantly different from the one of a system interacting solely with its environment. This was illustrated in the same paper by an example Hayek gave of a cybernetic system that regulates its stock of fuel through negative feedback. When the stock of fuel is low, the system responds so as to get more fuel from its environment. No additional difficulty arises if we suppose that the information about the fuel level is conveyed by another system. This second system would communicate a signal that could trigger a reaction from the first system, thus performing the stimulative function of language.

With his general scheme, then, Hayek was able to generate the first two functions of language. The paper ends abruptly, though, in the middle of his attempt to explain the third (descriptive) function of language, that is, explaining the communication of a symbol that evokes the same class of responses both in the emitter and the receiver. Even worse: Hayek does not mention the argumentative function, leaving unexplained two of Popper's four functions of language. Therefore, in his unfinished manuscript, Hayek "had failed to explain one or more higher functions of language within his theory – *as Popper had predicted!*" (Birner, 2009, p. 189, emphasis in the original).

Hayek ultimately did not succeed in explaining the principle of the highly purposive behavior displayed by human beings as illustrated by their uses of language. It seems like negative feedback was not enough to account for the workings of human purpose, which left a technically limited Hayek helpless when confronted with this huge challenge. Hayek's use of cybernetics, however, did not end there. When Hayek, after learning about this intellectual movement, turned his attention from the sensory order back to the social order, he saw that he could restate and further elaborate his old ideas using the same concepts he employed in TSO. Self-regulating machines and organisms, which Hayek had previously used as analogs for the human brain, would later be used by Hayek as analogs for human society.

CYBERNETICS IN THE SOCIAL ORDER

Brain, Society, and the Knowledge Problem

What does the human brain have in common with human society? A lot, Hayek would answer. After finishing TSO, he would use many ideas he developed in this book in the study of social phenomena and the methodology of science. However, we must avoid the temptation of describing TSO as some kind of foundation for his later works. The relationship between TSO and Hayek's other works is much more complicated. As Hayek himself pointed out, influences flow not only from TSO to his other works, but also the other way around:

> My colleagues in the social sciences find my study on *The Sensory Order* uninteresting or indigestible ... But the work on it helped me greatly to clear my mind on much that is very relevant to social theory. My conception of evolution, of a spontaneous order and of the methods and limits of our endeavours to explain complex phenomena have been formed largely in the course of work on that book. As I was using the work I had done in my student days on theoretical psychology in forming my views on the methodology of the social science[s], so the working out of my earlier ideas on psychology with the help of what I had learnt in the social science helped me greatly in all my later scientific developments. (Hayek, 1979, p. 199)

It is important to clarify this in order to guard against possible misunderstandings of the discussion that will be offered in this section. In the present work, we are not interested in tracing every relationship between TSO and Hayek's later works.[20] Our aim is the more humble one of analyzing this issue solely from the point of view of the ideas and concepts of cybernetics. Restricting the scope of analysis in this way, and recalling that Hayek makes no reference to this theory before he started working on TSO,[21] it becomes evident that the use of its ideas proceeded chronologically from TSO to his other works. Our task, therefore, will be to describe how the ideas of cybernetics, initially used by Hayek to understand the sensory order, became part of the way he would conceive of social orders (and spontaneous orders in general).

In 1977, Hayek was invited to present on "The Sensory Order after 25 Years" at a conference organized by psychologists interested in his long neglected book on theoretical psychology.[22] In the discussion that followed the presentation, a member of the audience asked Hayek to elaborate on the parallels between the human brain and the economic system that were implicit in his theory. His response was the following:

In both cases we have complex phenomena in which there is a need for a method of utilizing widely dispersed knowledge. The essential point is that each member (neuron, or buyer, or seller) is induced to do what in the total circumstances benefits the system. Each member can be used to serve needs of which he doesn't know anything at all. Now that means that in the larger (say, economic) order, knowledge is utilized that is not planned or centralized or even conscious [...] In our whole system of actions, we are individually steered by local information – information about more facts than any other person or authority can possibly possess. And the price and market system is in that sense a system of communication, which passes on (in the form of prices, determined only on the competitive market) the available information that each individual needs to act, and to act rationally. (Hayek, 1982, pp. 325–6)

According to Hayek, then, both society and the brain are complex self-organizing systems. But the keyword here is *information* – or, alternatively, *knowledge* (Hayek, 1973, pp. xvii–xix; Scheall, 2016). These are systems in which the information possessed by the whole is dispersed among its numerous parts and in which each part could not possibly grasp all the knowledge of the whole. In both systems, the mutual coordination of the parts (neurons or individuals) is reached not by each part's explicit mastery of a large amount of information of the system (brain or society), but by the tacit use of information implicitly conveyed by the operation of the rules that constrain the relationship between the parts (such as the structure of neural firing paths and the price system).[23]

This leads us back to Hayek's seminal article, "Economics and Knowledge" (1937/2014), in which he explicitly introduced the broad and interdisciplinary research program of coordination he would pursue until the end of his life.

Though at one time a very pure and narrow economic theorist, I was led from technical economics into all kinds of questions usually regarded as philosophical. When I look back, it seems to have all begun, nearly thirty years ago, with an essay on "Economics and Knowledge" in which I examined what seemed to me some of the central difficulties of pure economic theory. Its main conclusion was that the task of economic theory was to explain how an overall order of economic activity was achieved which utilized a large amount of knowledge which was not concentrated in any one mind but existed only as the separate knowledge of thousands or millions of different individuals. But it was still a long way from this to an adequate insight into the relations between the abstract overall order which is formed as a result of his responding, within the limits imposed upon him by those abstract rules, to the concrete particular circumstances which he encounters. It was only through a re-examination of the age-old concept of freedom under the law, the basic conception of traditional liberalism, and of the problems of the philosophy of the law which this raises, that I have reached what now seems to be a tolerably clear picture of the nature of the spontaneous order of which liberal economists have so long been talking. (Hayek, 1965/2014, pp. 49–50)

In this article, Hayek considers the difficulties for the concept of equilibrium posed by the subjectivity and dispersion of knowledge. At the level of society, equilibrium means mutual compatibility of individual plans. This compatibility, in turn, requires that each individual possess correct knowledge about the planned actions of others on which the execution of his plan depends. Hayek asks how this state of affairs is realized. How, starting from a situation of disequilibrium, is equilibrium approached? What process accounts for the acquisition and communication of "more correct" knowledge that enables a tendency to equilibrium? (Hayek, 1937/2014).

In "The Use of Knowledge in Society" (1945/2014), Hayek would make a first step in the direction of providing an answer to this problem by considering "the price system as such a mechanism for communicating information" (p. 100). The execution of the plans of the individuals determines the existing relative market prices. As these plans are based on each individual's knowledge of his particular circumstances of time and place, the price system is a reflection of private information dispersed among the many components of a society. Thus, prices implicitly convey important information to individuals that they could not acquire otherwise.

Cybernetics, with its emphasis on the relationship between information and organization, seemed to Hayek to provide a good approach to his problem of the emergence of social coordination. The way cybernetics was initially applied to the analysis of society, however, would not be very satisfactory from Hayek's perspective. None other than Wiener, the most central figure of the cybernetics movement, explicitly ridiculed the view that the market exhibited any self-regulating mechanism.

> There is a belief, current in many countries, which has been elevated to the rank of an official article of faith in the United States, that free competition is itself a homeostatic process: that in a free market, the individual selfishness of the bargainers, each seeking to sell as high and buy as low as possible, will result in the end in a stable dynamics of prices, and with redound to the greatest common good [...] Unfortunately, the evidence, such as it is, is against this simple-minded theory [...] There is no homeostasis whatever. We are involved in the business cycles of boom and failure, in the successions of dictatorship and revolution, in the wars which everyone loses. (Wiener, 1948a, p. 159)

Given Wiener's central role in the field of cybernetics, it is instructive to further explore his social theory and compare it to Hayek's. In spite of his critical remarks on free competition, Wiener's discussion of the cybernetics of society hints at some very important Hayekian points. Just as any organism, a society is held together "by the possession of means of acquisition, use, retention, and transmission of information" (Wiener, 1948a, p. 161). Besides, the information available to society has to be distinguished from the information available to the individual. Contrary to the information available only to the individual, the information available to society "can be recognized as a distinct form of activity by other members of the race, in the sense that it will in turn affect their activity, and so on" (Wiener, 1948a, p. 157).

The implications Wiener drew from all of this, however, were very different from Hayek's. The means of communication of a society too large for direct contact among its members, according to Wiener, would be the written word (books and newspapers), the radio, the telephone system, the telegraph, the posts, the theater, the movies, the schools, and the church. Each of these, besides their primary function as means of communication, also serves secondary functions determined by the private interests of their controllers (owners, administrators, advertisers, etc.). In a society strongly based on private property and monetary transactions, these secondary functions tend to encroach on the primary one of communication, thus making less information available at the social level and, consequently, hindering the attainment of social homeostasis (Wiener, 1948a, p. 161).

Contrasting Wiener's perspective with Hayek's, what attracts one's attention is not only their ideological differences, but what each of them took to be the main communication mechanisms that would promote social order. Wiener's discussion deals solely with *deliberately-created* information and its vehicles of communication. It seems like he did not consider that there existed important non-designed and tacit means of communication among men. What about, say, the price system? Despite its flaws, does it not convey indispensable information about the relative scarcities of different goods in an economy? From a Hayekian point of view, it could be said that Wiener took the explicit knowledge tip of a big tacit knowledge iceberg as if it was the whole thing.

Hardin and the Invisible Hand of Evolution

As we have seen, Hayek did not profit much from Wiener's particular views on social cybernetics. Closer to him on this issue was the cybernetic-inspired biologist and ecologist Garrett Hardin. In his famous book on the history of the theory of evolution, *Nature and Man's Fate* (1959), Hardin interpreted the Darwinian adaptation process as a cybernetic system and compared it to the natural price doctrine of classical economists such as

Adam Smith and David Ricardo. He maintains that "In the Darwinian scheme, the concept of the 'fittest' has the same normalizing role as that played by the 'natural' process of commodities or labor in economics" (Hardin, 1959, p. 55).

Both systems are organized not by the intentional action of its components, but by spontaneous regulating forces that act as negative feedback, as shown in Figs. 7 and 8. When a variable (market price or species' trait) deviates from its norm (natural price and fittest trait) in one direction, counteracting forces push this variable in the opposing direction, generating a tendency of gravitation toward the norm. In short, Smith's "invisible hand" was actually a "cybernetic hand," which had a very close analog in the Darwinian adaptation process.

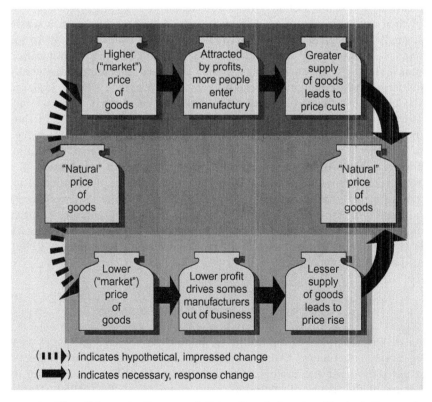

Fig. 7. The Cybernetic System of Price Regulation in Classical Economics (Hardin, 1959, p. 53).

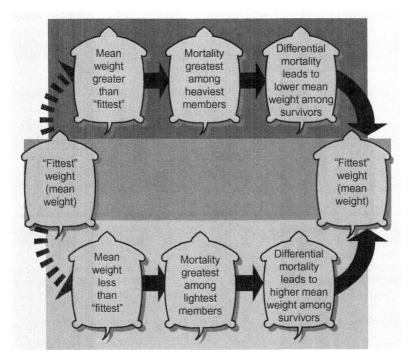

Fig. 8. The Cybernetic System of Trait Regulation in Darwinian Evolution (Hardin, 1959, p. 55).

These adjustment processes are not costless. They incur "waste" in the form, say, of bankruptcy of businesses and the death of fitness-deviating specimens. An infinitely wise designer could get rid of this waste by substituting the direct control of the variable (setting it to the level of its norm) for the indirect operation of the process of adaptation. But, as this wise designer is not to be found in either case, we must resort to the cybernetic scheme of adaptation and accept that the existence of some waste is not only inevitable, but a necessary condition for the regulation of the system.

The first glimmerings of the importance of waste are quite old, but waste did not really come into its own until the last of the eighteen century, with the work of economists, particularly of Adam Smith (and later Ricardo). Before them, many economists dreamed of a world made perfect and waste-free through law — through regulations governing the prices of commodities, for example. [...] In effect, Smith said that the world is best and most equitably governed when waste governs it. It does not matter if some men place too high and others too low a price on a commodity. The former goes bankrupt from too little business, the latter from too much; their wiser competitors survives. Through waste, we learn what is the "right" price. [...] That which man's poor intellect may be incapable of creating directly can be produced indirectly through the waste-actuated Smith-Ricardian cybernetic system. It was Darwin's genius to show that the same system would explain the fact of biological adaptation. (Hardin, 1959, pp. 326–327)[24]

The apparently incredible claim of evolution is that "In order to make a perfect and beautiful machine, it is not requisite to know how to make it ... Design emerges from blind Waste" (Hardin, 1959, pp. 301–302). But why is this waste not quickly eliminated by the selection process? The first reason is that mutations constantly occur, although not with a high frequency. The second and more important reason is that the selection process is not perfect because it lumps together genetically and environmentally determined variations.

Everyone knows that the size of an adult animal is determined by both its heredity and its environment, particularly by the nutrition received during youth [...] But the individual who successfully runs the gantlet can pass on to his offspring only what he possesses in the way of hereditary capabilities, divested of environmental "luck". This makes for a certain inexactness in the selective process; some might even use the word "injustice". Be that as it may, Nature's confounding of heredity and environment in the selective process is one of the explanations of the continuing variability of succeeding generations. [...] The generation of error is without end. (Hardin, 1959, p. 63)

Hayek read Hardin's[25] book and made very similar remarks about how the price mechanism operated as a cybernetic system. This would constitute an important part of the answer to the coordination problem he formulated in his 1937 article. Indeed, Hayek would argue that the mutual adjustment of individual plans he had previously talked about "is brought about by what, since the physical sciences have also begun to concern themselves with spontaneous orders, or 'self-organizing systems', we have learnt to call 'negative feedback'" (Hayek, 1968/2014 p. 309).[26] Besides, as some "intelligent biologists" like Hardin had recognized, "the idea of the formation of spontaneous or self-determining orders, like the connected idea of evolution, has been developed by the social sciences before it was adopted by the natural sciences" (Hayek, 1968/1978, p. 74).

At least in part because of his lack of adequate technical training,[27] Hayek would never develop a formal cybernetic model of the price system. The work in which he would best develop the understanding of price changes as conveying negative feedback is *Law, Legislation and Liberty*:

The correspondence of expectations that makes it possible for all parties to achieve what they are striving for is in fact brought about by a process of learning by trial and error which must involve a constant disappointment of some expectations. The process of adaptation operates, as do the adjustments of any selforganizing system, by what cybernetics has taught us to call negative feedback: responses to the differences between the expected and the actual results of actions so that these differences will be reduced. This will produce an increased correspondence of expectations of the different persons so long as current prices provide some indications of what future prices will be, that is, so long as, in a fairly constant framework of known facts, always only a few of them change; and so long as the price mechanism operates as a medium of communicating knowledge which brings it about that the facts which become known to some, through the effects of their actions on prices, are made to influence the decision of others. (Hayek, 1976, pp. 124–125)

Here Hayek goes beyond Hardin, developing his own theory of spontaneous plan coordination in cybernetic terminology. In this passage, he seems to be trying to provide an answer to the question he posed thirty years earlier about what are the conditions for a tendency to equilibrium.[28] Compare this to the following quote from "Economics and Knowledge":

... the assertion that a tendency towards equilibrium exists ... can hardly mean anything but that, under certain conditions, the knowledge and intentions of the different members of society are supposed to come more and more into agreement or, to put the same thing in less general and less exact but more concrete terms, that the expectations of the people and particularly of the entrepreneurs will become more and more correct. In this form the assertion of the existence of a tendency towards equilibrium is clearly an empirical proposition, that is, an assertion about what happens in the real world which ought, at least in principle, to be capable of verification [...] The only trouble is that we are still pretty much in the dark about (a) the *conditions* under which this tendency is supposed to exist and (b) the nature of the *process* by which individual knowledge is changed. (Hayek, 1937/2014, p. 68)

Thirty years later, he was no longer "pretty much in the dark" about (a) and (b). The nature of the process of change of individual knowledge would be provided by negative feedback, i.e., by the error correction that follows the contrast between expectations and reality. The conditions for the existence of a tendency to spontaneous ordering enumerated by Hayek, however, are in need of further clarification.

First, the price mechanism can only function properly as a "medium of communicating knowledge" if prices are let free to fluctuate according to the existing market conditions. Price controls undermine the knowledge-coordinating function of the price system because they restrict the amount of knowledge used in the determination of prices to that possessed by the few bureaucrats in charge. For this reason, we should not dispense with the free operation of the price mechanism, even when it leads to some unwanted outcomes:

> The frequent recurrence of such undeserved strokes of misfortune affecting some group is, however, an inseparable part of the steering mechanism of the market: it is the manner in which the cybernetic principle of negative feedback operates to maintain the order of the market. It is only through such changes which indicate that some activities ought to be reduced, that the efforts of all can be continuously adjusted to a greater variety of facts than can be known to anyone person or agency, and that that utilization of dispersed knowledge is achieved on which the well-being of the Great Society rests. (Hayek, 1976, p. 94)

Just as the actual fitness of a specimen is determined by the combination of its hereditary capabilities and its environmental luck, the reward of an individual in the market is the product both of his skills and of his individual luck. The market is no "meritocracy." On the contrary, often we see undeserving people being highly rewarded and deserving ones receiving very little remuneration. The attempt to remedy these seemingly unfair outcomes by interfering with the price system, however, is misguided, for it ignores that we cannot know enough to dispense with the coordination brought by freely adjusting prices.

> It may be difficult to understand, but I believe there can be no doubt about it, that we are led to utilize more relevant information when our remuneration is made to depend indirectly on circumstances we do not know. It is thus that, in the language of modern cybernetics, the feedback mechanism secures the maintenance of a self-generating order [...]. It is indeed *because* the game of catallaxy disregards human conceptions of what is due to each, and rewards according to success in playing the game under the same formal rules, that it produces a more efficient allocation of resources than any design could achieve. [...] It is not a valid objection to such a game, the outcome of which depends partly on skill and particular individual circumstances and partly on pure chance, that the initial prospects for different individuals, although they are all improved by playing that game, are very far from being the same. (Hayek, 1978, p. 64)

The second clarification regards what Hayek has in mind when he talks about the need of a fairly constant *framework* of known facts. Here he is referring to the institutional background of a society – its systems of laws, social norms, and customs – that may enable the individual to anticipate the likely outcomes of his actions (Vaughn, 1999a, p. 140). The degree of effectiveness of the price mechanism depends crucially on the society's system of rules of conduct, which can promote or preclude social coordination. For example, no one would deny the important role in the social order played by the enforcement of private property rights and contracts or by the degree in which people can be trusted to be honest and keep the promises they make.

To sum up: the existence and character of social orders in general (and of price-coordination in particular) depend on the *structure* of rules of conduct observed in society. Therefore, a satisfactory explanation of social order would need to address how these rules of conduct were originated, and how they are maintained or changed over time. This leads us to Hayek's theory of cultural evolution, in which he tries to explain exactly the origins and development of social rules of conduct.

Bertalanffy and the Appropriate Scope of Cybernetics

Given Hayek's endorsement of Hardin's analogies between the price mechanism and the Darwinian process of selection, one could expect that Hayek would also conceive cultural evolution as a cybernetic process regulated by negative feedback. Nowhere does he do that however. The reason for this seems to be that he had learned from his "Viennese friend" Ludwig von Bertalanffy that dynamic processes such as evolution could not be adequately analyzed solely with the tools of cybernetics.

Bertalanffy was an Austrian biologist and philosopher who created general system theory, a field of research aimed at extending analogies between disciplines even beyond those made by cybernetics. While the aim of cybernetics was to study systems that involved control and communication in the animal and machine, general system theory intended to study general properties that applied to systems *in general*.

We cannot go into detail here about the project of general system theory beyond pointing out its relationship with cybernetics as seen by Bertalanffy.[29] The relevant distinction here is between the cybernetician's view of goal-seeking behavior as the result of information and negative feedback, and the general system theoretician's view of equifinality as a result of open systems feeding from negative entropy.

According to the second law of thermodynamics, closed systems display a general tendency towards maximum entropy or disorder. In contrast, in the living world, there seems to exist a tendency to higher order, as organisms evolve and develop. How can both things be conciliated? Bertalanffy answers this question by conceiving living organisms as open systems. Differently from closed systems, where there is no exchange of matter between its inside and outside, open systems import and export materials from their external environment. Thus, by "importing complex organic molecules, using their energy, and rendering back the simpler end products to the environment" (Bertalanffy, 1950b, p. 26), the organism feeds from negative entropy.

For Bertalanffy, an important difference between open and closed systems is that the former can display equifinality. In closed systems, the final state of the system is always determined by its initial conditions. In this case, if initial conditions or the process are changed, so is the final state. In contrast, equifinality may be said to be present in a system where the same final state can be reached from different initial conditions and in different ways — that is, it does not presuppose a predetermined structure or mechanism. Only open systems, by exchanging materials with the environment and importing negative entropy, can display equifinal behavior (Bertalanffy, 1950b, p. 25). One example of equifinality is the growth of larvae, in which "the same final result, namely a typical larva, is achieved by a complete normal germ of the sea urchin, by a half germ after experimental separation of the cells, by two germs after fusion, or after translocations of the cells" (Bertalanffy, 1950a, p. 157).

Bertalanffy was aware of the cybernetics literature on goal-seeking behavior in feedback systems, but maintained that his concept of equifinality in open systems was the more general one. According to him, implicit in the explanation of purposive behavior as a result of feedback was the assumption of a fixed structure that guaranteed the desired result (Bertalanffy, 1950a, p. 159). This perspective, though, contrary to the open system's view, would not be adequate for dealing with cases where the structure itself evolves. In the case of organic systems, Bertalanffy differentiates between secondary regulations (due to feedback mechanisms) and primary regulations (due to equifinality in general):

> [...] the *primary regulations* in organic systems, i.e., those which are most fundamental and primitive in embryonic development as well as in evolution, are of the nature of dynamic interaction. They are based upon the fact that the living organism is an open system, maintaining itself in, or approaching a steady state. Superposed are those regulations which we may call *secondary*, and which are controlled by fixed arrangements, especially of the feedback type [...] Thus dynamics is the broader aspect, since we can always arrive from the general system of laws to machinelike function by introducing suitable conditions of constraint, but the opposite is not possible. (Bertalanffy, 1968, p. 44)

According to Bertalanffy, cybernetic models can only account for orders generated through the secondary regulations of a given fixed structure (in the case of Hayek's social theory, a given structure of rules of conduct). Those ordered processes that involve changes in the structure itself — such as evolution — should be conceived as the result of the primary regulations of open systems. In other words, negative feedback explained homeostasis, but not heterostasis:

> Concepts and models of equilibrium, homeostasis, adjustment, etc., are suitable for the maintenance of systems, but inadequate for phenomena of change, differentiation, *evolution*, negentropy, production of improbable states, creativity, building-up of tensions, self-realization, emergence, etc.; as indeed Cannon realized when he acknowledged, beside homeostasis, a "heterostasis" including phenomena of the latter nature. (Bertalanffy, 1968, p. 23, emphasis added)

Hayek makes very similar remarks about the limitations of homeostasis as a means of attaining and preserving order. Changes in the environment, says Hayek, sometimes require changes in the structure of rules of conduct if the order of the whole is to be preserved:

> From any given set of rules of conduct of the elements will arise a steady structure (showing '*homeostatic*' control) only in an environment in which there prevails a certain probability of encountering the sort of circumstances to which the rules of conduct are adapted. A change of environment may require, if the whole is to persist, a change in the order of the group and therefore in the rules of conduct of the individuals; and a spontaneous *change of the rules of individual conduct* and of the resulting order may enable the group to persist in circumstances which, without such change, would have led to its destruction. (Hayek, 1967a/2014, pp. 282–283, emphasis added)

Bertalanffy's conceptions of primary and secondary regulations had a counterpart in Hayek's discussion of what he called the twin ideas of evolution and spontaneous order. In short, the twin ideas thesis asserts that "the problem of the origin or formation and that of the manner of functioning of social institutions was essentially the same" (Hayek, 1967b/2014, p. 298). By that Hayek meant that the current structure of institutions of a group and the functions performed by those institutions are determined jointly by the evolutionary history of the group, in which structures of institutions that generated functional orders relative to the environment they encountered were selected instead of the competing ones.

Although Hayek attributes the original insight of the close relationship between evolution and spontaneous order to the thinkers of the Scottish Enlightment and to the later Carl Menger,[30] it was from Bertalanffy that he got the conceptual framework that enabled him to articulate and justify this alleged intimate relationship. Significantly, there is an apparent influence from Bertalanffy in the way Hayek links the "dynamics" of evolution to the "statics" of spontaneous orders. As Lewis pointed out:

> … some of the key components of the analytical framework in terms of which Hayek articulates and develops his Mengerian insight about the need to combine static and dynamic analysis—the conceptual glue that holds the notions of spontaneous order and evolution together, if you will—are, as we have seen, ones that Hayek obtains from

Bertalanffy. [...] Hayek used Bertalanffy's ideas to express and develop Menger's insight about the intimate connection between the origin and manner of functioning of social institutions in a modern idiom, namely the language of system theory. (Lewis, 2015, p. 22)

This influence from Bertalanffy had important consequences for the scope of cybernetics in Hayek's work. Just as Bertalanffy had argued before him, Hayek viewed cybernetics as enabling only the study of orders generated by a given static structure. According to Hayek, this is the case with respect to the price system, which, provided it is embedded in a larger framework of suitable social institutions, can maintain a reasonable degree of individual plan coordination These social institutions, in turn, are formed and changed over time through a larger dynamic process of cultural evolution.

CONCLUSION

In this chapter, we have seen how Hayek used cybernetic concepts and ideas from his book *The Sensory Order* in his later works on the nature and origins of social order. It was argued that Hayek's initial interest in this theory lay in its potential to explain purposive behavior and, thus, to provide a scientific justification for the subjectivist approach to the social sciences. This part of Hayek's project, however, could not be completed as Hayek was unable to provide a satisfactory answer to Popper's challenge.

Later, Hayek would use the framework of cybernetics to restate and further develop his ideas on the spontaneous formation of orders. One of the central institutions that allows social coordination – the price mechanism – would be described by Hayek as a cybernetic system. Consistent with Bertalanffy's assessment of the scope of cybernetics, Hayek's theory described the operation of feedback systems as depending on a given structure which is originated and changed by a dynamic process. Hayek's particular conceptualization of this dynamic process, in turn, would take the form of a theory of cultural evolution.

Recall that, in the epigraph of this chapter, Hayek said that investigations of the problem of complex self-organized orders had become so numerous that he had not been able to study more than a few of them closely. Among the few he did study closely were works from the field of cybernetics. By exploring how cybernetics influenced Hayek throughout his career, we hope to have contributed to a better understanding of Hayek's own conception of complexity and, ultimately, to a better understanding of Hayek's system of thought as a whole.

NOTES

1. Other important developments were general system theory, chaos theory, and catastrophe theory. For more on these other precursors of complexity, see Rosser (2009, pp. 171–175).

2. In this work we will focus mainly on the so-called "old" or "first-order" cybernetics. There is no evidence of significant influence on Hayek from the "new" or "second-order" cybernetics.

3. Heinrich Klüver was a psychologist and an important figure of the Macy Conferences of cybernetics. He was professor at University of Chicago during the 1950s, when Hayek worked on the Chicago Committee of Social Thought. Correspondence available between Hayek and Klüver suggests that they became close friends during this period. A letter from Klüver to Hayek in 1970 indicates that cybernetics was one of their main mutual interests: "If you were here there would be much to talk about. The American scene is rather interesting at the present time (to say at least) – economically, politically, psychologically and even cybernetically (although Warren McCulloch has seen fit to leave us forever on Sept 24 last year)" (Hayek Collection, Box 31, Folder 4).

4. Garrett Hardin was a biologist and ecologist whose work had cybernetics as one of its inspirations. He is widely known in the economics circles as the formulator of the problem of "The Tragedy of the Commons".

5. Ilya Prigogine was a physicist of the Free University of Brussels and associated with the cybernetics approach. Rosser (1999, p. 185) states that he learned of Hayek's approach to the "Brussels School" of cybernetics from Peter M. Allen, a student of Prigogine's

6. Cybernetics was explicitly inspired in the design of servomechanisms (or feedback-control systems) and in statistical mechanics (as we will see, information is defined as negative entropy).

7. The term homeostasis was coined by the physiologist Cannon (1932). Besides the temperature-regulating mechanism in a homoeothermic animal, other examples of homeostasis are the regulation of glucose and pH levels in the human blood.

8. These properties were:
   (1) $H(p_1, p_2, ..., p_n)$ should be continuous for each p_i;
   (2) if $p_i = \frac{1}{n}$ for every i, then H should be a monotonic increasing function of n;
   (3) $H(p_1, p_2, ..., p_n) = H(p_1 + p_2, p_3, ..., p_n) + (p_1 + p_2)H\left(\frac{p_1}{p_1 + p_2}, \frac{p_2}{p_1 + p_2}\right)$

Note also that, when $p_i = 0$ for some i, $p_i \log(p_i)$ is not defined, but as $\lim_{p_i \to 0+} p_i \log(p_i) = 0$, we can redefine $0\log(0) = 0$ and preserve the property of continuity (Kapur & Kevasan, 1992, p. 28).

9. According to Kapur and Kevasan (1992, p. 8), it was John von Neumann who supposedly advised Shannon to use the term entropy by saying that "First, the expression is the same as the expression for entropy in thermodynamics and as such

you should not use two different names for the same mathematical expression, and second, and more importantly, entropy, in spite of one hundred years of history, is not very well understood yet and so as such you will win every time you use entropy in an argument!". Avery (2003, p. 81) and Tribus and McIrvine (1971) report similar quotes from von Neumann.

10. Wiener, in turn, based his work on the pre-war literature on control engineering and communication engineering and, in particular, on servomechanisms.

11. The Macy Foundation was established in 1930 by a family of merchants with the mission of promoting "health and the ministry of healing." The foundation mainly funded medical research and medical schools (Tudico & Thibault, 2012). Frank Fremont-Smith, medical director of the foundation, had been a friend of Rosenblueth since their days at Harvard Medical School (Conway & Siegelman, 2005, p. 108).

12. Margaret Mead reported being so excited with what she heard at the conference that she did not notice she had broken one of her teeth until the conference was over (Conway & Siegelman, 2005, p. 95).

13. For a comprehensive history of the cybernetics movement, see Kline (2015). Mirowski (2002) is the seminal work on the influence of cybernetics and related developments on economics.

14. "Take such things as tools, food, medicine, weapons, words, sentences, communications, and acts of production − or any one particular instance of any of these. I believe these to be fair samples of the kind of objects of human activity which constantly occur in the social sciences. It is easily seen that all these concepts (and the same is true of more concrete instances) refer not to some objective properties possessed by the things, or which the observer can find out about them, but to views which some other person holds about the things.[...] They are all instances of what are sometimes called 'teleological concepts,' that is, they can be defined only by indicating relations between three terms: a purpose, somebody who holds that purpose, and an object which that person thinks to be a suitable means for that purpose" (Hayek, 1943/2014, p. 80).

15. That was the reason why he rejected Mach's theory according to which there existed such a one-to-one correspondence, with sensory qualities being all that ultimately existed.

16. In the passage quoted, Feser uses the term "mere mechanical operations" as the opposite of intentional or directed behavior. This usage, however, is somewhat misleading because, as we will see, Hayek sees some "mechanical" systems as displaying purposive behavior.

17. Besides cybernetics, Hayek (1952) also mentions an alternative approach to the explanation of purposive behavior given by "the more recent and most promising work of L. von Bertalanffy" (p. 83). He, however, did not make direct use of this approach in his argumentation in TSO.

18. Already in the first manuscript of "What is Mind?" dated in 1945, in which no sign of influence from cybernetics is found, Hayek writes that "it would seem to follow from our thesis that the difference between purely 'mechanical' and mental processes is not one of kind but merely one of degree, and that between the purely mechanical process of the simplest reflex type and the most complex mental process [...] there can be an almost infinite number of intermediate types [...] It is not likely

that we shall be able to understand the peculiar character of conscious processes until we have got a little further in understanding the working of the probably much more extensive basis of mental but not-conscious processes on which the super-structure of conscious processes rests" (Hayek Collection, Box 128, Folder 34, p. 30).

19. However, the similarities between human purposive behavior and negative feedback systems should not be overstated. From Hayek's perspective, the basic difference between systems such as Wiener's anti-aircraft machine and the human brain lies not in their nature, but in their different degrees of complexity. According to Hayek, a difference in degree of complexity can generate a difference in the kind of explanation appropriate to account for the phenomena. Both the anti-aircraft machine and the human brain are purposive and, in principle, entirely reducible to physics. However, as the human brain itself is the apparatus of explanation, we can only explain in detail phenomena having a degree of complexity lower than that of the human brain. Therefore, it is practically impossible to reduce the human brain to its physical properties. This is only possible with respect to simpler purposive systems like the anti-aircraft machine. On this, see Hayek (1952, pp. 184−190). Koppl (2005) interprets this aspect of TSO as a "scientific defense of methodological dualism" (p. 389). The opposite view − that TSO represents a de-emphasis of subjectivism in favor of a methodology more oriented to complexity − is advocated by Caldwell (2004a).

20. The interested reader should refer to the extensive discussion made by various authors in Butos (2010a), a volume of the book series *Advances in Austrian Economics* tiled *The Social Science of Hayek's 'The Sensory Order'*. Also relevant to this theme are Butos and Koppl (2007) and Gick and Gick (2001).

21. Interestingly, references to cybernetics are not to be found either in *The Constitution of Liberty* (1960/2011), the project Hayek started just after finishing TSO and which was published eight years after his book on theoretical psychology.

22. Walter B. Weimer, the cognitive psychologist who organized this conference, had an important role in bringing more attention to the relevance of *The Sensory Order* to modern cognitive psychology and to the social sciences. On this, see Butos (2010b, pp. 2−4).

23. Although society and brain are organized on similar principles, "society is not a brain and must not be represented as a sort of super-brain" (Hayek, 1967a/2014, p. 286). Contrary to the brain, which directs the organism, society does not work as a directing center.

24. Compare: "If anyone really knew all about what economic theory calls the *data*, competition would indeed be a very wasteful method of securing adjustment to these facts [...] Against this, it is salutary to remember that [...] competition is valuable *only* because, and so far as, its results are unpredictable and on the whole different from those which anyone has, or could have, deliberately aimed at" (Hayek, 1968/2014, pp. 304−305).

25. Hardin was also familiar with Hayek's works. There are a couple of letters from Hardin to Hayek in the Hayek Archives at the Hoover Institute. In one of them, dated in 1978, Hardin thanks Hayek for sending a copy of "The Three Sources of Human Values" (part of the postscript of *Law, Legislation and Liberty*), saying that he profited a lot from reading it. He also mentions a presentation by

Hayek on a Sociobiology meeting where the audience was "unequipped to appreciate the wisdom" of the speaker (Hayek Collection, Box 23, Folder 22). Later, Hardin wrote a review of Hayek's book *The Fatal Conceit*, mainly criticizing it for not taking seriously the population problem (Hardin, 1989).

26. See also: "It was the great achievement of economic theory that, 200 years before cybernetics, it recognized the nature of such self-regulating systems in which certain regularities (or, perhaps better, 'restraints') of conduct of the elements led to constant adaptation of the comprehensive order to particular facts" (Hayek, 1970/2014, p. 345) and "in the language of modern cybernetics, the feedback mechanism secures the maintenance of a self-generating order. It was this which Adam Smith saw and described as the operation of the 'invisible hand' – to be ridiculed for 200 years by uncomprehending scoffers" (Hayek, 1978, p. 63).

27. "By the late 1950s it appears that Hayek began to realize that he simply lacked the mathematical background to formalize his ideas within psychology. He then tried to express them within economics [...] again with at best limited success. Ultimately, he decided to express his ideas verbally by identifying a variety of fields that studied complex orders, and from which he drew conclusions about their characteristics" (Caldwell, 2015, p. 29).

28. Except that in LLL he substitutes the concept of order for the one of equilibrium. The difference between the two is that while equilibrium requires a perfect compatibility of plans, order requires only partial compatibility, so we "can meaningfully speak about an order being approached to various degrees, and that order can be preserved throughout a process of change" (Hayek, 1968/2014, p. 308). For a great discussion about Hayek's concept of order and its implications for economics, see Vaughn (1999a).

29. For more on Bertalanffy and general system theory, see Drack and Pouvreau (2007, 2015) and Pouvreau (2014). For a great discussion on the relationship between Hayek and Bertalanffy, readers should refer to Lewis (2015).

30. Hayek's linking of evolution to self-organization was not original even if we restrict ourselves to the cybernetics literature. Ashby (1947a, 1947b, 1948) had already made this connection and developed a complete theory of the relationship between both concepts in his paper "Principles of the Self-Organizing System" (Ashby, 1962). This paper was presented in the 1961 University of Illinois Symposium of Self-Organization, in which Hayek, Bertalanffy, and McCulloch were present. Unfortunately, Hayek did not present a work in this conference and the rather short transcripts of the discussions that followed the presentations do not contain any useful information regarding Hayek's opinions about the ideas exposed at the event. The symposium was organized by Heinz von Foerster and George Zopf Jr.

ACKNOWLEDGMENT

The author would like to thank Jorge Soromenho, Bruce Caldwell, Scott Scheall, Jack Birner, Barkley Rosser, Peter Boettke, Pedro Garcia Duarte, José Chiappin, the participants of the HOPE workshop and the participants of the INET Young Scholar Online Seminar in the History of

Economic Thought and Philosophy of Economics for helpful comments on earlier drafts. This work was enabled by the São Paulo Research Foundation (FAPESP) through the grant#2015/00352-0. The author thanks the Estate of F. A. Hayek for granting me permission to quote from his unpublished materials.

REFERENCES

Ahrendt, W. R., & Taplin, J. F. (1951). *Automatic feedback control.* New York, NY: McGraw-Hill.

Ashby, W. R. (1945). The physical origin of adaptation by trial and error. *The Journal of General Psychology, 32,* 13–25.

Ashby, W. R. (1947a). Principles of self-organizing dynamic systems. *Journal of General Psychology, 37,* 125–128.

Ashby, W. R. (1947b). Dynamics of the cerebral cortex. Automatic development of equilibrium in self-organizing systems. *Psychometrica, 12,* 135–140.

Ashby, W. R. (1948). Design for a brain. *Electronic Engineering, 20,* 379–383.

Ashby, W. R. (1949). Review of N. Wiener, cybernetics. *Journal of Mental Science, 95,* 716–724.

Ashby, W. R. (1956). *An introduction to cybernetics.* New York, NY: Wiley.

Ashby, W. R. (1960). *Design for a brain* (2nd ed.). New York, NY: Wiley.

Ashby, W. R. (1962). Principles of the self-organizing system. In H. v. Foerster & G. W. Zopf Jr. (Eds.), *Principles of self-organization* (pp. 255–278). New York, NY: Pergamon Press.

Avery, J. (2003). *Information theory and evolution.* River Edge NJ: World Scientific Publishing Co. Pte. Ltd.

Barbieri, F. (2013). Complexity and the Austrians. *Filosofía de la Economía, 1,* 47–69.

Bertalanffy, L. v. (1950a). An outline of general system theory. *The British Journal of Philosophy of Science, 1,* 134–165.

Bertalanffy, L. v. (1950b). The theory of open systems in physics and biology. *Science, 111*(January), 23–29.

Bertalanffy, L. v. (1968). *General system theory: Foundations, development, applications.* New York, NY: George Brazillier.

Birner, J. (2009). From group selection to ecological niches. Popper's rethinking of evolutionary theory in the light of Hayek's theory of culture. In R. S. Cohen & Z. Parusniková (Eds.), *Rethinking popper, Boston studies in the philosophy of science* (pp. 185–202). Dordrecht: Springer.

Butos, W. N. (Ed.). (2010a). *The social science of Hayek's 'The Sensory Order'* (Vol. 13). Advances in Austrian Economics. Bingley, UK: Emerald Group Publishing Limited.

Butos, W. N. (2010b). The unexpected fertility of Hayek's cognitive theory: An introduction to the social science of Hayek's the sensory order. In W. N. Butos (Ed.), *The social science of Hayek's 'The Sensory Order'* (Vol. 13, pp. 1–20). Advances in Austrian Economics. Bingley, UK: Emerald Group Publishing Limited.

Butos, W. N., & Koppl, R. G. (2007). Does the sensory order have a useful economic future? In E. Krecké, C. Krecké, & R. Koppl (Eds.), *Cognition and economics* (Vol. 9, pp. 19–51). *Advances in Austrian Economics.* Oxford: Elsevier Ltd.

Caldwell, B. (2004a). *Hayek's challenge: An intellectual biography of F. A. Hayek*. Chicago, IL: The University of Chicago Press.

Caldwell, B. (2004b). Some reflections on F. A. Hayek's the sensory order. *Journal of Bioeconomics, 6,* 239–254.

Caldwell, B. (2015). *F. A. Hayek and the economic calculus*. Working Paper.

Cannon, W. B. (1932). *The wisdom of the body*. New York, NY: W. W. Norton & Co.

Colander, D., Holt, R. P., & Rosser, J. B. (2004). *The changing face of mainstream economics*. Arbor, MI: University of Michigan Press.

Conway, F., & Siegelman, J. (2005). *Dark hero of the information age: In search of Norbert Wiener, the father of cybernetics*. Cambridge: Basic Books.

Drack, M., & Pouvreau, D. (2007). On the history of Ludwig von Bertalanffy's "general systemology", and on its relationship to cybernetics. *International Journal of General Systems, 36*(3), 281–337.

Drack, M., & Pouvreau, D. (2015). On the history of Ludwig von Bertalanffy's "general systemology", and on its relationship to cybernetics – Part III: Convergences and divergences. *International Journal of General Systems, 44,* 1–51.

Feser, E. (2006). Hayek the cognitive scientist and philosopher. In E. Feser (Ed.), *The Cambridge companion to Hayek* (pp. 287–314). Cambridge: Cambridge University Press.

Gaus, G. (2006). The evolution of society and mind: Hayek's system of ideas. In E. E. Feser (Ed.), *The Cambridge companion to Hayek* (pp. 232–258). Cambridge: Cambridge University Press.

Gerovitch, S. (2002). *From newspeak to cyberspeak: A history of soviet cybernetics*. Cambridge, MA: MIT Press.

Gick, E., & Gick, W. (2001). F. A. Hayek's theory of mind and the theory of cultural evolution revisited: Toward an integrative perspective. *Mind and Society, 2,* 149–162.

Hardin, G. (1959). *Nature and man's fate*. New York, NY: Rinehart & Company, Inc.

Hardin, G. (1989). Review of the fatal conceit: The errors of socialism, by F. A. Hayek. *Population and Development Review, 15,* 551–561.

Hayek, F. A. (1937/2014). Economics and knowledge. In F. A. Hayek (Ed.), *The market and other orders* (pp. 57–77). Chicago, IL: University of Chicago Press.

Hayek, F. A. (1943/2014). The facts of the social sciences. In F. A. Hayek (Ed.), *The market and other orders* (pp. 78–92). Chicago, IL: University of Chicago Press.

Hayek, F. A. (1945/2014). The use of knowledge in society. In F. A. Hayek (Ed.), *The market and other orders* (pp. 93–104). Chicago, IL: University of Chicago Press.

Hayek, F. A. (1952). *The sensory order: An inquiry into the foundations of theoretical psychology*. Chicago, IL: The University of Chicago Press.

Hayek, F. A. (1960/2011). In R. Hamowy (Ed.), *The constitution of liberty: The definitive edition*. Chicago: The University of Chicago Press.

Hayek, F. A. (1965/2014). Kinds of rationalism. In F. A. Hayek (Ed.), *The market and other orders* (pp. 39–56). Chicago, IL: University of Chicago Press.

Hayek, F. A. (1967a/2014). Notes on the evolution of systems of rules of conduct. In F. A. Hayek (Ed.), *The market and other orders* (pp. 278–292). Chicago IL: University of Chicago Press.

Hayek, F. A. (1967b/2014). The results of human action but not of human design. In F. A. Hayek (Ed.), *The market and other orders* (pp. 293–303). Chicago, IL: University of Chicago Press.

Hayek, F. A. (1968/1978). The confusion of language in political thought. In F. A. Hayek (Ed.), *New studies in philosophy, politics, economics and the history of ideas* (pp. 71–97). London: Routledge & Kegan Paul.

Hayek, F. A. (1968/2014). Competition as a discovery procedure. In F. A. Hayek (Ed.), *The market and other orders* (pp. 304–313). Chicago, IL: University of Chicago Press.

Hayek, F. A. (1970/2014). The errors of construtivism. In F. A. Hayek (Ed.), *The market and other orders* (pp. 338–356). Chicago, IL: University of Chicago Press.

Hayek, F. A. (1973). Rules and order: *Vol. 1. Law, legislation and liberty.* London: Routledge.

Hayek, F. A. (1976). *The mirage of social justice: Vol. 2. Law, legislation and liberty.* London: Routledge.

Hayek, F. A. (1978). The atavism of social justice. In F. A. Hayek (Ed.), *New studies in philosophy, politics, economics and the history of ideas* (pp. 50–56). London: Routledge & Kegan Paul.

Hayek, F. A. (1979). *The political order of a free people: Vol. 3. Law, legislation and liberty.* London: Routledge.

Hayek, F. A. (1982). Weimar-Hayek discussion. In W. B. Weimer & D. S. Palermo (Eds.), *Cognition and the symbolic processes* (Vol. 2, pp. 321–329). Hillsdale, NJ: Lawrence Erlbaum Associates.

Hayek, F. A. (1988). *The fatal conceit: The errors of socialism.* London: Routledge.

Heims, S. J. (1993). *Constructing a social science for postwar America: The cybernetics group, 1946–1953.* Cambridge, MA: The MIT Press.

Kapur, J. N., & Kevasan, H. K. (1992). *Entropy optimization principles with applications.* San Diego, CA: Academic Press.

Kline, R. R. (2015). *The cybernetics movement – Or why we call our age the information age.* Baltimore, MD: John Hopkins University Press.

Koppl, R. (2005). Review of Bruce Caldwell, Hayek's challenge: An intellectual biography of F. A. Hayek. *Journal of Economic Behavior and Organization, 59,* 287–291.

Lewis, P. A. (2015). *Systems, structural properties and levels of organisation: The influence of Ludwig von Bertalanffy on the work of F. A. Hayek.* Retrieved from http://ssrn.com/abstract=2609349. Accessed on October 2, 2015.

McCulloch, W. S. (1948). A recapitulation of the theory with a forecast of several extensions. In L. K. Frank (Ed.), *Teleological mechanisms* (Vol. 50, pp. 259–277). New York, NY: Annals of the New York Academy of Sciences.

McCulloch, W. S., & Pitts, W. (1943). A logical calculus of the ideas immanent in nervous activity. *Bulletin of Mathematical Biophysics, 5,* 115–133.

Mirowski, P. (2002). *Machine dreams: Economics becomes a cyborg science.* Cambridge: Cambridge University Press.

Mitchell, M. (2009). *Complexity: A guided tour.* New York, NY: Oxford University Press.

Popper, K. (1953). Language and the body-mind problem: A restatement of interactionism. *Proceedings of the 11th international congress of philosophy* (pp. 101–107). Brussels: North-Holland Publishing Company.

Pouvreau, D. (2014). On the history of Ludwig von Bertalanffy's "general systemology", and on its relationship to cybernetics – Part II: Contexts and developments of the systemological hermeneutics instigated by von Bertalanffy. *International Journal of General Systems, 43*(2), 172–245.

Rosenblueth, A., Wiener, N., & Bigelow, J. (1943). Behavior, purpose and teleology. *Philosophy of Science, 10,* 18–24.

Rosser, J. B. (1999). On the complexities of complex economic dynamics. *Journal of Economic Perspectives, 13*, 169–192.

Rosser, J. B. (2009). Introduction. In J. B. Rosser (Ed.), *Handbook of complexity research* (pp. 3–11). Cheltenham: Edward Elgar.

Rosser, J. B. (2010). How complex are the Austrians? In R. Koppl, S. Horwitz, & P. Desrochers (Eds.), *What is so Austrian about Austrian economics?* (Vol. 14, pp. 165–179). (Advances in Austrian Economics). Bingley, UK: Emerald Group Publishing Limited.

Scheall, S. (2016). A brief note concerning Hayek's non-standard conception of knowledge. *Review of Austrian Economics, 29*, 1–6.

Shannon, C. (1948). A mathematical theory of communication. *The Bell System Technical Journal, 27*, 379–423.

Tribus, M., & McIrvine, E. C. (1971). Energy and information. *Scientific American, 224*(September), 179–188.

Tudico, C., & Thibault, G. (2012). *The history of the Josiah Macy Jr. foundation.* New York, NY: Josiah Macy Jr. Foundation.

Vaughn, K. (1999a). Hayek's implicit economics: Rules and the problem of order. *Review of Austrian Economics, 11*, 129–144.

Vaughn, K. (1999b). Hayek's theory of the market order as an instance of the theory of complex, adaptive systems. *Journal des Economistes et des Etudes Humaines, 9*(2–3), 241–256.

Weaver, W. (1964). Recent contributions to the mathematical theory of communication. In C. Shannon & W. Weaver (Eds.), *A mathematical theory of communication* (pp. 1–28). Urbana, IL: The University of Illinois.

Wiener, N. (1948a). *Cybernetics.* Cambridge, MA: MIT Press.

Wiener, N. (1948b). Time, communication, and the nervous system. In L. K. Frank (Ed.), *Teleological mechanisms* (Vol. 50, pp. 197–278). New York, NY: Annals of the New York Academy of Sciences.

THE HISTORY OF A TRADITION: AUSTRIAN ECONOMICS FROM 1871 TO 2016

Peter J. Boettke, Christopher J. Coyne and Patrick Newman

ABSTRACT

This chapter provides a comprehensive survey of the contributions of the Austrian school of economics, with specific emphasis on post-WWII developments. We provide a brief history and overview of the original theorists of the Austrian school in order to set the stage for the subsequent development of their ideas by Ludwig von Mises and F. A. Hayek. In discussing the main ideas of Mises and Hayek, we focus on how their work provided the foundations for the modern Austrian school, which included Ludwig Lachmann, Murray Rothbard and Israel Kirzner. These scholars contributed to the Austrian revival in the 1960s and 1970s, which, in turn, set the stage for the emergence of the contemporary Austrian school in the 1980s. We review the contemporary development of the Austrian school and, in doing so, discuss the tensions, alternative paths, and the promising future of Austrian economics.

Keywords: Austrian economics; marginal revolution; market process theory; Carl Menger; F. A. Hayek

Research in the History of Economic Thought and Methodology, Volume 34A, 199–243
Copyright © 2016 by Emerald Group Publishing Limited
ISSN: 0743-4154/doi:10.1108/S0743-41542016000034A007

INTRODUCTION

This chapter provides a survey and overview of the contributions of the Austrian school of economics, with an emphasis on post-WWII developments. It is important for our narrative that readers keep some background information in mind. First, as the present symposium serves to substantiate, the Austrian school of economics experienced a great migration during the 1930s and 1940s out of Austria and the German-language scientific community in the direction of the English-language scientific community in Great Britain and the United States. Second, during the 20th century, the discipline of economics became increasingly professionalized and, as a result, scientific and scholarly work was performed almost exclusively within the institutional structure of higher education. The result was that published work moved from treatises and monographs to focused research articles in specialized journals. The idea of the amateur enthusiast and generalist as a significant contributor to the discipline was crowded out by the rise of the technical expert. Third, the professional fate of the Austrian school of economics ebbed and flowed with some considerable volatility throughout the period we will be surveying. Although this volatility is not solely a function of either the migration or some perceived flaw in the core of Austrian theory, the influence of these factors at particular points in time cannot be dismissed out of hand.

The Journal of Economic Literature classification system (i.e., JEL codes) was established to aid in the cataloging of scholarly contributions to economics. The characterization of the Austrian school in the JEL codes mimics the rise, fall, and rise again of the professional reputation of the school. Prior to 1925, the contributions of the Austrian school were captured under the banner of neoclassical theory, whereas, in the post-1950 period, they have been categorized as heterodox theory. What happened in the intervening years that influenced this perceived change in the mainstream status of the Austrian school? Today, Austrian economics is categorized alongside Marxism, Institutionalism, and Feminist Economics as part of the "Current Heterodoxy" (B53). At the same time, however, Austrian economics has recently been added to the category of macroeconomics and monetary economics as an alternative "General Aggregative Model" (E14). What has changed since 2000 that led to this development? Part of our purpose in this survey is to answer these questions.

Israel Kirzner, in discussing the strange professional fate of the Austrian school between 1925 and 1950, has added another twist to the mystery. Kirzner claims that precisely at the time the professional reputation of the Austrian school was at its nadir, members of the school were making their most original and profound contributions to the science. He highlights Mises's *Human Action* (1949) and Hayek's *Individualism and Economic Order* (1948) as the critical Austrian texts published in this period, and emphasizes the development of the central Austrian idea of the market as a process of the discovery and utilization of knowledge.

There have been three significant episodes for Austrian economics in the years following the immediate postwar era surveyed in the present symposium. The first concerns the breakdown of the Keynesian consensus in the 1970s and Hayek's receipt of the Nobel Prize in 1974. The second was the collapse of communism in the 1990s, and the belated recognition of the prescience of Mises and Hayek's critiques of central planning in the 1920s and 1930s. The third and most recent episode was the re-evaluation of Austrian business-cycle theory (ABCT) in the wake of the financial crisis of 2008 and ensuing "Great Recession." Each of these episodes brought increased attention to the contributions of the Austrian school, as well as increased scientific scrutiny of the core arguments and intellectual practices of the school.

A survey of the Austrian school could focus on personalities. Samuelson (1981), certainly no fan of Austrianism, nevertheless wrote an article detailing who he thought would have won the Nobel Prize in Economic Science had the award been established in 1901, at the same time as the other prizes. Among the names on his list were Carl Menger, Eugen Böhm-Bawerk, and Ludwig von Mises. So, a focus on personalities would certainly express much of interest to the history of economic thought and methodology.

Alternatively, a survey of the Austrian school could focus on the major methodological, theoretical, and political-economic debates in which members of the school figured prominently. The *Methodenstreit* of the late 19th century − prompted by the school's founder, Carl Menger − led to disputes over positivism and formalism that engaged later Austrian economists in the 20th century. Similarly, at various times in the first several decades of the school's history, Austrian economists played a critical role in debates with Walrasians, Marshallians, and Knightians over value theory, price theory, capital theory, and market theory. With the rise of the "New Economics" in the late-1930s and 1940s, Austrian economists discovered a new *bête noire*. And, of course, Austrian economists often sharpened their own analytical position in opposition to Marxists and market socialists. In the post-WWII period, these methodological, analytical, and political-economic debates would continue with novel twists and new central characters, but the essential Austrian perspective would remain a powerful antidote to whatever the prevailing professional consensus was at any given time.

Finally, one could survey the Austrian school by considering the various academic homes or the scholarly publications that have fallen under the editorial control of prominent members of the school. The school was of course born at the University of Vienna. For a time following Hayek's emigration to Great Britain in 1931, the London School of Economics (LSE) was the source of much of the most cutting-edge work in Austrian economics. In the postwar period, following the emigration of both Mises and Hayek to the United States, and, indeed, up to the present day, the academic contingent of the American revival of Austrian economics has resided primarily at New York University (NYU) and George Mason University (GMU). Moreover, Austrian economists have, at one time or another, exerted direct editorial responsibility over such prominent publications as *Archiv für Sozialwissenschaften*, *Economica*, *Il Politico*, and the *Review of Austrian Economics*.

Our approach is to blend these multiple approaches together to survey the history of the Austrian school and the prospects for its continued development. It is our contention that the best way to address Kirzner's conundrum is not merely to engage in improved scientific salesmanship of the existing body of Austrian thought, but to advance the ideas and use them to solve pressing methodological, theoretical, and practical problems. The professional reputation of the Austrian approach will rise through specific scholarly contributions. The gap that emerged in the 1930s and 1940s between the school and the mainstream was an aberration due to a variety of philosophical and historical contingencies of the time. Of course, the future is in part a function of the path-dependent past and the history of those fateful decades has yet to be completely overcome. Nonetheless, it is our position that the only way to place the discipline of economics back on a path more in harmony with Austrian masters is to actively use these tools to display the methodological, analytical, and practical power of the Austrian approach.[1]

THE THEORY OF PRACTICAL KNOWLEDGE AND THE PRACTICALITY OF THEORETICAL KNOWLEDGE

Since its founding, the Austrian school of economics has been both blessed and cursed by a mixed focus on purely scientific contributions to economic theory and practical engagement with public policy. As a student, Carl Menger (1840–1921) was a liberal activist. Menger was educated in Prague and Vienna, and eventually received his doctorate in jurisprudence from Krakow's Jagiellonian University. Prior to his scientific career, Menger had worked as a journalist reporting on daily market news, an experience that catalyzed his interest in economic theory. Menger found that the classical theory of price determination did not align with the way prices emerge in the real-world economy. He sought to align economic theory with the operations of markets he had observed as a journalist.

Menger was appointed to the faculty of law at the University of Vienna in 1871, and assumed the chair in economic theory in 1873. It was here that the Austrian school of economics was born. As can be seen in his *Lectures to the Crown Prince Rudolf of Austria* (1994), Menger's liberal activism never disappeared. However, Menger kept this activism separate from his scientific work. The next generation of Austrian school economists followed a similar approach.

Eugen von Böhm-Bawerk (1851–1914) rose to international prominence in the 1880s with his work *Capital & Interest* (1959 [1921]), as well the controversy that followed his *Karl Marx and the Close of His System* (1949). From the beginning of his career, Böhm-Bawerk worked both in the Austrian ministry of finance and as a professor of economics. He was first appointed Finance Minister in 1895 and would serve in this capacity in several separate terms over the next decade. Throughout his time in office, Böhm-Bawerk argued for sound money and fiscal responsibility. Indeed, when he became concerned that mounting military demands were encouraging fiscal profligacy, he resigned from this position in 1904. Friedrich Wieser (1851–1926), the other leading light in the second generation of the Austrian school, also balanced his purely scientific contributions with a commitment to public policy analysis. However, Wieser was more sympathetic to a version of Fabian socialism than the classical liberalism of Menger and Böhm-Bawerk.

The next generation of Austrian school economists included Ludwig von Mises (1881–1973) and Joseph Schumpeter (1883–1950). Both also forged a balance between scientific interests and practical policy concerns. This blend of the theoretical and practical continued with the final generation of Austrian school economists to be trained at Vienna – F. A. Hayek, Fritz Machlup, Gottfried Haberler, and Oskar Morgenstern.

Much of this admixture of the scientific and political can be explained by simple necessity. Scholarly life in Vienna existed largely outside of the university. The development and exchange of ideas was grounded in intellectual "circles" that met regularly, but whose members often held full-time jobs in business or government. As indicated by the example of Menger's journalistic experience spurring his scientific work, it was also the case that the research interests of many prominent Austrian school economists were the direct consequence of engagement with specific practical problems.

The economists of the Austrian school thus had multiple audiences including: (1) their scientific peers, (2) their students (for those in academia), (3) policy makers (for those who worked, officially or otherwise, on problems of policy), and (4) the general public. The blending of scientific and practical insights, as well as communication to multiple audiences, characterized many Austrian economists (then and now) and contributed to the revival of the tradition in America. We stress this point because it affects how we interpret the different paths that Austrian economics has taken over time.

These factors have been especially relevant in the new millennium. The Internet has broken down many of the old walls between academic research and popular writing. In the 1940s, when Hayek wrote "The Use of Knowledge in Society" (1945), he understood that he was addressing an audience of fellow professionals, just as Mises understood when he was writing for *The Freeman* in the 1950s that his audience was that of the interested layman. But the modern world of blogs and social media has complicated any such simple sorting. Not everyone is able to speak intelligently to multiple audiences, so intellectual markets historically sorted folks into teaching jobs, policy jobs, journalism jobs, and academic-research jobs. This has changed as today's modern technology has blurred the lines that could traditionally be drawn between these categories.

Any survey of the Austrian school of economics, therefore, must acknowledge that this intermingling of the scientific and the practical has been both blessing and curse. The blessing is evident in two points. First, Austrian economists believe that policy relevance is a virtue not a vice and, thus, they tend to focus their attention on pressing issues of public policy. Second, Austrian economists believe that engagement with issues of public concern means that Austrian ideas can be supported outside of the traditional sources of financial provision and intellectual encouragement. There are many amateur enthusiasts of Austrian economics and this fact sustained the tradition during the years when the economics profession had moved decidedly against the general thrust of the Austrian school in methodological, analytical and ideological terms. The Volker Foundation and the Foundation for Economic Education (FEE) played a critical role in the early period of the Austrian revival in post-WWII America. In the 1960s and 1970s, that same role came to be played by the Earhart Foundation, the Scaife Foundation, the Bradley Foundation, Liberty Fund, and the Institute for Humane Studies (IHS). Professional associations, such as the Mont Pelerin Society and the Philadelphia Society, played a more vital role in the communication of Austrian ideas among professional economists than did, say, the meetings of the American Economic Association. Without a dedicated audience of amateur enthusiasts, there is a strong possibility that the Austrian school of economics would have been simply relegated to a foregone chapter in the history of economic thought — albeit an illustrious chapter with many acknowledged contributions to the development of modern economic thought.

That said, there is also a sense in which this culture of amateur enthusiasts has cursed the subsequent development and absorption of Austrian ideas into in the economics mainstream. In America, in particular, the Austrian school became closely identified with the libertarian political movement. Perhaps an analogy might help clarify the relevant point here. It is amateur enthusiasts who make the National Football League the major industry that it is, but were these enthusiasts to take the field on Sundays, American football would surely lose much of its popular appeal. Science is a similar endeavor of expert discourse, and in the postwar period the expert discourse in economics has taken place among university professors and in specialized journals to which many of the central figures of the Austrian revival refused to contribute.[2] Instead, seeking to do an end-run around the academic establishment, they focused on publishing in general outlets and with non-academic publishers.

One relevant factor was that many figures of the Austrian revival held academic posts, but often not in PhD-granting institutions and, thus, they were not beholden to the publishing expectations and demands placed on research faculty. Of course, this also meant that many could not supervise graduate students and, were thereby severely limited in influencing the next generation of economic professionals. In America, during the 1950s and 1960s, the Austrian school could barely be maintained within the academic world. Things would change a bit in the late 1970s and early 1980s when an Austrian emphasis was established within the PhD programs at NYU, GMU, and Auburn University.

Prior to the advent of the Internet, the intellectual marketplace sent strong sorting signals so that anyone could understand the different kinds of contributions being made. So, while the amateur enthusiast might have liked to get on the field, the barriers were such that no amateur could simply replace the quarterback. However, the Internet now gives many the impression that anyone can play regardless of background and skill, and this has had a very confusing impact, especially as many policy issues — for example, former U.S. Congressman Ron Paul's political opposition to both American foreign policy and domestic economic policy in the wake of the "Great Recession" — have moved the Austrian school to the forefront of public discourse. It is important to keep these issues in mind as we assess the various contributions of the contemporary Austrian school.

THE HABSBURG YEARS: THE ORIGINAL THEORISTS

The marginal revolution in value theory can be traced to 1871 when Carl Menger, William Stanley Jevons, and Leon Walras independently discovered the concept of marginal utility. However, 1871 also marks the birth of the Austrian school. In his *Principles of Economics*, published that year, Menger provided the edifice that would define the Austrians and distinguish their approach from that of other contemporary schools.

Some of the uniquely Austrian concepts that Menger developed include the means-end framework, the relationship between the specificity of goods and their value, and the temporal distinction between goods of higher and lower orders. Menger's emphasis on the temporal element inherent in economic production would be an important distinguishing characteristic of the Austrian school. In addition, Menger stressed the marginal aspect of the value of goods which, in turn, led to the famous Law of Marginal Utility.[3] Finally, Menger described an innovative theory of exchange that stressed price formation in the real world as opposed to price determination in general equilibrium. This led Menger to criticize the pricing analysis of his contemporaries, as well as their use of the unrealistic assumption of continuous mathematical functions to describe exchange.

Menger's next book, *Investigations into the Method of the Social Sciences* (1985 [1883]) considered the methodological aspects of economic theorizing and sparked the infamous *Methodenstreit*, (in English, "battle over methods"). In this book, Menger first described spontaneous orders a concept that would be used by many later Austrians.[4]

The Mengerian legacy would be carried on by Eugen von Böhm-Bawerk and Friedrich von Wieser, Menger's two most prominent colleagues at the University of Vienna. Menger's defense of the place of deductive theory in economics would be taken up by Böhm-Bawerk in both German- and (via translation) English-language scientific discussions. However, both Böhm-Bawerk and Wieser were primarily concerned with working out the implications of Menger's insights in analytical economics rather than in methodology.

Böhm-Bawerk expanded the architectonic structure of Austrian theory originally set out by Menger. In *The Positive Theory of Capital* (1959 [1889]), Böhm-Bawerk built on Menger's price theory with his "marginal pairs" analysis, which describes the zone of an equilibrium price achievable in the real world without relying on continuous demand and supply schedules. Böhm-Bawerk also built off of Menger's distinction between goods of higher and lower orders in developing a capital theory that emphasized the temporality of production. Producing higher-order goods refers to engaging in roundabout (long-term) production processes, as their production is more temporally remote from final consumption than are lower-order goods (obtained through shorter production processes). Production in a society increases through the additional utilization of long-term production processes that are more productive than shorter ones. Böhm-Bawerk was instrumental in highlighting the fact that the economy is a structure of production consisting of heterogeneous (i.e., relatively specific) capital goods employed in production processes of varying degrees of roundaboutness.

In addition, Böhm-Bawerk developed an influential theory of interest. In his *History and Critique of Interest Theories* (1959 [1884]), Böhm-Bawerk dissected earlier explanations for interest. Böhm-Bawerk in turn emphasized time preference – that individuals prefer present consumption to future consumption, as one of the factors accounting for interest. He (1962 [1896]) used this to demolish the Marxian myth that interest was an exploitative phenomenon. Although there were disagreements between the two – for reasons that remain somewhat obscure, Menger famously described Böhm-Bawerk's capital theory as "one of the greatest errors ever committed" (Schumpeter, 1954, p. 847) – Böhm-Bawerk's canon is firmly within the approach originally laid out by Carl Menger.[5]

Wieser was instrumental in developing the concept of opportunity cost, which in turn led to the Law of Cost.[6] The value of factors of production used in a production process is in part determined by the various forgone alternatives of other consumer goods they could produce. The prices of consumer goods, which are based off of their utility, determine the cost of factors, and not the other way around.[7] Wieser's most famous works were *Natural Value* (1989 [1893]) and *Social Economics* (1927 [1914]). However, for various reasons, Wieser's works are fundamentally different than those of Menger and Böhm-Bawerk, and future advancements in the Austrian school did not build off of them.[8]

Other important theorists that could be counted among the second generation of Austrian economics include Philip Wicksteed and Frank A. Fetter.[9] Although he explicitly pledged allegiance to Jevons, a close reading of Wicksteed's economics places him more in the Austrian tradition. Among other insights, his *The Common Sense of Political Economy* (1910) made notable contributions to the theory of price. First, Wicksteed developed total demand-stock analysis, which shows that the traditional forward sloping supply curve is nothing but a reservation demand by sellers for an existing stock of a produced good; in the absence of this, Wicksteed showed, demand price is exclusively determined by consumer demand.[10] Second, Wicksteed analyzed the process by which disequilibrium prices (where shortages and surpluses exist) converge to equilibrium prices as market participants obtain greater knowledge and better appraise their situations, a particularly important point that foreshadows later Austrian analyses of uncertainty and the market process.[11] In various essays and in his *Economic Principles* (1915), Fetter contributed to the Austrian tradition via his work on the theory of rent and the pure time-preference theory of interest. In particular, Mises would build off of Fetter's work and argue that time preference is the sole determinant of interest, in contrast to Böhm-Bawerk, who defended a more eclectic approach.[12]

After WWI, the intellectual leadership of the Austrian school would shift to a new generation of scholars. By the 1930s, the unquestioned leaders of the school were Ludwig von Mises and F. A. Hayek.

THE INTERWAR YEARS: FROM MISES TO HAYEK

The next phase in the history of Austrian economics would mark both the rise and fall of the school. The Austrian approach was considered cutting-edge throughout the 1920s and into the early 1930s, but was already passé by the end of WWII. This sets up the Kirznerian conundrum and the future shift in the JEL codes discussed in the introduction. Many mainstream economists would argue that by this time all of the important Austrian insights had been incorporated into the body of Neoclassical thought.[13] However, as Kirzner (2014) has argued, this was in fact when the Austrians' most distinctive contributions were made. These contributions were in the fields of money and the trade cycle, economic calculation and the market process, and economic methodology. The main force driving all of these advancements was Ludwig von Mises.[14]

Böhm-Bawerk unexpectedly died in 1914, and Menger had stopped writing economics long before his death in 1921. This would open the door for the next generation to take over the scientific leadership of Austrian economics. Three names dominate this period in Austrian economics: Joseph Schumpeter, Hans Mayer, and Ludwig von Mises.[15] Mises had established himself as one of the leading voices of his generation of economists in the German-language scientific community with the publication of *The Theory of Money and Credit* (1953 [1912]). Although Mises' work was more closely allied with the Menger-Böhm-Bawerk approach, Böhm-Bawerk placed greater hope in Joseph Schumpeter for the advancement of economic theory at this time.[16] Böhm-Bawerk never developed a theory of money and appears to have not thought highly of Mises' work (see Garrison, 1999, pp. 119–120; Salerno, 1999b, pp. 41–42).

In his book, Mises advanced the Mengerian and Böhm-Bawerkian approach in many ways. These include the ordinal nature of marginal utility and its application to money, his regression theorem according to which money must originate as a commodity, and his monetary transmission mechanism, which showed that monetary injections were non-neutral. Mises' analysis stands in stark contrast to the contemporary works of Irving Fisher, who argued for an aggregative approach that relied on holistic concepts such as velocity and the price level, and who believed that money was neutral in the long run. Most importantly, Mises combined Böhm-Bawerk's capital theory with Knut Wicksell's natural rate of interest and developed his theory of the trade cycle, later known as Austrian Business Cycle Theory (ABCT). In this theory, Mises argued that the manipulation of money and credit by the central bank distorts interest rates and the structure of production, a process that inevitably leads to a bust.[17]

A critical part of Mises's work in *The Theory of Money and Credit* was a nascent theory of the role of monetary calculation in the coordination of economic affairs. Mises argued that the very phenomena of money presupposes an economic order based on productive specialization and private-property rights in producer as well as consumer goods. Money prices serve as guides to the human mind and as such are the essential tool in the economic calculation of alternative investment activities. After WWI, Mises further developed his ideas about the centrality of monetary calculation in coordinating advanced material production, first in his critique of "War Planning" in *Nation, State and Economy* (1983 [1919]), then with the theory of economic calculation he developed in "Economic Calculation in the

Socialist Commonwealth" (1935 [1920]) and, finally, with his more elaborate treatment in *Socialism* (1951 [1922]).[18]

In these works, Mises showed that the only way to rationally allocate
society's scarce means among competing ends — that is, the only way to
solve society's economic problem — was for entrepreneurs in the private-
property market economy to rely upon the knowledge provided by the
profit-and-loss signals indicated by changes in money prices. According to
Mises, private-property offers not only incentives to husband resources efficiently, but also provides the basis for exchange. It is in the market for the
means of production that exchange ratios are formed which constitute the
money prices that, by forming the basis for profit-and-loss accounting,
guide economic decisions. In socialist societies, economic calculation is rendered impossible because the abolition of private property in the factors of
production means that there is no market for these factors. Without a market, there will be no money prices that reflect the relative scarcities of the
factors. As a result, there will be no way to distinguish the most economical
projects from the array of those that are technologically feasible. Economic
calculation will be absent and, as a result, socialism cannot sustain a modern industrial economy. Mises's critique challenged how socialists understood the viability of their system and sparked the famous "socialist
calculation debate."

In his *Epistemological Problems of Economics* (1960 [1933]a, 1960 [1933]b),
Mises also made major contributions to the field of economic methodology.
Mises argued that sociology, or the general theory of human action, and its
most developed branch — economics — was a deductive system grounded on
the axiom of human action — which he argued was a priori — plus various
subsidiary empirical propositions. As, in his assessment, the field of sociology
had been diverted by the influence of Durkheim away from the more appropriate foundations laid by Max Weber, Mises adopted the term *praxeology*
to describe this science of human action. Mises's philosophical position stood
in stark contrast to the growing trend of his day toward, in one direction,
formalism, and, in another direction, positivism.

Mises's neighbors, the logical positivists of the Vienna Circle, argued for
the unity of science (rather than the methodological dualism advocated by
Mises), while the burgeoning formalist movement, perhaps best embodied
at the time by Karl Menger's (son of the Austrian school's founder)
Mathematical Kolloquium at the University of Vienna, insisted that economists should build formal models that would yield tentative hypotheses
that could be tested empirically and quantitatively (rather than the more

nuanced negation that might arise in the interpretation of history via theory that Mises envisioned).

During the second half of the 1930s, Mises published little technical economics as he was working on a planned treatise titled *Nationalökonomie*. It is also important to recall a critical point raised in the introduction, namely, the great migration from Vienna of Austrian economists throughout the 1930s. Moreover, Mises's works were not widely available in English, so the communication of his essential contributions to economics would be left to others in his Viennese research circle who moved to the United Kingdom and the United States in the 1930s. This opened the door for younger colleagues such as Fritz Machlup, Oskar Morgenstern, Gottfried Haberler, as well as contemporaries like Joseph Schumpeter, to convey the Austrian school's contributions to English-language scientific communities. The most prominent of the younger scholars, and the one most closely associated with Mises, was F. A. Hayek. Following his move to the London School of Economics in 1931, Hayek — along with the Englishmen Lionel Robbins, who headed the LSE economics department — would represent the ideas of the Austrian school in debate with both the market socialists and the Cambridge (U.K.) school best represented by John Maynard Keynes.

Although he was not among Mises' students, Hayek considered Mises his mentor and developed Mises' analyses in many ways, especially in the fields of trade-cycle theory and economic calculation. It was, in fact, Mises who provided Hayek with his first job as an economist at the Vienna Chamber of Commerce and the two worked in close collaboration for about a decade. Hayek would soon publish a number of essays and books on trade-cycle theory, particularly *Prices & Production* (1931a, 1935b), and *Monetary Theory and the Trade Cycle* (1933).[19]

In these works, Hayek expanded upon Böhm-Bawerk and Wicksell's theories, and refined the structure-of-production concept.[20] Hayek argued that the interest rate is really the price spread between various stages of production that capitalists would earn in long-run equilibrium. The interest rate would fall or rise depending on how the proportion of consumption to investment changed. He used this to show that the lengthening of the structure of production was either sustainable or not depending on whether it was caused by an increase in voluntary savings or by credit expansion. Mises and Hayek used ABCT to explain the onset of the Great Depression and the inability of governments to use deliberate policy to correct the misaligned structure. The Mises-Hayek explanation of the Great Depression was advanced in two works, *The Great Depression* (1934b) by Lionel Robbins and the unfortunately neglected *Banking and the Business Cycle* (1937) by the American economists Chester A. Phillips, T. F. McManus, and R. W. Nelson.[21] Further works in the ABCT tradition include: Fritz Machlup's *The Stock Market, Credit, and Capital Formation* (1940 [1931]), Richard von Strigl's *Capital and Production* (2000 [1934]) and Gottfried von Haberler's "Money and the Business Cycle" (1932).

In the 1930s, an English-language socialist calculation debate arose in response to Mises's original contribution. According to the market socialists, Mises' economic calculation problem could be overcome by solving, either via mathematics or trial-and-error, a Walrasian system of equations describing a general equilibrium condition. Hayek responded in *Collectivist Economic Planning* (1935a), a collection of essays on the controversy that he edited and to which he contributed two essays. Hayek soon wrote a third essay, included in his *Individualism and Economic Order* (1948), on the calculation debate. Hayek argued that solving such a system mathematically would be insuperably complex.[22] The socialists Oskar Lange and Abba Lerner responded that the managers of nationalized firms could "play market" and solve the economic problem via trial-and-error. However, Hayek argued that this "solution" still missed the fundamental properties of markets – that is, private property and market-determined prices – that allow for effective economic calculation. Hayek's point was that these attempted "solutions" to Mises' original socialist calculation critique presupposed the availability to the socialist policymaker or manager knowledge that could be *discovered* only in the marketplace. Hayek's "The Meaning of Competition" (1948 [1946]) would later deploy this same criticism against the sterile perfect competition model.

Unfortunately, by the beginning of WWII, the Lange-Lerner "solution" was widely accepted in the economics community, and Hayek's prescient warnings went unheeded. In addition, the perceived usefulness of ABCT went into decline throughout the decade, especially with the publication of John Maynard Keynes's *General Theory of Employment, Interest and Money* (1936), which forever altered the landscape of the economics discipline. Keynesian economics explained economic fluctuations using holistic macroeconomic aggregates that ignored the structure of production and the coordinating role of relative prices, as understood through the Hicksian IS-LM diagram. Keynes and Hayek had dueled earlier, beginning with Hayek's trenchant reviews of Keynes's previous *Treatise on Money* (1930) (Hayek, 1931b, 1931c, 1932; Keynes, 1931). By the end of the 1930s, it was generally accepted within the economics community that Keynes and his followers had won the debate. As a result, the Keynesian approach would dominate economic theory in the 1940s and beyond.[23] Other than Mises and Hayek, nearly all of the adherents of ABCT repudiated the theory and became Keynesians. The Austrians were consigned to the dustbin of history. Both Mises's *Nationalökonomie* (1940) and Hayek's *The Pure Theory of Capital* (1941) fell more or less stillborn from the press.

Mises would emigrate from Geneva (his home since leaving Vienna in 1934) to the United States in 1940. Though he struggled to find his way in an unfamiliar nation at the relatively advanced age of 60, Mises accepted an offer to work with the National Bureau of Economic Research, and soon published two books, *Bureaucracy* (1944a) and *Omnipotent Government* (1944b). Still in London, and convinced that the intellectual world had gone haywire due both to an epistemological attitude that refused to acknowledge human cognitive limitations with respect to social phenomena and an analytical error that ignored the role of institutions in social analysis, Hayek would soon embark on his, ultimately uncompleted, "Abuse of Reason" project. The sort of *epistemic institutionalism* that he had hinted at in his "Economics and Knowledge" (1937a) simply eluded his contemporaries. When he first embarked on this project with *Freedom and the Economic System* (1939a) and *The Road to Serfdom* (1944), Hayek was seen by his contemporaries as moving away from economics toward political theory and philosophy. There is a strong sense of intellectual isolation that both Mises and Hayek experienced in the immediate postwar era. It certainly seemed that the Austrians were down, but, as it happened, they would not be counted out.[24]

BEFORE THE REVIVAL: LACHMANN, ROTHBARD, AND KIRZNER

The decade of the 1940s is a critical time in our narrative because economics had abandoned the last vestiges of Austrian advancements in the past two decades and, by the early 1950s, had coalesced into the neoclassical synthesis. War-torn Europe would see a further migration of academic economists to the United States which, due to both the GI Bill and the Cold War, would experience a great expansion of higher education during the next three decades. The center of gravity within the science of economics moved decidedly to the United States after WWII, and to professional economists in the United States, the Austrian economists were simply outdated relics. It is not accurate to say that Mises and Hayek were unknown, but it is true that, by the 1950s, they were viewed as largely irrelevant to the further technical development of economics, an irrelevance fully captured in the JEL codes.[25]

The neoclassical synthesis was the post-WWII fusion of Walrasian and Marshallian microeconomics with Keynesian macroeconomics undergirded by increasingly mathematical methods in theory, and positivism in empirical research. The works that most contributed to this synthesis were Hicks' *Value and Capital* (1946), Stigler's *The Theory of Price* (1946), and Samuelson's *Foundations of Economic Analysis* (1947), the latter of which combined a coordinating Walrasian microeconomics with a discoordinating Keynesian macroeconomics (Boettke, 2012 [1997], pp. 272–73; Salerno, 2009, pp. xl–xlii, xxi–xxii).

However, even in this environment, Mises continued to work to advance Austrian economics. By far his most important work of the 1940s, and widely acknowledged to be the most important Austrian work of the 20th century, was his epochal *Human Action* (1949). An English-language revision of his earlier *Nationalökonomie* (1940), this sweeping treatise elaborated and refined his earlier advancements in money, calculation, and method, as well as in other fields (such as interventionism).[26] The bedrock of his system was his elucidation of the market process, where appraising entrepreneurs seek to make profits and avoid losses in accordance with the dictates of consumer sovereignty. In doing so he showed that the free market is the most effective institutional framework for the promotion of general welfare.

Although he mostly neglected his earlier work on capital theory, Hayek also continued to write in the 1940s and produced a collection of several of his most important early essays on knowledge, calculation, and the market process, titled *Individualism and Economic Order* (1948). In the 1950s, Mises and Hayek would continue to write about economics, especially its epistemology and methodology.[27] However, Hayek's focus was primarily on philosophy and legal theory, while the aging Mises concentrated on popular articles meant to articulate economic principles to the layman. It was ultimately in this decade that the responsibility for advancing technical Austrian economics would be passed to a new generation, best represented by Ludwig Lachmann, Murray Rothbard, and Israel Kirzner.

Lachmann had been a student of Hayek's at the LSE and his career in economics focused on capital and the theory of expectations, two fields also developed in Hayek's early work. Lachmann's most important work was *Capital and Its Structure* (1956), a book grounded in the structure-of-production tradition. He argued that the economy contained a vast network of heterogeneous capital goods constructed according to the various plans and forecasts of economic actors. Lachmann's work on expectations and their role with regard to convergence to general equilibrium would continue to evolve over the course of his career. He came increasingly under the influence of G. L. S. Shackle, and would eventually argue that divergent expectations prevent a convergence to equilibrium, a controversial position that became a particular bone of contention among later Austrians.[28] However, after *Capital and Its Structure*, Lachmann was drawn into university administration and only returned to research in the late 1960s. At the start of the next decade, Lachmann published *The Legacy of Max Weber* (1971).

In contrast to Lachmann, Rothbard and Kirzner, who were both a generation younger than Lachmann, were working on their PhD's in the 1950s and were taught (officially or otherwise) by Mises. Although not a formal student, Rothbard attended Mises' seminars throughout the 1950s, while Kirzner received his PhD directly under Mises. Both sought to position themselves firmly within the Misesian tradition.[29]

In the 1950s, Rothbard's most important essays in the Austrian tradition were "Towards a Reconstruction of Utility and Welfare Economics" (1956) and "In Defense of 'Extreme Apriorism'" (1957). The first, published in a *festschrift* honoring Mises, defended Austrian views on utility and offered a new welfare theory. The second was a response to a debate between Machlup and Hutchison on the relationship between positivism and Mises' apriorism. Machlup offered a defense of his former mentor against Hutchinson's critique. Rothbard argued against both Hutchinson and Machlup's interpretation and defended Mises' praxeological framework as one where economic laws are deduced from realistic self-evident axioms.[30]

Rothbard was commissioned by the Volker Fund, an institute that promoted the ideas of Austrians and likeminded scholars, to write a textbook version of *Human Action*. The underlying ideas was that Mises's treatise assumed an audience familiar with technical economics, so a more popular treatment was needed in order to communicate Mises's ideas to the laymen.[31] Rothbard worked on this project for several years and eventually decided to develop a full-blown treatise in the style of Mises' work. The result was *Man, Economy, and State* (1962a), a landmark book in Austrian economics and one of the core texts in the subsequent rival of interest in Austrian economics among younger research scholars in the 1970s.

Rothbard's work was both an alternative to Samuelson's *Economics* (1948) and an attempt to return to the older style 19th-century treatise in economics that proceeded in steps from the basics of economic reasoning to more advanced, and at points very controversial, positions in theory and public policy. Among Rothbard's many theoretical innovations was a production theory that synthesized earlier strands of thought in the Austrian tradition. Rothbard combined the structure-of-production theory of capital with the pure time-preference theory of interest to provide a unified position on the interest rate (Salerno, 2009, xxvii). Rothbard's production theory represented the Austrian middle ground between isolated Marshallian firms and holistic Keynesian aggregates. The theory was further distinguished from Walrasian general equilibrium in that it concentrated on real-world dynamic adjustment processes. Rothbard also resurrected Fetter's rent theory to help explain factor pricing and incomes.[32]

Rothbard wrote a second important book, *America's Great Depression* (1963a), which provided an up-to-date Mises-Hayek explanation of the Great Depression. *America's Great Depression* was meant to challenge the prevailing wisdom according to which the Great Depression demonstrated the inherent instability of free-market capitalism and the necessity of government management of the economy in order to avoid the social ills of economic volatility and mass unemployment. Rothbard argued that the Federal Reserve's inflationary credit expansion in the 1920s caused an unsustainable bubble that lead to the 1929 stock market crash. Rothbard further catalogued the litany of government interventions that exacerbated the subsequent depression. Needless to say, Rothbard's Austrian account stood in stark contrast to the prevailing Keynesian and Monetarist explanations of the Great Depression.[33]

Though four years younger than Rothbard, Israel Kirzner started publishing around the same time.[34] In his first book, *The Economic Point of View* (1960), a published version of the dissertation he had completed under Mises,[35] Kirzner provided an intellectual history of the evolution of the economics discipline, chronicling its transformation from the science of wealth to the science of welfare. At the pinnacle of this science was Mises' praxeological system. In this book, Kirzner briefly touched upon a point that he would later develop more fully, namely, the relationship between Robbinsian economizing and Misesian human action.

Kirzner's second book, *Market Theory and the Price System* (1963), was a textbook intended for the contemporary neoclassical audience of the 1960s that attempted to fuse older neoclassical price theory with Austrian insights. It marked the beginning of Kirzner's later efforts to use Austrian insights within a neoclassical system. Perhaps the most important insight was Kirzner's analysis, using the Böhm-Bawerkian marginal pairs and

Wicksteedian total demand-stock framework, of convergence to equilibrium. In fine Wicksteedian fashion, Kirzner showed that, in any given market, incorrect speculative forecasts lead to disequilibrium prices. Transactions at these disequilibrium prices lead to a revision of plans and encourage learning among market participants that direct prices towards equilibrium. This analysis concentrated on the equilibrating *process*, rather than the equilibrium *end-state*, an important point considering the Austrian emphasis on real-world disequilibrium pricing, and would lead directly to Kirzner's later work on the equilibrating entrepreneur.

While both Rothbard and Kirzner were able to penetrate the mainstream by publishing in academic journals such as the *American Economic Review*, *Journal of Political Economy*, and *Quarterly Journal of Economics*, this was *not* where they concentrated their efforts to communicate to fellow scholars. They aimed instead at producing scholarly monographs and textbooks; and they both wrote to a broader audience about the importance of economic thought for understanding the world and public policy. Compare these aims with the activities of contemporaries such as Gary Becker and James Buchanan — both methodological individualists and (more or less) free market advocates — and the point we raised in the introduction concerning the pre-Internet mechanism of sorting the scientific and the practical should become clear. Becker and Buchanan certainly produced scholarly monographs, but these were typically followed by detailed scientific studies published in professional journals; neither wrote textbooks or treatises, let alone popular essays, in the early years of their careers. Becker and Buchanan built their respective scientific careers during the 1950s and 1960s, and they faced the same hostility in terms of advancing their unique research agendas in the economics profession. Yet, unlike Rothbard and Kirzner, both would go on to win widespread professional acclaim, including Nobel Prizes.

Why did Rothbard and Kirzner pursue their careers in this unorthodox fashion? There's no need for psychological speculation here. It suffices to point out that the journals of the era were allergic (and increasingly so) to certain styles of economic argument. In such an environment, the decision to write books and popular essays was an obvious one.[36] For very personal reasons, both remained somewhat more distant from the economics profession than would be considered normal for a young research scholar. This is all the more puzzling considering that both had easy access to the mainstream in the form of Fritz Machlup, a very social person who was seriously engaged with the elite of the economics profession, and who certainly could have encouraged these young professors in their interactions with non-Austrian economists. Alas, such social aspects of science were not inculcated in the American Austrians. So it was multiple factors, both within the profession and through decisions taken by practicing Austrian economics during the third quarter of the 20th century, which tended to reinforce the *sub rosa* existence of the Austrian School.

Other important books in the Austrian tradition published during this period include Henry Hazlitt's *The Failure of the "New Economics"* (1959) and *The Critics of Keynesian Economics* (1960)[37] and W. H. Hutt's *Keynesianism-Retrospect and Prospect* (1963). Both Hazlitt and Hutt were consumed with bringing to light the defects of the Keynesian system. One could be forgiven for thinking that the torrent of books published by notable authors during these years might have sparked an Austrian revival in the 1960s, but this was not the case. These books were widely ignored by the profession. Moreover, little work was done in Austrian economics proper during the rest of the decade.[38]

However, those books − particularly Rothbard's *Man, Economy, and State* (1962a) − did inspire a renewal of interest in Austrian economics among libertarian scholars and younger students.[39] The mainline of Austrian economics had always been oriented toward the free market. Mises's work further encouraged the public perception of this orientation to such a degree that, during these years, he was commonly dismissed as an anachronistic free-market ideologue. Of course, Rothbard's writings, academic and popular, as well as his political activism, led him to an even more extreme *laissez-faire* stance. For better or worse, the future of Austrian economics was monogamously wedded to political libertarianism.[40] And by the early 1970s, a full-blown Austrian revival was on the horizon.

AUSTRIAN ECONOMICS THROUGH THE END OF THE 20TH CENTURY: NEW PATHS AND TENSIONS

Ludwig von Mises was named as a Distinguished Fellow of the American Economic Association in 1969. This was a considerable scientific honor, but the impression was that the award was for lifetime achievement and not an indication that future researchers should follow Mises on the Austrian path. Austrian economics had its time in the scientific limelight, and now that Mises was nearing his 90s, his peers could, without harm to their professional reputations, recognize his long illustrious career. Mises was always viewed as someone who belonged to the 19th century and the European culture of a bygone era, rather than the modern age of science. By this time, Hayek was retired not only from Chicago, but also from Freiburg, and had moved to a post in Salzburg that didn't have graduate students or even a functioning library. So, in effect, the two leading representatives of the Austrian school were retired, and younger scholars such as Rothbard and Kirzner were making little professional impact. From a scientific perspective, the Austrian school was at its nadir around the year 1970. However, things soon started to change in drastic ways.

The beginning of the 1970s marked a new, dramatically different, phase in Austrian economics. At this stage, the critical institutional actor was the Institute for Humane Studies and the critical individual influence was Murray Rothbard. Rothbard's blending, and at times blurring, of the lines between Austrian economics, revisionist history, and a radical and consistent libertarianism was always appealing to F. A. "Baldy" Harper, founder of IHS. Harper was a professor at Cornell University in the 1940s, when he was chastised for using Hayek's *The Road To Serfdom* in one of his classes. He was frustrated with what he saw as the closing of minds on campus — a manifestation of an earlier age's political correctness — and was lured away from academia to work for the Foundation for Economic Education (FEE) in New York, under the expectation that they would develop advanced educational and research programs. However, despite efforts by various staff members and longtime associates of FEE to establish a new "American Graduate School," the project never materialized.

So, by the end of the 1950s, Harper was looking to establish a new institute consistent with his own vision. In a lovely alcove, adjacent to the equally lovely Stanford University campus, he established the Institute for Humane Studies — the name was meant to reflect the 19th-century French liberal tradition of the *sciences humanies*. Harper's idea was to cultivate a new generation of scholars who would research topics of consequence, and once again colonize academic positions in philosophy, politics, economics, history, and law. The Institute continued many of the programs that the Volker Fund had sponsored in the 1950s to cultivate scholars working in political economy. The Volker Fund always had a strong commitment to Austrian economics and, in fact, was the main source of financial support for both Mises and Hayek following their arrival in America.

Starting in the 1970s, various conferences were organized devoted exclusively to Austrian economics, and with the success of these programs, plans were made to establish new institutes, as well as new graduate programs within which the Austrian tradition could play a significant role. Since

Rothbard was not a faculty member at a PhD-granting institution, but was well positioned within the Cato Institute[41] and the Libertarian Party, he tended to focus on ideological activities, while the effort to develop new graduate programs in Austrian economics were centered around Kirzner at NYU. It was the beginning of a new period when Austrians would attempt to seriously re-engage in academic discourse. This would soon lead to inter-necine debates that, at times, would appear to fracture the school.[42]

By the 1970s, the American revival of the Austrian school was firmly coupled with the libertarian movement intellectually, institutionally, and financially. A case in point was Rothbard's *Power and Market* (1970).[43] In this book, Rothbard provided Austrian critiques of *all* forms of government intervention. He included a brief analysis of stateless societies and the private provision of law, a system known as anarcho-capitalism, which would galvanize both Austrians and, more generally, libertarians, and serve as an important research topic for future generations of scholars.

Rothbard was having considerable success advancing Austrian ideas through the popular libertarian movement. Two publications founded by Rothbard, *Libertarian Forum* and *The Journal of Libertarian Studies*, frequently featured, in addition to Rothbard's own writings, essays by younger Austrian scholars. A mainstream publisher agreed to publish Rothbard's book *For a New Liberty* (1973), and he was profiled in several mainstream periodicals. Robert Nozick's *Anarchy, State and Utopia* (1974), heavily influenced by Rothbard, won the National Book Award, and Nozick was catapulted to superstar status within the discipline of philosophy.

At the same time, Kirzner continued to communicate the nuances of the Austrian approach to the market process in various essays and monographs. In 1973, the University of Chicago Press published Kirzner's highly influential *Competition and Entrepreneurship*, which described Kirzner's theory of the entrepreneur – a human actor alert to previously unrecognized opportunities for mutual gains from exchange – in its full efflorescence. In his earlier writings Kirzner had touched upon the idea that purposive human actors will be alert to that to which is in their interest to be alert to. He more fully developed these ideas in *Competition and Entrepreneurship*. The concept of the entrepreneur would be the central focus of Kirzner's scholarly activities for the rest of his career.

Kirzner emphasized that neoclassical price theory focuses on the end-state of general equilibrium rather than the process of equilibration. Arrow (1959) had earlier identified a central problem with the price-taking assumption at the heart of the Walrasian depiction of the market:

systematic market adjustment guided through relative price adjustments simply could not be modeled in the Walrasian fashion. Kirzner thought the Mises-Hayek theory of the entrepreneurial market process explained the equilibration process. Working within the neoclassical framework, Kirzner used his theory of entrepreneurship to fill in this lacuna in the theory of price adjustment. Kirzner's central insight, which he attributed to Mises, is that entrepreneurship is alertness to previously unknown profit opportunities. Entrepreneurs recognize profit opportunities and correct disequilibrium prices through arbitrage, thereby facilitating convergence to general equilibrium. Kirzner's book was initially highly praised within the Austrian movement, but would later stir some considerable controversy concerning the nature of both equilibration and the entrepreneur.

The year 1974 would prove to be a crucial year for the Austrian school. A cadre of young research scholars was posed to pursue advanced study in economics. The Austrian program at New York University was developing quickly, with a regular seminar, PhD fellowships, visiting professors, and post-doctoral fellowships. The time seemed right to bring students and faculty together to start a more organized scholarly movement. In June 1974, the IHS organized a conference in South Royalton, Vermont devoted exclusively to Austrian economics. Sadly, Mises had died the previous year and, for various reasons, Hayek could not attend the conference. Nonetheless, the South Royalton gathering was a rousing success. Papers by the next generation of Austrians, namely, Lachmann, Rothbard, and Kirzner were presented on diverse topics like method, capital, money, and equilibration. The conference produced a volume edited by Edwin G. Dolan titled *The Foundations of Austrian Economics* (1976). Shortly after South Royalton, Lawrence Moss organized a conference at the Southern Economics Association dedicated to the economics of Ludwig von Mises, and these papers were published in a volume edited by Moss titled *The Economics of Ludwig von Mises* (1976).

However, by far the most momentous event of 1974 − or, for that matter, most any other year − occurred in October when Hayek was awarded the Nobel Prize for his "pioneering work in the theory of money and economic fluctuations and ... penetrating analysis of the interdependence of economic, social and institutional phenomena" (Nobel, 1974). Hayek shared the Prize with Post-Keynesian Gunnar Myrdal, who was quite bothered to have to split the Prize with a déclassé Austrian economist − but Hayek didn't mind and the community of Austrians was elated. The world's attention was once again focused on the economic ideas of the Austrian school.

And so the burgeoning revival of the Austrian school received a further, and much-welcomed, burst of attention and expansion. The Institute for Humane Studies organized two further conferences on Austrian economics, the first, in 1975, in Hartford, Connecticut, and the second the following year at Windsor Castle in Scotland. The papers of the Hartford conference were gathered into a volume, edited by Louis Spadaro, titled *New Directions in Austrian Economics* (1978). This volume featured essays by the older generation of Austrian scholars as well as papers by younger scholars like Mario Rizzo, Dominick Armentano, Gerald P. O'Driscoll, and Roger Garrison. Further conferences in later years generated volumes edited by Rizzo (1979a, 1979b) and Kirzner (1982a, 1982b). Meanwhile, Hayek (1976) wrote a book outlining a new plan for monetary reform; O'Driscoll (1977a, 1977b) wrote on Hayek's conception of economics as a "coordination problem"; Kirzner (1979) compiled his 1970s essays on entrepreneurship; and Armentano (1982) developed a Rothbardian analysis of antitrust law.

Lachmann joined Kirzner at NYU as a visiting professor in 1975. Graduate programs soon started at Auburn University and George Mason University, the latter of which also created the Center for the Study of Market Processes. Finally, in 1982 Llewellyn Rockwell, with the assistance of Rothbard, founded the Ludwig von Mises Institute, which soon established *The Review of Austrian Economics* (RAE), a new academic journal devoted to Austrian economics.[44]

With this great proliferation of new forums for Austrian economics came various doctrinal disputes. The three main factions, headed, respectively, by Rothbard, Kirzner, and Lachmann, would debate three key issues for years to come.[45]

The first issue related to Kirzner's theory of the entrepreneur. A rift could already be noticed at South Royalton, when Kirzner and Lachmann presented papers that contained divergent positions on the nature of equilibration. Kirzner (1976) staked a position similar to his earlier work and argued that entrepreneurial alertness is the key to equilibration. From this perspective, in their search for profit opportunities, entrepreneurs correct market disparities and facilitate convergence of expectations to bring the economy closer to equilibrium. Lachmann (1976a), however, argued that entrepreneurial expectations could not only converge to bring the economy to equilibrium, but also diverge and lead the economy away from equilibrium. In the latter case, entrepreneurial activity would not correct previous errors but, instead, compound them and divert the market process from equilibrium. Lachmann's position led to a form of nihilism: the future was unknowable and so economists could predict little about it. The possibility of divergent entrepreneurial expectations was seen to run riot over previously held economic laws. O'Driscoll (1977a, 1977b) suggested that the resolution of the debate lay in the theory of spontaneous order.

Subsequent articles extended the discussion to the related Lachmannian themes of a "kaleidic" society (a term borrowed from Shackle) and radical subjectivism, a term used to describe the full implications of a main Austrian tenet.[46] Mario Rizzo and Gerald O'Driscoll published *The Economics of Time and Ignorance* (1985), a book strongly influenced by Lachmann. The book pursued subjectivism to its logical conclusion and restated Austrian principles using this new system. The reactions from both Rothbard and Kirzner were unenthusiastic, to say the least (Baird, 1987; Kirzner, 1985b). Lachmann (1985), however, praised the book, which would subsequently exert considerable influence on younger Austrians.[47]

A related point of disagreement related to aspects of Kirzner's entrepreneur. Kirzner (1973) argued that the entrepreneurial function could be analytically separated from the capitalist function (in the sense that entrepreneurs can be propertyless) and is characterized by being alert to profit opportunities and acting on that through arbitrage. Among others, Rothbard (1974, 1985) objected to the ownerless property and argued that entrepreneurship is better characterized by uncertainty bearing and appraisement rather than alertness. Kirzner (1982a, 1982b) defended his entrepreneur from his critics and continued to elaborate on his theory in future works (1985a, 1989, 1992).

The second debate concerned money. At South Royalton, Rothbard presented a paper on what he considered to be the major tenets of Austrian monetary theory. He posed three questions for future research: (1) What is the best route to free-market money?, (2) What is the relationship between a system of full reserves and one of free banking?, and (3) What is the Austrian definition of the money supply? The second question, in particular, led to considerable controversy. Rothbard favored a system of 100% reserves and argued for the illegitimacy of fractional-reserve banking. A free-banking system, though it would effectively limit credit expansion and tend to full reserves, was nevertheless second-best.

Against this position, Lawrence H. White articulated a theory of fractional reserve free banking, later to be elaborated by his student and future colleague George Selgin in *The Theory of Free Banking* (1988). White argued that credit expansion would be held in check in a system of free banking and that banks would tend to lower reserve ratios as the public grew more comfortable holding bank money. White cited the example of

Scotland in the late 18th and early 19th centuries as an approximation of this system. White (1985a, 1985b, 1986) further criticized Rothbard's position on the supposed illegitimacy of fractional reserves and his overly broad definition of the money supply (1978).[48] Rothbard (1988) and Sechrest (1988), a free banker otherwise sympathetic to White's monetary work, criticized White's position on the history of free banking in Scotland. Block (1988) and Salerno (1987) defended Rothbard, respectively, on the illegitimacy of fractional-reserve banking, and the broad definition of the money supply. Monetary debates continued well into the late 1990s and remain unresolved today.[49]

The last debate concerned the nature of calculation, coordination, and the respective views of Mises and Hayek on these matters, views that resurfaced to the forefront with the end of the communist countries around this time. One popular interpretation was that Hayek and Robbins retreated from Mises's arguments for the "impossibility" of socialism and the Lange-Lerner solution showed that socialism was possible. However, in his influential *Rivalry and Central Planning* (1985b), Don Lavoie maintained that Austrians had never retreated from the Misesian position and that the crucial concept, the entrepreneurial aspect of the competitive-discovery process, was always inherent in their works.

While applauding Lavoie's work, Kirzner (1988), stressed that Mises and Hayek's views did evolve over time – and for the better – from a static critique to a dynamic one, which later became the competitive-discovery process argument made explicit in Kirzner's works on entrepreneurship. This position was challenged by Salerno (1990a, 1990b, 1993) and Rothbard (1991). Salerno noted apparent differences between Mises and Hayek on knowledge and coordination. He argued that Mises's original static view, rather than the later uncertainty argument, was always, according to Mises, the key to the calculation problem.[50] Moreover, according to Salerno, Hayek and Robbins made a fateful error in retreating from the hardcore Misesian position to a defense based on the complexity of the relevant phenomena; properly understood, Hayek's knowledge problem described in "The Use of Knowledge in Society" (1945) was fundamentally different from the Misesian problem of economic calculation. Salerno's argument led to a lengthy debate (e.g., see Boettke, 1998, 2000, 2001; Caldwell, 2002; Herbener, 1996; Hoppe, 1996; Horwitz, 2004; Hulsmann, 1997; Kirzner, 1996; Salerno, 1994a, 1994b, 1996, 1999b, 2002; Yeager, 1994, 1997).[51]

By the 1990s a changing of the guard in the Austrian school was evident as many of the old guard passed away or retired and the generation of revival-era scholars assumed positions of intellectual leadership, often at research universities where, unlike in previous decades, they could train graduate students and chair doctoral dissertations. The Austrians who reached intellectual maturity in the last quarter of the 20th century had, by the end of this period, become elder statesmen of the tradition. Moreover, not only were they training graduate students, but they had succeeded in publishing their work in top journals and with respected academic presses. By the new millennium, there were more economists pursuing the Austrian approach than at any time since the interwar years, and this number has only increased in the last 15 years.[52]

AUSTRIAN ECONOMICS IN THE NEW MILLENNIUM AND BEYOND: THE BRIGHT PRESENT AND THE PROMISING FUTURE

There is no need for the new generation of Austrian economists to continue the internecine doctrinal disputes that have often hindered scientific progress. These young scholars should feel unencumbered by previous personality conflicts and focus instead on presenting the best arguments possible. But, of course, scars never fully heal and those who lived through them easily recognize traces of these debates in contemporary Austrian writings. Many of these issues have their roots in the intermingling of a scientific tradition with an ideological agenda, and the contentious idea that there is a coherent and intellectually respectable position called "Austro-Libertarianism."

With the advent of the Internet and social media, there has been an undeniable acceleration of the "democratization" of economic discourse in the new millennium. This democratization, we have emphasized, bears benefits as well as costs. From the perspective of the *academic project* of advancing Austrian economics, one potential cost is that of reinforcing the "outsider" status of the school. Of course it isn't an either-or decision and academics can take advantage of new technologies to engage a variety of audiences including: scientific peers, students, decision-makers in both the private and public sectors, and the general public. This approach requires an appreciation for engaging the academic community through academic outlets.

On the other hand, the combination of the Internet and the serious economic policy issues of the 2000s have brought many Austrian insights to public attention. The resurgence of ABCT as a viable theory towards understanding the 2008 financial crisis as opposed to alternative mainstream macroeconomic theories has led to renewed interest in Austrian economics in general and explains the recent reentry into the JEL codes.[53] The influence of U.S. Congressman Ron Paul and other libertarian organizations during the 2008 and 2012 Presidential elections also increased interest in the Austrian school. Many young scholars in the 21st century first encountered the Austrian school of economics not in a classroom lecture or an assigned reading by an economics professor, but through Google. Without a doubt, thanks to advances in modern technology, more students have watched interviews of Hayek on YouTube than have ever enrolled in his classes or attended his public lectures.

Buchanan (1979) taught that the most important function of an economist is didactic – to inculcate an appreciation of the spontaneous order of the market economy so that students become informed participants in the democratic process. If we take Buchanan at his word, then the democratizing aspects of new media must be judged a positive development. That said, we would be wise to keep in mind the warning from proto-Austrian Frédéric Bastiat: "The worst thing that can happen to a good cause is, not to be skillfully attacked, but to be ineptly defended" (Boettke, 2013, p. 45). While the Internet provides virtually unlimited access to information that would otherwise remain obscure, it requires disciplined judgment to truly learn from that information. A background in technical economics is an essential instrument of such discipline, but acquiring that background requires sustained study at a high intellectual level.

Important developments in the modern and contemporary Austrian school are adeptly summarized in *The Elgar Companion to Austrian Economics* (1994), *Handbook of Contemporary Austrian Economics* (2010), and *The Oxford Handbook of Austrian Economics* (2015).[54] However, these developments can also be seen in a survey of recent publications that have addressed, for example, problems of economic development (such as Coyne, 2007, 2013 and Powell, 2014), or works that consider the Global Financial Crisis (such as Koppl, 2014), and the various commentaries on the crisis and monetary economics in general (e.g., see Horwitz, 2012; Salerno, 2010, 2012; Selgin, 2010; Selgin, Lastrapes, & White, 2012; White, 2011). There are many scholars who have also made recent contributions to the fields of entrepreneurship and organization theory (e.g., see Foss & Klein, 2010; Foss, 2012; Holcombe, 2007; Klein, 2010; Langlois, 2013; Lewin & Baetjer, 2011; Lewin & Phelan, 2000; Sautet, 2000). Contemporary Austrian economists have made fundamental contributions to challenging new research programs concerning endogenous rule formation and self-governing social orders such as Leeson (2009, 2014), Skarbek (2014), and Stringham (2015). Finally, Austrians have made significant contributions to a growing "cultural economy" research program that considers (inter alia) the responsiveness of communities to devastating crises (Chamlee-Wright, 2010; Storr, 2013).

The contemporary Austrian school represents a thriving community. These scholars are constantly teaching, publishing, and promoting their work. Though points of emphasis and applications have shifted throughout the years, when the Austrian school celebrates its sesquicentennial in 2021, the core characteristics of the School will essentially be those that guided Carl Menger.

NOTES

1. In *Living Economics* (2012), Boettke argues that there is a "mainline" of economics and political economy that runs from Adam Smith and David Hume to Mises and Hayek, and from Mises and Hayek to Buchanan and Vernon Smith. This intellectual line is defined by substantive propositions about how the economic system works. There is also a "mainstream" of economics and political economy. However, Boettke argues that this is merely a "sociological" moniker that indicates nothing more than what is currently fashionable among elite economists. There have been several periods through the history of economics when the "mainline" and the "mainstream" were in close alignment, but there have been other moments of significant divergence. During these times of divergence, Boettke contends, various "schools of thought" emerge to act in an entrepreneurial fashion so as to bring them back into alignment. Recent examples of such entrepreneurial "schools" include "property rights economics," "public choice economics," "new institutional economics," and "market process economics." Of course, it should also be acknowledged that those who think the "mainline" is mistaken – Marxists, Historicists, Institutionalists, Keynesians, and Radicals – also engage in entrepreneurial acts to widen the divergence. See White's *The Clash of Economic Ideas* (2012) for a history of the main theoretical and policy-relevant debates of the 20th century.

2. On the other hand, part of the great attraction of the Austrian school of economics to the amateur enthusiast is that one of the main lessons of its teachings is that the conceit of the expert must always be held in check in the realm of public policy. Mises, in fact, argues in *Human Action* that the role of the economist is to challenge the conceit of those in power. And, a close reading of Hayek's Nobel Prize lecture, "The Pretence of Knowledge" (1989), as well as his *The Fatal Conceit* (1991) will reveal a similar indictment of the arrogance of the "expert." So how do you temper the conceit of the expert, but recognize the earned authority of the scientific expert? (see Levy & Peart, 2012).

3. Menger did not actually use the term marginal utility. The first Austrian to do so was Friedrich von Wieser. In contrast to his contemporaries, for Menger, marginal utility was a ranking, or a choice among two goods, and not a psychological concept measuring satisfaction.

4. Menger (1892, 1950 [1871]) described the formation of money in this way. The hallmark of this style of reasoning is that the analyst derives the "invisible-hand" theorem from the "rational choice" postulate via institutional analysis. In other words, the analyst begin with purposive actors then specify the institutional filter within which they pursue their purposes and interact with others pursuing their purposes, and then identify the equilibrating tendencies from the interplay of the logic of action with the logic of the situation. See Boettke, *Living Economics* (2012) for a discussion of this style of reasoning and its centrality to the "mainline" of economics and political economy.

5. Böhm-Bawerk would revise both books throughout his career. They were combined, with additional essays, into the three-volume treatise *Capital and Interest* (1959 [1921]). Mises considered Böhm-Bawerk's works "the most eminent contribution to modern economic theory" and strove to build off both his and Menger's insights (Mises, 1990b, p. 155). In addition, Hayek's work on capital and business-cycle theory in the 1930s was based off of Böhm-Bawerk's theories.

6. Böhm-Bawerk also substantially developed and explicated this theory (Böhm-Bawerk, 1962 [1894]).

7. This Austrian analysis of costs is fundamentally different from the Marshallian theory, which implied Neo-Ricardian real cost as the long-run determinant of the value of goods (Robbins, 1933, p. xvii).

8. For example, his theory of cost and value imputation is based on a nonmonetary communist economy. Mises harshly criticized Wieser and acknowledged that some of his theories could justify considering him more of a Walrasian than Austrian (Mises, 2009 [1978], pp. 27–28).

9. For more on Menger and Böhm-Bawerk, see Salerno (1999a) and Garrison (1999) respectively. For more on the distinctiveness of the founding Austrians in comparison to the Marshallians and Walrasians, see Endres (1997).

10. This is in sharp contrast to the Marshallian forward-sloping supply curve that is supposed to interact with an instantaneous demand curve. This Marshallian supply curve is particularly influential in modern partial-equilibrium analysis.

11. When discussing the Austrian qualities of Wicksteed, Kirzner (1999, p. 103), notes that both he and Rothbard relied upon Wicksteed's contributions in their respective price theories. Wicksteed's influence both at the LSE and, through Frank Knight, at Chicago is often overlooked in discussions of the subsequent development of economic theory. The "common-knowledge" of economists at different points in time and at different academic institutions is a topic that deserves much greater recognition and investigation. Irwin Collier's "Economics in the Rear-View Mirror" project is a potential corrective of this deficiency (see http://www.irwincollier.com/).

12. Rothbard built off of Fetter's rent theory. For a collection of his works, see Fetter (1977).

13. In 1932, Mises argued that the Austrian, Marshallian, and Walrasian schools were different only in their methods of presentation. However, his remarks should

be understood in context. What he meant was that Austrian and Neoclassical economists, as opposed to Historicists and Socialists, shared common ground with regard to the theoretical character of economics and their refutations of interventionist dogma. However, when focusing more on theoretical nuances, Mises acknowledged important differences between the schools (Boettke, 2012 [1997], pp. 268–260; Salerno, 2009, pp. xxviii–xxix).

14. This is the reason, we argue, for Hayek's statement in *The Counter-Revolution of Science* that Mises was ahead of his contemporaries (Hayek, 1952, p. 52).

15. Schumpeter moved to a teaching post in Bonn, Germany in 1925 and then to Harvard in 1932, so his role in the Austrian community of scientific economists was minimal after that time. Mayer assumed Wieser's chair at the University of Vienna and later ascended to the presidency of the Austrian Economics Society, as well as the role of main editor of *Zeitschrift für Sozialpolitik und Verwaltung*. Mayer is discounted historically due to his shameful accommodation of the Nazi regime. His career was typically judged by those were forced to migrate in the 1930s as a personal and professional failure. But, it must be acknowledged that, in the 1920s, he and Schumpeter were major influences in the community of Austrian economists.

16. Far from following in Böhm-Bawerk's footsteps, Schumpeter's work was closer in spirit to Wieser and Walras. Indeed, Böhm-Bawerk criticized Schumpeter's theories (Salerno, 1999b, pp. 39–41). Due to the educational-institutional structure of the Austro-Hungarian Empire, academic appointments to full-time chairs at the University of Vienna were both rare and political. Mises's failure to secure a chair must be interpreted in this context. In any case, it should be remembered that Mises was several times the second choice in such deliberations. Still, as has often been pointed out, a full-time chair for Mises was a hard sell because (a) he was Jewish, (b) he was a classical liberal, and (c) he didn't suffer fools. It has been pointed out that someone with Mises' considerable accomplishments could get a full-time appointment with any two of these traits, but not with all three. However, it is important to stress that Mises's position as *Privatdozent* at the University of Vienna did not limit his subsequent accomplishments. The international reputation of his research seminar was such that, through his connections with the Rockefeller Foundation, he was able to secure travel funding for several of his students and finance the operations of the Austrian Institute for Business Cycle Research.

17. Mises would continue to develop and refine his monetary theory throughout the 1920s and early 1930s. For collections of these essays, see Mises (1978, 1990a).

18. The seeds of economic calculation were in Böhm-Bawerk's description of the Law of Costs, and can also be seen in Wieser's discussion of the problem of economic planning.

19. Later essays can be found in Hayek (1939a, 1939b). See also his book on monetary theory (1937b).

20. Contrast the Austrian capital and interest theory with those of contemporary Marshallians and the Chicago school economist Frank Knight. Although Knight would influence later Austrians on the problems of entrepreneurship, profit and loss, and probability theory, his work on capital and interest is considered anathema. In particular, Knight argued that capital was a self-perpetuating homogenous fund and that time was not an important factor in production. He also banished

time-preference as a determinant of interest, something that Hayek initially accepted before returning to an eclectic Böhm-Bawerkian approach completely at odds with the Fetter-Mises pure time-preference theory of interest.

21. Robbins would be a particularly important colleague of Hayek at the London school of Economics. During the early 1930s in addition to the above book he wrote several Austrian essays on cost (1930, 1934a, 1934b, 1953 [1934]) and introductions to works of Mises, Hayek, and Wicksteed (1931, 1933, 1934a, 1934b). He also wrote *An Essay on the Nature and Significance of Economic Science* (1932), which was a methodological book grounded in the Misesian tradition.

22. Robbins (1934a, 1934b) also argued along similar lines. This method of argumentation was seen by many contemporaries as changing the Austrian position to one of the impracticability rather than, as argued by Mises, the impossibility of effective socialism.

23. For a comparison of Keynes' and Hayek's views, see White (2012).

24. It is important to remember that, at this time, Schumpeter, Morgenstern, Machlup, Haberler, etc. were all making their own way in their new academic homes. Machlup, in particular, is a case study of academic assimilation. To the discerning reader, Machlup's Misesianism is evident throughout his economics, but to those who think of Mises only in terms of a dogmatic insistence on *laissez faire*, Machlup might seem to have been cured of Misesianism. However, critics misunderstood the Misesian position on methodology and were completely unsympathetic to his politics, and so, neglected the profound affinities between Machlup and Mises.

25. This is something of an overstatement with respect to Hayek's "The Use of Knowledge in Society" (1945), which would in fact stimulate several generations of economic theorists, for example, the mechanism design work of Hurwicz, the information economics of Stigler, subsequent developments in information-theoretic economics by Stiglitz, and modern work on imperfect-knowledge economics by Frydman. This being said, Hayek's own unique understanding of the knowledge-generating role of the competitive market process would not be picked up in these rather "mainstream" efforts (Boettke & O'Donnell, 2013).

26. Mises wrote that only in *Nationalökonomie* did he fully explicate the theory of economic calculation and presented a unified price theory grounded in praxeology (2009 [1978], p. 95). This led to him describe the pricing process in terms of ordinal rankings of money and goods as opposed to the indifference curve barter framework which assumed a numeraire. Another important advancement was his elaboration of Fetter's pure time preference theory of interest to combat the eclectic Böhm-Bawerkian approach most recently developed by Fisher.

27. See Hayek's *The Counter-Revolution of Science* (1952), and Mises's *Theory and History* (1957) and *The Ultimate Foundation of Economic Science* (1962).

28. For a collection of Lachmann's various essays during this period, see (1977).

29. Hans Sennholz was another of Mises's students during this time and for many years represented the Misesian position from his faculty position at Grove City College, as well as in popular essays and books. However, all of his work was directed at students and interested laymen rather than scientific peers. His influence on the subsequent development of Austrian economics in the second half of the 20th century was channeled mainly through the legions of students he taught at

Grove City, many of whom would go on to academia, public foundations, and think tanks.

30. For a recent discussion of these issues see Zanotti and Cachanosky (2015).

31. Note how this stated purpose reflects back on our discussion in *The Theory of Practical Knowledge and the Practicality of Theoretical Knowledge*.

32. Mises praised the book, writing that "as the result of many years of sagacious and discerning meditation, [Rothbard] joins the ranks of eminent economists by publishing a voluminous work, a systematic treatise on economics ... adopting the best of the teachings of his predecessors, and adding to them highly important observations" (Mises, 1962a, 1962b). However, he criticized Rothbard's forays into philosophy and legal theory, disciplines that would consume much of Rothbard's later career.

33. Mises thought it was important enough to cite in a revised edition of *Human Action* (1966), and Hayek spoke highly of it in private conversations (Gordon, 2009). Rothbard published two additional essays on money during this time, the first a defense of gold against the Chicago monetarists, and the second an introductory monograph on money and inflation (Rothbard, 1962b, 1963b).

34. After delays due to conflicts with his first thesis advisor, Arthur Burns, forced Rothbard to switch to a second advisor, Joseph Dorfman, Rothbard finally earned his PhD from Columbia in 1956. Kirzner completed his PhD in 1957. Rothbard had published in the *American Economic Review*, *Southern Economic Journal*, and *Quarterly Journal of Economics* between 1950 and 1960 prior to publishing *Man, Economy, and State*.

35. Mises wrote a forward to the book, and had earlier recommended Kirzner for a position at NYU.

36. A bibliography of Rothbard's writings is available here: https://mises.org/library/rothbard-bibliography. An incomplete bibliography of Kirzner's writings that captures the critical first decade of his career can be found here: http://www.econ.nyu.edu/user/kirzner/. What these bibliographies reveal is that, while both Rothbard and Kirzner had some success in the professional journals, they devoted at least as much time writing for outlets such as *The Freeman* and *National Review*. Rothbard was always very comfortable in his role as radical heretic to the scientific orthodoxy. Kirzner was more focused on pure scholarship, but even his career reflected the common Austrian engagement with matters of public interest that we discussed in *The Theory of Practical Knowledge and the Practicality of Theoretical Knowledge*.

37. That Hazlitt, a well-known journalist and editorialist, made important, if non-academic, contributions to the Austrian tradition reinforces the mixed blessings of the Austrian tendency to intermingle the scientific with the popular.

38. Exceptions are Kirzner's monograph on capital theory (1966), which was strongly influenced by Lachmann (1956), and an essay on markets (1967), and some essays found in Lachmann (1977).

39. The collapse in the scientific development of Austrian economics within the profession during the 1960s was in part due to the collapse of the Volker Fund in the early part of the decade. Its termination weakened the strategic organization of scholars and financial resources dedicated to the revival, and the growth of other similarly-minded institutes was stunted until the early 1970s (Doherty, 2007,

pp. 292–297). The unrest of the 1960s, the anti-war movement, and the subsequent economic stagnation of the early 1970s proved to be fertile ground for young minds inclined to distrust so-called experts and to look outside the establishment for fertile insights, and it is here that the controversial idea of "Austro-Libertarianism" emerged with all its strengths and weaknesses.

40. At the University of Virginia's Thomas Jefferson Center for Political Economy the work of Mises and Hayek was taught as simply part of the common knowledge in political economy from a methodological individualist perspective, and several scholars would emerge from that who would develop these ideas in their own way. To name two, Paul Craig Roberts's work on market socialism and the Soviet system would challenge the conventional wisdom that the market socialist model answers the objections raised by Mises and Hayek as well as the way we understand Soviet economic planning. Craig Roberts worked closely with both Buchanan and G. Warren Nutter at University of Virginia. Richard Wagner also would emerge from the Jefferson Center working on themes influenced by Mises and Hayek at a methodological, analytical and practical policy level.

41. Rothbard helped establish the Cato Institute, a libertarian think tank that also promoted Austrian ideas, in 1974.

42. It is important to emphasize that Austrians have always had internal disagreements. In the post-WWII period, these controversies were mostly hidden from the public eye as the school itself existed only on an underground level.

43. Originally the third part of *Man, Economy, and State* (1962a), *Power and Market* (1970) was removed from the first edition because it was deemed too controversial and replaced with a short chapter on interventionism.

44. The *Austrian Economics Newsletter* and *Market Process* had both been publishing since the 1970s and 1980s, but were more newsletters than full-fledged academic journals. IHS published *Literature of Liberty*, which contained bibliographic essays focused on topics that appealed to both classical liberals and Austrian economists.

Rothbard served as editor of the RAE until his death in 1995 when editorial duties transitioned to Walter Block, Hans-Hermann Hoppe and Joseph Salerno. In 1997, Kluwer Academic Publishing made the decision to assign editorship to Peter Boettke. Block, Hoppe and Salerno would eventually start a new journal, *Quarterly Journal of Austrian Economics* (first issue published in 1998). Boettke continues as editor-in-chief of the RAE, a duty now shared with Christopher Coyne. Along with Israel Kirzner and Mario Rizzo, Boettke also established the book series *Advances in Austrian Economics* in 1994. *Advances* continues to publish with Christopher Coyne and Virgil Storr as co-editors.

45. Although Hayek was still writing in the 1970s and 1980s, he did not directly involve himself in these internal discussions. However Hayek's positions are closer to Kirzner than either Rothbard or Lachmann, and as a result the three groups can be characterized as Rothbardian, Hayekian-Kirznerian, and Lachmannian.

46. Among others, see White (1982), Lachmann (1976b, 1979, 1982), Littlechild (1979, 1982), Rizzo (1979a, 1979b), Shackle (1979), Boehm (1982), Selgin (1988 [1982]), and Boettke, Horwitz, and Prychitko (1986).

47. A related episode involving Lachmann concerns Don Lavoie's efforts to reconstruct Mises' apriorism and praxeological method from within the

philosophical framework of the hermeneuticist Hans-Georg Gadamer (see Ebeling, 1986; Lavoie, 1985a, 1986). Rothbardians reacted against this development (see Gordon, 1986; Hoppe, 1989; Rothbard, 1989). See Storr (2011) and the related symposium for a more appreciative view of Lavoie's efforts.

48. Further references to the Austrian theory of free banking include White (1989) and White and Selgin (1994). Horwitz (1992) and Sechrest (1993) were strongly influenced by the White-Selgin theory.

49. Among others, see White (1992), Salerno (1991, 1993, 1994a, 1994b), Hoppe (1994), De Soto (1995), Hulsmann (1996), White and Selgin (1996), and Hoppe, Hülsmann, and Block (1998). Horwitz (2000) deals indirectly with many of the relevant issues, as does much of the Austrian literature on capital and the business cycle. The main force behind much of the latter literature has been Roger Garrison, whose work is widely appreciated by both sides of the Austrian banking debate; see Garrison (1978, 1982, 1984, 1986, 1989, 1991, and esp. 2000). Other prominent books on capital and structure-of-production-theory include Skousen (1990), De Soto (2006 [1998]), and Lewin (1999).

50. See Mises (1951 [1922], pp. 120–121) where he argues that under stationary conditions "there no longer exists a problem for economic calculation to solve." The problem of economic calculation, Mises argued, "is of economic dynamics: it is not a problem of economic statics." Also see Mises (1935 [1920], p. 109). Furthermore, see Mises's (2005 [1927], p. 50) "the decisive objection that economics raises against the possibility of a socialist society [is that] it must forgo the intellectual division of labor that consists in the cooperation of all entrepreneurs, landowners, and workers as producers and consumers in the formation of market prices. But without it, rationality, i.e., the possibility of economic calculation, is unthinkable." As Hayek would later argue, not only does the price system coordinate the division of labor it does so through the utilization of the corresponding division of knowledge in society.

51. See also Thomsen (1992) and Rothbard (1992) for summaries of the respective lessons learned from the debates between, and among, Austrian economists and mainstream neoclassical economists since the 1970s.

52. The Society for the Development of Austrian Economics (SDAE) was founded in 1995 under the initiative of Karen Vaughn with an original membership of 25. There were more than 100 scholars in attendance at the most recent SDAE conference, which meets each November in conjunction with the annual meetings of the Southern Economic Association. Each year, the SDAE awards a Best Book and Best Article prize. Among the books that have won this award in recent years include treatises published by academic presses such as Cambridge, Princeton, Oxford, and Stanford – a far cry from publishing with Van Nostrand in the 1960s as both Kirzner and Rothbard did. We have, perhaps unfairly, excluded from our narrative the emergence of organized efforts to advance Austrian economics throughout Europe, Latin America, and Asia. A comprehensive accounting would include research and educational programs in Britain, Czech Republic, France, Germany, Guatemala, and Spain.

53. See Cachanosky and Salter (forthcoming) for a survey of some of the recent scholarly resurgence in ABCT.

54. Space constraints prevent a full list of the recent Austrian literature. See Evans and Tarko (2014) for a sample of recent work in Austrian economics in the 21st century.

ACKNOWLEDGMENT

We thank Scott Scheall for detailed comments and suggestions on multiple versions of this chapter. The financial support of the John Templeton Foundation and the Mercatus Center is gratefully acknowledged. The usual caveat applies.

REFERENCES

Armentano, D. (1982). *Antitrust and monopoly*. New York, NY: Wiley.
Arrow, K. (1959). Toward a theory of price adjustment. In M. Abramovitz (Ed.), *The allocation of economic resources: Essays in honor of Bernard Francis Haley*. Stanford, CA: Stanford University Press.
Baird, C. (1987). The economics of time and ignorance: A review. *The Review of Austrian Economics*, 1(1), 189–206.
Block, W. (1988). Fractional reserve banking: An interdisciplinary perspective. In W. Block & L. Rockwell (Eds.), *Man, economy, and liberty: Essays in honor of Murray N. Rothbard*. Auburn, AL: Ludwig von Mises Institute.
Boehm, S. (1982). The ambiguous notion of subjectivism: Comment on Lachmann. In I. Kirzner (Ed.), *Money, method, and the market process*. Lexington, MA: Lexington Books.
Boettke, P. (Ed.). (1994). *The Elgar companion to Austrian economics*. Aldershot: Edward Elgar Publishing.
Boettke, P. (1998). Economic calculation: The Austrian contribution to political economy. *Advances in Austrian Economics*, 5(1), 131–158.
Boettke, P. (2000). Towards a history of the theory of socialist planning. In *Socialism and the market: The socialist calculation debate revisited* (Vol. 1, pp. 1–39; 9 volumes). New York, NY: Routledge.
Boettke, P. (2001). *Calculation and coordination*. New York, NY: Routledge.
Boettke, P. (Ed.). (2010). *Handbook on contemporary Austrian economics*. Cheltenham: Edward Elgar Publishing.
Boettke, P. (2012). *Living economics*. Oakland, CA: The Independent Institute.
Boettke, P. (2012 [1997]). Where did economics go wrong? Modern economics as a flight from reality. In P. Boettke (Ed.), *Living economics*. Oakland, CA: The Independent Institute.
Boettke, P. (2013). Austrian economics. In B. Kaldis (Ed.), *Encyclopedia of philosophy and the social sciences*. London: Sage.
Boettke, P., & Coyne, C. (Eds.). (2015). *The Oxford handbook of Austrian economics*. New York, NY: Oxford University Press.
Boettke, P., Horwitz, S., & Prychitko, D. (1986). Beyond equilibrium economics: Reflections on the uniqueness of the Austrian tradition. *Market Process*, 4(2), 6–9, 20–25.
Boettke, P., & O'Donnell, K. (2013). The failed appropriation of F. A. Hayek by formalist economics. *Critical Review*, 25(3–4), 305–341.
Böhm-Bawerk, E. (1962 [1896]). Unresolved contradiction in the Marxian economic system. In *Shorter classics of Böhm-Bawerk*. South Holland, IL: Libertarian Press.

Böhm-Bawerk, E. v. (1949). Karl Marx and the close of his system. In P. Sweezy (Ed.), *Karl Marx and the close of his system and Böhm-Bawerk's criticism of Marx*. New York, NY: August M. Kelley Publishers.

Böhm-Bawerk, E. v. (1959 [1884]). A history and critique of interest theories. In *Capital and interest* (Vol. 1). South Holland, IL: Libertarian Press.

Böhm-Bawerk, E. v. (1959 [1889]). The positive theory of capital. In *Capital and interest* (Vol. 2). South Holland, IL: Libertarian Press.

Böhm-Bawerk, E. v. (1959 [1921]). *Capital and interest*. South Holland, IL: Libertarian Press.

Böhm-Bawerk, E. v. (1962 [1894]). The ultimate standard of value. In *Shorter classics of Böhm-Bawerk*. South Holland, IL: Libertarian Press.

Buchanan, J. (1979). *What should economists do?* Indianapolis, IN: Liberty Press.

Cachanosky, N., & Salter, A. (forthcoming). *The view from Vienna: An analysis of the renewed interest in the Mises-Hayek theory of the business cycle. The Review of Austrian Economics*.

Caldwell, B. (2002). Wieser, Hayek and equilibrium theory. *Journal des Économistes et des Études Humaines, 12*(1), 47–66.

Chamlee-Wright, E. (2010). *The culture and political economy of recovery*. New York, NY: Routledge.

Coyne, C. (2007). *After war*. Stanford, CA: Stanford University Press.

Coyne, C. (2013). *Doing bad by doing good*. Stanford, CA: Stanford University Press.

De Soto, J. H. (1995). A critical analysis of central banks and fractional-reserve free banking from the Austrian perspective. *Review of Austrian Economics, 8*(2), 25–36.

De Soto, J. H. (2006 [1998]). *Money, bank credit, and economic cycles*. Auburn, AL: Ludwig von Mises Institute.

Doherty, B. (2007). *Radicals for capitalism*. New York, NY: Public Affairs.

Dolan, E. (Ed.). (1976). *The foundations of modern Austrian economics*. Menlo Park, CA: Institute for Humane Studies.

Ebeling, R. (1986). Towards a hermeneutical economics: Expectations, prices, and the role of interpretation in a theory of the market process. In I. Kirzner (Ed.), *Subjectivism, intelligibility, and economic understanding: Essays in honor of Ludwig M. Lachmann on his eightieth birthday*. New York, NY: New York University Press.

Endres, A. (1997). *Neoclassical microeconomic theory: The founding Austrian vision*. New York, NY: Routledge.

Evans, A., & Tarko, V. (2014). Contemporary work in Austrian economics. *Journal of Private Enterprise, 29*(3), 135–157.

Fetter, F. (1977). In M. Rothbard (Ed.), *Capital, interest, and rent: Essays in the theory of distribution*. Kansas City, MO: Sheed Andrews and McMeel, Inc.

Fetter, F. A. (1915). *Economic principles*. New York, NY: The Century Co.

Foss, N. (2012). *Organizing entrepreneurial judgement*. Cambridge: Cambridge University Press.

Foss, N., & Klein, P. (2010). Alertness, action, and the antecedents of entrepreneurship. *Journal of Private Enterprise, 25*(2), 145–162.

Garrison, R. (1978). Austrian macroeconomics: A diagrammatical exposition. In L. Spadaro (Ed.), *New directions in Austrian economics*. Kansas City, KC: Sheed Andrews and McMeel.

Garrison, R. (1982). Austrian economics as the middle ground: Comment on Loasby. In I. Kirzner (Ed.), *Method, process, and Austrian economics: Essays in honor of Ludwig von Mises*. Lexington, MA: Lexington Books.

Garrison, R. (1984). Time and money: The universals of macroeconomic thinking. *Journal of Macroeconomics*, 6(2), 197–213.

Garrison, R. (1986). Hayekian trade cycle theory: A reappraisal. *The Cato Journal*, 6(1), 437–453.

Garrison, R. (1989). The Austrian theory of the business cycle in the light of modern macro-economics. *Review of Austrian Economics*, 3(1), 3–29.

Garrison, R. (1991). New classical and old Austrian economics. *Review of Austrian Economics*, 5(1), 91–103.

Garrison, R. (1999). Eugen von Böhm-Bawerk: Capital, interest, and time. In R. Holcombe (Ed.), *The great Austrian economists*. Auburn, AL: Ludwig von Mises Institute.

Garrison, R. (2000). *Time and money: The macroeconomics of the capital structure*. New York, NY: Routledge.

Gordon, D. (1986). *Hermeneutics versus Austrian economics*. Working Paper Series. Mises Institute.

Gordon, D. (2009, May 8). *Frederich Hayek as a teacher*. Retrieved from http://mises.org/daily/3458

Haberler, G. v. (1932). Money and the business cycle. In Q. Wright (Ed.), *Gold and monetary stabilization*. Chicago, IL: University of Chicago Press.

Hayek, F. (1931a). *Prices and production*. London: Routledge.

Hayek, F. (1931b). Reflections on the pure theory of money of Mr. J.M. Keynes. *Economica*, 11, 270–295.

Hayek, F. (1931c). A rejoinder to Mr. Keynes. *Economica*, 11, 398–403.

Hayek, F. (1932). Reflections on the pure theory of money of Mr. J.M. Keynes (continued). *Economica*, 12, 22–44.

Hayek, F. (1933). *Monetary theory and the trade cycle*. London: Jonathan Cape.

Hayek, F. (1935a). *Collectivist economic planning*. London: George Routledge & Sons.

Hayek, F. (1935b). *Prices and production* (2nd Rev. ed.). London: Routledge.

Hayek, F. (1937a). Economics and knowledge. *Economica*, 4(13), 33–54.

Hayek, F. (1937b). *Monetary nationalism and international stability*. New York, NY: Longmans, Green.

Hayek, F. (1939a). *Freedom and the economic system*. Chicago, IL: University of Chicago Press.

Hayek, F. (1939b). *Profits, interest, and investment*. London: Routledge.

Hayek, F. (1941). *The pure theory of capital*. Chicago, IL: University of Chicago Press.

Hayek, F. (1944). *The road to Serfdom*. Chicago, IL: University of Chicago Press.

Hayek, F. (1945). The use of knowledge in society. *American Economic Review*, 35(4), 519–530.

Hayek, F. (1948). *Individualism and economic order*. Chicago, IL: University of Chicago Press.

Hayek, F. (1948 [1946]). The meaning of competition. In *Individualism and economic order*. Chicago, IL: University of Chicago Press.

Hayek, F. (1952). *The counter revolution of science*. Glencoe, IL: The Free Press.

Hayek, F. (1976). *Denationalisation of money*. London: The Institute of Economic Affairs.

Hayek, F. (1989). The pretence of knowledge. *American Economic Review*, 79(6), 3–7.

Hayek, F. (1991). *The fatal conceit: The errors of socialism*. Chicago, IL: University of Chicago Press.

Hazlitt, H. (1959). *The failure of the "new economics"*. Princeton, NJ: D. Van Nostrand.

Hazlitt, H. (Ed.). (1960). *The critics of Keynesian economics*. Princeton, NJ: D. Van Nostrand.

Herbener, J. (1996). Calculation and the question of arithmetic. *Review of Austrian Economics*, 9(1), 151–162.

Hicks, J. (1946). *Value and capital* (2nd ed.). Oxford: Oxford University Press.

Holcombe, R. (2007). *Entrepreneurship and economic progress.* London: Routledge.

Hoppe, H.-H. (1989). In defense of extreme rationalism: Thoughts on Donald McCloskey's the rhetoric of economics. *Review of Austrian Economics*, 3(1), 179–214.

Hoppe, H. H. (1994). How is fiat money possible?-or, The devolution of money and credit. *Review of Austrian Economics*, 7(2), 49–74.

Hoppe, H. H. (1996). Socialism: A knowledge or a property problem? *Review of Austrian Economics*, 9(1), 143–149.

Hoppe, H.-H., Hülsmann, J. G., & Block, W. (1998). Against fiduciary media. *Quarterly Journal of Austrian Economics*, 1(1), 19–50.

Horwitz, S. (1992). *Monetary evolution, free banking, and economic order.* San Francisco, CA: Westview Press.

Horwitz, S. (2000). *Microfoundations and macroeconomics: An Austrian perspective.* New York, NY: Routledge.

Horwitz, S. (2004). Monetary calculation and the unintended extended order: The Misesian microfoundations of the Hayekian great society. *Review of Austrian Economics*, 17(4), 307–321.

Horwitz, S. (2012). Causes and cures of the great recession. *Economic Affairs*, 32(3), 65–69.

Hulsmann, G. (1996). Free banking and the free bankers. *Review of Austrian Economics*, 9(1), 3–53.

Hulsmann, G. (1997). Knowledge, judgement, and the use of property. *Review of Austrian Economics*, 10(1), 23–48.

Hutt, W. (1963). *Keynesianism: Retrospect and prospect.* Chicago, IL: Regnery.

Keynes, J. M. (1930). *A treatise on money.* London: Macmillan.

Keynes, J. M. (1931). The pure theory of money: A reply to Dr. Hayek. *Economica*, 11, 387–397.

Keynes, J. M. (1936). *The general theory of employment, interest, and money.* New York, NY: Macmillan.

Kirzner, I. (1960). *The economic point of view.* Princeton, NJ: D. Van Nostrand.

Kirzner, I. (1963). *Market theory and the price system.* Princeton, NJ: D. Van Nostrand.

Kirzner, I. (1966). *An essay on capital.* New York, NY: A.M. Kelley.

Kirzner, I. (1967). Methodological individualism, market equilibrium and market process. *Il Politico*, 32, 787–799.

Kirzner, I. (1973). *Competition and entrepreneurship.* Chicago, IL: University of Chicago Press.

Kirzner, I. (1976). Equilibrium versus market process. In E. Dolan (Ed.), *The foundations of modern Austrian economics.* Menlo Park, CA: Institute for Humane Studies.

Kirzner, I. (1979). *Perception, opportunity, and profit.* Chicago, IL: University of Chicago Press.

Kirzner, I. (Ed.). (1982a). *Method, process, and Austrian economics: Essays in honor of Ludwig von Mises.* Lexington, MA: Lexington Books.

Kirzner, I. (1982b). Uncertainty, discovery, and human action: A study of the entrepreneurial profile in the Misesian system. In I. Kirzner (Ed.), *Method, process, and Austrian economics: Essays in honor of Ludwig von Mises.* Lexington, MA: Lexington Books.

Kirzner, I. (1985a). *Discovery and the capitalist process.* Chicago, IL: University of Chicago Press.

Kirzner, I. (1985b). Review of the economics of time and ignorance. *Market Process*, 3(2), 1–4, 17–18.

Kirzner, I. (1988). The economic calculation debate: Lessons for Austrians. *Review of Austrian Economics*, 2(1), 1–18.

Kirzner, I. (1989). *Discovery, capitalism and distributive justice*. Oxford: Basil Blackwell.

Kirzner, I. (1992). *The meaning of market process, essays in the development of modern Austrian economics*. London: Routledge.

Kirzner, I. (1996). Reflections on the Misesian legacy in economics. *Review of Austrian Economics*, 9(2), 143–154.

Kirzner, I. (1999). Philip Wicksteed: The British Austrian. In R. Holcombe (Ed.), *The great Austrian economists*. Auburn, AL: Ludwig von Mises Institute.

Kirzner, I. (2014, October 2). *Dr. Israel Kirzner's keynote address on F. A. Hayek and the Nobel prize*. Retrieved from http://mercatus.org/events/40-years-after-nobel-fa-hayek-and-political-economy-progressive-research-program

Klein, P. (2010). *The capitalist and the entrepreneur*. Auburn, AL: Ludwig von Mises Institute.

Koppl, R. (2014). *From crisis to confidence*. London: The Institute for Economic Affairs.

Lachmann, L. (1956). *Capital and its structure*. London: London School of Economics.

Lachmann, L. (1971). *The legacy of Max Weber*. Berkeley, CA: The Glendessary Press.

Lachmann, L. (1976a). On the central concept of Austrian economics: Market process. In E. Dolan (Ed.), *The foundations of modern Austrian economics*. Menlo Park, CA: Institute for Humane Studies.

Lachmann, L. (1976b). From Mises to Shackle: An essay on Austrian economics and the Kaleidic society. *Journal of Economic Literature*, 14(1), 54–62.

Lachmann, L. (1977). *Capital, expectations, and the market process*. Menlo Park, CA: Institute for Humane Studies.

Lachmann, L. (1979). Comment: Austrian economics today. In M. Rizzo (Ed.), *Time, uncertainty, and disequilibrium*. Lexington, MA: Lexington Books.

Lachmann, L. (1982). Ludwig von Mises and the extension of subjectivism. In I. Kirzner (Ed.), *Money, method, and the market process*. Lexington, MA: Lexington Books.

Lachmann, L. (1985). Review of the economics of time and ignorance. *Market Process*, 3(2), 5–6.

Langlois, R. (2013). The Austrian theory of the firm: Retrospect and prospect. *Review of Austrian Economics*, 26(3), 247–258.

Lavoie, D. (1985a). *The interpretive dimension of economics-science, hermeneutics, and praxeology*. Center for the Study of Market Process Working Paper Series.

Lavoie, D. (1985b). *Rivalry and central planning*. New York, NY: Cambridge University Press.

Lavoie, D. (1986). Euclideanism versus hermeneutics: A re-interpretation of Misesian apriorism. In I. Kirzner (Ed.), *Subjectivism, intelligibility, and economic understanding: Essays in honor of Ludwig M. Lachmann on his eightieth birthday*. New York, NY: New York University Press.

Leeson, P. (2009). *The invisible hook*. Princeton, NJ: Princeton University Press.

Leeson, P. (2014). *Anarchy unbound*. Cambridge: Cambridge University Press.

Levy, D., & Peart, S. (2012). If germs could sponsor research: Reflections on sympathetic connections among subjects and researchers. In R. Koppl, S. Horwitz, & L. Dobuzinskis (Eds.), *Experts and epistemic monopolies* (Vol. 17). Advances in Austrian Economics. Bingley, UK: Emerald Group Publishing Limited.

Lewin, P. (1999). *Capital in disequilibrium: The role of capital in a changing world.* New York, NY: Routledge.

Lewin, P., & Baetjer, H. (2011). A capital-based view of the firm. *Review of Austrian Economics*, *24*(4), 335–354.

Lewin, P., & Phelan, S. (2000). An Austrian theory of the firm. *Review of Austrian Economics*, *13*(1), 59–80.

Littlechild, S. (1979). Comment: Radical subjectivism or radical subversion? In M. Rizzo (Ed.), *Time, uncertainty, and disequilibrium.* Lexington, MA: Lexington Books.

Littlechild, S. (1982). Equilibrium and the market process. In I. Kirzner (Ed.), *Method, process, and Austrian economics: Essays in honor of Ludwig von Mises.* Lexington, MA: Lexington Books.

Machlup, F. (1940 [1931]). *The stock market, credit, and capital formation.* London: William Hodge.

Menger, C. (1892). The origins of money. *Economic Journal*, *2*, 239–255.

Menger, C. (1950 [1871]). *Principles of economics.* Glencoe, IL: Free Press.

Menger, C. (1985 [1883]). *Investigations into the method of the social sciences.* New York, NY: New York University Press.

Mises, L. v. (1935 [1920]). Economic calculation in the socialist commonwealth. In F. Hayek (Ed.), *Collectivist economic planning.* London: George Routledge & Sons.

Mises, L. v. (1940). *Nationalökonomie.* Geneva: Editions Union.

Mises, L. v. (1944a). *Bureaucracy.* New Haven, CT: Yale University Press.

Mises, L. v. (1944b). *Omnipotent government.* New Haven, CT: Yale University Press.

Mises, L. v. (1949). *Human action.* New Haven, CT: Yale University Press.

Mises, L. v. (1951 [1922]). *Socialism.* New Haven, CT: Yale University Press.

Mises, L. v. (1953 [1912]). *The theory of money and credit.* New Haven, CT: Yale University Press.

Mises, L. v. (1957). *Theory and history.* New Haven, CT: Yale University Press.

Mises, L. v. (1960 [1933]a). *Epistemological problems of economics.* Princeton, NJ: D. Van Nostrand Co.

Mises, L. v. (1960 [1933]b). The controversy over the theory of value. In *Epistemological problems of economics.* Princeton, NJ: D. Van Nostrand Co.

Mises, L. v. (1962a). *The ultimate foundation of economic science.* Princeton, NJ: D. Van Nostrand.

Mises, L. v. (1962b). Man, economy, and state: A new treatise on economics. *New Individualist Review*, (Autumn), 39–42.

Mises, L. v. (1966). *Human action* (3rd ed.). Chicago, IL: Regnery.

Mises, L. v. (1978). In P. Greaves (Ed.), *On the manipulation of money and credit.* New York, NY: Free Market Books.

Mises, L. v. (1983 [1919]). *Nation, state, and economy.* Indianapolis, IN: Institute for Humane Studies.

Mises, L. v. (1990a). In R. Ebeling (Ed.), *Money, method, and the market process.* Norwell, MA: Kluwer Academic Publishers.

Mises, L. v. (1990b). *Economic freedom and interventionism: Anthology of articles and essays.* Irvington-on-Hudson, NY: Foundation for Economic Education.

Mises, L. v. (2005 [1927]). *Liberalism: The classical tradition.* Indianapolis, IN: Liberty Fund.

Mises, L. v. (2009 [1978]). *Memoirs.* Auburn, AL: Ludwig von Mises Institute.

Moss, L. (Ed.). (1976). *The economics of Ludwig von Mises*. Menlo Park, CA: Institute for Humane Studies.

Nozick, R. (1974). *Anarchy, state, and Utopia*. New York, NY: Basic Books.

O'Driscoll, G. (1977a). *Economics as a coordination problem: The contributions of Frederich A. Hayek*. Kansas City, KS: Sheed Andrews & McMeel.

O'Driscoll, G. (1977b). Spontaneous order and the coordination of economic activities. *The Journal of Libertarian Studies*, *1*, 137–151.

Phillips, C., McManus, T., & Nelson, R. (1937). *Banking and the business cycle*. New York, NY: Macmillan.

Powell, B. (2014). *Out of poverty*. Cambridge: Cambridge University Press.

Rizzo, M. (1979a). Disequilibrium and all that: An introductory essay. In M. Rizzo (Ed.), *Time, uncertainty, and disequilibrium*. Lexington, MA: Lexington Books.

Rizzo, M. (Ed.). (1979b). *Time, uncertainty, and disequilibrium*. Lexington, MA: Lexington Books.

Rizzo, M., & O'Driscoll, G. (1985). *The economics of time and ignorance*. Oxford: Basil Blackwell Ltd.

Robbins, L. (1930). On a certain ambiguity in the conception of stationary equilibrium. *Economic Journal*, *40*, 194–214.

Robbins, L. (1931). Foreword. In F. Hayek (Ed.), *Prices and production*. London: Routledge.

Robbins, L. (1932). *An essay on the nature & significance of economic science*. London: MacMillan & Co.

Robbins, L. (1933). Introduction. In P. Wicksteed (Ed.), *The common sense of political economy*. London: George Routledge & Sons Ltd.

Robbins, L. (1934a). Remarks upon certain aspects of the theory of costs. *Economic Journal*, *44*, 1–18.

Robbins, L. (1934b). *The great depression*. London: Macmillan.

Robbins, L. (1953 [1934]). Introduction. In L. v. Mises (Ed.), *The theory of money and credit*. New Haven, CT: Yale University Press.

Rothbard, M. (1956). Towards a reconstruction of utility and welfare economics. In M. Sennholz (Ed.), *On freedom and free enterprise*. Princeton, NJ: D. Van Nostrand.

Rothbard, M. (1957). In defense of "extreme apriorism". *Southern Economic Journal*, (January), 314–320.

Rothbard, M. (1962a). *Man, economy, and state*. Princeton, NJ: D. Van Nostrand.

Rothbard, M. (1962b). The case for a 100 per cent gold dollar. In L. Yeager (Ed.), *In search of a monetary constitution*. Cambridge, MA: Harvard University Press.

Rothbard, M. (1963a). *America's great depression*. Princeton, NJ: D. Van Nostrand.

Rothbard, M. (1963b). *What has government done to our money?* Colorado Springs, CO: Pine Tree Press.

Rothbard, M. (1970). *Power and market*. Menlo Park, CA: Institute for Humane Studies.

Rothbard, M. (1973). *For a new liberty*. New York, NY: Macmillan.

Rothbard, M. (1974). Review of competition and entrepreneurship. *Journal of Economic Literature*, *12*(3), 902–903.

Rothbard, M. (1978). Austrian definitions of the supply of money. In L. Spadaro (Ed.), *New directions in Austrian economics*. Kansas City, KC: Sheed Andrews and McMeel.

Rothbard, M. (1985). Professor Hebert on entrepreneurship. *Journal of Libertarian Studies*, *7*(2), 281–286.

Rothbard, M. (1988). The myth of free banking in Scotland. *Review of Austrian Economics*, *2*(1), 179–187.

Rothbard, M. (1989). The hermeneutical invasion of philosophy and economics. *Review of Austrian Economics*, *3*(1), 45–59.

Rothbard, M. (1991). The end of socialism and the calculation debate revisited. *Review of Austrian Economics*, *5*(2), 51–76.

Rothbard, M. (1992). The present state of Austrian economics. *Journal des Economistes et des etudes humaines*, *6*(1), 43–89.

Salerno, J. (1987). The "true" money supply: A measure of the supply of the medium of exchange in the U.S. economy. *Austrian Economics Newsletter*, *6*(4), 1–6.

Salerno, J. (1990a). Ludwig von Mises as a social rationalist. *Review of Austrian Economics*, *4*(1), 26–54.

Salerno, J. (1990b). Postscript: Why a socialist economy is "impossible". In L. v. Mises (Ed.), *Economic calculation in the socialist commonwealth*. Auburn, AL: Ludwig von Mises Institute.

Salerno, J. (1991). The concept of coordination in Austrian macroeconomics. In R. Ebeling (Ed.), *Austrian economics: Perspectives on the past and prospects for the future*. Hillsdale, MI: Hillsdale College Press.

Salerno, J. (1993). Mises and Hayek dehomogenized. *Review of Austrian Economics*, *6*(2), 113–146.

Salerno, J. (1994a). Ludwig von Mises's monetary theory in light of modern monetary thought. *Review of Austrian Economics*, *8*(1), 71–115.

Salerno, J. (1994b). Reply to Leland B. Yeager on Mises and Hayek on calculation and knowledge. *Review of Austrian Economics*, *7*(2), 111–125.

Salerno, J. (1996). A final word: Calculation, knowledge, and appraisement. *Review of Austrian Economics*, *9*(1), 141–142.

Salerno, J. (1999a). Carl Menger: The founding of the Austrian school. In R. Holcombe (Ed.), *The great Austrian economists*. Auburn, AL: Ludwig von Mises Institute.

Salerno, J. (1999b). The place of Mises's human action in the development of modern economic thought. *The Quarterly Journal of Austrian Economics*, *2*(1), 35–65.

Salerno, J. (2002). Frederich von Wieser and Friedrich A. Hayek: The general equilibrium tradition in Austrian economics. *Journal des Economistes et des etudes humaines*, *12*(2), 357–377.

Salerno, J. (2009). *Introduction to the second edition of man, economy, and state with power and market*. Auburn, AL: Ludwig von Mises Institute.

Salerno, J. (2010). *Money: Sound and unsound*. Auburn, AL: Ludwig von Mises Institute.

Salerno, J. (2012). A reformulation of Austrian business cycle theory in light of the financial crisis. *Quarterly Journal of Austrian Economics*, *15*(1), 3–44.

Samuelson, P. (1947). *Foundations of economic analysis*. Cambridge, MA: Harvard University Press.

Samuelson, P. (1948). *Economics*. New York, NY: McGraw-Hill.

Samuelson, P. (1981). Bertil Ohlin (1899–1979). *The Scandinavian Journal of Economics*, *83*(3), 355–371.

Sautet, F. (2000). *An entrepreneurial theory of the firm*. New York, NY: Routledge.

Schumpeter, J. (1954). *A history of economic analysis*. New York, NY: Oxford University Press.

Sechrest, L. (1988). White's free banking thesis: A case of mistaken identity. *Review of Austrian Economics*, *2*(1), 247−257.

Sechrest, L. (1993). *Free banking: Theory, history, and a Laissez Faire model.* Westport, CT: Greenwood Publishing Group.

Selgin, G. (1988). *The theory of free banking.* Totowa, NJ: Rowman and Littlefield.

Selgin, G. (1988 [1982]). Praxeology and understanding. *Review of Austrian Economics*, *2*(1), 19−58.

Selgin, G. (2010). The futility of central banking. *Cato Journal*, *30*(3), 465−473.

Selgin, G., Lastrapes, W., & White, L. (2012). Has the fed been a failure? *Journal of Macroeconomics*, *34*(3), 569−596.

Shackle, G. (1979). Imagination, formalism, and choice. In M. Rizzo (Ed.), *Time, uncertainty, and disequilibrium.* Lexington, MA: Lexington Books.

Skarbek, D. (2014). *The social order of the underworld.* Oxford: Oxford University Press.

Skousen, M. (1990). *The structure of production.* New York, NY: New York University Press.

Spadaro, L. (Ed.). (1978). *New directions in Austrian economics.* Menlo Park, CA: Institute for Humane Studies.

Stigler, G. (1946). *The theory of price.* New York, NY: Macmillan.

Storr, V. (Ed.). (2011). Special issue: Don Lavoie's "the interpretive dimension of economics". *The Review of Austrian Economics*, *24*(2), 85−233.

Storr, V. (2013). *Understanding the culture of markets.* New York, NY: Routledge.

Streissler, E., & Streissler, M. (Eds.). (1994). *Carl Menger's lectures to the crown prince Rudolf of Austria* (E. Streissler, & M. Streissler, Trans.). Aldershot and Brookfield: Edward Elgar.

Strigl, R. v. (2000 [1934]). *Capital & production.* Auburn, AL: Ludwig von Mises Institute.

Stringham, E. (2015). *Private governance.* New York, NY: Oxford University Press.

The Prize in Economics 1974 − Press Release. (1974, October 9). Retrieved from http://www.nobelprize.org/nobel_prizes/economic-sciences/laureates/1974/press.html

Thomsen, E. (1992). *Prices and knowledge: A market process perspective.* New York, NY: Routledge.

White, L. (1982). Mises, Hayek, Hahn, and the market process: Comment on Littlechild. In I. Kirzner (Ed.), *Method, process, and Austrian economics: Essays in honor of Ludwig von Mises.* Lexington, MA: Lexington Books.

White, L. (1985a). Free banking and the gold standard. In L. Rockwell (Ed.), *The gold standard: An Austrian perspective.* Lexington, MA: Lexington Books.

White, L. (1985b). *Free banking in Britain.* Cambridge: Cambridge University Press.

White, L. (1986). A subjectivist perspective on the definition and identification of money. In I. Kirzner (Ed.), *Subjectivism, intelligibility, and economic understanding: Essays in honor of Ludwig M. Lachmann on his eightieth birthday.* New York, NY: New York University Press.

White, L. (1989). *Competition and currency.* New York, NY: New York University Press.

White, L. (1992). Mises on free banking and fractional reserves. In M. Spangler & J. Robbins (Eds.), *A man of principle: Essays in honor of Hans F. Sennholz.* Grove City, PA: Grove City College Press.

White, L. (2011). A gold standard with free banking would have restrained the boom and bust. *Cato Journal*, *31*(3), 497−504.

White, L. (2012). *The clash of economic ideas.* Cambridge: Cambridge University Press.

White, L., & Selgin, G. (1994). How would the invisible hand handle money? *Journal of Economic Literature, 32*(4), 1718–1749.

White, L., & Selgin, G. (1996). In defense of fiduciary media-or, we are not devo(lutionists), we are Misesians! *Review of Austrian Economics, 9*(2), 83–107.

Wicksteed, P. (1910). *The common sense of political economy.* London: Macmillan.

Wieser, F. v. (1927 [1914]). *Social economics.* London: George Allen and Unwin.

Wieser, F. v. (1989 [1893]). *Natural value.* London: Macmillan & Company.

Yeager, L. (1994). Mises and Hayek on calculation and knowledge. *Review of Austrian Economics, 7*(2), 91–107.

Yeager, L. (1997). Calculation and knowledge: Lets write finis. *Review of Austrian Economics, 10*(1), 133–136.

Zanotti, G. J., & Cachanosky, N. (2015). Implications of Machlup's interpretation of Mises's epistemology. *Journal of the History of Economic Thought, 37*, 111–138.

PART II
ESSAYS

THE GREAT DEPRESSION OF 1873–1896 AND PRICE FLUCTUATIONS: BRITISH FORERUNNERS OF THE LONG WAVES PERSPECTIVE

Daniele Besomi

ABSTRACT

This chapter enquires into the contribution of two British writers, Herbert Somerton Foxwell and Henry Riverdale Grenfell, who elaborated upon the hints provided by Jevons towards a description of long waves in the oscillations of prices. Writing two decades after Jevons, they witnessed the era of high prices turning into the great depression of the last quarter of the nineteenth century, the causes of which they saw in the end of bimetallism. Not only did they take up Jevons's specific explanation of the long fluctuations, but they also based their discussion upon graphical representation of data and incorporated in their treatment a specific trait (the superposition principle) of the 'waves' metaphor emphasized by the Manchester statisticians in the 1850s and 1860s. Their contribution is also interesting for their understanding of crises versus depressions at the time of the emergence of the interpretation of

Research in the History of Economic Thought and Methodology, Volume 34A, 247–292
ISSN: 0743-4154/doi:10.1108/S0743-41542016000034A008

oscillations as a cycle, which they have only partially grasped − as distinct from the approach of later long wave theorists.

Keywords: Augustus Sauerbeck; business cycles; bimetallism; waves metaphor; graphical representation of time series; Manchester bankers

JEL classifications: B22; B31; E31; E32; E50; Y10

The history of the long waves theory in the modern sense of the term is customarily narrated as beginning from van Gelderen (1913), de Wolff (1924) and especially Kondratiev (1926, 1928), preceded by a handful of forerunners: the engineer Hyde Clarke, who suggested a fixed-period cycle of 54 years based on external, unspecified physical causes (1847); Jevons (1865), then Tugan-Baranovsky (1894),[1] Parvus (1901), with a few other names being cited as having reflected on the long-term development of the economy, less systematically, at the beginning of the twentieth century.[2] In this chapter, I examine the arguments of two writers who, contributing in 1886, deserve to be included in this list: Henry Riverdale Grenfell and Herbert Somerton Foxwell. These two writers belong to the lineage that stems from the reflections of William Langton, further elaborated by Jevons, on the coexistence of fluctuations of different periods and the relationship between them. Like Jevons, Grenfell and Foxwell recognized tidal waves of prosperity and depression related to the abundance or scarcity of gold, and they extended his arguments and data taking into account the developments of the two decades after Jevons's contribution. One of them (Foxwell) presented these data in a graphical form and, like Jevons had done earlier and Kondratiev had done later, he identified waves of different lengths from these diagrams − a method that, at the time, was still far from common.

In the first section, I am going to discuss the setting of the problem by Jevons, who identified long periods in which prices tended to increase and equally long periods when they tended to fall, based on price statistics he elaborated and presented diagrammatically starting from Newmarch's data. Jevons discussed these movements in conjunction with two oscillations of a shorter period, decennial and seasonal. He argued that they ride on top of each other, describing this situation by means of the 'wave' metaphor: he relied on the superposition property of waves. We find the same specific usage of this trope by two like-minded Manchester bankers who were members, like himself, of the Manchester Statistical Society: William Langton and John Mills. The second section deals with the perception, permeating the last quarter of the nineteenth century, that crises where changing their character, from sudden and violent outbreaks of panics and failures into sluggish and persistent depressions. This provides the context for the third section, where the contribution of Henry Riverdale Grenfell is discussed. Based on the *Economist*'s continuation of Newmarch's statistics on prices, Grenfell extended Jevons's description of long waves into the next descending cycle of years. This description, diagnosed as being caused by changes in the value of gold, was instrumental to the bimetallist policy proposal supported by Grenfell and other writers. This includes Foxwell, the editor of the book collecting Jevons's papers on this subject. The fourth section will deal with his contribution to the debate, focusing in particular on his graphical depiction of the three superposed price waves, while the following section will be devoted to some later statements by the same writer, extending a few years the series of data by means of Sauerbeck's index.[3]

A number of issues are inextricably interwoven in this episode of the history of long waves theories. There is the unfolding of the lineage of writers originating from Langton, followed by Jevons and Mills and eventually by Grenfell and, in much more detail, by Foxwell, who treated fluctuations of different periodicity as superposable and due to independent causes. Another matter in question is the specific usage of the wave metaphor precisely to stress this point, and to represent the undulating nature of the time-series diagrams depicting price indexes. The very history of the usage of such diagrams, and of the recognition of long-period fluctuations, is also an interesting point. Finally, there is also the place of all these writers in the history of the theory of crises, some still interpreting them as recurrent phenomena with a common morphology without, however, closing the circular causal chaining of all phases, while others saw the cycle as the normal dynamics of economies based on credit. In the concluding section I will therefore place these contributions in context, comparing them with Kondratiev's.

JEVONS AND THE MANCHESTER BANKERS

Hyde Clarke is mentioned as a forerunner of long waves theory, thanks to a notice by Jevons, who referred to the assumption of the existence of a

54-year cycle as of being of interest and deserving to be examined in depth. Jevons's interest in Clarke's contribution, however, was less focused on the longer cycles than on Clarke's division into shorter cycles of a periodicity fitting with Jevons's inquiries into sunspot-created decennial crises (Jevons, 1878, in 1884, pp. 222–223) and his attribution of the origin of this cycle to physical causes (p. 224). Here we will not deal with Clarke in detail (see Black, 1992; Henderson, 1992), as his approach was along a different line from the one followed by the writers with whom we are concerned here. Our story begins with Jevons, who is usually given a passing (and sometimes frankly misleading) reference. Yet he deserves more accurate treatment, as he clearly distinguished between a long-period movement of prices and shorter fluctuations superposed onto the former, for his usage of the wave and tide metaphors, for his recognition of the main cause of the long fluctuation, and because he set the standards for procedures used by later writers to further discuss the relationship of short and long waves.

Jevons's inquiry began in 1863, when he set to ascertain whether the gold discoveries in 1849–1851 in California and in Australia had affected the price of gold – a very popular issue at the time.[4] He proceeded by calculating a geometrical mean ratio of the price movements of 118 commodities, which he also represented in graphical form. It was clear to him that prices are subject to various influences, in particular due to alternation of inflationary and speculative prosperities and deflationary depressions. Accordingly, he discriminated 'the various causes of *temporary* fluctuations in prices, in order [to] more surely recognize the effect of the *permanent* cause in question' (Jevons, 1863, in 1884, p. 16, emphasis added). His method was (following Newmarch) to compare prices from 1851 to the average price during the previous full commercial fluctuation (1844–1850): 'we must then form the best judgement as we can to the part of the commercial tide in which any year since 1851 is situated, and allowing for the height of the tide, judge how far the level of prices has been permanently altered by the gold discoveries' (*ibid.*, p. 35). He confidently concluded that after 1850 prices had generally increased, and therefore gold had indeed depreciated; he was more cautious about the amount of the rise, which he estimated at a minimum of 9 per cent, or more probably at about 15 per cent.

Two years later, Jevons extended his series of data (elaborating on Tooke's *History of prices*) beginning from 1782; he followed the same method and focused on about 40 commodities. Again the results were plotted into diagrams for some of the commodities or groups of commodities, one of which represented the general variations of the entire set of commodities. Jevons relied on the graphs to draw his inference regarding the movement of general prices, as 'the eye easily compares any year or period with any other year or period,[5] (Jevons, 1865, in 1884, p. 129).

In his diagram of general prices (Fig. 1), Jevons clearly recognized a long-period fluctuation onto which the decennial commercial fluctuations were superposed:

> The curve of the general variation of prices is perhaps the most interesting. In this we detect a series of smaller undulations, *riding*, as it were, on one very great one. We see elevations of prices probably due to speculation, and reaching their highest points in the years 1796, 1801, 1809, 1814, 1818, 1825, 1836, 1839, 1847, and 1857. The speculation of 1793 is hardly perceptible, and the extraordinary rise of prices in 1825 is chiefly marked by a pause in the very rapid downward course of prices about that time. From 1833 to 1843, there is an elevation of prices of a more extensive character than can well be assigned to speculation alone. Since 1852, lastly, prices have risen in a permanent manner, which points to the effect of the Californian and Australian discoveries.
>
> It is, however, the general form of the undulation of prices which is most remarkable. After the year 1790 an enormous and long-continued elevation presents itself. And when prices had reached their highest, about the year 1809, a still more surprising fall commences, reaching its lowest point in 1849. Between 1809 and 1849, prices fell in the ratio of 100 to 41 (Jevons, 1865, in 1884, p. 129; emphasis added).

Although he declared that he would not undertake to explain the facts, he disputed the major explanations offered by other writers of the state of prices in the first half of the century: the derangement of the currency, an

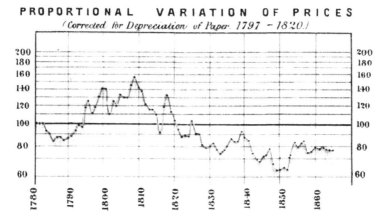

Fig. 1. Jevons's Diagram Depicting the General Variation of Prices of 40 Commodities (1780–1865). *Source*: From Jevons (1865) (1884 reprint, facing p. 150; the original figure included three more time-series graphs, omitted here).

unusual frequency of bad seasons, or improvements in production techniques (pp. 130–132). He suggested instead that the production of gold,
together with the flow of gold between countries, had changed roughly in
accordance with the fluctuations in the general price level – his conclusion
being however marred by gaps in the data concerning the flow of specie to
and from Britain, but supported by the direction of price changes of foreign vegetable products (pp. 132–138).

In a further contribution on the fluctuations of prices and trade, Jevons
also inquired about annual fluctuations, observing that frequently the
money market is subject to autumnal drains of currency and capital, most
notably in the month of October. Jevons's explanation relied on seasonal
trades: agriculture, outdoor activities and tourism take place mostly in the
summer months, and labourers are paid at that time. The cash reserves of
the firms after paying their workers run low at that time of the year, and so
do the reserves of country banks. They both replenish their reserves of
notes and coins by withdrawing the October dividends, rather than placing
them in deposits (Jevons, 1866, in 1884, p. 170).

For our theme, the interesting aspect here is not much Jevons's explanation, but rather the idea that there are yearly periodical fluctuations superposed onto the decennial alternation of prosperities and crises. This
characterization of the composite movement consisting in fluctuations with
different causes was expressed, taking up the words of two other writers, in
terms of the waves and tides metaphors. In October 1865, a correspondent
to *The Economist*, initialled G. F., pointed to an 'annual tide' in the movement of money:

> [T]here is an *annual tide* in the cash transactions of this country, and I believe of all
> countries. The currency generally, including bank-notes of all our banks, gold coin and
> silver coin, expands from July to the end of October or beginning of November; it con-
> tracts from the middle of November to the end of March, and is, on the whole, station-
> ary in April, May, and June. ... Such is the annual tide, masked to some extent by the
> action of the quarterly tides.[6] I believe that observations in the direction I have indi-
> cated would be found to confirm the law of annual tides arising from agricultural as
> distinguished from manufacturing causes; and to prove that they are a periodical source
> of disturbance in the money markets of the world, of greater force and importance than
> has hitherto been acknowledged (cited in Jevons, 1866, in 1884, p. 163).

Jevons then reported that he had recently learned about William Langton's
paper presented at the Manchester Statistical Society in December 1857.[7]
Jevons only cited a passage concerning the Autumnal pressure, but
Langton's argument was more complex. He drew a diagram with weekly
figures from 1844 to 1857 representing the difference between the bills

discounted at the Bank of England and the securities temporarily deposited at the Bank by private individuals on the one hand, and the private deposits at the Bank on the other. Langton's diagram 'shew[s] to the eye' three distinct fluctuations accompanying each other: the first was a 'quarterly fluctuation, exhibiting an almost invariable increase in the demands of the public upon the Bank, from the second week in each quarter up to the first week in the following one' (Langton, 1858, p. 10). The second one was described as follows (this is the passage cited by Jevons):

> This short and superficial wave *is accompanied* by another, not so easily detected (because sometimes absorbed in a larger movement), and more difficult to account for. It has an annual increment and collapse, and is doubtless connected with the action of the seasons upon trade. In the midst of other disturbances, this wave may be traced in the magnitude of the operations of the third and fourth quarters, and the almost invariable lull in the second quarter of each year; the third quarter being generally marked by rapid increase in the demand for accommodation at the Bank. The culminating point of the movement, originating in the third quarter of the year, appears to be a moment favourable to the bursting of those periodical storms, in which the commercial difficulties of the country find their crisis (Langton, 1858, pp. 10–11; cited by Jevons, 1866, in 1884, pp. 164–165; emphasis added).

The third undulation consists in the decennial periodical crises that at the time were recognized by most writers on the subject (see Besomi, 2010a), and it is on these fluctuations that the remainder of Langton's paper focused: 'These disturbances are *the accompaniment* of another wave, which appears to have a decennial period, and in the generation of which moral causes have no doubt an important share' (Langton, 1858, p. 11; emphasis added).

A few years later, shortly after Jevons's writings on this subject, another Manchester banker and member of the local Statistical Society, John Mills, took up Langton's waves and tides metaphor, giving it a new twist. Mills compared the annual and quarterly oscillations to '"waves," as distinct from the current or the tide' (Mills, 1868a, p. 13), or 'decennial tide' (p. 30), fluctuations that are not rooted in the peculiarities of the calendar but constitute 'facts of a new order', the causes of which lie at a deeper level (p. 13). Mills's passage is momentous, as his distinction between waves and tides expresses in metaphorical form the recognition of the existence of a primary cyclical movement with minor oscillations around it, their causes being entirely independent of each other. This is part of his recognizing the *entire cycle* as the *normal* state of the economic system, while other writers on the subject treated prosperity as the normal state of the system, the boom as an anomalous deviation from it and the crisis as the violent return to the normal. With Jevons's help, Mills drew diagrams of the movements of some variables in the course of the cycle, the shape of which clearly resembles waves — these diagrams differ from Jevons's time-series representations in being idealizations: in Mills's words, 'type-cycles' exhibiting the ' "*general* character" of such a cycle of fluctuation' (p. 30; see Fig. 2).

Around the time of Jevons's writings, then, a number of authors had recognized the existence of fluctuations with different periodicity: quarterly, yearly, decennial and spanning over decades. In his 1865 article Jevons focused on the yearly and decennial ones, in his 1866 contribution on the decennial and long-period ones; he refrained from drawing and discussing all three at once. Yet his usage of the waves metaphor would

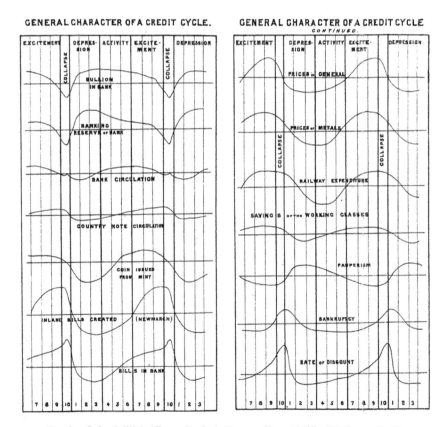

Fig. 2.   John Mills's 'Type-Cycles'. *Source*: From Mills (1868, pp. 8–9).

have allowed him easily to do so, for waves can be linearly superposed: their combined effect is the sum of their separate undulations, and the behaviour of each wave is independent of the other waves fluctuating simultaneously.[8] Thus Langton wrote about waves *accompanying* each other, Jevons's decennial undulations *ride* on the great wave (Jevons, 1865, in 1884, p. 129; the full passage is cited above), and their combined effects aggravate the distress that each of them would create separately, explaining why the outbreaks of commercial crises coincide with the autumnal pressure of the annual waves (Jevons, 1862, in 1884, p. 8; taken up in Jevons, 1866, in 1884, p. 164). Mills's distinction between 'waves' and 'tides' also permits the superposition of the shorter waves onto the decennial tide. The stage was thus set for other writers to pursue the metaphor on the basis of expanded series of data. But Langton, Jevons and Mills's arguments were not mentioned again in the literature. The Manchester bankers were mostly ignored,[9] and Jevons's views were taken up only two decades later, when the economic conditions were perceived to have radically changed.

NEW AND OLD CRISES: THE GREAT DEPRESSION

Between the Napoleonic wars and the time of Jevons's writings cited in the previous section, crises followed one another with some rough regularity. One can safely claim that after the 1847 panic most commentators were convinced that crises showed a periodical character with a roughly decennial frequency – the adjective 'periodical' being used to stress the recurrence of crises rather than a strict astronomical periodicity.[10] After the 1873 panic in the United States, however, the character of crises was quickly perceived as having changed: instead of manifesting themselves suddenly and violently, they became sluggish and persistent. The terminology adapted to the new situation: by the end of the decade the term 'crisis', which had been predominantly used to describe the phenomenon since 1837, was substituted by the term 'depression'[11] till the end of the century (Besomi, 2011, pp. 74–78).[12]

A few examples will suffice to illustrate not only the switch in terminology but also two opposite interpretations of the difference between the old and the new crises. On the one hand we have some writers, such as Edward Atkinson and Friedrich Engels, who saw a deep qualitative difference between the old crises and the situation in the late 1870s and 1880s. The former wrote:

> Any lack of occupation which deprives a large number even of common laborers of their customary supply of such [necessities of life] will affect the trade of the merchant, the traffic of the railway, and the sale of the products of the manufacturer in vastly greater measure than a temporary commercial crisis which only changes the ownership of realized wealth. The present period of depression must be considered in this light; it is very different from the ordinary commercial crises such as those of 1836 and 1857 (Atkinson, 1885, p. 313).

Similarly, and more in detail, Friedrich Engels stated in the Preface to the English edition of Marx's *Capital*:

> The decennial cycle of stagnation, prosperity, over-production and crisis, ever recurrent from 1825 to 1867, seems indeed to have run its course; but only to land us in the slough of despond of a permanent and chronic depression. The sighed-for period of prosperity will not come; as often we seem to perceive its heralding symptoms, so often do they again vanish into air (Engels, 1887, pp. xiii–xiv).

Again, in the appendix to the 1886 new edition of *The Condition of the Working Class in England*:

> The recurring period of the great industrial crises is stated in the text as five years.[13] This was the period apparently indicated by the course of events from 1825 to 1842. But the industrial history from 1842 to 1868 has shown that the real period is one of ten years; that the intermediate revolutions were secondary and tended more and more to disappear (Engels, 1886, p. v).

> This then, was the position created by the Free Trade policies of 1847, and by twenty years of the rule of the manufacturing capitalists. But then a change came. The crash of 1868 was, indeed, followed by a slight and short revival about 1873; but that did not last. We did not, indeed, pass through the full crisis at the time it was due, in 1877 or 1878; but we have had, ever since 1876, a chronic state of stagnation in all the dominant branches of industry. Neither will the full crash come; nor will the period of longed-for prosperity to which we used to be entitled before and after it. A dull depression, a chronic glut of all markets for all trades, that is what we have been living in for nearly ten years (*ibid.*, p. viii, citing from his own 'England in 1845 and in 1885', *Commonweal*, March 1885, pp. 12–14).

On the other hand, some writers maintained instead that the difference was not qualitative but only a matter of degree. For instance, Samuel Dana Horton[14] wrote:

> The difference [...] between the crises of 1797, 1847, and 1866, on one side, and, on the other side, of the decade now closing, is, in important phases of the matter, a difference in degree; the first mentioned crises being acute, intense, but very short, the latter

making up for its comparative mildness by a phenomenal duration, by the cumulation of distress, and by uncertainty of its reaching an end (Horton, 1887, p. 37).

As we shall see, the British forerunners of the long waves theory also understood the difference between the crises in the central part of the century and the deep depressions of the last quarter as differing in quantitative rather than qualitative terms.

The metaphorical usage changed as well as the terminology: while towards the middle of the century the prevalent tropes used to describe crises emphasized their devastating and abrupt character (financial and commercial storms,[15] 'tradequakes', avalanches tearing down credit, explosions blowing apart commercial houses and so on), the depression in the later part of the century was characterized by means of different images. In France, a number of writers referred to the state of the economy from the late 1870s as an anaemic condition. The propounder of this image seems to have been Émile de Laveleye, who distinguished between inflammatory and anaemic diseases. At first his distinction was generic:

> Crises are the diseases of credit, for countries where credit is little used escape them. Sometimes they are as sharp as an inflammation, sometimes as slow and insidious as an anemic (Laveleye, 1882, p. 238; English transl. 1884, p. 223).

Later, he applied it to the different character of crises in the middle and in the last quarter of the century:

> Crises are sometimes acute but short-lived, like those of 1847 and 1857, and sometimes they are persistent like those of 1874 and 1888. If one wishes to compare the diseases of the circulation to those of the human body, one can say that the former have the nature of inflammations, the latter of an anaemia (Laveleye, 1890, p. 380).[16]

Laveleye's expression was taken up by Gide, who compared short crises to outbursts of fever and longer ones to an anaemic state (1891, p. 364; also in the following editions), and later by Raffalovich:[17]

> We will call 'crisis' the perturbations disturbing the regular progress of business .... [The crisis is] the outbreak of the illness and the acute point of a previously existing disease. The word 'crisis' would make no sense if applied to a protracted state of idleness and stagnation, to a chronic morbid condition for which the word 'depression' is better used in English. In this language, the word 'crisis' indicates a sudden occurrence, often having the character of a panic (Raffalovich, 1898, p. 1127).[18]

In English, the emphasis was on the transmission of the effects of depressions. They were described as expanding like tidal waves, moving slower yet as powerfully as panics and crises.[19] A few examples will suffice to illustrate this usage. An article in the *Memphis Daily Appeal* reported that 'The general wave of commercial depression is now seriously felt in England' (Anonymous, 1876). A year and a half later, *The Morning Star and Catholic Messenger* hoped that the wave had exhausted its force and was about to give way to a new prosperous era:

> Many reasons could be adduced to show that the slow but steady improvement in business affairs which we have of late from time to time recorded in these columns, is likely to continue and increase till the recovery is complete and permanent. The wave of commercial depression has been rolling steadily toward the Pacific, where it is beginning to waste its force, and may be expected soon to disappear (Anonymous, 1878).

Yet the following year a new 'wave of business depression ... appeared to be passing over the whole of the civilized world' (Anonymous, 1879). A few years later, the *Midland Figaro* noted that 'the present "wave of unparalleled trade depression" has had its effect upon merchants, large and small' (Anonymous, 1885), and in the mid-1890s *The Record-Union* reported that the Secretary of the U.S. Treasury John Calisle had declared: 'A great wave of depression has swept over the industrial commercial and financial world, more injurious in its effects in some places than in others, but entailing great loss and distress nearly everywhere' (Anonymous, 1895).[20]

Later literature has stressed that while there had actually been a depression in agricultural output and prices, overall the British economy had grown just the same in real terms, even if at a reduced pace (for references and an assessment, see Capie & Wood, 1997). Nevertheless, the general perception at the time was that the last decades of the century were 'hard times',[21] characterized by falling prices.[22] The latter are explained today by the inflow of cheap agricultural products from abroad together with a shortage of gold supply.

In contemporary debates, the emphasis was on the redistributive effects of deflation − commentators were concerned in particular with the increasing burden of debt − and on the missing (or, at any rate reduced) stimulus of high prices on the speculative activity characterizing prosperity. The widely prevalent explanation of crises and their recurrence in mid-nineteenth century Britain relied on the credit-overtrading-speculation mechanism, in which prices played a crucial role. Credit enables merchants to trade beyond their capital; this excess of trade makes prices rise, in turn inducing speculation. This stimulates trading further, in increasingly implausible enterprises and in a spiral supported by continuous increase in prices. This situation, however, is fragile. Credit relies on mutual trust, and as soon as this lacks, the entire system collapses: credit is halted, people need cash to repay their debts, they rush to sell but nobody wants to buy.

Prices fall, affecting profitability and expectations, with their corollary of failures and distress. These circumstances eventually weed out the businesses that have extravagantly speculated to excess, preparing the ground for a return to a normal economic activity – until optimism pushes again into overtrading (for an overview of this approach, see Besomi, 2010b, pp. 198–202).

Clearly, with the prevalence of a trend of falling prices the incentive to speculate was too modest and the few years of prosperity were not as lively and long-lasting as before, and the consequent reaction (as it was called) was less violent and originated more persistent depressions. The relationship between falling prices and depression of trade was made explicit by numerous commentators: some viewed it in terms of cause and effect,[23] others in terms of co-occurrence[24] and others still in terms of equivalence.[25] In any interpretation, the problem was to identify the causes of falling prices and suggest a remedy.

HENRY RIVERSDALE GRENFELL AND THE BIMETALLISM DEBATE

One of the strains of the debate on the Great Depression concerned the monetary standard. Most writers saw the cause of falling prices in the scarcity of gold compared to its demand. Bimetallists blamed the gold standard, to which a number of countries switched around 1873, the year of a panic in the United States, and as a matter of fact the beginning of the depression. Germany adopted the gold standard in 1873, the Scandinavian countries followed between 1873 and 1876, Holland did in 1875, the United States by 1876 and the Latin Monetary Union in 1878. Bimetallists argued that the demonetization of silver increased the demand for gold which – as a direct consequence of the quantity theory – implied a fall of prices. Moreover, this caused a fall in the price of silver by about 20 per cent, with the consequence that countries on the silver standard – India, in particular – saw their international purchasing power reduced and were no longer able to purchase goods from countries on the gold standard. Their suggested solution, therefore, was to establish an international standard based on both gold and silver that would be less liable to fluctuations and not subject to constant appreciation.[26]

Among the writers arguing in favour of a bimetallist solution, an eminent figure was Henry Riversdale Grenfell. Grenfell (1824–1902), from a prominent London family of merchants, succeeded his father as a director of the Bank of England from 1865 to his death, and served as deputy governor and as governor of the Bank from 1879 to 1883 (Howe, 2004). He was a very active advocate of the bimetallic standard, and it is precisely in a pamphlet devoted to this subject that he suggested the interpretation of the great depression as the descending phase of a long wave.

In an address delivered in May 1886 before a meeting of the Bi-Metallic League in Birmingham, Grenfell argued, on the basis of *The Economist*'s index numbers, that Britain was experiencing 'a considerable fall in prices of all commodities'. He maintained that this fact 'is synonymous with a rise in the price of gold'. He recollected that after the demonetization of silver in Germany, the French mint ceased to offer a fixed price for silver in gold and restricted the coinage of silver, thereby factually interrupting the bimetallic standard. He pointed out that, as a consequence, the exchange ratio between gold and silver, which had remained constant on average since 1801 to that point, started to fall. Finally, he noted that the supply of gold had diminished after 1852. Thus the supply of gold had fallen while its demand was increasing, also because Scandinavia, Italy and the United States started absorbing gold (Grenfell, 1886, pp. 7–8).

If this situation explained why prices were falling, it still provided no inescapable reason why anything should be done about it. Grenfell noticed that there had been depressions in the past, without however necessarily requiring specific action. He argued, however, that previous depressions were different in depth, and it was precisely in this difference that laid the necessity of intervening:

> ... we must enquire whether there is anything in this particular depression, making it essentially different from previous depressions[.] ... I am sorry to say that I have lived long enough to recollect three or four of these trade depressions. From 1815 to the present time we have had a great many; indeed, one has occurred almost every ten years. After great inflations of prices, caused by over speculation, great depression of trade follows. Almost every ten years these fluctuations have occurred, and I think the Government were right in refusing to be easily alarmed or aroused when these alterations in trade were observed, seeing that they had generally sprung from natural causes, such as an over sanguine disposition at one time followed by a depressed state of men's minds in another. But the present depression in trade is almost unprecedented in length and severity (Grenfell, 1886, p. 9).

At this point, Grenfell advanced the suggestion that there were two distinct undulatory movements at play, one superposed onto the other: the decennial crises run on top of alternating swings of increasing or decreasing prices of much longer duration. Just like Jevons and the Manchester bankers, he found it convenient to use the waves metaphor to describe this effect:

> We will attempt to examine and to come to some right judgement on it. Many of you have crossed the Atlantic Ocean, and have observed the great Atlantic rollers, with smaller waves *riding, so to speak*, upon them. I may venture to compare the decennial depressions to the small waves, and the present depression to the large rollers. I think I may say that we had a long wave of depressed trade and unremunerative operations from the peace of 1815 up to the time of the gold discovery, then a long wave of prosperity up to the demonetization of silver, and a long, trying, dragging trade from 1873 to the present date (p. 9, emphasis added).

Grenfell's 'long wave' is only slightly more explicit than Jevons's, and although it claims to be based on price data, it is not depicted graphically. The idea of the shorter waves being independent of the great rollers and *riding* upon them (the same verb used by Jevons), however, is expounded very clearly.

FOXWELL ON PRICE FLUCTUATIONS, 1886

Shortly after Grenfell's speech, Herbert Somerton Foxwell — the editor of Jevons's (1884) *Currency and Finance*[27] in which the papers on gold mentioned above had been reprinted — took part in a series of lectures delivered in various Scottish locations on *The claims of Labour* (Oliphant, 1886). His contribution 'Irregularity of employment and fluctuations of prices' (Foxwell, 1886) was republished separately. As the title of the lecture suggests, Foxwell's main concern was the effect of price fluctuations on the stability of employment: 'interruptions of employment are to a great extent directly caused by disturbances originating in prices' (p. 25).

While Grenfell cited the *Economist*'s data without actually listing them, Foxwell presented data from an unspecified source in graphical form.[28] He presented diagrams of the index numbers of the prices of tin, iron, cotton and general wholesale prices from 1870 to 1886, and another curve of general wholesale prices from 1782 to 1886. The latter is reproduced as Fig. 3. Foxwell's reading of the latter is of interest:

> [The variation of general prices] is not a simple movement, due to a single set of causes, but a complex movement, made up, as we shall find on examination, of three kinds of movements, each due to a different set of causes (Foxwell, 1886, p. 31).

The most striking feature consists in

> the regular recurrence of a wave or undulation, once every ten years or so. This is the commercial fluctuation so well known in the business world by the crisis in which it

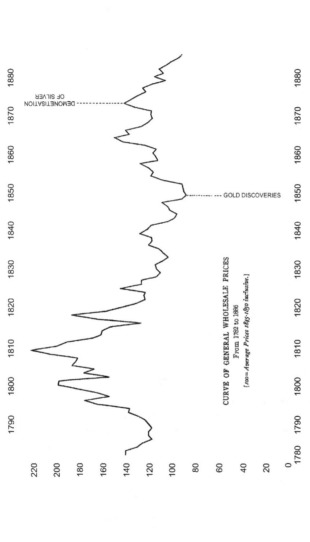

Fig. 3. Foxwell's Curve of the Index of General Wholesale Prices, 1782–1886, indicating the Gold Discoveries in 1850 and the Demonetization of Silver in 1873. *Source:* From Foxwell (1886, insert).

usually culminates. It has been distinguished as the 'credit cycle,'[29] because it is the result of the expansion and contraction of commercial credit. Jevons has calculated the average period of this cycle as about 10.6 years (*ibid.*, p. 32).

This 'wave occurring about every ten years', however, is irregular in shape. The elements giving rise to such unevenness and asymmetries are the curve's second component:

> This irregularity arises from movements in the general money market, due either to speculation in the money market itself, or to the effects on the money market of movements originating in the great wholesale markets. We must add, then, to the credit cycle, irregularities arising from the general markets, as a second element of the general price curve (*ibid.*).

These two movements are accompanied by a 'very impressive − to my mind almost awe-inspiring −... vast ground-swell, the greatest rhythm known to economic science' (p. 31). This is

> a more fundamental movement, underlying both those I have noticed,—the ground-swell, as I have called it, of the general price curve. The oscillations of the credit cycle, and of the general markets, do not take place about a horizontal level of prices, but about a base or standard of prices, which sometimes rises and sometimes falls, and whose movements retain the same direction for long periods of time. These fundamental movements of prices are caused by changes in the demand or supply of the monetary metals. We may speak of them as variations in the standard of value. I have already pointed out the general character of these variations. From 1785 to 1810 the value of money fell, and prices rose. From 1810 to 1850 the value of money rose, and prices fell. From 1850 to 1873 the value of money fell, and prices rose. Since 1873, the value of money has been rising again, and prices have fallen to the level of 1850 (pp. 32−33).

In Foxwell's description we have decennial waves, to which irregularities are additively superposed, both taking place on top of deep swells. The general movement results from the simple summation of three independently caused curves, of which Foxwell gives an idealized graphical rendition: the credit cycle is represented in the form of a smooth and symmetrical sine-like wave, the ground-swells are represented as angular trend lines, while the market disturbances are depicted as irregular and aperiodic vibrations (Fig. 4). Foxwell's use of annual data prevented him from considering the seasonal fluctuations detected by Jevons, which could have provided the fourth layer.

Foxwell drew two implications from his argument. The first one is that one can expect a credit wave to reverse its course fairly shortly and adapt one's business policy accordingly; but if the price fall is due to alterations in the monetary standard, low prices may be followed by still lower prices. Foxwell suggested that this was precisely the situation at the time when he was writing (p. 33). The second corollary is that the general trend of falling

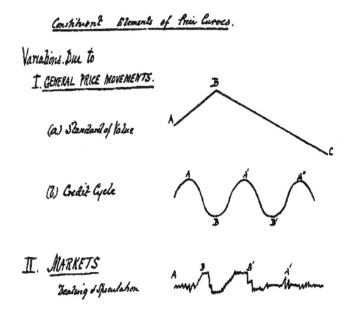

Fig. 4. Foxwell's Idealized Curves Representing Oscillations of Different Length: the Long Swells, the Decennial Credit Cycle and Short-Term Market Fluctuations. *Source*: From Foxwell (1886, insert).

or rising prices influences the relative length and depth of the decennial crises – a point he had earlier attributed to Hyde Clarke:[30]

> When the value of money is falling, the general basis of prices, about which the credit wave undulates, is an ascending line. Consequently, the years of rising prices are more numerous than those of falling prices; and the extent of the rise is increased, while the fall is broken. This was the case from 1850 to 1873; trade increased by leaps and bounds. Since 1873 the value of money has been rising. The basis of prices is a descending line. The situation is reversed (pp. 33–34).

SAUERBECK'S PRICE INDEX, AND FOXWELL'S EVIDENCE BEFORE THE ROYAL COMMISSION ON AGRICULTURE

After another few months, Augustus Sauerbeck[31] published a paper in the *Journal of the London Statistical Society* offering a fresh set of data illustrating the extent of the price fall. Drawing from various sources, Sauerbeck constructed index numbers of the average value of prices each year, rather than of prices taken at single points (Sauerbeck, 1886, appendix A); he took the average prices of the period 1866–1877 as a base. The general price index included the prices of 45 commodities from 1845 to 1885. Sauerbeck also offered a diagram with the index number of prices since 1820 (data before 1846 only include 31 commodities), to which a line representing the 10-year moving average since 1822 was added. Again, the now familiar undulatory long-term movement (once more qualified as 'wave') stands out, even better than in the diagrams by Jevons and Foxwell thanks to the smoothing effect of the moving average line:

> [The diagram illustrates] the up and down movements of the average prices in each year, and the principal political and commercial events. A second line (dotted) is inserted showing always the average of ten years. It obliterates still further the ordinary fluctuations, and gives a clear picture of the gradual movement of the average prices of whole periods, indicating the great downward course during the first half of the century, which reached its lowest point in the decade 1843–52 (= 82), the upward wave with the highest period from 1864–74 (= 102), and the retrograde movement since (Sauerbeck, 1886, p. 594).

Sauerbeck's index number, updated to 1912 in a yearly article in the same journal (renamed in 1887 *Journal of the Royal Statistical Society*), quickly became the standard reference for British prices. When, in 1894, Foxwell was called as a witness before the Royal Commission on Agriculture appointed to inquire about the agricultural depression, he produced Sauerbeck's diagram[32] as evidence, stating that among the seven or eight index numbers of prices available at the time he considered Sauerbeck's series to be 'the most carefully prepared and the one which best represents the general movement of prices' (Royal Commission on Agriculture, 1894, Q. 23,558; see also Q. 23,563), although all showed the same kind of movement (Q. 23,564). Foxwell objected to the significance of the moving average line, because by incorporating the prices of the previous 10 years 'when prices are descending the average is a little too high, and when prices are rising the average is a little too low'. He reported that, having consulted various authorities, the President of the Royal Statistical Society asserted that 'there was only one satisfactory way' of representing a good average line of a changing line, 'namely, by a hand drafted average; and ... to avoid suspicion of bias it was better to get the drafting done by a person who had nothing before him but the simple diagrammatic expression of the curve' (Q. 23,571). Foxwell thus asked Sauerbeck to draw a curve of the average manually, and had it before him when discussing the data; he did not, however, give a copy to the Commissioners, as there was no time to have the diagram corrected and reprinted) (Fig. 5).[33]

There are some differences between Foxwell's reading of his own diagram in 1886 and the evidence he gave based on Sauerbeck's diagram. One concerns the periodization of the first wave. While in 1886 Foxwell thought that the first general fall of prices had started in 1810, in 1894 he placed the beginning of the descent in 1817 or 1818, 'at the time when the resumption of cash payments was in contemplation':[34] 'The course of prices before that had been much higher during the Great War; but, starting from that point, we find a general tendency to a fall' (Q. 23,571). Sauerbeck's graph obviously does not support such a reading, for it only begins from 1820. A year later, Foxwell thought the fall had begun in 1815: he maintained, in fact, that it was accepted as 'a fact beyond dispute' and 'perhaps matter of common knowledge' that

> Setting aside the movements due to periodic outbursts of speculation, we find that after a persistent fall of prices from the Peace of 1815, to the gold discoveries of 1848, there followed a rise, rapid at first, and afterwards more gradual, which culminated in 1873; from which year to the present time there has been an almost continuous fall, only broken by slight recoveries about the dates 1880 and 1890 (Foxwell, 1895, p. 3).

Further slight differences in emphasis can be found in Foxwell's description of the causes of fluctuations – again, in the form of three independent sets of causes of fluctuations. Let me quote at length:

> Q. 23,573: Would you state what are the causes to which you attribute the various fluctuations? — I wish to say that for the purpose of analysis, I think it is sufficient to remark upon three different causes of the fluctuations which we see given us in any such curve of prices. In the first place, you have fluctuations which are of a more or less accidental and temporary kind, due to fluctuations in demand and supply of commodities, and so forth, which we may describe as market causes, causing the peculiarly characteristic shape of that curve in particular places. Then it has been pointed out by economists for a long time past that there has been a tendency—at all events, there was a tendency up to year 1873—to a fluctuation of a longer period, and, generally speaking, cyclic or periodic in its nature—a speculative fluctuation: a rise of prices during one portion of the period, followed by a fall, after the collapse of the speculative prices, and generally speaking occupying a period of some 10 years—or something like 10½ years as the late Professor Jevons thought. I think that that is pretty obvious upon the curve. It is pretty obvious that, besides those peculiar market fluctuations which give it an irregular character, there is a wave, a periodic fluctuation, every 10 years. That is fairly marked until you get to 1873, after which the curve becomes very continuous, I admit. I do not attribute that variation to the causes of which I wish to speak particularly to-day. I attribute that mainly to a speculative movement which seems to recur in that way; it has recurred, at all events, in the past at something like the interval of 10 years. But after setting aside the

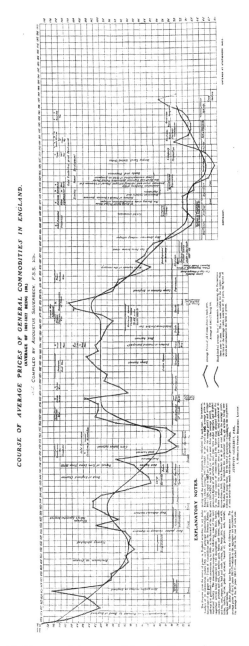

Fig. 5. Sauerbeck's Course of Average Prices of General Commodities in England.
Source: From Sauerbeck (1908).

fluctuation due to market causes, and the fluctuation due to this speculative cycle, there still remains an underlying movement, a sort of tidal movement, which has been called by the French mathematician and economist Cournot a great secular movement,[35] because it goes on for long periods of time in the same direction. I wish to lay very great stress upon the character which distinguishes that movement: that is not a movement which, as a rule, tends to correct itself. After the rise of prices owing to the speculative causes, you will probably get a fall. It was put to me once, I remember, by a merchant in Sheffield: 'We are accustomed to expect four or five good years, and then four or five bad years, and that we understand and are able to deal with; but here we have a persistent movement.' That persistent movement is in my opinion the underlying current movement; and if you take the whole period before us here, from 1817 down to 1893 or 1894, you will see that from 1817 to 1850 there was a general current movement in the direction of a fall of prices—at all events, a general movement which I will attribute as a matter of opinion to currency causes. After 1850 there is again a general movement, quite apart from the speculative movement to which I have referred, in the direction of a rise, terminating in 1873. After 1873 it is equally evident that there is a general movement in the direction of a fall (Royal Commission on Agriculture, 1894).

One of the peculiarities of this description, in contrast with the approach of 8 years before, is that Foxwell suspected that the 'credit cycle' (the expression was not used by him, but by one of the questioners: Q. 23,575) had become less conspicuous after 1873, as suggested by a visual inspection of Sauerbeck's graph (Fig. 5). He did not, however, elaborate on that.

A second feature is the stress on the self-correcting character of the speculative cycle, in contrast with the persistent nature of the effect of currency disturbances causing the secular movement.[36] The difference with the former version mostly consists in emphasis, as this argument was already clearly implicit in 1886 – even the anecdote about the Sheffield merchant had already been cited (Foxwell, 1886, p. 33). The explicit reference to self-correction, however, is interesting and rather revealing. Most writers in the second half of the nineteenth century would have agreed in interpreting crises not as aberrant disturbances to the 'normal' course of events, but as the painful yet necessary correction (sometimes called 'reaction') to the exaggerations that take place during prosperity, when 'feverish' speculation raises prices and induces further speculative trading on credit. This approach to crises, however, was not fully cyclical: the focus of the analysis was on crises, their causes and their consequences. The depression only set the stage for the next boom by eliminating the over-speculative trades and bringing the economic system back to its normal state; it did not, however, actively launch it. The causal chain is interrupted at this point: re-launching speculation requires some impulse, such as the 'passion for gambling' or the sanguine attitude of the public. The idea of recovery as being stimulated by the conditions of the depression was absent in most nineteenth-century writers, the asymmetry being apparent in the odd number of phases of the cycle to which a name was given, such as in Juglar's and Sauerbeck's three-fold denomination (prosperity, crisis, liquidation, and development of trade, crisis, depression, respectively; see Fig. 5) where an expression for recovery was missing. Foxwell's reference to self-correction belongs precisely to this tradition, as he clearly writes about 'speculative fluctuations', and refers to the fall of prices after the collapse of speculative rash, implying the idea of reaction, but does not mention any reason why there should be recovery after the fall.[37]

In the following years Foxwell made two additional passing references to Sauerbeck's data again hinting at the tidal movement of prices, which is worth recording for the sake of completeness. He reproduced Sauerbeck's diagram once more in a discussion about *The monetary situation*, an address before the Political Economy Circle of the National Liberal Club delivered in March 1895 (Foxwell, 1895a). The paper restated Foxwell's bimetallist position;[38] in particular, the diagram was juxtaposed with another graph depicting the fluctuation of the exchange rate of gold and silver, and the production of the two metals, in order to demonstrate that the value of silver fluctuated roughly in accordance with the general price level and that therefore the cause of price fluctuations after 1873 (their tendency to fall, in particular) resided in the oscillations of the value of gold. In this essay Foxwell did not discuss the decennial crises but focused exclusively on the long swings in prices; the paper is thus much less interesting than Foxwell's previous contributions on the subject. It is notable, nevertheless, that he had again slightly changed the periodization of the phases of rising and falling prices (see Table 1).

Two decades later, when discussing the inflation that took place during the war, Foxwell referred again to Sauerbeck's index numbers. He did not take up the general perspective on long-term oscillations, but he noticed that in 1896 the fall of prices was reversed, and again he attributed the cause of the movement to fluctuations to the supply of gold:

> Prices have been rising on the average, ever since 1896, at about the rate of 2 per cent per annum. That rise is explained by the large increase in the gold supplies (Foxwell, 1917, 1919 reprint, p. 232).

The sharper inflation since the beginning of the war, on the other hand, could not be accounted for by gold supplies: Foxwell saw its main cause in 'the enormous expenditure of the Governments', which occurred by means

Table 1. Periodization of Ascending and Descending Waves.

	High Prices/ Prosperous Trade	Low Prices/ Depressed Trade	High Prices/ Prosperous Trade	Low Prices/ Depressed Trade	High Prices/ Prosperous Trade	Low Prices/ Depressed Trade
Jevons	Enormous and long-continued elevation of prices 1790–1809	Fall in prices 1810–1849	1850–			
Grenfell (1886)		Long wave of depressed trade and unremunerative operations 1815–1850	Long wave of prosperity 1850–1873	Dragging trade 1873–		
Foxwell (1886)	Rising prices 1785–1810	Falling prices 1810–1850	General rise of prices 1850–1873	Downward movement of prices 1873–		
Sauerbeck (1886)		Great downfall course of 10-year average prices: first half of the century (data begin in 1822) to 1843–1853	1843–1853 to 1864–1874	From 1864–1874		
Foxwell (1894)		1817–1850	1850–1873	1873–		
Foxwell (1895)		1815–1849	Rapid increase in 1851, then high prices 1853–1873	1873–		
Foxwell (1919) Kondratiev (1926)	1780s–1810/1817	1810/1817–1844/1851	1844/1851–1870/1875	1870/ 1875–1890/1896	1896– 1890/1896–1914/1920	1914/1920–

of 'enormously increased issues of notes' (pp. 234–235), accompanied by a shortage of productive power.

CONCLUSION: WAVES, CYCLES AND FLUCTUATIONS

With their references to 'long waves' as distinct from decennial fluctuations, these English writers anticipated some of the themes that constitute Kondratiev's thesis, but surely not all of them.

Firstly, the British pioneers set a standard, concerning the periodization and the reliance on long-term data, which they used to give a statistical form to the general impression that during the last quarter of the nineteenth century Britain was undergoing a great depression the features of which were quite different from the periodical crises that had marked the previous decades. Rather than arguing that crises had evolved into something qualitatively different,[39] they identified an underlying movement taking place in the long run, upon which the recurrence of crises was superposed and which affected their characteristics, in particular their intensity and duration.[40]

Secondly, the British writers examined above only used statistics concerning British prices, and their reflections were limited accordingly. Kondratiev accepted their dataset, as he also referred to Jevons's series and Sauerbeck's updating (Kondratiev, 1928, English transl. p. 38n); but he also referred to data on France and considered other variables as well: interest rates, foreign trade turnover, production and consumption of coal, pig iron and lead. Kondratiev found that the movement of these variables largely corresponded with the wave suggested by price fluctuations; nevertheless, it required considering intervals rather than specific years to determine the turning points.[41] Nevertheless, the dating of the various ascending and descending phases of the waves offered by the Britons first and by Kondratiev later is fairly consistent; opinions only diverged concerning the turning point marking the beginning of the descent of prices in the second decade of the nineteenth century[42] (see Table 1). The British writers were clearly convinced that raising and falling prices are concomitant with (or have a causal relationship with) prosperity and depression. But their claim that there were long waves of prosperity and depression could only be based on price fluctuations, while the arguments of Kondratiev (and, before him, van Gelderen) were more general in scope and based on wider empirical grounds.

The third aspect to be compared concerns the wave metaphor. Previously and contemporarily to our writers, this trope was frequently used in the context of crises and economic fluctuations, but with emphasis on different traits of the comparison term. A first metaphorical usage of 'waves' indicated the existence of a mechanism of transmission from cause to effect, through space (e.g., from country to country or from centres to the periphery) or from one branch of business to another, the intensity of which decreases on the base of the distance travelled, as in the following examples: '... the tide of England's commercial prosperity, whose enriching wave, though more attenuated as more widely extended from the centres of commercial circles, has nevertheless reached the most distant agricultural districts' (Heyworth, 1841, p. 9); or 'England ... suffers from crises, panics, and times of terror—the effects of which reverberate all over the world. Other countries suffer from crises, but they do not affect England, for frequently they are but the consequence of the wave which first rises in England. If this wave can travel so fast, what must be its height at the centre, in the country where it comes from?' (Seyd, 1875, p. 77). A second usage of the wave metaphor, incorporating both the idea of transmission and the idea of an overwhelming and all-encompassing effect, is that of the tidal wave, often taking the form of the expression 'wave of depression' – which, not surprisingly, had a surge in usage at the end of the 1870s to a peak in the mid-1880s in the United States and at the end of the decade in Britain (see, for a few examples, the second section above).[43] Other writers used the wave metaphor for a third purpose, to indicate that trade alternates between good times and bad times, so that prosperity must be followed by depression and conversely,[44] as in the following examples: George Wilson pointed out that 'Nothing in nature can be forever increased. The physical law of the "rhythm of motion" applies everywhere. We ride up on a wave of apparent prosperity for everybody, but we must stop some time to reach the top of the wave: and then we cannot stop on it always. Some cause will bring us down, sooner or later' (Wilson, 1880, p. 27), while an anonymous contributor to *Capital and Labour* stressed that 'There have always been waves and cycles of success and failure, alike in agriculture and in commerce, and notwithstanding the prolonged season of depression and failure through which the country has passed, we may yet anticipate speedy improvement' (Anonymous, 1881). Accordingly, waves have crests that must be taken advantage of ('It is the opinion of many real estate men that the crest of the present wave of high prices will come next summer. Many real estate speculators who bought up cheap property during the dull season are preparing to unload then':

Anonymous 1, 1886) before they break ('It is our duty to make the most of the wave of prosperity, which would be broken on the rock of political disturbance': Anonymous 2, 1886). Typically, such waves are irregular and unpredictable ('We have suffered periodically financial crashes and revulsions, tossed upon its uncertain waves, blown up and down by the breath of speculation': Spaulding, 1869, p. 115). Most notably, the alternance of ups and downs of the waves was used to indicate that a series of prosperous years will be followed by a number of years of depression, without any causal implication, precisely as a string of heads must come after a string of tails in the tossing of a coin.

Fourthly, the waves metaphor was occasionally employed in a more technical way. Some writers used waves to represent fluctuations around the average or true level: Danson diagrammatically represented the variations of the price of wheat in France, obtaining a 'waved line ... [indicating] the variations of the annual price, above and below the average' (Danson, 1850, p. 158), while a correspondent of the *New-York Tribune* argued that the waves of market prices did not alter the intrinsic value of gold: 'Leaving out of the calculation the little ups and downs of market prices, which, like the waves of the sea, do not affect the general level, no nation and no government can raise or sink the value of a definite quantity of gold' (Anonymous 1, 1874). It was only much later, in the interwar years, that waves were used in a fifth meaning to refer to a proper cycle, with causally connected phases, in the sense of undulatory motion as described by physics − similarly to the analogous way of using the pendulum metaphor in the same years: see Louçã (2001, 2007). Hansen and Tout, for instance, explained that

> To understand the business cycle it is necessary first, to examine the internal structure of the present order, which 'causes' economic life to move in a wave-like manner in the same sense that the internal structure of the pendulum 'causes' it to swing in definite periods; and second, to examine into those initiating forces which 'cause' the cycle movement in the same sense that a kick 'causes' the pendulum to swing (Hansen & Tout, 1933, p. 120).

Similarly, Irving Fisher pointed out that

> There are two sorts of cyclical tendencies. One is 'forced' or imposed on the economic mechanism from outside. Such is the yearly rhythm; also the daily rhythm. Both the yearly and the daily rhythm are imposed on us by astronomical forces from outside the economic organisation; and there may be others such as from sunspots or transits of Venus. Other examples of 'forced' cycles are the monthly and weekly rhythms imposed on us by custom and religion.

> The second sort of cyclical tendency is the 'free' cycle, not forced from outside, but self-generating, operating analogously to a pendulum or wave motion (Fisher, 1938, p. 338).

The use of the waves metaphor by Jevons and the other Britons discussed in this chapter is not only descriptive as the previous and contemporary references to this trope, but couples it with a very specific physical property of waves:[45] that of not disturbing other waves travelling on the same medium, so that their movement remain mutually independent and their resulting amplitude is simply the sum of the amplitudes of the individual waves, each one retaining its own periodicity. These writers all stressed that the waves with different periodicity are subject to different causes independent of each other. It is also interesting that their use of the waves metaphor was connected to the image of undulation as it appeared in diagrams, of which these writers were among the early users for argumentative purposes (see note 5): the analogy was therefore both visual and functional.

Not for Kondratiev. He argued that the dynamics of the 10-year cycle and the long waves are not independent:

> I did not touch on the question of the relationship between the two aforementioned types of process. This does not mean that I thought that evolutionary processes go their own way and that fluctuating processes go their own way, the two being in reality, different and independent. That is not my opinion. The process of the real dynamics is unified. But it is not linear, it is not represented by a simple ascending line. On the contrary, it is formed non-uniformly by shocks and fluctuations. Only for the purposes of study and analysis can we focus our attention either on the processes of general development and the stages and forms of this development or, conversely, on fluctuating processes, by adopting a conventional scientific approach (appropriate to the solution of analytic problems) (Kondratiev, 1926, 1998, translation p. 25).

Kondratiev's theory of long cycles was an extension of Tugan's theory of the business cycle based on the accumulation of loanable funds to very durable forms of capital (see e.g., Reijnders, 1993). In this perspective, one can indeed hardly separate 10-year cycles from long ones, as free loanable funds are in liquid form that can be channelled either towards shorter- or longer-run investments precisely because they are free. Kondratiev was therefore correct in claiming that, in his theoretical perspective, the dynamics of short and long cycles are to be treated as united. It is doubtful, however, that he was justified in separating them for the sake of analysis and focus only on one of them.[46] Such a separation would be possible only if the two processes were independent, that is, linear (Goodwin, 1953, in 1982 reprint p. 113) − not in Kondratiev's sense in the citation above of giving rise to straight lines, but meaning that equations are linear. Thus, far from rejecting the property of waves superposition which the Britons referred to, Kondratiev's separation of long and short cycles presupposed it.

The fourth aspect to be stressed in the comparison of the forerunners of the long wave theory and Kondratiev's approach is that, as a consequence of applying to dynamics of prices and crises the superposition principle of waves the writers considered in these pages could interpret the depressions of the 1870s and 1880s as belonging to the same qualitative kind as the previous crises, differing only in severity, in contrast with the view of writers such as Atkins and Engels cited in section 'Henry Riversdale Grenfell and the Bimetallism Debate' above. Accordingly, they could explain the difference of intensity and in the relative length of prosperities and depressions in different periods without resorting to ad hoc or topical assumptions, but within a unitarian framework. Kondratiev similarly stressed that the phase of the long cycle onto which the decennial cycle is threaded affects the features of the latter, thereby interpreting prolonged depressions within the same framework as successions of periods characterized by numerous ample booms interrupted by short and shallow crises (Kondratiev, 1926, 1998 translation, pp. 47–48).

This leads to the fifth and final aspect to be compared concerning the status of long waves. The approach of the British pioneers was surely more descriptive than theoretical. They did identify a cause of fluctuations, which regarded policy issues and the supply of gold rather than the dynamics of capitalist economies. Although they identified and quite precisely periodized prolonged times of inflation alternating with times of falling prices, respectively corresponding to prosperities and depressions, and insisted that such fluctuations were clearly recognizable from the tabular data and from the diagrams, they never claimed that they were part of a cycle. On the contrary, Kondratiev and van Gelderen considered the waves as constituting a cycle, which they not only described in its features, but tried to explain, by extending Tugan-Baranovsky's theory of the 10-year cycle based on the fluctuations of free loanable funds to the long run. Kondratiev, probably aware of the debates at the end of the previous century – at least by reading Jevons's and Sauerbeck's contributions – endogenized the fluctuations of the supply of gold, arguing that periods of scarcity of gold would exert a strong pressure towards improving extractive methods and searching for new sources. He maintained that attributing the long waves to fluctuations in the gold supply was just mistaking the effect for the cause (Kondratiev, 1926, English transl. p. 49). Jevons was aware that the increase in production driving the demand for gold was affected by technological progress, but discarded its influence on price fluctuations, arguing that inventions had to be distributed more or less evenly in time (Jevons, 1865, pp. 131–132). Kondratiev countered that 'from the scientific point of view it would be even more wrong to think that the direction and intensity of these discoveries and inventions were completely random', and that they should be considered instead as driven by the needs of production (Kondratiev, 1926, English transl. p. 49).

This difference in approach needs to be set in context. The idea that the economic system revolves in cycles, with each phase causing the next one, had only very few representatives in Britain in the last quarter of the nineteenth century.[47] The two notable exceptions were John Mills and Walter Bagehot.[48] While most writers at the time maintained that the normal state of an economic system consisted in prosperity, the abandonment of which, due to excessive greediness or passion for gambling, set up a (usually sudden and violent) reaction bringing the system back to normal, Mills suggested instead that the normal state of the system consisted in a cycle during which

> commercial Credit runs through the mutations of a life, having its infancy, growth to maturity, diseased over-growth, and death by collapse; and that each cycle is composed of well-marked normal stages, corresponding to these ideas in nature and succession. And as Credit is a thing of moral essence, the external character of each stage of its development is traced to a parallel change of mental mood, and we find the whole subject embraced under the wider generalisation of a normal tendency of the human mind (Mills, 1868, p. 17).

Mills insisted on the importance of the successional order of this cycle of development (p. 17), and that 'it is of importance to carry with us this idea of the normalism of the successive phases,—because accidental modifications frequently occur which may distract attention from the main line of the case' (p. 22). His contribution is more important for the idea of the normality of the entire cycle rather than its specific explanation (probably the first one based on a psychological mechanism), as illustrated in the idealized graphs reproduced as Fig. 2.[49]

On the other hand, Bagehot suggested a theory of the cycle based on fluctuations in the availability of loanable funds: during prosperity, the accumulation of capital after a while absorbs the savings that have piled up during depression and requires even more. The supply of savings, however, cannot keep the pace, for increased activity in one trade induces further increases in other trades, and consequently the cost of money rises. But this strains trade, and any incident eventually blocking the advance in one branch, and consequently in all its suppliers, eventually affect the entire economy. The value of, and the demand for, loanable funds drops, and saving increases again at a rate faster than investment. When a large amount of free capital has accumulated and interest rates are low, sooner or later investment is bound to restart a new cycle (Bagehot, 1873a, 1873b; for a discussion see O'Brien, 2001). In Britain, however, Bagehot's suggestion was not explored any further, and was rescued by Tugan-Baranovsky only two decades later.[50]

However, by the end of the century a number of German-speaking authors were heading towards the understanding of the dynamics of capitalist economies in terms of cycles – most notably Tugan-Baranovsky, who was Kondratiev's mentor.[51] By the time Kondratiev was writing, in the 1920s, the cyclical approach – business cycle theory, as it was called by then in the United States following the terminology used by Mitchell, or trade cycle theory in Britain, following the title of Lavington's book – was almost universally accepted. Business cycle institutes were active throughout the western world and in Soviet Russia, and it is precisely from the Moscow institute that Kondratiev was writing. Business cycles theory had not yet turned mathematical, but the idea that the dynamics of capitalist economies revolve in cycles, each phase of which is rooted in the previous one and causes the following stage, was widespread, and there were a number of theories upon which one could elaborate when thinking of a cycle with different frequency. The very idea of the simultaneous existence of cycles of different periods was not new either, as the article by Kitchin illustrating the short cycles, later eponymously named after him, was published in 1923, and had been cited by Kondratiev himself.[52]

The interpretation of long waves as cyclical, rather than as fluctuations driven by some exogenous cause combined with a policy factor, was surely facilitated by Kondratiev's intellectual environment more than it could have been for Foxwell (let alone Grenfell). Foxwell was in a way caught in the middle. On the one hand, his idealized representation of the cycle (Fig. 3) took up Mills's (Fig. 2) and reflected a symmetrical understanding of the phenomenon. On the other hand, the analytical mechanism he envisaged revealed an asymmetrical interpretation. His formulation (in the long quotation on pp. 266–268) of the self-correcting character of the credit cycle[53] meant, in fact, that excessive prices due to speculation caused a reversal, while Foxwell did not give any indication of the reasons why the opposite deviation should have brought about a further inversion and why such a movement should have been self-sustaining. In the lecture on unemployment, where he dwelled a bit longer on the decennial fluctuations, he blamed the depression on 'the misdirection and unintelligent development of industry' and financial crises on 'rash speculation, fostered by bad banking' (Foxwell, 1886, pp. 55–56): a diagnosis that does not permit a symmetrical explanation of recovery and progress or for a complete circular chain of causation between phases.

The long waves of Jevons, Foxwell and Grenfell are thus only fluctuations, not cycles. They are exogenously caused tidal waves on the top of which the decennial crises can run their repetitive course, without affecting the long-run development while being affected by it only in the obvious mechanical sense that prosperities are longer and more marked than depressions during the ascending phase of the long wave and conversely. Kondratiev's long cycle instead is a genuine cycle, in which phases are causally chained to each other. It is thought to be endogenously caused by the same factors determining the decennial cycle, yet Kondratiev treated it as independent from it.

This difference in perspective, deep as it is, is nevertheless nothing more than a reflection and a projection in the long run of the gap between the understanding of crises and of business cycles prevalent in the last quarter of the nineteenth century in Britain on the one hand, and almost everywhere in the 1920s on the other. Far from being an anachronism or merely based on similarity in the terminology, the inclusion of Grenfell and Foxwell (and Sauerbeck to a smaller extent) in the narrative of the history of long waves theory fills the gap between Jevons's contributions in the 1860s and Tugan's in 1894 and Parvus's in 1901:[54] chronologically, as it shows that the discussion was not interrupted after Jevons, but was resumed, building further upon his data and arguments; theoretically, as the long-run approach to the problem of recurring crises mirrored the status of the reflection on the same issue in the decennial perspective; epistemologically, as there is a continuum in the increased reliance on empirical data in research on this subject and in the use of the graphical method of representation; and historically, as the reflections and the debates on the Great Depression were seen as both a practical and theoretical problem, requiring at once a policy solution and a new framework to understand the changing characteristics of crises.

NOTES

1. Judging from the table of contents, Tugan's discussion of long-run factors in the background of English crises in the first part of the German and French editions

(1901 and 1913) were already present in the first Russian version of 1894. I am grateful to François Allisson for having translated the table of contents for me.

2. See for example, van Duijn (1983), Ch. IV; Mager (1987), pp. 21–24; Barnett (1998), pp. 106 and 115–118; Boccara (1993); Fontvieille (1993); Reijnders (1990), Ch. 2; Reijnders and Louçã (1999); Kleinknecht (1987); Freeman (1996); Makasheva (1993) refers to Kondratiev's Russian predecessors and contemporaries.

3. The line of thinkers beginning with Langdon, followed by Jevons and Mills and eventually reaching Foxwell, who emphasized the coexistence and superposition of independent fluctuations of different periods ascribed to different causes, has already been noted by Eugen von Bergmann in his brilliant history of the theories of crises published in 1895 (pp. 240–255).

4. Jevons himself later described it as a 'much-questioned' issue that called forth 'hundreds of publications' and created 'incessant discussion', the opinion about the subject being 'divided' (Jevons, 1865, in 1884, p. 119).

5. This remark by Jevons, as well as other similar ones cited below in the text, witnesses that graphical representations of data were rather uncommon at the time. Despite early usage by Playfair (1785–1786, 1798, 1805) of diagrams to depict the movement of economic variables in time and occasional occurrence of time-series graphs in the first half of the nineteenth century (Galton, 1813; West, 1826; the astonishing Cooke, 1828; Danson, 1850; Jones, 1845; Thorburn, 1854), the usage of this tool remained uncommon until the 1870s. Several of these writers had to publish their diagrams at their own expenses, as Jevons had to do in order to print his 1862 charts (for a history of graphical representations of data see Funkhouser, 1937; for a discussion more specifically focused on economics, see e.g., Klein, 2001; Maas & Morgan, 2002).

6. G. F. refers here to the opinion of the editor of *The Economist* according to whom there is 'a sort of tide in the cash transactions of the country', with an outgoing current at the end of each quarter, while there is an incoming flow at the middle of each quarter (14 October 1865, cited in Jevons, 1866, in 1884, p. 162).

7. Jevons was elected a member of the Society in 1865–1866 session, and became vice-president in 1868–1869 and president in 1869–1871. He was very active, and contributed with several papers: see Ashton (1934), chapter VIII.

8. A few years later, Edgeworth explained the relationship between waves of different length, namely, the decennial fluctuations and the oscillations resulting from the action of the law of errors operating on the summation of random shocks as follows: 'We must distinguish the undulations which have not been reduced to law from the *tides* which Jevons analysed. The normal law of fluctuation applies not so much to the ebb and flow of tides, as to the undulatory motion which is relative to, superadded on, those periodic movements' (Edgeworth, 1888, pp. 114–115).

9. The learned Bergmann (1895) is an exception (see note 3). For an assessment of their contribution and influence, essentially exerted on Jevons, see Ashton (1934), chapter VI.

10. Before the late 1870s, 'periodicity' was used mostly as 'recurrence'. After Jevons's inquiry on solar activity as the cause of crises in the late 1870s, the term referred more often to a fairly strict chronological regularity: see Besomi (2010a).

11. Meteorological terminology may have helped the transition. Although the Oxford English Dictionary dates in 1881 the first occurrence of 'depression' as 'A

lowering of the column of mercury in the barometer or of the atmospheric pressure which is thereby measured' (*OED*, 2014), the term seems to have been introduced gradually, as the expression 'depression of the barometer' was already used in the 1820s (e.g., in the title of an article by Howard in 1822), with several occurrences appearing regularly in later years. In 1878 the usage was established enough to induce Arthur Crump to write about 'unprofitable transactions originating with traders who have little or no capital that constitute the great depression, to use a meteorological phrase, which culminates in the whirlwind of a commercial crisis' (Crump, 1878, p. 216).

12. Besides the analysis of frequency of the occurrence of the terms 'crisis' and 'depression' in the title of writings on the subject as conducted in Besomi (2011), it is also possible to examine the normalized frequency of the expressions containing these two words by means of Google n-grams (https://books.google.com/ngrams), a tool that searches through a sample of the books digitized by Google. Considering the expressions 'commercial crisis', 'financial crisis', 'monetary crisis', 'economic crisis'; and 'commercial depression', 'trade depression', 'economic depression', 'financial depression', 'industrial depression', 'depression of trade', 'agricultural depression', in singular and in plural, individually or grouping those based on 'crises' separately from those based on 'depression', one notices that, both in British and in American English, the expressions based on 'depression' have been in use since the 1820s, but have had a sudden increase in frequency of usage since the late 1870s. While in American English the terms based on 'crisis' remained predominant from the 1837 panic till the end of the nineteenth century and again after the mid-1940s, in British English the expressions based on 'depression' became dominant in the late 1870s to be used less frequently than 'crises' from the late 1930s. In British English the expressions concerning 'depression' used more frequently in the late 1870s and responsible for surpassing 'commercial' and 'financial crises', were 'commercial depression' and 'depression of trade' and, towards the end of the century, 'agricultural depression'; in the United States, the favourite expressions using 'depression' took the adjectives 'financial' (from the mid-1870s) and 'industrial' (from the early 1880s).

13. In the original edition of 1845, Engels had probably taken the figure from John Wade's *History of the Middle and Working Classes* (Wade, 1833): see Besomi (2008), pp. 629–631.

14. Horton was a friend of Foxwell: see note 38.

15. The changing status of this image is discussed in Besomi (2014).

16. 'Les crises sont parfois aiguës mais de courte durée, comme celles de 1847 et de 1857, parfois persistantes comme celles de 1874, 1888. Si on veut comparer les maladies de la circulation à celles du corps humain, on peut dire que les premières ont le caractère d'une inflammation et les secondes celui d'une anémie' (my translation).

17. Juglar instead used a similar metaphor to distinguish the crisis from its successive liquidation. When 'disappointment begins and everybody complains; high prices have melted away; nothing can be sold except at a loss, and all aspects of social life bear a mark of this situation. It is no longer an acute disease, but a chronic illness that undermines an entire nation by causing falling prices, the slowing down of business and unemployment' ('C'est alors [during the liquidation] que

les désillusions commencent et que les plaintes s'élèvent de toutes parts; partout les hauts prix ont disparu; on ne peut rien réaliser sans perte et toutes les manifestations de la vie sociale en portent la trace; ce n'est plus une maladie aiguë, c'est une maladie chronique qui mine une nation par la baisse des prix, le ralentissement des affaires et les chômages qui en sont la conséquence': Juglar (1886), p. 6 of the offprint; my translation).

18. 'Nous appellerons "crise" les perturbations qui viennent troubler la marche régulière des affaires ... la crise [constitue] l'explosion du mal, le point aigu d'un état maladif préalable; [le terme 'crise'] n'aurai aucun sens si on voulait l'appliquer à un état prolongé de langueur, de marasme, à une condition morbide chronique, pour laquelle les Anglais emploient le mot de *depression*, tandis qu'ils réservent l'expression de 'crise' aux accidents subits, qui ont souvent un caractère de panique' (my translation).

19. As explained by Gibbs, 'The main reason why a continuous or prolonged fall in prices causes depression in trade and industry is, that it discourages enterprise on the part of capitalists, whether large or small; and by increasing the burden of their obligations gradually deprives them of the power to extend or even to carry on productive industries. This state of things sooner or later must rob an increasing population of wage earners of the opportunities of labour. This, in its turn, must react prejudicially on the army of distributors (sometimes called middlemen), whether merchants, brokers or shopkeepers, and on the auxiliary businesses of bankers, stockbrokers and others. The process by which the wave of depression, caused by the failure and inability of capitalists to keep the wheels of industry going, reaches these latter classes, may be a slow one. But it will reach them at last' (Gibbs, 1894, p. 107).

20. The symmetrical concept to the 'wave of depression' is naturally a 'wave of prosperity'. In the last quarter of the century, however, such tides were more often wished for than actually witnessed. In 1874 *Capital and Labour* expressed the 'hope that the tide will turn, and that there will be once more a wave of commercial prosperity' (Anonymous 2, 1874, p. 1010); three years later someone writing for the same periodical was still optimistic: 'Advices from the United States report that trade there is unquestionably improving ... Perhaps the wave of returning prosperity will gradually approach our shores' (Anonymous, 1877). John Miller, writing retrospectively at the end of the century observed that 'there are ebbs and flows, and when each wave of prosperity has flowed to us during the last twenty years many hopes have been raised that at last it had come to go forward and grow in volume as it rolled, but these hopes have not been realised' (Miller, 1894, p. 16).

21. The expression 'hard times', not specifically tied to economic conditions, was naturally used more often than 'depression of trade' (as indicated by Google n-grams: see note 12). The frequency diagram of its usage in British English, however, shows a rapid increase in the late 1870s.

22. Shrewd contemporary observers were aware that conditions were not worse (and probably better) in terms of production and employment than during the liquidation of previous crises. Nevertheless, it was argued that ' "Depressions" ... may exist when almost all the statistical sign point the other way'. The gloomy feeling of depression is generated by falling prices that hit merchants and capitalists (Giffen, 1885, pp. 801–804). Also see note 19.

23. For instance, Archibald Alison discerned in the falling prices consequent to the 'diminution of the supplies of the world's currency ... one of the causes of the extraordinary depression of trade' of the first half of the nineteenth century: reported in Patterson (1882), p. 20, who also cites Newmarch (1878) to the same effect. Sauerbeck, with reference to the 1870s and 1880s, also wrote about 'The extraordinary and almost unprecedented fall of prices which has characterized the commercial history of the last twelve years, and the consequent depression of trade' (1886, p. 1). More pointedly and precisely, Giffen argued that the general fall of prices 'produces much of the gloom. Merchants and capitalists are hit by it. At their stock-takings, with the same quantities of goods, or even with greater quantities, their nominal capital appears reduced. In falling markets their operations result steadily in loss for a considerable period. Many who have conducted operations with borrowed money are cleaned out; and fail. The community need be none the poorer. The goods themselves are not destroyed. Somebody gets the benefit of the lower prices. But the leaders of industrial enterprise, those who run the machine, are all poorer, and feel even poorer than they really are, as they are accustomed to look mainly at nominal values, and not at the quantities of the things themselves which they possess'. Again: 'A fall of prices ... is a usual feature in every depressed period, and accentuates and very largely creates the depression' (pp. 803, 806 and *passim*). Giffen's conclusion is subscribed to by Smith, 1887, pp. 85–88). Henry Meysey-Thompson similarly stressed the role of indebtment: a persistent fall in the price level 'constantly increases the burden of all debts. Every manufacturing concern with heavy debenture or mortgage debts would eventually fail. Every shop-keeper who had a lease and had borrowed some money would break; every landowner who had heavy family charges would be swept away; every farmer who had borrowed money from the bank must go into the bankruptcy court. It has been said that there is a time in the history of a nation when no one can afford to be idle; meaning, of course, that the rewards of industry are so great. But there is also a time when no man can afford to be busy. In a time of increasing currency and rising prices the man who works hardest, and embarks most capital in his business, makes most; but in a time of decreasing currency and falling prices the man who works hardest and embarks most capital loses most. What we call prosperous times are times when everyone can work his hardest and produce with both hands, and exchange what he produces at a profit; but that can only happen when currency increases as fast as the demands of increasing population and increasing trade' (Meysey-Thompson, 1888, pp. 50–51). Finally, a leaflet by the Bimetallic League maintains that 'writers on money from Hume to Walker [have argued] that rising prices encourage and falling prices discourage industry' (London Bimetallic League circa, 1896, p. 4).

24. For example, Thomas Wilson stated that 'it is generally admitted' that 'our present currency system ... has caused depression of trade and great depression in the prices of commodities': in Grenfell (1886), p. 19.

25. For instance, William Houldsworth was 'disposed to hold that Falling Prices and Depression of Trade are synonymous terms' (1895, p. 215).

26. For a summary of the bimetallist position, see Green 1998, pp. 588–593.

27. In 1881 Foxwell had succeeded Jevons in the University College Chair in London. For a biographical portrait see Keynes (1936).

28. Foxwell's graph, however, probably combines the diagram plotted by Jevons (1865) for the interval 1782–1850, and a graphical rendition of the *Economist*'s figures. A similar curve had been previously drawn by Laughlin in 1886 (between pages 38 and 39), who explicitly cited both Jevons and the *Economist* as his sources. Laughlin's line, however, showed the discontinuity between the two sources, while Foxwell seems to have adjusted the baseline.

29. The expression seems to be due to Mills (1868); Foxwell may have picked it up from Jevons, who attributed it to Mills in his *Primer of political economy* (1878), p. 121.

30. In his introduction to Jevons's *Currency and Finance*, Foxwell noted that 'reference was made by Mr. Hyde Clarke to the probability that some longer periodicity (e.g., a period of 26½ years) might overlie and interfere with the recurrence of the decennial period principally considered by Mr. Jevons', lamenting however that reliable statistical materials were not available for long enough periods for an adequate inquiry (Foxwell, 1884, p. xxxv).

31. Little is known about Augustus Sauerbeck: De Gruyters's World Biographical Information System online does not carry any entry on him; there only seems to be a one-page obituary in the *Journal of the Royal Statistical Society* (Anonymous, 1929), focusing on his contribution on price indexes. No birthdate is reported.

32. Presumably in the updated version Sauerbeck had privately published in 1894, as requested by Foxwell (Sauerbeck, 1894; Royal Commission on Agriculture, 1894, Q. 23,560); Sauerbeck's diagram omitted the annotations indicating the phases of 'development of trade', 'crisis' and 'depression'. The graph was meant to be printed in an appendix of the *Report*, but apparently it was not.

33. In reprinting and updating his data in a separate print in 1908, reproduced here as Fig. 5, Sauerbeck substituted the moving average line with a 'hand-drafted average line of movements eliminating the fluctuations from year to year. This is more suitable for the diagram than the line of average index numbers of 10 years' (Sauerbeck, 1908).

34. The Act for the Resumption of Cash Payments, which resumed the convertibility of banknotes into gold, suspended by the Bank Restriction Act in 1797, had been under consideration for some time but was eventually passed only in 1819 to become effective in 1821. Meanwhile under this temporary paper-standard régime the bimetallism standard was officially abandoned and the gold standard was adopted with the 1816 Coinage Act (see Redish, 1990, 2000, chapter 5), ratifying an effective situation since 1774 when payments in silver had been limited to a maximum of 25£.

35. Cournot (1838), § 11: 'Cela n'empêche pas que la valeur moyenne ainsi déterminée ne puisse éprouver et n'éprouve en effet, sur une échelle de durée plus grande encore, des variations absolues. Ici, comme en astronomie, il faut reconnaitre des variations *séculaires*, indépendamment des variations *périodiques*.'

36. Weaker formulations of this thesis also circulated at the time. For instance, Giffen spoke of it focusing only on the possibility of weathering oscillating prices versus persistently falling prices: 'The point to which I would draw special attention is, that ... the most disastrous characteristic of the recent fall of prices has been the descent all round to a lower range than that of which there had been any previous

experience. It is this peculiarity which—more than anything else—has aggravated the gloom of merchants and capitalists during the last few years. Fluctuations of prices they are used to. Merchants know that there is one range of prices in a time of buoyancy and inflation, and quite another range in times of discredit. By the customary oscillations, the shrewder business people are enabled to make large profits, but during the last few years the shrewder as well as the less shrewd have been tried. Operations they ventured on when prices were falling to the customary low level have failed disastrously, because of a further fall which is altogether without precedent. The change is more like a revolution in prices than anything which usually happens in an ordinary cycle of prosperity and depression in trade' (Giffen, 1885, p. 809).

37. Foxwell's use of the term 'cycle' should not mislead into suggesting that he thought of a complete causal circle: see note 53.

38. Foxwell was the vice-president of the Bimetallic League (Spahr, 1893, p. 402). Keynes reports that Foxwell 'took a leading part in the Bimetallic controversy, as one of the outstanding academic supporters of change, and as a friend and helper of the American authorities, General F. A. Walker and Dana Horton' (Keynes, 1936, p. 599; CW X, p. 278).

39. Foxwell, however, was open to some doubt in his 1896 witness before the Agriculture commission when he admitted that the amplitude of decennial fluctuations had considerably diminished after 1873 (Q. 23,573, cited in previous section).

40. The contributions of these writers fit well with the observation that the interest in long waves is itself cyclical, as the hypothesis is usually discussed during the descending phase (Boccara, 1993; Freeman, 1996, p. xiv). Jevons, however, is a notable exception.

41. On Kondratiev's dating of long cycles, see Barnett (1998).

42. On the one hand, data for the earliest wave could have been poorer than for successive periods (Sauerbeck's series only begins in 1820). On the other hand, writers who believed that the currency has something to do with fluctuating prices would look for some relevant date in that connection. Both 1810 and 1817 were significant, the former being the peak of the inflationary pressure that induced the Parliament to establish a Select Committee to inquire into the high price of bullion (the result being the Bullion Report), and the latter being the year following the official establishment of the gold standard (Coinage Act of 1816).

43. Google n-grams show later peaks in 1918 (absolute maximum) and again in 1934 for British English, while in American usage only one peak followed in 1922.

44. Other tropes to express the same notion were the turning tides and the pendulum swinging back.

45. While they focused on the superposition property of waves, the British pioneers ignored other features that could have been implied by the same metaphor: for instance, they did not stress regularity, did not focus on their amplitude (whether constant or decreasing or wildly changing) and were not interested in their capacity of transmitting vibrations at a distance.

46. On the lack of realism of the assumption that loanable funds would remain waiting for an employment for as long as a quarter of a century, see Garvy (1943), p. 219.

47. On the theoretical triviality of the approach summarized in the main British dictionary of economics of that era, Palgrave's, see Bridel (2011).

48. Hyde Clarke also interpreted the 54-years cycle as being truly cyclical, because he believed that nature revolves cyclically and could actually be reduced to elementary laws (Clarke, 1838). The economy reflects this periodicity as it is subject to the influence of these physical recurrences, in particular meteorological ones affecting the abundance or scarcity of crops (Clarke, 1847).

49. It should be noted that the wave metaphor was not used in this connection, but only in the sense discussed above.

50. Bagehot was quoted by Tugan, but not in this connection.

51. Not surprisingly, Kondratiev's contribution was acknowledged earlier in Germany than it was in English-speaking countries: his 1926 article was first translated into German as 'Die langen Wellen der Konjunktur' (i.e., 'The long waves in the conjunctural cycle') in the same year, from which it was translated into English as 'The long waves in economic life' in 1935. The mistaken translation of Kondratiev's terminology originated here, 'long cycles' being rendered as 'long waves', surely taking up the tradition stemming from Kautsky, who wrote of the 'Wellenbewegung der kapitalistischen Industrie' (1901), an expression cited by Tugan (1901, p. 403), Dietzel (1909, p. 1091), Weber (1910, p. 25) and Schumpeter's 'Wellenbewegung des Wirtschaftslebens' (1914). Kondratiev himself used the term 'wave' but only to indicate the long upswings and downswings (Barnett, 1998a, pp. 106–107), thus applying it in the sense of advancing and regressing tidal waves as discussed above.

52. Kitchin described the short cycle as depending on psychological causes, the major cycle as consisting in an aggregation of two or three short cycles, and the trend as being linear and depending on variations in the volume of the world's money. He denied that the trend was cyclical in nature (Kitchin, 1923, p. 14), a position explicitly rejected by Kondratiev (1926, 1998 English translation p. 25).

53. The use of the word 'cycle' itself does not indicate a cyclical approach. Among its meanings recorded in the *Oxford English Dictionary* there are intervals of time, the execution of a specific pattern, or a recursive repetition of such patterns. Business cycles as they were understood in the first half of the twentieth century imply interpreting the word in the third sense, while the indication of a specific pattern followed by the economic system as *starting* from quiescence, slipping into excitement, culminating in a crisis, followed by a depression *ending* again in quiescence, as in the famous passage by Overstone (quoted by Foxwell in 1886, p. 55), underlies understanding the term 'cycle' in the second sense. For a more detailed discussion see Besomi (2011, pp. 89–94).

54. This is not to suggest that these writers exerted any influence upon the later development of long cycles theories. Grenfell's pamphlet is unlikely to have been read by many people, excluding the keenest debaters on bimetallism, the literature on the subject being very vast and topical. Foxwell may have read Grenfell's contribution, but there is no evidence to support this hypothesis. Foxwell's paper, although later deemed by Keynes as being his 'main original work' (Keynes, 1936, p. 612), seems to have been scarcely quoted (JSTOR only finds a handful of occurrences). Sauerbeck's price index, on the contrary, was one of the standard references for British prices, and was certainly used by Kondratiev. As pointed out by one of

the economic dictionaries of the time that cited it, 'the index numbers that Sauerbeck has calculated following those supplied by *The Economist* have been much exploited by bimetallists' (Guyot, 1901, p. 490: 'Les bimétallistes ont beaucoup exploité les *Index numbers* que M. Sauerbeck a établis à l'imitation de ceux de *The Economist*'). Commentators, however, were interested in the actual index rather than in the distinction between ordinary fluctuations and long-term movement.

ACKNOWLEDGMENT

I am grateful to Giorgio Colacchio, Francisco Louçã, Sonya Marie Scott and the journal's referees for helpful comments on the first draft of this chapter. The usual disclaimers apply.

REFERENCES

Anonymous 1. (1874). Gold and greenbacks. *New-York Tribune*, 13 August, p. 4.
Anonymous 2. (1874). The coal and iron trades. *Capital and Labour, 44,* 23 December, 1009–1010.
Anonymous. (1876). Finance and trade. *Memphis Daily Appeal*, 25 July, p. [3].
Anonymous. (1877, November 14). Board of trade returns for october. *Capital and Labour*, (195), 594.
Anonymous. (1878). The business outlook. *The Morning Star and Catholic Messenger*, 17 February, Morning, 6.
Anonymous. (1879). The unemployed in Victoria. *Capital and Labour: An Economic, Commercial, and Mechanical Journal, 301,* 26 November, 678.
Anonymous. (1881). Harvest prospects. *Capital and Labour: An Economic, Financial, and Commercial Journal, 391,* 17 August, 470.
Anonymous. (1885). Continental cuttings. *The Midland Figaro, 478,* 18 December, 14.
Anonymous. (1895). Sound money. Secretary Carlisle addresses the people of Kentucky. Why he is opposed to the free coinage of silver. *The Record-Union, LXXXIX,* 76, 21 May, 1.
Anonymous. (1929). Augustus Sauerbeck. *Journal of the Royal Statistical Society, 92*(2), 300.
Anonymous 1. (1886). Rambler's note book. *Springfield Globe-Republic*, 14 November, 5.
Anonymous 2. (1886). Mr. Service' speech. *The Australasian, 1033,* 16 January, 120.
Ashton, T. S. (1934). *Economic and social investigations in Manchester, 1833–1933. A centenary history of the Manchester statistical society.* London: King. Reprinted Hassocks: The Harvester Press, 1977.
Atkinson, E. (1885). *Addenda to the second edition of the distribution of products.* New York, NY: G. P. Putnam's Sons.
Bagehot, W. (1873a). *Lombard Street: A description of the money market.* London: King.
Bagehot, W. (1873b). The very peculiar position of the year 1873 (unsigned leader). *The Economist, 31,* (4 January), 1–3.

Barnett, V. (1998). Dating the long cycle turning points: Kondratiev and after. In N. Makasheva, W. J. Samuels, & V. Barnett (Eds.), *The works of Nikolai D. Kondratiev* (Vol. 1, pp. xxxv–xxx). London: Pickering & Chatto.

Barnett, V. (1998a). *Kondratiev and the dynamics of economic development: Long cycles and industrial growth in historical context*. London: Macmillan.

Bergmann, E. von (1895). *Geschichte der nationalökonomischen Krisentheorien*. Stuttgard: Kohlhammer.

Besomi, D. (2008). John Wade's early endogenous dynamic model: 'Commercial cycle' and theories of crises. *European Journal of the History of Economic Thought, 15*(4), 611–639.

Besomi, D. (2010a). The periodicity of crises. A survey of the literature before 1850. *Journal of the History of Economic Thought, 32*, 1 March, 85–132.

Besomi, D. (2010b). 'Periodic crises': Clément Juglar between theories of crises and theories of business cycles. *Research in the History of Economic Thought and Methodology, 28A*, 169–283.

Besomi, D. (2011). Naming crises. A note on semantics and chronology. In D. Besomi (Ed.), *Crises and cycles in economic dictionaries and encyclopedias* (pp. 54–132). London: Routledge [Chapter 3].

Besomi, D. (2014). Tempests of the business world: Weather metaphors for crises in the nineteenth century. In R. Baranzini & F. Allisson (Eds.), *Economics and other Branches – in the shade of the Oak Tree. Essays in honour of Pascal Bridel* (pp. 291–308). London: Pickering & Chatto.

Black, R. D. C. (1992). Dr. Kondratieff and Mr. Hyde Clarke. In W. J. Samuels (Ed.), *Research in the history of economic thought and methodology* (Vol. 9, pp. 35–58). Greenwich, CT: JAI Press.

Boccara, P. (1993). Poussées périodiques de la pensée sur les cycles longs, récurrence et irréversibilité: De l'apparition des fluctuations de période Kondratieff vers leur mise en cause radicale. *Economies et Sociétés, 27*(7–8), July–August, 73–139.

Bridel, P. (2011). "Of the 'old' Palgrave on crises". In D. Besomi (Ed.), *Crises and cycles in economic dictionaries and encyclopedias* (pp. 332–342). London: Routledge [Chapter 16].

Capie, F., & Wood, G. E. (1997). Great depression of 1873–1896. In D. Glasner (Ed.), *Business cycles and depressions. An encyclopedia* (pp. 287–288). New York, NY: Garland.

Clarke, H. (1838). On the mathematical law of the cycle. *The Railway Magazine and the Annals of Science V*, November, pp. 378–380.

Clarke, H. (1847). Physical economy – A preliminary inquiry into the physical laws governing the periods of famines and panics, Railway Register [reprinted in F. Louçã and J. Reijnders (eds.) *The foundations of long wave theory: Models and methodology*. Volume 1, Cheltenham: Edward Elgar, 1999, pp. 3–20].

Cooke, L. (1828). *A series of statistical charts shewing the fluctuations in quantity and value of the products of the soil, with various ascertainments obviously influential on the husbandry of the British Empire, founded on official and other authentic documents*. London: The Author.

Cournot, A. (1838). *Recherches sur les principes mathématiques de la théorie de la richesse*. Paris: Hachette.

Crump, A. (1878). *A new departure in the domain of political economy*. London: Longmans, Green, & Co.

Danson, J. T. (1850). On the fluctuations of the annual supply and average price of corn, in France, during the last seventy years, considered with particular reference to the political periods of 1792, 1814, 1830, and 1848. *Journal of the Statistical Society of London, 13*(2), May, 152–167.

Dietzel, H. (1909). Ernten (Erntzyklus und Wirtschaftszyklus). In J. Conrad et al. (Eds.), *Handwörterbuch der Staatswissenschaften* (3rd ed., pp. 1091–1102). Jena: Fisher.

Edgeworth, F. Y. (1888). The mathematical theory of banking. *Journal of the Royal Statistical Society, 51*(1), March, 113–127.

Engels, F. (1886). *Appendix to the condition of the working class in England in 1844*. New York, NY: John W. Lovell Company. Originally published in German in Leipzig: Otto Wigand, 1845.

Engels, F. (Ed.) (1887). *Editor's preface to K. Marx, Capital: A critical analysis of capitalist production*. London: Swan Sonnenschein, Lowrey, & Co.

Fisher, I. (1938). The debt-deflation theory of Great Depressions. *Econometrica, 1*(4), October, 337–357.

Fontvieille, L. (1993). Les débats théoriques à propos des mouvements longs. *Economies et Sociétés, 27*(7–8), July–August, 11–37.

Foxwell, H. S. (1884). Introduction to Jevons 1884, pp. xix–xliv.

Foxwell, H. S. (1886). *Irregularity of employment and fluctuations of prices*. Edinburgh: Co-operative Printing Company.

Foxwell, H. S. (1895). A criticism of Lord Farrer on the monetary standard. *National Review*, January (cited as reprinted in pamphlet form, London: Effingham Wilson).

Foxwell, H. S. (1895a). *The monetary situation*. Read before the Political Economy Circle of the National Liberal Club, March 27, 1895. London: Effingham Wilson. Translated as "La situation monetaire", *Revue d'Économie Politique*, vol. IX, 1895, pp.

Foxwell, H. S. (1917). Inflation: In what sense it exists; how far it can be controlled. *Journal of the Institute of Actuaries, October*, Reprinted in Foxwell, *Papers on Current Finance*, London: Macmillan, 1919, 220–262.

Freeman, C. (1996). Introduction to C. Freeman. In C. Freeman (Ed.), *Long wave theory* (pp. xiii–xxxvi). Cheltenham: Edward Elgar.

Funkhouser, H. G. (1937). Historical development of the graphical representation of statistical data. *Osiris, 3*, 269–404.

Galton, S. T. (1813). *A chart, exhibiting the relation between the amount of Bank of England notes in circulation, the rate of foreign exchanges, and the prices of gold and silver bullion and of wheat; with explanatory observations*. London: J. Johnson & Co.

Garvy, G. (1943). Kondratieff's theory of long cycles. *Review of Economic Statistics, 25*(4), November, 203–220.

Gibbs, H. H. (1894). The effects of the fall in the general level of prices, in: *International Bimetallic Conference. Mansion House, London. May 2nd and 3rd, 1894. Report of Proceedings*. London; Manchester: Effingham Wilson & Co.; Waterlow & Sons Limited, J. F. Cornish, pp. 106–162.

Gide, C. (1891). *Principes d'économie politique* (3rd ed.). Paris: Larose et Forcel.

Giffen, R. (1885). Trade depression and low prices. *Contemporary Review, 47*, June, 800–822.

Goodwin, R. M. (1953). The problem of trend and cycle. *Yorkshire Bulletin of Economic and Social Research, 5*(2), 89–97. Reprinted in Goodwin, *Essays in economic dynamics*, London: Macmillan, pp. 112–121.

Grenfell, H. R. (1886). *The silver question. Address delivered at Birmingham*. May 28th, 1886, Birmingham: Buckler Brothers.

Guyot, Y. (1901). Index numbers. In Y. Guyot & A. Raffalovich (Eds.), 1898–1901, *Dictionnaire du commerce, de l'industrie et de la banque* (Vol. 2, p. 490). Paris: Guillaumin.

Hansen, A. H., & Tout, H. (1933). Annual survey of business cycle theory: Investment and saving in business cycle theory. *Econometrica, 1*(2), April, 119–147.

Henderson, J. P. (1992). Astronomy, astrology and business cycles: Hyde Clarke's contribution. In W. J. Samuels (Ed.), *Research in the history of economic thought and methodology* (Vol. 9, pp.1–34). Greenwich, CT: JAI Press.

Heyworth, L. (1841). *To the working classes ... on the natural law of wages.* Manchester: J. Gadsby.

Horton, S. D. (1887). *The silver Pound and England's monetary policy since the Restoration; Together with the history of the Guinea, illustrated by contemporary documents.* London: Macmillan.

Houldsworth, W. H. (1895). Trade and industry, in U. C. Gibbs et al., The currency question for laymen. *The National Review, 25*(146), (April), 213–219.

Howard, L. (1822). On the late extraordinary depression of the barometer. *Philosophical Transactions of the Royal Society of London, 112*, 113–116.

Howe, A. C. (2004). Grenfell, Henry Riversdale (1824–1902). In *Oxford Dictionary of National Biography*. Oxford: Oxford University Press. online edn, May 2009. Retrieved from http://www.oxforddnb.com/view/article/38687. Accessed on November 5, 2014.

Jevons, W. S. (1862). *Diagram showing the price of the English funds, the price of wheat, the number of bankruptcies ... since 1731. [And] Diagram showing all the weekly accounts of the Bank of England since the passing of the Bank Act of 1844.* London: Edward Stanford.

Jevons, W. S. (1863). *A serious fall in the price of gold ascertained, and its social effects set forth* (pp. 13–118). London: Edward Stanford. Reprinted in Jevons 1884.

Jevons, W. S. (1865). The variation of prices and the value of the currency since 1782. *Journal of the Statistical Society of London, 28*, June, 294–320. Reprinted in Jevons 1884, pp. 119–150.

Jevons, W. S. (1866). On the frequent autumnal pressure in the money market, and the action of the Bank of England. *Journal of the Statistical Society of London, 24*, June, 235–253. Reprinted in Jevons 1884, pp. 160–187.

Jevons, W. S. (1878). Commercial crises and sun-spots, *Nature* 14 November (reprinted in Jevons 1884, pp. 221–243).

Jevons, W. S. (1884). In H. S. Foxwell (Ed.), *Investigations in currency and finance.* London: Macmillan.

Jones, J. A. (1845). *A statistical chart shewing the comparative amounts of the revenue expenditure, exports, imports, and land sales of New South Wales, the quantities of wool, oil and tallow exported, the price of wheat, and the increase of the population from 1822 to 1844.* Sydney: W. Colman.

Juglar, C. (1886). La liquidation de la Crise et la reprise des affaires. *L'Economiste Français*, 6 February. Offprint published in Paris: Chaix.

Keynes, J. M. (1936). Herbert Somerton Foxwell. *Economic Journal, 46*, 184, December, pp. 589–619; reprinted in *The collected writings of John Maynard Keynes*, vol. X: *Essays in biography*, London: Macmillan, 1972, pp. 267–296.

Kitchin, J. (1923). Cycles and trends in economic factors. *Review of Economic Statistics, 5*(1), January, 10–16.

Klein, J. L. (2001). Reflections from the age of economic measurement. In J. L. Klein & M. S. Morgan (Eds.), *The age of economic measurement* (pp. 111–136). Durham: Duke University Press.

Kleinknecht, A. (1987). *Innovation patterns in crisis and prosperity: Schumpeter's long cycle reconsidered.* London: Macmillan.

Kondratiev, N. D. (1926). Long cycles of economic conjuncture [in Russian], *Vosprosy Konyunktur* I: 1. German translation as "Die langen Wellen der Konjunktur" in *Archiv für Sozialwissenschaft und Sozialpolitik*, 1926; abridged English translation of the German translation as "The long wave in economic life", in *Review of Economic Statistics*, 1935. New English translation from the reprint in Kondratiev 1928 as *The long wave cycle* by G. Daniels (New York, NY: Richardson and Snyder, 1984). A further English translation as "Long cycles of economic conjuncture" in *The works of Nikolai D. Kondratiev*, ed. by N. Makasheva, W. J. Samuels, and V. Barnett, London: Pickering & Chatto, vol. 1, 1998, pp. 25–63.

Kondratiev, N. D. (1928). In N. D. Kondratiev & D. I. Oparin (Eds.), Long economic cycles *[in Russian]*. Moscow: Russian Association of Social Science Research Institutes. (reprints Kondratiev 1926). English translation as *The long wave cycle*, New York, NY: Richardson & Snyder.

Langton, W. (1858). Observations on a table shewing the balance of accounts between the mercantile public and the Bank of England. *Transactions of the Manchester Statistical Society*, 1857–58 Session, 9–22.

Laughlin, J. L. (1886). *The history of bimetallism in the United States*. New York, NY: D. Appleton and Company.

Laveleye, É. de (1882). *Eléments d'économie politique*. Paris: Hachette (Engl. transl: *The elements of political economy*, London: Chapman and Hall, 1884).

Laveleye, É. de (1890). Crise. In *La grande encyclopédie: inventaire raisonné des sciences, des lettres et des arts* (Vol. 13, pp. 380–385). sous la dir. de MM. Berthelot, Hartwig Derenbourg, F.-Camille Dreyfus ... [et al.], Paris: Lamirault, 1885–1901.

London Bimetallic League, circa. (1896). Reply to leaflet no. 2 of the Gold Standard Defence Association. In London Bimetallic League, *Leaflets 1–28, bound together*. London: Bimetallic League, 1896–1899.

Louçã, F. (2001). Intriguing pendula: Founding metaphors in the analysis of economic fluctuations. *Cambridge Journal of Economics*, *25*(1), January, 25–55.

Louçã, F. (2007). *The years of high econometrics. A short history of the generation that reinvented economics*. London: Routledge.

Maas, H., & Morgan, M. S. (2002). Timing history: The introduction of graphical analysis in 19th century British economics. *Revue d'Histoire des Sciences Humaines*, *7*, 97–127.

Mager, N. H. (1987). *The Kondratieff waves*. New York, NY: Praeger.

Makasheva, N. (1993). The beginning of long wave theory: A Russian story. *Economies et Sociétés*, *27*(7–8), July–August, 247–260.

Meysey-Thompson, H. (1888). [untitled speech], in *The proceedings of the bimetallic conference held at Manchester, 4 and 5 April, 1888*, Manchester: The Bimetallic League, pp. 48–56.

Miller, J. W. (1894). *The distribution of wealth by money*. London: Effingham Wilson.

Mills, J. (1868). On credit cycles and the origin of commercial panics. *Transactions of the Manchester Statistical Society for the Session 1867–68*, 5–40. Reprinted in H. Hagemann (ed.), *Business cycle theory: Selected texts 1860–1939*, London: Pickering & Chatto, vol. 1, 2002, pp. 57–88.

Newmarch, W. (1878). On the progress of the foreign trade of the United Kingdom since 1856, with especial reference to the effects produced upon it by the protectionist tariffs of other countries. *Journal of the Statistical Society of London*, *41*(2), June, 187–298.

O'Brien, D. P. (2001). Bagehot's Lombard Street and macroeconomic stabilisation. *Scottish Journal of Political Economy*, *48*(4), 425–441.

Oliphant, J. (Ed.). (1886). *The claims of labour. A course of lectures delivered in Scotland in the summer of 1886, on various aspects of the labour problem by John Burnett,... Benjamin Jones,... Patrick Geddes,... Alfred Russel Wallace,... William Morris; and Herbert Somerton Foxwell.* Edinburgh: Co-operative Printing Company Limited.

Oxford English Dictionary. (2014). Depression, *OED Online version* September 2014. Retrieved from http://www.oed.com/view/Entry/50451. Accessed on 4 November 2014.

Parvus, A. (1901). (I. L. Helphand). *Die Handelskrisis und die Gewerkschaften.* Munich: Ernst. (Partial English translation as 'The Sturm und Drang period of capital', in F. Louçã and J. Reijnders (Eds.) *The foundations of long wave theory: Models and methodology.* Volume 1, Cheltenham: Edward Elgar, 1999, pp. 21–24.

Patterson, R. H. (1882). *The new golden age and influence of the precious metals upon the world.* Edinburgh: William Blackwood and Sons.

Playfair, W. (1785–1786). *The commercial and political atlas; representing by means of stained copperplate charts, the exports, imports, and general trade of England, at a single view.* London.

Playfair, W. (1798). *Lineal arithmetic; applied to shew the progress of the commerce and revenue of England during the present century; which is represented and illustrated by thirty-three copperplate charts. Being a useful companion for the cabinet and counting house.* London, printed for the author [etc.].

Playfair, W. (1805). An inquiry into the permanent causes of the decline and fall of powerful and wealthy nations, illustrated by four engraved charts. In *Designed to shew how the prosperity of the British empire may be prolonged.* London: Greenland and Norris.

Raffalovich, A. (1898). Crise. In Y. Guyot & A. Raffalovich (Eds.), *Dictionnaire du Commerce, de l'industrie et de la banque* (pp. 1127–1129). Paris: Guillaumin.

Redish, A. (1990). The evolution of the Gold Standard in England. *The Journal of Economic History, 50,* 4 (December), 789–805.

Redish, A. (2000). *Bimetallism. An economic and historical analysis.* Cambridge: Cambridge University Press.

Reijnders, J. (1990). *Long waves in economic development.* Aldershot: Edward Elgar.

Reijnders, J. (1993). Pioneers of long waves research: Van Gelderen, Kondratieff and the intellectual heritage of Tugan-Baranowsky. *Economies et Sociétés, 27*(7–8), July–August, 261–293.

Reijnders, J., & Louca, F. (1999). One and a half centuries of controversy on long waves and the dynamics of capitalism: An introduction. In F. Louca & J. Reijnders (Eds.), *The foundations of long wave theory: Models and methodology* (Vol. 1, pp. xi–xxxiii). Cheltenham: Edward Elgar.

Royal Commission on Agriculture. (1894). *First report of Her Majesty's commissioners appointed to inquire into the subject of agricultural depression. Presented to both Houses of Parliament by command of Her Majesty,* London: H.M. Stationery Office.

Sauerbeck, A. (1886). Prices of commodities and the precious metals. *Journal of the Statistical Society of London, 49*(3), September, 581–648. Reprinted London: Edward Stanford, 1886.

Sauerbeck, A. (1894). *Course of average prices of general commodities in England.* [from 1818 to 1893]. London: Privately printed. Reprinted in *The Journal of Commerce and Commercial Bulletin,* 4 October 1894, pp. 4–5.

Sauerbeck, A. (1908). *The course of average prices of general commodities in England.* London: King.

Schumpeter, J. A. (1914). Die Wellenbewegung des Wirtschaftslebens. *Archiv für Sozialwissenschaft und Sozialpolitik, 39*(1), 1–32.

Seyd, E. (1875). *The banks of issue question. Memorial addressed to the Governor and Court of Directors of the Bank of England, and submitted to the Select Committee of the House of Commons of 1875.* London: Edward Stanford.

Smith, S. (1887). *The bi-metallic question.* London: E. Wilson.

Spahr, C. B. (1893). Giffen's case against bimetallism. *Political Science Quarterly, 8*(3), September, 401–425.

Spaulding, E. G. (1869). *A resource of war − The credit of the government made immediately available. History of the legal tender paper money issued during the great rebellion. Being a loan without interest and a national currency.* Buffalo, NY: Express printing company.

Thorburn, T. (1854). *Diagrams: Corn-trade, and other subjects.* Edinburgh: The Author.

Tugan-Baranovsky, M. I. (1894). *Promyshlennye krizisy v sovremennoi Anglii, ikh prichiny i blizhaishie vliyaniya na narodnuyu zhizn,* St. Petersburg. 2nd ed. 1900, enlarged German translation as *Studien zur Theorie und Geschichte der Handelskrisen in England,* Jena: Fisher, 1901; enlarged and revised French translation as *Les crises industrielles en Angleterre,* Paris: Giard & Brière, 1913.

van Duijn, J. J. (1983). *The long wave in economic life.* London: Allen & Unwin.

van Gelderen, J. (J. Fedder), (1913). Spring tides of industrial development and price movements [in Dutch]. *De Nieuwe Tijd, 18,* 253–277, 369–384, 445–464. English transl. in C. Freeman, ed., *The long wave theory,* Cheltenham: Edward Elgar, 1996.

Wade, J. (1833). *History of the middle and working classes; with a popular exposition of the economical and political principles which have influenced the past and present condition of the industrious orders. Also an appendix of prices, rates of wages, population, poor-rates, mortality, marriages, crimes, schools, education, occupations, and other statistical information, illustrative of the former and present state of society and of the agricultural, commercial, and manufacturing classes.* London: Effingham Wilson (reprinted New York, NY: Kelley, 1966). 2nd edition 1834, 3rd edition 1835.

Weber, A. (1910). *Der Kampf zwischen Kapital und Arbeit. Versuch einer systematischen Darstellung, mit besonderer Berücksichtigung der gegenwärtigen deutschen Verhältnisse.* Tübingen: J. C. B. Mohr.

West, E. (1826). *Price of corn and wages of labour, with observations upon Dr. Smith's, Mr. Ricardo's, and Mr. Malthus's doctrines upon those subjects and an attempt at an exposition of the fluctuation of the price of corn during the last thirty years.* London: John Hatchard and Son. [Reprinted (without diagram): London: Routledge/Thoemmes Press, 1993].

Wilson, G. (1880). *National banking examined.* Kansas, MO: Press of Ramsey, Millett & Hudson.

Wolff, S. de (1924). Prosperitäts- und Depressionsperioden. In O. Jensen (Ed.), *Der lebendige Marxismus.* Jena: Thüringer Verlagsanst. (Engl. transl. as 'Phases of prosperity and depression' in F. Louçã and J. Reijnders (Eds.) *The foundations of long wave theory: Models and methodology.* Volume 1, Cheltenham: Edward Elgar, 1999, pp. 25–44).

NO PLACE FOR LAW AND ECONOMICS: THE CONTROVERSY OVER RAILROAD REGULATION BEFORE THE HEPBURN ACT

Nicola Giocoli

ABSTRACT

At the turn of the 20th-century railroad regulation was hotly debated in the United States. Railways were accused of abusing of their monopolistic position, in particular by discriminating rates. Public opinion's pressure for tighter regulation led to the 1906 enactment of the Hepburn Act, which strengthened the powers of the Interstate Commerce Commission. American economists actively participated in the debate. While most of them sided with the pro-regulation camp, the best economic analysis came from those who used the logic of modern law and economics to demonstrate how most railroads' practices, including rate discrimination, were simply rational, pro-efficiency behavior. However, as relatively unknown Chicago University economist Hugo R. Meyer would discover, proposing that logic in public events could at that time cost you your academic career.

Research in the History of Economic Thought and Methodology, Volume 34A, 293–338
ISSN: 0743-4154/doi:10.1108/S0743-41542016000034A009

Keywords: Railway economics; rate regulation; Hepburn Act;
A. T. Hadley; F. W. Taussig; H. R. Mayer

JEL classifications: B13; K23; L51

INTRODUCTION: A POPULAR (AND RISKY) THEME

Presenting his paper on "Government regulation of railway rates" in the
early afternoon of December 27, 1905, at the special session on railroad
regulation organized during the 18th Annual Meeting of the American
Economic Association (AEA), Hugo Richard Meyer was probably quite
optimistic about his academic future. Already a mature scholar, his linger-
ing academic career had finally taken a positive bend the year before, with
an appointment as assistant professor of Political Economy at the
University of Chicago.[1] Between 1905 and 1907 he would publish inten-
sively, including four books and several scientific papers, on his preferred
subject of railroad and public utility regulation. And now he was about to
give his most important talk, in front of the country's best economic minds.

The topic Meyer was going to cover was high on the list of economic
debates at the time. Always a thorny issue, railroad regulation had become
the object of heated controversy in the months before the passing of the
Hepburn Act (June 1906). Strongly endorsed by US President Theodore
Roosevelt, the Act would beef up the power of the Interstate Commerce
Commission (ICC), establishing, among other things, the Commission's
authority to fix maximum railroad rates.

American economists took an active part to the discussions preceding
the enactment of the bill. At the 1904 meeting, the AEA had already
hosted a special session, jointly organized with the American Political
Science Association, about "Corporations and Railways." Now another
special session, this time on "The Regulation of Railway Rates," had
been set up. Beyond publishing the material from the two sessions, the
AEA would also dedicate one of its monographs to a long essay on
"Railroad rate control in its legal aspects," by Michigan economist and
former ICC member Harrison Standish Smalley. Overall, railroad economics would occupy more than 250 pages of the *Publications of the
AEA* – the forerunner of the *American Economic Review* – between May
1905 and May 1906.

No doubt, Meyer's paper dealt with a hot topic. What he could not figure out yet was how hot it would turn out to be — indeed, so hot that it would burn his dreams of an academic career and de facto force him into exile.

By the end of the 19th century, the classical faith in the market's self-policing ability had almost vanished in the economic profession. The US economists' take on the regulatory issue focused on the allocative function rate regulation should accomplish, downplaying the classical themes of justice and equality.[2] And railroads were of course *the* issue, as far as regulation was concerned. Already by the 1860s, they represented the most important institution in America in terms of employees, capitalization, and social influence.[3] No surprise, then, that the first comprehensive regulatory measure passed by Congress, the 1887 Interstate Commerce Act, was designed to regulate the railroad industry, via the institution of the ICC. Indeed, by that date, states had already been regulating railroads for the previous half century and courts had been called to adjudicate law several times in regulatory conflicts between the states, the railroads, and the other subjects having an interest in railway services.

Every economist agreed that, in theory, free markets would determine normal price as the long-run equilibrium value of railway services and that this normal price would conform to production cost. At the same time, almost[4] everybody recognized that, *against* classical economics, in the case of railroad monopolies competitive forces would *fail* to exercise sufficient pressure to push the prices down to cost; in this failure of competition to properly work lay the rationale for rate regulation. American city planner Robert Harvey Whitten, who uniquely combined legal expertise and economic literacy, explained this rationale most effectively: "In the case of unregulated virtual monopoly the force that tends to limit prices charged to the cost of production is lacking. This creates the necessity for public regulation of the rates of charge of public service companies. The aim of public regulation is to accomplish what in other industries is assumed to be accomplished automatically by free competition, that is, to limit the price charged to the normal cost of production" (Whitten, 1914, p. 422).

In the early years of the 20th-century, Whitten's belief in the necessity of railroad regulation was shared by almost the entire profession. Not only the so-called "new schoolers," who had founded the AEA in 1885 in open polemic against the classical orthodoxy, subscribed to it, but more traditional economists could also themselves endorse some limited regulatory activity. In offering the earliest complete analysis of natural monopolies — those, as he wrote, "which are created by circumstances, and not by law"

(Mill, *Principles*, II.15.9)[5] – John Stuart Mill had already explained that, in "the case of a road, a canal, or a railway," which are "always, in a great degree, practical monopolies," the government, by granting "such monopoly unreservedly to a private company, does much the same thing as if it allowed an individual or an association to levy any tax they chose, for their own benefit, on all the malt produced in the country, or on all the cotton imported into it." For this reason, he continued, "To make the concession for a limited time is generally justifiable, on the principle which justifies patents for invention: but the state should either reserve to itself a reversionary property in such public works, or should retain, and freely exercise, *the right of fixing a maximum of fares and charges*, and, from time to time, varying that maximum" (*ibid.*, V.11.36; emphasis added). The classical school thus admitted some railroad rate regulation, at least from 1848.

Classical liberals would have little to object either. Free resource mobility – the analytical touchstone of classical economics – was obviously out of question in the case of railways. Hence, the "right of exit" – the possibility of opting out of a certain regulatory framework by moving business somewhere else – offered no defense against misguided regulation. Moreover, protection of the national market against the risk of excessive fragmentation caused by excessive state control over businesses was a traditional concern for those who wanted to "constitutionalize the free market." Finally, efficiency required that network industries, such as railways, be managed at a national level. Combining these features together, even classical liberals could recognize a limited form of federal regulation over railways and similar industries as the lesser evil – surely superior, as a regulatory solution, to state-based regulation that would likely undermine both nationwide networks and the national market.[6]

Alas, railroad regulation was no easy task. During the Gilded Age, the problem had at least two facets: how should the railroads be regulated and who, between the states and the federal government, should regulate them. The latter was as delicate as the former – possibly more, in that it touched the constitutionally sensitive issue of the division of power between Washington and the states. The stakes were so high, both economically and constitutionally, that the jurisprudential answers given to both prongs of the railroad regulation problem shaped all the other areas of regulatory activity in the United States.

Given the prevailing views and the subject's importance, Meyer was aware that his argument against railroad regulation and the pending bill, and in defense of railroads' rate-setting freedom, would probably meet strong opposition from the economists' audience at the 1905 meeting. Still, he felt confident enough to propose it, if only because he could invoke in its defense two of the discipline's leaders. His analysis of the regulatory problem – in particular of the most controversial issue of all, railway rate discrimination – would in fact track that of Arthur Twining Hadley and Frank William Taussig. Beyond relying on up-to-date economic theory (viz., newly forged neoclassical micro), his essay cleverly blended it with legal reasoning, in order to ground his policy conclusion on rigorous juridical and efficiency basis: a brilliant display of *law and economics*, had the term already been coined.[7] Yet, neither the appeal to authority nor the use of the smartest analytical tools could rescue Meyer's career after he spoke. Simply, railroad regulation was not a matter of applying correct economics. It was rather an issue of bending economic analysis to achieve predefined political goals.

The chapter builds on Meyer's sad tale to review the pre-1906 American debate on railroad rate regulation. My goal is to show how a few economists had at the time already embraced the gist of what would later become law and economics, but also how the majority of the discipline, as well as the legislators and the public opinion, rejected this approach and, with it, what most readers would today consider sound economic analysis. I take the Meyer incident, on which available information are indeed scant (exception being made for the public reactions his arguments provoked), as an excuse to illustrate a broader point, namely, that economic ideas never fail or succeed in a vacuum. Regardless of their intrinsic validity, they are only accepted when their end-users – be they other economists, or policy- and law-makers – find them persuasive in terms of a broader socio-political framework. The economists' power to persuade is, in short, always contextual.

The next section gives a bit of information about the origin of the railroad regulation problem. Sections "Railroads as Natural Monopolies – or Just 'Particular' Ones?" and "Regulation as a Problem of Federalism" present the natural monopoly and federalist sides of the issue. In sections "The Evils of Railroads: Extortion and Instability" and "Pro-efficiency Pooling?" I examine some of the evils allegedly caused by railways' practices and a possible solution, pooling. Sections "The Third Evil: Rate Discrimination" and "A Classical Rationale for Discrimination" cover the worst such evil, rate discrimination, and the pro-efficiency explanation of the practice given by Hadley and Taussig. Section "In the Lion's Den: Meyer's AEA Paper" deals with Meyer's paper at the AEA and the furious reactions it triggered. The last section concludes, showing how the episode is also illustrative of the wider problem of preserving academic freedom.

THE ORIGINS OF RAILROAD REGULATION

The free play of market forces would benefit society as a whole – that was one of the main messages of classical *political economy*. This particular message was supported by a theoretical apparatus – that is, classical *economics* – where perfect capital mobility and the profit equalization theorem occupied center stage.[8] The economics of the railroad industry presented post–Civil War Americans with a wholly different scenario, one where, because of the enormous amount of fixed capital required, firms could not easily enter and exit the market, while competition led active firms towards either financial ruin or absolute monopoly. The underlying assumptions and fundamental theorems of classical economics simply made no sense in the railroad industry, or so it seemed.[9] "The railway system is not one which is amenable to the laws of supply and demand," Charles Francis Adams observed. "It is an undisputed law of railway economics that *the cost of movement is in direct inverse ratio to the amount moved.*" When scale economies where sufficiently large, competition simply did not apply. The inverse relation between cost and traffic pointed to "a conclusion which is at the basis of the whole transportation problem: *competition and the cheapest possible transportation are wholly incompatible*" (Adams, 1870, pp. 233–234; original emphasis).

Adams was under many respects the founder of modern regulation. He realized from the beginning that a general view of the railroad problem was necessary in order to pursue that very public interest competitive forces were unable to safeguard. Under his decade-long leadership (1869–1879), the Massachusetts Board of Railroad Commissioners experimented a new approach that aimed at reconciling the interests of all the parties involved – railroad owners, customers, workers, and local communities.[10] In particular, Adams had a clear understanding of two basic facts. First, that the development of an efficient railway network was essential to promote public welfare, even more essential than, say, moderate transportation rates; hence, proper incentives had to be furnished to guarantee the necessary level and quality of investments in the business. Second, that the usual methods by which this result had been pursued in the past had failed. Neither unbridled competition, nor direct public ownership, nor the free exercise of monopoly power could work in the railroad case.[11]

Huge scale economies of course meant that complete monopoly was the best way to achieve "the cheapest possible transportation," but that solution was unacceptable to Americans, who traditionally loathed the privilege associated with monopoly, and even more so in the case of a very crucial industry like railways. Placing limits in the railroads' special charters was of no avail either, Adams observed. Apart from the lack of effective enforcement of charter provisions, even the most frequently used restraints, profit ceilings, had been ineffective, if not deleterious. It was very easy to circumvent them (by, say, stock watering); worse, they had reduced the railroads' incentive to invest in the expansion and improvement of service. Other solutions worked no better. Public ownership was disqualified on practical grounds: public authorities lacked the ability to manage complex businesses such as railroads. As to free competition, it had been the option embraced by several states. Following the classical recipe, legislators had openly encouraged entry in the railroad business. Unfortunately, the dismal record of bankruptcies, outstanding debt, and price wars showed that, in the light of the industry's peculiar economics, having new railroads to compete with existing ones was simply nonsense. As Michigan economist and ICC statistician Henry Carter Adams (no relation to Charles) would proclaim two decades later: "where the law of increasing returns works with any degree of intensity, the principle of free competition is powerless to exercise a healthy regulating influence" (Adams, 1887, p. 60).

The Adams of Massachusetts conceived of only one solution: the creation of a state railroad commission composed of industry specialists. The gap between public and private interests in so complex an industry required special expertise to be closed. Legislators could never rise to the task, if only because their terms in office were brief and uncertain. Intelligent regulation could only be implemented by making this special expertise a permanent part of government, detached from electoral contingencies: "Work hitherto badly done, spasmodically done, superficially done, ignorantly done, and too often corruptly done by temporary and irresponsible legislative committees, is in future to be reduced to *order and science* by the labors of permanent bureaus, and placed by them before legislatures for intelligent action" (Adams, 1868, p. 18; emphasis added).

Adams's approach at the Massachusetts Commission has been aptly defined "regulation by publication" (McCraw, 1984, p. 23). Lacking any real power beyond that of requiring information from railroad corporations, he tried to apply "order and science" to bend both the industry and state policy towards a more rational approach to the subject. Such an approach, in his views, coincided with the general goal of promoting public welfare via a stable and efficient system of railroad transportation. Informed persuasion was the Commission's main tool. In the case of rate regulation, this boiled down to three broad premises: that scientific precision in rate setting was impossible to achieve; that the pricing function had, with good reasons, better be left to corporate managers; that railroad rates were the outcome of the peculiar intermingling of competition and monopoly that characterized the industry (*ibid.*, p. 31). The key task for the Commission was to educate both the corporations and the public of the basic principles of railroad economics, including the natural monopoly character of the business and the fact that some consolidation was actually inevitable − indeed, desirable on efficiency grounds.

Rate regulation had therefore to be addressed towards the functional goal of systemic efficiency. The latter should be achieved trying to avoid recourse to courts, whose constitutional concerns would inevitably interfere with the grand goals of railroad policy, but also rejecting the use of "flat, across-the-board statutory rate[s]" (*ibid.*, p. 34), which would clash with the intricacies and needs of railroad management. It was, in short, a case-by-case approach to regulation, driven by the few principles of railroad economics Adams had managed to grasp by so early a date. Chief among them was the idea that regulators should exploit market forces, rather than fight them, in order to provide regulated businesses with the right incentives (*ibid.*, p. 39). These, together with the notion that no ideal pattern of regulated rates existed, were Adams's key messages to future regulatory endeavors − messages that even transcended the limits of his own analysis, which for instance led him to sponsor a 1871 Massachusetts statute prohibiting rate discrimination between short-haul and long-haul services. It would not take long for some smarter economists to understand that even this kind of seemingly unjust discrimination had strong efficiency reasons.

RAILROADS AS NATURAL MONOPOLIES − OR JUST "PARTICULAR" ONES?

After the 1880s, every American economist became aware of the peculiarities of the railway industry. The other Adams, Henry Carter, was archetypal of the almost universal recognition that competition could not bestow its wonders when powerful scale effects existed. "The capacity of the old road," he wrote, "may be extended at a cost comparatively less than would be required by the building of a new road; and, so decided are the advantages of an established business over one struggling into existence, that it is fair to regard the old road as practically free, for a long time at least, from the competitive interference of new capital" (Adams, 1887, pp. 61–62). Railroads were not unique in this feature. He acknowledged that, too: "There are many other lines of business which conform to the principle of increasing returns, and for that reason come under the rule of centralized control. *Such businesses are by nature monopolies.* We certainly deceive ourselves in believing that competition can secure for the public fair treatment in such cases, or that laws compelling competition can ever be enforced" (*ibid.*, p. 64; emphasis added).

Unsurprisingly, natural monopolies were a prominent subject on the economists' agenda. This was not an absolute novelty. Four decades before, John Stuart Mill had already explained that natural monopoly could well be accommodated within the classical model. His analysis encompassed those monopolies resulting from the technological characteristics of the production process itself – railways being the most obvious example. "When, therefore, a business of real public importance can only be carried on advantageously upon so large a scale as to render the liberty of competition almost illusory," he remarked having in mind the railway case, "it is an unthrifty dispensation of the public resources that several costly sets of arrangements should be kept up for the purpose of rendering to the community this one service. It is much better to treat it at once as a public function" (*Principles*, I.9.24). While Mill suggested that this kind of public utilities be owned and managed by public authorities, possibly in the form of a decentralized service performed at local level, American economists could still invoke his authority to justify alternative solutions to the natural monopoly problem – first and foremost, rate regulation – without trespassing the bounds of classical orthodoxy. Not a bad idea, politically speaking, given the delicate nature of the railroad problem.

However, not everyone recognized that railroads constituted a natural monopoly. No less than the most famous railway economist of the period, Yale professor Arthur Twining Hadley denied that. Perfectly aware of the decreasing pattern of railroad costs, Hadley did not believe that this feature automatically defined them as natural monopolies.[12] Were this the case, he argued, one would observe much merger activity and a dearth of new entrants. Neither was observed, though, for the simple reason that railroad costs were *not* perpetually declining.

Hadley conceived of railroads as "particular monopolies," rather than natural ones, characterized by peculiar short-run problems, due to their high fixed costs and limited ability to discriminate. As a consequence of these peculiarities, railroad rates would always oscillate between the minimum of short-run variable cost (say, during price wars) and the maximum monopoly level. Most significantly, Hadley was among the earliest economists to recognize that the structure of the market was unrelated to the effectiveness of competition. Competition was to him both an institution (i.e., a method to set prices different from custom, ethics, politics, etc.) and a process: in this, his analysis lay fully within classical political economy.[13] Accordingly, he thought the market power of railroads and other "particular monopolies" was always constrained by competitive pressure, in the form of potential competition, the rise of substitute products or, at the very least, the necessity to keep alive the local shippers who were the monopolist's best customers.[14]

Though minoritarian, Hadley's combination of a correct analysis of scale effects with a belief in the perennial power of competitive forces was not unique. Even when substantial evidence indicated that competition brought dismal results, as in the railroads case, other economists continued to assert their faith in the classical model. For example, in 1884, Gerrit L. Lansing argued against regulation of railroad rates on account of the ability of competitive forces to keep the monopoly problem under control. In the purest classical spirit, Lansing believed capital flows would always guarantee the long-run equalization of returns even in the railway case, both intra- and interindustry (Lansing, 1884, p. 463).[15] Two decades later, in his presentation at the AEA meeting, Meyer would proclaim that "upon examination [railway rates] prove to be not arbitrary but compelled, that is, fixed by competition between the railways and the waterways, the competition of rival railways, and, most frequently, by the competition between rival producing centers and distributing points" (H. R. Meyer, 1906a, p. 61). The upshot of Meyer's analysis was clear: if competitive processes were still effectively setting railroad rates, no reason existed for extending regulatory powers upon the latter.

Who was right? The majority of economists invoking some form of rate regulation in the spirit of Mill's analysis of natural monopolies or those minoritarian, albeit authoritative, voices still reposing their faith in the long-run equilibrating effect of competition? Was the heuristic power of classical economics still of any use or should classical analysis be replaced by new ideas, more attuned to modern industrial conditions? And what about the belief in the desirable properties of the classical "system of natural liberty", as Adam Smith called it? Could the Smithian system still represent a reference point in a world of big business and enormous capital investments?

REGULATION AS A PROBLEM OF FEDERALISM

In an outstanding 1988 essay published in the *Yale Law Journal*, law historian Herbert Hovenkamp has explained how the uncertainty surrounding railroad economics at the end of the 19th century also affected the history of regulatory efforts in the United States. In particular, Hovenkamp's thesis is that the less-than-complete agreement about the correct theory of railroad markets and behavior had the unfortunate effect of making regulators blind to the key feature of the American railroad system, namely, it being a network that simultaneously pertained to two markets: a market of short-haul, generally intrastate, services and a market of long-haul, generally interstate, services (Hovenkamp, 1988, pp. 1018–1019).

The two markets gave rise to regulatory problems of very different nature. Hovenkamp summed them up in these terms: "In the 1880s, states had jurisdiction only over intrastate routes, where rates tended to be very high. On the other hand, the federal government had jurisdiction only over interstate routes, where competition had driven rates on most routes so low that they were unremunerative. As a result, the problem Congress faced in the final decades of the 19th century was not high railroad rates but rather the potential collapse of the national railroad system as a result of rate wars or overzealous state regulation" (*ibid.*, p. 1026). Devoid of adequate economic tools to understand, let alone handle, this complex dichotomy, American regulators of the Gilded Age could only perform poorly. The only way to take hold of these problems together, Hovenkamp claimed, is by conceiving of the late 19th-century regulation of railroads as a fundamental problem of federalism (*ibid.*, p. 1020). Yet, very few economists of the time were up to the analytical challenges raised by the dichotomic nature of railroad competition within a federalist institutional framework.

The economic problem was intermingled with the constitutional problem. Classical competition seemed not to work properly in the presence of massive investments in fixed capital. Some railroads earned permanent monopoly profits at the same time that others were driven into bankruptcy by cutthroat competition. None of these phenomena could be prima facie reconciled with classical market theory. Their consequences being clearly undesirable for society, some kind of sovereign intervention seemed necessary to counter them. Unfortunately, Hovenkamp complained (*ibid.*, p. 1035), prevailing constitutional theory hindered the proper kind of intervention.

Building a railway was a very expensive venture. Private banks, fearing that railroad companies would need a long time to pay off their debts, if

ever at all, were reluctant to lend them money. To remedy the situation,
Congress provided assistance to the railroad companies. Between 1850 and
1871, railroads received millions of acres of land grants, which they mostly
sold, using the revenue to offset a significant portion of construction costs.
Moreover, the 1862 Pacific Railway Act established that companies agreeing to undertake the construction of transcontinental lines would be eligible
for loans from the federal government at a moderate interest rate. Without
the assistance of the federal government, the construction of main transcontinental railroads would probably not have been possible. However, it
would be wrong to conclude that the American railroad system was mainly
built on the basis of federal aid. In fact, less than 10 percent of total railroad mileage built in the United States between 1860 and 1920 came as a
direct result of federal land grants and loans. The government program
was obviously important in promoting new settlements in the West, but
most of the railroads were built by private enterprises, almost always with
the fundamental support of states and local communities – a support that
came as well in the form of loans and land grants.[16]

Not only were states crucial in the development of the largest chunk of
the American railway system, but they also had almost exclusive regulatory
control over the whole system, both intrastate and interstate. A troublesome circumstance because, under the existing theory of federalism, states
could only control *intrastate* transactions; likewise, the federal government
had exclusive control over *interstate* movement, but not, in general, over
transactions within a single state that merely affected interstate commerce.
In short, orthodox federalism could only encompass a regulatory model
that gave neither the states nor the federal government effective control
over what, economically speaking, were spillover effects between intra- and
interstate networks. This despite the latter being an essential – and seemingly obvious – element of any railway system.[17]

The great jurist – and future first ICC chairman – Thomas McIntyre
Cooley was among the few who had a clear grasp of where the core of the
regulatory problem resided. As he wrote of railroad competition: "What is
a fatal impediment to its control by law is, that the States and the nation
have, in respect to it, a divided power; and while it is for the interest of the
nation at large to encourage the competition which favors long hauls, it is
for the interest of localities to make competition most active in short hauls"
(Cooley, 1883, p. 215). He explained the troubles that could arise with an
example that, as we learn below, would occupy a central position in the
economists' reflections: "State is therefore likely to favor legislation which
compels proportional charges, or something near such charges, for all

distances; but this, if it could be adopted and enforced, would preclude the great through lines of New York and Pennsylvania from competing at Chicago, St. Paul, and St. Louis in the grain-carrying trade of the North west, and would reduce such links as are wholly within a State, to the condition of mere local roads, compelled to make high charges or go into bankruptcy" (*ibid.*).

Cooley's example was not just hypothetical. State regulations – especially when they interfered with the twin nature of the railway service – had actually contributed to the railroads' financial troubles. Yet, railway transportation was too strategic for the nation's economic development to be allowed to collapse. A process of federal regulation began in the late 1880s to take regulatory authority away from the individual states and ensure that a more systemic view be adopted. Cooley anticipated the innovation: "But whenever State power should thus be exerted prejudicially, it can hardly be doubted that Congress would interfere, under its authority over inter State commerce, in aid of those competitive forces which silently but steadily have forced down the charges for railway service" (*ibid.*, pp. 215–216). The 1887 Interstate Commerce Act – which forbade rebating, pooling, and, with some exceptions, rate discrimination; prescribed that rates be "just and reasonable"; and empowered the ICC to determine reasonableness – was the first step in this direction. Yet, as noted by Hovenkamp, two obstacles hindered the centralization process: the extant theory of federalism driving judicial review and the lack of proper understanding of railway economics.

THE EVILS OF RAILROADS:
EXTORTION AND INSTABILITY

In a lengthy 1906 essay commissioned by the AEA, Michigan economist and former ICC member Harrison Smalley listed three major kinds of abuses committed by railroad managers as the motivation behind the rise of state and federal regulation, as well as for the extensive case law dealing with it. The three "evils" of railroads – as he called them (Smalley, 1906, pp. 5–11) – were rate discrimination, monopolistic extortion, and instability of rates. The latter two captured the above-mentioned failure of classical competition in the presence of massive capital investments.

"The imposition of exorbitant charges is in large measure a consequence of monopolistic elements in the railroad industry," Smalley wrote to explain the railroad's extortionate power. "Even potential competition," he continued, "almost wholly fails as a restraining force, because of the immense cost of duplicating a railroad's plant and equipment, and because of the long time which the process of duplication must consume. The railroads are consequently free, in the absence of government control, to fix rates on the monopoly principle of maximum net return" (*ibid.*, p. 8). Many states followed the classical playbook and believed competition could provide a solution to this first evil. State legislatures attempted to eliminate extortionate rates by promoting the creation of more railroads. Accordingly, since the mid-19th century the majority of railroad charters contained no monopoly provisions. Railroad routes, particularly along longer hauls, became increasingly competitive in the three decades after the Civil War. The consequences for railroads were disastrous.

Under competitive conditions, costs did not determine rates, but rates determined what part of total costs a railroad could actually cover. Economic logic made any price above the short-run marginal cost "profitable," in the sense that it covered the direct costs of transportation and contributed something to the amortization of fixed costs. As in many other cases, the theoretical argument explaining this logic came from Hadley.[18]

In his 1885 masterpiece, *Railroad Transportation*, Hadley had criticized David Ricardo's analytical notion of competition for its reliance upon the classical hypothesis of perfect capital mobility among different businesses. A pillar of classical economics, the Ricardian assumption dictated that supra-competitive profits would quickly attract new capital in a business, while whenever price fell below cost production would stop and capital would exit.[19] The assumption, Hadley remarked, likely stemmed from Ricardo's experience as a banker, which had led him "to treat capital as something not fixed, but freely circulating, which could be at once withdrawn from a business when it became unprofitable." The problem was that "[i]n the case of a factory this is by no means true; in the case of a railroad it is absolutely untrue" (Hadley, 1885, p. 41).

The failure of Ricardo's assumption in the railway industry rested on objective grounds: "A railroad differs from many other business enterprises, in the existence of a large permanent investment, which can be used for one narrowly defined purpose, and for no other. The capital, once invested, must remain. It is worth little for any other purpose than the one in question. A railroad cannot contract its capital merely because it does not pay; nor can it be paralleled at short notice when it happens to pay remarkably well. In these respects it differs quite sharply from a bank or store; and, to a certain extent, from a factory" (*ibid.*, p. 40). Analytically speaking, the consequences were huge: "This is why it is so often said that *the ordinary laws of political economy do not operate in the case of railroads*" (*ibid.*, p. 41, emphasis added).[20] In the railroad case, any rate larger than average variable cost would help defray overhead; hence, it would result in a smaller loss than Ricardo-style shutdown. As a consequence of rational loss-minimization, capital would not exit the industry and production would go on.

While he emphasized the role of loss-minimization behavior in any industry with large fixed costs, Hadley did not believe that the latter automatically created a natural monopoly *à la* Mill − that is, a situation demanding some form of regulation or public ownership. Instability, rather than the impossibility of competition, was to his view the main trait of "particular monopolies," like those in the railroad industry.[21] Rates permanently oscillated from a high to a low extreme. At the high extreme, monopoly railroads would make huge profits, causing in due time the entry of new capital. The latter would in turn trigger a price war, with rates pushed down to their lowest level, which meant negative profits, eventual exit and a new monopoly. The industry thus lacked any tendency towards stable rates and normal profits; on the contrary, it exhibited an innate propensity to ruinous competition. "[Ricardo's] theory fails," Hadley proclaimed, "because far below the point where it pays to do your own business, it pays to steal business from another man. The influx of new capital will cease; but the fight will go on, either until the old investment and machinery are worn out, or until a pool of some sort is arranged" (*ibid.*, p. 72).[22] During these frequent bursts of cutthroat competition, even the limited margin over variable cost, guaranteed by loss-minimization behavior, disappeared. The rates' lowest extreme was indeed barely sufficient to cover operating expenses, but wholly inadequate to repay a single bit of the fixed costs. As a consequence, railroads were unable to service the (usually huge) long-term debts that burdened their financial structure.

Experience showed that entry could even generate rates *higher* than before. Because of the doubling or trebling of fixed costs, the price of shipping a package could indeed rise despite the fact that competing railroads still lost money. Hence, competition was not only bad for the railroads, but also often bad for costumers too.[23] While they benefited in the short run from very low rates, costumers might be called to endure the long-run outcomes of such "forced" competition, as they would eventually bear the cost of needless additional capacity. Under this respect, not even price regulation would help them much, because regulators had to set rates at a level sufficient to guarantee a reasonable return on capital to *each* railroad; rates would be higher when two or more rail-roads existed rather than only one.

Price wars brought forth the second of Smalley's evils, the instability of rates Hadley had already complained of. A theme that had come especially to the fore in the earliest cartel cases under the Sherman Act,[24] unstable rates damaged industrial interests almost as much as high rates. "The industrial interests of every community demand that railroad charges shall be stable," Smalley observed. "The transportation factor is an essential one in all industries, and accordingly an element of transportation expense is present in the cost of practically every commodity. For railroad rates, therefore, to be unstable is to introduce an element of serious uncertainty into all business" (Smalley, 1906, p. 9).

That railroad cartels featured prominently in early antitrust case law was not casual. Cooperation rather than rivalry among railroads was the easiest solution to cure both evils: extortion and instability. The well-known peculiarities of railroad competition actually led many US economists in the 1880s to deem combinations inevitable in that industry. The privileged kind of cooperation was not fully-fledged cartelization, though, but rather *pooling*, a looser form of agreement that divided traffic and income among participating railroads. As usual, Hadley saw it most lucidly.

PRO-EFFICIENCY POOLING?

His analysis of "particular monopolies" had led Hadley to conclude that railway rates would continuously oscillate between the level of short-run variable cost and monopoly. Yet, unwelcome as they might be, price instability, and the related destructive effects of competition, did not necessarily require government's intervention. A market-based solution existed, in the form of some kind of agreements between competing railroads. "There is but one way to prevent" the undesirable outcomes of competition, Hadley wrote. "If competition is ruinous to all parties, all parties must stop competing. If it finds no natural limit, it must be artificially limited; it must end in combination" (Hadley, 1885, p. 74). As he explained: "This agreement may take any one of four forms. 1. Agreement to maintain rates. 2. To divide the field. 3. To divide the traffic. 4. To divide the earnings. The last three are commonly known as pools" (*ibid.*).

The reason pools were preferred to cartels — that is, straightforward price-fixing agreements — lay in the latter's extreme fragility. Once again, the logic of railway economics drove this outcome. The rate set by a cartel was obviously designed to cover both fixed and variable costs of each participating railroad. It was therefore higher than short-run marginal cost, namely, the minimum acceptable threshold for each company. The temptation for each cartel member to shave the agreed rate to get more business, while still partially contributing to cover its fixed expenses, proved irresistible. Obeying the cartel was not equilibrium behavior, a modern economist would say.[25]

Hadley knew this phenomenon all too well: "The first [form of agreement] is the simplest, but least effective." Echoing a famous passage in the *Wealth of Nations*,[26] he noted: "There is scarcely an organized industry where the dealers do not meet and settle upon a schedule of rates and discounts, agreeing that no one shall sell below these prices." Yet, he added: "Such agreements are rarely kept. It is for the interest of all that rates in general should be maintained; but it is for the interest of each concern to secure business for itself by not quite maintaining them. This constitutes a great temptation to depart from schedule prices; a temptation all the stronger because it is so easy to violate the agreement indirectly, and so hard to detect any such violation. The result is apt to be a system of underhand competition, worse in many respects than the open competition which existed before there was any agreement at all" (*ibid.*, pp. 74–75).[27] Railroads then had recourse to the other forms of agreement, whose varying advantages and costs (especially, policing ones) Hadley described in his works. The biggest such gain was, in his view, rate stability. At the same time, actual and potential competition guaranteed that the monopoly power of the pool be always limited, thereby effectively solving the extortion evil.

In the end, Hadley had a fairly positive view of pooling, which he saw as a market-based solution to the peculiar problems of the railroad industry — that is, a solution preserving a role for market forces and voluntary behavior, with no outside coercion by the law. As he put it: "Combination does not produce arbitrary results any more than competition produces uniformly beneficent ones. [...] It is usually far-sighted policy for a combination to put its rates so low as not to tempt new capital too rapidly into the field. If that lesson is learned, the public gets the benefits of competition without its disadvantages" (*ibid.*, pp. 76–77). The policy prescription was clear enough: "Unluckily, we place these combinations outside of the protection of the law, and by giving them this precarious and almost illegal character we tempt them to seek present gain even at the sacrifice of their own future interests. We regard them, and we let them regard themselves, as a means of momentary profit and speculation, instead of recognizing them as responsible public agencies of lasting influence and importance" (*ibid.*, p. 77). Railroad pooling looked like the only way the stability of so crucial an industry could be reconciled with the core ingredient of the classical view of economic freedom, namely, freedom from government coercion.

Hadley wrote these words in 1885, that is, two years before the enactment of the Interstate Commerce Act that formally prohibited railroad pools. As we said, he was not the only economist of the time who supported pooling: many others shared his views, though most did so on the grounds of the standard, natural monopoly argument. Their voices got louder in the wake of the anti-pooling provision. For example, Henry Carter Adams wrote: "If it is for the interest of men to combine no law can make them compete. For all industries, therefore, which conform to the principle of increasing returns, the only question at issue is, whether society shall support an irresponsible, extra-legal monopoly, or a monopoly established by law and managed in the interest of the public. In this latter way may the benefits of organization in the form of monopoly be secured to the people, and in no other" (Adams, 1887, p. 64). Pooling found supporters throughout the economists' spectrum, politically speaking.

Columbia economist Edwin Robert Anderson Seligman – one of the brightest economic minds of the Gilded Age and a leader of the "new school" progressives – devoted most of a two-part, 85-page essay in the *Political Science Quarterly* to demolish the rationale of the 1887 Act's anti-pooling provision. He did not pull his punches, both against Congress and, perhaps even more, against those fellow economists who were still after the competitive ideal of classical theory. "We must recognize the monopolies as existing facts," he wrote, "but hold them under control. We have in general gone on the opposite theory. We have believed in the universal existence and beneficence of free competition; we have willfully blinded our eyes to what was taking place about us; and today we wake up only to recognize the existence of these gigantic combinations. To legislate against them and fall back again on the specific of free competition would be absolutely futile. Competition has had its day and has proved ineffective. Let us be bold enough to look the facts straight in the face and not shrink from the logical conclusions of our premises. Recognize the combinations but regulate them" (Seligman, 1887, p. 374).

Faithful to the mantra of the German Historical School that "experience is no less convincing than theory,"[28] Seligman went on for several pages describing the experience with pooling of American as well as European railroads. The conclusion was unambiguous: "All the European countries, therefore, inculcate the same lesson. Unjust discriminations and especially preferential rates are found in inverse ratio to the pools. Where the pools are legalized and most effective, as in Germany and Belgium, the abuses are least; where the pools are less frequent, as in England, the abuses are greater; where the pools are rare and ineffective, as in Holland, the abuses are scandalous" (*ibid.*, p. 388). Economic laws made the trend towards pooling unstoppable: "Nothing will be gained by the attempt to stop pools. We may prohibit them, but cannot prevent them. And if they could be prevented, they would simply disappear for a time; the causes which rendered their existence necessary would reassert themselves, and in the long run prove invincible, with the only result that in the meantime the country would have been exposed to an intensification of the very evils which it was desired to suppress" (*ibid.*).

Perhaps the most significant page of Seligman's essay came when he proposed a new argument in favor of the pools. In his view, pooling agreements actually stimulated – rather than stifled – competition among railroads. They did so by redirecting companies away from cutthroat pricing and towards more virtuous forms of non-price competition, like quality in service. The passage deserves to be quoted in full, because it shows better than any other the efforts many late 19th-century economists made to reconcile their deep faith in competition[29] and distrust of state interferences with their awareness that the theoretical underpinnings of both this faith and this distrust did not apply anymore: in short, the struggle to preserve classical *political economy* while abandoning classical *economics*.

"One misconception more fatal than any yet discussed still remains," Seligman wrote. "It is commonly supposed that pooling entirely prevents competition. This is a mistake. Pooling maintains the advantages of *a healthy competition* and at the same time prevents the dangers of an utterly unrestricted or 'cutthroat' competition. The mere agreement to divide traffic or earnings in certain percentages does not put a stop to all competition. Each of the various roads will still attempt to procure as much business as can possibly be obtained in a fair and open manner. If any line while maintaining the published rates is yet enabled to run above its allotted percentage, this surplus will justify the railway in demanding an increased percentage in the new allotment that is to be made at the expiration of the monthly or yearly pooling arrangement. The incentive to *fair and healthy competition* is not removed; each line will endeavor to vie with its rival in accommodations and facilities. But the temptation to take unfair advantages of its rivals is diminished, for an increase of traffic due to rebates or violations of the pooling agreement manifestly cannot justify a claim for increased percentages. A successful pool prevents railway wars with the accompanying discriminations, but does not prevent healthy emulation to attract business. *It simply raises the plane of competition to a higher level*" (*ibid.*, p. 389; emphasis added). In the case of railroads, price competition was harmful, but other, "superior" forms of competition did exist; public authorities should simply let railroad companies free to discover and exploit them. Regardless of the distance separating a "new schooler" like Seligman from the economists of the old guard, passages like this confirm that, as far as the essence of competition was concerned, he still subscribed to the classical idea of competition as an open-ended, dynamic process – a rivalry in service, not a state.

Even jurists recognized that pooling was indeed desirable and that the law should not prohibit it. Remarkably, these were the 1905 views of no less than Martin Augustine Knapp, the then-chairman of the ICC.[30] The paper he delivered at the 1904 meeting of the AEA was, quite understandably, a eulogy of rate regulation and the Commission's activity. Yet, after having complained, like many economists had done, that "[t]he evils which have attended the growth and operation of our railway systems, and which have given rise to so much public indignation, have their origin and inducement for the most part in the competition of carriers which our legislative policy seeks to enforce,"[31] Knapp manifested a frank preference for pooling: "I advocate the legal sanction of associated action by rival carriers in the performance of their public functions. This is the one sensible and practicable plan, adapted to existing conditions and suited to the requirements of a public service. Such a policy would promote and invite the conduct of railway transportation in the manner most beneficial to the people and the railroads alike" (Knapp, 1905, pp. 29–30).

From the vantage, and authoritative, point of his high office, Chairman Knapp could then declare that: "The true theory of public regulation, therefore, the theory which is best calculated to produce useful results, is to allow the railways to unite with each other in the discharge of their public duties, thereby making it feasible and for their interest to conform, in all cases to their published schedules, and to invest the regulating body with authority, after investigation of complaints upon due notice and hearing, to condemn the rates found to be actually or relatively unreasonable and to prescribe, subject to judicial review, a substituted standard to be thereafter observed" (*ibid.*, p. 30). Knapp sounded here much like the Charles Adams of almost four decades before. They both envisioned regulation as a mere support to free market behavior. They both believed regulators should only intervene when the regulated subjects abused of the freedom to self-organize their business enlightened legislators had − or should have − accorded them. Even in the seemingly lost case of railways, the distance separating these views from the Smithian version of classical political economy was not so great.

Knapp's views were not idiosyncratic. Notwithstanding the express anti-pooling provisions of the Interstate Commerce Act, the ICC had since the start been more sympathetic to the railroads on this issue. Accordingly, it had encouraged a certain amount of controlled pooling throughout the 1890s. While the ICC's overall record is very controversial − with critics from opposing fields accusing the Commission of being, alternatively, excessively friendly or excessively hostile to railroad companies − there is no doubt that on allocative efficiency grounds its performance was mixed at best. On one hand, the ICC recognized that pooling was necessary to preserve the railroads' financial integrity and, even more importantly, the lawfulness of some coordination − all the more indispensable given the interconnected nature of large part of the railway business.[32] On the other hand, especially as far as the rate-assessment part of its activity was concerned, the ICC's policies often prevented the best allocation of transport services, by letting fairness concerns prevail over efficiency ones (McCraw, 1984, pp. 63−64). Once again, this was due to a lack of proper understanding of the economics of rate-making.

The "protection" of the ICC and the favor of a large and influential part of the economists' and jurists' community did not suffice to preserve the legality of pooling. The provision in the 1887 Act spoke clearly against this kind of agreements.[33] Most commentators, then and now, agree that the Act answered the needs of both shippers − who were obviously hostile to pooling − and railroads. The latter, at least according to some accounts, had invoked the intervention of Congress in order to curb the excesses of state regulations, on the one side, and obtain some legal sanction to that rate stability that cartels and other private arrangements were unable to guarantee, on the other.[34] What is certain is that all the debate about pooling ended in 1897, when the Court applied the Sherman Act to declare all railroad cartels and pools unlawful.[35]

Seligman had been a good prophet a decade before. "The abolition of pooling would in fact hasten the very result which it is desired to avoid," he wrote. "Division of the traffic and the earnings" were to his views just penultimate steps "in the progress of combination." "The final steps," as he foresaw them, "are lease and absolute consolidation. [...] If therefore pools, which still permit competition to a limited degree, be abolished, the process of complete consolidation, which utterly precludes competition, will be accelerated" (Seligman, 1887, pp. 389–390). In fact, the Court's 1897 decision gave further impetus to the great railroad merger movement that had already started in the previous decade and that would eventually transform America's network of hundreds of small railroads into a half dozen giant systems by the 1920s.[36]

THE THIRD EVIL: RATE DISCRIMINATION

The third evil identified by Smalley's (1906) essay was also the worst. Neither monopoly pricing nor rate instability raised so much passion and complaint in American society as the discrimination of railway fares: "In any statement of railroad evils attention is most naturally directed first to unjust discrimination, as the most serious of all" (Smalley, 1906, p. 5). The public opinion's fury against rate discrimination verged on hysteria. The practice even featured in popular novels – such as Frank Norris's *The Octopus*[37] – as the epitome of the railroads' rapacious and ruthless attitude towards customers and competitors. Simply said, rate discrimination was the single most important and controversial problem of railroad regulatory policy during the Gilded Age.

Among the various forms of discrimination, the one attracting most attention, and protest, was the so-called short-haul/long-haul discrimination, which occurred when a railroad charged a higher price per mile for a short distance than it did for a long one. Net of the fixed cost of loading and unloading the trains, which explained part of the differential, long- and short-haul rates were often far away from any proportion to actual direct costs of service. As Hovenkamp (1988, pp. 1049–1050) remarked, it was not just a matter of short hauls costing *proportionally* more than long hauls. The loudest complaints arose from the fact that short hauls frequently cost *absolutely* more than long hauls, even though the short haul was completely contained within the long-haul route: little surprise that the practice could stimulate the fantasy of talented writers.

Novelists are not always good economists, though. What the American public failed to understand was that competition, rather than cost, determined railway rates. As even ICC chairman Knapp recognized: "The power to compete is the power to discriminate, and it is simply out of the question to have at once the presence of competition and the absence of discrimination. To my mind the legislation which decrees that all rates shall be just and reasonable, and declares unlawful every discrimination between individuals or localities, is plainly inconsistent with competitive charges" (Knapp, 1905, p. 29). The full understanding of the rationale of rate discrimination was among the most valuable contributions of the late 19th-century marginalist techniques. Yet again, the new economics did not necessarily entail discarding the core message of classical political economy.

The economic basis for short-haul/long-haul rate discrimination had already emerged before the advent of marginalism.[38] Starting from the late 1860s, the argument had been made that railroad lines between distant points were much more competitive than commonly believed precisely because variable costs were so small, almost insignificant. Frequently, competing lines existed that connected the same commercial centers – the main industrial cities – but passed through different points en route. It followed that competition for traffic between the centers was far greater than competition for traffic between the points along the way. This simple empirical observation, that railway lines did not have to be "parallel" in order to compete, lay at the heart of the short-haul/long-haul problem. By the turn of the century, it was well-known that indirect routes between two points might have an economic advantage over direct routes between the same two points, for the simple reason that the railroads stopped at more towns on the longer routes. As a result, companies had more opportunities to fill their cars than they would on the direct route. Again, the fact that the actual cost of running extra miles was comparatively low, usually lower than the opportunity cost of traveling with less than a full load, was crucial to make the indirect route more profitable than the shorter one.

The other well-established principle was that the portion of fixed costs borne by any class of railroad traffic was price-determined rather than price-determining.[39] Whenever no competition existed on a certain route, railroads set a rate high enough to cover both variable and fixed costs. This was typically the case for short-haul rates – that is, for traffic between local points almost always connected by a single, monopolistic railroad. It followed that those fixed costs that were not covered by the rates charged on more competitive, long-haul traffic were repaid by the short-haul rates charged upon monopoly routes. Several observers, including smart ones like Charles Adams,[40] concluded that railroads were using their monopolistic short-haul overcharges to cross-subsidize their competitive long-haul expenses. Short-haul shippers seemed therefore unjustly discriminated to the benefit of long-haul ones. Regardless of its efficiency, discrimination would then deserve reproach as a sheer matter of justice. Technically speaking, however, no cross-subsidization was involved in the practice, at least as long as long-haul rates exceeded direct operating costs. As always, the implied economics found exhaustive explanation in Hadley.

The 1885 treatise clarified that even the shippers who paid the high local rates actually benefited from the short-haul/long-haul discrimination. "The points where there is no competition," Hadley conceded, "are made to pay the fixed charges, while the rates for competitive business will little more than pay train and station expenses." Still, everybody gained. Long-haul shippers enjoyed the benefits of competition, because for the railroads "it is better to have business on those terms than to have it go by the rival route" (Hadley, 1885, p. 114). As to short-haul customers, their gain stemmed from the fact that "the local business at intermediate points is so small that this alone cannot support the road, no matter how low or how high the rates are made. In other words, in order to live at all, the road must secure two different things − the high rates for its local traffic, and the large traffic of the through points which can only be attracted by low rates. If they are to have the road, they must have discrimination" (ibid., p. 115). The moral of the story was clear: cancel the long-haul traffic and the short-haul customers would have no railway at all to ship their goods. Who was actually subsidizing whom, then?

The same logic held in the case of discrimination based on the nature of the products. Railroads were accused of using artificially high rates on first-class goods to subsidize low rates on cheaper goods, where competition was much stronger. With his famous oyster example,[41] Hadley showed that even those who paid high rates on first-class goods benefited from the practice. Any rate higher than average variable cost contributed to repay the railroad's fixed costs, and thus to reduce all other rates. Thus, shippers of first-class goods benefited if the railroads also shipped cheap goods at any rate higher than direct operating costs, regardless of whether the rate differential was in any sense justified by differences in cost of service. As in the oyster "all-or-none" case, cheap goods traffic could even be necessary condition for the existence of the first-class service. Again, Hadley's economics showed that discrimination benefited everyone, railroads and shippers.

Analytically, his presentation of the subject was a major step forward in the history of economics. Hadley was the first economist to link the necessary conditions for successful price discrimination − monopoly power and the ability to separate markets − with a simple elasticity specification.[42] In his "Theory of railroad rates" − which he developed in Appendix II of the 1885 book − the relationship between traffic carried and the rate charged was given both a mathematical statement and a diagrammatic illustration by way of a traffic demand curve. The basic assumption of his analysis was that railroads are profit-maximizers: "The practical railroad manager has one general principle in this matter. He lowers rates whenever he thinks it will increase net earnings – in other words, as long as it will increase gross earnings faster than it increases operating expenses" (*ibid.*, p. 261). The principle – which in the appendix took the form of a differential equation – led the manager to lower rates "until the differential of gross earnings on a particular line of traffic ceases to be greater than (i.e., becomes equal to) the differential of the operating expenses" (*ibid.*). Under the implicit assumption of elastic demand, Hadley applied the marginalist principle to conclude, both in words and in formulas, that railroads would seek new traffic as long as the increase in revenues brought about by additional traffic exceeded the increase in cost (*ibid.*, p. 263).[43]

Hadley presented a *competitive* theory of rate discrimination, in that he explained the phenomenon as an essential part of the competitive process in the railroad industry. The railroads' financial health, their ability to expand service to new markets and lower the average price of transport (thanks to market expansion under decreasing costs), even the possibility itself of their supplying any service at all – everything depended upon the adoption of well-designed discriminatory practices. This was the sense of his statement that "there are many instances where the railroads are not responsible for [local discriminations]": it was the inexorable logic of competition ("the natural causes," as he called them) that led to these practices. Accordingly, he explained that "it is worse than useless to try to prohibit them by law. We are not arguing in favor of this system, but against the popular remedy – a statute" (*ibid.*, pp. 114–115). As he wrote in a comment to the Interstate Commerce Act: "There is not in American railroad practice a collision of interest between shippers as a class and railroad owners as a class. Laws based on the supposition that there was, have done much more harm than good" (Hadley, 1888, p. 181).

More specifically, Hadley's hostility against rate regulation of the kind envisioned by the 1887 Act rested on two reasons. He was worried, first, that regulation without the possibility of pooling would fail to produce rate stability, and, second and more importantly, that the ICC or any other regulator could cause massive allocative distortions – all the bigger were regulation to be driven by the "cost of service" principle, that is, the notion of charging for each transportation its actual cost. "There was never a more mistaken idea than the idea that rates would be reduced if they were based upon cost of service," he complained, deeming the principle and its consequences "bad for the railroads, bad for the shipper, and bad for the prospect of low average rates" (*ibid.*, p. 250).[44] As to other forms of regulation, clear to his mind was the "maze of absurdities" generated by the profit limits imposed to British utilities (Hadley, 1896, p. 167). In pure classical spirit, Hadley believed government regulation always provided a very poor alternative to competitive market forces. In particular, tampering with rate discrimination would inevitably redirect resources away from their optimal investment. In short, railroad regulation was unnecessary and, in the long run, potentially deleterious for economic progress (Hadley, 1888, p. 186).

Hostile to regulation, Hadley was on the contrary sympathetic to a judicial approach, if based upon a clear definition of property rights and the common law standard of reasonableness of rates. Reasonableness had of course to be evaluated according to economic logic − that is, upon the principle of competitive discrimination, not cost of service.[45] Additionally, he favored the legalization of pooling and a duty of disclosure for railroads' data and activities. The overall goal was to favor a limited degree of stability in the industry, without hindering the free play of the competitive forces he saw at work even in the presence of railroad monopolies. Notwithstanding the marginalist character of his analysis and the explicit abandonment of classical analytical principles, Hadley's recipe lay therefore well within the boundaries of classical political economy.

A CLASSICAL RATIONALE FOR DISCRIMINATION

Hadley was not alone to fight the battle for correct economic thinking. Another seminal contribution to the development of regulatory economics came in 1891, when Harvard economist Frank William Taussig gave his own version of why price discrimination was important for industries with high fixed costs.[46] Different from Hadley, his approach rested on the traditional premise that railroads be natural monopolies. Thus the peculiar structure of their production costs, rather than competitive effects, drove Taussig's analysis, which borrowed from classical economics much more than Hadley's.

Railroads were an industry subject to joint, indivisible costs. This was, generally speaking, the case of "any industry in which there is a large plant, turning out, not one homogeneous commodity, but several commodities, subject to demand from different quarters with different degrees of intensity" (Taussig, 1891, p. 443). As Taussig recognized, Mill had already studied this case,[47] including its main economic implication, namely, that each commodity or service contributed to these joint costs "in proportion to the demand for it. It will contribute more and sell proportionately high if the demand does not need to be tempted by low prices, and will contribute less and sell proportionately low if a high price tends to choke off the demand" (*ibid.*, p. 444).[48]

Mill's principle had a straightforward implication on railroad rate-making: "It is, therefore, in accord with what we might expect from general theory that the different sorts of traffic contribute in very different proportions towards paying the fixed charges, or the return to capital, – the element in railway operations which represents joint cost. Traffic which will continue to come even at comparatively high rates will continue to be taxed high, and will contribute largely towards fixed charges. Traffic for which the demand is sensitive to price, and which can be got only at low rates, will contribute little" (*ibid.*). Classical economists knew this phenomenon well, Taussig remarked. Even Smith had acknowledged that turnpike tolls were differentiated on a willingness-to-pay basis (*ibid.*, p. 445).[49]

Railroads were a joint cost industry like no other. In their case, not only fixed costs, but also the largest part of operating expenses "represents outlay not separate for each item of traffic, but common to the whole of it or to great groups of it" (*ibid.*). A careful analysis of the different components of these expenses led Taussig to claim that only a very small portion of total railway costs was directly dependent on the amount of traffic. "Railways present on an enormous scale a case of the production at joint cost of different commodities," he concluded (*ibid.*, p. 453).

Competition entered into play here. The joint nature of most railway costs increased "[t]he fierceness of railway competition, due in part to the fact that the enormous plant is irrevocably committed to that particular business." Under competitive conditions, only variable costs would be calculated into price: "a railway will not retire from the competitive business as long as it yields anything above the small fragment of expense directly traceable to that particular traffic" (*ibid.*, p. 456). But if fixed costs were not accounted for, the railroads would be unprofitable and there would be no new investment in them, to the detriment of the entire economy. Since the competitive pricing mechanism contributed nothing to fixed costs, how could they be repaid? Taussig's first conclusion was that *cost of service* – the beloved notion of supporters of anti-discrimination rules – had nothing to do with rational rate-making, if not for the (usually tiny) part related to variable costs. The pervasiveness of the joint cost phenomenon entailed that no cost-based rule could determine railroad rates.

Even more explicitly than Hadley, Taussig foreran here what is modernly called the second-best approach to efficient pricing. Today we know that in the presence of a multiproduct firm, whose overheads need to be covered by total revenues but cannot be assigned to individual products, a proper use of differential pricing can raise total output, spreading the joint costs' burden among more customers. The idea is that the firm would set each product's price above its marginal cost, at a level sufficient to cover overheads and obtain a normal return on investment. An optimal set of markups exists that would generate the required total revenue with a minimum loss of output with respect to the first best. These efficient markups depend on the elasticities of demand and are known in modern jargon as Ramsey prices. Of course, whenever total revenues are larger than total costs, including overheads and a normal return, the firm is earning supracompetitive profits. Hence, the proper test for monopoly power looks at total revenues and total costs, not at the size of the markup on any specific product: even a very high markup is not by itself an indicator of monopolistic profit.[50]

Taussig had a clear understanding of the technique and its implications. In his terminology, the most efficient way to repay railroad investments meant charging "what the traffic will bear" – that is, what Seligman called *value of service*.[51] The principle aimed at maximizing railroad traffic on the basis of the customers' willingness-to-pay, that is, of the different elasticity of the various portions of demand. Taussig's second conclusion was therefore that price discrimination – whatever its basis: freight classification, geography, or the amount of competition along a particular route – was sensible economic behavior, and an efficient one at that. "This seems to me to be the fundamental explanation of the classification of freight," he concluded. "As time went on, experience forced on managers, whether in charge of public or of private railways, that adaptation of rates to demand which is the inevitable outcome of the peculiarities of the industry" (*ibid.*, pp. 454–455). All instances of discrimination, even the most despised ones, stemmed from the inexorable logic of joint costs, viz., a purely technological feature: they were all "cases in which the explanation of apparent anomalies lies in the fact that by far the greater part of the cost of rendering the service is incurred, not for the particular traffic in hand, but for the traffic as a whole" (*ibid.*, p. 456).

If railroads' rate-making practices were efficient, then the best public policy was simply to encourage the largest amount of shipping of all kinds of products, even if they had to be shipped at widely disparate rates. This would permit the spreading of fixed costs over the largest amount of cargo and, consequently, would lower freight rates overall. The policy suggestion was not a mere add-on. Taussig had written the 1891 essay with the express goal of countering the mounting challenge of the so-called "ethical approach" to railway rates. The latter's core idea was that railway rates were like taxes and, therefore, should be set according to principles of justice akin to those used in taxation policy.[52]

Taussig's emphasis on the technological peculiarities of the railway industry, on its being affected by the joint cost phenomenon "on an enormous scale," thus had an additional rhetorical motivation. It aimed at demonstrating the objective – that is, inevitable – character of current rate-making practices more effectively than any argument based upon competitive considerations à la Hadley. The latter relied upon a profit-maximization assumption Taussig did not want to employ, lest his thesis be undermined by the easy (albeit wrong)[53] criticism that profits were precisely what a publicly-owned, ethically-driven railroad would *not* pursue. On the contrary, classical economics – with its focus upon objective production conditions – was wholly adequate to the task. Hence, his exclusive recourse to Millian principles, rather than to the marginalist techniques he, like Hadley, perfectly mastered.[54]

Of course, Ramsey pricing only addresses efficiency concerns, but does not necessarily satisfy fairness criteria. The practice can easily lead to high markups on the transport of, say, food and other necessities and low markups on the transport of, say, luxury goods. This would happen whenever the former's demand is relatively inelastic and the latter's elastic: an outcome that many at Taussig's time (and even today) would consider unfair. Yet, Taussig thought that joint costs analysis provided a strong counter-argument to the ethical approach.

Rate discrimination had nothing to do with justice, but with technical necessities: "I trust I have succeeded in showing that the main peculiarities in railway rates, *those which have appeared under government management as well as under private management*, are not to be explained on a supposed basis of justice and right, by which the well-to-do are charged high, and the needy are left off easily" (*ibid.*, p. 461; emphasis added). No form of railroad ownership – public or private – which aimed at preserving financial integrity could be exempt from applying this iron logic: "The financial interest of the government would inevitably push it to making rates on this elusive traffic [of bulky goods and long-distance hauls] low enough to attract it: the traffic would be charged what it would bear. It is the nature of the industry which explains the fact, abundantly proved by experience, that government management does not lead to the disappearance of classification and apparent discrimination in rates" (*ibid.*, p. 459). Claiming, as in popular discussions, that "it is 'right' that expensive goods should pay high rates, and cheap goods low rates" was therefore only a manifestation of that "disposition, common among those untrained in economic reasoning, to accept as right and just that which has worked itself out in the long run from the play of ordinary economic forces" (*ibid.*, p. 462).

Like public ownership, not even regulation could neglect the reality of joint costs. Here Taussig's target was the "fair and reasonable" principle for railway rates established by Section 1 of the Interstate Commerce Act. He complained that the ICC "has been led by this provision, among others, to the slippery problem of directly fixing rates" (*ibid.*, p. 458). The most dangerous slip would of course consist of surrendering to the cost of service principle, especially when interpreted in pursuit of ethical goals like fairness or justice. Though "the difficulties of saying what are 'reasonable' rates seem well-nigh insuperable," he, like Hadley, had rejoiced at the commissioners' wisdom: "The Inter-state Commerce Commission, in its interpretation of the phrase ['reasonable and just'], has wisely refrained from putting the test of reasonableness in any assumed cost of services, and in practice has accepted the existing system of rate-making as on the whole reasonable" (*ibid.*). Once again, the wisest form of regulation was -- as classical political economy required – to conform to the insight of those who knew the industry best, namely, the railroad companies themselves and their customers.

IN THE LION'S DEN: MEYER'S AEA PAPER

By the turn of the century it was clear that, their intellectual authority notwithstanding, Hadley and Taussig had failed to reposition the debate on railway rate discrimination upon more solid economic basis. In fact, they had not even managed to persuade the totality of their fellow economists. A sign of their failure was the circumstance that, as late as 1906, Smalley felt the necessity to explain once again, in an AEA official publication, the logic behind the railroads' rate-making practices.[55]

"Under the conditions of competition as it prevails among railroads," Smalley duly reported, "there is no alternative except between discrimination and speedy insolvency. The explanation of this fact is found in one of the characteristic features of the railroad industry, namely, the relation between expenses and volume of traffic. Expenses increase but slightly when traffic increases greatly" (Smalley, 1906, p. 6). Thus, "railroad managers are under a constant and powerful incentive to get business even at reduced rates"; moreover, "it is utterly impossible to determine what any given service will cost the company" (*ibid.*). The combination of these two circumstances explained why a railroad manager was willing to offer "whatever rate is necessary to get the business away from his rivals, devoutly hoping all the time that the rate will not prove injurious to his road, but utterly without means of judging its effect. The outcome is that traffic managers are swayed by an impulse to accept traffic at almost any rate, if compelled to do so by competition" (*ibid.*, p. 7). It followed that: "Competition between railroads is fierce and intense, and constantly tends to develop into the 'cutthroat' variety, ending perhaps in the all too familiar 'rate wars'. Dominated by the passion for traffic, eager to snatch it from competing lines, each road cuts rates wherever necessary, or offers other advantages to get the traffic for itself. And thus swarm into industrial life that horde of evils [...] of unjust discrimination" (*ibid.*). The latter "is not only a possibility in railroad management – it is a natural and inevitable consequence of all unrestricted railroad competition," Smalley concluded. "Railroads do not usually wish to discriminate, but they are compelled to do it. Discrimination may drive them into bankruptcy, but abstinence from it is sure to do so, so long as competition persists. They discriminate in order to live – though their discrimination may sometimes kill them" (*ibid.*). Hadley and Taussig could not have said it better. Yet, they *had* said it, long before. Had two decades passed in vain?

The point is that by 1906 the controversy about railroad regulation in general, and rate discrimination in particular, was as intense as ever. The passions raised by these issues were such that some of the economists who dared oppose the populist calls for tighter restraints on the railroads' rate-making freedom "were identified as nothing more than mouth-pieces for the railroad interests" (Hovenkamp, 1988, p. 1050). The principle that competition and technology, rather than cost of service, determined the rates was a dangerous one to defend. Smalley could afford upholding it on behalf of the AEA because the policy proposals of his essay (he favored strict regulation, aimed at promoting public interest over railroads' rights) counterbalanced – in fact, contradicted – the analytical part.[56] As Chicago economist Hugo Meyer experienced, no such escape existed when the policy conclusions more consistently followed the analysis.

His was one of the two papers presented in December 1905 at the AEA session on railroad regulation. Meyer had learned the lesson of Hadley and Taussig well. Economic logic led him to claim that only "upon superficial examination" could "the railway rates of this country [...] appear to be arbitrary, inconsistent, and grossly discriminating." Proper inquiry revealed that they were "not arbitrary but compelled, that is, fixed by competition between the railways and the waterways, the competition of rival railways, and, most frequently, by the competition between rival producing centers and distributing points. [...] examined more carefully, they cease to appear grossly discriminating, and prove to be honestly and intelligently discriminating. Moreover, they prove to be marvelously well adapted to the needs of our country" (H. R. Meyer, 1906a, p. 61). Yet, Meyer went beyond the mere repetition of economic principles. He brilliantly mixed legal and economic arguments, providing an excellent application of what we would now call the law and economics point of view. The notions that the law should never disregard the efficiency considerations stemming from economic analysis and that, conversely, economists should always keep an eye at how legal rules affect the economy were the guiding lights of Meyer's argument — only a few decades too early.

Meyer stressed that correct economic reasoning had found support in judicial decisions. "For eighteen years we have had in force the act to regulate commerce, which forbids not all discrimination, but only undue and unjust discrimination," he reminded his audience. "Under that statute the federal courts have sustained every great American railway rate practice brought before them for adjudication; and the characteristic feature of those practices is discrimination, intelligent and honest, made for the purpose of meeting the needs of trade and industry" (*ibid.*, p. 62). Data showed that railroads disobeying the ICC's rate-related orders had won almost every time (32 of 35) the controversy had reached a federal court (*ibid.*).[57] Against "the statesmanlike spirit in which the federal courts have construed the act," and contrary to what the ICC itself had done in its early years, the Commission was now reading "at its pleasure" into the same act "political and economic theories, none of which the Congress had made a part of the established law of the land, and at least one of which is in direct conflict with the intentions of the framers of our federal constitution." The principles followed of late by the ICC — like, for example, "to grant each community the rightful benefit of location," or "to keep different commodities on an equal footing" — found no legitimacy in economic theory, nor in express Congress provisions. These principles "one and all, have meant: not the promotion of trade, but the restraint and the partial destruction of trade and of competition" (*ibid.*, pp. 63–64).

Abusing its limited power to prescribe railway rates, and notwithstanding its nature of pure administrative body, the ICC had become, in fact, "a deputy Congress, free to make and unmake the public policy as well as the law of the land" (*ibid.*, p. 64). This exercise of a quasi-legislative function seemed to contradict established constitutional doctrines.[58] But even before than a problem of dubious constitutional legitimacy, it was a matter of bad economics: "All of the foregoing attempts at legislation rest upon the doctrine that railway rates must be based upon respective costs of service, that they may not be made upon 'commercial considerations', *i.e.*, in obedience to the competition of the markets" (*ibid.*, p. 66). The outcome, to Meyer's view, had been dismal: "Restraint of competition and trade, and disregard of the rights of several of the parties to each controversy over railway rates, has been the characteristic feature of every decision in which the Commission has condemned a great American railway rate practice" (*ibid.*, p. 67). The bottom line of Meyer's presentation was crystal clear. While a new statute, like the future Hepburn Act, could settle the legitimacy issue by formally granting rate-setting powers to the ICC, use of these very powers without a proper understanding of the economics of railroad pricing would spell disaster for the American economy.

Unsurprisingly, Meyer's tirade against the ICC met hostile reactions, both at the AEA meeting and elsewhere. The discussant, Dartmouth economist Frank Haigh Dixon, simply called his ideas unacceptable. The political climate of the period, in general, and of the AEA, in particular, led Dixon to proffer words that would have sound abomination just a couple of decades before: "the views of Mr. Hugo Meyer [...] lead inevitably to the policy of extreme laissez-faire, to the general conclusion that the interaction of competitive forces, undisturbed by state interference, has led and will lead to beneficent results to the people and industries of this country, and that any governmental interference must have a tendency to thwart the working of this beneficent policy" (Dixon, 1906, p. 84).

Having so dismissed the classical system of natural liberty, Dixon moved on to defend the cost of service principle of rate-making, which he called "the distance tariff." He turned Meyer's argument against the principle, and in favor of rate discrimination, on its head, arguing that "the policy of disregarding distance which is carried to such an extreme by American roads" had actually been deleterious for the US economy. As he put it: "the country has been obliged to bear the burden of indirect shipments on differential roads, and cross-shipments of goods of the same character to

markets far removed from producing sections" (*ibid.*, pp. 86–87). Once
again, what benefited railroads was not necessarily good for the country as
a whole: "The traffic manager obviously looks at the question from the
point of view of his own road alone. It does not at all follow that his stren-
uous efforts to develop territory and secure business that leads him even to
invade the territory of another system, is for the best economic interest of
the country as a whole. Rate wars and patched up peace treaties may be
regarded by some as automatic and beneficent adjustments of the rate question, but they involve unquestionably great economic waste" (*ibid.*, p. 87).

Sadly for Meyer, the negative reactions did not end with an unfavorable
discussant. Even the second paper presented at the session read more as an
attack to his own one than an independent contribution. The author was
another Meyer, Balthasar Henry, an economist and sociologist at the
University of Wisconsin, who was also a member of the state's railroad
commission and a future ICC commissioner. The Meyer of Wisconsin
defended the work of regulatory bodies. The final sentence of his paper
said it all: "there are two, and only two, alternatives before the world today
with respect to railways: either government ownership and operation, or
rigid governmental control. My choice is the second alternative" (B. H.
Meyer, 1906a, p. 83). Like Dixon, Balthasar Meyer had no faith in the beneficial effects of competition: "competition as a regulator of rates and a
protector against unreasonable or unjust rates has proven itself a failure in
every country in which railway systems have been developed" (*ibid.*, p. 74).
The reason was simply that railways were enterprises like no others: "in
current discussions it is frequently asserted that railway enterprise is like
every other business enterprise, and that no more legislation is needed for a
railway than for a soap factory. This paper assumes that the railway differs
in many of its most vital aspects from other commercial enterprises, and
that upon these differences, well understood by *nearly* every member of this
Association, but not by many *outside* of the association, rests the necessity
of more far-reaching restrictive legislation. The conditions of today
demand an effective control of all railway rates" (*ibid.*, p. 69; emphasis
added). One may not fail to notice the polemics implicit in the two itali-
cized words. How could an economist deserving his name fail to understand that railways were not like soap factories?[59]

The failure of competition went hand in hand with the evils of rate discrimination: "There is, perhaps, no state in the union in which there are
not hundreds of misfits in the rate" (*ibid.*). "The mere fact of their existence," Balthasar Meyer continued, "is sufficient ground for the demand to
give a commission power to fix rates within limitations prescribed by law.

[...] To give a commission power over the rate and service does not necessarily mean the frequent or continual exercise of such power. In fact, the possession of power may be the safest guarantee against the necessity for the constant exercise of it" (*ibid.*, p. 72). Skepticism about market forces, and a barely concealed polemic against the other Meyer, was the leading trait: "We are told that no such tribunal is needed, for the reason that railway rates are beyond the power of control by traffic men; that railway rate-makers are generally passive and merely 'register' the commercial forces which are continually being reflected into their brains; that commercial conditions and the competition of markets determine rates. [...] That railway rates are in many cases the result of nicely balanced commercial conditions is demonstrable. That they are in other cases violating commercial conditions is equally demonstrable. The appeal to commercial conditions is sometimes a fact and sometimes fiction" (*ibid.*, p. 71).

Then, as if he were himself discussing Hugo Meyer's paper, Balthasar Meyer proceeded to defend the work of enlightened railway regulators – like himself. "It is argued that if a commission is given power to prescribe a rate, either on complaint or on its own initiative, the result will be a general remodeling of all rates in accordance with theoretical or political considerations controlling the commission," he noted in apparent reference to the other presentation. His reply was that: "Generally speaking, this position assumes ignorance, dependence, and lack of energy on the part of commissions. [...] The conflict of sectional interests is a reality. The impotence of the commission in the face of sectional interests is largely a myth" (*ibid.*, pp. 74–75). As to the role of courts, so praised in the other Meyer's work, Balthasar was skeptical that they could ever replace expert commissioners: "Proposed federal legislation cannot, therefore, create this sectional rivalry. It already exists; but there exists no tribunal with power over the rate to which an appeal may be taken for the establishment of a just and reasonable basis upon which to continue the rivalry" (*ibid.*, p. 77). Indeed, one such tribunal did exist: "A railway commission is peculiarly well fitted to arbitrate and decide questions arising from antagonistic interest" (*ibid.*, p. 76). Experience showed that regulators were not going to abuse of their quasi-legislative power: ICC's decisions "from the time of its organization to the present show no dogmatic adherence to any one principle of rate-making" (*ibid.*, p. 78).[60]

Next came a defense of the distance tariff. Rather than bringing new economic arguments, he resorted to ridicule the critics, thus implicitly including in his mockery the likes of Hadley and Taussig: "One feature of the controversy with reference to this phase of government rate-making is most extraordinary. It is this: The railway was created to overcome distance and to create place utilities; and now it is urged that a general regard for distance in making rates would bring ruin! [...] many sane men in the United States fail to understand the 'beneficent' effects of a system of rate-making which absolutely neglects an extra distance of a thousand or fifteen hundred miles!" (*ibid.*, pp. 79−80). That a link existed between the *function* of railways and the best way of *pricing* their services was only clear to Balthasar's mind. Undeterred, he assaulted another pillar of the Hadley−Taussig edifice, namely, the notion that rate-making had better be left to the railway managers' determination. "[T]he danger of disturbing so-called fundamental rates is largely a myth," Balthasar wrote, "But even the challenge of a basal rate does not necessarily bring harmful results to the house of cards of rate schedules. *Until railway rates are made in a more scientific manner, and rest upon foundations which can be tangibly described and determined*, it is well not to manifest too much anxiety regarding the inviolability of their present frail foundations" (*ibid.*, p. 77; emphasis added). Once again, the implication was immediate: no solid economic theory of railway rates existed; hence, regulators could have a free hand at establishing them. Any "sane man" denying this was either a bad economist or a puppet in the railroads' hands − probably both.[61]

FINALE: A CAREER-ENDING INCIDENT

The onslaught at Hugo Meyer's views did not remain a mere academic controversy like many others. Because of his ideas, the Chicago economist was directly charged with corruption by a prominent member (and future chairman) of the ICC, Judson Claudius Clements, and by a US Senator, Iowa Republican Jonathan Prentiss Dolliver. The defamatory indictment followed Meyer's presentation of his views about railway regulation before the US Senate Committee on railways. His testimony was so badly received that it triggered accusations of bribery by railroad companies. This further incident took place a few months before the AEA meeting[62] and caused great agitation in the academic community, especially because of the allegation that railroads and, more generally, big business were influencing education in top American universities as a strategy to further their interests.

Commissioner Clements declared that "Wealth always finds it is easy to employ men of theory and doctrine and ability to express its views, and they are often directed to educating the public up to the idea of the superior sanctity of vested rights as against individual rights and individual opportunities in the contests in which engage in the different walks of life. It is ordinarily to be expected that these gentlemen would attack a doctrine or practice that was at variance to the doctrines dear to the patron saint." As to Senator Dolliver, he fused in the indictment Meyer and his new department colleagues by publicly proclaiming that "the University of Chicago smelled of oil like a Kansas town" – this, of course, in reference to the munificent sponsor that University was allegedly subservient to.[63] So reckless was Dolliver's attack that he even incurred in an incredible blunder. In the same speech, he scorned Meyer for his about-face on railroad regulation, which had allegedly followed his appointment to Chicago. Meyer had surely been bribed into becoming a defender of railroads: how else could one explain the reneging of his earlier, strong pro-regulatory views? Alas, the Senator's venom was misplaced: the Meyer he referred to for having previously invoked regulation was Wisconsin Balthasar, not Chicago Hugo!

The public at large liked the latter's ideas no better. "Partisan and untrustworthy": with these words the April 4, 1906, issue of the *Boston Evening Transcript* informed its readers of Hugo Meyer's recent monograph on *Government Regulation of Railway Rates* (Meyer, 1905).[64] Such was the measure of popular tolerance for any law and economics reasoning that, regardless of its merit, did not conform to the dominant view that competition could not work in the case of railways and that government intervention was compulsory to protect public interest against railroad practices.

In June 1906, President Roosevelt's pressing eventually prevailed. Congress passed the Hepburn Act, empowering the ICC to declare an existing rate unreasonable and prescribe a new one – that is, a full rate-making power. Despite the economists' massive involvement in the debates, the enacted solution was not the one suggested by the best law and economics scholarship. The time for accepting the legal implications of efficiency-based economic reasoning had not come yet. In the hands of the ICC, "just and reasonable" rates could be twisted to pursue goals other than economic efficiency and, sometimes, also other than US constitutional values.

Already less than outstanding,[65] Meyer's academic career ended there. Following these episodes, he left for Australia in 1907, where he died in 1923 without ever returning to the United States. While we cannot be sure about the motives for this decision, it is a fact that he never had an academic affiliation again. In his new country, he continued to do research on British public utilities and the history of state ownership in Victoria, but he never became a university professor.[66] The assault against his academic integrity did not remain unanswered, though. The powerful head of Chicago Economics Department, James Laurence Laughlin, published a short note in Meyer's defense in the January 1906 issue of the *Journal of Political Economy*, of which he was editor.[67] Laughlin's words are a good yardstick for appreciating what railroad regulation could actually mean in early 20th-century America.

"On the railway question the prevailing tone is one of general hostility to large corporations," Laughlin complained. "In some academic circles the necessity of appearing on good terms with the masses goes so far that only the mass-point-of-view is given recognition; and the presentation of the truth, if it happens to traverse the popular case, is regarded with something akin to consternation" (Laughlin, 1906, p. 41). Yes, academic freedom was at risk, but the threat did not come from the railroads' or oil barons' money: "it is not amiss to demand that measure of academic freedom that will permit a fair discussion of the rights of those who do not have the popular acclaim. It is going too far when *a carefully reasoned argument* which happens to support the contentions of the railways is treated as if necessarily the outcome of bribery by the money kings" (*ibid.*, emphasis added). Apparently, the law and economics point of view was still far from gaining acceptance — and with it the idea that theoretical controversy should be kept separate from political ones.

NOTES

1. Born in 1866, before moving to Chicago, Meyer had been instructor in Political Economy at Harvard (where he had graduated in 1892) from 1897–1903.

2. On the relationship between American jurisprudence on railroad regulation and classical political economy, see Giocoli (2017). By classical political economy it is meant here the Smithian, non-utilitarian version of the approach, namely, the one that dominated the American economic discourse for the good part of the 19th century, as epitomized by the most diffused textbook of the pre– and post–Civil War era, Francis Wayland's *Elements of Political Economy* (Wayland, 1837). On the incredible sale numbers of Wayland's text, see Frey (2002) and Colander (2011).

3. See for example, Perelman (2006, pp. 70–71). As historian of regulation Thomas McCraw put it: "Railroading influenced American society in the late nineteenth century as only television would in the late twentieth — or as the Roman Catholic Church had influenced the life of medieval Europe" (McCraw, 1984, pp. 4–5).

4. The *almost*, as we argue below, refers to no less than the father of modern railway economics, Arthur Twining Hadley, who remained optimist about the

effectiveness of competition to curb monopoly power in the railroad industry, at least in the long run. At the bottom of this view, which Hadley held from his first major work in 1885 (Hadley, 1885, pp. 101–105) until the end (see, e.g., Hadley, 1928), lay his pioneering intuition about the absence of any necessary relation between the structure of a market and the effectiveness of competition.

5. "There are many cases in which the agency, of whatever nature, by which a service is performed, is certain, from the nature of the case, to be virtually single; in which a practical monopoly, with all the power it confers of taxing the community, cannot be prevented from existing" (Mill, *Principles*, V.11.36). On Mill's analysis of natural monopoly, see Mosca (2008).

6. See Epstein (2014, pp. 152–153); Giocoli (2017).

7. By law and economics I mean the study of the interaction between legal institutions and the economy, that is, an economics-driven investigation of how law affects the organization and functioning of economic systems. This is a broader, and partially different, research program than Posner-style economic analysis of law, namely, the application of neoclassical tools to evaluate the law's efficiency and its impact upon incentives. See Medema (2009), chapter 7.

8. The distinction between political economy and economics follows Schumpeter, who defined a system of political economy as "an economics that includes an adequate analysis of government action and of the mechanisms and prevailing philosophies of political life," "an exposition of a comprehensive set of economic policies" that are advocated "on the strength of certain unifying normative principles" (Schumpeter, 1986 [1954], pp. 22, 38).

9. The same problems of massive investments in fixed capital, huge scale economies, and natural monopoly power affected other industries too. Not only the usual suspects, like waterways, toll bridges, or street lights, but also wholly private businesses like, say, grain elevators or slaughterhouses. In all these cases, the principles of classical economics seemed not to work. Still the issues raised by railroads were unique on account of the industry's importance for the whole economy and of the intermingling of public and private activities that characterized it. In fact, every legal or jurisprudential development in any of the above-mentioned sectors was invariably read in terms of its eventual impact on the railroads. On sheer theoretical terms, what made railway economics truly special was the centrality of the problem of multiple pricing. Railroads were the quintessential example of multiproduct enterprises, but traditional economic theory was ill-equipped to deal with it. For a history-driven summary of the main issues in railway economics, see Waters (2007).

10. See McCraw (1984, pp. 7–44).

11. See McCraw (1984, pp. 10–15).

12. See Cross and Ekelund (1980, p. 227).

13. See Giocoli (2013), Morgan (1993, pp. 572–573).

14. See for example, Hadley (1896, p. 165).

15. A life-long officer at the Southern Pacific Railroad Co., Lansing was, like Hadley, quite optimist about the effectiveness of market forces, but lacked the Yale professor's analytical insight. Thus, his classical conclusion that "[t]he best possible results to all will follow where there is the freest operation of the natural forces of competition," with no "interference," "restriction," or "injury" by the state (Lansing, 1884, p. 475), was based on a simple faith in the virtues of capital mobility.

16. See Henry (1945, p. 182).

17. Hovenkamp (1988, pp. 1033–1034).

18. See Cross and Ekelund (1980, pp. 225–226).

19. "Ricardo's theory was based upon the assumption that when payment fell below cost of service active competition would cease" (Hadley, 1885, p. 72).

20. By "the ordinary laws of political economy," Hadley obviously meant classical economics.

21. Instability, Hadley believed, was much higher in the American case because, different from other countries (like e.g., Britain), Americans had not built their railway system "to accommodate and extend existing business," but rather "with a view to the development of new lines of traffic, new establishments, or even new cities. [...] This hope of future gains, out of all proportion to present traffic, of necessity gave railroad business in America a more speculative character than in England" (Hadley, 1885, p. 147). In his view, even managerial and legislative choices were the effect, rather than the cause, of the peculiar origin of American railroads.

22. On Hadley's views about railroad pools, see next section.

23. See Hovenkamp (1988, p. 1037).

24. The leading cases were United States v. Trans-Missouri Freight Association, 166 US 290 (1897) and United States v. Joint Traffic Association, 171 U.S. 505 (1898).

25. Still, railroads made recourse to elaborate internal enforcement devices to ensure conformity to cartelized rates. For an example of these devices, see Ulen (1980, p. 308).

26. "People of the same trade seldom meet together, even for merriment and diversion, but the conversation ends in a conspiracy against the public, or in some contrivance to raise prices" (Smith, *Wealth of Nations*, I.10.82). One might indeed argue that the forced competition state legislatures had somehow imposed to railroad markets was an instance of the danger Smith envisioned in the rest of the passage: "But though the law cannot hinder people of the same trade from sometimes assembling together, it ought to do nothing to facilitate such assemblies; *much less to render them necessary*" (*ibid.*, emphasis added).

27. The Elkins Act of 1903, which forbade rebating and required railroads to file their rates with the ICC, made cartel arrangements more stable. Once filed, the rates became mandatory, and railroads were forbidden to deviate from them. Since joint rate-making was legal under the Act, its overall effect was to make cheating more difficult. See Hovenkamp (1988, p. 1067).

28. Seligman (1887, p. 388). Like many of his contemporaries, Seligman had completed his economics training in Germany. On Seligman, see Dorfman (1949, pp. 254–256) and Asso and Fiorito (2006).

29. Though not necessarily in *price* competition, as the next quote shows.

30. Knapp's spell at the ICC, first as a member (since 1891) and then as chairman (since 1898), lasted until 1910, when he became a federal judge at the Court of Appeals of the Second Circuit.

31. "A mistaken and mischievous policy," he called it (Knapp, 1905, p. 29).

32. See Hovenkamp (1988, p. 1041).

33. The Fifth Section recited: "That it shall be unlawful for any common carrier subject to the provisions of this act to enter into any contract, agreement, or

combination with any other common carrier or carriers for the pooling of freights of different and competing railroads, or to divide between them the aggregate or net proceeds of the earnings of such railroads, or any portion thereof; and in any case of an agreement for the pooling of freights as aforesaid, each day of its continuance shall be deemed a separate offense."

34. The latter was for instance Hadley's interpretation of the true motivations behind the Act. The railroads "were tired of fighting, and were glad to make the law for the time being a pretext for the cessation of rate wars. The danger of disobeying the law was greater than the danger of suffering from the cut rates of a rival" (Hadley, 1888, p. 184). This interpretation is modernly associated to the name of Gabriel Kolko: see Kolko (1965). For a skeptical view, see Ulen (1980, pp. 308–309).

35. The case was *Trans-Missouri Freight Association*, quoted in note 24.

36. For an assessment of the actual impact of the Court's decision upon what already looked like an irreversible phenomenon, see Hovenkamp (1988, pp. 1042–1043).

37. See Hovenkamp (1988, p. 1049).

38. See Hovenkamp (1988, pp. 1050–1052).

39. "Railroad profits are to a large extent of the nature of rent rather than interest. They represent excess of market value above operating expenses" (Hadley, 1885, p. 123, fn. 1).

40. See McCraw (1984, pp. 39–40).

41. Hadley (1885, pp. 116–118). Cross and Ekelund (1980, p. 223) call the example "a classic in railway rate theory."

42. See Cross and Ekelund (1980, pp. 217–222), whose presentation I follow here.

43. Hadley further noted that "Each class of articles has a curve of its own" (Hadley, 1885, p. 263). The remark entails that his theory captured what is today called third-degree price discrimination (or group pricing), that is, the practice of dividing the market in segments and charging the same price for everyone in each segment. All necessary elements were there. His reference to a demand curve for each item of traffic clearly defined the separate markets of a monopolist. In the railroad case these markets could be separated by identifiable characteristics, like product classifications, or by distances, like long and short haul. A simple manipulation of Hadley's equations also shows that equilibrium prices in the separate markets were directly related to the demand elasticities of each market. Indeed, price elasticity of demand was an essential, though implicit, part of Hadley's model. More generally, Hadley showed in these pages a clear intuition of the basic rationale of the Ramsey pricing technique, on which see next section. Surveying the literature on railroad rates in the early 1930s, Illinois University transportation economist Philip Locklin indeed wrote: "No one reading Hadley's explanation of the theory of rates would ever make the error of considering the practice of charging what the traffic will bear as extorting the highest possible charge" (Locklin, 1933, p. 181).

44. Examining the first months of activity of the ICC, Hadley was relieved to acknowledge the commissioners' efforts to perform their duties following as much as possible "the broader principles of political economy," away from nefarious ideas like forcing railroads to base their rates on cost of service (Hadley, 1888, p. 181). The praise to ICC members (see e.g., *ibid.*, p. 172) did not extend to the content of the 1887 Act that he considered extremely dangerous for the future of American

economic development. A few years later, the ICC's changed attitude would confirm Hadley's fears: see next section.

45. Under this respect, Hadley very much appreciated the quasi-judicial character of the ICC's activity in its first months, and even more the fact that, contrary to most US courts, the Commission had applied what he deemed sound economic principles to assess the violations of the anti-discrimination provision of the Act (Hadley, 1888, p. 167 ff.).

46. The influential editor of the *Quarterly Journal of Economics* for forty years, Taussig had been the first "old school" economist to join the then-radical AEA, paving the way to the subsequent rapprochement between the two sides. See Dorfman (1949, p. 265). On the importance of Taussig's 1891 paper, see Locklin (1933, pp. 182–184).

47. See Mill, *Principles*, III.16.4–8. Taussig noted that even Smith had hinted at the problem of allocating joint costs in the *Wealth of Nations* (Taussig, 1891, pp. 461–462, footnote).

48. The latter sentence hinted, as in Hadley, at the price elasticity notion. Indeed, Taussig used the terms "sensitive" and "insensitive" to characterize what we modernly call "elastic" and "inelastic" demand. See for example, Taussig (1891, p. 454).

49. "When the toll upon carriages of luxury, upon coaches, post-chaises, etc. is made somewhat higher in proportion to their weight, than upon carriages of necessary use, such as carts, wagons, etc. the indolence and vanity of the rich is made to contribute in a very easy manner to the relief of the poor, by rendering cheaper the transportation of heavy goods to all the different parts of the country" (*WN*, V.1.75). Taussig noted that this passage lent itself to an explanation on purely economic grounds as much as to one based upon ethical criteria – that is, having everyone pay for the service according to his means (Taussig, 1891, pp. 461–462, footnote).

50. See Waters (2007, pp. 17–21), Baumol and Bradford (1970), esp. 277–280.

51. See Seligman (1887, p. 397). Taussig was wary of the latter expression, fearing that it might be misinterpreted in terms of the service's intrinsic utility (Taussig, 1891, p. 463). At the same time, he knew that even "charging what the traffic will bear" was a potentially troublesome expression. "That obnoxious phrase," he admitted, "is used to describe two distinct things; on the one hand, the adaptation of rates to demand which results from joint cost; on the other hand, the adaptation to demand which results from monopoly" (*ibid.*, p. 457). The latter use made the expression suspect, although the meaning was much about the same: "To the extent to which the element of monopoly enters, rates are again permanently affected by demand, or by what the traffic will bear. Any particular rate may be the result of the working of the two factors of monopoly and joint cost. [...] The traffic is charged what it will bear in two distinct senses" (*ibid.*). The expression captured a broad rational rate-making practice, of which classification of freight was just an example (*ibid.*, p. 456).

52. Taussig's specific target was a 1883 book by German economist Gustav Cohn, *Die englische Eisenbahnpolitik der letzten zehn Jahre (1873–1883)*. Under this approach, he complained, the problem of railway rates "is at bottom one of ethics, involving those considerations of public policy and of right and wrong which recur in the discussions of proportional or progressive taxation." It was this link between ethics and economics that led supporters of the approach to the conclusion

that "public ownership of railways, or at least public regulation of rates, is impera-tive" (Taussig, 1891, pp. 438–439).

53. A leader of the earliest generation of American neoclassical economists, Taussig knew well that profit maximization was tantamount to allocative efficiency.

54. This is a nice illustration of the circumstance that for American economists of the Gilded Age marginalism was still just *a* tool, not *the* tool, of analysis. See Yonay (1998), chapter 2.

55. Not that modern economists did much better. Introducing the logic of Ramsey pricing, Baumol and Bradford (1970, p. 265) complained that "the results which [this paper] describes have appeared many times in the literature and have been reported by most eminent economists in very prominent journals. Yet these results may well come as a surprise to many readers who will consider them to be at variance with ideas which they have long accepted." These words were printed in the 1970 *American Economic Review*!

56. See Smalley (1906), chapter VII.

57. For a possible explanation of the federal courts' attitude, see Giocoli (2017).

58. By the Commerce Clause of the US Constitution, the regulation of interstate commerce is one of Congress's enumerated powers.

59. Logan Grant McPherson, lecturer at Johns Hopkins University on transpor-tation economics and discussant of Balthasar Meyer's paper, could not miss the chance to reply that: "The fact is that in so far as its balance sheet is concerned a railroad company is exactly like a soap factory: if it spends more than it earns it cannot like the Post Office Department make up the deficit from taxation, but it is sold out just like a soap factory or any other business concern" (McPherson, 1906, p. 89). McPherson's discussion was a summary of economic principles along Taussig's lines: see *ibid.*, pp. 89–91.

60. Balthasar was pretty right here, in that the ICC's views on the issue had oscil-lated back and forth along the years. Yet, Hugo's point was precisely that no such oscillation was justified because there was only one correct economic explanation of railroad pricing: his (and Hadley's and Taussig's) own one.

61. Balthasar would reiterate his critiques, this time expressly targeting Hugo's theory, in B. H. Meyer (1906b). The violence of the attack, which bordered on libel, and even more the fact that it appeared as a book review of Mayer (1905) in the Chicago-based *Journal of Political Economy*, is further evidence that the fate of Hugo's academic career had been sealed by the controversy. Also see below, note 67 and the accompanying text.

62. Meyer gave his Senate testimony in May 1905.

63. Both quotes are from Laughlin (1906, pp. 42–43). Oil baron John D. Rockefeller had almost single-handedly financed the new University of Chicago (see Van Overtveldt, 2007, pp. 20–25). Railroads were tightly connected with the oil industry, which was one of their best customers, often to the point of monopsony.

64. For a deeper evaluation of the book, the article referred readers to – what else? – the scathing review by Balthasar Meyer mentioned above, note 61.

65. Remember that at the time of the Senate and AEA incidents, assistant profes-sor Meyer was already thirty-nine.

66. See the entries "Meyer, H. R." in *Who's Who in the World* (1912) and *The Encyclopedia Americana* (1920).

67. Laughlin also gave Hugo the opportunity to offer a convincing reply to Balthasar Meyer's critiques in the same journal: see H. R. Meyer (1906b). Unfortunately, the issue could not be settled on pure scientific grounds anymore.

ACKNOWLEDGMENTS

I thank Andreaa Cosnita Langlais, Tom Firey, Paul Moreno, Russell Pitman, Peter van Doren, and this journal's editors and referees for their useful comments and suggestions. I also thank Simon Cook for his invaluable help in revising my English. I am of course responsible of all remaining mistakes. A shorter version of this work has been published as Giocoli (2015–2016). The financial support of the *INET – Institute for New Economic Thinking* grant "Free from what? Evolving notions of 'market freedom' in the history and contemporary practice of US antitrust law and economics" (grant # INO1200015/033) is gratefully acknowledged.

REFERENCES

Adam, C. F., Jr. (1868). Boston. *North American Review, 106*(218), 1–25.

Adams, C. F., Jr. (1870). Railroad commissions. *Journal of Social Science, 2*, 233–236.

Adams, H. C. (1887). Relation of the state to industrial action. *Publications of the American Economic Association, 1*(6), 7–85.

Asso, P. F., & Fiorito, L. (2006). Introduction to Edwin Robert Anderson Seligman, *Autobiography* (1929). *Research in the History of Economic Thought and Methodology, 24-C*, 149–187.

Baumol, W. J., & Bradford, D. F. (1970). Optimal departures from marginal cost pricing. *American Economic Review, 60*(3), 265–283.

Colander, D. (2011). The evolution of U.S. economics textbooks. In M. Augello & M. E. L. Guidi (Eds.), *The economic reader: Textbooks, manuals and the dissemination of the economic sciences during the 19th and early 20th centuries* (pp. 324–338). London: Routledge.

Cooley, T. M. (1883). State regulation of corporate profits. *North American Review, 137*(32), 205–217.

Cross, M., & Ekelund, R. B. (1980). A.T. Hadley on monopoly theory and railway regulation: An American contribution to economic analysis and policy. *History of Political Economy, 12*(2), 214–233.

Dixon, F. H. (1906). Discussion on papers on railway rate regulation. *Publications of the American Economic Association*, 3rd Series, *7*(1), 84–89.

Dorfman, J. (1949). *The economic mind in American civilization* (Vol. III, pp. 1865–1918). New York, NY: The Viking Press.

Epstein, R. A. (2014). *The classical liberal Constitution. The uncertain quest for limited government*. Cambridge, MA: Harvard University Press.

Frey, D. E. (2002). Francis Wayland's 1830s textbooks: Evangelical ethics and political economy. *Journal of the History of Economic Thought, 24*(2), 215–231.

Giocoli, N. (2013). British economists on competition policy (1890–1920). *Research in the History of Economic Thought and Methodology, 31*(A), 1–57.

Giocoli, N. (2015-2016). When law and economics was a dangerous subject. *Regulation, Winter*, 32–38.

Giocoli, N. (2017). The (rail)road to *Lochner*: Reproduction cost and the Gilded Age controversy on rate regulation. *History of Political Economy, forthcoming*.

Hadley, A. T. (1885). *Railroad transportation. Its history and its laws* (1903 ed.). London: Putnam's Sons.

Hadley, A. T. (1888). The workings of the interstate commerce law. *Quarterly Journal of Economics, 2*(2), 162–187.

Hadley, A. T. (1896). *Economics: An account of the relations between private property and public welfare*. London: Putnam's Sons.

Hadley, A. T. (1928). The meaning of valuation. *American Economic Review, Papers and Proceedings, 18*(1), 173–180.

Henry, R. S. (1945). The railroad land grant legend in American history texts. *Mississippi Valley Historical Review, 32*(2), 171–194.

Hovenkamp, H. (1988). Regulatory conflict in the gilded age: Federalism and the railroad problem. *Yale Law Journal, 97*(6), 1017–1072.

Knapp, M. A. (1905). The regulation of railway rates. *Publications of the American Economic Association, Papers and Proceedings*, Part II, 3rd Series, *6*(2), 20–30.

Lansing, G. L. (1884). The railway and the state. *North American Review, 138*(330), 461–475.

Laughlin, L. J. (1906). Academic liberty. *Journal of Political Economy, 14*(1), 41–43.

Locklin, P. D. (1933). The literature on railway rate theory. *Quarterly Journal of Economics, 47*(2), 167–230.

Kolko, G. (1965). *Railroads and regulation 1877–1916*. Princeton, NJ: Princeton University Press.

McCraw, T. K. (1984). *Prophets of regulation*. Cambridge, MA: Belknap Press.

McPherson, L. G. (1906). Discussion on papers on railway rate regulation. *Publications of the American Economic Association*, 3rd Series, *7*(1), 89–94.

Medema, S. (2009). *The hesitant hand. Taming self-interest in history of economic ideas*. Princeton, NJ: Princeton University Press.

Meyer, B. H. (1906a). Government regulation of railway rates. *Publications of the American Economic Association*, 3rd Series, *7*(1), 69–83.

Meyer, B. H. (1906b). Government regulation of railway rates. *Journal of Political Economy, 14*(2), 86–106.

Meyer, H. R. (1905). *Government regulation of railway rates. A study of the experience of the United States, Germany, France, Austria-Hungary, Russia, and Australia*. New York, NY: Macmillan.

Meyer, H. R. (1906a). Government regulation of railway rates. *Publications of the American Economic Association*, 3rd Series, *7*(1), 61–68.

Meyer, H. R. (1906b). A reply to professor B. H. Meyer, privy councilor Von Der Leyen, professor Willard Fisher. *Journal of Political Economy, 14*(4), 193–223.

Mill, J. S. (1848). *Principles of political economy with some of their applications to social philosophy* (7th ed., p. 1909). London: Longmans, Green and Co.

Morgan, M. (1993). Competing notions of competition. *History of Political Economy*, *25*(4), 563–604.

Mosca, M. (2008). On the origins of the concept of natural monopoly: Economies of scale and competition. *European Journal of the History of Economic Thought*, *15*(2), 317–353.

Perelman, M. (2006). *Railroading economics. The creation of the free market mythology.* New York, NY: Monthly Review Press.

Schumpeter, J. A. (1986 [1954]). *History of economic analysis.* London: Routledge.

Seligman, E. R. A. (1887). Railway tariffs and the interstate commerce law. *Political Science Quarterly*, *2*:2(June), 223–264 (Part I); 2:3 (September), 369–413 (Part II).

Smalley, H. S. (1906). Railroad rate control in its legal aspects: A study of the effect of judicial decisions upon public regulation of railroad rates. *Publications of the American Economic Association*, 3rd Series, *7*(2), 4–147.

Smith, A. (1776). *An inquiry into the nature and causes of the wealth of nations* (5th ed., p. 1904). London: Methuen & Co.

Taussig, F. W. (1891). A contribution to the theory of railway rates. *Quarterly Journal of Economics*, *5*(4), 438–465.

Ulen, T. S. (1980). The market for regulation: The ICC from 1887 to 1920. *American Economic Review, Papers and Proceedings*, *70*(2), 306–310.

Van Overtveldt, J. (2007). *The Chicago school.* Chicago, IL: B2 Books.

Waters, W. G. (2007). Evolution of railroad economics. *Research in Transportation Economics*, *20*, 11–67.

Wayland, F. (1837). *Elements of political economy.* New York, NY: Leavitt, Lord & Co.

Whitten, R. H. (1914). Fair value for rate purposes. *Harvard Law Review*, *27*(5), 419–436.

Yonay, Y. P. (1998). *The struggle over the soul of economics. Institutional and neoclassical economists in America between the wars.* Princeton, NJ: Princeton University Press.

TOWARDS A RATIONAL RECONSTRUCTION OF PIGOU'S 'THEORY OF UNEMPLOYMENT'

Massimo Di Matteo

ABSTRACT

The chapter examines the core framework of A. C. Pigou's Theory of Unemployment (TU) with the aim of providing a rational reconstruction of his analysis of the determinants of unemployment in the short period. This is accomplished without any comparison with Keynes's criticism of TU, as often found in the previous literature.

I reconstruct Pigou's two-sector model, which only accounted for output in the wage good sector but not in the non-wage good sector, as a complete two-sector model to reveal his implicit assumptions about the passive behaviour of non-wage earners in the non-wage good sector. I also find classical elements, most notably the wage fund doctrine and the hypothesis on profits, in Pigou's approach, which partly explains why the model is incomplete when viewed in terms of its neoclassical elements. In the "A Rational Reconstruction of the Two-Sector Model" section, I sketch a mathematical model to make Pigou's analysis consistent.

Research in the History of Economic Thought and Methodology, Volume 34A, 339–356
ISSN: 0743-4154/doi:10.1108/S0743-41542016000034A010

The chapter shows how unemployment is determined and how economic policy to deal with it is conceived in the work of a major exponent of the pre-Keynesian approach.

Keywords: Neoclassical theory of unemployment; classical theory of unemployment; Pigou; wage fund; two-sector economy

JEL classifications: B22; B31

INTRODUCTION

The aim of the chapter is to analyze Pigou's core framework (Pigou, 1933) and discuss his arguments on the determinants of unemployment in a given short period. This is accomplished without any comparison with Keynes's criticism of the Theory of Unemployment (TU) as often found in the previous literature. I reconstruct Pigou's two-sector model, which only accounted for output in the wage good sector, but not in the non-wage good sector, as a complete two-sector model to reveal his implicit assumptions about the passive behaviour of non-wage earners in the non-wage good sector. I also find classical elements, most notably the wage fund doctrine and the hypothesis on profits, in Pigou's approach, which partly explains why the model is incomplete when viewed in terms of its neoclassical elements. In this reconstruction, I reveal the implicit assumptions behind TU and build a simple mathematical model to complete Pigou's analysis.

The plan of the chapter is as follows. In the 'Brief Review of Pigou's Two-Sector Model section, I outline Pigou's core approach.[1] This is done by eliminating all complications and qualifications not essential to the thesis and which distract from the main argument. In the 'What's Missing from the Two-Sector Model in *TU*' section through a careful analysis I reveal the implicit assumption in his theory. This part is enriched with a description of Pigou's analysis of the effects of different levels of demand for labour at a given real wage on employment and of the effects of real wage variations on employment. In the 'A Rational Reconstruction of the Two-Sector Model section, a simple mathematical model is constructed to make Pigou's analysis consistent. The last section concludes by showing that Pigou's approach, as reconstructed in the chapter, is very different from Keynes's and has roots in the classical as well as neoclassical schools, which is not surprising for the successor of Marshall.

BRIEF REVIEW OF PIGOU'S TWO-SECTOR MODEL

Let me start by reminding the reader that Pigou's exposition is irritating because, instead of setting the model in its simplest form to derive its main results and only then adding complications, he adds various qualifications[2] and discusses them in turn. The end result is that Pigou makes it difficult for the reader to obtain a clear idea of the concepts.[3] I therefore set out what appears to be the core of TU, hoping to clarify Pigou's views and elucidate the essential features of his approach. Pigou discusses the problem in a two-sector real framework composed of wage goods (WG) and non-wage goods (NWG).[4] He also lumps luxury consumption and capital goods together in NWG because they can be considered on the same footing (p. 75, 145–146) in the short, though not in the long, period. In TU, the short period[5] is defined as a situation where industrial equipment, both in form and quantity, may properly be regarded as more or less fixed[6] and the real wage is given and equal in both sectors.[7]

In this chapter, I limit consideration to the real analysis of wage and non-wage good markets. According to Pigou, monetary considerations can be discussed at the end (in Part IV) as they do not modify the conclusion in any essential way.[8] In his work, Pigou is interested in discussing what determines the level of unemployment in the short period, clearly having in mind that the level of unemployment can be different in each different short period.[9] To keep the analysis as simple as possible, Pigou maintains that would-be wage earners (the labour force in modern language) are more or less fixed in number[10] so that unemployment is simply the difference between them and employed workers.[11] The latter are determined by the demand for labour.[12] Throughout the book attention is therefore concentrated on the latter variable. If we add the hypothesis[13] that non-wage earners in the WG sector maximise profits, then the amount of WG produced can immediately be computed.[14]

How much employment is forthcoming in the economy as a whole? To answer this question Pigou reminds the reader, first, that non-wage earners are assumed (pp. 21–25) to consume a certain amount of WG (C in Pigou's notation)[15] and second that the WG can be increased or diminished (S in Pigou's notation) out of stocks already held.[16] If we add the WG paid to workers employed in the WG sector itself, there remains a quantity of WG that sets what I will call the maximum amount that can be used in the NWG industry, and accordingly the maximum amount of NWG that can be produced, given the technical conditions and the real wage in the NWG industry. Pigou argues as if actual and maximum employment were equal. The model is thus very simple, having a recursive structure. Given technical conditions[17] and the real wage in the WG sector, the amount of WG that maximises profits is produced. Given consumption of these goods (and a hypothesis on the destination of profits) by non-wage earners, changes in stocks, the real wage in both sectors and technology in the NWG sector, employment in the NWG sector is determined. So far Pigou's analysis, which is less than complete, could be considered a description of (short period) equilibrium.

WHAT'S MISSING FROM THE TWO-SECTOR MODEL IN *TU*

Let us see what is actually implied in Pigou's argument that actual is equal to maximum employment, according to my terminology. Indeed, the above means that all profits (net of C, consumption of wage goods by non-wage earners) obtained in the WG sector are available for the consumption of workers in the NWG sector. At time 0 in the WG sector we have[18]

$$W_{\text{WG}} + R_{\text{WG}} = \text{WG}_0 = C + W_{\text{WG}} + W_{\text{NWG}}$$

where WG_0 is total product of wage goods at time 0, R_{WG} profits in the WG sector, W_{WG} wage goods paid to workers of the WG sector, W_{NWG} wage goods paid to workers in the NWG sector, and C consumption of wage goods by non-wage earners. Clearly after profits in the WG sector have been maximised by equating the given real wage to the marginal productivity of labour, W_{WG} is known; Pigou considers that C is also determined, therefore all profits net of consumption will buy W_{NWG}.

At the same time in a two-sector model in equilibrium, we require that production be absorbed by demand in the NWG sector: this means that all profits made in the economy are spent in the NWG industry, partly as wage goods transferred from the WG sector to workers employed in NWG sector, partly as demand for NWG sector output (luxury and investment goods). In the sequel, I will refer to this as the macrobalance condition, a condition that appears to be implicitly assumed by Pigou. In other words, the macrobalance condition states that the NWG sector must employ a number of workers whose production of luxury and investment goods completely exhausts the profits of the WG sector (after taking into account consumption of these goods by non-wage earners) and the profits of the NWG sector itself. The wage fund[19] sets an upper limit to the amount of employment that results in the NWG industry. Non-wage earners maximise profits in the WG sector and, if all profits are spent in the way just described, the actual amount of employment equals the maximum amount allowed by the wage fund.

This is taken for granted by Pigou in his reasoning without any explicit discussion. In TU everything is described in real terms. The gist of Pigou's argument is revealed by the answer to the following question. What else could non-wage earners do with their profits in a non-monetary economy? After consuming a given part (C), they can only employ them in the NWG sector, namely invest and buy luxury goods. And what can they do with the profits obtained in the NWG sector? They can only consume them by buying the goods produced: this must be true whatever relative prices are (although Pigou never mentions prices in this respect).

But are they willing to do that? The answer we derive from Pigou is affirmative, as they have no other option. Non-wage earners do not hoard goods, as the cost of storage is (presumably) assumed to be higher than any appreciation in value. The introduction of money will not matter because, for followers of the quantity theory of money, a preference for liquidity is not justified. In the NWG sector, the real wage is given, as are technical conditions and industrial equipment. If, as just said, non-wage earners spent all the profits earned in the WG sector in the way just indicated (similar to the classical idea that all profits are reinvested), it is not certain however that they would be maximising profits in the NWG sector, as wage and employment are already determined. In other words, Pigou's assumption that non-wage earners spend all their profits in the NWG sector implies that they are content with whatever return they get in the sector. In contrast to the WG sector, rather passive behaviour of non-wage earners is assumed when producing investment and luxury goods. One could perhaps envisage this position as one in which equilibrium cannot be reached, as prices are not allowed to change and correct imbalances. However, asymmetry between the two sectors remains, or rather between the behaviour of NW earners in the two sectors.

In the following two subsections, I will show in detail the points of Pigou's argument that are subject to the above criticism.

Effects of a Change in the Demand for Labour

Let us start first with his analysis of the effects of a different level of demand for labour at the prevailing real wage on employment. It is appropriate to remember here that Pigou (p. vi) is not concerned with the broader influences that govern movements of demand, as already discussed at length in his *Industrial Fluctuations*.[20] In TU, Pigou examines this situation after his analysis of the effects of changes in the real wage on labour demand, but for my purpose it is more convenient to start with this case and treat the other later. Pigou argues[21] that a change in the aggregate demand for labour cannot lead to a change in employment, unless the wage fund can expand or contract: if it cannot, a decision to engage more labour in one occupation has to be compensated by an equivalent decrease in employment in another occupation, even if there is unemployment (p. 143).[22] Although Pigou does not say it explicitly, here he seems to mean that the real wage has to fall in the WG sector so as to provide extra wage goods to the extra workers in order to satisfy the increased demand for labour. Incidentally this would be true even if the real wage in NWG sector remained constant. In my opinion, however, the fall in wage in the WG sector is a sufficient but not necessary condition. Indeed, if on the contrary the real wage fell in the NWG sector only, the unchanged amount of profits of the WG sector would employ more people in the NWG sector and accommodate the increased demand. By the way, this could increase the total amount of profits in the NWG sector. As we shall see later in the chapter, Pigou objects to this line of thought.

To confirm my analysis it is important to go through the various steps of Pigou's argument. If the real wage is given, an increase in the demand for labour in the NWG sector will give rise to one of two possibilities, according to Pigou: (a) the wage goods needed are taken from other occupations in the NWG sector, or (b) there is a reduction in C and/or S. Under (a), aggregate employment does not change: it is revealing that Pigou does not describe a mechanism whereby an increase in the demand for labour in one sector of NWG could lead to a decrease in another sector of NWG. [23] Under (b), employment can increase but it is a very unlikely outcome because non-wage earners do not reduce their consumption of wage goods (pp. 146–147). On the other hand, stocks cannot be depleted unless for a minor amount: 'Plainly, however, this source of supply being a fund and not a flow it cannot be drawn for long (...)'. He concludes (p. 147): 'Hence reactions on S, like reactions on C, are not, in general, important'.

In principle, Pigou does not exclude the possibility of an increase in the demand for labour in NWG sector leading to an increase in employment, provided there is a reduction in the consumption of WG by non-wage earners, namely an increase in their savings. In this way, he makes it clear that the important factor for the increase in employment is what item is reduced: if non-wage earners agree to reduce their consumption of WG and increase the demand for luxury consumption goods or for capital goods, employment can increase; if, on the contrary, the reduction comes from a fall in luxury good consumption in favour of an increase in capital goods, this will not alter short run employment in Pigou's model. This derives from the assumption of lumping luxury consumption goods and capital goods together in the short period,[24] which Pigou (p. 145) exemplifies in the context of the (then) ongoing discussion about the so-called 'Treasury view': '(...) Just as there is no net addition to the aggregate demand for labour, and so to employment, if wage goods are shifted to road making from machine making, so also there is no net addition if they are shifted to it from the making of luxury motor cars or silk dressing-gowns or other articles of consumption too costly to enter into wage goods'. What about stocks? It is clear that Pigou appears to miss the fact that a reduction in inventories signals an increase in the aggregate demand (as we would say today) and concerns himself only with the limited amount of them that can be used to back an increased demand for WG. It is also clear that in the above circumstances there is no reason for *planned* stocks to fall in the face of an increase or a steady level of economic activity: but Pigou is not saying this, as we have just seen. A symmetric argument can be worked out for the case of reduction in the demand for labour.[25]

As a further point it can be inferred that Pigou does not take the macro-balance condition (introduced in the previous section) into account in a proper way from his discussion (p. 159) of the effects of an autonomous increase in C, the demand for wage goods by non-wage earners.[26] This, he maintains, will not have any effect on the quantity of labour demanded anywhere.[27] He appears to overlook that in this case the surplus available for employment in the NWG sector is reduced, as the macrobalance condition immediately reveals. So what is happening implicitly, according to Pigou, is that stocks must be falling: again an example of passive behaviour. Since they cannot fall further once they have reached zero, what will happen? Pigou does not tell us.

Effects of a Change in the Real Wage

Let us now come to the effects of real wage reduction discussed at length in the second part of TU. As in the previous subsection, here a fall (increase) means a lower (higher) level of the real wage: in other words, we are performing a comparative statics exercise. According to Pigou (pp. 38–39), in the short run an increase (fall) in the real wage does not induce the substitution of capital (labour) for labour (capital), this being a long run result which is arrived at step by step. Therefore, the overall effect on employment of such a change may be decomposed into the direct effect on the amount of WG produced and an indirect effect on the amount of NWG. The total effect can be computed to obtain a numerical value for the overall elasticity of the demand for labour with respect to a change in wages, the elasticity accordingly being composed of two parts. Following back on the envelope calculations,[28] Pigou (p. 89) asserts that during marked depressions the direct elasticity is much larger than one whereas in booms it is almost negligible. On this basis, he argues that WG production will increase, as a fall in the real wage induces profit maximising firms in the WG industry to demand more labour with a substantial increase in employment (pp. 96–97).

Pigou then examines what happens in the NWG sector as well. He proceeds by steps. First he supposes (p. 73) that the production of WG is not altered, in which case the only effect of a fall in the real wage is that the reduction in workers income be exactly matched by an increase in the income of non-wage earners. This can either be wholly consumed (an increase in C, but Pigou considers this to be rather rigid), added to stocks (again not plausible for reasons already given) or destined to increase the wage bill of the NWG sector. However, we know that there will be an increase in the production of wage goods and therefore, Pigou asserts, in the production of NWG. Again here to have an equilibrium we have to postulate that the macrobalance condition applies. A similar effect on employment can be achieved via an improvement in the technology of the WG industry.[29] Let us finally discuss the case (pp. 74–75) in which the real wage falls in the NWG sector, a situation we have already hinted at. Pigou maintains that there cannot be an increase in overall employment (p. 175 emphasis in the original): '*When the real—not the money—rate of wages ruling in the wage good industries is given*, the quantity of labour demanded in these industries is determined (...) by the wage rate in relation to their productivity functions (...). Nothing that happens in the non-wage good industries can, from the short-period standpoint (...), benefit the wage good industries (...)' Pigou's argument is that otherwise an infinite amount of employment is implied (p. 175): 'The people set to work on road making (...) have, *pro tanto*, more money to spend; they spend it, and so set to work more makers of the wage goods that they buy; these, by spending their money, set to work more makers of the wage goods that *they* buy; and so on indefinitely. Indeed, (…) it is only because some of the wage earners' goods are bought from abroad that the setting of a single new man to work on road making does not cause an infinite number of men to obtain employment in making wage goods'.

Finally, Pigou concludes with a sentence that is really the most synthetic expression of his viewpoint (pp. 75−76): again he postulates passive behaviour of non-wage earners in the NWG sector: ' (…) the thousand extra £ spent by the new employees taken on for road making goes to buy wage goods which would have been created anyhow and which, if not so bought, would have employed other labour, have been consumed by non-wage earners, (…) or have been placed in store'. This feature of Pigou's approach certainly has an anti-Keynesian flavour. Far from being those who rule the roost, non-wage earners, both as producers and *qua* investors, display rather passive behaviour and adapt to what is happening in the rest of the economy, namely to the decisions of producers in the wage good sector.

A RATIONAL RECONSTRUCTION OF THE TWO-SECTOR MODEL

Can we make Pigou's argument as reconstructed consistent with profit maximisation in the NWG sector? One could assume that entrepreneurs in the NWG sector can select the capital/labour ratio in the short run. This is not possible, however, given Pigou's definition of the short run. It would also imply that given the real wage and total employment, firms can vary the capital/labour ratio almost without limit to reach the preferred position.[30] In particular, there could be cases in which capital falls short of the amount required or alternatively is too much. The same argument applies, *mutatis mutandis*, if we refer to a variable degree of capacity utilisation.[31] On the other hand, if non-wage earners maximise profits in the NWG sector as well, it is not certain that all profits made in the WG sector will be invested in the NWG sector. This is a dilemma.

Can one complete Pigou's analysis in a consistent way that solves the dilemma? The crucial point, that Pigou apparently misses, is that if they want to maximise profits, non-wage earners in the NWG sector must equate the physical marginal productivity of labour with the *product wage* which differs in value from the real wage in the WG sector. So relative prices should be included in the analysis, if the process of profit maximisation in the NWG sector is to be properly accounted for. Let us set up a little recursive model to *complete* Pigou's approach in a consistent way. Here, it is an example of how this can be accomplished

$$F'(x) = \left(w/p_x\right)^0 \tag{1}$$

where F is the production function of the WG sector, F' the derivative of F with respect to labour, x employment in the WG sector, $\left(w/p_x\right)^0$ the given real wage (money wage divided by the price of WG) at time 0. Since marginal productivity of labour in the WG sector and the real wage are equal, we determine x, the level of employment in the WG sector, namely x_0

$$F(x_0) = \left(w/p_x\right)^0 E + C_0 \tag{2}$$

where E is the total employment and C_0 is the amount of WG consumed by non-wage earners and fixed in real terms (irrespective of prices). This expresses the wage fund doctrine in Pigou's version. From this relation, we find E, namely E_0

$$E_0 = x_0 + y \tag{3}$$

where y is the employment in the NWG sector. From this, we determine y, namely y_0. Then, since WG and NWG are different goods, profit maximisation in the NWG sector gives

$$G'(y_0) = \left(w/p_x\right)^0 \left(p_x/p_y\right) \tag{4}$$

where G' is the physical marginal productivity of labour in the NWG sector which is equal to the product wage. From this, we determine relative prices (p_x/p_y). Finally

$$G(y_0) = \left(w/p_x\right)^0 y_0 \left(p_x/p_y\right) + R_y \tag{5}$$

where R_y is the profit earned in the NWG sector and G is the production function in the NWG sector. From this we find R_y.

Since total production and total income are equal and, as stated in 'Brief Review of Pigou's Two-Sector Model' section, the real wage is given and equal in both sectors, it is apparent that the wages paid in the NWG sector are equal to the profits in the WG sector

$$F(x_0) - \left(w/p_x\right)^0 x_0 - C_0 = R_x = \left(w/p_x\right)^0 y_0$$

Namely

$$F(x_0) = \left(w/p_x\right)^0 [x_0 + y_0] + C_0$$

In this way the model is complete, but as shown, it requires endogeneity of the price of NWG, relative to the price of WG. This can be perfectly consistent with a short run analysis, if we are prepared to assume that prices are less sticky than wages. The reason why Pigou offers no such analysis is probably the habit of thinking in real terms that leads him to overlook the fact that the *value* of all profits has to be equal to the *value* of the NWG product. Relative prices are not taken into consideration by Pigou in this analysis.[32]

CONCLUSIONS

Pigou's theory as expressed in this chapter has to be considered a step in his lifelong task of analysing the actual determinants of unemployment. How can we characterise it? His methodology is Marshallian, at least if we accept Boland's (1992) reconstruction of Marshall's methodology. Alfred Marshall was always looking for a framework in which he could determine one variable at a time in order to make the analysis clear: he framed the discussion in such a way that everything else was for the moment fixed, either because it was determined in another context or was considered constant in the time period chosen. The same appears to be valid in Pigou's case, as exemplified by the recursive nature of his short-period theory. In addition, Pigou makes wide use of another typical Marshallian concept, namely the representative firm or worker.

A brief summary of the main features of Pigou's approach is as follows. At least in the WG sector, there is a downward sloping demand curve for labour and profits are maximised by equating the physical marginal productivity of labour to the given real wage: certainly a neoclassical feature. On the one hand, the idea of wage goods is classical in nature.[33] Some

members of the classical school (notably John Stuart Mill) also advanced
the concept of wage fund to argue that there is an inverse relation between
wages and employment. However, one cannot say that there is a uniform
position among them in this respect: it is still controversial whether
Ricardo's wage fund is (in)consistent with other parts of his theory.[34]
Although Marshall (1920, Appendix J) rejects the extreme version of the
wage fund theory, he appears to accept that there is something valuable in
it. He further argues that it was applied in support of some important theses that could be defended without it. Indeed, in his *Employment and
Equilibrium*, Pigou would defend the classical theory without the wage fund
theory.[35] How does Pigou reinterpret the wage fund theory? By fixing the
real wage in the short run, he takes the wage fund to determine employment rather than wages. Instead of considering the amount of capital given
by the output of previous year, he obtains his result by assuming maximisation of profits in the wage good industry. In this way he obtains a similar
consequence, namely, output of luxury and investment goods depends on
the wage goods produced, but the original version of the wage fund theory
is substantially altered.[36] However, all this would not be sufficient to determine overall employment unless supplemented by an appropriate hypothesis regarding profits. He adds what can be regarded as a classical
ingredient, namely that wage earners do not save and non-wage earners
spend all their profits[37] in the non-wage good industry, without however
paying any attention to the return obtainable. In particular, they spend
everything obtained in the NWG sector in the purchase of NWG goods:
these were brought to market by spending all the profits (save a given
amount) earned in the WG sector. Thus, the WG sector actually rules the
roost, since the conditions prevailing there determine the size of the other
sector and consequently overall employment. Also for classical economists,
production conditions in wage goods played an important role in the determination of the rate of profits; in Pigou their role is crucial in the determination of employment in the short run. In this respect, Pigou appears to
accept the classical vision of the existence of two kinds of goods, wage
goods and all other goods. One needs a surplus of the first to produce the
latter: the relation between the two types of goods is asymmetric. This concept, although declined in various ways by different classical authors, fades
away with the predominance of the neoclassical school.

The nature of the short-period equilibrium described by Pigou is such
that, although full employment does not necessarily result, it does not follow
that there is room for extensive State intervention to increase employment.
More generally, according to Pigou, unless you change the conditions in the

WG sector, employment cannot be increased: this will happen either through a reduction of the real wage rate and/or an improvement in the technical conditions of producing wage goods (with no change in the real wage). Viewed in this light it appears to be a short run version of a macro model concerned with quantities produced and assigning a central role to the WG sector. David Ricardo thought that if one could improve technical conditions in the WG sector, for any given real wage, then profits would be higher and growth (and possibly employment) sustained.[38]

This is not to blur the differences between classical and neoclassical schools, which are large not only regarding their theories of value and distribution, but also their characterisations of the long period and in their general visions. As for the latter, many interpreters (though not all)[39] think that Ricardo did not envisage a long period characterised by full employment: technical progress and/or lack of good quality land might produce persistent unemployment. On the other hand, Pigou thought that in the long period the real wage was so adjusted to the demand for labour that a position of (nearly) full employment was reached. As for the former, it must be admitted that the reason why the real wage is taken as given is very different in Pigou and in the classical economists. In the former it is simply the result of a bargain between trade unions and employers.[40] In the latter it was assumed to be valid in the long run for the analysis of value and distribution: the mechanism that keeps the wage linked to the subsistence value being that of induced changes in population.[41]

It emerges that Pigou mixes neoclassical features (decreasing marginal productivity and maximisation of profits) with classical features (centrality of wage goods production and a hypothesis on profits destination) in the field of macroeconomics and employment. This should not come as a surprise for a devoted pupil of Marshall.[42] On the other hand, according to Keynes what happens in the NWG sector, in particular, investment is the *primum mobile* and the WG sector is the rest, exactly the opposite of what Pigou argued.[43] This is made clear in this chapter when we refer to the macrobalance condition that expresses the relation between the two sectors and shows the passive behaviour of non-wage earners in the NWG sector implicit in TU. The change in vision could not have been greater.[44]

NOTES

1. This is useful because Pigou's is 'an exceedingly difficult book' (Hicks, 1937). A similar opinion is advanced by Sweezy (1934).

2. They include consideration of different centres of production, the fact that wage good (WG) and non-wage good (NWG) sectors include several items, the existence of monopolistic elements, the fact that production processes take time, substitution/complementary relations between goods, foreign relations, welfare provisions, expectations of future price changes, etc.

3. All quotations from TU omit reference to the book, giving only the page number. Another disturbing feature is that at p.109 we read that the first 182 pages (out of 319) are preparatory! As well, a huge number of misprints have been spotted by Sweezy (1934) and Opie (1935).

4. With respect to the fundamental problem determining employment, Hicks (1937, Section I) noticed the close relation between the theory of the 'ordinary classical economist' and the real approach expressed in TU.

5. The definition is different from Marshall's both with regard to supply of labour and to the real wage but the context is also different, as Marshall refers to the problem of value. In the Principles V, V, 7 (Marshall, 1920, pp. 312–313) we read: 'To sum up then as regards short periods. The supply of specialized skill and ability of suitable machinery (...) has not time to be fully adapted to demand; (...) on the other hand if the supply is excessive some of them must remain imperfectly employed since there is no time for the supply to be much reduced by gradual decay and by conversion to other uses'. See also Marshall (1920, p. 412).

6. Pigou (pp. 39–40).

7. Pigou (p. 33, 63). Later in the book (p. 253) he writes: 'The wage policy is sometimes exercised through collective bargaining on the part of Trade Unions, sometimes through State action establishing minimum rates of pay'. The technology is also given, as emerges from what Pigou says in discussing changes in labour productivity later in TU. One can speculate that the assumption on real wages comes from Marshall, who, in the concluding chapter of his *Principles*, appears to argue that real wages *do* in fact change slowly and that it is also sensible behaviour on the part of the trade unions to allow them to do so.

8. 'In recent years (...) economists have been inclined to concentrate attention on the money end. The result (...) has been to overstress somewhat the role that money plays in more normal times and to put in the background very important factors of a non-monetary character. For this reason, among others, I have chosen to write my book from the real end and to bring in the monetary factor only at a fairly late stage' (Preface). Pigou (p. 236) on the whole argues that the monetary factor does not exert a very great influence: this aspect is severely criticised by Hawtrey (1934). Although there is a hint already in *Employment and Equilibrium* (Pigou, 1941, p. 128), Pigou's (1943) effect is still to come, signalling a change in Pigou's assessment of the relative importance of real and monetary factors. Pigou's effect will make a real difference, rendering the classical analysis consistent though probably unrealistic, after Keynes's attack.

9. On the relation between unemployment at $t = 0$ and that at different periods, see the discussion in Chapter VI, Part I.

10. See in particular §6 in Chapter I of Part I where Pigou argues that a change in the real wage can alter the willingness of wage earners to work, but does not explicitly refer to a supply of labour function.

11. 'A man is only unemployed when he is both not employed and also desires to be employed' (p. 3) and later (p. 4) Pigou specifies that 'desire to be employed must be taken to mean desire to be employed at current rates of wages (...)'.

12. Leaving aside, once again, the complications induced by unfilled vacancies, discouraged and additional workers, all diligently discussed by Pigou.

13. '(...) the quantity of labour demanded (...) at any given rate of real wage is such that the value in terms of wage goods of its marginal net product (...) approximates to that rate of wage (...)' (p. 41).

14. If the marginal productivity of labour is decreasing as it is usual under assumption 1. (p. 51).

15. Irrespective of income and relative prices.

16. As I said, qualifications such as welfare provisions and foreign sector are disregarded.

17. With decreasing marginal returns to each factor.

18. My notation is different from Pigou's. Please note the classical way of defining profits as net revenues minus wages.

19. Later I will discuss the extent to which the wage fund doctrine is accepted by Pigou. In places he appears to be thinking in terms of a wage fund (e.g. p. 21, 143) as argued also by Sweezy (1934, p. 801).

20. See the excellent analysis in Zenezini (2010).

21. In Chapter IX ('Changes in particular non-wage good and non export industries in relation to the real demand for labour in the aggregate') of Part III.

22. More workers cannot be employed in the WG sector if the stock of capital and the real wage are constant and profits are maximised.

23. Pigou (p. 144) is well aware that in the face of increased demand, credit can be obtained, but this, to him, will not make any difference to the substance of the argument.

24. As mentioned, this overlooks the possibility that the same profits can buy more workers if the wage is reduced in the NWG sector alone.

25. For a detailed analysis see Di Matteo (2013).

26. The context is still that of a given real wage.

27. The point has already been noted by Cottrell (1994a) in the context of the validity of Keynes's criticism of Pigou. However, it is surprising that years later in the context of an evaluation of Mill's wage fund doctrine, Pigou writes (1949, p. 177): 'we encounter at once the objection that non-wage earners, employers or others, when the wages fund is given, may, if they choose, make the wages flow larger or smaller by varying the amounts of their own consumption; by, for example, in any year cutting down their consumption and handing over what they would have consumed in extra real wages to work-people. This objection is plainly fatal. How was it that Mill prior to his recantation failed to see the force of it?' And later he remarks (1949, pp. 178–179): 'There is, however, in the way of the wages fund doctrine a difficulty more deep seated than this; (...) that while a capital of goods in process is always essential, there is no need for any stock of wage goods at all – for any wages fund, predetermine or otherwise'. Here he admits (1949, p. 180) that this *can* lead to more employment in the NWG sector: 'It may be added to or subtracted from [wages flow] according as non-wage earners purchase and consume a smaller or a larger quantity of wage goods. (...) If, throughout, employment is held fixed,

this is all. Variations in the wages flow are simply reflected in equi-proportionate variations in the real wage rate. An increase in the wages flow may, however, well be partly taken out in an increase (...) of employment'. Pigou seems to be going back to his previous view (1927, p. 108), where he noticed a drawback of the wage fund theory in the presence of unemployment.

28. According to the meticulous and detailed review of the TU by Opie (1935, p. 299) all Pigou's calculations are really pure guesswork so that the exercise of estimating the elasticity of demand for labour using his model is worthless.

29. Indeed, according to Pigou (p. 160), an improvement in the productivity conditions of the WG sector leads to an increase in employment.

30. In addition, investment goods are actually bought for their prospective return, a concept absent from Pigou's short run considerations in the TU in which the stock of capital is assumed constant: indeed it would imply a totally different approach. Incidentally, these observations cast some doubt on the validity, even in the short period, of the assumption of lumping capital goods and luxury consumption goods together in the same sector because demand reflects different considerations for the two types of goods.

31. One can imagine another situation in which only labour is employed with constant returns in the NWG sector and the price of the good is equal to the wage. However, this hypothesis cannot be found in Pigou.

32. In order to complete Pigou's analysis Klausinger (1998) not only introduces relative prices, but he also includes other elements, such as the rate of interest and the expected yield of investment goods, that represent extensions of Pigou's analysis. Ambrosi (2003) also completes Pigou's analysis, but among other things, appears to argue as if the position reached by the economy were on the production possibility curve that entails full employment (a situation only conceivable in the long run, according to Pigou's analysis).

33. It is well known that for Marshall, the theory of demand is somehow linked to the classical theory of needs.

34. For Schumpeter (1954) it is consistent, for Garegnani (1984) inconsistent.

35. In addition, Marshall states that the wage fund doctrine relates only to the demand side of the question, a viewpoint shared with Pigou, as discribed in this chapter. He also argues that capital applied to support labour in any new industry, as a consequence of government intervention, must be withdrawn from some other industry, so the policy cannot change overall employment: a thesis completely shared by Pigou as reconstructed in this chapter.

36. In other words, it becomes a logical condition rather than a chronological one.

37. Except a fixed amount.

38. Pigou too (in Part III.11, especially pp. 159–160 and in III.12, pp. 167–168) deals with improvements in the WG sector .

39. Garegnani (1984) and Stigler (1952) are exponents of the two contrasting views.

40. When Marshall (Principles VI; II; 3) deals with the 'general rate of wages' he refers to the long period (Marshall, 1920, pp. 439–440).

41. It serves the analytical purpose of eliminating the effect of another element, besides rising rents, that could prevent accumulation, namely the increase in real wages.

42. Hicks (1983, essay 5) noticed how much Marshall and Pigou owed to Mill.

43. This is also Cottrell's (1994a) position, reached by a different route.

44. Cottrell (1994a, 1994b) already noted this in discussing Brady (1994) and Aslanbeigui (1992).

ACKNOWLEDGEMENT

I am extremely grateful to two referees for many useful suggestions. I thank Mauro Caminati who read previous drafts and discussed the theses I advance at length on several occasions. I am also indebted to Maurizio Zenezini and Annalisa Rosselli for their detailed comments on a previous draft. The paper was presented at the conference 'New Developments on Ricardo and the Ricardian Traditions' in Lyon (September 2013). I am grateful to all the participants and in particular Gilbert Faccarello and Antonella Palumbo for their comments.

REFERENCES

Ambrosi, G. M. (2003). *Keynes, Pigou and Cambridge keynesians. Authenticity and analytical perspective in the keynes-classics debate*. Basingstoke: Palgrave.

Aslanbeigui, N. (1992). Pigou's inconsistencies or Keynes' misconceptions? *History of Political Economy, 24*(2), 413–433.

Boland, L. (1992). *Principles of economics*. London: Routledge.

Brady, M. E. (1994). A note on the Keynes-Pigou controversy. *History of Political Economy, 26*(4), 697–705.

Cottrell, A. (1994a). Keynes' appendix to chapter 19. A reader's guide. *History of Political Economy, 26*(4), 681–695.

Cottrell, A. (1994b). Brady on Pigou and Keynes: Comment. *History of Political Economy, 26*(4), 707–711.

Di Matteo, M. (2013). Pigou's *theory of unemployment*: What "classical" macroeconomics really was, *STOREPapers*, 2013/4, 73–93. Retrieved from [http://www.storep.org/wp/wp-content/uploads/2013/08/STEP-2013-04-DiMatteo.pdf]

Garegnani, P. (1984). Value and distribution in the classical economists and marx. *Oxford Economic Papers, 36*(2), 291–325.

Hawtrey, R. G. (1934). The theory of unemployment by Prof. A.C. Pigou. *Economica, 1*(2), 147–166.

Hicks, J. R. (1937). Mr. Keynes and the classics. *Econometrica, 5*(2), 147–159.

Hicks, J. R. (1983). *Classics and moderns*. Oxford: Basil Blackwell.

Klausinger, H. J. (1998). Pigou on unemployment. In P. Fontaine & A. Jolink (Eds.), *Historical perspectives on macroeconomics: Sixty years after the general theory* (pp. 37–51). London: Routledge.

Marshall, A. (1920). *Principles of economics*. London: Macmillan.

Opie, R. G. (1935). Professor Pigou's theory of unemployment. *Zeitschrift Fuer Nationaloekonomie, 6*(3), 289–314.

Pigou, A. C. (1927). *Industrial fluctuations*. London: Macmillan.

Pigou, A. C. (1933). *Theory of unemployment*. London: Macmillan.

Pigou, A. C. (1941). *Employment and equilibrium. A theoretical discussion*. London: MacMillan.

Pigou, A. C. (1943). The classical stationary state. *Economic Journal, 53*(December), 343–351.

Pigou, A. C. (1949). Mill and the wages fund. *Economic Journal, 59*(June), 171–180.

Schumpeter, J. A. (1954). *History of economic analysis*. London: George Allen & Unwin.

Stigler, G. J. (1952). The Ricardian theory of value and distribution. *Journal of Political Economy, 60*(3), 187–207.

Sweezy, P. M. (1934). Professor Pigou's theory of unemployment. *Journal of Political Economy, 42*(6), 800–811.

Zenezini, M. (2010). Unemployment and full employment. A retrospective view. *Rivista Internazionale di Scienze Sociali, 118*(2), 225–262.

ROMANCE OR NO ROMANCE? ADAM SMITH AND DAVID HUME IN JAMES BUCHANAN'S "POLITICS WITHOUT ROMANCE"

Andrew Farrant and Maria Pia Paganelli

ABSTRACT

Can we model politics as exclusively based on self-interest, leaving virtue aside? How much romance is there in the study of politics? We show that James Buchanan, a founder of public choice and constitutional political economy, reintroduces a modicum of romance into politics, despite claiming that his work is the study of "politics without romance": Buchanan's model needs an ethical attitude to defend rules against rent-seeking.

We claim that Adam Smith, more than David Hume, should be considered one of the primary intellectual influences on Buchanan's public choice and constitutional political economy. It is commonly believed that Hume assumes in politics every man ought to be considered a knave, making him an influence on Buchanan's idea of politics without romance. Yet, it is Smith who, like Buchanan, describes rent-seeking and suggests that public virtues may be the remedy through which good rules maintaining liberty and prosperity can be generated and enforced. Smith, like

Research in the History of Economic Thought and Methodology, Volume 34A, 357–372
ISSN: 0743-4154/doi:10.1108/S0743-41542016000034A013

Buchanan, rejects sole reliance on economic incentives: the study of politics needs some romance.

Keywords: James Buchanan; David Hume; Adam Smith; benevolence; constitutions

Can we meaningfully model politics with a completely self-interested rational choice framework? Can we model politics as exclusively based on self-interest? Can we model politics leaving virtue aside? Can we model politics "without romance"? We suggest that even a father of the study of "politics without romance" ends up relying on something other than self-interest to ultimately enforce a set of supposedly knave-proof rules.

James Buchanan − the recipient of the Nobel Memorial Prize in Economic Sciences in 1986 for his path-breaking work on "the theories of political and economic decision-making (Public Choice)" (Nobelprize.org "The Prize in Economics 1986 − Press Release") − introduces the economic method to the analysis of political phenomena. "Politics without romance," as Buchanan called it, means that we need motivational homogeneity when analyzing market and non-market decision-making so as to prevent any biases in the analysis. The idea of analyzing policy-makers as self-interested, rather than public-spirited, is usually attributed to the 18th-century Scottish philosopher David Hume and his dictum that one should presume that every man is a knave when designing political institutions and should thus design the constitution to assure that it is by and large knave-proof. Buchanan's analysis, allegedly following Hume, similarly starts with the assumption that every man is to be supposed a knave.

Adam Smith, the 18th-century Scottish social philosopher (often viewed as the father of economic analysis), analyzes many of the government policies of his time in a way that would prove readily familiar to anyone acquainted with Buchanan's work. For instance, Smith's analysis of mercantilism in his *Wealth of Nations* provides a vivid description of what we would today recognize as rent-seeking behavior. Indeed, Smith − much like Buchanan − suggests that the remedy to rent-seeking behavior lies in the adoption of good "rules of the game." Smith, however, suggests that public virtue may provide the instrument by which a high-quality set of rules of the game, or institutional framework, ultimately keeps rent-seeking behavior squarely in check.

We argue that Smith's emphasis on the importance of public virtue links James Buchanan's constitutional political economy more closely to Smith's analysis than to Hume's alleged analysis, and that Adam Smith, more than David Hume seems to provide the intellectual influence on James Buchanan. Linking Buchanan more to Smith than to Hume helps us highlight that even Buchanan seemingly needs to reintroduce romance into politics. We argue indeed that Buchanan does not embrace a complete and sole reliance on assuming that every man is a knave. Instead, Buchanan claims that "good" constitutional rules alone may not be enough to make a free and prosperous society a reality: an underlying set of appropriate ethical norms is essential. In contrast to the alleged Humean assumption of universal knavery, Buchanan believes a strong ethical attitude is what would generate and ultimately defend rules against rent-seeking. This is far closer to the Smithian tradition than the allegedly Humean one, and brings Smith to a much more prominent role in the intellectual roots of the analysis of Buchanan's style "politics without romance." Similarly, Buchanan was heavily influenced by Smith's focus on exchange and Buchanan famously modeled politics as a complex multi-party exchange (see, e.g., Buchanan & Tullock, [1962] 2004).[1] In this chapter, however, we focus on the commonalities between Buchanan and Smith's emphasis on the complementarity between ethical norms and institutional constraints.

By understanding the intellectual influence and similarities of Buchanan with other thinkers, we suggest that we can better address the question of whether the allegedly knave-proof constitutional checks are sufficient to guarantee a system of natural liberty and constrain government – as Hume seems to suggest in the eyes of much of the literature on the topic – or if some public spirit and the virtue of the legislator are necessary instead – as Smith seems to suggest.

The chapter develops as follow. In the next section, there is an account of the relevant features of Buchanan's thinking that are often associated with Hume. In the following section, there is an analysis of the differences between Buchanan and Hume. Finally, we present the similarities between Buchanan and Smith, showing that Buchanan is rather closer to Smith than to he is to Hume. Concluding remarks end the chapter.

BUCHANAN AND "POLITICS WITHOUT ROMANCE"

Public choice theory and constitutional political economy are often conflated, even if they generally are separate bodies of analysis.

Public choice theory – the economic analysis of in-period political decision-making – provides an economic analysis of the workings of bureaucracy, voting rules, and the public sector more broadly understood. By contrast, constitutional political economy studies the choice among alternative sets of political rules and constraints (hence the emphasis on the constitutional rules of the game per se). As Buchanan often emphasized, one's choice among differing sets of rules would be heavily informed by the model of politics one utilized when making predictions about the working properties of these alternative sets of rules. For instance, someone who placed much weight on the benevolent-despot model as descriptive of in-period political reality would probably see little necessity to overtly limit the range and scope of governmental discretionary power. By contrast, an individual who was influenced by public choice theory – the analysis of in-period political reality without romance (Buchanan, 1979) – would favor a set of constitutional rules and constraints that would more sharply constrain the in-period exercise of discretionary governmental power.

Buchanan characterizes his work as the study of politics without romance (Buchanan, 1979, p. 211). Traditionally when politicians buy a car, they are assumed to be self-interested, but the very same politicians are assumed to drop their self-interest and to become public-spirited when they are faced with lobbyists who want a particular piece of special interest group legislation to pass in exchange for their political support. Buchanan argues for the theorist to make a supposition of motivational homogeneity when analyzing private and public choices. Consequently, a theorist who argues that material self-interest generates pervasive market failure is analytically obligated to assume that a politician is just as self-interested when he or she deals with self-seeking lobbyists as is the case when they buy a car as a private chooser.

Accordingly, we may try to reduce the negative effects of rent-seekers with knave-proof rules of the political game, including the constitution. Thus, constitutional rules can be viewed as akin to a "minimax strategy aimed at securing protection against the worst-case outcomes that might emerge" (Brennan & Buchanan, [1985] 2000, p. xxiii). Indeed, Faria (1999) shows that, given the assumptions that Buchanan uses, his constitutional equilibrium is the best option available to deter self-interested politicians. Levy (2002) develops this idea further by arguing that for Buchanan constitutional rules provide insurance against the potential worst-case disaster that results when we assume that individuals are public-spirited when they turn out to be knaves instead.

Buchanan often appears to suggest that the rules of the game are de facto self-enforcing or inherently binding. For instance, Buchanan ([1981] 2001, p. 46) claims indeed that we should have little "or no concern with replacing 'bad,' 'evil,' or 'incompetent' politicians with others who may be 'good.'" We should instead focus on "setting up rules or constraints within which politicians must operate, rules that will make it a relatively trivial matter as to the personal characteristics of those who happen to be selected as governors" (Buchanan, [1981] 2001, p. 47). Consequently, Buchanan may appear to believe that good institutions per se will suffice to check knavery.

If we assume knavery at all levels of analysis, however, the rent-seeking conundrum appears insoluble. Unless we suppose that the rules of the game are self-enforcing, it is unclear why a self-interested citizenry would adequately produce the public good of constitutional enforcement.

Buchanan uses a Rawlsian type "veil of ignorance" mechanism to deter rule designers from creating rules that benefit them at the expense of societal well-being. However, the problem of self-enforceability was immediately apparent. The Buchanan archival manuscripts contain a grant proposal that Buchanan prepared as early as 1970, to fund what seems like the second part of *The Calculus of Consent* ([1962] 2004). The proposed book was to be titled "The Calculus of Control" and would deal with the self- and external enforceability of rules. Gordon Tullock, James Buchanan's co-author of the *Calculus of Consent* ([1962] 2004) explicitly identifies the problem in a retrospective analysis of the *Calculus* 25 years after its original publication: "the view that the government can be bound by specific provisions [constitutional rules] is naïve. Something must enforce those rules, and whatever enforces them is itself unbounded" (Tullock, 1987, p. 87). That is to say: we are not given any reason to believe that the "right" rules will be enforced. Enforcement is a public good: it has a private cost and a public benefit. Giving up rents now increases someone else's payoff in the future (Levy, 1991). The incentives do not promote rule enforcement.

There are two possible solutions to the problem of enforceability: assume the problem away or introduce public spirit. Buchanan, writing with Geoffrey Brennan, candidly notes that "There is ... one *crucial assumption* which clearly underlies the whole constitutional construction – that of *enforceability*" (Brennan & Buchanan, [1980] 2000, p. 13. Italics added). And elsewhere he tells us that a modicum of public-spiritedness is necessary: "Formal constraints on behavior, as laid down in legal and constitutional structures, can *never alone* be sufficient to insure viability in social order. An underlying set of ethical norms or standards seems essential, although we recognize that formal and informal constraints become substitutes at some margins of adjustment" (Buchanan, [1981] 2001, p. 25). Consequently, as Buchanan himself puts it, the viability of a free society is apparently predicated upon the "widespread adoption of a 'constitutional attitude,' a proclivity or tendency to examine issues from a constitutional perspective, as opposed to the pragmatic, short-run, utilitarian perspective that seems to characterize ... day-to-day political discussion and action" (Buchanan, [1981] 2001, p. 42). And again, writing with Brennan, Buchanan admits that something akin to a "new civic religion" (Brennan & Buchanan, [1985] 2000, p. 166) will have to emerge. In 1996, he repeats and strengthens the claim: "As the historical experience of many countries suggests, constitutions can be reformed without being effectively enforced. Perhaps more *important than formal constitutional changes are changes in ethical attitudes that would make attempted reforms workable*" (Buchanan, [1996] 2001, p. 275. Italics added).

Does Buchanan, then, allow romance back into the analysis? (See, among others, Brennan, Hamlin, & Goodin, 2000; Farrant & Paganelli, 2005; Frey, 1997).

BUCHANAN, HUME, AND "POLITICS WITHOUT ROMANCE"

Credit for the intellectual origins of the motivational homogeneity postulate at the base of the idea of "politics without romance" − "all men are knaves" − is commonly attributed to David Hume's essay *Of the Independency of Parliament*. This attribution, though, may come more from the secondary literature and an oral tradition than from Buchanan himself. In the *Calculus of Consent* ([1962] 2004, pp. 313−314), in a passage which is worth citing in full, Buchanan writes:

> [Hume] states that the purpose or aim of the checks and controls provided by the political constitution should be that of making it "the interest, even of bad men, to act for the public good." It is in this respect that the conceptions of David Hume appear most helpful, and they seem to have much in common with our own. Our basic analysis of the individual calculus that is involved in choosing among alternative organizational rules, in selecting a political constitution, has demonstrated that it will often be to the rational self-interest of the individual to select a particular rule that can be predicted to produce results on occasion that run counter to the self-interest of the individual calculated within a shorter time span. By shifting the choice backward from the stage of the specific collective decision to the stage of the constitutional decision, we have been able to incorporate the acquiescence of the individual to adverse collective action into a calculus that retains an economic dimension and that can still be analyzed in non-moral terms. In this respect our immediate precursor is Hume, who quite successfully was able to ground political obligation, neither on moral principle nor on contract, but on

self-interest. Hume did this by resorting to the idea that the self-interest of each individual in the community dictates the observance of conventional rules of conduct. These
rules, which may or may not have been formalized in contract, are necessary for the
orderly conduct of social affairs. This argument, which does not base political obligation on contractual obligation, allows the primary difficulty of the contract theorists to
be neatly surmounted. Not only is it to the initial interest of parties to agree on conventional rules if such rules do not exist, but it is also to the continuing interest of individuals to abide by the conventional rules in existence. Hume recognized, of course, that,
were it possible, the individual's own interest would best be served by the adhering to
the conventional rules of all other persons but himself while remaining free to violate
these rules. However, precisely because such rules are *socially* derived, they must apply
generally. Hence each individual must recognize that, were he to be free to violate con-
vention, others must be similarly free; and, as compared to this chaotic state of affairs,
he will rationally choose to accept restrictions on his own behavior.

The claim is loud and clear. Yet, this is the *only* place in the *Calculus*
where Buchanan cites Hume.[2] Note also this is in an appendix: "Appendix
1: marginal notes on reading political philosophy."

A second explicit reference indicating the relevance of Hume on
Buchanan is to be found in *The Reason of Rules* ([1985] 2000, p. 68), coau-
thored with Geoff Brennan. Here, Brennan and Buchanan claim:

Using the Homo economicus behavior model in constitutional analysis, and justifying
this use on analytic rather than empirical grounds, is a procedure we have borrowed
from the classical political economist-philosophers in their analysis of political institutions. And we can, perhaps, do no better in this connection than appeal to David
Hume: "In constraining any system of government and fixing the several checks and
controls of the constitution, every man ought to be supposed a knave and to have no
other end, in all his actions, than private interest."

Meanwhile, commentators such as Sutter (1998), Faria (1999), and
Besley (2007) credit, with much emphasis, Hume, as the intellectual root of
Buchanan. Kliemt (2005, p. 204) even calls Buchanan "'David Immanuel
Buchanan' (for James Buchanan building on David Hume and Immanuel
Kant) since this indicates the intimate theoretical relationship between the
founding fathers of both modern political philosophy and Public Choice."
The oral tradition at the Public Choice Center in Fairfax Virginia where
Buchanan spent his last decades supports this interpretation.

So Buchanan's "politics without romance" seems often to be interpreted
as grounded in Hume's having urged that one suppose universal knavery.
But is this really the case?

If Hume is indeed the intellectual father of Buchanan's "politics without
romance," the child is not as trenchant strong as the father. Hume, again,
allegedly, consistently assumes knavery at all levels. But Buchanan does

not. In addition, in an approach that differs from Buchanan's contractarian design of a constitution, Hume reminds us that nobody wrote the "antient constitution" of Britain. The "antient constitution," with its checks and balances, emerged unintended from centuries of compromises, bargaining and negotiations between rival parties and political bodies. Paley, a contemporary of Hume, has the clearer exposition of what Hume calls "the antient constitution": the "constitution of England, like that of most countries of Europe, hath grown out of occasion and emergency; from the fluctuating policy of different ages; from the contentions, successes, interests, and opportunities, of different orders and parties of men in the community. It resembles one of those old mansions, which, instead of being built all at once, after a regular plan, and according to the rules of architecture at present established, has been reared in different ages of the art, has been altered from time to time, and has been continually receiving additions and repairs suited to the taste, fortune, or conveniency, of its successive proprietors" ([1785] 2000, p. 328).

This patch-work of history and chance is unintended but may yet prove able to prevent the knavery of one group from prevailing. On the other hand, relying on one constitutional author or a small group of them, under the veil of ignorance or not, implies that his/their knavery would go unchecked, resulting in tyranny: "If any single person acquire power enough to take our constitution to pieces, and put it up a-new, he is really an absolute monarch; and we have already had an instance of this kind, sufficient to convince us, that such a person will never resign his power, or establish any free government" (Hume, [1752] 1985, p. 52).

Hume's account of the "antient constitution" therefore does not need a veil of ignorance differently from Buchanan's, nor does it have an enforcement problem, again differently from Buchanan's. In Hume's view, the accidental division and separation of power generates a system of checks and balances. An unintentional and "accidental" process of competing knavery generates the rules that allow knavery to play against knavery. With several knavish players, the attempts of a single knave to acquire too much power would be prevented by the knavery of others. Similarly, knavery checks knavery because any single member of a given faction has a mighty temptation to defect, weakening the power of the faction. So where "power is distributed among several courts, and several orders of men, we should always consider the separate interest of each court, and each order; and, if we find that, by the skillful division of power, this interest must necessarily, in its operation, concur with public, we may pronounce that government to be wise and happy" (Hume, [1752] 1985, p. 43).

What is relevant for us is that, if we take the alleged Humean assumption seriously, we avoid Buchanan's problem at its root. Knavery checks knavery by maintaining a multiplicity of competing self-interests; with separation and division of power, knavery offers enough incentives to write, enforce, and maintain knave-proof rules; power does not ineluctably gravitate to one constitutional player. This does not imply that the checks and divisions are going to work every single time, as the Cromwell[3] episode teaches, but for Hume this is as good as it gets. We may get something like a second- or third-best Nash equilibrium. But a better equilibrium cannot be attained without a mighty and therefore unlikely improvement in the "manners" (morals) of mankind.

Marciano (2005) goes through great effort to show that Hume does not quite present the view of mankind that many of today's scholars working in the field of constitutional political economy appear to want him to have. Hume does not assume narrow rationality nor does he assume that self-interest is exclusively a motivational force. The assumption that in politics every man ought to be considered a knave is not Hume's, but it is what Hume attributes to "political thinkers." Smith (2013) also makes the point that Hume's essay *Idea of a Perfect Commonwealth* may be a "case for the identification of a model of political order that might inspire reform rather than provide a precise blueprint to be enforced. Perhaps these aspects of Hume's project are closer in spirit to Buchanan's project ... than they are to anything in Smith." Be that as it may, Buchanan's followers do credit Hume for the intellectual origins of Buchanan's "politics without romance," and what they credit Hume for is his reliance on the worst-case assumption about human behavior in imperfect commonwealths. Yet, Buchanan himself, differently from his commentators, seems to be more aware of the influence that Adam Smith had on his thinking than the influence of David Hume.

BUCHANAN, SMITH, AND "POLITICS WITHOUT ROMANCE"

The claim that Adam Smith should be more openly recognized as an important intellectual influence on James Buchanan is based not just on the distance between Buchanan and the alleged position of Hume, but also on the closeness of Buchanan and Smith (Evensky, 2005). Buchanan himself recognizes the relevance of Adam Smith to his thought. Indeed, Buchanan claims that Smith is one of the ten thinkers who influenced his intellectual development the most. Hume does not make that list (Buchanan, 1992).[4]

In the *Calculus of Consent* ([1962] 2004) Smith appears in more sections than Hume. Smith is cited in the conceptual framework, the orthodox model of majority rule, and the appendix, while Hume is cited only in the appendix. Yet, with the exception of the appendix, where Smith and Hume are bundled together with Spinoza as early thinkers who recognize the role of institutions in human behavior, the other mentions of Adam Smith strictly refer to his economic theory.

In *Limits of Liberty* ([1975] 2000, pp. 214–215), Buchanan recognizes the role of Adam Smith in the intellectual foundation of his work:

> Adam Smith sought to free the economy from the fetters of mercantilist controls; he did not propose that the specific goals of policy be laid down in advance. He did not attack the failures of governmental instruments in piecemeal, pragmatic fashion; he attacked in a far more comprehensive and constitutional sense. He tried to demonstrate that, by removing effective governmental restrictions on trade, results would emerge that would be judged better by all concerned. Precisely because of this comprehensiveness, this concentration on structural-institutional change, Adam Smith deservedly won acclaim as the father of political economy. He and his compatriots proposed genuine "constitutional revolution," and their proposals were, in large part, adopted over the course of a half-century.

Also in *Reason of Rules* ([1985] 2000), Buchanan recognizes the role of rules to check the avarice of rent-seekers in Smith. In the preface, we read:

> The notion that rules may substitute for morals has been familiar to economists and philosophers at least since Adam Smith. And, of course, the great intellectual discovery of the eighteenth century was the spontaneous order of the market, the discovery that within an appropriate structure of rules ("laws and institutions" in Adam Smith's phraseology), individuals in following their own interests can further the interests of others.... What it [the cooperation of agents in a market] does require is an appropriate "constitutional context" – a proper structure of rules, along with some arrangements for their enforcement. All of this was once the centerpiece of "political economy," and even today economics textbooks retain vestiges of such principles. But at one time an economist was literally defined as a person who "knows how markets work," with "work" being understood in terms of the coordination of individual behavior through the institutional structure. (Preface XVI-xvii)

At page 4, and then in the following several pages, we find again Smith and his focus on "laws and institutions":

> At least since the eighteenth century, and notably since Adam Smith, the influence of rules (Smith's term was "laws and institutions") on social outcomes has been understood, and this relationship has provided the basis for a central theme in economics and political economy, particularly as derived from their classical foundations. If rules

influence outcomes and if some outcomes are "better" than others, it follows that to the extent that rules can be chosen, the study and analysis of comparative rules and institutions become proper objects of our attention.

Buchanan therefore recognizes Smith as providing much of the intellectual foundation for his work. In the rest of the chapter, we show characteristics of Adam Smith – the analysis of interest groups and of the reliance of good institutions on public spirit – which seem to link him to Buchanan.

BUCHANAN, SMITH, AND "ROMANCE"

There are at least two aspects of Smith's writing that link him with Buchanan's: Smith's understanding of what we would now describe as rent-seeking behavior and his argument that public-spiritedness is a necessary ingredient in a constitutional recipe for the design of knave-proof institutions.

Stigler (1971, p. 266) describes the depth of Smith's understanding of rent-seeking as follows: "The merchants and manufacturers are singled out [in *The Wealth of Nations*] for the unusual combination of cupidity and competence which marks their legislative efforts." Anderson (1989) reinforces Stigler's arguments, making a stronger case that Smith's commitment to the scrutiny of rent-seeking was indeed complete. Evensky (2005) elaborates further.

For Smith, big merchants and manufacturers are what we would call a powerful and well-organized interest group, able to lobby successfully (WN I.x.c.27, 145). Big merchants and manufacturers are few and know each other well. In contrast to other groups, according to Smith, they also know their interest well. With their sophistry, they manage to use rational ignorance in their favor and convince others that what benefits them benefits the country, even if it imposes a cost on everybody else. Merchants and manufacturers are, in fact, "an order of men whose interest is never exactly the same with the public, who generally have an interest to deceive and even oppress the public, and who accordingly have, upon many occasions, both deceived and oppressed it" (WN I.xi.p. 10, p. 267). "Their interest is, in this respect, directly opposite to that of the great body of the people" (WN IV. iii.c.9–10, pp. 493–494). The problem would not arise if their concentrated interest would not be able to access a political power which is willing to give out monopoly privileges. But granted that access, their power becomes formidable.

The laws that the big merchants and manufacturers are able to "extort from the legislature" (WN IV.viii.3, p. 643, IV.viii.4, p. 644, IV.viii.17, p. 648) benefit a few at the expense of many. Because of their inefficiency, these laws are also unjust: "[t]o hurt in any degree the interest of any one order of citizens, for no other purpose but to promote that of some other, is evidently contrary to that justice and equality of treatment which the sovereign owes to all the different orders of his subjects" (WN IV.viii.30, p. 654). These are the laws the special interests of the great merchants and manufacturers lobby for and obtain in exchange for political support: "The member of parliament who supports every proposal for strengthening this monopoly, is sure to acquire not only the reputation of understanding trade, but great popularity and influence with an order of men whose numbers and wealth renders them of great importance. If he opposes them, on the contrary, and still more if he has authority enough to be able to thwart them, neither the most acknowledged probity, nor the highest rank, nor the greatest publick services can protect him from the most infamous abuse and detraction, from personal insults, nor sometimes from real danger, arising from the insolent outrage of furious and disappointed monopolists" (WN IV.ii.43, p. 471).

For Smith, would-be rent-seekers are sufficiently powerful to be able to intimidate the legislature. Indeed, Smith charges that the cruelty of the "revenue laws ...[is rather] mild and gentle, in comparison of some of those [laws] which the clamor of our merchants and manufacturers has extorted from the legislature, for the support of their own absurd and oppressive monopolies" (WN IV.viii.17, p. 648). Moreover, Smith claims that the rent-seeking clamour of rapacious merchants and manufacturers will seek to drive the country into a war in order that they attain "that little enhancement of price which this monopoly might afford our producers" (WN IV.viii.53). They impoverish society (WN IV.viii.c.43, p. 604. see also WN, IV.i.10; IV.ii.38; IV.iii.c.10), but they do not care. Self-interest prevails over public-spirit among big merchants and manufacturers as well as legislators.

Smith's analysis of rent-seeking includes not only the generation of rents but also the consequences of the attempts to take them away. For Smith, the losses that rent-seeking generates are going to last. Once privileges are granted, they will not be taken away: "[t]o expect, indeed, that the freedom of trade should ever be entirely restored in Great Britain, is as absurd as to expect that an Oceana or Utopia should ever be established in it. Not only the prejudices of the publick, but *what is much more unconquerable, the private interests of many individuals, irresistibly oppose it*" (WN IV.ii.43, p. 471. Emphasis added). The damage great merchants and manufacturers inflict upon society is permanent (Tullock, 1975).

Finally, the similarity between Buchanan and Smith sound presents even on the backdoor re-entrance of public-spiritedness. Once again, Stigler picks up on this aspect of Smith. Smith has an account of what laws ought to be and an account of what laws actually are. The two are not the same. Stigler (1971, pp. 268–274) notes that "appropriate or not, Smith implicitly rejected the use of self-interest as a general explanation of [how] legislation [ought to be]," meaning that "in the political scene … reforms must be effected, if effected they can be, by moral suasion. At best this is an extraordinarily slow and uncertain method of changing policy; at worst it may lead to policies which endanger the society." In fact, Smith seems to admit that in a system with "police, revenue, and arms," there are no real protections against some of the abuses of knavery but our sense of beauty and our weak civic spirit (TMS, IV.1.11 pp. 184–187). A system of natural liberty is a beautiful system and it would be a pity to ruin it by interfering with it. The legislator should not fall for the flattery of the self-interested merchants but should preserve the system of natural liberty out of reverence toward its beauty (Hanley & Paganelli, forthcoming). While politicians and lobbyists are self-interested and the policies one observes are the result of their self-interest, one should hope for public spirit in the legislator to try to develop and enforce rules to contain that self-interest (Hanley, 2009). Peart and Levy (2008, p. 5) hint in a similar direction when, in a very different context, they claim "Buchanan resides squarely in a Smithian framework (and … depart[s] from Hume)" when "generosity fills the gaps in the development of 'law' or contracts." Smith, like Buchanan, but not Hume, after closing the door to public-spirit, opens a window to it. Smith, more than Hume, seems to be closer to Buchanan.

CONCLUSIONS

James Buchanan, a founding father of the analysis of "politics without romance," extends the assumption that every man ought to be considered a knave to the political context. The intellectual origins of knave-proof institutional design a-la-Buchanan are usually attributed to the Scottish philosopher David Hume. Yet, Buchanan differs from the alleged position of

Hume as he falls back on having to assume public spirit at the pre-constitutional design and enforcement levels, while Hume, using a model of accidental checks and balances, is able to avoid it. Adam Smith, on the other hand, who also has an analysis of rent-seeking and knave-proof institutions, needs to rely on the public-spiritedness of the legislator, in a way that is not far from Buchanan. The similarities between Adam Smith and James Buchanan should be more thoroughly recognized. And Buchanan should be recognized as reintroducing romance into politics.

In times of political turmoil and of the redesign of institutions, it is vital to understand what may help to generate and sustain robust and stable institutions. Having a clear understanding of a theory may help in using the theory in an effective way, and studying the intellectual origins of a theory may offer a clearer understanding of the theory. In looking at the intellectual origins of Buchanan's study of "politics without romance," we propose that Adam Smith should be considered as its true intellectual father. Buchanan, like Smith, has to admit that the need for a strong ethical attitude is what would defend the rules that generate prosperity against rent-seeking. By looking at the influence of Smith on Buchanan we are able to highlight that Buchanan has a larger component of romance than if Hume alone is considered.

NOTES

1. We thank an anonymous referee for emphasizing the importance that Buchanan placed on the idea of politics as exchange.

2. On the page before this there is actually another mention of Hume. "His work on the political order anticipates, in many respects, that of David Hume and that of Adam Smith on the economic order. Spinoza deliberately sets out to construct political institutions in such a fashion that individuals acting in pursuit of their own interests will be led, by the institutional structure within which such action takes place, to further the interests of their fellow members in the political group" (p. 312).

3. It is noteworthy that Hayek – a great admirer of Hume's thinking – would invoke Cromwell as a model "liberal" dictator (Farrant & McPhail, 2014; Farrant, McPhail, & Berger, 2012).

4. A reader has wondered whether sympathy might help to disentangle the commonalities between Buchanan and Hume's analysis of politics. Although any adequate consideration of this important issue is beyond our scope here we do note how much of Hume's analysis of politics centers upon the way in which sympathy (only applying to those who enjoy perceived equal status) systematically skews

approbational incentives and increases intra-factional solidarity. This, in turn, intensifies factional struggles for power. Marciano (2005) provides an excellent analysis of Hume and sympathy.

ACKNOWLEDGMENTS

We wish to thank two anonymous referees, Alain Marciano and John Berdell, the participants of 2013 HES, ESHET, and the Summer Institute for the Preservation of the History of Economic Thought for useful feedback and comments. All mistakes are ours.

REFERENCES

Anderson, G. M. (1989). The butcher, the baker, and the policy-maker: Adam Smith on public choice. *History of Political Economy, 21*(4), 641–659.

Besley, T. (2007). The new political economy. *The Economic Journal, 117*(524), F570–F587.

Brennan, G., & Buchanan, J. M. ([1985] 2000). *The reason of rules: Constitutional political economy/Geoffrey Brennan, James M. Buchanan.* Indianapolis, IN: Liberty Fund.

Brennan, G., & Buchanan, J. M. ([1980] 2000). *The power to tax: Analytical foundations of a fiscal constitution/Geoffrey Brennan and James M. Buchanan.* Indianapolis, IN: Liberty Fund.

Brennan, G., Hamlin, A., & Goodin, R. (2000). *Democratic devices and desires: Theories of institutional design.* Cambridge: Cambridge University Press.

Buchanan, J. M. ([1975] 2000). *The limits of liberty: Between anarchy and Leviathan.* Indianapolis, IN: Liberty Fund.

Buchanan, J. M. (1979). *What should economists do? Preface by H. Goeffrey Brennan and Robert D. Tollison.* Indianapolis, IN: Liberty Press.

Buchanan, J. M. ([1981] 2001). Constitutional restrictions on the power of government. In *Choice, contract, and constitutions.* Indianapolis, IN: Liberty Fund.

Buchanan, J. M. (1992). *Better than plowing, and other personal essays/James M. Buchanan.* Chicago, IL: University of Chicago Press.

Buchanan, J. M. ([1996] 2001). Distributional politics and constitutional design. In *Choice, contract, and constitutions.* Indianapolis, IN: Liberty Fund.

Buchanan, J. M., & Tullock, G. C. ([1962] 2004). *The calculus of consent: Logical foundations of constitutional democracy.* Indianapolis, IN: Liberty Fund.

Evensky, J. (2005). *Adam Smith's moral philosophy.* Cambridge: Cambridge University Press.

Faria, J. R. (1999). Is there an optimal constitution? *Constitutional Political Economy, 10*(2), 177–184.

Farrant, A., & McPhail, E. (2014). Can a dictator turn a constitution into a can-opener? F.A. Hayek and the alchemy of transitional dictatorship in Chile. *Review of Political Economy, 26*(3), 331–348.

Farrant, A., McPhail, E., & Berger, S. (2012). Preventing the 'Abuses' of democracy: Hayek, the 'military usurper' and transitional dictatorship in Chile? *American Journal of Economics and Sociology, 71,* 513–538.

Farrant, A., & Paganelli, M. P. (2005). Are two knaves better than one? Hume, Buchanan, and Musgrave on economics and government. *History of Political Economy, 37,* 71–90.

Frey, B. S. (1997). A constitution for knaves crowds out civic virtues. *The Economic Journal, 107*(443), 1043–1053.

Hanley, R. P. (2009). *Adam Smith and the character of virtue.* New York, NY: Cambridge University Press.

Hanley, R. P., & Paganelli, M. P. (forthcoming). Adam Smith on money, mercantilism and the system of natural liberty. In D. Carey (Ed.), *Money and the enlightenment.* Oxford: Voltaire Foundation.

Hume, D. ([1752] 1985). *Essays, moral, political, and literary.* Indianapolis, IN: Liberty Fund.

Kliemt, H. (2005). Public choice and political philosophy: Reflections on the works of Gordon Spinoza and David Immanuel Buchanan. *Public Choice, 125*(1/2), 203–213.

Levy, D. M. (1991). *The economic ideas of ordinary people: From preference to trade/David M. Levy.* London: Routledge.

Levy, D. M. (2002). Robust institutions. *Review of Austrian Economics, 15*(2–3), 131–142.

Marciano, A. (2005). Benevolence, sympathy, and Hume's model of government: How different is new political economy from classical political economy? *History of Political Economy, 37,* 43–70.

Paley, W. ([1785] 2000). *The principles of moral and political philosophy.* Indianapolis, IN: Liberty Fund.

Peart, S. J., & Levy, D. M. (2008). Discussion, construction and evolution: Mill, Buchanan and Hayek on the constitutional order. *Constitutional Political Economy, 19*(1), 3–18.

Smith, A. ([1759] 1984). *The theory of moral sentiments [TMS].* Indianapolis, IN: Liberty Classics.

Smith, A. ([1776] 1981). *An inquiry into the nature and causes of the wealth of nations [WN].* Indianapolis, IN: Liberty Classics.

Smith, C. (2013). Adam Smith and the new right. In C. J. Berry, M. P. Paganelli, & C. Smith (Eds.), The *Oxford* handbook of Adam Smith (pp. 539–558). Oxford: Oxford University Press.

Stigler, G. J. (1971). Smith's travels on the ship of state. *History of Political Economy, 3*(2), 265–277.

Sutter, D. (1998). Leviathan at bay: Constitutional versus political controls on government. *Economic Inquiry, 36*(4), 670–678.

Tullock, G. (1975). The transitional gains trap. *Bell Journal of Economics, 6*(2), 671–678.

Tullock, G. C. (1987). The calculus after 25 years. *Cato Journal, 7*(2), 313–321.

PART III
FROM THE VAULT

'THE CAUSE OF YE WAST OF THE SILVER OR BULLION OF ENGLAND': A NEW DOCUMENT FROM THOMAS MUN'S AGE

Salim Rashid

ABSTRACT

A hitherto unknown manuscript from the 1620s, whose only extant copies appear to be in Dublin, shows the balance of trade being forcefully developed, without the concern for the East India Trade that marks Thomas Mun. It goes on to consider economic and monetary policy, particularly the relative valuation of gold and silver, more closely.

Keywords: Economic policy; scarcity of coin; balance of trade

Item Ms Z.3.5.32(1) in the catalogue of Marsh's library, Dublin, refers to a manuscript, 'The cause of ye *wast* of the silver or bullion of England,' dated 1619, (hereafter, *Wast*[1]) which appears out of place with all surrounding

Research in the History of Economic Thought and Methodology, Volume 34A, 375–401
Copyright © 2016 by Emerald Group Publishing Limited
All rights of reproduction in any form reserved
ISSN: 0743-4154/doi:10.1108/S0743-41542016000034A011

material. It happens to be a copy of a manuscript in the Ussher collection
at Trinity College Dublin, but the version at Trinity College was so faint
that I found it unreadable. The title sounds like an anti-consumption tract
bemoaning English luxury, but it happens to be much more than that. The
Wast sets out a programme of economic development. Here are the principal themes

It is the Balance of Trade that determines the scarcity of silver in England

A commonwealth may continue a losing trade, if the trade increases employment and
retains skills

Short-run losses by tráders have to be absorbed in order to achieve long-run gains

England has surplus labor (with zero opportunity cost)

Import substitution is strongly urged

The East India trade is justified, despite the export of silver

Dutch fishing needs emulation

Productivity will improve with higher wages, which the poor deserve and
because ... Land is the ultimate repository of wealth

At the very start the manuscript states the primacy of the Balance of trade
in determining the scarcity of silver in England, a position soon to be associated with Thomas Mun. It then goes on to reflect on a variety of economic issues and comes close to setting up a rough plan for the economic
development of England. Despite the constant association of the balance of
trade with Mun's name, this wider argument regarding economic development was also the intent of Mun, as a close reading of either the famous
England's Treasure by Foreign Trade, or the earlier *Discourse of Trade*
(1621), will show. But the *Wast* shows no clear links to Mun. The language,
the style and the emphasis are all entirely different. While Mun is forcefully
didactic, the *Wast* makes a greater attempt to be logical about issues, so
much so, that when the author gets entangled in an illustration, he
promptly informs the reader that examples should not be pushed beyond
the purpose they were chosen for. The primacy given to the balance of
trade in determining the [foreign]exchanges, the comprehensive framework
for economic development, including the development of 'infant industries',
the advocacy of higher wages and the self-conscious attempt to set up a framework for discussing such issues gives the *Wast* much of its interest.

The date given in the library catalogues is 1619, which would make it
much earlier than Mun, but unless we have a revised manuscript, the internal evidence clearly indicates a later date. To illustrate the strictness with

which vigilant States enforce monetary laws, *Wast* refers to the case of Bartholomew (Bartholomeus) Munter, brother to an influential Dutch merchant, who was convicted of forgery in 1621. As the *Wast* gets the punishment wrong, it may be that the *Wast* was written before the trial was concluded. There is another hint given on folio 23^2 in the following sentence referring to the making of Dutch cloth: 'Which making of cloth it may be they must now cease from because they are cut off from Spain which did give them much wool'. This is almost certainly a reference to the ending of the 12 years truce in late 1621; as the onset of hostilities between Spain and the Netherlands had been anticipated for some time, the *Wast* is either being written just as the Treaty expired or in anticipation of the imminent expiry. Both lines of evidence suggest late 1621 as the date for the *Wast*.

This is an attempt at economic analysis contemporaneous with Mun, by an author who is conscious of his own understanding of the subject, yet struggles with both the words and the style in which to express himself. He was probably a self-taught merchant. The greater merchants associated with the Merchant Adventurers or the East India Company, were typically more educated in rhetoric and made some occasional references to the Hellenes or the Romans. He was probably someone of considerable experience in dealing with Holland and northern Europe, as the numbers given for profit rates correspond with those used by merchants in the Eastland trade.[3] Lionel Cranfield is a possibility, but it is hard to believe that someone in his high position would leave us something so unfinished, nor does it have the telltale columns of figures said to be characteristic of Cranfield. Since the author suggests that trades which make short-run losses should be pursued, it may be that he was no longer an active merchant.

For at least 150 years there has been a debate between economists and economic historians on the value of the category 'Mercantilism', which was invented by Adam Smith to differentiate between his predecessors and the economic thought in the Wealth of nations. Among the many points raised in opposition to Adam Smith's characterization are; there was no uniformity of thought in the 150 years between Mun and Smith, there is little attention paid to the specific problems out of which the policies of 'Mercantilism' arose, the appropriateness of the policies are not judged in context and so on. Reviewing the themes of a large literature on this debate is needless here, but there is a need to say something further about the period 1620–1630. Between 1954 and 1960, a number of economic historians – Barry Supple, R. W. K. Hinton, J. D. Gould and Lynn Muchmore – made a determined effort to correct the presuppositions of historians of economic thought. It was shown how Mun wrote in the context of vigorous policy debates, that some important parts of his famous *Englands Treasure* were taken directly from some memos he wrote for the Council of Trade, that the major ideas were not arrived at through some dispassionate or even disinterested analysis of the economy but were forged in the context of arguing immediate policy problems. In recent years, it has led to a more active consideration of the 'bureaucrats', to use an anachronistic term, in trying to understand economic thought.[4]

This reliance of economic thought on current problems, in this case perceived by the scarcity of coin, is heightened by a look at the Commons Debates – see the notes on the speeches of Cooke on 26 February 1621 and of Cranfield on 13 March 1621 – or in the State Papers Domestic. On going through calendar SPD, there are not only many references to the scarcity of coin as well as recognition of pamphlets being published on Trade, but the contents of item 130 on p. 210 for 1620 [no further date given] seem to match the content of the *Wast*

> Tract on the modes by which treasure is wasted, viz, the export of coin, superfluity in expenditure, especially at christenings, &c, with suggestions for remedy thereof, viz: – edicts against excess in apparel, &c; raising the value of coin; making copper moneys; encouraging trade at home by making it free; encouraging fishing; the working of the silver, lead, coal and alum mines; suppression of beggars, particularly a class called canters, who have a government, language, and religion of their own &c

Despite the differences in the latter half of the title,[5] which may be due to our selection of what is significant in the manuscript, the description seemed to agree quite well with the *Wast*. The title of the tract is 'Some Few remedies to prevent the *wast* of Treasure, at home and abroad' If it was an early version of the *Wast,* the date at Marsh's would be justified. However, the contents again differ in style, content and emphasis. This tract is also quite short – barely 10 folio pages compared with the 37 folio pages of the *Wast*. The principal points it makes are

1. Laws cannot prevent the profitable flow of treasure
2. Treasure is vital to Trade
3. The King is most affected and must control enhancement of coin
4. Real wealth is recognized
5. England should follow the Dutch
6. Companies are harmful – grant a free trade
7. Domestic resources – fishing, lead, copper, coal, need to be developed.

The *Wast* is perhaps best seen as part of a trio of analyses for
1620–1621 available to us – 'The causes of the scarcity of coin' [reprinted
in Thirsk & Cooper, 1972], 'Some few remedies to prevent the *wast* of treasure at home and abroad' and the *Wast*. The first item, 'The causes', is just
a listing of a variety of factors to be blamed for the scarcity of coin; the second, 'Some few remedies', provides a paragraph on each issue, with most
attention paid to curbing excessive spending. So the pamphlet tran-
scribed here is the most developed presentation of a theme common to
several analysts of this period. At first, many different factors were listed
as causes of the economic difficulties faced by England. Gradually, the
many were narrowed to a few and then to one, the balance of trade, as
the primary cause of the scarcity of coin or bullion. What is notable
about the *Wast* is the immediate focus upon the balance of trade, a position that Mun would gradually adopt. The sequence of three manuscripts noted above suggests how analysts, most probably merchants,
were both finding a voice and arriving at a consensus about the economic problems of England. Perhaps the entries in the calendar SPD is
the best single source for the economic thought of England in the years
prior to the Civil War.

EVALUATION

In assessing the importance of the *Wast* one must resist the temptation to
consider the phrase or the concept of the 'balance of trade' to be of particular importance because of its novelty. Even though historians of economic
thought have married the phrase to Thomas Mun, J. D. Gould has noted
that,[6] already in 1612 a Report noted of the balance of trade as one of
several 'commonplace so well knowne ... as it is enough to mention them
only'. As the Royal accounts were frequently presented, and the surplus or
deficit became matter for debate or policy, the only novelty lay in applying
the same concepts to Foreign Trade.[7] The balance would also arise naturally in considering the amount of bullion in a country. Since England had
no mines of gold or silver, and since these metals constituted the means of
payment, the only way the stocks in England could change would be by the
net balance of imports and exports. So the balance of trade can be seen as
having several sources and hence a 'commonplace'. In other words, it is the
use that the 'balance of trade' is put to that directs our attention. The issue
being debated in the 1620s was whether the exchanges moved the balance

of trade or vice versa. Tawney's characterization of the intellectual scene just prior to this period is as follows:[8]

> The traditional prophylactic against 'the over-balancing of the kingdom ... with foreign commodities' consisted in the antiquated system of exchange controls known, for the mystification of osterity, as the Statutes of Employment.

It will be desirable to know who wrote the *Wast*. It must have been perceived to have some merit to be copied and taken to the Ussher collection in Dublin; and then copied again for the Marsh library. The *Wast* takes a strong stand on the Balance of Trade causing the exchanges, [not vice versa], it advocates a development bank, it argues for higher wages, it claims that wealth returns to the land, so landlords should encourage general economic growth. It defends the East India Company but briefly, perhaps because the concerted attacks of 1624—1628 had not begun, or because Mun was already writing his defence at this time.

It may be useful to see the *Wast* in the light of other contemporary analyses, such as those of Edward Misselden and Thomas Mun. Edward Misselden (1622) reviews the main ideas of his monograph, *Free Trade*, by telling us on pp. 102—03 that he 'considered the causes of the decay of Trade, in the matter and form thereof' — such references to Aristotlean logic, plus many other indications of being learned in the classics, is quite missing in the *Wast*, whose object is always to get straight to the point. Thomas Mun is also rarely distracted from addressing the economic issue. Misselden continues to review the causes of the scarcity of money:

> The immediate causes [are those that] either hinder the importation; or such as cause the Exportation; and both in the under-valuation of His Majesties coine.

Changing the valuation of coin is an important item on Missleden's agenda, a point the *Wast* considers to be of minor importance. The *Wast* does not deny that foreign devaluations hurt, but argues that the effect is not quantitatively sufficient. Misselden then goes on to review the remedies and provides a comprehensive list; notable in this list is the Statute of Employments, which the *Wast* pays almost no attention to. Both the style and the focus of the *Wast* sufficiently separates it from Misselden and points towards the later formulation of Mun (1664).

There is much that is similar between Mun's *Discourse* of 1621 and the *Wast*. Mun pp. 5—6 begins his *Discourse* by describing clearly the balance of trade, which he deals with separately as imports and exports, as being the touchstone of treasure, then he gets involved in the specifics of the East India trade. Mun returns to general principles again on pp. 39—47, where he begins by agreeing that the valuations of foreign coin do hurt, and his last point is that any trade that does not bring in money, after re-export, is hurtful. Mun's purpose in 1621 was to defend his company, the East India company, which he does by using the net balance of coin (or bullion) of any company as the criterion of benefits. Mun decides on the benefits of each trade by balancing the long-run cash account for each trading company and not a global balance of trade, that is, involving all trading companies simultaneously, for England.

Finally, a few thoughts on the significance of these materials for our understanding of the economic acumen of that age. Apart from the 'Cause', each of the others clearly describes real wealth as that which is ultimately desirable. Adam Smith recognized this and went on to observe that while 'some of the best English writers upon commerce' begin by noting the items of real wealth, 'in the course of their reasonings' the items of real wealth 'seem to slip out of their memory'.[9] As there is considerable support for reading the early authors in this way, we have to ask, what caused the deflection of attention away from real wealth? Smith hinted that it was an identification of the precious metals with real wealth, as though they believed that 'all wealth consists in gold and silver', a characterization that was too delicious for later economists not to embellish.[10]

If we grant the authors of the 1620s some insight and read them carefully, it is possible to see that their 'error' lay elsewhere than in the confusion between bullion and wealth. They really believed that money 'created' activity. Misselden waxes warmly on Money as the life of Trade, and Mun explains the same point carefully in Englands Treasure, but even in 1621 he comments that

> England is endowed with such an abundance of rich commodities, that ... it hath beene much inriched with treasure brought in from forrain parts; which hath given life unto so many worthy trades. (p6)

So money begets Trade. Hence, acquiring gold and silver is the essential first step in gaining new trade.

Once we read the materials of the 1620s in context, two important points arise. First, in the short run the arguments of Barry Supple on the importance of the currency devaluations in Europe as preventing successful exports and leading to a persistent deficit in the balance of trade, acquire force. Secondly, J. D. Gould pointed out that the long-run specie-flow mechanism of classical economics would not have occurred to those in the 1620s because contemporaries would have seen how, despite a continual influx of money, Holland was enjoying constant or falling prices. In conclusion, the literature leading up to the *Wast*, as well as the *Wast* itself, seem to confirm the characterization of Lars Magnusson regarding four original points about the 'mercantilistic revolution' in economic thinking during this period:[11]

> [It] implied the emergence of an explicit and principled discussion on how wealth was created as well as distributed
>
> [It] implied the application of, for want of a better name, a Baconian scientific programme in which logical argumentation should prevail
>
> Most writers ... argued on the basis of a 'material' interpretation of man and society
>
> Perhaps the most important ... was the view that the economy must be perceived as a system.

A warning is essential for any reader of the transcription below: Deciphering and reading this manuscript was hard. Numbers get changed within an illustration, words and perhaps even a paragraph, gets repeated; the use of a single bracket, that is no closing bracket, almost no punctuation and no paragraphing may force the reader to guess. The author frequently starts a thought with 'which', 'and' or 'but' etc. So it is easy to misread. On a first reading, I gave the author the benefit of the doubt and assumed that he made sense, then I went back and rechecked my reading with the general sense of the paragraph and by confirming my rendering of a particular word by referring to other parts where the same word was used and written with less ambiguity. Sometimes this was not possible, though the sense requires, for example, 'importing', the word could only be read as 'exporting'. As these surprises spoil the flow of the argument, which was otherwise building up carefully, the temptation to impose meaning by exchanging words was great. I have resisted the temptation in the hope that a more readable version of the *Wast* will be found and these surprises shown to be the result of copying errors. If such a version is found and the conjecture is justified, the importance of the *Wast* will increase greatly. For ease of reading, I have provided headings, where feasible, for many sections of the transcription. [?] indicates those words or phrases I am still doubtful of. Page numbers in bold are the original folio pages. The interested reader may wish to see if some variant punctuation makes a difference.

> Some optional notes to help the reader of the *Wast*. Page numbers refer to folio page numbers
>
> What is real wealth? **p1**
>
> England is wealthy yet wanting in coin **p1**
>
> This is due to the balance of trade **p2**

The cause of ye *wast* of the silver or bullion of England; The means to remedie ye same; The good effect yt will follow the remedie. Ms Z 3.5.32(1) Marsh's Library

All common wealths must have those things within themselves as shall sustain the same or else find some other commodity which another country has need of and so by exchanging each with other many countries are supplied with – of that which themselves want by yielding another commodity which themselves have not. This traffic is so ordinary that there is no need to speak further of the same. The commodity which are of absolute necessity for a country to have are coin and cattle for fooding, wool and flax for clothing, coals or wood for burning, timber and stone for building, salt for preserving and keeping of meat, as also iron to bring those materials in to such form as they may be unto man useful.

Now by how much the more any kingdom doth exceed another in these things by so much hath it advantage to be richer in all other things, that

are esteem of man, than that kingdom that is his inferior in the same: and
seeing that it cannot be denied that England doth herein exceed many
nations, and in the plentie of the same is made almost equal to any: so that
for daintie fooding, rich clothing, (if we would but esteem our own as others
do) sumptuous building we have of ourselves to serve ourselves, and as we
do to spare great store of the same to others. But what is the reason then
that our land so exceeding other in the materials aforesaid should be in
comparison of others so needy in the want of money **P2**, as at preisent it is?

The only cause I can command [?] is that our commodities that go out
from us pay not for them which are brought in unto us, so that our
commodity falling short of this performance the supply of necessity must be
silver. For this there needs no other proof (being such a one as is undeniable)
than other nations (especially the Dutch) have infinite store of our coin, and
we have none of them, and very little or none if any others. Another proof
may be to consider the abundance of foreign commodities which we spend,
which, if I should go to name them particularly, It would ask a whole volume,
and the few we have to bring those in, so that we may wonder that we feel
not the waste more than we do, although it is wonderful enough.

Now there is three objections which being answered will make the
conclusion aforesaid more plain yet. The first is an answer to a question,
which I myself have often demanded, namely how the low countries do
come to have so much of our English coin. The answer hath been that they
making our money to go so high with them as it doth is the means by
which they have so much of our coin as they have. For prof thereof it is
said that a merchant having sold the low countries commodities he cannot
find anything to carry back again from us so beneficial as money. The same
being made to give five or six in the hundred higher then own coin. And so
likewise when any merchant shall go from us to buy their commodities if
he consider what commodity to carry he cannot find any so profitable as
money for the cause aforesaid. Also it is said this doth follow that our
money being **P3** so profitable and altogether without trouble it makes the
merchant careless to take our commodity yet diligent to bring over and sell
the wares of the low countries. It may be well said of this as of all other
cases where there is the cause given which is not the cause, it make us apply
a remedy but so far will it be from helping the same as if it do no hurt it is
well. It is sure it can never do good, for the raising of our gold it was a very
good thing, and made gold to go in more abundance than it did before
among ourselves, yet not one foote lesse did it hinder his going from our
self; nay, whereas before they went forward to use the help of the gold
smith to get them gold, by which means there was a discovery made of the

abundance old Dutch men carried out of the land. Whereupon they were fined in many thousand pounds, whereas now it is carried as frequently as before and no need to be beholding to the goldsmiths, by reason the raising doth make men give out their gold rather than silver. And so their carelessness to carry our commodities and their diligence to put off foreign.

Let us raise those commodities they bring to us amongst ourselves, and their diligence will quickly be prevented, for a merchant considering what he should carry out of England to make profit of he cannot find above two or three sorts. The rest which we have, they have them also, and many hundreds sorts more than we have. Now of those two or three sorts one is restrained as to the dealing of our own nations as to the staples of woolen cloth the rest his rates go so high amongst ourselves as they are prohibited not go out from ourselves as corn, hides, tallow, and so of the rest. On the contrary our commodities bring forth among them, there may be found with them a hundred sorts, which they make, we not, and yet we use the same so that a merchant having sold our commodities with them **P4**. can say, I can carry this or that commodity and so speak of diverse which he may say I can get so many in the hundred by the same; whereas the low countries commodity being sold with us, when a merchant shall cast what to return thither, he cannot find any artificial commodity with us, except woolen cloth, which is made with themselves. Now to carry any commodity over will be at the least ten in the hundred charges, and the same being made among themselves is as good cheaper with them as with us. How is it otherwise possible now [?] but they of necessity must carry over ready money so that if we raise those artificial commodities among ourselves which now they bring us, we should then make their case just the same that ours now is, and although there were five in hundred lost in the money yet any merchant would rather lose five in the hundred then ten in the hundred. So that our country giving utterance of the commodities they bring unto us is the cause of their diligence and consequently of the having of our money and not the making of our money five in the hundred better than their own.

For let it be considered that any having sufficient of our commodity will not give so much for the same by twenty, thirty, or forty in the hundred as when they have need. Now if you make the raising of our money to five in the hundred the cause, you make five in the hundred to do that as twenty thirty forty in the hundred cannot do. **P5**. Again if a merchant bringing over foreign commodity, if he did not return make his return of them in a less a year!, he is not such a fool but will quickly cast a figure and find that notwithstanding he has lost five in the hundred in bringing over money.

Yet he might have gained more by the interest of the same than to bring over commodities to lie upon his hand a whole year. Seeing that in England he could have gained after ten in the hundred by the same. But whereas we think that they make our money to go higher five in the hundred than their own they are not so unwise. Well foreseeing, nay have good experience of the evil of the same. For if this were so a merchant had presently matter to work upon for gain as to do nothing, but to give out our money for their and to bring it to his Majesty's mint so to melt the same down, paying the Mintmasters for the coining and so give out the same again for theirs by which means in time their bullion and coin might be clean sucked from them. So that our money doth not go five in the hundred higher than theirs. But their money in his alloy[?] is five in the hundred before than ours. Now if they did alloy it fifty in the hundred and so accordingly to let it go, will you say hereupon they have ours better than their own by fifty in the hundred. If any should so think they would be in errs as now we are in thinking so of the other. But the States are so careful that- forayne money shall go no higher than as to hold correspondence with their own as that they will prevent any trick to be put upon them herein. For which I alledge a late proof of the States preceding against Bartholomew Munter, a great merchant of Amsterdam, who seeing there came in to Holland coin which by reason of his late coining the true value of the same was set[?], so that it went much higher than it was worth wch Munter quickly spied and so agreed with the prince from whence this coin came to have certain thousands coined, and so to pay a reasonable good profit for the coining much of which being put forth by him in the low countries. The same was quickly found out and the said Munter punished with fire and banishment so that if they had not thus prevented this evil, Munter was in a course quickly to have sucked the low countries of infinite treasure. So that it is clear a State cannot more endanger itself and make loss of treasure than to make the set[?] coin to go higher then it is worth. For by this means there is a fair opportunity afforded for others to coin of the same, and by it to draw out the commodity of a country, for much less than in itself it is worth. Therefore the Low countries are so careful in this that the brass money itself which the coin is very near worth to be sold. For as it is brass as it is coin so that none can coin the same because it will hardly pay for the labor. **P7.** of the coining.

Contrariwise in Spain where there is made brass money to go very high, if hath been a means that infinite store of this brass money hath been coyned by others and brought into Spain and put of, and their silver pieces of eight brought away for it, And when there was copper money in Ireland which went much higher than its value Tyrone took presently the advantage and more it may which are not known and had great store of it coined in Antwerp, in Flanders which he pay his fellow rebels with all, which had it not been prevented he might have had money to this day to have continue his rebellion, if he could have lived so long. Again many places in Germany which make their money go much higher then its true value is at the least by thirty in the hundred, and if the low countries by this means gain such great store, than their by this reason should gain much more, yet this hath being a means so to waste them of their coin as themselves do wonder at it. By reason that their commodities are drawn from them much less than their worth in their value, and whereas much of the money is brought into the low countries they will receive the same as his true value is worth, which is afterwards gathered up and returned again from whence it came; so that one told me that did deal in this kind by the return of five hundred pounds he hath gain one hundred and fifty. And how can this but waste p**8** a country to give out their money low and to receive the same high, if there were no danger of others to take benefit of the coining, and although foreign coin is some time wasted in the low countries higher than his true value is, yet this is never done by authority. But merchants that receave the same in foreign countrys for their commoditys, do labor to put forth the same again at as high a rate as they can for their own particular profit, which when it is perceived it is presently set at his true or rather to be less in value then their own.

And this is well proved by the banks that are erected in any city, for the security whereof the whole city standeth bound. Now any man is to receive money in the time of this improvement occasioned as aforesaid if he will received the money by assuming the payment of the same for his use into the bank the party which is to pay the same cannot deny so to pay it. Now the bank will not receive the same any higher than authority hath established his value so that as our case doth stand this our money going high with them is our profit and their loss which none would deny if they did give us money for money, which is all one with commodities. For by this means we have the more of their commodities for the less of our moneys by so much as the difference **P9**. is in the rise of their making our money to go higher than their own. By this which hath been spoken it doth appear that it is not the raising of our money that doth take the same from us but the venting of their commodities. And I have staid [?] the longer upon the same because many will hardly be removed from this conceipt.

The second objection may be made from the examination of the kings custom books that if few goods outgate there is more money received than few goods ingate. One might conclude from hence that our commodities going out do pay for them which do come in from foreign parts according as the books of ingate and outgate shall stand in relation each to other. It is to be noted that I do but imagine this relation not as granting it true which if it be yet I shall prove it is not sufficient to disprove what I have formally concluded. And so much as it shall be found short of that which is granted so much the more shall it be found as a help to prove what I spoke for. For I know by my own experience that upon goods outwards value for value the are rated higher than upon goods inwards. As for example any man entering goods ingate shall receive more for them twenty or thirty in the hundred than they stand rated for in the Kings books. Let any that hath so entered goods ingate lay out of this hundred and twenty or hundred and thirty which he has received for that which was in the Kings book of rates. But at an hundred one hundred of the same upon the commodities that go out from us and enter these outgate and it will be found that rates are upon those goods as much as he paid for them or rather higher. **P10** Now by this rule any may carry twenty or thirty in the hundred out of the land and it shall never be missed so that notwithstanding the value of customs for goods outgate doth exceed that of ingate, yet it doth prove against me except it make good this difference. As also another difference which will be made to appear from the grossness of our commodities that go out from us. And The finest of them which we receive from foraigne and likewise a difference betwixt the going out of goods and their coming in. For all merchants know by experience that in a gross commodity there cannot be saved that in customs as there may be done in the fine. Inso much that the cause that many merchants enter any fine is not that they cannot save the custom but by entering of small[?] quantity they may under pretense of the same utter abundance without being suspected not to have paid his customs. For a gross commodity cannot be hid in such a small corner as a fine may. For silks, velvets, teince gold cambrick's lawns and many other costly commodities, tenne thousand pounds worth will not take up so much room as one hundred pounds worth of our cloths will do, which is the finished commodities we export, and for their difference of going out and coming in. In their going out there must be an entry made of the same before it can be let aboard otherwise it is presently forfeited; whereas ingate it may be left aboard and taken thence[?] at our best leisure for pg **11** no forfeiture can be except it be caught upon the land so that here is a wonderful benefit of having and not the having of it, as also betwixt folks and folks, so that I may say the truth, nay the hundred part which is sold in England of fine commodities his Majesty doth not receive any impost for. So that by these reasons it doth appear that this question of the custom books is so far from making against the former conclusion as that by a true a consideration of them it may be made more clearer.

The third objection is that it may said there is no silver mine found in England but all that we have is given unto us by other nations for our commodities. For the answer of which I may compare England to a man being a great gatherer of wealth but leaves the same to his son which doth not add to his fathers getting but consume what is gotten for him. For if we consider the abundances of foreign commodities that are spent by us over that which was spent by our forefathers we shall find the difference so great in diverse things as it is in this. One only thing for money which I will name which is sacke being used by our forefathers as an apothecary drug whereas now our abundance of exporting the same doth make it a staple commodity unto that nation from whom we fetch it. Many other things might be named but this difference is confessed by all. Therefore I say no more of it and we are not only hurt by this but our cloth which was a trade but of late peculiar to ourselves hath now his practice in other kingdoms as namely Spain, Venice, the low countries. Now if we consider the frugalness of our forefathers living and the trade of clothing peculiar to them which is (and daily more and more will be) diminished with us the matter is nothing **P12**. hard to see that they might gather and we waste that which is so left us.

Having made clear the cause of wasting of our silver the remedy doth now the easier appear. And so, those that must be the doctors [?] of the same must be the commonwealth in general. The reason is because a commonwealth exercising a practice may in the same be great gainers although losers in that kind. As a particular must find his gain without which although he may begin yet it is not possible he should continue any practice. As for example let it be supposed that the commonwealth should make a bank of eleven hundred pounds with which they intend to make some artificial work for sale. For which there is giving out of the bank the said eleven hundred pounds unto several particulars of the commonwealth. They having given nothing for the same but their art and labor. Coming to make sale of this commodity in another Kingdom there can be gotten no more for it than ten hundred. Now here in the practice is immediately an hundred pound loss yet mediately a thousand pounds gain. For the commonwealth hath made itself to have by his art and labor one and twenty hundred pounds for his eleven hundred pounds.

Again let us consider this contrary; as if now you should go into another kingdom and take this eleven hundred pounds and give into the same for their art and labor bringing in the same home unto your own country and receive for it twelve hundred pounds. Here in the immediate practice is eleven hundred pound less for there is lesse[?] in this commonwealth by this eleaven **P13**. hundred pounds that you did so give out for the art and labor yet was done in another Kingdom then was before you brought the said commodity.

And to apply this unto England it may be proved to have at this day many courses afoot which will give the practice there in a hundred pounds gain by leaving in the Kingdom less a thousand pounds than it had before he had his hundred of gains. On the contrary many practices are neglected by us by which we might gain to ourselves many thousands of pounds without losing of one hundred in his immediate practice itself. For there might be named two (beside those which are to keep in our money) which would be in his mediate profit unto us from other nations at the least three hundred thousand pounds every year (in a short time which now as our case is cannot have the practice by a particular. Because a particular taking in hand any course notwithstanding there should be a profit to him in his immediate practice yet if it answers not in proportion the stock he shall so employ he cannot continue it. Whereas a commonwealth finding a great profit in one kind can easily give a little out of the same profit to make good the same loss in the other. Howsoever we see this, yet the not practising of the same hath hindered us of infinite treasure which otherwise we might have. Yea there were courses that we were wont all together to raise them amongst ourselves. Now by reason **P14**. particulars find more profit to buying the same from other nations they are neglected to be raised among us by which, unspeakable hindrances will increase among us in time if the commonwealth lay not to a helping hand for the commodities that take our money, or commodities which would otherwise yield us money being such as other nations cannot well be without and of three kinds.

The first is such as may all together be raised within ourselves. Both the matter and form of which many particulars might be named which do take our commodities or money from us. The second sort is such as our country doth noth yield the matter of the first principles yet it might give at his forms[?] the difference being as much between the first principle and forms as ten or twenty shillings is to one. As for example one pound of silk in his first principle is not worth the tenth part of that it is having past the workers hand and so it is in a pound of flax in his first principle. It is not worth sixpence which by workmanship may be made worth forty shillings so that we should labor that our own people should have the working of all things we spend which is not a matter of impossibility but easily to be affected. The third **P15**. kind is that which the nature of our country afford not, neither can there be any edition. The matter be natural and no otherwise useful as wine, oil, grocery, spicery, in which two courses might be used. The one is that there should be laid a good excise unto his Majesty's use upon all commodities of this kind which are to be spent with ourselves that we may be the more sparing in the use for the lesser we spend of these the more is the gain of our commonwealth. Always provided that as little charges as might be should be laid out upon these goods or any others that brought In to the land with purpose to carry out again for to trade and traffic. For otherwise great excise may cut us off from the trading with others by which means we must be driven to bring in to the country but just as much as might be to save the same and soe[?] quite loss that which would redowned to no profit to his Majesty but loss. And others by this means taking the whole benefit of that which we might otherwise share with all. The second is for that for these and all other commodities our own shipping may have the benefit of their fetching from foreign parts for it is well known that the fetching of a commodity is many times two three yea ten times dearer than the commodity itself. And although it might be said there is good order taken from this **PG16** because no Englishman may freight a stranger if he can get a <u>native</u> yet I heard a great cry against the East Indian trade that hath now his exercise with us by which means we fetch those spices at the best hand. For many that I have heard speak against it I have asked them whether they would suffer <u>spicery</u> to come into the land — they answered they thought it as absurd. To say against that but they reply that we carry out only silver for the same whereas we might have them for our commodity from other nations when as it is not considered that if a peppercorn or clove were not brought in unto us to take our money from us yet our commodities pay not for the *wast*. This being accepted excepted for now we carry no money for the same but into the East Indies. Yet, as I have before showed, others have infinite store of our coin which is gone to supply that which our commodities do fall short to perform (as I have said, this being excepted). Now if it were granted true that our commodities did over balance those which do come in unto us. Notwithstanding it easy to make it appear that the commonwealth will receive great hurt by the same for there is at the least **P17** ten times more spent for their fetching than they cost where they are bought, all which ourselves have the benefit of. As namely for the building of the shipping, wages of marriners and other offices being very many that have employed herein. Now it is possible to sell our commodities to countervail this loss for our commodities which will not by this means yield twenty shillings in the hundred more than now we have therefore same (nay it is not hard show that in a very short time we shall get more loss for them than now we sell them for). Whereas the commonwealth is so much a loser as the difference is betwixt that which is spent amongst ourselves and that which we give only for the commodities from whence we fetch it.

So that four great evils will fall upon us by this neglect. The first is that we with our money shall build shipping, maintain mariners and officers in the same, to the strengthening of others and weakening of ourselves. Secondly we shall pay three times custom, for the same, as namely ingate and outgate into the province into which it shall be imported as also when we bring the same home. Which how great it will arise unto let but the third part which is now paid be considered and it will **P18** appear that this difference only should make us continue the trade. Thirdly the trade resting in one or two nations hands they many raise the same as it is the ordinary course of merchants to do) to be dearer twenty thirty forty in the hundred then now at this present they are sold for[?]; Fourthly, this shall be another canker to waste our treasure for if our commodity doth at this present pay for the rest that do come in unto us for much as our commonwealth hath the benefit of in their fetching will be quite carried out from us and it cannot be determined how much more soe[?] That for every ten pounds they do carry from us they will then take at the least an hundred.

By this it may be perceived how good it is for commonwealths to gain everything at the first hand now there is three objections to be removed that —seem [This is torn and can't be seen] against the strict observing of this practice. The first and principal is that our raising so of commodities within ourselves may hinder his Majesty of his customs that is received for those commodities that are so imported; but this may easily be remedied[?] by making all such wares so raised unsalable until it doth pass under some saling house, where such impositions may be paid to his Majesty as now are upon the same in the book of rate. Wherein there may be an easier course taken for the due payment of the same then is possible to be taken for the same in the custom house. In which there might be wonderful great difference of profit to his Majesty and not alloane as it shall afford an easier means for the true payment of such impost as shall be laid upon the same **P19** But in many things might our practice exercise itself in as one only Kingdom might take as much from us now we do from others much more from others several Kingdoms might take of more than now we only of ourselves spend. So that whereas his Majesty cannot receive now but for so much as doth just come in unto ourselves the same might be paid as aforesaid and much more that might go out from us ourselves. The second objection is that we not taking other nations commodities from them they will not take ours. And so by seeking of gain in one kind we may sustain greater loss in another. As the case of late in the restraining of our white cloths to the end they might be colored and dressed by ourselves which did seem to be a great good, but experience did show it to be otherwise in his proof. Afore I answer this objection I will show that it is an error to think we are well if we receive commodity for commodity being as much as if a man should say I will get no more than I spend or spend no more than I get. **p20** By which resolution any can conclude such a one shall never add anything to his estate. Therefore it is better for a commonwealth to sell a commodity rather for fifty Pounds in ready money then to receive a hundred pounds worth in commodities, as for example our woolen cloth art -doth then improve it to be ten times better then it -is in his first principal bringing the same into another Kingdom there is receaved for − [?] this commodity which they have improved by their labour to tenne times better than it was [?this is torn]' in his first princpal; also now can it be said how is one penny gained by this meanes into the commonwealth. For howsoever you did improve our commodities by the labour of the people to make the commonwealth richer than it was before by the difference of his worth of that it was in his first principal and of that it is worth −being so improved yet this counterchecked − y^t you have received no more than labour for labour. Just as if one should say if you will do a day's labour for me I will do **P21** another for you. Whereas a commodity being sold for fifty pounds ready money there is added to the commonwealths enriching about forty pounds clear by the art and labour which if commodity be received for the same ninety pounds of this is added unto the same by art and labour also so that in affect there is but ten pound given for it. But some may say here I reckon art and labour worth nothing. For an answer it is but an example therefore not to be extended farther than the drift of it, which is to show that we should still rather labour to have money coming unto us from others than to go out from us to others. Which cannot be without raising the commodities within ourselves that take it away and again though scarcity of labour in any are not now profitable to themselves or commonwealth insomuch that I have heard some pray earnestly that God would take them and their children out of the world. Because their misery hath been such as not knowing what to turn themselves upon to get bread to put in their mouths.

Now I come to the objection in which we must understand that our **P22** Undertaking of those courses cannot make the matter worse possible or as bad as now it is (for- as hath formerly been declared, now our commodity for commodity is wholly eaten up and also our coin wasted to supply that

which our commodity come short[?] to perform so that if they should refuse
our commodities, which indeed will never be if we order our courses as we
may. The worst that can arise from the same is that now those people that
have their employment for making of woolen cloth for which we have their
artificial commodities those people employed to the making up of that
which now we receive from others. The difference proving our advantage in
that our people shall in change of exercise save [?] that in the commonwealth which is now and hath been this long time been wasting out of it.
And whereas it may be said that in this change of exercise we shall change
for a practice we are very expert in to that we are altogether contrary, for
this let it be likewise considered that other nations have no advantage of us
herein, their case being one with ours. For it being made plain that our
condition is such as doth call for a remedy shall this fear hinder us from
the same. Cannot we live as well nay better without the commodities of
other nations then they can live without ours. So shall we make **P23** void
this truth that England needes not to be beholding to other nations yet
other nations must be beholding to it. For that if this feare take place it
must needs be said we are in bondage which will every year prove to be
greater and greater upon us, Which I think the stomach of our nation is it
so great as they will deny this conclusion in words. Which, if we will have
remedy, it must be done in deeds.

Now for the proof to strengthen this objection brought from the example of our white clothes from whence it may be considered which is the
thing I will plead for. That a course of trading shall be better gained without prohibiting any other then it can be to practice in that kind. For prohi-
bitions must exercise themselves either upon such that do go out from us or
come in unto us. Now if the prohibition be made upon foreign commodities because we would raise the same within ourselves then shall other
nations work upon us by prohibiting of ours. So that a part or that particular of our commonwealth which is exercised wherein the alteration shall be
made will suffer that which the commonwealth in general ought to do. So
if it be our own commodity that is prohibited thinking thereby to add [?]
that unto it ourselves which is now done by other nations the case will be
just one with the former and this the experience of this ordinance made
about the cloth doth prove. For this which is the staple of England being
stopped from his wanted course the sense of which evil appearing so grossly
P24 to the low countries that without any intermission two main trades
would be wrung out of their hands. Whereupon they presently made an
order that not any of this colored cloth should be bought upon pain of
the loss of the cloth so bought and a great fine besides. And where did

the weight of this evil waste but upon them which were exercised in this practice only. So that we practicing our courses without opposing others we may gain our ends without being opposed. For it is never seen that any course by another nation is so much taken to heart where there is lyberty suffered to any to bring in his commodity freely.

And we do not gain ours by prohibiting of theirs. Which I may prove by the low countries now making of cloth which we never grudge at being noo [?] are suffered to carry ours thither freely and to sell the same as well as we can. Which making of cloth it may be they must now cease from because they are cut of from Spain which did give them much wool. But then the question may be whether a course can be gained by us in this manner or not. I answer with less loss then if we practice otherwise, for as I have said we not opposing others our courses may go on. Soe if we shall not find any jott of loss now we having raised a commodity within ourselves it may be quickly considered what they can afford the same commodity which do bring it from foreign. And p**25** so we without fail to undersell them although the commodity so raised with us be sold unto loss of that which the making of the same cost for this is not to be accompted loss because ourselves have the gain of this loss. And how great shall the gain be which doth prevent another nation from bringing in that to us as we must either give our money or commodity. Which otherwise would bring us in money and this will not only be without loss but it will not carry so much as evil mixt with it and yet the restraint shall be more effectual then is possible to make the same in any other kind whatsoever. And experience hath well showed that to get a practice as heretofore we have labored to do is as it hath proved hurtful. For whereas there hath been great privileges given (to a very good intent of the giver) to some particulars of a commonwealth to gain a practice being once made their own carvers[?] fopr to enrich themselves they care not to animate another. Which doth make them so exercised in the courses prohibited to neglect their practice because they cannot afford it as those which are now made. The buyers must have it. The buyers well knowing their advantage and this was just the case of the stopping our woolen cloth. It was made so cheap that many left of to make the same and to this day never returned to it again which is such a hurt to a commonwealth as cannot be reckoned or easily imagined and thereupon such arts are faine to have their repeale without effecting anything except that hurt which **P26** causeth it again to be repealed.

A second reason that should make us to gain our ends without the alteration of any courses is that so we may dispose of our course as that it may be known to pay the loss or gain. As also the discerning of advantages as the time when and how to make the same in the first <u>practice</u> profitable and when to neglect the same for a greater advantage. Whereas <u>laboring</u> in the other kind it is a mere impossibility to know loss or profit. Now when a course shall be arrived[?] at all adventures it can give no encouragement to the prosecuting of it. If it be demanded how it can appear such certainty in one and not in the other, I answer as it hath been before showed, there being no alteration made all thing go on in their current as if we did not meddle with any practise) then for the practise we labour to gain. It is easy to keep reckoning so much such a commodity cost the making or raising and so much is made of the same so that the going out and coming in compared each to other the difference doth presently appear.

A third reason that many plead for this form, a stop of a sudden being made we cannot have the use of that we may necessarily need. For a practise must have some time to be such as to serve us with that which now we have from others. As the third objection is it may be said that many merchants that are exercised in foreign traffic being raised amongst ourselves their traffic in those things will cease if there were no other. **P28** Answer, But a public is to be prefered before a private. It were sufficient if I said no more but as I said before concerning his Majesties customs so it may be said to such merchants that their trade may be more gainful to export the same to many nations than now. It can be by only bringing in the same only to ourselves for what doth beget a great traffic and great store at Merchants but by making a commonwealth rich as the contrary doth make a nullity of both. The proof of which is evidently to be seen if we do but cast our eyes upon a commonwealth that is poor which yieldeth neither trade nor Merchant. For any commonwealth being drained dry of her treasure will fail at the last to give the merchant himself supply which is the instrument to draw the same out. So that it will be far from doing hurt that in all kinds it will do good and this will necessarily follow that when the commonwealth shall by this means drive the merchant from a traffic which is hurtful unto it he will be driven upon which shall be benefit unto the same.

Now to propound by way of example one particular. Not that but our practise should with all convenience enter upon as many as we can and that for these reasons. The first is that so many as we leave will be such suckers that they will be great hinderers to our fruitfulness. They second is that our abundance of people. One or two particulars will not yield them employment **P29** The third is when we have raised so much as is for our own lands, use the overplus, being of several kinds, shall the better be vented to other nations unto the continuing and increasing of our own peoples employment. For this all men know that he which hath but one or two commodities cannot take so much as he that hath many.

And for this particular it is Hollands and cambricks which doth take ten times more money out the land than the East Indian Trade. Especially now we are given to were (wear) such great ruffs both men and women. So that there may be many that their whole apparel is not so costly as the bands about their necks. Yet a great clamour is made against the East Indian Trade and for this nothing said now. There are two causes that hinder the one and not the other from us. The one is that the East Indian Trade professeth that he cannot trade without the carrying out of money whereas for the other it is thought that we give commodity for commodity. The second cause is a practise of both which − seemeth[?] a confirmation of the first that is one carryeth out money apparently in one or two ships in the year which doth make a great show. The other carryeth out money covertly and by stealth not in one or two ship in the year or out of one port only, **P30**, by one company of dealers alone, but all the year long it is carried out of many of his Majesty's ports and by many hundreds of men. Which being so divided an hundred (thousands)? pounds doth not appear, whereas ten thousand pounds going in that manner as the East Indian trade doth carry it, it is as an wonder to us. And the difference afore being made but ten to one if we consider what we spend one of the one and of the other we shall finde it at the least an hundred to one.

Now the means to boost our practise in this may be two ways. The one is the commonwealth might set apart a bank of which money which might be such as to employ such as which we might fetch over from other nations skilful in this trade to teach ourselves. The second way is to propound the example of the late King of France which finding the clothes of Arras took abundance of silver out of his kingdom. To prevent which he agreed to lend a Dutch man some twenty thousand pound for certain years by which means he gained this trade into France which after the expiration of the term agreed upon returned to the king again. So for the remedy.

Now to speak of the benefits which will ensue upon the remedy, which will be that which the drift of all the discourse doth tend unto. Namely to keep in our silver with ourselves and to bring in from others. Which will prove the proverb of Solomon to be such to our sovereign as now by reason of want of employment **pg31** the multitude is counted rather a burden then a blessing. And not only shall it be his Majesty's strength, as it is a multitude. But many thousands of men that now cannot eat their own bread may be made able to be subsidy men in the Kings books. The second benefit shall prove to pay great profit to those which might be chief authors of this under our sovereign as namely the nobility, gentry and yeomanry making the revenue of their land much greater than now it is. For I may call the nobility gentry and yeomanry the sea of our land, into which all the rest as rivers do empty themselves in giving to them their silver those commodities which do arise out of those lands. Now it cannot be denied but they do return to those rivers against that which they have for all tradesmen whatsoever have their livelihood from the land, but the evil of it is that they empty themselves abundantly into foreign rivers which do never run into them again. For when we buy Holland's cambricks and diverse other kinds of stuff is it not all one almost as if we went into Holland to bestow our money when we buy silk, velvets and satins; is it not as if we went into Italy to bestow our money. When we drink any kind of wine is not as if we went into Spain or France to bestow our money, I speak not this as if I would have men forbear the use of those things. That is far from my meaning but to show that the **P32** raising of those commodities amongst ourselves will so divert the current that when the sea doth so give to his own rivers it is impossible but that it must receive still from their own again to the keeping of themselves full.

And for those things we are mere natural as wine and such like, to let our practise be such towards other nations as to suck upon them. That which shall pay for the same with a great overplus there being many practises neglected which by a particular cannot be acted yet by the commonwealth it might be done to great profit. Although as I have said before there was but little profit yea if it were but some small loss in his immediate course yet when it shall be gained in his mediate practise many thousand pounds which might be done by one of two practices, much more by many. Whether shall this have his current upon the owners of land for those commodities that are raised upon their land. So that when there is an increase of silver in the land it shall not work an increasment in the revenues of land as now the diminishing doth made it contrary it being not possible it should be otherwise. And if we would hear but of gold or silver mine we would presently run into the West Indies for the same **P33** and with good reason too. Yet we have both gold and silver mines at our doors and we pass by it taking little notice of the same out of which the low countries dig at least two millions every year. The farthest place they go to is Hitland. Having done their fishing there they come into the narrow sea; this being neglected or very weakly followed by us because a particular cannot find that profit as to encourage him in the prosecuting of it which the commonwealth might do to the setting of infinite store of their people at work and find some profit in the practise itself.

Many other practices might be acted by us to the great enriching of the commonwealth and whereas we once were afore in all the world in shipping the low countries having in such a sudden got the start both in shipping silver and in other commodities and riches as that all man would not think that possible true to have the same we ported (exported) of them except their own dyes do for it so might it plainly be demonstrated that England in a short time might increase in shipping in treasure and other riches to the wonderment of others as now we and others do at the low countries. **P34**

If the commonwealth did but do what it might wherein itself should be the only gainer and principal stich (?) as should be the principal doers of the same. Now if we turn our eyes but upon two sorts of people which if their condition were remedied the same would return as a present profit to the commonwealth. First the abundance of poor which are not able to eat their own bread in every parish (perish) in England which if they were employed as they might be the same poor would give money for that which is now given unto them for nothing. The remedying whereof would give such a profit as that if it where justly considered many practices might be begotten with us with less loss than this is to the commonwealth at this day in one year. The second sort of people are them whose employment are so scarce as that their living is a very oppressing of nature so that let their poor hungry bellies cry never so loud upon them they cannot give it supply of what it would have. **P35** And whereas we attribute the happiness other commonwealths to industry as if they were greater labourers than we which is not so. For I will have done more labour in England for sixpence than I can have done in another country for two shillings. For many with us would fain work but they cannot tell where to get it who might be so employed that in short time we might have as few poor as their countries have. As also to make our mens labour at as high rates as it is other where. Which being effected who show[shoud] have profit but the owners of land. For if men now out of such miserable necessity live after the rate of six-pence a day, if they get two shillings, would they not live after the same rate? Which would soon make a rise of lands revenues improving those commodities which do arise upon the same double of what it is now worth, and yet no man feel the hurt of it. And for this matter of industry **P36** we suppose to <u>exceed</u> us it is well known to many in England that a particular man being exercised in a <u>practise</u> by which it may be that he doth keep a work some hundred two or three (which is ordinary with great cloth work-ers). Those which he doth so keep a work do constantly follow their labour from five in the morning till eight at night, some working for three pence and some for four pence and the best hath not above eight pence a day. Now if this practise fail to yield this particular profit he then succeasseth [?] whereupon those that took so great labour for so little wages do want employment and to come to look it from others that are in the like practice.

They are already full rather ready to put of some of their own they had before then to take more. So that my heart cannot think of it but with grief. How I see how those have with lamentable prayers and tears and wringing of hands beg for such a hard labour for so little a profit and yet no supply could be given unto them. Will you say now how that **P37** they want industry? Get them but practise and there will be industry found in abundance for those being put out from this labour, which did support them although very meanly yet now wanting the same they must needs become impudent beggars. And this will increase more and more in England if it be not remedied.

I might go forward so much to show that the commonwealth by not looking so much to profit immediately in a course might not only gain courses which it hath not but might by the same rule wholly extinguish a practise in another country, getting the same alone unto itself but because it is better to labour to keep that which we have than to take from other I will say no more but here end.

NOTES

1. The OED lists '*Wast*' as an obsolete form of 'Waste'.
2. I am grateful to a referee for pointing out this.
3. See the appendix to Hinton (1959).
4. On Mun, see Muchmore (1970). On bureaucrats, primarily Suprinyak (2011) but also Cramsie (2002), Finkelstein (2000) and Wennerlind (2011).
5. It is unclear why there is a reference to the beggars known as canters in the SPD since the document seems to devote no space to them at all.
6. Gould (1954, p. 83 fn1).
7. Dietz (1964).
8. Tawney (1958, p. 129), Lipson (1915–1931) considers the interest to lie in the belief that the exchange rate was being manipulated, p. 74, notes how there was a strong move to regulate the exchanges, but comes to the odd conclusion that the main interest of the debates lay in their giving birth to the balance of trade theory, p. 84.
9. Smith (1981, p. 450).
10. See J. R. McCulloch's Introduction (1856, p. vii).
11. Magnusson (1994, p. 11).

ACKNOWLEDGEMENTS

I am deeply grateful to the Mccarthy Fellowship of Marsh's Library for the support that led to the discovery of this manuscript and wish to give my grateful thanks to the Library and its staff for their continual help.

Marja Smolenaars, Maureen Mulvhill, 17th C specialist with the Princeton Research Forum, Princeton, and Mary Beth de Filippis, curator of the show on a 17th C Dutch merchant, Margrieta van Varick at Bard Gallery, NYC, for Munter. Mark Rankin of James Madison university taught me that '*Sacke* is a Spanish sweet wine that was popular in the sixteenth and seventeenth century'. Carlos Suprinyak has done significant new work on the economic thought of this era and provided useful comments. Geoffrey Ross of the History library at the University of Illinois was very helpful with getting me online copies of manuscripts at the British Library. Two anonymous referees made some very useful and constructive suggestions.

REFERENCES

Cramsie, J. (2002). *Kingship and crown finances under James VI and I. 1603–25.* Suffolk: Boydell Press.

Dietz, F. C. (1964). *English public finance, 1485–1641* (2nd ed.), New York, NY: Barnes and Noble.

Finkelstein, A. (2000). Harmony and balance: *An intellectual history of seventeenth century economic thought.* Ann Arbor, MI: University of Michigan Press.

Gould, J. D. (1954). The trade depression of the Earky 1620's. *The Economic History Review,* 7(1), 81–90.

Hinton, R. W. K. (1959). *The eastland trade and the commonweal.* Cambridge: Cambridge University Press.

Lipson, E. (1915–31). *An economic history of England* (Vol. 3). London: A & C Black.

Magnusson, L. (1994). *Mercantilism: The shaping of an economic language.* London: Routledge.

Misselden, E. (1622). *Free trade.* London: Printed by IohnLegatt for Simon Waterson.

Muchmore, L. (1970). A note on Thomas Mun's 'England's Treasure by Forraign Trade. *The Economic History Review,* 23(3), 498–503.

Mun, T. (1621). A discourse of trade. In J. R. McCulloch (Ed.), (1856). *A select collection of tracts upon commerce.* London: Political Econmy Club.

Mun, T. (1664). Englands treasure by foreign trade. In J. R. McCulloch (Ed.), (1856), *A select collection of tracts upon commerce.* London: Political Econmy Club.

Smith, A. (1981). *An inquiry into the nature and causes of the wealth of nations.* Indianapolis, IN: Liberty Classics. Original edition 1776.

Suprinyak, C. E. (2011). *The role of experts in the public assessment of England's trade crisis of the early 1620s.* Cedeplar/UFMG Working Paper No. 421. Belo Horizonte.

Tawney, R. H. (1958). Business and politics under James I: *Lionel Cranfield Merchant and minister.* Cambridge: Cambridge University Press.

Thirsk, J., & Cooper, J. P. (1972). *Seventeenth-century economic documents.* Oxford: Clarendon.

Wennerlind, C. (2011). *Casualties of credit: The English financial revolution, 1620–1720.* Cambridge, MA: Harvard University.

PART IV
REVIEWS

REVIEW OF THE NEW ENGLISH TRANSLATION OF HEINRICH VON STACKELBERG (1934, 2011) *MARKET STRUCTURE AND EQUILIBRIUM*, TRANSLÀTED BY DAMIEN BAZIN (SCIENTIFIC DIRECTOR), LYNN URCH AND ROWLAND HILL, BERLIN, SPRINGER, 2011

Jan Horst Keppler

ABSTRACT

This English translation of Heinrich von Stackelberg's Marktform und Gleichgewicht *will be welcomed by economists working in the field of industrial organisation and beyond. It has been overdue for more than 80 years. This translation will allow matters to be set straight concerning a number of fundamental theoretical issues connected to Stackelberg's*

Research in the History of Economic Thought and Methodology, Volume 34A, 405–411
Copyright © 2016 by Emerald Group Publishing Limited
ISSN: 0743-4154/doi:10.1108/S0743-41542016000034A012

*work as well as allow to clarify a number of misunderstandings that go
back to the first reviews of Stackelberg's 1934 classic on competition theory.*

Keywords: Monopolistic competition; duopoly; conjectural variation;
corporatism

JEL classifications: B21; B31; D21; D43; L13

This English translation of Heinrich von Stackelberg's *Marktform und
Gleichgewicht* will be welcomed by economists working in the field of industrial organisation and beyond. It has been overdue for more than 80 years.
This translation will allow matters to be set straight concerning a number
of fundamental theoretical issues connected to Stackelberg's work as well
as allow to clarify a number of misunderstandings that go back to the first
reviews of Stackelberg's (1934) classic on competition theory.

The translation as such is well done. *Market Structure and Equilibrium*
overall reads fluently and does justice to the German original. Perhaps it
sticks occasionally even too closely to the initial German vocabulary and
grammar. A phrase describing firm behaviour under Cournot assumptions
thus becomes 'each company orientates itself to its rival's supply' instead of
the more straightforward 'each company takes its rival's output as given
(p. 57)'.

Stackelberg, who appreciated Anglo-Saxon economics, would have
approved to make his text as easily accessible as possible to English-speaking readers even if that would have meant moving slightly further
from German original. It sometimes shows that the actual translation was
undertaken by two non-economists, Lynn Urch and Rowland Hill, while
an economist, Damien Bazin, provided the scientific oversight. The economic and theoretical content of *Marktform und Gleichgewicht* is well preserved and this is at the end the decisive point. Yet not every sentence has
been couched in an idiom familiar to today's economists. The latter will, of
course, perfectly understand the new English text but to do so will require
an effort greater than with a less literal translation. Just choosing the word
'duopoly' rather than the fancy 'dyopoly' would have helped matters in
this respect.

Why does this matter? It matters because it is important is to get
Stackelberg's *Market Structure and Equilibrium* read by industrial

economists and game theorists rather than by historians of economic thoughts, who are by and large better equipped to read texts that go against the habitual grain. The ambition must be to include *Market Structure and Equilibrium* in a standard reading list of English-speaking monographs of the 1930s at a par with Edward Chamberlin's *Theory of Monopolistic Competition* or Joan Robinson's *Economics of Imperfect Competition*.

Despite these quibbles, this translation should finally allow integrating Stackelberg's theories into the mainstream of industrial economics. While the name of Heinrich von Stackelberg is well recognised, his theory itself leads at best a partial existence. In particular, the leader-follower equilibrium connected with his name was explicitly designated as a special case:

> It shows that for a dyopoly ... the 'Bowley dyopoly' is the rule, the 'Cournot dyopoly' is the special circumstance ... and the 'asymmetrical dyopoly' is the exception. (p. 49)

It is, in fact, little known in the English-speaking world that the famed Stackelberg leader-follower equilibrium with differentiated conjectural variations is but a rare exception in Stackelberg's theory. For Stackelberg, the standard case was the symmetric Bowley duopoly, in which *both* competitors include their rival's profit (or optimal response) function rather than his output into their profit functions. This leads to a constellation in which *both* firms put their so-called 'independence output' on the market which leads to oversupply and negative profits for both companies. This case is sometimes referred to in the English-speaking literature as 'war of attrition' with absolutely no reference to Stackelberg.

Ironically, the name 'Bowley duopoly' that Stackelberg chose for this case was a misnomer. Arthur Bowley's original development of duopoly in his *The Mathematical Groundwork of Economics* (1924) is considerably less precise (Bowley, 1924). His great merit was to have first introduced the notion of 'conjectural variation' (later so termed by Ragnar Frisch), yet without following up any particular case:

> To solve these [two equations for profit-maximizing] we should need to know x_2 as a function of x_1, and this depends on what each producer thinks the other is likely to do. There is then likely to be oscillation in the neighbourhood of the price given by the equation,
>
> $$\text{marginal price for each} = \text{selling price}$$
>
> unless they combine and arrange what each shall produce so as to maximize their combined profit. (Bowley, 1924, p. 38)

Bowley thus loosely combines the ideas of Edgeworth (oscillation) and Bertrand (marginal cost equals price) and indeed leaves room for conjectural variations other than the one postulated by Stackelberg. Quite understandably Wicksell considers Bowley's views on the matter 'rather vague' (Wicksell, 1958, p. 216) and Stackelberg's attribution of the 'Bowley duopoly' to the author of *Mathematical Groundwork* is more an act of generosity, than one of genuine intellectual indebtedness (Wicksell, 1958).

However, as the 'Bowley duopoly' remains the central case, structural oversupply, cut-throat competition and instability are the corollaries of competition between firms with homogenous goods. This is important, since it provides the underlying motivation for the sulphurous concluding chapter of *Market Structure and Equilibrium* on 'Market Structure and Economic Policy', where Stackelberg argues in favour of systematic cartelisation under state supervision to limit oversupply and guarantee stability. Modern economists tend to shrug off Chapter 6 as a tribute to the economic and political circumstances of the time by a fundamentally liberal economist.

This means underestimating the structuring force of the critical fault-line in Stackelberg's work, which is defined by the difficulties of attaining and preserving economic equilibrium. Later works show much sympathy for factors such as product differentiation, frictions or bounded rationality to explain why markets with profit-maximising competitors can maintain a degree of stability. However, in 1934 Stackelberg was still driven by the ambition to develop *his* pure theory of duopoly with the appropriate policy implications to boot.

Coming back to the 'asymmetrical case', very closely connected to Stackelberg's name, it should be noted that the asymmetry is neither due to a fundamental cognitive difference between the two competitors (many economic textbooks refer to a higher rationality of the Stackelberg leader) nor to sequential decision-making; that is the leader having a first mover advantage in choosing his output (as modelled for instance in Tirole (1988). This has led to an explicit criticism by modern neoclassical economists that Stackelberg did not adequately model sequential behaviour of 'leaders' and 'followers' in a dynamic context (Friedman, 1983). James Friedman, for instance, writes that:

> It is true that leadership is meaningless if decisions are simultaneous. So a discussion of leadership is meaningful only within a dynamic model. (Friedman, 1983, p. 109)

This criticism, however, is unfounded and due to the common misperception that Stackelberg's work is built around an equilibrium model. For

Stackelberg, instability is intrinsic due to the desire of *both* firms to establish themselves as 'leaders' by putting forward their profit-maximising output. With Stackelberg, both competitors are equally intelligent and decide on their output simultaneously in full knowledge of their competitor's cost and profit functions. Their only difference consists in the structure of their cost functions; that is their respective fixed and variable costs.

The asymmetric equilibrium is the result of a special case, in which a firm with low fixed and high variable costs would indeed maximise its profits by assuming the 'dependence position', which means limiting its output by integrating only its competitor's output into its profit function rather that the latter's best response function. Given that such differences in the structure of costs are rare, the 'asymmetrical duopoly', which by a quirk of the history of ideas has become the emblematic case connected with Stackelberg's name, is indeed an exception. The classic 'Cournot case', to which Stackelberg adds nothing other than a thorough exposition, is then confined to cases in which both companies have strongly increasing marginal costs.

The translation by Bazin, Urch and Hill will now allow laying these misconceptions to rest. The latter are due mainly to the first reviewers of *Marktform und Gleichgewicht*, Nicholas Kaldor, John Hicks and Wassily Leontief. Astonishing from today's point of view, all three of them were capable of reading German (Hicks, 1935; Kaldor, 1936; Leontief, 1936). All three welcomed the book as an important contribution to the theory of imperfect markets. For Nicholas Kaldor it was 'much the most comprehensive work, that has yet appeared on imperfect markets (Kaldor, 1936, p. 227)', while Leontief praised it for its 'skill and elegance (Leontief, 1936, p. 554)'. Both warmly advocated a translation into English, which had to wait until today. Stackelberg's sympathies for a corporatist order in Chapter 6 were ridiculed by Hicks as a 'pæan to the Corporate state', drawing an indignant rejoinder from the author, whose admiration for the work of J. R. Hicks is well documented in Stackelberg's obituary by Eucken (1948).

Despite this success, unusual for a non-English writer, these three reviews also marked the beginning of the misunderstandings concerning Stackelberg's duopoly theory. Kaldor thus sees differences in conjectural variations as responsible for the different outcomes, not differences in cost functions, a misunderstanding that has proven influential. Hicks half-heartedly defends an earlier approach by Harrod's that had gone nowhere and Leontief, who has by far the best understanding of the work, comes up with an equilibrium solution that amounts to joint profit maximisation, this time by market forces rather than by political fiat. Leontief's solution would possibly be the outcome of a reformulation of Stackelberg's model as a repeated game.

Finally, this new translation will allow a more serene assessment of the limits of Stackelberg' analysis. These limits are aptly summarised by Kaldor's observation that

> ... though unfortunately nearly all his [Stackelberg's] conclusions are vitiated by a certain irrational interpretation of the nature of rational behaviour. (Kaldor, 1936, p. 227)

This is quite true. The key question that poses itself when considering the implications of the symmetric Bowley duopoly is indeed why profit-maximising competitors would want to behave in a manner that leads to negative profits with a high probability of bankruptcy? Is this rational or irrational? It is rational from a myopic point of view that never looks beyond the current period. In multi-period models very strong rationality assumptions would have to be made in order to maintain the instability result (Keppler, 1994 for a discussion). Without product differentiation the alternative of explicit or tacit collusion, Marshall's 'fear of spoiling the market', would always be superior. This was also pointed out by Hicks (Hicks, 1935, p. 335). A strict theoretic formulation of a one-shot game, would probably arrive at a mixed-strategy equilibrium. While neither company would like to commit to its 'dependence output' in advance, in the case that A plays his 'independence output', it would indeed be better for B to play its 'dependence output' rather than to go for an all-out war of attrition.

The question is whether such rationalisation would capture the essence of Stackelberg's work. The Darwinian impetus to ever and always insist on the independence output to prove one's fitness in the economic struggle for survival might have appealed to the East Prussian nobleman in a broader sense. These and other fascinating research questions can now be fruitfully pursued on the basis of the timely and competent translation by Bazin, Urch and Hill.

REFERENCES

Bowley, A. L. (1924). *The mathematical groundwork of economics*. Oxford: Clarendon.
Eucken, W. (1948). Obituary: Heinrich von Stackelberg. *Economic Journal, 58*, 132–135.
Friedman, J. W. (1983). *Oligopoly theory*. Cambridge: Cambridge University.

Hicks, J. R. (1935). Review of H. von Stackelberg, Marktform und Gleichgewicht. *Economic Journal, 45*, 334–336.

Kaldor, N. (1936). Review of Von Stackelberg 1934. *Economica, 3*, 227–230.

Keppler, J. (1994). *Monopolistic competition theory: Origins, results, implications.* Baltimore, MD: The Johns Hopkins University Press.

Leontief, W. (1936). Stackelberg on monopolistic competition. *Journal of Political Economy, 44*, 554–559.

Stackelberg, H. V. (1934). *Marktform und gleichgewicht.* Berlin: Springer.

Tirole, J. (1988). *The theory of industrial organization.* Cambridge, MA: MIT Press.

Wicksell, K. (1958). *Selected papers on economic theory.* London: Allen and Unwin.